LIFE AND TIMES

OF

NICCOLÒ MACHIAVELLI.

MACHIAVELLI

from a bust in the possession of Count Bentivoglio

The Life and Times

OF

Niccolò Machiavelli

BY

PROFESSOR PASQUALE VILLARI

TRANSLATED BY

MADAME LINDA VILLARI

A NEW EDITION

(AUGMENTED BY THE AUTHOR. REVISED BY THE TRANSLATOR)

ILLUSTRATED

VOLUME I

GP

**GREENWOOD PRESS, PUBLISHERS
NEW YORK**

Originally published in 1892 by T. Fisher Unwin

First Greenwood Reprinting, 1968

Library of Congress Catalogue Card Number: 68-31007

PRINTED IN THE UNITED STATES OF AMERICA

PREFACE TO THE NEW EDITION.

HIS is the first complete English version of my book on "Machiavelli and his Times," the original translation, in four volumes, produced between the years 1878–83, having been considerably shortened to suit the convenience of its publisher. Whereas the two first volumes were issued intact with all the documents appertaining to them, the rest of the work was deprived of two entire chapters, and every document suppressed. One of the eliminated chapters treated of Art, and it was precisely in the Fine Arts that the Renaissance found its fullest and most distinctive expression. Niccolò Machiavelli, it is true, had no personal concern with the Arts, but they are so essential a feature of the national development of his period, and so closely connected with our literature, that it is impossible to understand either theme without considering the artistic life of the age. The second chapter omitted was of greater length, and even greater importance, being a careful account of all that has been written and thought regarding Machiavelli by critics of all countries at different times. It was therefore a necessary aid towards the due comprehension and appreciation of the man and his works. The political doctrines of the Florentine Secretary are not altogether individual creations of his own. To no small extent they were the product of his times, and exercised a noteworthy influence on the events of subsequent ages. It was requisite, therefore, to examine the nature of this constant, yet ever-varying influence on the deeds and thoughts of those who have pronounced very contradictory verdicts on Machiavelli. Without such examination, the reader's mind would be inevitably perplexed by the crowd of conflicting opinions.

Hence, all will understand how gladly I accepted Mr. Fisher Unwin's proposal of bringing out a complete translation of my book, accompanied by all the more important documents, and particularly by some newly discovered private correspondence, and other inedited letters, written by Machiavelli when Secretary to the Republic. The whole translation has been again revised and collated with the original text, while, on my part, I have been enabled to insert a few corrections in historical details.

Strictly speaking, this is all that need be said. Nevertheless, I venture to add a few brief remarks.

So many books on the Renaissance have appeared of late, that it is only natural to regard the public as almost wearied of the theme, and on the point of refusing attention to anything connected with it. Therefce, I believe it may be useful to indicate what are the points of permanent value—not, assuredly, of my own work, but of its subject. I have shown elsewhere that I was impelled to study the Renaissance not only because we find in that period the primary source of many national qualities and defects, but because we may likewise discover therein the cause of many erroneous judgments passed on us by foreigners. Accordingly, the study of the Renaissance appeared to me to offer the best means of teaching us Italians to know ourselves, correct our faults, and tread the path of progress.

The Renaissance, however, was not isolated to Italy; it was also a period of much importance in the history of the rest of Europe. It was then that, by the revival of classic learning, reason was emancipated, and the modern individual first born and moulded into shape; hence investigation into the circumstances of the modern man's birth teaches us how to comprehend his character. If this may be said of man-kind and civilization in general, it may be still more stoutly asserted with regard to the conception and character of politics. The Middle Ages had no idea of the modern State, of which the Renaissance laid the first stone ; no idea of the science of politics. Theoretically, the Middle Ages admitted no difference between the conduct of in-dividual and of public life, between private and political morality, although, practically, the difference was then more marked than at any other time. In those days men often wrote like anchorites, while fighting tooth and nail like savages. The Renaissance, on the contrary, recognized, and even exaggerated, this difference ; Machiavelli tried to for-mulate it scientifically, and, by force of his new method founded political science. But, absorbed in pondering the divergences between public and private action, he pushed on relentlessly to extreme conclusions, without pausing to observe whether some link of connection might not be hidden beneath such divergence ; whether both public and private conduct might not proceed from a common and more elevated principle. It was this that gave birth to the innumerable disputes, which, even at this day, have not yet come to an end. Nor is it easy for them to come to an end, when we remember, while admitting, in real life, that public morality truly differs from private, that on the other hand, we are sufficiently ingenuous—not to say hypocritical—to maintain that the essential characteristic of modern politics consists in conducting public business with the same good faith and delicacy which we are bound to observe in private affairs. This, as every one knows, is always the theory, not always the practice. Yet, unless voluntarily inconsistent, we are forced by this theory to judge Machiavelli with increasing severity, and his memory, therefore, is still held accursed. Often, too, we find him most cruelly condemned in the words of those whose deeds are most accordant with his views. As the matter now rests, the Machiavelli question is reduced, for many minds, to the single inquiry whether he was an honest or a dishonest man.

Hence, it was, first of all, necessary to separate the verdict to be passed on the man, accordingly as he should be proved honest or dishonest, from that to be pronounced on his doctrines; since of these it is requisite instead to ascertain the truth or the falsity, and to what extent they are true or false. This question, as I have endeavoured to prove, has a practical, as well as a scientific value at the present day. If in real life we recognize a difference between public and private morality, then—since no one doubts the duty of always being honest—it becomes necessary to define the limits of this difference and investigate the true principles of political integrity. If, on the contrary, we deny this difference—which really exists—it follows that, in practice, everything must be left to chance. And this would be a triumph for those *politicians* who, while feigning the highest and most immaculate virtue, succeed in perpetrating actions equally condemned by every rule of public and private morality. The consequences of all this were far less noticeable in the past, when all States, not excepting Republics, were governed by a limited political aristocracy. Tradition and education then served as substitutes for principles. But in modern society, where all men may rise to power from one moment to another, the more tradition and education are lacking, the more urgent the need for principles. Hence, the best way to reach a final solution, is to study the problem from its birth, tracing its course, and noting what modifications it underwent both in theory and practice. At any rate, it is impossible to form an accurate judgment of Machiavelli without first arriving at a sufficiently clear conception of this problem.

Also, in examining a question of this kind, we are driven to investigate many others dating from the same period, and equally agitating to the modern conscience. It was during the Renaissance that unlimited faith in the omnipotence of reason first arose and led to the belief that society, human nature, history, and the mystery of life, could be success-fully explained without the slightest reference to religion, tradition, or conscience. Endeavours were made, in fact, to explain all those problems, while taking for granted that neither the eternal, the supernatural, nor the divine, need be even hypothetically admitted. Then, for the first time, was asserted the vain pretence that it was possible for us to construct and destroy human society at our own pleasure : the very theory afterwards put to so fatal a test by the French Revolution, and of which a no less fatal experience is offered to ourselves, by those who still maintain that new states of society may be founded with the same ease with which new systems of philosophy are invented. And as all these ideas simultaneously flashed on the human mind, after the close of the Middle Ages, men rushed at once to the logical consequences deduced from them, and with the greater serenity, because incapable of foreseeing eventual results. By examining these doctrines in the age of their birth we are better enabled to judge them, since, besides witnessing their logical consequences, we also perceive what direct or indirect influences they speedily brought to bear upon practical life. For we see the spectacle of a great people who founded the grand institutions of the Universal Church and the Free Communes, struggled victoriously against the Empire, created Christian Art, poetry, the *Divina Commedia*—and then note how that same people, changing its course, emancipated human reason, initiated a new science, a new literature, modern civilization, yet simultaneously destroyed its political institutions and its liberty, corrupted the Church, fell to the lowest depths of immorality, and became a prey to foreign conquest.

For all these reasons the biography of Niccolò Machiavelli cannot be restricted to the treatment of his individual work. It must necessarily investigate the rise and development of a new doctrine, manifesting in no small degree the spirit of an age, and personified in a man. This it is that constitutes Machiavelli's historical importance. Hence, a complete comprehension of the man is only to be obtained by clearly distinguishing that which was the product of his times from his personal achievement, even as it is necessary to distinguish between his individual character and the worth of his doctrines. We shall then more plainly discern the reason of certain contradictions to be found in Machiavelli. The deductions of the thinker are sometimes in tragical conflict with the forecasts and aspirations of the patriot, and an impartial study of this conflict will throw a new light on the man, his age, and his doctrines. Only thus, it seems to me, is it possible to arrive at the truth, and estimate Machiavelli with the strict justice that is the chief purpose of history. To what extent I have succeeded or failed in this, my readers must decide.

PASQUALE VILLARI.

PREFACE TO THE FIRST EDITION.

IN offering to the public a fresh biography of Niccolò Machiavelli, I feel that it is needful to state my reasons for adding another to the many works upon the same subject already before the world.

Throughout a long series of years the Florentine Secretary was regarded as a species of Sphinx, of whom none could solve the enigma. By some he was depicted as a monster of perfidy ; by others as one of the noblest and purest of patriots. Some looked upon his writings as iniquitous precepts for the safe maintenance of tyranny ; others, on the contrary, maintained that the "Principe" was a sanguinary satire upon despots, intended to sharpen daggers against them, and incite peoples to rebellion. While one writer exalted the literary and scientific merits of his works, another would pronounce them a mass of erroneous and perilous doctrines, only fitted for the ruin and corruption of any society foolish enough to adopt them. And thus the very name of Machiavelli became, in popular parlance, a term of opprobrium.

In course of time, and through the development of criticism, not a few of these exaggerations have disappeared, but it would be a great mistake to suppose that any unanimity of opinion has as yet been obtained on the points of highest importance. Many of my readers may remember the indignant outcry raised, especially in France, against the Provisional Government of Tuscany, when it initiated the revolution of 1859, by decreeing a new and complete edition of Machiavelli's works. To the insults then hurled against Italians in general, and the Florentine Secretary in particular, others retorted by lauding his political genius and purity of mind. Only a few years have elapsed since the appearance of a new " History of the Florentine Republic," written by one whose name is cherished and venerated throughout Italy. This work contains a very eloquent parallel, full of just and ingenious observations, between Guicciardini and Machiavelli. And the comparison concludes, not only to the advantage of the former writer, but also with the assertion that the latter was " malignant at heart, malignant of mind, his soul corrupted by despair of good." [1]

Nor was this a hasty judgment ; on the contrary, it was the fruit of careful study, of long meditation, and pronounced by one whose word had no slight weight in Italy. The two Tuscan scholars who, in 1873, commenced the publication of the newest edition of Machiavelli's works, frequently allude to the close and cordial friendship they suppose him to have felt for Cæsar Borgia, even at the moment when the latter's hands were stained by the most atrocious crimes ; and they even publish some inedited documents, the better to confirm their assertion.

On the other hand, more recent biographers, although not always agreeing upon other points, exalt the patriotism no less than the genius of Machiavelli, while some of them, after careful study of his works and of inedited documents, even praise his generosity, nobility, and exquisite delicacy of mind, and go so far as to declare him an incomparable model of public and private virtue. It seems to me that this is a proof that we are still far removed from harmony, and that new researches and fresh studies may not be altogether superfluous.

There were various reasons for this great and continual dissension. The times in which Machiavelli lived are full of difficulties and contradictions for the historian, and these are embodied and multiplied in the person of the Secretary, after a fashion to really makes him sometimes appear to be a sphinx. It is naturally perplexing to behold the same man who, in some pages, sounds the praises of liberty and virtue in words of unapproachable eloquence,

---

[1] Gino Capponi, "Storia delle Repubblica di Firenze," vol. ii. p. 368, Florence, Barbéra (2 vols. 8vo), 1875.

teaching elsewhere principles of treachery and deceit, how best to oppress a people and secure the impunity of tyrants. Nor are these doubts dissipated by first seeing him faithfully serving his Republic for fifteen years, then sustaining misery and persecution for his love of liberty, and afterwards begging to be employed in the service of the Medici, were it but "*to turn a stone.*" Yet the contradictions of history and of human nature are manifold, and in the present case would have been much more easily explained, were it not that most writers have sought to be either accusers or defenders of Machiavelli, judges—too seldom impartial—of his morality and of his patriotism, rather than genuine biographers. To many—particularly in Italy—it appeared sufficient to have proved that he loved liberty, and his. country's unity and inde- pendence, in order to be lenient upon all other points ; therefore they praise both his doctrines and his morals, even previously submitting them to a diligent critical examination, almost as though patriotism were a sure evidence of political and literary capacity, and necessarily exempt from vice and crime in private life.

This inevitably called forth opposite opinions, for which the contradictions noted above furnished abundant food. So that little by little the whole question seemed limited to an endeavour to ascertain whether the "Principe" and the "Discorsi" had been written by an honest or a dishonest man, by a republican or by a courtier, whereas what it really concerned us to know was the measure of scientific value of the doctrines contained in. them ; whether they were true or false, did or did not comprise novel truths, did or did not serve for the advancement of science? None can deny that if those doctrines were false, no virtue of the writer could make them true ; if true, no vices of his could make them false.

Undoubtedly there has been no lack of influential writers who have undertaken an impartial and rational examination of Machia- velli's works, but these have almost always given us critical essays and dissertations rather than real and complete biographies. Absorbed in a philosophical examination of his theories, they either gave too little attention to the times and character of the author, or spoke of them as though every dispute might be settled by stating that Machiavelli represented the character of his age and faithfully depicted it in his own writings. But in a century there is space for many men, many ideas, many different vices and different virtues, nor do the times alone suffice to render clear to us all that is the work, the personal creation of genius. Nevertheless, it is, of course, necessary to study them in order to form a complete judgment of the doctrines of a writer who—as in Machiavelli's case—derives so much from them and yet puts so much of himself in his works. This is not, however, the place for entering upon an examination of biographers and critics, of whom it will be my duty to speak farther on, in making use of their writings and giving frequent quotations from them. My present object is simply to announce that I have no intention of being either the apologist or the accuser of the Florentine Secretary. I have studied his life, his times, and his writings, in order to know and describe him as he really was, with all his merits and demerits, his vices and his virtues.

This may probably appear to be a needless presumption, after the attempts already made by writers of greater authority than myself. But thanks to historical materials of recent accumulation, and others which, though still unexplored, are now easily accessible, we have increased facilities for solving many of those doubts which previously seemed to present insurmountable difficulties. It is certain that publications such as the ten volumes of Guicciardini's inedited works,[1] the diplomatic correspondence of almost every province of Italy, an infinite number of other documents, not to mention the original works of Italian and foreign writers, have dissipated many obscurities and contradictions both in the literary and political history of the Italian Renaissance. Also the rapid progress of social science in our own days, naturally makes it much easier to determine the intrinsic value and historic necessity of that which many have called Machiavellism. And for all that relates to the Secretary personally, there are the papers which passed at his death into the hands of the Ricci family, then to the Palatine Library in Florence—where for a long time they were very jealously kept—and now, in the National Library, are accessible to all, and even partly published. In the five volumes already issued by Signori Passerini and Milanesi of their new edition of Machiavelli's works, many useful documents selected from Florentine archives and libraries are comprised. Nevertheless a very considerable mass of highly important papers still remained unexplored. For instance, to my certain knowledge, there are several thousands of Machiavelli's official letters still inedited, and

[1] Guicciardini, " Opere Inedite."

—as far as I know—never before examined by any biographer. This being the case, it seemed to me that there would be no undue presumption in venturing upon another trial.

Were all biographies necessarily planned upon the same model, then indeed I might be exposed to severe blame. But I have thought it right to choose the form best adapted to the nature of the subject. So little is known of Machiavelli during the years in which he completed his studies and his character was in course of formation, that I have tried, in part at least, to fill the great gap, by a somewhat prolonged study of the times. I have endeavoured to examine the gradual rise in that century of what may be called the Machiavellian spirit, before he himself appeared upon the scene to give it the original imprint of his political genius, and to formulate it scientifically. Then, after having to a certain extent studied Machiavellism before Machiavelli, I drew near to him as soon as he became visible in history, seeking to learn his passions and his thoughts, as far as possible, from his own writings, and those of his most intimate friends and contemporaries. For without neglecting the examination of modern authors, I have always preferred to depend upon the authority of those closer to the events which I had to relate.

And this too has contributed in no slight degree to give a special form to this biography. Among the documents of most importance for the comprehension of Machiavelli's political life, the "Legations" must certainly be included, since these contain not only the faithful history of all his embassies, but likewise the earliest germs of his political doctrines. But although their value with this had been already noted—among others by Gervinus—these "Legations" had never been much read, partly because they are, of necessity, full of repetitions, and partly because, in order to be generally liked and understood, they would require a running commentary upon the events to which they allude. Therefore, to enable the reader to perceive with his own eyes the way in which our author's ideas were formed, I have frequently had to give summaries of, and even *verbatim* extracts from many of his despatches. And this far oftener than I could have wished— swiftness of narration in view of, but never oftener than I considered necessary for a full knowledge of the subject.

Then, too, the official letters written by Machiavelli in the Chancery form the indispensable complement of the "Legations." If the latter make us acquainted with his political life away from the Republic, the former teach us to know what it was at home. Many, of course, are of no value whatever, being simple orders given to this or that Commissary, and hastily repeating the same things over and over again. There are others, however, in which we find frequent flashes of the great writer's style, ideas, and originality. And the majority of these letters being—as we have shown—still unpublished, it was requisite to examine all with great care and attention. I therefore undertook this tedious and often ungrateful task, copying, or causing to be copied, some thousand letters, certain of which I have quoted in the foot-notes, from others given important extracts, while some few again I have transcribed *verbatim* in the Appendix, so that the reader might be able to have a clear idea of their general nature. This, too, contributed to slacken the pace of the narrative, and try as I might, there was no remedy for it. It was impossible to leave unmentioned that which was, for so many years, Machiavelli's principal work ; nor was it possible to speak of so vast a mass of unpublished letters without often quoting and inserting here and there a few sentences, especially since there is small hope that any one will undertake to publish them in full. It is useless to enumerate here all the other documents which I sought out and read ; they can easily be ascertained from the notes and appendix. I will merely remark that during these researches I was enabled to give to the world three volumes of Giustinian's despatches, which were collected and examined by me, not only because of the fresh light they threw upon the times occupying my attention, but also because they enabled me to place in juxtaposition with the Florentine secretary and orator, one of the principal ambassadors of the Venetian Republic, and thus institute a comparison between them. When in 1512 the Medici were reinstated in Florence, liberty was extinguished, and Machiavelli being out of office, and fallen into the obscurity of private life, his biography then changes its aspect and is almost exclusively limited to the examination of his written works and the narration of the events in the midst of which they were composed. This, however, is the principal subject of the second volume, which, being still incomplete, cannot be placed before the public as soon as I should have desired. For my own part I should have preferred waiting until both volumes could have been published simultaneously. But in the long years during which my studies have been carried on, I have witnessed the publication of many fresh dissertations on, and biographies of

Machiavelli, of documents, in many instances discovered and transcribed by myself ; and so many other works bearing on the same subject are already announced, that it appears best to publish this first volume without further delay. Besides, this method of publication is now so general that many excellent precedents justify my adoption of it.

I must notify to my readers that in quoting from the works of Machiavelli, I have made use of the Italian edition, dated 1813, one of the best at present completed. I have, however, been careful to collate it with the more recent edition commenced at Florence in 1873, but still far from completion, and deprived, by the death of Count Passerini, of its most energetic promoter. In this, a very praiseworthy attempt has been made to give a faithful reproduction of Machiavelli's original orthography. But in the many quotations inserted by me in the present work, I have occasionally thought it advisable to expunge certain conventional and well-known modes of speech which were out of place in a modern work. This, however, I have done with great caution and solely to avoid the inconvenience of changing too often or too rapidly the material form of diction. In the Appendix, on the contrary, I have scrupulously and entirely adhered to the original orthography. The reader will also see that I have been frequently forced to disagree with the two learned gentlemen who bestowed their labours on the new edition, especially with regard to the importance and significance they have sought to attribute to some of the documents which they have already published. But to this I shall refer elsewhere, merely remarking here that I have no intention of questioning their undoubted merit, nor their care and diligence in publishing the documents, seeing that these are of great value to the biographer, and have frequently been made use of by myself.

To one erroneous notice it is imperative however to refer. In the Preface to the third volume, published in 1875, after deploring the loss of many of Machiavelli's letters, the editors go on to say : "It is a known fact that many volumes of his private letters, which were in the hands of the Vettori family, were for ever lost to Italy by being fraudulently sold by a priest to Lord Guildford, from whom they passed into the hands of a certain Mr. Philipps, who, during his life, preserved them and other precious things in his possession with such extreme jealousy, as to even refuse to let them be examined, much less copied, for the new edition of the Works of Machiavelli decreed in 1859 by the Tuscan Government, when a request to that effect was made to him by the Marquis of Lajatico, special ambassador to London. And although he (Philipps) is now dead and has legally bequeathed these letters and other things to the British Museum, we are still unable to make use of them, his creditors having come forward to prevent his will from being executed." Now it was impossible for me to write a biography of Machiavelli, without making every effort to gain a sight of the "many" volumes of private letters of which the existence was thus positively asserted. Setting inquiries on foot, I ascertained that Lord Guildford had really purchased in Florence three volumes of manuscript letters, the which were indicated in his printed catalogue as inedited letters of Machiavelli, and further described as a *literary treasure* of inestimable value. These letters were afterwards purchased by the great English collector of manuscripts of all kinds, Sir Thomas Phillipps, and were by him bequeathed, with the rest of his library, to his daughter, the wife of the Rev. E. Fenwick, and now resident in the neighbourhood of Cheltenham. To Cheltenham I accordingly went and at last held in my hands the three mysterious volumes. The reader will readily appreciate my surprise, my disappointment, on discovering that in the whole three volumes there was only a single letter which could even be supposed to have been written by Machiavelli !

The volumes in question are in ancient handwriting, are marked in the Phillipps' catalogue, No. 8238, and are entitled : "Carteggio Originale di Niccolò Machiavelli, al tempo che fu segretario della Repubblica fiorentina. Inedito."

The first letter—which has no importance—bears date of the 20th of October, 1508, is written in the name of the Ten, and at the bottom of the page has the name Nic° Maclavello, appended to it, according to the usual custom of the coadjutor who copied the registers of the Chancery. This is the sole letter of which the minute may possibly have been his, but we cannot be quite sure even of this. All the other letters—beginning with the second of the first volume—are dated from 1513, when he was already out of office, and the Medici reinstated in Florence, down to 1526. Always addressed to Francesco Vettori, now ambassador to Rome, now envoy elsewhere, always written in the name of the Otto di Pratica who succeeded to the Ten in 1512, the initials N. M. are to be found at the bottom of almost every page. Occasionally, however, we find the name of Niccolò Michelozzi, sometimes abbreviated, sometimes in full, and it was Michelozzi who was Chancellor of the Otto di Pratica during that period. The first letter, therefore, extracted from some register of the Republic, was placed at the beginning of these volumes, for the sole purpose of deceiving the too credulous purchaser, who had he taken the trouble to look at the dates, must have understood that the others could not possibly be by Machiavelli. So, having examined the catalogue of the enormous Phillipps's library and taken a few notes from other Italian manuscripts contained in it, I went back to Florence with nothing gained save the certainty of the non-existence of the supposed correspondence.

And now one last word only remains to be said. It frequently happens that authors are pushed by some secret idea to the choice of their subject. What chiefly urged me to mine was, that the Italian Renaissance, of which Machiavelli was undoubtedly one of the principal representatives, is the period in which our national spirit had its last really original manifestation. It was followed by a prolonged slumber from which we are only now awakening. Hence the study of this period of our history may, if I am not mistaken, prove doubly useful to us, not only by acquainting us with a very splendid portion of our old culture, but likewise by offering us more than one explanation of the vices against which we are still combating at the present day, and of the virtues which have assisted our regeneration. And the lesson will be all the more valuable, the better the historian remembers that his mission is not to preach precepts of morality and politics, but only to endeavour to revive the past, of which the present is born, and from which it derives continual light, continual teaching. This at least is the idea that has given me encouragement and comfort, by keeping alive in me the hope that, even far from the world and shut up with my books, I am not forgetful of the mighty debt, which now more than ever—in the measure of our strength —we all owe to our country.

1878.

CONTENTS.

———◆———

CONTENTS.

BOOK THE FIRST.

LIST OF ILLUSTRATIONS.

THE LIFE AND TIMES

OF

NICCOLÒ MACHIAVELLI.

INTRODUCTION.

I.

THE RENAISSANCE.

IT would be difficult to find any period in the history of modern Europe equal in importance with that distinguished in History under the name of the Renaissance. Standing midway between the decay of the Middle Ages and the rise of modern institutions, we may say that it was already dawning in the days of Dante Alighieri, whose immortal works while giving us the synthesis of a dying age herald the birth of a new era. This new era—the Renaissance—began with Petrarch and his learned contemporaries, and ended with Martin Luther and the Reformation, an event that not only produced signal changes in the history of nations which remained Catholic, but transported beyond the Alps the centre of gravity of European culture.

During the period of which we treat, we behold a rapid social transformation in Italy, an enormous intellectual activity. On all sides old traditions, forms, and institutions were crumbling

and disappearing to make way for new. The Scholastic method
yielded the place to philosophy, the principle of authority fell
before the advance of free reason and free examination.

Then the study of natural science began ; Leon Battista
Alberti and Leonardo da Vinci hazarded the first steps in search
of the experimental method ; commerce and industry advanced ;
voyages were multiplied, and Christopher Columbus discovered
America. The art of printing, invented in Germany, quickly
became an Italian trade. Classical learning was everywhere diffused, and the use of the Latin tongue,—now more than ever the
universal language of civilized people—placed Italy in close relation
with the rest of Europe, as its accepted adviser and mistress
of learning. Political science and the art of war were created ;
chronicles gave way to the political histories of Guicciardini
and Machiavelli ; ancient culture sprang into new life, and amid
many other new forms of literary composition the romance of
chivalry came into existence. Brunelleschi created a new architecture, Donatello restored sculpture, Masaccio and a myriad of
Tuscan and Umbrian painters prepared the way, by the study of
nature, for Raphael and Michel Angelo. The world seemed
renewed and rejuvenated by the splendid sun of Italian culture.

But, in the midst of this vivid splendour, strange and inexplicable contradictions were to be found. This rich, indus-
trious, intelligent people, before whom all Europe stood, as it
were, in an ecstasy of admiration — this people was rapidly
becoming corrupt. Everywhere liberty was disappearing, tyrants
were springing up, family ties seemed to be slackened, the domestic
hearth was profaned : no man longer trusted to the good faith
of Italians. Both politically and morally the nation had become
too feeble to resist the onslaught of any foreign power ; the first
army that passed the Alps traversed the peninsula almost without
striking a blow, and was soon followed by others who devastated
and trampled the country with equal impunity.

Accustomed as we are now to hear daily that knowledge and
culture constitute the greatness and prove the measure of a
nation's strength, we are naturally led to inquire how Italy could
become so weak, so corrupt, so decayed, in the midst of her
intellectual and artistic pre-eminence !

It is easy to say, that the fault lay with the Italians, who tore
each other to pieces instead of uniting for the common defence.
But to assert their guilt does not explain it. Was not the Italy

of the Middle Ages more divided and yet stronger ? were not the civil wars and reprisals of those days even blinder and more sanguinary ? Nor is it enough to say that the country had been exhausted by the struggles and dearly-bought grandeur of the Middle Ages. How can we call a nation exhausted at the very moment when its intelligence and activity are transforming the face of the world ? Instead of wearily trying to formulate general judgments, it is better to turn our attention to the observation and description of facts. And the principal fact of the fifteenth century is this : that Italian mediæval institutions having engendered a new state of society and great civil progress, suddenly became not only insufficient, but dangerous. Hence a radical transformation and revolution became unavoidable. And it was precisely at the moment when this social convulsion was going on in Italy, that foreign invaders fell upon the land and checked all internal progress.

The Middle Ages were ignorant of the political organism known to us as the State, which unites and co-ordinates social forces according to precise rules. Instead, society was then divided into Fiefs and Sub-fiefs, into great and little Communes, and the Commune was merely a truss of minor associations, badly bound together. Above this vast and disordered mass stood the Papacy and the Empire, which, although increasing the general confusion by their frequent wars against each other, still gave some rough unity to the civilized world. In the fifteenth century all this was entirely changed. On the one hand, great nations were gradually coming into shape ; on the other, the authority of the empire was restricted in Germany, in Italy little more than a memory of the past. The Pontiffs, occupied in constituting an actual and personal temporal power, although still at the head of the universal Church, could no longer pretend to the political dominion of the world, but aspired to be as other sovereigns. In this state of things, the Commune which had formed the past grandeur of Italy, entered on a substantially new phase of existence to which historians have attached too little importance.

The Commune had now obtained its long-desired independence, and had only its own strength to rely upon : in all wars with its neighbours it could no longer hope nor fear the interposition of a superior authority. Hence it became necessary to enlarge its own territory and increase its strength, the more so, since in whatever direction it looked, it beheld great States and military monarchies in process of formation throughout Europe. But owing to the political constitution of the Commune, every extension of territory evoked dangers of so grave a nature as to imperil its very existence. We may really say that a fatal hour had struck in which exactly what was most necessary to it, threatened the gravest danger. The Commune of the Middle Ages was ignorant of representative government, and only understood a government directed by its free citizens ; therefore, it was necessary to restrict these to a very small number, in order to avoid anarchy. For this reason the right of citizenship was a privilege conceded to only a few of those who dwelt within the circuit of the city walls. Florence, the most democratic republic in Italy, which in 1494 attained to its most liberal constitution, numbered at that date about 90,000 inhabitants, of whom only 3,200 were citizens proper.[1] Even the Ciompi, in their disorderly revolt, had not claimed citizenship for all. As to the territory outside the walls, it was considered enough to have abolished servitude ; no one contemplated giving it a share in the government. This state of things was based, not only on the statutes, laws, and existing customs, but also in the profound and radical convictions of the most illustrious men. Dante Alighieri, who had taken no small part in the very democratic law of the *Ordinamenti di Giustizia* (Rules of Justice) at the time of Giano della Bella, speaks with regret in his poem of the days when the territory of the Commune only extended a few paces beyond the walls, and the inhabitants of the neighbouring lands of Campi, Figline, and Signa had not begun to mix with those of Florence ;

> " Sempre la confusion delle persone
> Principio fu del mal della cittade." [2]

And Petrarch, who dreamed of the ancient empire, and was so enthusiastic for Cola di Rienzo, advised that in reorganizing the Roman republic, its government should be confided to the citizens proper, excluding as foreigners the inhabitants of Latium, and even the Orsini and the Colonna, because these families, although Roman, were, in his opinion, of foreign descent.

Accordingly, whenever the territory of one Commune became

---

[1] Villari, " The History of G. Savonarola," translated by L. Horner, London. Longmans, 1863.

[2] " Paradiso," xvi. 66–8. See also the lines 42–72.

enlarged by the submission to it of another, this latter, however mildly governed, found itself completely shut out from political life, and its principal citizens driven forth into exile in foreign parts. The spectacle of a Pisan or a Pistoian in the Councils of the Florentine republic would have been as extraordinary as now-a-days that of a citizen of Paris or Berlin seated on the benches of the Italian Parliament. It was far preferable then to fall under a monarchy, since all subjects of a monarchy enjoyed equal privileges, and every inhabitant of every province was eligible for public offices. In fact, Guicciardini remarked to Machiavelli, when the latter was sketching the plan of a great Italian republic, that such a form of government would be to the advantage of a single city and the ruin of all others ; since a republic never grants the benefit of its freedom " to any but its own proper citizens," whereas monarchy " is more impartial to all." [1] And no terror could equal that experienced by the Italian republics when Venice,—who yet granted greater freedom to her subjects than any other,— turned her attention to the mainland, and aspired to the dominion of the peninsula. They would have preferred, not monarchy alone, but even foreign monarchy, since then they might preserve some local independence, which in those days could not be hoped for in Italy under a republic. Guicciardini considered that Cosmo dei Medici, in aiding Francesco Sforza to become Lord of Milan, saved the liberty of all Italy, which would otherwise have fallen under Venetian domination.[2] And Niccolò Machiavelli, who so frequently sighed for a republic, yet in all his official letters, in all his missions, always speaks of Venice as the chief enemy of Italian freedom.

In this condition of things, with these convictions, it was impossible to hope that the Commune could unite Italy by the formation of a strong republic. One might hope in a confederation or in a monarchy ; but the first presupposed a central government different from that of the Communes, in which the city was no longer the state, and was in opposition with the Papacy and the kings of Naples. A monarchy instead, found arrayed against it, on the one hand that ancient love of liberty which had made Italy

---

[1] Guicciardini, " Opere Inedite," published by Counts Piero and Luigi Guicciardini, in Florence, from 1857 to 1866, in ten vols. See in vol. i. (" Considerazioni intorno dei Discorsi di Machiavelli ") the consideration on chap. xii. of the " Discourses." Guicciardini at this point styles kingdom what we call monarchy, and monarchy the union of many Communes in one republic.

[2] " Opere Inedite," vol. iii. ; " Storia di Firenze," pp. 8, 9.

glorious, and on the other the Popes, who, placed in the centre of the Peninsula, too weak to be able to unite it, but strong enough to prevent others from doing so, from time to time called in foreigners who came to turn all things upside down. For all these reasons the Commune, once the strength and greatness of Italy, may be said to have outlived itself in presence of the novel social problems now arising on all sides, and among the thousand dangers welling up in its own bosom. The Commune had proclaimed liberty and equality. How then could the lower classes, who had fought and conquered feudalism side by side with the wealthy merchant class, be content to be excluded from the government ?

Neither could the inhabitants of the territory without the walls, who were bound to take arms in the defence of their country, be disposed to tolerate entire exclusion from every public office, from every right of citizenship. And as the territory extended, and new cities were vanquished, the number of the oppressed increased, and passions became inflamed as the disproportion between the small number of the governing and the great number of the governed continually augmented, and all equilibrium became impossible. Had a skilful tyrant then stepped forward, he would have been supported by an infinite multitude of malcontents, to whom he would have appeared in the light of a liberator, or at least in that of an avenger.

And if we turn our eyes from political conditions to social, we shall notice a transformation of equal gravity and equal danger. Looked at from afar, at first sight, the Communes of the Middle Ages appear to be small states in the modern sense of the word ; yet in reality they were merely agglomerations of a thousand different associations. Greater guilds (Arti), and lesser guilds, societies and leagues all arranged as so many republics with their assemblies, statutes, tribunals, and ambassadors. These were sometimes stronger than the central government of which they did the work when—as often happens in times of revolution —that government was entirely suspended. We might almost say that the strength of the Commune consisted entirely in the associations that divided and governed it. To these the citizens were so tenaciously attached that often they gave their lives in defence of the republic, merely because it shielded the existence of the association to which they belonged, and prevented it from falling a prey to others.

Hence the Middle Ages have justly been called the ages of associations and castes. The great number and variety of these produced an infinite variety of characters and passions unknown to the ancient world ; but the modern individual, independence, was not yet created, every individual being then absorbed as it were, in the caste in which and for which he lived. In fact, during a very long period, Italian history seldom records the names of the politicians, soldiers, artists, and poets who were the founders and defenders of the Communes, the creators of Italian institutions, letters and arts. They were Guelphs and Ghibellines, major and minor arts or trades, wandering poets, master masons, always associations or parties, never individuals. Even the colossal figures of popes and emperors derive their importance, less from their personal characteristics and qualities, than from the system to which they belonged, or the institution they represented.

All this rapidly disappeared in the fifteenth century. Dante's Titanic form stood out from the mediæval background, in the midst of which he still lived, and he boasted with pride of having been his own party. The names of poets, painters, and party leaders were now frequently heard, and individual characters began to be seen in distinct prominence above the crowd. We behold a general transformation of Italian society, which, after having destroyed feudalism and proclaimed equality, found itself compelled to dissolve the associations that had helped to constitute it in its new form. And more than elsewhere this is most clearly seen in Florence where the *Ordinamenti di Giustizia* (1293) abased the nobility and drove them from the government ; suppressed certain of the associations ; rendered *cliques* impossible ; and for the first time placed a Gonfalonier [1] at the head of the Commune. The necessity of beginning to constitute the unity of the modern state was a natural result of the increasing democratic form assumed by the Commune ; this was indeed the weighty problem Italy had to solve in the fifteenth century. But the period of change and transition was beset by a thousand dangers ; old institutions fell to pieces before new arose, each individual, left to his own guidance, was solely ruled by personal interest and egotism ; hence moral corruption became inevitable.

Morality, in the Middle Ages, had its chief basis in the closeness

[1] I have treated this argument at length in an article entitled "La Republica Florentina al tempo di Dante Alighieri," published in the " Nuova Antologia," vol. xi. pp. 443 and following (July, 1869).

of family bonds and class ties. Of such bonds both law and custom were very jealous guardians : they kept up family inheritances, prevented their removal by marriage to another Commune ; and moreover rendered marriage extremely difficult between persons, not only of different Communes, but even of opposing parties in the same city. Hence in the bosom of each caste we find a great community of interests ; tenacious affection and great spirit of sacrifice ; much jealousy and frequent acts of hatred and revenge against neighbours. Little by little all this vanished, owing to the snapping of old ties by political reform, by increased equality, and by the increased application of the imperial Roman law rendering women less subject to the domination of their male relatives. And precisely as the Commune had been suddenly left to rely upon its own resources on the cessation of Imperial or Papal supremacy, so the citizen, released from all bonds, found himself in isolated dependence on his own strength. He could no longer feel the old interest in the fate of neighbours who no longer concerned themselves with him ; his future, his worldly condition, now solely depended on his own individual qualities. Thus at one and the same time egotism became a power in society and human individuality developed in ever fresh and varying forms. Not only did individual names multiply and ambitious faction-leaders arise on all sides ; but the civil wars of the Communes seemed to be converted into personal feuds ; cities were divided by the names of their most powerful and turbulent citizens ; families split asunder and tore each other to pieces ; men no longer recognized the sanctity of any bond. The prejudices, traditions, virtues and vices of the Middle Ages all disappeared to make way for another state of society and other men.

All who take into consideration the double transformation which our Republics have undergone will perceive that while on the one hand they were weakened by the aggrandisement of their territories, and felt increasing need of a central government of greater strength, bearing more equally upon all, on the other hand in proportion to the loosening of the bonds of caste, the number increased of ambitious and audacious individuals whose only object was the acquisition of power. The outbreak of these ambitions at the very time in which the Communes were naturally tending towards monarchial forms, constituted a very serious danger ; and thus, as at one time Communes had sprung up all over Italy, so now the hour had struck for the uprising of tyrants.

But whatever his vices, the Italian tyrant had a certain individuality of character, a real historical importance. It was not necessary for him to be of noble or powerful descent, nor even to be the first-born of his house. A tradesman, a bastard, an adventurer of any kind, might command an army, head a revolution, become a tyrant, provided that he had audacity and the talent of success. History records many strange tales of this sort, and the Italian novelists who so faithfully depicted the manners of their times, often cut jests about obscure persons who took it into their heads to try and become tyrants ; as, for instance of that shoemaker who, as Sacchetti tells us, "wished to possess himself of the lands of Messer Ridolfo da Camerino." [1] The fifteenth century was rightly styled the age of adventurers and bastards. Borso d'Este at Ferrara, Sigismondo Malatesta at Rimini, Francesco Sforza at Milan, Ferdinand of Aragon at Naples, and many other lords and princes were bastards. No one was longer bound by any conventions or traditions ; everything depended on the personal qualities of those who dared to tempt fortune, on the friends and adherents whom they knew how to gain.

Compelled to snatch their power from the midst of a thousand risks and a thousand rivals, they lived in a state of perpetual warfare and licence : no scruples forbade them the use of violence, treason, or bloodshed. For these men, wrong-doing had no limits save those imposed by expediency and personal needs ; they looked upon it as a means adapted to reach a desired end. To exceed those limits was regarded not as a crime but as a folly unworthy of a politician, since it brought no advantage. Their conscience ignored remorse, their reason calculated and measured everything ; but even when all difficulties were overcome, and success attained, their dangers were by no means at an end. It was necessary to struggle against the fierce discontent of those who, by force of habit, could not bear to live without taking part in the government ; against the savage disappointment of those rival aspirants to tyrannical power who had been forestalled or defeated. When a popular rising was put down by force, daggers were secretly pointed from every side, and plots were all the more cruel, since they bore the stamp of

---

[1] Novella XC. edit. Le Monnier, Florence, 1860–61.

personal revenge ; were woven by friends, by members of the family : the nearest relations,—often brothers,—were seen contending for the throne with steel and poison. Thus the Italian tyrant was, as it were, condemned to reconquer his kingdom daily ; and to this end he considered any and every means justifiable.

In this miserable state of things, personal courage, military valour, and a remorseless conscience were not the only qualities required ; it was also needful to have great presence of mind, astute cunning, profound knowledge of men and things, and above all complete control of personal passions. It was necessary to study social, as we study natural phenomena, to have no illusions, to depend upon nothing but reality. It was imperative for every tyrant to thoroughly understand his own kingdom, and the men among whom he lived, in order to be able to dominate them, to discover a fitting form of government, to build up an administrative system, justice, police, public works, everything in short, on the ruins of the past. All substantial power was concentrated in the tyrant's hands, and the unity of the new state came into birth as his personal creation. And with him were born the science and the art of government ; but at the same time an opinion was diffused, that afterwards became a very general and fatal error—namely, that laws and institutions are inventions of the statesmen, rather than the natural results of the nation's history and social and civil development. During the Middle Ages, state and history were believed to be the work of Providence, in which human will and reason had no part ; during the Renaissance, on the contrary, everything was thought to be the work of man, who, if foiled in his intents, could blame none but himself and Fortune, which was held to have a large share in the ordering of human destinies. In a country so divided and subdivided as Italy, these vicissitudes were everywhere multiplied and repeated ; and it is easy to imagine how much and in how many different ways they contributed to the corruption of the country. Tyrants sprang up among republics, popes, and Neapolitan kings, and all being jealous one of the other, sought the friendship of neighbours and foreigners, in order to weaken and divide their enemies. Thus plots and intrigues increased *ad infinitum*, and at the same time a strange network of political interests was formed which multiplied the international relations of the different states, caused the first idea of political balance to arise in Italy, and endued our diplomacy with marvellous activity, intelligence, and wisdom. Those were days in which every Italian seemed a born diplomatist : the merchant, the man of letters, the captain of adventurers, knew how to address and discourse with kings and emperors, duly observing all conventional forms, and with an admirable display of acumen and penetration. The despatches of our ambassadors were among the chief historical and literary monuments of those times. The Venetians stood in the first rank for practical good sense and observation of facts, the Florentines for elegance of style and subtle perception of character, but they had worthy rivals in the ambassadors of other states. Thus, the art of speaking and writing became a formidable weapon, and one that was highly prized by Italians.

It was then that adventurers, immovable by threats, prayers or pity, were seen to yield to the verses of a learned man. Lorenzo dei Medici went to Naples, and by force of argument persuaded Ferrante d'Aragona to put an end to the war and conclude an alliance with him. Alfonso the Magnanimous, a prisoner of Filippo Maria Visconti, and whom all believed dead, was instead honourably liberated because he had the skill to convince that gloomy and cruel tyrant that it would better serve his turn to have the Aragonese at Naples than the followers of Anjou, winding up his argument by saying : "Would'st thou rather satisfy thy appetite than secure thee thy State?"[1] In a revolution at Prato, got up by Bernardo Nardi, this leader, according to Machiavelli, had already thrown the halter round the neck of the Florentine Podestà when the latter's fine reasoning persuaded him to spare his life ; and thus nothing more went well with him.[2] Such facts may sometimes be exaggerations or even wholly fictitious ; but seeing them so constantly repeated and believed, proves what were the ideas and temper of these men.

Therefore it is not astonishing if even tyrants loved study and ardently encouraged art, literature, and culture in every shape. And they did this, not merely from a keen perception of the art of governing or as a means for turning the people's attention from politics ; it was likewise a necessity of their condition, a true

[1] Machiavelli, "Storie," vol. xi. lib. v. p. 11. We generally quote the works of this author from the edition of 1813.
[2] Machiavelli, "Storie," lib. vii. p. 184.

and real intellectual need. A well-written diplomatic note, a skilful discourse, could resolve the gravest political questions. To what did the Italian tyrant owe his dominions, if not to his own intelligence ? How could he be indifferent to the arts which educated it and increased his importance ? His happiest hours of rest from state affairs were passed among books, literati, and artists. The museum and the library were to him that which the stable and the cellar were to many feudal lords of the north ; everything that could cultivate or refine the mind was a necessary element of his life : in his palace the perfect courtier was formed, the modern gentleman came into existence.

There was, however, a strange contradiction in the men of that period, a contradiction that often appears to ¡us an insoluble enigma. We can forgive the savage passions and crimes of the Middle Ages, or can at all events understand them, but to behold men who speak and think like ourselves, men who experience genuine delight before a Madonna by Fra Angelico or Luca della Robbia, before the aerial curves of Alberti's and Brunelleschi's architecture, men who show disgust at a coarse attitude, at a gesture that is not of the most finished elegance ; to behold these men abandon themselves to the most atrocious crimes, the most obscene vices ; to behold them using poison to dismiss from the world some dangerous rival or relative : this it is that we cannot comprehend. It was a transitional period in which it may be said that the passions and characteristics of two different ages had been grafted one upon the other, in order to form before our eyes a mysterious sphinx which excites our wonder and almost our fear. But we should be too severe towards it were we to forget that one age may not be judged by the creeds and rules of another.

In whatever direction we turn our eyes, we behold the same facts reproduced under different forms. The military forces of the fifteenth century were no longer those of the Middle Ages, and, though widely different from, gave birth to the modern army. In the times of the Communes, wars were carried on by lightly armed foot-soldiers. Every spring the merchant, the artizan, buckled on their breastplates, marched outside the walls to the attack of baronial castles and neighbouring lands, and then went quietly back to their workshops. Very little importance was given to cavalry, which, for the most part, consisted of nobles. But as time went on all this entirely changed. Wars became much more complicated, and an army's main strength consisted in the heavy cavalry, or, as the phrase went, in the men-at-arms. Each one of these was followed by two or three horsemen, bearing the heavy armour, which he and his charger only donned in the hour of action, for its weight was so terrible, that if they fell to the ground with it, they could not rise again without help. And this species of iron-clad tower wielded a lance of enormous length, with which he could overthrow a foot-soldier before the latter could reach him with halberd or sword. One squadron of this cavalry was always enough to rout an army of infantry, until the invention of gunpowder and improvement of firearms again transformed the art of war. The Florentines learnt this to their cost, when on the field of Montaperti (1260) a handful of German cavalry, joined to the Ghibelline exiles, put to rout the strongest infantry force ever collected in Tuscany. And at Campaldino (1289) the Tuscan foot had to throw themselves under the horses of the men-at-arms and rip them up before they could win the battle. This new method of fighting had a fatal result for our republics. It required long training and continual practice to form a good man-at-arms ; how could artizans and merchants find time for that ? There were no standing armies in those days, and the aristocracy, which alone could have been trained to live under arms, had been destroyed in the Italian Communes. What then was to be done ? Recourse was had to foreigners, and the use of mercenary troops began.

In other countries the aristocracy preserved its power ; and accordingly there were plenty of men who made fighting their trade. These were always nobles with a following of vassals. Every time that the Emperor descended upon Italy, every time that the party of Anjou resumed their continual enterprises upon Naples, or the Spaniards made some new raid, there remained behind at the end of the campaign a number of soldiers and disbanded troops, who, eager of adventure, sought and took service under the different lords and Republics. The first arrivals always attracted others, for bountiful pay was given, and foreigners found us easy prey by reason of our lack of men-at-arms. Bands of adventurers began to be formed who sold their swords to the highest bidder. These soon became insolent bullies, dictating laws to friends and enemies alike. But little by little the Italians began to enrol themselves under these banners, and fascinated by the new way of life, multiplied so rapidly and succeeded so well that they soon set about forming native companies. Certainly there was no lack of material among us for captains and soldiers. What better career for party leaders who had been defeated in their ambitious design by still more ambitious rivals? They hurried to join the first band of adventurers they could find, and trained themselves to arms in order to command later a squadron or company of their own. By serving under a noted leader, or forming a band, the pettiest tyrants were enabled to defend and aggrandize their own State. When one Republic was conquered and subdued by another, the citizens who had ruled and then unsuccessfully defended it, sometimes emigrated *en masse* to wander about as adventurers, and sought in warfare the liberty they had lost at home. Thus did the Pisans when their Republic fell into the hands of the Florentines, and thus did many others. Country districts gave a good number of soldiers, and certain provinces like Romagna, the Marshes, and Umbria—where anarchy was so great that men seemed to live by rapine, vengeance, and brigandage—were a nursery and mart of mercenary leaders and soldiers.

These bands can neither be called a mediæval nor a modern institution. Peculiar to a transitional period, they had a temporary character, being composed of fragments of all the recently destroyed old institutions, and were altogether disastrous ; but nevertheless they were imbued with the spirit of the new Italian Renaissance, and owed their importance to it. Our Italian companies soon began to gain the upper hand over the foreign—especially after Alberico da Barbiano had created his new art of war—and assumed a different form and character. For the foreign bands were commanded by a council of leaders, each one of whom had great authority over his own men, who were generally, at least in part, his private vassals, and were ready to follow him and separate from the others whenever required. In Italy, on the contrary, the importance and strength of the band depended entirely on the valour and military genius of the man who commanded and almost personified it. The soldiers obeyed the supreme will of their head, without, however, being bound to him by any personal fealty or submission, and were ready to forsake him in favour of a more famous leader or higher pay. War became the work of a directing mind ; the army was held together by the name and courage of its commander ; every battle was, as it were, his own military creation.

Thus was formed the school of Alberico da Barbiano, to be speedily followed by those of Braccio da Montone, the Sforza, the Piccinini, and many more, each learning his trade in another's ranks. The Italian captain created the science and art of war, as the prince created the science and art of government. Both in one and the other were the highest manifestations of talent and individuality; in both the one and the other the moral strength was lacking which alone can give true stability to the works of man. The individual was nowhere more free from the conventional ties of the Middle Ages than in these bands; his fame and power alike depended solely on his own courage, his own genius.

Muzio Attendolo Sforza, one of the most terrible captains of his time, and who became High Constable of the Kingdom of Naples, had originally been a field-labourer, and began his military career as a stable-boy. His natural son, Francesco, was Duke of Milan. Carmagnola, commander-in-chief of the Venetian's most formidable armies, and lord of many estates, began life as a herdsman. Niccolò Piccinini, before becoming a famous captain, was a member of the guild of butchers in Perugia. Nor did these things cause the smallest surprise to any one. The free company was an open field to individual activity; strength, luck, and talent alone commanded in it; there were no traditional nor moral trammels of any sort. The Free Companies made war without serving any principle or any fatherland, transferring their aid from friends to enemies for higher pay or finer promises. As for military honour, maintenance of oaths, fidelity to his own banner, all such things were unknown to the free captain, who would have deemed it puerile and ridiculous to allow such obstacles to stop him on the road to fortune and power,—the sole objects of his life.

In many respects his career and character resembled those of the Italian tyrant. At the head of a complicated and difficult administration, he had daily to collect new soldiers, in order to fill vacancies in his ranks, caused more frequently by desertion than by the sword of the enemy, and he had daily to find the money for paying his men in peace and war. He was in continual relations with the Italian States, seeking employment and gaining money by threats or promises, and corresponding with those who made the highest bids to carry him off from their adversary. In fact, he resembled the lord of some city that moved from place to place, a circumstance that did not make it easier to govern ; even as the tyrant, he lived in perpetual danger, and more so when at peace than at war. He was constantly threatened by the jealousies of the other leaders of bands or companies ; by the ambition of his subordinates, who often plotted conspiracies against him ; also by fear of being left without an engagement, and having to disband his army for want of funds. Having no certainty of his good faith, the States he served always held him in suspicion, and from doubts passed readily to deeds, as was seen by the fate of Carmagnola and Paolo Vitelli, suddenly seized and beheaded, the one by the Venetians, the other by the Florentines, at the head of whose armies they fought. It was singular, too, to see these men—generally of low origin and devoid of culture—surrounded in their camps by ambassadors, poets, and learned men, who read to them Livy and Cicero, and original verses, in which they were compared to Scipio and Hannibal, to Cæsar and Alexander. When, as very often happened, they conquered some territory on their own account, or received it in return for their services, they were really captains and princes at the same time.

Thus, then, war became a kind of diplomatic and commercial operation for the Italian States ; he was the conqueror who could find most money, procure most friends, and best flatter and reward the celebrated captains whose fidelity was only to be kept alive by fresh money and fresh hopes. But soon the true military spirit began to perish among these soldiers, who fought to-day against their comrades of yesterday, with whom they might be again united in the next four-and-twenty hours. Their object was no longer victory, but spoil. Later the Free Companies disappeared altogether, to be replaced by the standing armies for whom they had prepared the way ; but they left behind them a load of heavy calamities, during which Italians gave proof of much talent and great courage ; founded the new art of war ; manifested an infinite variety of aptitudes, qualities, and military characteristics ; and yet became continually weaker, continually more corrupt.

In literature we see more clearly than elsewhere the general transformation that took place at this time. Our historians in general deplore, without seeming to understand why the Italians, after having created a splendid national literature by the " Divina Commedia," the " Decamerone," and the " Canzoniere," [1] should

---

[1] The Sonnets of Petrarch.

have gone astray from the glorious path, by turning to the imitation of ancient writers, almost despising their own tongue, and upholding the use of Latin. But on reading the works of Dante and Petrarch and Boccaccio, it is easy to perceive that these authors opened the path trodden by the fifteenth century. In the " Divina Commedia " antiquity holds throughout a post of honour, and is almost sanctified by a boundless admiration ; in the " Decameron " Latin periods already transform and transplace Italian periods ; Petrarch is undoubtedly the first of the men of learning.

Whoever compares Italian writers of the thirteenth century with those appearing at the end of the fifteenth and the beginning of the sixteenth centuries, will speedily see that the time spent upon the classics during that interval had not been thrown away. In fact, in reading, I will not say the " Fioretti di San Francesco " and the " Vite " of Cavalca, but the " Monarchia " and the " Convito " of Dante, and even the " Divina Commedia," we must, as it were, transport ourselves into another world ; the author frequently reasons in the old scholastic style ; neither observes nor sees the world as we see it. If, on the other hand, we look at the works of Guicciardini, Machiavelli, and their contemporaries, we find men who, even with different opinions, think and reason like ourselves. The scholastic systems, mysticism, and allegories of the Middle Ages have so entirely disappeared that no memory of them seems any longer to exist. We are on this earth, in the midst of reality, with men who no longer look upon the world through a fantastic veil of mystic illusion, but with their own eyes, their own reason, unenslaved by any authority. And thus the question arises : in what way did the scholars of the fifteenth century contrive to discover a new world by means of classical studies, almost as Columbus discovered America in seeking a fresh passage to the Indies ?

The Middle Ages, in order to re-awaken a new spiritual life in mankind, had despised earthly concerns and the needs of society, had subjected philosophy to theology, the State to the Church. The real was only considered useful as a symbol or allegory to express the ideal, the earthly city merely a preparation for the heavenly ; there was a reaction against all that had been the essence of Paganism, the inspiration of ancient art. Thus human reason remained shut up in scholastic syllogisms, in the clouds of mysticism, in the fantastic and complicated creations of the romances of chivalry and minstrelsy of Provence. But when with a sudden rush of new inspiration, Italian poetry and prose sprang up to describe the real passions and affections of mankind, sentence of death was passed on the world of the Middle Ages.[1] The old vague and fantastic forms could not stand against these new and precise analyses, this splendid imagery, this style and language, through which thought shines as through the purest crystal. This literature, however, in giving a new direction to the human mind, soon gave birth to new needs, all of which it could not satisfy. It is true that a poetic language was now in existence, that incomparable forms had been found for the tale, the sonnet, the song, and the poem : but the new philosophical, epistolary, oratorical, and historical styles were still unborn. For this reason the writer of the thirteenth century very often resembled a man who, in spite of having strong limbs, travels a road so narrow and so beset with obstacles, that he cannot walk without help ; in order to keep his feet he is obliged from time to time to support himself on scholastic crutches. Who can help perceiving that Dante himself had still one foot in the Middle Ages, when in his " Monarchia " we find him disputing whether the Pope should be compared to the sun, the Emperor to the moon : whether the fact of Samuel deposing Saul, and the offerings of the Magi to the infant Saviour, can prove the dependency of the Empire on the Church ? In reading the " Cronaca " of Giovanni Villani, we find not merely a writer of much graphic power, but a most acute observer, whom nothing escapes, a man practised in the world and its affairs. He sees and notes everything ; battles, revolutions both political and social, forms of government, new buildings, pictures and literary works, the industry, commerce, taxes, expenditure, and revenues of the republic ; for he sees that human society is composed of all these things, and that from them is derived the power and prosperity of States. Yet never once does he hit upon the logical unity of historic narration that connects all these

---

[1] My excellent colleague and friend, Professor A. Bartoli, in one of his "Memorie" among the "Pubblicazioni della Sezione di Filosofia e Filologia dell' Instituto Superiore" (Florence, Le Monnier and Co., 1875, vol. i. p. 351 following), has recently shown that the study of nature, as well as of the classics, had followers throughout the Middle Ages, and hence that the realism of the Renaissance had a more ancient origin than is generally believed. We, however, only treat of this historical period after it had already assumed a definite and determined form ; we do not explore its more remote origin.

elements together, and makes the connecting bond visible ; his work never rises above the modest limits of a chronicle. And whenever the writer of the thirteenth century treats of philosophy or politics, whenever he tries to compose an oration or a letter, he seems condemned to resume the fetters he has snapped.

It was necessary, therefore, to enlarge the limits of style ; to spread the language ; to render it more universal, more flexible ; to find out new literary forms which were still wanting, and had now become necessary. And this want began to be felt at the very moment when the young and vigorous growth of the national strength had been arrested by the political and social complications which we have already noted. Thus the spring of originality suddenly failed which had already created our litera-ture, and which alone could complete it, by leading it towards the new forms it sought. But as these forms are not changeable at pleasure, but determined by the laws of nature and of thought, and were first discovered by the Greeks and the Romans, in whose writings they still maintain all the vigour, splendour, and originality which works of art possess only at the moment of their first creation, a return towards the past presented itself as a natural means of progress, and the close relation of Italian culture to Latin made it seem like a new draught from the primal source, a return to the old national grandeur. The Greeks and the Latins offered to Italy a literature inspired by nature and reality, guided by reason alone, neither subject to any authority, nor veiled in the clouds of allegory or of mysticism ; to imitate this literature, then, was to break the last fetters of the Middle Ages. Thus in all things the impulse was towards the ancient world. It was there that painting and sculpture found perfected study of the human form and faultlessness of design ; it was there that architecture discovered a more solid mode of construction, and one better adapted to the various needs of social life ; it was there that the man of letters found the mastery of style of which he was in search, and the philo-sopher, independence of reason and observation of nature ; it was there, in the Roman world, that the politician beheld that State unity which not only science, but society itself, was then seeking as its necessary aim.

Imitation of the antique became a species of mania that seized upon all men ; tyrants sought to copy Cæsar and Augustus, republicans Brutus, free captains Scipio and Hannibal, philosophers Aristotle and Plato, men of letters Virgil and Cicero, even the names of persons and places were changed for Greek and Latin ones.

Yet the Middle Ages had certainly not ignored all ancient writers, and held some of them in almost religious respect. But mediæval classic learning was, with slight exception, very different from that which now arose. It had been restricted to a small number of the more recent Latin writers, who having lived under the Empire which still seemed to dominate the world, and was deemed immutable and immortal, were less removed from Christian ideas, were read almost as contemporary authors ; and whose works were twisted and bent to support the tenets of Christianity. Virgil prophesied the coming of Christ ; Cicero's ethics must be identical with those of the Gospels ; and Aristotle, known only in Latin translations and garbled by his commentators, was made to maintain the immortality and spirituality of the soul in which he had no belief. The tastes and desires of the fifteenth century were widely different. There was no desire now to transform the Pagan into the Christian world ; this century wished to recur to the former and be thus led back from the city of God to that of men, from heaven to earth. Therefore a knowledge of the more recent classic writers was no longer sufficient ; it was necessary to read all and the more ancient with most ardour, since they demanded a greater mental effort, and rendered necessary a longer ideal journey. For that reason ancient manuscripts were eagerly hunted for and commented upon, ancient monuments discussed with a feverish activity unexampled in history. It seemed as though the Italians wished not only to imitate the ancient world, but to raise it from the tomb and bring it to life again, since they felt that in it they learnt to know themselves, and entered, as it were, into a second life ; it was a true and genuine renaissance. Nor did they perceive that their imitations and reproductions were animated by a new spirit that went on gradually developing, at first in an invisible and hidden way, till at last it burst suddenly from its chrysalis, and shone forth in a national and modern shape. Thus it was by study of the ancients that the Italians were enabled to free themselves and Europe from the fetters of the Middle Ages, and instead of interrupting, they continued and completed in a different form the work begun by the writers of the thirteenth century.

The new literary and artistic productions were not, however, the result of a young and vigorous inspiration, born of a young and vigorous society,—such as that in which Dante lived,—full of ardour and faith, abounding in strong characters and stern passions. Produced at a period in which a feverish activity of the mind still continued, but the nobler aspirations of the human heart had ceased to exist, they showed the consequences of this state of things. Marvellous success is attained in all branches in which visible nature and the outer study of man and man's actions have the principal part. The fine arts, still plastic in their nature, lost the epic grandeur of Giotto and Orcagna, the religious inspiration of the old Christian cathedrals ; and assimilating classical forms—although unconsciously altering them— they were inspired by Grecian genius to imitate nature and reproduce it in new and spontaneous creations, surrounded by an ethereal veil, with colours of unequalled brilliancy and freshness. It was an art that, through the ingrafting of Christian upon Pagan forms, acquired new spontaneousness and purity ; shed immortal glory on its age and nation, and was the most complete manifestation of the Renaissance from which it was derived and to which it communicated its own special character. The poetry of this period was also unrivalled in its descriptions and reproductions of the real which stood out clear and well defined, even amidst the most fantastic creations of the chivalric and tragi-comic poem. Political science, treating of human actions in their objective and exterior value, in their practical consequences, almost apart from the moral character they acquire in the human conscience, and the intentions by which they are inspired, not only flourished, but was the most original creation of the fifteenth and sixteenth centuries.

Men worked with irresistible energy ; they sought and found every possible form of literature ; they acquired immense truth and facility in prose and poetry ; they created the language and style of oratory, diplomacy, history, and philosophy, but the religious sentiment disappeared ; moral sensibility was weakened, and the cultivation of form often increased to the disadvantage of substance, a defect which has endured for centuries in Italian literature, almost as a witness of the conditions under which it took its definite form. In considering this prodigious intellectual activity, that reappeared with increasing splendour in a thousand different shapes, yet always accompanied by moral decay, the historian of those times is struck with terrified amazement, recognizing the presence of a mysterious contradiction, prophetic of future ills. When the evil secretly corroding this nation came to the surface, a tremendous catastrophe was inevitable ; and its continual advance side by side with so much intellectual progress, is precisely the history of the Renaissance. For the better comprehension of this, it is needful to examine matters still more closely.

II.

THE PRINCIPAL ITALIAN STATES.

1. *Milan.*

T Milan, for the first time, we find an Italian Commune transformed, through tyranny, into a modern State. Having become the centre of a vast agglomeration of republics and lordships, now united and now separated by different interests and jealousies, there arose in its midst the power of the Visconti, who were divided among themselves by private and bloody dissensions. In 1378, Bernabò Visconti was in conflict with his nephew Giovan Galeazzo, better known by his title of Count of Virtù. Both equally ambitious and equally wicked, the first was a blind slave to his passions, and in consequence fell a victim to his nephew, who knew how to direct his own towards a given end. The latter succeeded in 1378 in throwing him and his children into a dungeon, which they never left alive ; and these obstacles removed, he began vigorously to re-organize the State and put down anarchy.

Beset by a thousand enemies, Giovan Galeazzo had no army, and was even deficient in military courage ; but he joined to grea' cunning a profound knowledge of mankind, and real political genius. Shut up in his castle of Pavia, he took into his service the first captains in Italy, and the most renowned diplomatists, weaving, with the help of the latter, the threads of his dark policy all over the Peninsula, which he quickly filled with intrigues and wars ; he, the while, directing military operations in the solitude of his cabinet.

Thanks to his sureness of eye and promptness of will, he succeeded in making a complete hecatomb of the petty tyrants of Lombardy, allying himself with one to ruin another, and finally turning against those who had helped him, and assuming possession of their States. Thus he formed the Duchy of Milan, of which he received the investiture from the Emperor. He then extended his dominions to Genoa, Bologna, and Tuscany, and hoped to place the crown of Italy upon his head, after defeating Florence, which he had already worn out by continual wars. But on the 3rd of December, 1402, death put an end to all his projects. It is marvellous to observe how, in the privacy of his cabinet, he undertook many skilfully conducted wars, and brought them to a successful close, while at the same time engaged in creating and ordering a new State. Although the chief object of his government was the imposition of taxes to pay for his incessant warfare, justice was generally well administered, the finances were well regulated, and general prosperity was on the increase. The free assemblies were converted into councils of administration and police, and every city had a *Potestà*, elected, no longer by the people, but by the Duke; the Commune was no longer a State, but, as in modern times, an organ of administration; a *collegio*, or council of men of authority in the capital, already shadowed forth the modern cabinet. Surrounded by *literati* and artists—initiator of great public works, among which are the two noblest monuments in Lombardy—the Cathedral of Milan and the Certosa of Pavia, where, too, he gave new life and renown to the university — Gian Galeazzo Visconti is the first of modern princes. Under his rule mediæval institutions entirely disappeared, and the unity of the new State was established. This, however, being an altogether personal creation, with no object beyond the individual interest of the prince, after his death the State quickly lapsed into anarchy, torn by the contending ambitions of mercenary leaders.

Later, Filippo Maria, son of Giovan Galeazzo, took in hand the reins of government, and followed in his father's footsteps. He had been compelled to share the State with his brother Giovanni Maria, a ferocious man, who threw his victims to be torn to pieces by the large pack of dogs he kept for that purpose; but the daggers of conspirators came to Filippo's aid, and on the 12th of May, 1412, Giovanni was stabbed in a church. Filippo was a degenerate copy of his father, cunning, false, traitorous, and cruel; he did not possess Giovan Galeazzo's political faculty, but he united perfect control over his passions to a wide knowledge of mankind. Timid even to cowardice, he had the strangest passion for rushing into continual and dangerous wars. These, however, he conducted by means of the first captains in Italy, selected with admirable discrimination, and whom he contrived to make each in turn suspicious of the other, in order to secure his own safety from their ambition. Surrounded by spies, shut up in his castle of Milan, which he never left, he duped everybody, always finding fresh opportunities of deceit ; he lived in perpetual conflict with other States, yet always escaped defeat by craft. The Florentines were routed by him at Zagonara in 1424 ; by the Venetians, whom he always opposed, he was defeated over and over again ; but after making peace—not always on honourable terms—he quickly collected more money and again declared war. He even threw himself into the Neapolitan struggle between the Angevins and the Aragonese, and succeeded in capturing Alphonso of Aragon, whom he afterwards liberated, in order to deprive the Angevins of complete victory. In the midst of the great tumult of events and enemies that he had provoked, he reconquered and reorganized the paternal State, holding it securely by force of his diabolical cunning down to the day of his death in 1447.

Having no legitimate heirs, and only one natural daughter, Bianca, had made his condition all the more perilous, since there were many who aspired to succeed him. Among them was one, recognized throughout Italy as the first captain of his time, to whose aid Visconti was continually obliged to recur, as he found himself perpetually at his mercy. Francesco Sforza was a lion who knew how to play the fox, and Filippo Maria was a fox who liked to don the lion's skin. They went on for many years, each lying in wait for the other, and each thoroughly aware of the other's secret designs. Often and often Sforza was on the brink of total ruin, ensnared in the plots of Visconti, who then came to his assistance. In 1441 Filippo gave him his daughter in marriage, thus nourishing his most ambitious hopes, the better to make use of him in war, yet always weaving fresh plots against him, from which, on his side, Sforza as often escaped without ever yielding to any wish for revenge. And in this way, when, after a reign of nearly fifty years, Visconti died a natural death, Sforza had power enough to succeed in his long meditated design.

And now one dynasty is replaced by another, and the Italian

prince is presented to us under a totally different aspect. The Visconti had been a great family, and by cunning, daring, and political genius, had become masters of the Duchy they had built up. The Sforza, on the contrary, were new men, of obscure origin, and fought their way with the sword. Muzio Attendolo, the father of Francesco Sforza, was born of a Romagnol family, living a life of semi-brigandage and hereditary *vendette* in Cotignola. It is said that the kitchen of their house looked like an arsenal : among dishes and smoky saucepans hung breastplates, swords, and daggers, which the family, men, women, and children, all used with equal courage. While yet a mere lad, Muzio was carried off by a band of adventurers, and being shortly afterwards joined by his own people, he took the command of his company, and was known by the name of Sforza, which was given to him in the field. Possessed of indomitable courage, strength, and energy, he was less a general than a soldier who joined in the *mêlée* and killed his enemies with his own hands. Of a very impetuous disposition, some of his actions were those of a brigand, as for instance when he ran his sword through Ottobuono III. of Parma, while parleying with the Marquis of Este. Yet by perpetually transferring his services from one master to another, carrying disorder and devastation wherever he went, he succeeded in becoming lord of many lands, which he kept for himself and his faithful followers. It was in the kingdom of Naples, while in the pay of the capricious queen, Joanna II., that he passed through his chief and strangest vicissitudes : first general, then prisoner, now High Constable of the kingdom, then once more in prison, he was on the point of perishing miserably, when at Tricarico his sister Margherita, sword in hand, and a helmet on her head, so thoroughly frightened the royal messengers that she obtained her brother's release. He was again given the command of the royal forces, and afterwards died near Aquila, drowned in the Pescara river, while swimming across it to urge his men to follow him on to a victory that seemed already assured. And thus ended a life no less stormy than the sea in which his body found a grave (1424).

Francesco, his natural son, a youth of twenty-three years, instantly took command of his father's troops, and led them on from victory to victory, giving proof of true military genius and great political acumen. Always master of himself, he never gave way to his passions, excepting when it was expedient to do so. He served the Visconti against the Venetians, the Venetians against the Visconti ; he first attacked the Pope, depriving him of Romagna, and giving his orders, *invitis Petro et Paulo*, and then defended him. Through his military genius he became the man whom all desired to have in their service, for it seemed as though no power in Italy could be victorious without him, although captains such as the Piccinini and Carmagnola were then flourishing. But amidst all these vicissitudes he kept his eye upon one fixed point, and on the death of Filippo Maria, it was quickly seen how a free captain could change into a statesman.

A Republic had been proclaimed in Milan ; its subject cities had thrown off the yoke ; Venice was threatening, and internal dissensions had broken out. He offered the aid of his sword to the tottering city which believed it had found in him an anchor of safety, and then gradually found itself besieged by its own captain, who, on the 25th of March, 1430, made his triumphal entry, with an already arranged court. His first act was to ask the people whether, to defend themselves against the Venetians, they would prefer to rebuild the fortress of Porta Giovio, or maintain a permanent army within the walls. They voted for the fortress, which soon became the strongest bulwark of tyranny against the people. Friends and enemies alike, if formidable, were quickly imprisoned, deprived of everything they possessed, and even put to death without hesitation. All the State territories were reconquered, rebellion was suppressed, order, administration, and common justice were re-established with marvellous rapidity. And in all these acts Sforza proceeded with the calmness of a man who knows his own strength, and desires to gain a reputation for impartiality and justice. Yet, whenever it seemed opportune, no one knew better than he how to get rid of friends and enemies with perfidious cruelty.

The Revolt of Piacenza was suffocated in the blood of his faithful captain, Brandolini. When the slaughter had reached its climax, and everything was pacified, Brandolini was thrown into prison, to the general amazement, as a suspected person, and was afterwards found with his throat cut and a blunted and bloody sword by his side. The populace said that the Duke had thus punished his captain's excessive cruelty ; the keener witted declared that the Duke, after having used him to the utmost, had got rid of a useless instrument, so that on the latter alone the odium of the enormous bloodshed might fall. Born and

reared in war, the Duke now wished to be a man of peace, and
aimed only at the consolidation of his own State within its
natural boundaries, totally abandoning the ambitious and perilous
designs of the Visconti. And when, after an almost universal,
but not very important war, the Italian potentates concluded a
general peace in 1454, Sforza contrived to make himself implicitly
recognized by all, and retained the territories of Bergamo, Ghiara
d'Adda, and Brescia. Noted as one of the most audacious and
turbulent free captains, he was in a position to know what heavy
calamities they bring upon orderly and pacific States ; hence he
was one of those who chiefly contributed, if not to put them
down, at least to deprive them of much of their past importance,
as indeed was already happening by the natural force of events.
Jacopo Piccinini was now the sole survivor of the old school of
mercenary leaders, and truly one who had only to raise his
standard to assemble a formidable army. He was living quietly
in Milan, when he was seized by a desire to visit his lands in
the kingdom of Naples, and was much encouraged in this by
the Duke, although every one knew how sorely he was hated by
Ferrante d'Aragona. No sooner did he reach Naples than he
was received with open arms by the king, who took him to see
the palace, and then threw him into a dungeon, where he soon
died. Sforza protested loudly against this breach of faith ; but
all men believed that by agreement with the king, he had thus
freed himself of an inconvenient neighbour.

Francesco Sforza was, as a modern historian [1] happily expresses
it, a man after the heart of the fifteenth century. A great
captain and an acute politician, he knew how to play both the
lion and the fox ; when bloodshed was necessary, he did not
shrink from it, but at other times he sought to distribute impartial justice, and even showed himself capable of generosity
and pity. He founded a dynasty, conquered a dominion, which
he left secure and well governed, and constructed great public
works, such as the Martesana Canal and the chief hospital of Milan.
Surrounded by Greek exiles and Italian scholars, the Court of the
whilom adventurer speedily became one of the most splendid in

---

[1] Burckhardt, "Die Cultur der Renaissance in Italien :" Basle, 1860. Since
then a second edition of this important work, with several changes and additions,
has appeared, and now a very faithful Italian translation has been published by
Professor D. Valbusa, with many original additions and corrections by the
author, "La Civiltà del secolo del rinascimento in Italia ec." Florence, Sansoni,
1876.

all Italy, and his daughter Ippolita was renowned for her Latin
discourses, which were universally extolled. The famous Cicco
(Francesco) Simonetta, a most learned Calabrian, and a man of
proved fidelity, was the Duke's secretary, his brother Giovanni
was his historian, and Francesco Filelfo, the courtier poet, sang
his praises in the " Sforziade." Thus, celebrated in prose and verse
as the just, the great, the magnanimous, Francesco Sforza breathed
his last on the 8th of March, 1466. He had attempted all things,
succeeded in all things, therefore his contemporaries believed him
the greatest man of the age. But of what nature was the State
that he had actually constituted ? A society whose every element
of strength was rapidly exhausted ; a people whom its sovereign
believed he could mould into any form he would, as .if they were
plastic material in the hands of a new artist, whose sole merit
consists in carrying out the ends he proposes, whatever those
ends may be. Neither the Visconti nor Sforza ever conceived
any truly great or fertile political idea, for they never identified
themselves with the people, but only made it an instrument of
their own interests. They were masters in the art of governing,
but they never succeeded in founding a true government, for by
their own tyranny they had destroyed its essential elements. The
fatal consequences of their policy, which was too truly the
Italian policy of the fifteenth century, were to be speedily made
apparent throughout the Peninsula, just as on the Duke's death
they began to be manifested in Milan.

Sforza's dissolute and cruel son, Galeazzo Maria, had so depraved
a disposition that he was even accused of having poisoned his
own mother. In the belief that all was lawful and possible for
a prince, he, in an age that might almost be called civilized,
caused several of his subjects to be buried alive, others, on the
most frivolous pretexts, he condemned to death amid lingering
tortures, and only spared those who could redeem their lives with
gold. He dissipated treasures in his festivals at Milan, and
his cavalcades all through Italy, spreading corruption wherever he went. Not content with seducing the daughters of the
noblest Milanese houses, he himself exposed them to public contempt. Neither public institutions nor popular indignation
imposed a check upon his unbridled licence, for the people no
longer existed, and all institutions had become mere engines of
tyranny.

At last an end was put to this state of things by one of the

most singular and noteworthy of the many conspiracies for which
this age was remarkable.

Girolamo Olgiati and Giannandrea Lampugnani, pupils of
Niccola Montano, who had trained them by classical studies to
love, liberty, hate, and tyranny, being injured by the Duke,
resolved on revenge, and found in Carlo Visconti a third companion moved by the same motives. They strengthened their
zeal for the enterprise by the study of Sallust and Tacitus, they
practised stabbing with the sheaths of daggers, and, having
arranged everything for the 26th of December, 1476, Olgiati
went to the church of St. Ambrose, threw himself at the Saint's
feet, and prayed for success. On the morning of the chosen
day the three conspirators attend divine service in the church
of St. Stephen, and recited a Latin prayer expressly composed
by Visconti : "If thou lovest justice and hatest iniquity,"
they besought the Saint, "fashion our magnanimous enterprise, and be not wrathful if we must presently stain thy altars
with blood, in order to free the world of a monster." The
Duke was killed, but Visconti and Lampugnani fell victims to
the fury of the populace, who wished to revenge their own
executioner. Olgiati sought safety in flight, but was soon
captured and condemned to a cruel death. When shattered by
torture, he called to his aid the shades of the Romans, and
commended his soul to the Virgin Mary. Being urged to repent,
he declared that had he to die ten times over amid those tortures,
ten times would he cheerfully consecrate his blood to so heroic a
deed. Up to his last moments he continued to compose Latin
epigrams, congratulating himself when they were neatly turned ;
and as the headsman drew near, his last words were :—" *Collige
te, Hieronyme, stabit vetus memoria facti. Mors acerba fama
perpetua.*" [1] Here we see that while all political feeling was
extinguished in the people, there were a few individuals in whom
Christian and profane sentiments, love of liberty, and ferocious
personal hatred, heroic resignation and unquenchable thirst for
blood, vengeance, and glory, were all mingled in the strangest
way. Ruins of old systems and remains of various civilizations

---

[1] Machiavelli says instead : *Mors acerba, fama perpetua, stabit vetus memoria
facti.* "Storie," vol. ii. lib. vii. p. 203. Olgiati's confession is found in Corio.
See also Rosmini's "Storia di Milano," vol. iii. p. 23 ; Gregorovius, "Geschichte
der Stadt Rom" (zweite Auflage), vol. vii. p. 241 and fol. ; "Cola Montano,
Studii storici" di Gerolamo Lorenzi Milan, 1875.

were confused together in the Italian mind, while the germ was budding of a new individual and social form, which had as yet no well-defined outline. Later, Lodovico il Moro, the late Duke's brother, an ambitious, timid, restless man, usurped his nephew Galeazzo's dominions, and, to keep up his unjustly acquired power, threw all Italy into confusion, as we shall have occasion to notice, when, after examining the condition of the different States, we give a general glance at the whole Peninsula.

2. *Florence.*

The history of Florence shows us a condition of things widely different from that of Milan. At first sight it seems as though we were plunged in a huge chaos of confused events of which we can understand neither the reason nor the aim. But on closer examination we find a clue, and can perceive how the Florentine Republic, amid an infinite series of revolutionary changes, and every political institution known to the Middle Ages, steadily aimed at the triumph of the democracy, the total destruction of feudalism, and achieved these objects by means of Giano della Bella's *Ordinamenti della Giustizia* in the year 1493. From that date Florence became exclusively a city of traders, was no longer divided between nobles and burghers, but between *fat* people and *small* people (*popolo grasso* and *popolo minuto*), into major and minor arts or guilds. Of these, the former were engaged in wholesale commerce and the great business of exportation and importation, while the latter carried on the retail traffic and internal trade of the city. From this arose division and often collision of interests, and thence the formation of new political parties. Whenever it was a question of aggrandizing the territory of the Republic ; of making war upon Pisa to keep open the way to the sea, or upon Sienna to monopolize trade with Rome ; or of repulsing the continual and threatening attacks of the Visconti of Milan, government invariably fell into the hands of the Arti Maggiori, who were richer, more enterprising and better able to comprehend and guard the important interests of the State beyond its boundaries. But, when war was at an end, and peace re-established, then immediately the Arti Minori, spurred on by the lowest populace, rose in rebellion against the new aristocracy of wealth which oppressed them with continual wars and taxes, and demanded increased liberty and more general equality.

These continual alternations lasted more than a century, namely, down to the time when the territory of the Republic was constituted, and the prolonged wars with Milan came to an end. Then the final triumph of the minor guilds became inevitable, and it was their inexperience and intemperance that smoothed the way for the establishment of the tyranny of the Medici.

It would, however, be a mistake to imagine that the Medici rose to power by the same means and artifices employed by the Visconti and the Sforza. Had any one arbitrarily attempted to torture the citizens of Florence, to bury any of them alive, or to have them torn to pieces by dogs, as did the Lords of Milan, he would have been instantly swept away by the popular indignation, and by the union of the Greater and Lesser guilds. The importance and political speciality of the Medici consisted precisely in the fact that their victory was the result of traditional rules of conduct carried out by that family, for more than a century, with unrivalled constancy and acuteness, so that they contrived to consolidate their power without having recourse to violence. And to have succeeded in this in a city so acute, so restless, so jealous of its ancient liberties, was a proof of true political genius. As far back as 1378, during the disorderly revolt of the Ciompi, we find the hand of Salvestro di Medici, who, although belonging to the greater guilds, assisted and spurred on the lesser to overthrow their power, thus achieving great popularity. That tumult being suppressed, and war having again broken out—the greater guilds and the Albizzi family being therefore once more in power—we find Vieri dei Medici leading a quiet life, always devoted to money-making. He never ceased, however, to show himself favourable to the popular party, in which he contrived to gain so much influence that Machiavelli said of him :—"That, had he been more ambitious than good, he might, without hindrance, have made himself master of the city." [1]

But Vieri understood too well the temper of the times, and was content to wait and prepare the way for Giovanni di Bicci, who was the true political founder of his house. This latter clearly saw the impossibility of changing the government of Florence by violent means, and that no object was to be gained by holding power, even repeatedly, in a Republic which changed its chief

[1] Machiavelli, " Storie," vol. i. lib. iii. p. 193.

magistrates every two months. There was but one method of obtaining real and assured predominance, namely, by marshalling under his orders a party of sufficient strength and prudence to guarantee the highest offices of the Republic to its own adherents in perpetuity. And the Albizzi had soon occasion to perceive that this design was prospering, for their adversaries—notwithstanding perpetual admonishments and sentences of exile—were always elected in increasing numbers. In vain the former attempted to countermine Giovanni dei Medici's work by inopportune proposals of laws intended to weaken the Lesser Guilds, for they could not get them passed in Council without their adversary's help, and this he openly refused them, thus continually increasing his power with the people (1426). It was Giovanni dei Medici who proposed and supported the law of *Catasto*,[1] by which it was ordained that the amount of every citizen's possessions should be verified and registered, a law which prevented the powerful from levying taxes *ad libitum* to the oppression of the weak. The law was carried, the authority of the Medici was thereby much increased, and, while really making a rapid flight towards power, they seemed to be wholly intent on giving a more democratic form to the Republic. This, both then and afterwards, was their favourite device.

When Cosimo dei Medici succeeded his father in 1429, he was forty years of age, and being already a man of great authority and fortune on his own account, found his way clear before him. He had largely increased his paternal inheritance by commerce, and he used his means so generously, lending and giving on all sides, that there was hardly any man of weight in Florence who had not sought and received help from him in moments of need. Thus, without ever laying aside, at all events in appearance, the modesty of the private citizen, every day saw the increase of his influence, which was employed by him to destroy the last remains of the power of the Albizzi and their friends. These, goaded to desperation, rose in rebellion, and drove him into exile, not daring to do worse (1433). But Cosimo still preserved his prudent calm. He went to Venice in the attitude of a benefactor repaid by ingratitude, and was everywhere received like a prince. The following year a popular revolt, fomented by a countless number of those whom he had benefited—or who hoped for benefits on the fall of

[1] Upon this point there has been much controversy. *Vide* " Archivio Storico Italiano," series v. vol. i. p. 185.

the Albizzi—recalled him to Florence.   If powerful at his departure, he was much more powerful on his return, and was, moreover, animated by a spirit of revenge.   He now threw aside his former reserve in order to profit by the favourable moment.   Without shedding too much blood, he thoroughly broke up the adverse party by means of persecution and exile, abasing the great and exalting men "of low and vile condition." [1]   To those who accused him of excess, and of ruining too many citizens, he was accustomed to answer : that States could not be governed by paternosters, and that with a few ells of crimson cloth, new and worthy citizens could easily be manufactured. [2]

Cosimo dei Medici was now *de facto* master of Florence, but he was still, *de jure*, a private citizen, whose power, based solely and wholly on his personal influence, might fail at any moment. Therefore, he set to work to consolidate it, by a method as novel as it was sagacious.   He brought about the creation of a *Balìa,* empowered to elect chief magistrates for a term of five years. Composed of citizens devoted to himself, this Balìa secured his position for a long time ; and by having it renewed every five years in the same way, he was able to solve the strange problem of being for all the rest of his life, Prince and absolute master of a Republic, without ever holding any public office, or discarding the semblance of a private citizen.   This did not, however, prevent him from occasionally having recourse to bloodshed.   When he beheld in the city the daily increasing power of Neri dei Gino Capponi, that sagacious politician and valiant soldier, who had the support of Baldaccio d'Anghiari, Captain of the infantry forces, Cosimo, not daring to attack him openly, determined to do so through his friends.   Accordingly, no sooner was a personal enemy of Baldaccio elected Gonfaloniere, than, during a sudden tumult, Baldaccio was thrown from a window of the palace of the Signoria ; and all men suspected, though none could prove, that Cosimo was the chief instigator of the crime. [3]   But after this he continued to govern with what were then called *modi civili*, or gentle means, and which were always the device of the Medici.

[1] Guicciardini, "Storia di Firenze," p. 6.

[2] He meant by this that given the cloth necessary for robes of office, all men could be citizens.

[3] Machiavelli, who in his "Storie Florentine" frequently tries to exculpate the Medici, considers the Gonfalonier Bartolommeo Orlandini sole author of the crime. Guicciardini, on the contrary, who in his "Storia di Firenze," judges the Medici much more impartially, attributes everything to Cosimo.

FRANCESCO SFORZA.

(*From the relief in the National Museum of Florence.*)

Though possessed of but little culture, this sagacious merchant, nailed to his office desk, this unscrupulous politician, surrounded himself with artists and men of letters. Frugal to meanness in his personal expenditure, he lavished treasures in encouraging the fine arts, in constructing churches, libraries, and other public edifices : he passed the most delightful hours of his life in listening to and commenting on Plato's "Dialogues ;" he founded the Platonic Academy. Thus it is in great measure owing to him that Florence now became the principal centre of European culture. He had divined that in modern society, arts, letters, and science were becoming a power which every government ought to take into account.

Nor was his foreign policy less sagacious. Having protected Nicholas and helped him with money when he was a Cardinal, he found him most friendly as Pope ; and thus the business affairs of the Curia were entrusted to the Medici's bank in Rome, no little to their profit. Sooner than other men, Cosimo had foreseen the future destiny of Francesco Sforza, and had gained his friendship : so that the latter on becoming Lord of Milan, proved a powerful and faithful ally. Then the continual wars with Milan came to an end, and Florence owed to Cosimo a long enduring peace. So it is not surprising if, after his death, the rule of the Medici still going on, he should be styled *Pater patriae*. Machiavelli declares that he was the most renowned citizen, " for a civilian " " d'uomo disarmato " that Florence, or any other city, ever possessed. In his opinion, no man ever equalled Cosimo in political insight, for he discerned evils from afar, and provided against them in time ; thus he was able to hold the State for thirty-one years, "through so great variety of fortune, in so restless a city, with citizens of so changeable a temper." (" In tanta varietà di fortuna, in sì varia città, e volubile cittadinanza.") [1]. Nor was the equally authoritative opinion of Guicciardini different from this. Yet under his course of policy all the old Florentine institutions were reduced to empty names, without one new one springing up ; thus continual vigilance and an inexhaustible series of ever fresh contrivances were required to carry on the machinery of the State.

The last years of Cosimo's life passed very dismally for Florence, since the adherents of the Medici, no longer restrained by the prudence of their chief, who was now overcome by the infirmi-

[1] Machiavelli, " Storie," vol. ii. pp. 148–52.

ties of age, began to show their partizanship ; and to persecute and exile their enemies to excess. Nor were things changed during the short rule of Cosimo's son Piero. But at his death (1469), Lorenzo and Giuliano appeared upon the scene : and the first of these, though only twenty-one years old, was already a notable personage. Educated by the first men of letters of the age, he had proved himself the equal of many of them in wit and learning ; in travelling through Italy to visit the different courts and gain experience of mankind, he had left everywhere a great opinion of his talents. He resolutely seized the reins of government, and foreseeing that the election of the new Balìa would not be certain in the Council of the Hundred, he managed, with the help of his most trustworthy friends, and as if by surprise, to have the Signori in office and the old Balìa empowered to elect the new. Having in this manner secured a five years' term of power, he was able to set to work without anxiety.

Lorenzo inherited his grandfather's political sagacity and far surpassed him in talent and literary culture. In many respects too he was a very different man. Cosimo never left his business office ; Lorenzo neglected it, and had so little commercial aptitude that he was obliged to retire from business, in order to preserve his abundant patrimony. Cosimo was frugal in his personal expenses and lent freely to others : Lorenzo loved splendid living, and thus gained the title of the Magnificent ; he spent immoderately for the advancement of literary men ; he gave himself up to dissipation which ruined his health and shortened his days. His manner of living reduced him to such straits, that he had to sell some of his possessions and obtain money from his friends. Nor did this suffice ; for he even meddled with the public money, a thing that had never happened in Cosimo's time. Very often, in his greed of unlawful gain, he had the Florentine armies paid by his own bank ; he also appropriated the sums collected in the *Monte Comune* or treasury of the public debt, and those in the *Monte delle Fanciulle*, where marriage portions were accumulated by private savings—moneys hitherto held sacred by all.

Stimulated by the same greed, he, in the year 1472, joined the Florentine contractors for the wealthy alum mines of Volterra, at the moment in which that city was on the verge of rebellion in order to free itself from a contract which it deemed unjust. And Lorenzo, with the weight of his authority, pushed matters to such a point that war broke out, soon to be followed by a most cruel sack of the unhappy city, a very unusual event in Tuscany.[1] For all this he was universally blamed. But he was excessively haughty, and cared for no man : he would tolerate no equals, would be first in everything—even in games. He interfered in all matters, even in private concerns and in marriages : nothing could take place without his consent. In overthrowing the powerful and exalting men of low condition, he showed none of the care and precaution so uniformly observed by Cosimo.

It is not then surprising if his enemies increased so fast as to lead to that formidable conspiracy of the Pazzi of the 26th of April, 1478. In this plot, hatched in the Vatican itself where Sixtus IV. was Lorenzo's decided enemy, many of the mightiest Florentine families took part. In the cathedral, at the moment of the elevation of the Host, the conspirators' daggers were unsheathed. Giuliano dei Medici was stabbed to death, but Lorenzo defended himself with his sword and saved his own life. The tumult was so great that it seemed as though the walls of the church were shaken. The populace rose to the cry of *Palle ! Palle !* the Medici watchword, and the enemies of the Medici were slaughtered in the streets or hung from the windows of the Palazzo Vecchio. There, among others, were seen the dangling corpses of Archbishop Salviati and of Francesco Pazzi, who, gripping each other with their teeth in their last struggle, retained that posture for a time. More than seventy persons perished that day, and Lorenzo, taking advantage of the opportunity, pushed matters to extremity by his confiscations, banishments, and sentences of death. Thereby his power would have been infinitely increased if Pope Sixtus IV., blinded by rage, had not been induced to excommunicate Florence, and make war against it, in conjunction with Ferdinand of Aragon. On this Lorenzo, without losing a moment, went straight to Naples, and made the king understand how much better it would serve his interests for Florence to have but one ruler, instead of a republican government always liable to change and certainly never friendly to Naples. So he returned with peace re-established and boundless authority and popularity. Now indeed he might have called himself lord of the city, and it must have seemed easy to him to destroy the republican government altogether. With his pride and ambition it is certain that

[1] *Vide*, among other Florentine historians of the time, the "Cronache Volterrane," published by Tabarrini in the "Archivio Storico," vol. iii. p. 317 and fol.

he had an intense desire to stand on the same level with the other princes and tyrants of Italy, the more so as at that moment success seemed entirely within his grasp. But Lorenzo showed that his political shrewdness was not to be blinded by prosperity, and knowing Florence well, he remained firm to the traditional policy of his house, *i.e.*, of dominating the Republic, while apparently respecting it.

He was well determined to render his power solid and durable ; and to that end had recourse to a most ingenious reform, by means of which, without abandoning the old path, he thoroughly succeeded in his aim.

In place of the usual five-yearly Balìa, he instituted, in 1480, the Council of Seventy, which renewed itself and resembled a permanent Balìa with still wider powers. This, composed of men entirely devoted to his cause, secured the government to him for ever. By this Council, say the chroniclers of the time, liberty was wholly buried and undone,[1] but certainly the most important affairs of the State were carried on in it by intelligent and cultivated men, who largely promoted the general prosperity. Florence still called itself a republic, the old institutions were nominally still in existence, but all this seemed and was no more than an empty mockery. Lorenzo, absolute lord of all, might certainly be called a tyrant, surrounded by lackeys and courtiers—whom he often rewarded by entrusting them with the management of charitable funds ;—leading a life of scandalous immorality, keeping up continual and general *espionnage ;* interfering in the most private affairs ; forbidding marriages between persons of condition that were not to his taste, and bestowing the most important offices on the lowest men, who thus, as Guicciardini puts it, " had become rulers of the roast." [2] Yet he dazzled all men by the splendour of his rule, so that the same writer observes, that though Lorenzo was a tyrant, " it would be impossible to imagine a better and more pleasing tyrant."

Industry, commerce, public works had all received a mighty impulse. In no city in the world had the civil equality of modern States reached the degree to which it had attained not merely in

[1] " Diarii di Alamanno Rinuccini," published by Ajazzi, Florence, 1840, pp. cx-xii. In the " Archivio Storico," vol. i. pp. 315 and fol., are the two *Provisions* that instituted the Council of Seventy, published and annotated by the Marchese Gino Capponi.

[2] " Storia Fiorentina," chap. ix. p. 91.

Florence itself, but in its whole territory and throughout all Tuscany. Administration and secular justice proceeded regularly enough in ordinary cases, crime was diminished, and above all, literary culture had become a substantial element of the new State. Learned men were employed in public offices, and from Florence spread a light that illuminated the world. Lorenzo, with his varied and well-cultivated talents, his keen penetration and unerring judgment in all departments of knowledge, was no ordinary patron and Mæcenas ; he stood among the first *literati* of his age, and took an active part in the labours he promoted, not only in the interests of his government, but also from real and undoubted intellectual taste. Nevertheless, in order to turn letters to political uses, he endeavoured by his festivals and his carnivalesque songs to enervate and corrupt the people, and succeeded only too well. Thus, without an army, without the lawful command of the State, he was master of Florence and of Tuscany, and moreover exercised immense influence over all the Italian potentates. His enemy, Sixtus IV., was dead. Pope Innocent VIII. was not only his friend, but married a relation into his family, bestowed a Cardinal's hat on his infant son Giovanni, and always turned to him for advice. The inextinguishable hatred that burned between Lodovic the Moor and Ferdinand of Aragon, a hatred which threatened to set all Italy ablaze, was held in bounds by Lorenzo—for that reason rightly called the balancing needle of Italy—and it was not till after his death that it led to fatal consequences. His political letters, frequently examples of political wisdom as well as elegance, were pronounced by the historian Guicciardini to be among the most eloquent of the age.

But Lorenzo's policy could found nothing that was permanent. Unrivalled as a model of sagacity and prudence, it promoted in Florence the development of all the new elements of which modern society was to be the outcome, without succeeding in fusing them together ; for his was a policy of equivocation and deceit, directed by a man of much genius, who had no higher aim than his own interest and that of his family, to which he never hesitated to sacrifice the interests of his people.

3. *Venice.*

The history of Venice stands in apparently direct contradiction with that of Florence. The latter, in fact, shows us a series of revolutions which, starting from an aristocratic government, reached the extreme point of democratic equality, only to fall later under the despotism of a single head ; while Venice, on the contrary, proceeded with order and firmness to the formation of an increasingly powerful aristocracy. Florence vainly sought to preserve liberty by too frequent changes of magistrates ; Venice elected the Doge for life, rendered a seat in the Grand Council an hereditary honour, firmly established the Republic, became a great power, and retained her liberty for many centuries. This enormous divergence, however, is not only easily explained, but is much reduced in our eyes when we examine the special conditions amid which the Venetian Republic grew into shape. Founded by Italian refugees, who settled in the lagoons to escape the tide of barbarian invasion, it was exposed but little, if at all, to the influence of Feudalism and the other Germanic laws and institutions which had so widely penetrated into many parts of Italy. Thus in Venice from the very beginning there were seen opposed to each other the people engaged in industry and commerce and the old Italian families, who without the support of the empire, or the strength of the feudal order, were very easily overruled and conquered.

An aristocracy of wealth was quickly formed, and these new nobles had no difficulty in taking possession of the government and holding it for ever. This triumph which, in Florence, was the slow result of many and frequent struggles, was in Venice as permanent as it was rapid. From the first, the prosperity of the lagoons was entirely dependent upon the distant expeditions and far-spreading commerce which everywhere formed the strength of the burghers or *popolo grasso*. Then, while on the one hand the energies of the people or *popolo minuto* were employed for many months of the year in lengthy voyages, on the other the government of the colonies gave opportunities of command to the more ambitious citizens, without any danger to the Republic.

Thus the Venetian Constitution, in its first origin but little different from that of other Italian Communes, went on from change to change owing to the widely different conditions by which it was surrounded. From the beginning the Doge was elected for life, because the city being divided in many islands, all tending to render themselves independent of one another, the need of greater centralization was soon made manifest. But the Doge was surrounded by nine citizens who composed the *Signoria*, and there were, as in other cities, two Councils, the Senate or *Pregati*, and the Grand Council. On solemn occasions, an appeal was made to the people collected in a public assembly called Arrengo, answering to the Parliament of Florence. Had things stood still at this point, the Venetian Constitution, with the exception of the Doge for life, would not have been radically different from that of Florence. But the far greater strength quickly acquired by the aristocracy of wealth, for the reasons above mentioned, gradually concentrated nearly all the power of the State in the Grand Council, which, on the abolition of the Arrengo and the narrowing of the Doge's authority, was the true sovereign power, and became hereditary through a series of slow reforms between the years 1297 and 1319, leading to what was called the *Serrata* of the Grand Council. Thus the circle was closed, and government was in the hands of a powerful aristocracy that later on instituted a Golden Book.

But although here, in Venice, there was no feudal principle to be fought against, these reforms were not carried without much opposition on the part of the old families, who, seeing themselves excluded from the government, sought and found adherents among the lowest classes. The conspiracy of Tiepolo Baiamonte (1310) was formidable enough for a few days to place the very existence of the republic in extremity of peril. But after a fierce conflict within and without the city, it was suffocated in bloodshed, and followed by the creation of the Council of Ten, a terrible tribunal which, by summary trials, but always in accordance with the laws, punished by death every attempt at revolt. Then, indeed, all danger was warded off from the aristocratic government, and it daily gained fresh strength. The solidity of Venetian institutions favoured the progress of Venetian commerce, and increased riches gave courage for new undertakings in the East, the field of Venetian glory and Venetian gain.

In the East the republic had encountered two powerful rivals, Pisa and Genoa; but the maritime power of the Pisans was shattered at the Meloria (1284) by the Genoese, who in their turn after a long and sanguinary struggle were irreparably defeated by the Venetians at Chioggia in 1380. And thus by the end of the fourteenth century Venice was free from all rivals, mistress of the seas, in the enjoyment of internal security, and most prosperous in commerce. Then she aspired to conquest on the mainland, and entered upon a second period of her history, during which she found herself involved in all the intrigues of Italian politics, lost her primitive character of an exclusively maritime power, and began to be corrupt. Hence the weighty accusations brought against her by contemporaries and posterity alike, but it was irresistible necessity that had forced her into the new path. In fact, when great States were springing up on all sides, the dominion of the lagoons was no longer secure, and it was no longer enough to watch over her own commerce on the mainland. The Scaligeri, the Visconti, the Carrara, the Este, detested the thriving Republic. They threatened it and isolated it in its own lagoons precisely when it most needed new markets for its superior wares ; for its trade with the East which was only to be fed by that with the West. And when the Turks advanced and began to check the conquests of the Republic and threaten its colonies for other reasons, this need became still more pressing.

It is true that Venice was then attacked by a thousand dangers on both sides ; but these dangers were inevitable, and she met them, fighting by land and by sea, with heroic ardour, and at first with unexpected good fortune. Venice certainly was somewhat unscrupulous in promoting her new interests ; often compelled in Italy to combat disloyal enemies, she too made use of violence and fraud. Yet it was never the personal caprice of an individual subjecting all things to his own will ; it was a patriotic aristocracy giving its blood for its country. In the fifteenth century the first to feel the claws of the lion of St. Mark were the Carrara, lords of Padua, who were strangled to death in 1403. After that, Venice sent to Padua a *Rector* for civil, and a Captain for military affairs, leaving intact all old laws and local institutions. The same took place, or had already taken place, in Friuli, Istria, Vicenza, Verona, Treviso. It was a very intelligent and liberal policy for those times ; but with their independence, the new subjects lost for ever all hope of liberty. The conquered territories certainly derived great advantages from being under a strong and just government and sharing in the immense trade of Venice ; but although material well-being might make the multitude forget their love of liberty and independence, there remained in all the powerful families who had held or hoped to hold rule, an intense hatred for the new tyrant, who was envied for the stability and strength of her government, and considered the most formidable enemy of all the other Italian States.

She proceeded on her course of conquest, and the fifteenth century, in which Italy began rapidly to decline, seemed on the contrary to open to Venice an era of increased prosperity. Her nobles had made men forget the irregularity of their origin, by the enormous sacrifices they had made for their country, and by the valour they had shown in the naval battles in which they commanded. Absorbed in political life, they freely left to the people all commerce and industry, which prospered miraculously under the shelter of a fixed government and victorious arms.

Even the advance of the Turks, which later wrought such terrible harm on the republic, seemed at this period almost to turn to its advantage. In fact, many islands of the archipelago, and other States, finding themselves in great danger through the impotence of the Greek Empire to defend them from the terrible hurricane that was drawing near, invoked the protection of Venice and gave themselves into her hands. Thus her dominions were enlarged and fresh subjects acquired, ready to pour out their blood in combating the common enemy, who, in the earlier encounters, suffered very heavy losses. All these things helped to rouse the spirit of the Venetians, who at this time believed themselves destined to be the bulwark of Christendom and the dominant power in Italy. Throughout their political dealings, in the correspondence of their ambassadors, in their continual wars by sea and land, patriotic feeling over-ruled every other, and inspired a noble boldness of language in citizens who were ever ready to lay down their lives for their country. The honour, the glory of Venice, was always their dominant motive ; and in their struggle against the advancing Turks they gave continued proofs of heroism. When the Venetian fleet encountered its formidable enemy near Gallipoli, in May, 1416, Pietro Loredano, its commander, wrote to his government : " Boldly did I, the captain, crash against the foremost of the enemy's galleys, full of Turks, who fought like dragons. Surrounded on all sides, wounded by an arrow which had passed through my jaw beneath the eye, by another through my hand, as also by many more, I did not cease from fighting, nor would I have ceased till death. I captured the first galley and planted my flag upon it. The Turks who were on board were cut to pieces, the rest of the fleet routed." [1] Venice alone, in the Italy of the fifteenth century, was capable of enterprises so daring and language so frank. The little republic of the lagoons had become one of the greatest potentates of Europe. But the dangers closing in around her were immense and waxing greater on all sides.

The Doge Tommaso Mocenigo foresaw these dangers, and on his death-bed, in April, 1423, prayed and entreated his friends not to be tempted to undertake wars and conquests, and above all not to elect as his successor Francesco Foscari, whose immoderate ambition would certainly drag them into the most audacious and perilous enterprises. But these prudent counsels were uttered in vain. Filippo Maria Visconti was then threatening all Northern and Central Italy ; the Turks were on the advance. Francesco Foscari was duly elected, and he certainly was not the man to bring back into harbour a vessel already launched on the open sea. No sooner did the Florentines implore help against the Visconti, than he exclaimed in the Senate :—" Were I at the end of the world and saw a people in danger of losing its liberty, I would hasten to its assistance." " Nu patiremo che Filippo tuoga la libertà ai Fiorentini ? Sto furibondo tiran scorrerà per tutta Italia, la struggerà e conquasserà senza gastigo ? " [2] Thus, in 1426, began the formidable struggle which, frequently interrupted and renewed, only ended with the death of Visconti in the year 1447.

In these twenty-one years Foscari showed a truly Roman patriotism and energy, struggling against external and internal dangers of every kind. Each year the Visconti's treasures enabled him to bring fresh armies into the field, and the Venetian Republic was always ready to meet them. Carmagnola, who had come over to the Venetians, gave cause for suspicion immediately after his first victories, and was, without hesitation, brought to a regular trial and condemned to death. On the 5th of May, 1432, *cum una sprangha in bucha, et cum manibus ligatis de retro juxta solitum,*[3] he was led between the columns of the Piazzetta and there beheaded. In 1430 there was an attempt against the Doge's life, and

---

[1] Romanin (" Storia documentata di Venezia," vol. iv. lib. x. chap. 3) quotes from Sanuto all this account, of which we have given a brief summary.

[2] Romanin, " Storia documentata di Venezia," vol. iv. p. 108.

[3] The words of the sentence as given by Romanin.

in 1433 a conspiracy against his government : the Ten brought swift and exemplary justice to bear upon the guilty parties. Later, at the instigation of the Visconti, the last of the Carrara tried to reconquer his lost dominions, and persuaded Ostasio da Polenta, lord of Ravenna, to throw off his allegiance to Venice. Carrara lost his head between the columns of the Piazzetta (1435), Polenta died in exile at Crete, and Ravenna was added to the Venetian territory. After Visconti's death, and shortly after the cessation of hostilities with Milan, there occurred the fall of Constantinople (1453), in which so many Italians, especially Venetians, lost their lives. This event, marking a new epoch in the history of Europe, was a mortal blow to Venice. Yet, in 1454, she succeeded in making a treaty, which ensured free trade to her subjects, and gave her time to prepare for new conflicts.

But the chief danger to the Republic sprang from the fresh germs of corruption, now beginning to threaten it with internal discord. Foscari's enemies, not content with having plotted against his life and his government, now assailed him by bitter persecution of his last surviving son, Jacopo, a man of very frivolous character, but blindly beloved by his father. Exiled, in 1445, for having accepted gifts, which the laws strictly forbade to the Doge's son, he, after having obtained pardon, was again condemned to exile in Canea in 1451, for supposed connivance in the assassination of one of his former judges. Recalled from his place of exile in 1456, he was subjected to a fresh trial, for having maintained a secret correspondence with the Duke of Milan, and condemned to a longer term of banishment. Entering the prison, the old Doge, unmoved by the sight of his son imploring pardon at his feet, exclaimed :—"Go, obey the will of thy country, and seek for nought else." But hardly had he tottered from the prison, leaning on his staff, than he fell into a swoon.[1] Shortly afterwards Jacopo Foscari died in exile (12th January, 1457), and the paternal heart of the man, who had sustained with an iron resolution, a gigantic struggle in defence of the Republic, broke down under the persecutions heaped upon his son. Aged, worn out, crushed, he had no longer the strength required to conduct State affairs, and to defend himself from his enemies. On being invited to resign, and refusing to do so, he was formally deposed. His ring having been broken off, the ducal cap removed

[1] " Diarii " di Marin Sanuto, and the " Cronaca " of Delfin. See the fragments cited by Romanin, vol. iv. p. 286, and fol.

from his head, he calmly descended the same stairs by which he had mounted on his accession to the Dogeship, quietly conversing with those who were near, and without accepting any offered arm. His successor was elected on the 30th October, and he died of a broken heart on the 1st of November, after a thirty-four years' reign. Francesco Foscari was certainly one of the greatest political characters of his time.[1] With him, Venice attained the height of her power ; after him she soon began to decline, though remaining heroic even in decay.

Forsaken by all the rest of Italy, she was left alone to confront the Turks, who were advancing with formidable forces. The *sopra-comito* (or admiral) Girolamo Longo wrote in 1468 that the Turkish fleet which he had to encounter was of four hundred sail, and six miles in length. " The sea seemed a forest. This may seem an incredible thing to hear, but it is a marvellous thing to behold ; . . . now see if by stratagem it be possible to gain an advantage. Men and not words are what is required." [2] These seem almost like accents of fear beside those words of Loredano, which we have already quoted. Times, in fact, were changed : the Republic continued to send forth fresh fleets, which fought heroically ; it organized the resistance of all Christian populations, who freely gave their blood for the cause ; it sent arms and money to the Persians, so that they too might aid to check the threatening march of Mahomet II. ; but all was in vain. Negroponte, Caffa, Scutari, other cities and possessions, fell one after another, in spite of their valiant defence. And at last Venice, weary of always standing alone to combat the enemy of Christianity, in January, 1479 made a peace, which guaranteed her own commerce, and which, seeing the sad state to which she was reduced, might be considered honourable. Then the rest of Italy joined in violent abuse of Venice, the more so when their alarm reached its climax in 1480 by the taking of Otranto by the Turks. But shortly after, the death of Mahomet II., and the consequent disorders at home, recalled the Turkish invaders from our shores, and Italy thought no more upon the subject.

From this time forward the horizon of the Republic grows narrower and narrower. Solely occupied by material interests,

---

[1] The following inscription was placed upon his tomb : "*Post mare perdomitum, post urbes marte subactas, Florentem patriam, longævus pace reliqui.*"

[2] This letter is in the *Annali* of Malipiero, and is also quoted by Romanin, vol. iv. pp. 335, 336.

MARZOCCO.

(From the relief by Donatello in the National Museum of Florence)

involved in the intrigues of Italian policy, it no longer assumes the guardianship of the Peninsula, and of all Christendom, against the Moslem, and every fresh event of the world's history seems to be to the injury of Venice. The discovery of America, and of the Cape of Good Hope, removed her from the principal highways of commerce. Reduced on all sides, she lost, together with her great gains, the historical importance which had been hers as the connecting link between the East and the West. Now she was reduced to snatching this or that scrap of territory from her neighbours, and imposing on them her still great and powerful trade. Her dominions now extended on one side to the Adda, on the other she held Ravenna, Cervia, Rimini, Faenza, Cesena, and Imola in the Romagna : in the Trentino she held Roveredo and its dependencies ; she had carried her arms as far as the Adriatic coast of the Neapolitan kingdom, and held some lands there. But this very fact of her having taken something from all, had gained her the fear and hatred of all.

Then again, this vast State was all under the rule of one city, in which but a small proportion of the citizens had a hereditary right to command. Not even in Venice, therefore, was it possible to hope for the wide and organic development of a modern State ; she remained rather as a survival of old republican institutions, outliving itself, and condemned to perish for want of nourishment. Meanwhile, it was still the strongest, most moral government in Italy ; but as its circle of activity diminished, so too diminished the magnanimous virtues, the heroic characters, born of the great perils they had had to struggle against, and of the continual sacrifices to which they were summoned. Instead of these, there ensued in the ruling class an enormous growth of egotism, luxury, and greed for gold. The jewel-loaded, satin-clad wives of the Venetian patricians, inhabited during the fifteenth century abodes of greater richness than any that were to be found in the palaces of Italian potentates. " The men," says the Milanese writer Pietro da Casola, " were more modest and austere ; they dressed like so many doctors of the law, and those who dealt with them had to keep both eyes and ears wide open."[1] But their policy, if less egotistical than that prevalent in the rest of Italy, was still that of a narrow local and class interest. They looked almost with

[1] See the " Viaggio " of Brother Pietro da Casola, a Milanese, published by G. Porro, Milan, Ripamonti, 1855. Romanin, vol. iv. pp. 494, 495, quotes some fragments.

pleasure on the ruin of Italy, hoping thus to insure their own power over it. And when foreign armies approached the Alps, they allowed them free passage, in the belief that they could later drive them back, and command in their place. The contrary ensued ; this selfishness of theirs, which helped no man and threatened all, led to the League of Cambray, in which nearly the whole of Europe arrayed itself against the little Republic, which, in spite of its gallant resistance, could not, as it had hoped, secure its own safety in the midst of the general ruin of the whole country.

4. *Rome.*

Amid the infinite variety of characters and institutions presented to us by Italy in the fifteenth century, the history of Rome forms almost a world apart. Chief centre of the interests of all Christian lands, the Eternal City was more sensitive than any other to the great transformations going on in Europe. The formation of great and independent States had broken up and rendered for ever impossible the universal unity of which the Middle Ages had had some prevision, and had even partially fulfilled. The Empire was becoming more and more restricted within the German frontiers, and the aim of the Emperor was to strengthen his position by settled and direct dominion within his own proper States. Therefore the Papacy, henceforward condemned to renounce its pretensions to universal sovereignty in the world, felt the urgent necessity of constituting a secure and genuine temporal kingdom. But the transfer of the Holy Seat to Avignon, and the long-enduring schism had thrown the States of the Church into disorder and anarchy. Rome was a free Commune, with a similar constitution to that of the other Italian Republics, but industry and commerce had not flourished there, nor had its political organism ever attained a vigorous development, chiefly in consequence of the exceptional supremacy exercised by the Pope, and the excessive power of the nobles who threw everything into confusion. The Orsini, the Colonna, the Prefetti di Vico, were sovereign rulers in their immense domains, in which they had stores of arms and armed men ; they nominated judges and notaries, and sometimes even coined money. Besides, there were also cities who were, or were continually trying to render themselves independent within the Roman territory, which extended from the Garigliano to the confines of Tuscany.

Every one, too, can imagine to what condition the Papal sway was reduced in cities like Bologna, Urbino, Faenza, and Ancona, all independent Republics or Lordships. Therefore, in order to form a temporal kingdom, a war of conquest was necessary. This Innocent VI. (1352–62) had attempted to begin, by means of Cardinal d'Albornoz, who, by fire and sword, brought a great portion of the State into submission. But this boasted submission was in fact reduced to the construction, in all principal cities, of fortresses held in the Pope's name ; to transforming the tyrants into vicars of the Church, and compelling the Republics to take an oath of obedience, while their statutes were left intact. In this way the Este, the Montefeltro, the Malatesta, the Alidosi, the Manfredi, the Ordelaffi, were legitimate lords of Ferrara, Urbino, Imola, Rimini, Faenza, Forli ; while Bologna, Fermo, Ascoli, and other cities remained Republics. The political constitution of Rome then began to be changed into an administrative constitution by the destruction of ancient liberties, and Popes Urban V. and Gregory XI. continued in the same path ; but the prolonged schism in the Church again plunged everything into anarchy, and prevented the formation of any strong government or any stable authority.

At last, in the year 1417, the Council of Constance put an end to the schism, by deposing three Popes and electing Oddo Colonna, who took the name of Martin V. Thus the history of the Papacy enters on a new period which lasts until the beginning of the following century, and during this time the successors of St. Peter seem to put aside all thought of religion, and devote themselves exclusively to the construction of a temporal kingdom. Having become exactly similar to other Italian tyrants, they profited by the same arts of government. Still the great diversity of their station in the world, and the peculiar temper of the State they tried to rule, endued their proceedings with a special character. Generally elected at a very advanced age, the Popes suddenly found themselves in the midst of a riotous and powerful nobility, at the head of a disordered and loosened State, in a turbulent city where frequently they were without adherents, and not seldom complete strangers. Therefore to gain strength, they favoured and enriched nephews who were often their own sons ; and thus originated the great Church scandal, known as Nepotism, and which specially appertains to this century. Then having once been drawn into the tumultuous vortex of Italian politics, the

Popes found themselves compelled to promote simultaneously two different interests, not unfrequently at variance the one with the other, *i.e.*, the political and the religious interest. Religion became an instrument for the advancement of their political ends, and thus, though only rulers of a small State, they were able to turn all Italy upside down, and without succeeding in bringing it into subjection, to keep it weak and divided until it fell a prey to the foreigners, whom they continually called to their aid. On the other hand, brute force and political authority were used to keep alive the religious prestige which had no longer any root in men's minds. Such a state of things confused all conscientious feeling in these representatives of God upon earth, and made them gradually fall into so horrible a delirium of obscenity and crime, that all decency was forsaken, and the Vatican became the scene of every imaginable orgy and outrage, of plots and poisonings. It seemed as though the Papacy desired to extirpate all religious feeling from the mind of man, and overthrow for ever every basis of morality.

The first germs of this fatal corruption of the Papacy originated in the conditions in which it then was, and quickly bore fruit under Martin V., who was, however, the best Pope of that century. He arrived from Constance,—according to the expression of a modern writer,—like a lord without lands, so that in Florence the street-boys followed him with jeering songs. Entering Rome on the 28th of September, 1420, with the aid of Queen Giovanna of Naples, the Roman people, having by this time lost all their free institutions, presented themselves to him as a throng of beggars. War, pestilence, and famine had ravaged the eternal city for many years ; monuments, churches, and houses were alike in ruin ; the streets full of heaps of stones and boggy holes ; thieves robbing and pillaging by day as well as night. All agriculture had disappeared from the Campagna, and an immense extent of land had become a desert ; the cities of the Roman territory were at war with each other, and the nobles, shut up in their strongholds which were mere robbers' dens, despised all authority, would submit to no control, no law, and led the lives of brigands. Martin V. set to work with firmness, and first of all completed the destruction of Roman freedom, by changing the city into an administrative municipality. Then many rebel domains were subjected, many leaders of armed bands taken and hung ; order thus began to be re-established, and a form of regular government inaugurated. But this end was attained by the means we have alluded to above. The Pope, to gain adherents, threw himself entirely into the arms of his relatives, the Colonna, arranged wealthy marriages for them, conceded to them vast feuds in the States of the Church, or obtained the concession of others equally large in the kingdom of Naples. In this way he increased their already enormous power, and was the initiator of Nepotism. In order to keep up the asserted supremacy of the Popes in the kingdom of Naples, and get all possible advantages from it for his own friends, he gave his support, first to Giovanna II., who had assisted him to enter Rome ; then to Louis of Anjou, her adversary ; lastly, to Alfonso of Aragon, who triumphed over all. And this fatal system of policy, continued by his successors, was the principal cause of the almost utter destruction of the Neapolitan kingdom and of the ruin of Italy. Yet in Rome there was seen at last some show of order and of regular government. Streets, houses, and monuments were partially restored ; for the first time for many years it was possible to walk through the city and out for some miles into the Campagna, without fear of robbery and assassination. Therefore after the Pope's death (20th Feb., 1431), his tomb bore these words : *Temporum suorum felicitas ;* and the inscription cannot be said to be altogether un-merited, especially when we consider how speedily all his sins were thrown into the shade, by the far greater crimes of his successors.

Eugene IV., who leant upon the Orsini, thereby making deadly enemies of the Colonna, was quickly driven out of Rome by a revolution, and pursued with volleys of stones as he fled down the Tiber, cowering in a boat (June, 1434). Arrived in Florence, he had to re-establish his government over again and sent to Rome the patriarch, afterwards Cardinal Vitelleschi, who, at the head of armed bands, carried on with fire and sword a real war of exter-mination. The family of the Prefetti di Vico was extinguished by the execution of its last representative Giovanni ; that of the Colonna was partly destroyed by the hardy prelate ; the Savelli underwent the same fate. Many castles were razed to the ground, many cities destroyed, and their inhabitants scattered hunger-stricken over the Campagna where they wandered about in misery, sometimes even offering to sell themselves for slaves. When at last Vitelleschi, at the head of a small army, made a triumphal entry into the Eternal City, that trembled at his feet, the Pope, seized with suspicion, sent Scarampo, another prelate of the same stamp, to supersede him.   Vitelleschi, who attempted resistance, was surrounded, wounded, taken prisoner, and confined in the castle of St. Angelo, where he died.   Then Eugene IV. was able to return quietly and safely to Rome, and died three years afterwards in 1447.

There was some singularity in the destiny of this Pope, who finally subjected the Eternal City.   While Vitelleschi and Scarampo were shedding rivers of blood, he remained in Florence enjoying festivals and the society of learned scholars.   Without having much culture or love of letters, he found it necessary, when attending the Council of Florence, to employ interpreters to discuss and treat with the representatives of the Greek Church, and was therefore obliged to admit into the Curia learned men who quickly overran it, not without certain noteworthy changes in the history of the Papacy.   A solemn funeral oration in classic Latin was recited beside his bier by the celebrated scholar Tommaso Parentucelli, who was chosen as his successor, without being possessed of other merits than his erudition.   He took the name of Nicholas V., and it was a general saying that, in his person, learning itself had ascended the chair of St. Peter.   Finding the Papal power sufficiently firm, Nicholas, who although devoid of original talent, and also—gravest of defects in a scholar of the fifteenth century — ignorant of Greek, but nevertheless the greatest existing collector and arranger of ancient codices, carried this passion with him to the Apostolic Chair, and made it the sole object of his pontificate.

His dream was to convert Rome into a vast centre of learning, into a great monumental city, with the finest library in the world. Had it been possible, he would have transported all Florence to the banks of the Tiber.   He scattered agents all over Europe to collect and copy ancient codices ; scholars of all kinds were offered large salaries as translators, without any regard to their religious or political opinions.   Valla, who had written most noisily against the temporal power, was one of the first to be summoned. Stefano Porcaro, who, like Cola dei Rienzo, had become, through his classical studies, infatuated for the Republic, was also overwhelmed with honours.   However, after he had entered into a conspiracy for firing the Vatican, and restoring republican institutions, the Pope lost patience with him, and let him be condemned to death.   But nothing could cool the ardour of Nicholas for learning ; he thought that all things might be remedied by a few Latin speeches, even the fall of Constantinople ; and he never ceased to collect manuscripts and summon men of learning to Rome. The Curia became an office for translators and copyists, and the Vatican library was rapidly collected and enriched by many splendidly bound volumes. At the same time new roads were opened, fortresses built, churches and monuments of all kinds erected. There reigned a perfect fever of activity, for the Pope, with the assistance of the first architects in the world, among whom was Leon Battista Alberti, had conceived a design, according to which Rome was to eclipse Florence. The leonine city was to be transformed into a great Papal fortress, in which St. Peter's and the Vatican were to be rebuilt from the very foundations. And although Nicholas V. did not succeed in completing this colossal enterprise, for which several generations would barely have sufficed, yet he initiated it with so much ardour, that during his reign the whole aspect of Rome was changed, and the immortal works executed in the times of Julius II. and Leo. X. were but the fulfilment of his own design.

On the 24th of March, 1455, Nicholas V. died the death of a true scholar, that is, after having pronounced a Latin oration to his Cardinals and friends, and was succeeded by Calixtus III., a Spaniard, and able jurist, who had first found his way to Italy as a political adventurer in the suite of Alphonso of Aragon. Calixtus was already seventy-seven years of age ; he belonged to the corrupt Spanish clergy, not yet tamed and disciplined by the politic measures of Ferdinand and Isabella, and he bore the ill-omened name of Borgia ; his brief Papacy was, like a meteor, the herald of coming evils. He had no concern with codices and scholars. With a blind cupidity, unrestrained by any trace of decency or shame, he loaded with honours, land and gold those nephews, of whom one was destined later to assume the triple crown under the notorious name of Alexander VI. He filled the city with Spanish adventurers, entrusting them with all duties of administration and police, thereby causing an enormous increase of crime. Blood was shed on all sides ; anarchy again threatened to rule in Rome, when old Calixtus died (6th August, 1458), whereupon a sudden burst of popular indignation put the Spaniards to flight, and the Pope's nephews themselves barely escaped with life.

Another scholarly Pope now ascended the throne, Enea Silvio

Piccolomini, of Sienna, a man of varied and versatile talent and character. His early life was passed in pleasure, then amid the controversies at Basle, where he upheld that Council's authority in opposition to the Pope's ; later, among the affairs of the imperial chancery in Germany, where he was the first to propagate Italian learning, he recanted his bold doctrines, renounced his juvenile errors, and thus was able to rise step by step in ecclesiastical rank until he reached the Papal Chair (19th August, 1458), and assumed the name of Pius II. He still continued to study and compose works of merit, but he did not patronize learned men, as all had hoped, employing himself instead in bestowing offices and patronage on his relations and his Siennese friends. Rome had once more fallen a prey to anarchy, in consequence of the mad policy of Calixtus III., who, although a creature of the Aragonese, had favoured the Angevins ; but Pius II., with greater shrewdness, favoured the Aragonese, and thus, assisted by them, was able to conquer the rebels. This Pope's ruling idea was that of a general crusade against the Turks ; only as a man of his day, and a scholar, he was more stirred by rhetorical enthusiasm than by religious zeal. In Mantua, whither he invited all Christian princes to a solemn congress (1459), many Latin discourses were pronounced ; but in point of fact this great meeting was a mere literary display, with many high sounding promises never destined to be carried into effect. Notwithstanding all this, the Pope wrote a Latin letter to Sultan Mahomet II. expecting to convert him by that means. And when, on the contrary, fresh Greek exiles were perpetually arriving, flying before the Turks, who had invaded the Morea, and Thomas Paleologus was the bearer of the head of St. Andrew, all Rome was, as it were, turned into a temple to receive the sacred relic, which was accompanied by thirty-five thousand torches. The Pope seized this occasion to deliver another solemn discourse in favour of a crusade, to a sceptical people, many of whom only felt an interest in the relic because it was brought by persons who spoke the language of Homer.

In 1462, Pius II. had collected a large sum of money through the unexpected discovery of rich alum mines at Tolfa, and again took up the idea of a crusade, inviting all Christian princes to straightway set out for the East. Old and suffering as he was, he caused himself to be carried in a litter to Ancona, where he expected to find armies and fleets, intending to go with them and bestow his blessing on their arms, like Moses when Israel fought against Amalek. But he found the port entirely empty ; and when at last a few Venetian galleys arrived, the Pope drew his last breath, gazing towards the East, and urging the pursuance of the crusade (15th August, 1464). His life, which to some may perhaps seem a worthy subject of romance, or even of epic narration, was in reality devoid of all true greatness. Pius II. was a scholar of considerable talent, who wished to do some heroic deed, without possessing in himself the heroic element. Although, doubtless, the most noteworthy pontiff of this century, he had no deep convictions ; he reflected the opinions and feeble desires of the men among whom he lived, changing perpetually, according to the times and conditions in which he was placed. His reign seemed to have a certain splendour, to hold out many hopes, but he left nothing durable behind him. After popes who had established the temporal power by force, and popes who had caused art and letters to flourish in Rome ; after Pius II. who had not only re-established order, but had even seemingly inaugurated a religious awakening, it might have been hoped that a better era of peaceful security was at hand. But it was now, on the contrary, that all passions ran riot, and the worst crimes, the most horrible obscenities of the Papacy, were near at hand.

Paul II., consecrated on the 16th of September, 1464, approached this period without beginning it, and we may say that he was better than his reputation. Yet he, too, careless of learning, was given up to the pleasures of life, and without being devoid of political qualities, considered it a part of the art of government to corrupt the people by festivities on which he squandered treasures. His name has come down to posterity with hatred, because he roughly expelled all the scholars of the Segreteria to make room for his own adherents. And when the learned world raised its voice still louder, and in the Roman Academy of Pomponio Leto, speeches were made recalling those of Cola dei Rienzo and Stefano Porcaro, he broke up the academy and imprisoned its members. It was then that Platina, confined and tortured in the Castle of St. Angelo, swore to have revenge, and obtained it by depicting his persecutor as a monster of cruelty in his " Lives of the Popes," a very widely known work. But Paul II., without being in the least a good Pope, was not without certain merits. He re-ordered justice, severely punishing the bravos who filled Rome with their crimes, he had a new compilation of Roman law drawn up, he fought energetically against the Malatesta of Rimini, and put down the arrogance of the Anguillara family, who owned a great part of the Campagna, and of the territory of St. Peter. Neither must his offences be too severely blamed when we remember the times and the men who came after him.

The three following Popes, Sixtus IV., Innocent VIII., and Alexander VI., are those filling the most degraded period in papal history, and proving to what a state Italy was then reduced. The first of these men was a Genoese friar, who immediate after his election (9th August, 1471) exhibited himself as a violent despot, devoid of all scruples and all decency. He needed money, and therefore put up to sale offices, benefices, and indulgences. He showed a downright mania for the advancement of his nephews, some of whom were, according to the general verdict, his own sons. One of these, Pietro Riario, was made Cardinal, with an income of sixty thousand crowns, and plunged so desperately into luxury, dissipation, and debauchery of all kinds, that he soon died, worn out by his vices, and overwhelmed with debts. The other brother, Girolamo, as zealously patronized, led the same sort of life. The Pope's whole policy was ruled by his greed of fresh acquisitions for his sons and nephews. It was solely because Lorenzo dei Medici had crossed these designs that the conspiracy of the Pazzi was hatched in the Vatican, and that on its failure the Pope made war upon Florence, and launched a sentence of excommunication against that city. Later, he joined the Venetians in their expedition against Ferrara, always with the same object of snatching some province for his family. A general war was the result, in which even the Neapolitans took part, by making an attack upon Rome, where fresh feuds among the nobility quickly broke out. Roberto Malatesta, of Rimini, was summoned to the defence of the eternal city, and when he died of a low fever, contracted during the war, the Pope tried to recompense his services by despoiling his heir of his State. This design, however, the Florentines managed to defeat.

The Pope, perceiving his danger, now changed his policy, and joined the Neapolitans against Ferrara and the Venetians, since these latter seemed disposed to conduct the war solely for their own advantage. He then began to revenge himself upon the nobles, especially the Colonna. Girolamo Riario, the blood-

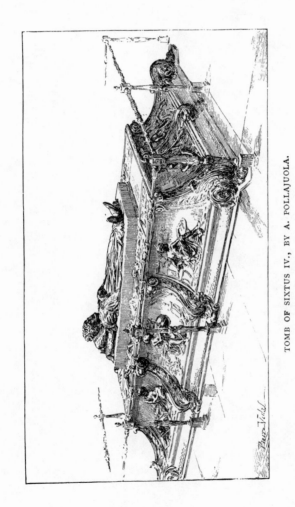

TOMB OF SIXTUS IV., BY A. POLLAJUOLA.

thirsty, commanded the artillery,—which had been blessed by
the Pope—gained possession of the Castle of Marino by promising
to spare the life of his prisoner the Protonotary Lorenzo Colonna,
and nevertheless caused his head to be cut off. During the
funeral ceremony in the church of the Holy Apostles, the infuri-
ated mother held her son's head up by the hair, and displaying
it to the people, exclaimed, " Behold how the Pope keeps faith ! "
But these scenes of bloodshed in no wise disturbed the mind of
Sixtus IV. When, however, he suddenly received intelligence
that the Venetians whom he had abandoned, had, without consulting him or taking his concerns in account, concluded the
peace of Bagnolo (7th August, 1484), he was seized with a violent
attack of fever, and died (12th August, 1484), as men said, of the
pains of peace.

> " Nulla vis saevum potuit extinguere Sixtum
> Audito tantum nomine pacis, obit." [1]

The palaces of the Riario were being sacked, the Orsini and
the Colonna in arms, when the Cardinals hurriedly assembling
in conclave, succeeded in patching up a truce. Then began a
most scandalous traffic in votes for election to the Papal chair,
which was sold to the highest bidder. The fortunate purchaser
was Cardinal Cibo, who was proclaimed Pope on 29th August,
1484, under the name of Innocent VIII. Hostile to the Aragonese,
he soon joined the conspiracy of the Neapolitan barons, promising
men, arms, money, and the arrival of a new Angevin pretender.
The city of Aquila began the rebellion by raising the standard
of the Church (October, 1485) ; Florence and Milan declared for
the Aragonese ; Venice and Genoa, on the other hand, declared
for the Pope and the barons, who had the aid of the Colonna,
while the Orsini, taking up arms in the Campagna, marched
straight to the walls of Rome. Confusion was at its height ; the
Pope despairing of succour, armed even the common felons ; the
Cardinals were at variance, the people terror-stricken, and
Cardinal Giuliano della Rovere alone paced the walls, and prepared for their defence. An attack was momentarily expected
from the Duke of Calabria. But the Pope's invitation to Renè
II. of Lorraine had the effect of bringing about a peace, compell-

[1] Guicciardini, " Storia Fiorentina," p. 70.

ing Ferrante to pay an annual tribute, and grant an amnesty to the barons, who, however, were put to death shortly afterwards.

During all this confusion, anarchy had again broken loose in Rome, nor was any way found to restrain it : no morning passed without corpses being found in the streets. Malefactors who could pay, obtained safe conducts ; those who could not were hung at Tor di Nona. Every crime had its price, and all sums over one hundred and fifty ducats went to Franceschetto Cibo, the Pope's son ; smaller amounts to the Chamber. Parricide, violation, any sort of crime, could obtain absolution for money. The Vice-Chamberlain used to say laughing, " The Lord desireth not the death of the sinner, but his life and his purse." The houses of the Cardinals were crammed with weapons, and gave shelter to numerous assassins and malefactors. Nor was the state of things in the country very different from this. At Forlì Girolamo Riario was assassinated (1484), men said, because the Pope wished to give that State to Franceschetto Cibo ; at Faenza, Galeotto Manfredi was murdered by his own wife. Dagger and poison were everywhere at work, the most diabolical passions were unchained in Italy, and Rome was the headquarters of crime.

Meanwhile, Innocent VIII. passed his time in festivities. He was the first Pope who openly acknowledged his own children, and celebrated their wedding feasts. Franceschetto espoused Maddalena, daughter of Lorenzo dei Medici (1487), and by way of recompense, her brother Giovanni was made a Cardinal at the age of fourteen. In the midst of these and other sumptuous family rejoicings, a singular personage arrived who completed the strange spectacle offered by Rome in those days. This was Djem, or as he was called by the Italians, Gemme, who had been defeated and put to flight in struggling against his brother Bajazet for the succession to the throne of Mahomet II. At Rhodes the knights of that order had made him prisoner, extorting from Bajazet thirty-five thousand ducats a-year, on condition of preventing his escape. Later, Pope Innocent contrived to get this rich prey into his own hands, and obtained forty thousand ducats yearly from Bajazet, who offered to pay a much larger sum on receipt of his brother's corpse, but this last arrangement did not suit the Pope's purpose. So on the 13th of March, 1489, Djem, seated motionless in his saddle, dressed in his native costume, and wrapped in his austere Oriental melancholy, made his solemn entrance into Rome, and was lodged in the Vatican, where he passed his time in studying music and poetry.

The taking of Granada, the last stronghold of the Moors in Spain, the arrival of holy relics from the East, all gave occasion for festivals, processions, and bacchanalian orgies. There was a very imposing ceremony on the arrival of the youthful Cardinal, Giovanni dei Medici, then only seventeen years of age, and to whom his father, among other useful advice, wrote that he must bear in mind that he was about to inhabit the sink of all iniquity. And this Rome certainly was. The Pope's sons and nephews made the town ring with the scandal of their daily life. Franceschetto Cibo lost fourteen thousand florins in a single night at play with Cardinal Riario, whom he accused to the Pope of cheating at cards ; the money, however, had already disappeared. The Eternal City had become a great market of offices and posts, often only created in order to be sold. And not only offices, but false bulls, indulgences to sinners, impunity for assassins, could be had for money : a father, by payment of eight hundred ducats, obtained absolution for the murder of his two daughters. Every evening corpses found about the streets were thrown into the Tiber.

In the midst of these diabolical orgies, the Pope every now and then fell into a lethargy that was mistaken for death, and then his relations and the cardinals hurried to secure their treasures and the precious hostage Djem, and all Rome was in a tumult. The Pope would awake from his trance, and thereupon the merry-makings went on as before, and assassination was the order of the day. At last a fresh attack of the Pope's malady left little room for hope. Anxious relations crowded round the bed of the dying man, who could take nothing but woman's milk ; then, it was said, transfusion of blood was tried and three children sacrificed to the experiment.

But all was in vain, and on the 25th of July, 1492—the same year in which Lorenzo dei Medici had died—Innocent VIII. breathed his last at the age of sixty. At the death of Sixtus IV., Infessura had blessed the day that freed the world from so great a monster, and the following Pope was much worse than his predecessor. Nobody now believed that a worse than Innocent could be found, yet the infamy of the new Pope Alexander VI., caused that of his predecessors to be totally forgotten. Of this monster it will be time to speak in narrating the catastrophe, which, during his pontificate, and partly through his misdeeds, overwhelmed the whole of Italy.[1]

5. *Naples.*

The kingdom of Naples resembles a perpetually stormy sea, which becomes monotonous by the changeless uniformity of its motion. It is true that the Hohenstauffen period had been one of glory ; but it closed with Manfred's noble death and the tragic end of Corradino (29th October, 1268), a drama of which the lugubrious echo resounds throughout the Middle Ages. The triumph of the Angevins, summoned across the Alps by the Popes—always the bitterest enemies of the mighty Frederic II. and his successors—was the beginning of endless calamities. The bad government of Charles I. of Anjou soon drove the people to rebellion ; in order to subdue them it was necessary to lean upon the barons, who, becoming exceedingly powerful, split up into factions, tore the miserable country to pieces, and were a powerful weapon in the hands of the Popes, who always hastened to call in a new pretender whenever they beheld any one prince becoming formidable. In this way they sought to acquire territory for their nephews, and maintain their pretended supremacy in the kingdom, which they devastated and plunged into anarchy with infinite harm to all Italy. Nevertheless they also had to pay the penalty of this iniquitous system of policy, for the Roman nobles having extended their dominions down into the south, and being therefore subjects of two States, became a lever used by turns to the hurt of one or the other, with fatal results for both. Accordingly the whole kingdom of Naples was subjected to a process of dissolution. New pretenders arose every day, the people were always oppressed, the barons always in revolt, no institutions could acquire stability or firmness, no individual character could long succeed in dominating and guiding the rest.

Under Joanna I., who had four husbands, and was murdered by suffocation under a feather bed, the kingdom had fallen into complete anarchy, and the Court turned into an assemblage of dissolute adventurers. Later King Ladislaus seemed about to initiate a

[1] For the history of Rome, besides older works, see Gregorovius's " Geschichte der Stadt Rom.," vol. vii., and Reumont's " Geschichte der Stadt Rom.," vol. iii., parts 1 and 2.

new era. He had subjugated the barons, conquered internal
enemies, placed a garrison in Rome itself, and was advancing at
the head of a powerful army, after inspiring all men with the
belief that he was willing and able to make himself king
of all Italy, when he died suddenly at Perugia, as all believed
of poison, in 1414. With Joanna II., the sister of Ladislaus, a
fresh period of indecency and chaos began. A widow, elderly,
dissolute, the mistress of her own steward, she allowed the State
to fall a prey to the nobility, mercenary leaders, and courtiers of
the lowest stamp. Martin V., who had had her crowned in 1419,
sent the following year for Louis III. of Anjou to come and assert
his claims to the throne. Joanna in her turn invited Alfonso of
Aragon over from Spain and proclaimed him her successor, but
shortly nominated in his stead René of Lorraine, who was
supported by Pope Eugene IV. and the Duke of Milan. Then
followed a long and ruinous war, which only came to an end
when Alfonso of Aragon, after winning many battles, entered the
capital by the aqueducts of the Capuan Gate on 2nd of June, 1442,
and became at last master of the kingdom that he had conquered at the price of so long a war and such enormous efforts.
This was the foundation of the Aragonese dynasty.

It is hardly necessary to say in what a miserable condition the
State then was, and how universal was the desire for peace.
Alfonso's triumph was hailed as the beginning of a new era.
He had left Spain to come and carry on in our country an
adventurous war, in which, after dangers and hardships of every
description, he had conquered a vast kingdom, struggled with
numerous foes, and defeated the first captains of the age.
A stranger in Italy, he now ruled provinces which had been long
harassed and domineered over by strangers. He had besides
rapidly lost all foreign characteristics, and become in all things
similar to our princes, with the addition of a warlike and
chivalric spirit that they very seldom possessed. He went
about unarmed and unattended among his people, saying that
a father should have no fear of his own children. His Court
was crowded with learned men, and a thousand anecdotes are
related in proof of his extraordinary admiration of ancient
writers. Happening to march with his army past a city, the
birthplace of some Latin writer, he halted as before a sanctuary ;
he never made a journey without having a copy of Livy or Cæsar
with him. His panegyrist Panormita pretended to have cured

him of an illness, by reading to him a few pages of Quintus
Curtius ; Cosimo dei Medici had concluded a peace with him, by
sending him one of Livy's codices. A warrior and a man of
unprejudiced mind, he gave a welcome to all scholars who were
persecuted elsewhere. This was the case with Vallá when he
had to fly from Rome on account of his pamphlet against the
temporal power of the Popes ; the same with Panormita when
his " Ermafrodito," although much lauded for the facile elegance
of its versification, excited scandal by an obscenity which had not
yet become familiar to men of learning, and was publicly anathe-
matized from the pulpit. These and many other *literati* were
cordially received at the Neapolitan Court, and splendidly rewarded with large salaries, houses and villas.

Exalted to the skies by the learned, Alfonso gained the title of
the Magnanimous through his generosity and knightly spirit.
But as a statesman, as founder of a dynasty and pacificator of a
kingdom, one cannot accord him much praise. After having
ravaged the unfortunate southern provinces with war, he drained
them by taxes levied to pay his soldiery and reward his adherents
the nobles, whom he loaded with favours and rendered more
tyrannical than they were before. Given up to the pleasures of
life, he never succeeded, during the sixteen years of undisputed
rule that remained to him, in founding anything durable, in
doing anything to relieve the people from the depth of misery
in which his wars had plunged them, or to secure his dynasty
by the consolidation of the kingdom. Dying, 1458, at the
age of sixty-three, he bequeathed his hereditary states in Spain
together with Sicily and Sardinia to his brother ; while the
kingdom of Naples, fruit of his victories, he left to his natural
son Ferdinand, whose maternal origin is involved in mystery.

Heir to a vast kingdom, conquered and pacified by his father,
Ferdinand, or Ferrante as he was called, had a right to expect
that he might quietly enjoy its possession ; but, on the contrary,
he was obliged to re-conquer it all again by force of arms, for the
latent disorder now quickly broke out. The first spark of discord
was lit by Pope Calixtus, who owed everything to Alfonso, and
had himself legitimized Ferrante's birth. But he now declared
the Aragonese line extinct, and claimed the kingdom as a fief
of the Church. The Angevin barons were in arms, René of
Lorraine landed between the mouths of the Volturno and the
Garigliano ; revolutions broke out in Calabria and elsewhere.

FERRANTE OF NAPLES.

(*From the bronze bust in the National Museum of Naples.*)

Yet, with enemies on all sides, Ferrante, by 1464, had succeeded in again subjugating the whole kingdom ; and then, instead of establishing order, thought of nothing but revenging himself upon his foes. He was accustomed to destroy his enemies by treacherous means, and, with cynical cruelty, would embrace them, caress them, and entertain them gaily at dinner before sending them to their death. A man of remarkable ability, of great courage and political penetration, but full of vices and contradictions, he governed in a most ruinous manner, and even traded on his own account. He would collect a stock of merchandise and then forbid his subjects to sell their theirs until he had disposed of his at his own price. All his transactions were based upon a false and artificial system, which ended by destroying the strength of the State, although the king had chosen very able men as ministers. Of these the best known are his secretary, Antonello Petrucci, and Pontano, who, besides being one of the finest scholars of his age, was also a very acute diplomatist, and Ferrante's prime minister ; it was he who conducted all affairs with the other Italian States, wrote all diplomatic despatches, and concluded all treaties. Francesco Coppola, the very rich and powerful Count of Sarno, carried on commercial operations in quest of money, unhampered by scruples of any sort. But these clever ministers were but the tools of the false policy of a crafty and ingenious tyrant, who looked upon his State and his people in the light of a property from which it was his duty to squeeze as much as possible during his life, and leave his heirs to take care of themselves. Then, ·too, his son Alfonso, Duke of Calabria, was prouder, more cruel, and more tyrannical than his father, without possessing either his ability or courage, and disgusted all who approached him. When the Turks who were occupying Otranto, suddenly withdrew, on account of the death of Mahomet II., it appeared as though they were flying before Alfonso, the which so increased his pride and made him so much more unbearable, that Antonello Petrucci himself and the Count of Sarno, immeasurably disgusted, and foreseeing the evils that the character of the heir to the throne would bring about in the future, placed themselves at the head of the malcontents and determined to attempt a revolt. Pope Innocent fanned the flame, and the result was that great conspiracy of the barons which set the kingdom of Naples ablaze and threatened to cause a general war throughout Italy (1485). Ferrante's craft and courage sufficed to calm even this tempest ; he concluded a treaty of peace, and, as usual, succeeded in revenging himself upon his enemies. But his was a policy that could only be successful while it was a question of keeping under a turbulent and exhausted kingdom by still further exhausting it. When, however, dangers attacked it from abroad, matters were beyond remedy.

And such a danger was now at hand, for Charles VIII. of France was making preparations for the fatal expedition that was to herald the renewal of foreign descents upon the Peninsula. Ferrante, now an old man, quickly took alarm, and warned all the princes of Italy of the coming calamity, entreating them to unite for the common defence. The letters he wrote at that time have a painful tone, a passionate eloquence which seems to elevate and ennoble his mind, and an extraordinary political acumen that is almost prophetic.[1] He perceived and described to admiration all the calamities which awaited his country and the princes who, like himself, blinded by their own cunning, had rendered unavoidable the common misfortune. But it was already too late. Italy could not escape the abyss into which she was already falling. Ferrante had to go down to his grave with his conscience tortured beforehand by the fall of his kingdom and of his dynasty, a fall that was already seen to be inevitable when death closed his eyes on the 25th of January, 1494.

The whole lengthy drama that we have so far described is but a preparation for the coming catastrophe. And if we were to turn our attention from the greater to the minor States into which the Peninsula is divided, we should find at Ferrara, Faenza, Rimini, Urbino, everywhere, the same series of crimes, the same corruption. Indeed, the petty princes, exactly because they were weaker and involved in greater dangers, often perpetrated more numerous and grosser acts of cruelty in order to save their threatened power. Still, they never neglected the encouragement of literary culture, of the fine arts, of the most exquisite refinements of civil life, thus bringing out still more forcibly the singular contrast, that is one of the special characteristics of the Italian Renaissance, and one of the greatest difficulties it offers to our comprehension.

Many Italian writers, animated by a spirit of patriotism that is

---

[1] *Vide* the "Codice Aragonese," published by Cav. Prof. F. Trinchon, Superintendent of the Archivi Napolitani, in three vols., Naples, 1866–74.

not always the most trustworthy guide in judging of historical facts, have tried to prove that the social and political condition of Italy in the fifteenth century was similar to that of the rest of Europe, and need, therefore, excite no astonishment. Louis XI., they remind us, was a monster of cruelty, and author of the most fraudulent intrigues ; the poisonings of Richard III. are not unknown ; Ferdinand the Catholic prided himself on having duped Louis XII. ten times ; the great Captain Consalvo was a notorious perjurer, &c., &c.[1] It is but too true that the formation of the greater European States was accomplished by destroying local governments and institutions by treachery and violence ; and, in these conditions of warfare, the blackest crimes and most atrocious acts of revenge everywhere took place ; and although such deeds seem almost natural in the general barbarity of the Middle Ages, they appear utterly monstrous and unwarrantable amid the mental culture of the Renaissance. And in Italy such crimes were certainly less excusable than elsewhere, since there culture had reached a higher pitch, and the contradiction presented by this mixture of civilization and barbarism was more plainly evident.

Nor must it be forgotten that monarchs such as Louis XI. and Ferdinand the Catholic, notwithstanding their crimes, completed a national work, making of France and Spain two great and powerful nations, while our thousand-and-one tyrants always kept the country divided with the sole and personal object of maintaining themselves on their sorry thrones. And if the policy of the fifteenth century was everywhere bad, it must be acknowledged that it originated in Italy, who taught it to other nations, and the number who pursued it in Italy was infinitely greater than in any other country. At every step we come upon tyrants, faction-leaders, conspirators, politicians, diplomatists ; indeed, every Italian seemed to be a politician and diplomatist even in his cradle. Thus corruption was more universal than elsewhere, spreading in wide circles from the government through society at large ; and so it happened that this Italian policy which brought into action such prodigious intellectual forces, and produced so great a variety of characters, ended here in Italy by building only upon sand. It is true that, looking lower

---

[1] " Considerazioni sul libro del Principe," added by Professor A. Zambelli to the volume containing " Il Principe i Discorsi di N. Machiavelli." Florence, Le Monnier, 1857.

down in the social scale, we find the ties of kindred still respected, ancient customs still preserved, and a far better moral atmosphere. And if we turn away from regions where, as in the case of Naples, Rome, and the Romagna, a continued series of revolutions had upset and thrown everything into confusion, we find in Tuscany, in Venetia, and elsewhere, a population far more civilized, milder, and more cultivated than in the remainder of Europe, and far fewer crimes committed. Historians, especially foreign ones, have never taken this fact into account, and, judging the whole nation by the higher classes, who were also the more corrupt, they have formed mistaken conclusions as to the moral condition of Italy, who would have fallen to an even lower depth, and could never have come to life again, had she been altogether as bad as they have described.

It must, however, be confessed that it was not merely because political life was reserved for the few in France, Spain, and Germany, that the corruption caused by it was less diffused. The reason lay deeper : in those countries there were institutions and traditions that still stood firm, opinions that were never discussed, authorities that were always respected. These naturally created a public strength and morality altogether wanting among ourselves, where all things were submitted to the minutest analysis by the restless Italian mind, which, in seeking the elements of a new world, destroyed that in which it existed. The Venetian and Florentine ambassadors at the Court of Charles VIII., or of Louis XII., appeared to turn everything into ridicule. They found the monarch without ability, the diplomatists untrained, administration confused, business conducted at hazard ; but they were amazed by observing the immense authority enjoyed by the king. " When His Majesty moves," said they, " all men follow him." And in this consisted the great strength of the French nation. Guicciardini, in his despatches from Spain, plainly shows his hatred and contempt for that country, yet he cannot abstain from noticing that the personal interests of Ferdinand the Catholic being in agreement with the general interests of the nation, the royal policy derived enormous strength and value from that fact. The customs of Germany and Switzerland appeared to Machiavelli similar to those of the ancient Romans whom he so heartily admired. Had the disorder and moral corruption of other nations been altogether identical with that which one found in Italy, how could we interpret these judgments of highly competent men? How could it be explained that Italy was already decaying, even before being overrun by foreigners, while other nations were budding into new life? But, as we have before remarked, it is necessary to guard against all exaggeration, or it would be impossible to understand the great vitality that the Italian nation undoubtedly possessed, and, above all, its marvellous progress in art and letters. It is to this latter subject that we will now turn.

III.

I. PETRARCH AND THE REVIVAL OF LEARNING.[1]

O great distance of time separates Dante Alighieri (1265–1321) from Francesco Petrarca (1304–74), but whoever studies their life and writings might almost believe them to belong to two different ages. Dante's immortal works are the opening of a new era, but Dante still stands with one foot in the Middle Ages. He has made himself "parte per se stesso," and has a supreme disdain for the bad and iniquitous company ("compagnia malvagia e scempia ") that surrounds him,[2] but he is always a most

[1] Regarding Petrarch as a man of learning, our best sources of information are his own letters, well edited and annotated by Fracassetti—" Epistolæ de rebus familiaribus et variæ ' · Florentiæ, Typis Felicis Le Monnier, 1859–63, 3 vols. ; " Lettere Familiari e Varie " (translation, with notes), 5 vols. : Florence, Le Monnier, 1863–64 ; and "Lettere Senili ": Le Monnier, 1869–70. Besides this, a valuable study upon Petrarch is to be found in Dr. Georg Voigt's " Die Wiederbelebung des classischen Alterthums, oder das erste Jahrhundert des Humanismus " : Berlin, Reimer, 1859. This work, and that of Burckhardt, " Die Cultur der Renaissance in Italien," are of the greatest importance for the history of Italian learning. Other interesting books on the same subject are : " Petrarque, Etude d'apres de nouveaux documents," par A. Mézières : Paris, Didier, 1868 ; and the "Petrarka " of Ludwig Geiger : Leipzig, Duncher und Humblot, 1874. Professor Mézières makes much use of the letters published by Fracassetti, but hardly any of Voigt and Burckhardt's estimable works. Geiger's work, on the other hand, is a synthesis of all that others had written before him, and was published on the occasion of the centenary celebrated in Arquà, the 18th of July, 1874, when two very interesting speeches, one by Carducci, the other by Aleardi, were also published. Of other recent works on Petrarch, such as that of De Sanctis ("Critical Essay on Petrarch," Naples, 1869), it is unnecessary to speak here, since they treat of the Italian poet, and not of the man of learning.

[2] " Paradiso," canto xvii. 61-63, 67-69.

energetic partisan, fighting sword in hand amid the Guelph and Ghibelline factions. The Empire that he desires and invokes is always the mediæval Empire, and he defends it with arguments borrowed from the scholastic philosophy, which even penetrates into his " Divine Comedy." Thus Dante's image remains as though hewn in marble by Michael Angelo, in the midst of the tumultuous passions of his age, against which he fights, but out of which he has not yet found escape. Petrarch, on the contrary, is of weaker mould, of less original poetical genius, is neither Guelph nor Ghibelline ; he despises scholastic philosophy ; feels that literature is becoming a new power in the world, and that he owes all his force to his own genius ; he has almost forgotten the Middle Ages, and comes before us as the first modern writer. It is, however, singular to observe how together with all this he was an almost fanatical enthusiast for the Latin writers whom he studied and imitated all his life, neither imagining nor desiring anything better than the revival of their culture, their ideas, and even their policy. The explanation of how these same continual efforts to return to the ancient world led instead to the discovery of a new is, as we have already remarked, the problem that has to be solved by the historian of the revival of learning in the fifteenth century. The singular phenomenon is already clearly visible in Petrarch, for in him we find the germ of the whole following century, and the many men of learning who succeed him seem only to take, each one of them, some one portion of the multiple work which he embraced in its entirety, excepting the study of Greek that he could only encourage by his advice. From his early youth Petrarch forsook law and scholastic philosophy for Cicero and Virgil ; he travelled about the world, employed all his friends in obtaining ancient manuscripts for him, and formed a very valuable collection of them. He transcribed much with his own hand, sought out unknown or forgotten authors ; but his special quest was for works of Cicero, who was his idol, of whom he discovered two orations at Liège, and some private letters at Verona.[1] This was a great literary event, for the flowing and

---

[1] It is known that Petrarch believed that he had once possessed Cicero's " De Gloria," and then lost it through lending it to his master, who, pressed by poverty, sold it, to Petrarch's life-long regret. Voigt, in his " Wiederbelebung," pp. 25, 26, expresses his belief that Petrarch was mistaken upon this point. The volume he had lent contained many treatises ; it is possible, therefore, says Voigt, that the title " De Gloria " was given by the copyists, as often happened, to one or more chapters of some other work—the " Tusculane," for instance. This is the

somewhat pompous eloquence of Cicero became the constant model of Petrarch and other learned men, and his epistles were in especial favour as being the most diffuse form of literary composition. The letters of Petrarch inaugurate the long series, they form his best biography, and are a literary and historical monument of sovereign importance. They are addressed to his friends, to princes, to posterity, to the great writers of antiquity. Every affection, every thought, finds a place in them ; and the author exercises himself, under Cicero's faithful guidance, in every literary style. History, archæology, philosophy, are all treated of in these letters, which thus, on the one hand, form an encyclopedic manual admirably fitted for the collection and diffusion of a new culture, too young to support as yet a more scientific treatment. On the other hand, the author displays his own intellect in these letters, gives free vent to his affections, describes people and princes, different characters, and different lands. In Petrarch, the scholar and the practical observer of reality are united ; indeed, we can discern how one was born of the other, and how antiquity, leading the man of the Middle Ages by the hand, guides him from mysticism to reality, from the city of God to that of men, and helps him to acquire independence of mind.

If, however, we examine the form of these epistles of Petrarch, we find that his Latinity is often both inelegant and incorrect ; no one would dare to place it on a level with that of the classic writers, and it is inferior to that used later by Poliziano, Fracastoro, and Sannazzaro. We must compare it with that of the Middle Ages to see the immense stride that he has made, and the superiority of his Latin even to that of Dante. But Petrarch's highest merit by no means consists in this new classic elegance ; it consists in the fact that he was the first to write freely of all things in the same way that a man speaks. He was the first to throw aside all scholastic crutches, and prove how much more swiftly a man could walk without leaning upon them. Sometimes a little too proud of this, he occasionally abuses his facility, falls into artifices that are mere *tours de force*, or allows himself to

learned writer's hypothesis, and is founded on the observation that Petrarch lent the work when very young, at a time when he knew but little of Cicero's writings, and that later he was never able to make any exact statements about that work. If ever really possessed by Petrarch, concludes Voigt, it is hardly credible that, even if missing for a time, it should have been lost for ever.

chatter like a child who, having made the discovery that his tongue can express his thoughts, goes on talking even when he has nothing more to say.[1]

Petrarch, in short, broke through the mediæval meshes, in which man's intellect was still entangled, and by means of his new style showed the way to treat of all subjects in a clear and spontaneous manner. In reading his epistles, we are often amazed by the fervour of his almost Pagan love of glory. It sometimes seems to be the principal motive of his actions, the scope of existence substituted by him for the ancient Christian ideal. Dante had already learned from Brunetto Latini how man may make himself eternal ; but although in his " Inferno " the condemned think much of their earthly glory, in the " Purgatorio " there is far less anxiety about it ; we are told that Oderisi da Gubbio was punished "*per lo gran desio dell' eccellenza*," [2] and it disappears entirely in the " Paradiso," where the things of earth are almost forgotten. The Middle Ages sought for eternity in another world, the Renaissance sought it in this, and Petrarch had already embraced this new order of ideas. In his opinion, it was the desire for glory that inspired all eloquence, all magnanimous enterprises, all virtuous deeds ; and he was never weary of seeking glory, was never satiated with it, although no man ever attained to so much during his life. The rulers of the Florentine republic wrote to him " obsequiously and reverently " (*ossequenti e riverenti*), as to one " whose equal the past knew not, nor would future ages know." [3] Popes and cardinals, kings and princes, alike deemed it an honour to have him for their guest.[4] A tottering old man, deprived of sight, traversed the whole of Italy, leaning on one of his sons and one of his pupils, in order to embrace the knees of the immortal man and print a kiss upon the brow that had conceived so many sublime things ; and it is Petrarch himself who tells us this with great satisfaction. [5] The day on which he received the poet's crown on the Capitol (8th April, 1341) was the most solemn and happiest of his life : " not

[1] Voigt makes this comparison.

[2] " For his great desire of excellence."

[3] " Lettere Familiari," Italian edition. *Vide* note to the fifth letter of the eleventh book. Petrarch received the invitation on 6th April, 1351. *Nota bene* that we always quote from Fracassetti's edition of Petrarch's letters.

[4] "*Et ita cum quibusdam fui, ut ipsi quodammodo mecum essent,*" he himself says in his Letter *ad Posteros.* " Fam. et Variæ," Latin edition, vol. i. p. 3.

[5] " Lettere Senili," bk. xvi. ep. 7, vol. ii. pp. 505–507.

so much on my own account," he says, "as an incitement to others to attain excellence."

This sentiment becomes sometimes, as it were, the familiar spirit (or Daemon) of the Renaissance. Cola dei Rienzo, Stefano Porcaro, Girolamo Olgiati, and many others, were less stirred by a veritable love of liberty than by a wish to emulate Brutus. At the scaffold's foot, it was no longer the faith in another world, but only the hope of glory in this, which gave them courage to meet death. And Machiavelli expresses the ideas of his age, when he says that men, if unable to obtain glory by praiseworthy deeds, seek it by vile, since to make their names live after them is their sole desire.[1]

All things tend to urge Petrarch, and after him, his contemporaries and successors, towards the world of reality ; he has a great passion for travelling, on purpose to see, and describe what he sees : *multa videndi amor ac studium.*[2]

He goes to Paris, to ascertain the truth of the marvels told of that city ; at Naples he visits in detail the enchanting environs, with the Æneid as his guide. He seeks out the lakes of Avernus, Acheron, and Lucrinus, the Sybil's cavern, Baiæ and Pozzuoli, and describes everything minutely, equally delighted with their natural beauties and classic memories.[3] Virgil had been Dante's guide in the three kingdoms of the unseen world ; Virgil is Petrarch's guide in the study of nature. A fearful storm breaks over the bay one night, and he leaps from his bed ; goes all over the city and down to the beach ; watches the shipwrecks ; observes the sea, the sky, and all the other phenomena ; strolls into the churches among the praying people, and then writes one of the most celebrated of his letters.[4] All this has no longer any novelty for us, born amid modern realism ; but we must remember that Petrarch was the first to quit the mysticism of the Middle Ages, and in order to quit it, was obliged to don a Roman toga.

Dante it is true sometimes describes nature with a few marvellous touches, but all such descriptive bits are used by him as comparisons and accessories the better to bring his ideas and his personages into relief ; Petrarch was the first writer to give to nature a value of her own, as in the pictures of the masters of the

[1] " Opere," vol. i., proem to the " Storie," p. clv.

[2] " Epistola ad Posteros," at the beginning of the " Familiares."

[3] " Lettere Familiari," book v. ep. 4.   [4] Ibid., book v. ep. 5.

fifteenth century. In his descriptions of character there is a down-right realism that recalls the portraits painted in later years by Masaccio, Lippi, and Mino da Fiesole. We find him drawing and colouring the truth just as it is, and because of its truth, without any other object. He is told of a certain Maria of Pozzuoli, a woman of enormous strength, who lives always armed, and is carrying on a hereditary feud, and he makes a journey on purpose to see her, speak with her, and describe her.[1]

He gives a lively description of the dissolute licence of the Court of Joanna I., and of the sway exercised over it by the Franciscan friar Robert of Hungary—" Of low stature, bald, red-faced ; with swollen legs ; rotten with vice ; leaning bent upon his staff from hypocrisy rather than infirmity : dressed in a filthy frock, which leaves half his person uncovered, in order to feign poverty ; that man strides through the palace with an air of command, despising all men, trampling justice under foot, con-taminating all things. Almost like a new Tiphys or Palinurus, he steers through the tempest this vessel that must speedily sink." [2]

Elsewhere he brings before us with singular graphic power the stern figure of Stefano Colonna, saying, that, "although old age had somewhat cooled the spirit in his fierce breast, yet even when seeking peace, he always finds war, since he would rather go down to the tomb fighting than bend his unconquered head." [3] These plain and speaking outlines, intermingled with continual quota-tions from the classics, and almost with fragments of antiquity, gain even greater force by the contrast, and make us see with our own eyes, touch with our own hands, the new world that is being born of the revival of the old.

If, too, we seek in Petrarch no longer the man of letters but the individual, then we find that, in spite of his own goodness and sincere admiration for virtue in others, there was already apparent in him that weak changeableness of character, that excitable vanity, that attributing to words almost the same importance as to facts and actions, which subsequently formed the usual temper of the learned men of the fifteenth century. He is one of those who have most loudly extolled friendship, pouring out treasures of affection in his letters to his friends ; but it would not be easy to

[1] " Lettere Familiari," book v. ep. 4.
[2] " Lettere Familiari," book v. ep. 3. Fracassetti gives this letter the date of 23rd November, 1343.
[3] " Lettere Familiari," book viii. ep. 1.

find in his life any example of a deep and ideal friendship, such as that, for instance, manifested in Dante's expressions about Guido Cavalcanti. A great deal of this expansive affection of his vented itself in the literary exercise to which it gave rise. Some may think that this was contradicted by Petrarch's constant passion for Madonna Laura, who inspired him with those immoral verses, which, in spite of his own contempt for them, form his greatest glory. It is certain that in his "Canzoniere," we find the truest, most refined analysis of the human heart, a diction free from all antiquated forms—even more modern than the language of many writers of the Cinquecento—and so transparent that the writer's thoughts shine through it, as through purest crystal. It is certainly impossible to doubt the existence of true and sincere passion ; but this Canon who proclaims his love to all the winds of heaven, publishes a sonnet for every sigh, tells all the world how great is his despair if his Laura will not look upon him, and all the time is making love to another woman, to whom he addresses no sonnets, but by whom he has several children—how can he make men believe that his passion is really as he describes it, eternal, pure, and sole ruler of his thoughts ? [1]

And here again the noble figure of Dante shines before us with increased brightness ; Dante, who concealed himself lest other men should guess the secret of his love, and who only wrote when his passion, having mastered his strength, burst from his lips, in the shape of immortal verse. Yet Dante's Beatrice is ever wrapped

---

[1] Prof. Mézières, in the fourth chapter of his work on Petrarch, relates how the poet began to love Laura in 1330, that she was the wife of Hugh de Sade since 1325, and died in 1348, leaving a large family. In 1331, according to Mézières, Petrarch's passion was very strong, and continued the same until after Laura's death. Then the French biographer, obliged to admit that Petrarch, Canon of Lombez, and Archdeacon of Parma, did not content himself with this species of affection, but at the same time loved another woman by whom he had a son in 1337, and a daughter in 1343, makes the following remarks :—" Ce n'est pas *une des particularités les moins curieuses* de son amour pour Laure qu'au moment où il éprouvait pour elle une passion si vive, il fût capable de chercher ailleurs ces plaisirs des sens qu'elle lui réfusait obstinément. C'est une histoire analogue à celle d'un grand écrivain de nôtre siécle, qui au sortir du salon d'une femme célèbre où il était réduit, malgré lui, à aimer platoniquement, se dedommageait dans des amours plus faciles, des privations qu'il subissait auprès de sa maitresse " (p. 153). But it is by such *particularités curieuses* that one judges a man's character ; and Prof. Mézières, who wished to prove the seriousness and depth of Petrarch's love, and of his general character, would have done better to refrain from alluding to Chateaubriand, whose character showed much frivolity and inconsistency.

in an ethereal veil of mysticism, and finally transfigured into theology, is removed even farther from us ; Petrarch's Laura, on the contrary, is always a real woman of flesh and blood ; we see her close to us, her voluptuous glances fascinate the poet, and even in his moments of greatest exaltation, he remains of the earth, earthly.

In his political career too, Petrarch's mutability—to call it by no harsher name—is also plainly apparent. He was a friend of the Colonna, to whom he professed to owe everything, " body, soul, fortune," [1] and by whom he was beloved as a son, and received as a brother, yet after he had overwhelmed them with exaggerated praises, he forsook them in the moment of their peril. In fact, when Cola dei Rienzo began the extermination of that family in Rome, Petrarch, who entertained a boundless admiration for the classical Tribune, encouraged him to persevere in the destruction of the nobility : " Towards them every severity is a religious duty, all pity an inhumanity. Pursue them sword in hand, even could you only overtake them in hell itself." [2] But this did not prevent him from writing, almost at the same moment, pompous letters of condolence to Cardinal Colonna : " Though your house have lost a few of its columns, what matters it ! It will ever have in thee a solid foundation. Julius Cæsar was one man, yet sufficient for all." [3] Later on he again considered the Colonna as Massimi and Metelli ; [4] but he did not therefore refrain from calling the Tribune to account for his weakness in not having rid himself of his enemies when able to do so. [5] It is true that he tried to excuse himself by saying that he did not fail in gratitude ; *sed carior Respublica, carior Roma, carior Italia.* [6] But what prevented him from keeping silence ? And yet this very republican, so ardent an admirer of the third Brutus, " who unites in himself, and surpasses the glory of his two predecessors," [7] shortly afterwards entreated the Emperor Charles IV. to come into Italy, saying that : " Italy invokes her spouse,

---

[1] " Lettere Senili," book xvi. ep. 1. See also " Lettere Familiari," book v. ep. 3 ; book vii. ep. 13 ; book xiii. ep. 6 ; " Epist. ad Posteros," and in the Italian edition of the " Lettere Familiari " the two notes to the 1st and 12th epistles in book viii.

[2] " Epistolæ de rebus famil. et variæ," vol. iii. ep. 48, pp. 422-32. This epistle is addressed to Cola dei Rienzo and the Roman people.

[3] " Lettere Familiari," book viii. ep. 1.　　　[4] Ibid., book viii. ep. 1.

[5] Ibid., book xiii. ep. 6.　　　[6] Ibid., book xi. ep. 16.

[7] " Epistolæ de rebus famil. et variæ," vol. iii. ep. 48, pp. 422-32.

her liberator, and waits impatiently to see his first footstep printed on her soil,[1] and who before had chosen even Robert of Naples as the subject of his praise, declaring that monarchy alone could save Italy.[2]   It is also well known how many reproofs he addressed to the Popes for leaving Rome, which could not exist without them.

We cannot judge Petrarch otherwise than leniently when we see that he himself was unaware of these contradictions, because in point of fact all these speeches of his were nothing but literary exercises, never the expression of a sincere and profound political passion desirous to translate itself into action.   Given a subject, his pen ran most swiftly in Cicero's track, and followed the harmonious cadence of his periods.   But—and here we again meet with Petrarch's most original characteristic—in treating of either republic, monarchy, or empire, he never speaks as a Florentine, always as an Italian.   It is true that the Italy of his desire is often to. be confounded with the ancient Rome that he yearns to revive, but for that very reason he is the first to see in his learned dreams the unity of the State and of the country.   Dante's Italy is always mediæval ; Petrarch's, although majestically enfolded in the toga of the Scipios, and the Gracchi, is nevertheless a united and modern Italy.   Thus in this, as in all else, we see that our author was even here a true representative of his times : in endeavouring to return to the past, he opened a new future.   He seems always old, and is ever new ; but we must never forget that the primary source of his inspiration is a literary one, otherwise we shall be led into continual mistakes and unjust judgments.

Petrarch is a fierce assailant of jurisprudence, medicine, philosophy, of all the sciences of his day, because they do not fulfil their promises, but rather keep the mind enchained amid a thousand sophistries. . His writings are often directed against scholastic philosophy, alchemy, astrology, and he is also the first who dared openly to revolt against the unlimited authority of Aristotle, the idol of the Middle Ages.   All this does the greatest honour to the good sense, that raised him above the prejudices of his day.   But it would be a gross error to seek to find in him a

---

[1] "Lettere Familiari," book xii. ep. 1, 24th February, 1350.

[2] "Epist. de rebus famil. et variæ," book iii. ep. 7 : "Monarchiam esse optimam relegendis, reparandisque viribus Italis, quas longus bellorum civilium sparsit furor.   Haec ut ego novi, fateorque regium manum nostris moribus necessariam, etc."   This was written in 1339 according to Fracassetti.   See his note in the Italian edition.

daring scientific innovator. Petrarch does not fight in the name
of a new principle or new method, but in the name of beauty of
form and of true eloquence, which he cannot find in those sciences,
and cannot discover in the ill-translated and mutilated Aristotle
of his times. Scholastic philosophy and its barbarous phraseology
were incorporated in all the knowledge of the Middle Ages, and
this barbarous phraseology was the enemy Petrarch fought against
in all branches of learning. The Italian Renaissance was a
revolution brought about in the human mind, and in culture by
the study of beauty of form inspired by the ancient classics. This
revolution and all the perils occasioned by starting from form to
arrive at substance are clearly and strikingly manifested in the
writings of Petrarch, the man of learning, who has therefore been
styled by some, not merely the precursor, but the prophet of the
following century.

2. LEARNED MEN IN FLORENCE.[1]

The work initiated by Petrarch speedily found a very large
number of followers in Florence, and thence spread rapidly
throughout Italy. In Florence, however, it was the natural outcome of the political and social conditions of a people, in whose
midst even the learned of other provinces came to perfect themselves in their studies, and gained, as it were, a second citizenship.
In our histories of literature, which are frequently too full of

---

[1] One of the most important works on the history of the learned men is the
"Vite di uomini illustri del secolo," xv., written by Vespasiano Bisticci, published
for the first time by Mai, and then by Professor Adolfo Bartoli, Florence, Barbéra,
1859. Bisticci, although a most valuable authority for the width and certainty of
his information, must, however, be examined with caution, on account of his
excessive ingenuousness and want of critical faculty. His statistics are not trustworthy, and he seldom troubles himself to give dates. Tiraboschi's " Storia della
Litteratura Italiana " (Florence, Molini, Landi and Co., 1805–13) contains a truly
precious harvest of facts regarding the learned men. Voigt and Burckhardt,
frequently quoted, offer important remarks. Nothing, however, but an examination
of the works of the learned men allow us to form an exact judgment of their
respective value. Nisard's work, " Les Gladiateurs de la Republique des lettres
aux, xvme, xvime, xviime siécles" (Paris, Levy, 1860), contains, notwithstanding the
oddity of its title, very valuable observations. A vast miscellany of notices is to
be found in the "Epistolæ " of Ambrozio Traversari, published by Mehus, with
a memoir of the author ; the numerous biographies written by Carlo de Rosmini
are very useful also, not as criticisms, but for exactness of facts. Other special
works will be mentioned in the proper place.

biographical anecdotes and external 'facts, the names of these scholars are given in a mass, so that they all seem to be first-rate men, to have the same physiognomy and the same merits, and to hold the same object in view. To us, however, it is only important to know those who showed true originality amid the thousand others already fallen or now falling into deserved oblivion, who with feverish activity repeated the same things over and over again. Our object is not to give a catalogue of the learned men and their writings, but to study the literary and intellectual transformation that their work brought about in Italy.

The first learned men who offer themselves to our notice are friends, pupils, or copyists of Petrarch. Boccaccio was one of his most diligent assistants, as a collector of numerous codices, an admirer and imitator of the Latin classics, and as promoter of the study of the Greek tongue, of which he was one of the first students. The works which were fruits of his learning are however lacking in true originality. His Latin writings on the "Genealogy of the Gods," on "Illustrious Women," on the "Nomenclature of Mountains, Forests, and Lakes," &c., are little else than a vast collection of antique fragments, without much philological or philosophical value. But his mind was saturated with the spirit of antiquity in so great a degree, that it shows itself in all his works, even in those written in Italian. In fact, his Italian prose shows too great an imitation of the Ciceronian period, and seems to intimate that the triumph of Latin will soon be universal.

After two men like Petrarch and Boccaccio had once started upon this road, Florence appeared suddenly tranformed into a hive of learned men. Learned meetings and discussions were held on all sides, in palaces, convents, villas,[1] among wealthy people, tradesmen, statesmen : all wrote, travelled, sent messengers about the world to discover, buy, or copy ancient manuscripts. All this did not result as yet in any original work ; but an enormous mass of material was collected, and the necessary

---

[1] Many notices on this head are collected in the volume divided into two parts, which Alessandro Wesselofsky has added to his edition of the " Paradiso degli Alberti." *Vide* " Il Paradiso degli Alberti, ritrovi e ragionamenti del 1389, romanzo di Giovanni da Prato," edited by Alessandro Wesselofsky : Bologna, Romagnoli, 1867. These meetings took place now in the house of Coluccio Salutati, now at the Paradiso, a villa belonging to Antonio degli Alberti, outside the San Niccolò Gate.

means prepared for a thorough revolution in the field of letters. The importance of this activity did not consist in the immediate results obtained, but in the energy and power in this wise employed and developed. The city of art and trade associations had now become the centre of literary associations. The first of these reunions was held in the convent of Santo Spirito, by Luigi Marsigli or Marsili, an Augustine friar and doctor of Theology, who lived in the second half of the fourteenth century. He had been the friend of Petrarch, was a man of mediocre ability, but to a great admiration for the ancients, he united an extraordinary memory, that gave him much aptitude for learned conversation ; and for a long period Florentine scholars mentioned in their letters the profit derived from those discussions. The commentary written by Marsigli on Petrarch's " Ode to Italy," shows that he had not yet quite cut himself loose from the literature of the thirteenth century.[1] The two most noted frequenters of his cell,[2] Coluccio Salutati and Niccolo Niccoli,[3] had, however, already entered on the new path. Salutati, born in the Val di Nievole in the year 1330, was also the friend and admirer of Petrarch, an earnest promoter of erudition, and a great collector of codices. He was the author of numerous Latin orations, dissertations, and treatises, and in consequence received from Filippo Villani, as a title of honour, the name of "real aper of Cicero." But his inflated and incorrect style, and his confused erudition, would not have sufficed to hand his name down to posterity, had not his moral qualities given even to his literary work an original stamp. Of exemplary character, and a lover of liberty, he was elected secretary of the Republic in 1375, and served it with the utmost zeal and ardour to the time of his death. Animated by patriotism and the love of letters, he freed the Florentine official style of writing from all scholastic forms, trying instead to render it

---

[1] " Comento a una canzone di Francesco Petrarca," by Luigi Marsili : Bologna, Romagnoli, 1863. Wesselofsky has been one of the first to remark that there was a period of transition between the " Trecentisti " and the learned men.

[2] Voigt, at p. 115, also mentions Gianozzo Manetti as one who frequented these reunions ; but it is a mistake. Luigi Marsigli was born about 1330, and died on the 21st of August, 1394 (Tiraboschi, vol. v. p. 171 : Florence, Molini, Landi and Co., 1805–13). Manetti was born in 1396 (Tiraboschi, vol. vi. p. 773), and belongs to a later generation. The origin of this mistake is, because after Marsigli's death, Vangelista da Pisa and Girolamo da Napoli taught at St. Spirito, and Manetti studied under them.

[3] Also known as Lino, Niccoluccio, Niccolino.

classical and Ciceronian, and thus he was the first to write diplomatic and business documents like works of art, and he wrote them with singular success. Galeazzo Maria Visconti is said to have declared himself more afraid of one of Salutati's letters than of a thousand Florentine knights ; and it is an undoubted fact that when the Republic was at war with the Pope, the letters written by Salutati, who, in a magniloquent style evoked the ancient memories of Rome, had the effect of stirring to revolt, in the name of liberty, many territories belonging to the Church. Classic names, reminiscences and forms, had the power of arousing a truly wonderful enthusiasm in the Italian mind.

And Salutati's work had very noteworthy consequences even in the future. The enlistment of literature in the service of politics, increasingly bound up the former with the public life of the Florentines, and prepared the way for a radical transformation in the latter. The old forms and conventionalities were gradually replaced by true and precise formulas, which, just as they had forced literary men to turn their eyes from heaven to earth, and from mysticism to reality, also induced statesmen to treat affairs from a natural point of view, and to rule men by studying their passions, without allowing themselves to be shackled by prejudice and traditional usage. This way led by gradual steps to the political science of Machiavelli and Guicciardini, that owes to learning not a few of its merits and defects. From this moment dates the introduction of that use and abuse of eloquence, logic, and subtlety, to forward certain political ends, which later became cunning and deceit. Salutati, however, never ceased to preserve his sincerity and open habit of mind.[1]

Up to the last day of his life he continued to study and to encourage youth in his own love for the classics.[2] He was sixty-

---

[1] Voigt has been the first to notice this point respecting Salutati.

[2] Leonardo Aretino has recorded that he owed to Salutati his knowledge of Greek and thorough study of Latin. " Nemo unquam parens in unico diligendo filio tam sedulus fuit quam ille in me." And Coluccio mentions this friendship with great delicacy and much nobility of language : " Continua et studiosa nobis consuetudo fuit, et cum de cunctis quæ componerem judex esset, et ego suarum rerum versa vice, nos mutuo, sicut ferrum ferro acuitur, exacueramus ; nec facile dixerim ex hoc dulce et honesto contubernio, uter nostrum plus profecerit. Uterque tamen eruditior evasit, fateri oporteat mutuo nos fuisse vicissim discipulus et magister." These two fragments of letters are given in Moreni's preface, p. xi, of the " Invectiva Lini Coluccii Salutati in Antonium Luscum Vicentinum,"

five years old when a rumour that Emmanuel Crisolora, of Constantinople, was about to come to Florence to teach Greek, intoxicated him with joy, and seemed to give him back his youth. In 1406 he died at the age of seventy-six, and was buried in the Cathedral with much solemnity, after his deeds had been celebrated in a Latin oration, and his corpse crowned with the poet's laurel. From that time the Republic always chose celebrated men of letters for her secretaries. The long series beginning with Salutati, comprised Marcello Virgilio, Machiavelli, and Giannotti,[1] and all the Italian Courts followed the example of Florence.

Niccolo Niccoli was a celebrated man in his day, although no author, and only an intelligent collector of manuscripts, which he often copied and corrected with his own pen. Yet, for the sake of classical studies, he put himself to infinite trouble and expense, and made many sacrifices. His researches after ancient manuscripts extended to the East and the West, for he gave letters and commissions to all travelling Florentines and those resident in

---

Florence, 1826. Loschi, or Lusco, as P. Bracciolini calls him, was learned in Latin and civil law, was chancellor to Gio. Galeazzo, then Secretary at Rome from the times of Gregory XII. to those of Nicholas V. Having spoken ill of Florence, Coluccio retorted with his "Invectiva," an example of the exaggeration and inflation sometimes reached by the learned style of writing. "Quænam urbs, non in Italia solum, sed in universo terrarum orbe est moenibus tutior, superbior palatiis, templis ornatior, formosiora edificiis ; quæ porticu clarior, platea speciosior, viarum amplitudine laetior : quæ populo maior, civibus gloriosior, inexhaustior divitiis, cultior agris ; quæ situ gratior, salubrior coelo, mundior caeno ; quæ puteis crebior, aquis suavior ?" &c., &c. And he goes on in this style for many pages (see p. 125 and fol.). According to P. Bracciolini (see note to p. xxvii of the preface to the "Invectiva "), Salutati had a collection of 800 codices, a very extraordinary number in those days. And this is how Leonardo Aretino speaks of the liberality with which Salutati gave copies of these to all his friends, after again repeating his praises of the disposition of his friend and master : " Ut omittam quod pater communis erat omnium, et amator bonorum . . . omnes in quibus conspiciebat lumen ingenii, non solum verbis incendebat ad virtutem, verum multo magis cum copiis, tum libris suis juvabat, quos ille pleno copia cornu non magis usui suo quam ceterorum esse volebat." (See p. xxvii of the above-quoted preface.) Afterwards Salutati's library was dispersed, being sold by his sons (Ibid., pp. xxvii–viii). Shepherd, in his "Vita di Poggio Bracciolini," gives various notices of Salutati, a few of his letters, and a catalogue of his works. See the edition of Salutati's "Epistolæ," prepared by Mehus, which is not, however, very correct. Many of Salutati's writings still remain unedited in the public libraries of Florence.

[1] After Coluccio Salutati, the following were successively among the secretaries of the Republic : Leonardo Bruni, Carlo Marsuppini, Poggio Bracciolini, Benedetto Accolti, Cristoforo Landino, Bartolommeo Scala, Marcello Virgilio Adriani, who was first secretary while Machiavelli was second, Donato Giannotti, and not a few others.

foreign countries. A frugal liver, he spent his whole fortune, and ran heavily into debt, in order to purchase books. His energy was so great that applications were made to him from all quarters respecting ancient codices, and it is chiefly owing to him that Florence then became the great book centre of the world, and possessed librarians as intelligent as Vespasiano Bisticci, who was also the biographer of all the learned men of his day. Niccoli was also most indefatigable in attracting the most reputed scholars of Italy to Florence, in order to have them employed in the Florentine University,[1] or in other ways. It was through his efforts that Leonardo Bruni, Carlo Marsuppini, Poggio Bracciolini Traversari, Crisolora, Guarino, Filelfo, were summoned to Florence and given employment. But being of an irritable disposition, his friendship easily changed to aversion, he then persecuted those whom he had previously protected, and as he enjoyed the favour of the Medici, his power of persecution was very great. To him and to Palla Strozzi is to be ascribed the reform of the Florentine University, and the encouragement of the study of Greek. So intense was his ardour for the propagation of learning, that after the fashion of a religious missionary, he would stop rich young Florentines in the street, exhorting them to devote themselves to *virtue*, *i.e.*, to Greek and Latin literature. Piero dei Pazzi, a youth who only lived, as he himself said, to enjoy himself ("per darsi bel tempo"), was one of his converts, and became a man of learning.[2]

Niccoli's house was a museum and ancient library, Niccoli himself, a living bibliographical encyclopedia. He had a collection of eight hundred codices, valued at six thousand florins.[3] In these days it is easy to realize the importance of a good library in an age when printing was unknown, and the price of a single manuscript was very often quite beyond the means of students, even when they knew where to seek it. Niccoli's library was thrown open to all, and all came to his house to study, to make researches, to copy, to ask help and counsel that was never with-

---

[1] Then known as the Studio Fiorentino.

[2] *Vide* Vespasiano's "Vita dei Piero dei Pazzi."

[3] In his "Vita di N. Niccoli," 8th paragraph, Vespasiano gives the number of volumes at eight hundred; other writers state that they barely exceeded six hundred. Poggio Bracciolini (see preface to Salutati's "Invectiva," before cited, p. 27) also says that they were eight hundred. Neither can their precise value be ascertained.

COSIMO DEI MEDICI.

(After the fresco by Benozzo Gozzoli, representing the Tower of Babel, in the Campo Santo of Pisa.)

held. Even at his frugal table he surrounded himself with objects of antiquity, and Vespasiano tells us, that "it was a rare sight to see how ancient he made himself."[1] The frivolous points of his character, and the somewhat ludicrous scandals of his private life, caused by a female servant who ruled him entirely, were passed over on account of his sincere, constant, and disinterested zeal for letters. When on his death-bed, at the age of seventy-three, in 1437, his only anxiety was to guarantee to the public the free use of his books, which, in fact, formed the first public library in Europe. This was owing to the care of his executors and the munificence of Cosimo dei Medici, who renounced his credit of five hundred florins, paid other of Niccoli's debts, and retaining a portion of the codices for himself, placed four hundred of them in S. Marco for the public use, and afterwards increased their number at his own expense.[2]

---

[1] Vespasiano.

[2] *Vide* Vespasiano, "Vita di N. Niccoli"; Mehus, "Ambr. Camaldulensis Epist." prefatio, pp. 31, 63, 82; Tiraboschi, vol. vii. p. 125, and fol. Cosimo dei Medici had the books placed in St. Mark's in the year 1444 in the grand hall built at his expense by the Architect Michelozzi, which was restored and enlarged after the earthquake of 1433 (P. Marchese, "Scritti Varii": Firenze, Le Monnier, 1855, p. 135). Later, that is after the overthrow of Piero dei Medici, in 1494, the friars of St. Mark's bought the codices in the private library of the Medici, which were afterwards bought back by Cardinal Giovanni dei Medici, who later became Pope Leo X. At his death, Cardinal Giulio dei Medici, afterwards Pope Clement VII., his executor, carried them back to Florence, and commissioned Michael Angelo with the construction of the building in which they were to be placed, in the cloister of St. Lorenzo. The edifice was completed under Cosimo I., after the death of Clement VII., and thus was founded the famous Laurentian library. According to Padre Marchese, Cosimo dei Medici, having paid Niccoli's debts, and added codices of his own to those of his deceased friend in St. Mark's, his sons and grandsons had a certain right over them, and, therefore, when they re-purchased from the brethren the private Medici collection, they included among them many of Niccoli's. Upon the history of these collections various notices are to be found in Vespasiano's "Vita di N. Niccoli" and "Vita di Cosimo di Medici"; Tiraboschi, vol. vi. p. 128, and fol.; "Poggio Opp."; Basle, 1538, p. 270, and fol.; Mehus, "Ambr. Camaldulensis Epist.," prefatio, p. lxiii, and fol., lxxvi, and fol.; P. Marchese, "Scritti Varii," p. 45, and fol. I have already published several documents in my "Storia di Frate G. Savonarola ed i suoi tempi." A short report—"Delle Biblioteca Mediceo, Laureziana di Firenze," Firenze, Tofani, 1872—was published by the librarian, Cav. Ferrucci, and its author, Signor Anziani, under-librarian. But everything relating to the history of the private Medici collection has been narrated at length and illustrated by new and important documents by Professor E. Piccolomini, in the "Archivio Storico," vol. xix., 1, 2, and 3 Nos. of 1874, and vol. xx. No. 4 of 1874. This same work has also been published separately, and entitled—"Intorno alle condizioni ed alle vicende della libreria Medicea privata," by E. Piccolomini: Firenze, Cellini and Co, 1875.

A third resort of learned men was the convent of the Angioli, the abode of Ambrogio Traversari, native of Portico, in Romagna, born in 1386, and nominated General Head of the Camaldolesi in 1431. An able and ambitious man, he was a great favourite with the Medici who, together with Niccoli, Marsuppini, Bruni, and not a few others, were frequent visitors to his cell. He had the faculty of preserving the friendships of even the touchiest of the set ; he knew how to keep a discussion alive, but he had very little literary originality. He made translations from the Greek ; wrote a work entitled " Hodæporicon," containing various literary notices and descriptions of his travels ; but his " Epistolæ " are his principal work, on account of his intimate relations with the scholars of his time, and form an important contribution to the history of that century. All this, however, is not enough to justify the great reputation that he then enjoyed, and that lasted after his death, for Mehus, in the preface and biographical sketch attached to his edition of the " Epistolæ," tried to concentrate round them the literary history of that century.

It would be an endless task to enumerate all the meeting-places of the learned ; but we must not forget to mention the house of the Medici, where all and every one of them found welcome, patronage, and employment. There, too, were to be found all artists and foreigners of any merit. Almost all the richer Florentines of the fifteenth century were patrons and cultivators of letters. Roberto dei Rossi, the Greek scholar, passed a celibate life in his study, and gave lessons to Cosimo dei Medici, Luca degli Albizzi, Alessandro degli Alessandri, Domenico Buoninsegni. The Nestor of these aristocratic scholars was Palla Strozzi—he who aided Niccoli in his reform of the Florentine University— who paid out of his own pocket a large portion of the sum required to tempt Crisolora to come and teach Greek in Florence, and who spent much gold in obtaining ancient codices from Constantinople. When most iniquitously driven into exile, at the age of sixty-two, by Cosimo dei Medici, he found courage to bear up under this misfortune, and the subsequent loss of his wife and all his children, by studying the ancient writers at Padua up to the age of ninety-two years, when he went to his grave.[1]

And lastly, it is necessary to mention the University of Florence. In general, the Italian universities had been seats of mediæval and scholastic culture ; learning had commenced outside, and not

[1] Vespasiano, " Vita di P. Strozzi."

seldom in opposition to them. But it was otherwise in Florence, the *Studio* almost rose and fell with the rise and fall of erudition. It did not come into existence until the December of 1321, dragged on languidly enough, now closed, now reopened, until 1397, when Crisolora, by his teachings in the Greek tongue, made Florence the centre of Hellenism in Italy. Later, the University again began to languish, but was renovated in 1414 by the efforts of Niccoli and of Strozzi, who, taking advantage of an ancient law, decreeing that none of the teachers should be Florentines, invited the most celebrated men in Greece and Italy ; thus forwarding more than ever the union of Latin and Greek culture, and that of Florentine learning with Italian. In 1473, Lorenzo dei Medici transferred the Studio to Pisa ; but Florence was allowed to retain a few chairs of literature and philosophy, which were always filled by celebrated men.[1] The great literary movement, that we have been employed in examining, produced no man of commanding talent after Petrarch and Boccaccio. All was confined to collecting, copying, correcting codices ; materials were prepared for a fresh literary advance, which, however, had not yet begun. Italian composition had decayed, and Latin had as yet no original merits ; we find grammarians, bibliophiles, and bibliographers in the place of real writers. But by slow degrees a new generation of learned men sprung up, showing a genuine, and, up to that date, unusual originality. This fact was the result of a natural process of things ; writers who had at last thoroughly mastered the Latin tongue, began to express themselves with an ease and spontaneity which gave rise to new literary qualities, even to a new literature. Grammatical questions, when examined and discussed by men of the acute intellect and fine taste at that time possessed by Italians, were inevitably transformed into philosophical questions, thus laying the foundation of fresh progress in science.

But extraneous causes were also at work to hasten and provoke so notable a transformation, and foremost among these was the study of Greek. It was the means of bringing into contact, not merely two languages, but two different literatures, philosophies,

---

[1] The decree was signed in 1472—Prezziner, " Storia del Pubblico Studio," &c. : Florence, 1812, in 2 vols. This work has not much historical value ; but notices concerning the Studio are to be found scattered among the writings of the learned men, and one can also consult the work entitled—" Historia Academiæ Pisanæ," auctore Angelo Fabronio : Pisis, 1791-95, in 3 vols.

civilizations. Thus the horizon was suddenly enlarged, and besides the greater originality of Greek thought and language, the mere fact of their great difference from Latin thought and language was of immense importance. The Italian mind found itself constrained to higher effort, to a longer and more difficult mental flight, requiring and developing greater intellectual energy. During the Middle Ages the Greek language had been very little known in Italy, and the knowledge of it possessed by the monks of St. Basilio, in Calabria, was much exaggerated by report. Two Calabrians, Barlaam and Leonzio Pilato, had picked up the language at Constantinople ; and the former of these taught its rudiments to Petrarch, who, notwithstanding his ardent desire to learn it, could never understand the Homer that he kept spread open before him.[1] The second was Professor in Florence for three years, thanks to Boccaccio, who thus brought about the foundation of the first Greek chair in Italy. But from 1363 to 1396 this instruction, in itself poor enough, failed entirely. Italians desiring to obtain it were compelled, like Guarino and Filelfo, to seek it at Constantinople. And the first Greek refugees who came among us were of far less use than is commonly supposed ; for being ignorant of Italian, having only a smattering of Latin, and not being men of letters, they were quite incapable of satisfying a passion to which, however, their very presence was a lively stimulus. It was the election of Emanuele Crisolora to a professorship in the Studio, in 1396, that really marked the beginning of a new era of Hellenism in Italy. Previously a teacher at Constantinople, he was a true man of letters, he was capable of teaching scientifically, and he numbered among his pupils the first *literati* of Florence. Roberto dei Rossi, Palla Strozzi, Poggio Bracciolini, Giannozzo Manetti, and Carlo Marsuppini immediately came to attend his lessons. Leonardo Bruni, then engaged in legal studies, no sooner heard that it was at last possible to learn Homer's tongue, and drink of the first fountain of knowledge, than he forsook everything in order to become one of the best Hellenists and *literati* of his time.[2] From that moment, he who was ignorant of Greek was esteemed but half educated in Florence, for that study made

---

[1] Petrarca, "Lettere Senili," bk. iii. lett. 6 ; bk. v. lett. 1 ; bk. vi. lett. 1, 2.
[2] Leon. Bruni, " Rerum suo tempore in Italia gestarum, Commentarius," apud Murat. Script., Tom. xix. p. 920.

rapid strides, and it was likewise greatly aided by the arrival of other refugees, generally of higher cultivation, and who found a better prepared soil.[1] Another important aid was the Florentine Council of 1439, which, intended to reunite the Greek and Latin Churches, served instead to unite the literary spirit of Rome and Greece. The Pope had need of Italian interpreters to understand the representatives of Greece, and both parties, equally indifferent to religious questions, at the first meeting leapt from theology to philosophy, which was usually among the Greeks more widely cultivated than letters. Giorgio Gemisto Pletone, the most learned of those who came at this time to Italy, and an enthusiastic admirer of Plato, succeeded in inspiring Cosimo dei Medici with the same admiration ; hence the origin of the Platonic Academy. An enormous enthusiasm, a prodigious literary activity then began in Florence, and at last we see the appearance of a new literary originality, and the beginning of a revival of philosophy.[2]

The first scholar to prove himself an original writer was Poggio Bracciolini, born at Terranova, near Arezzo, in 1380. After studying Greek with Crisolora, he went with Pope John XXIII. to the Council of Constance as a member of the Curia, and wearing the ecclesiastical dress, without, however, being in holy orders. This was a common custom among the learned, who— if unmarried—could in this manner obtain many advantages reserved for the clergy, of whom, however, they generally spoke much evil. Soon wearying of religious controversies and disputes, Bracciolini set out upon a journey, and in one of his letters gave an admirable description of the Falls of the Rhine and of the Baden springs ; indeed, of these latter he gives a picture so vivid that to this day we can recognize its fidelity.[3] His Latin, though far more correct than that of his predecessors, is full of Italianisms and neologisms ; but it has the spontaneousness and vivacity of a living language ; instead of a mere reproduction, it is a real and genuine revival. Therefore it is in Poggio and some of his contemporaries that we must look for the flower of the Humani-

---

[1] Tiraboschi, "Storia della Letteratura Italiana" ; Gibbon, "Decline and Fall," &c. ; Voigt, " Die Wiederbelebung," &c.

[2] *Vide* Voigt, Gibbon, and also my " Storia di G. Savonarola," vol. i. chap. iv.

[3] G. Shepherd, " Vita di Poggio Bracciolini," translated from the English by T. Tonelli, with notes and additions. Florence : Ricci, 1825, 2 vols. *Vide* vol. i. p. 65 and fol. the translation of the letter quoted from.

ties, not in those who, like Bembo and Casa, gave us an imitation which, if more faithful, is also more mechanical and material. Poggio, throwing aside dictionaries and grammars, feels the need of writing as he speaks ; is enthusiastic in the presence of Nature ; seeks truth, and laughs at authorities ; but still remains a man of learning, and this fact must ever be kept in sight. In the year 1416 he was present at the trial and execution of Jerome of Prague, and described everything in full in one of his best known letters to Bruni. The independence of mind with which this learned member of the Papal Curia dared to admire the heroism of Luther's precursor, and proclaim him worthy of immortality, is truly remarkable. But what was it that he admired in him ? Not the martyr, not the reformer ;—on the contrary, he asserts that if Jerome had indeed said anything against the Catholic faith, he well deserved his punishment. What he admired in him was the courage of a Cato and of a Mutius Scævola ; he extolled "his clear, sweet, and sonorous voice ; the nobility of his gestures, so well adapted either to express indignation or excite compassion ; the eloquence and learning with which, at the foot of the pile, he quoted Socrates, Anaxagoras, Plato, and the Fathers." [1]

Soon we find Poggio leaving Constance altogether, for the purpose of making long journeys. He traversed Switzerland and Germany, hunting through monasteries in search of old manuscripts, of which he was the most favoured discoverer in that century. To him we owe works of Quintilian, Valerius Flaccus, Cicero, Silius Italicus, Ammianust Marcellinus, Lucretius, Tertullian, Plautus, Petronius, &c. When the news of these discoveries reached Florence, the city was wild with joy, and Bruni wrote to him, that above all, by the discovery of Quintilian, he had made himself the second father of Roman eloquence. " All the people of Italy," wrote he, " should go forth to meet the great writer whom thou hast delivered from the hands of the barbarians." [2] Many others then followed his example in searching for manuscripts. It was said that Aurispa had brought from Constantinople no less than two hundred and thirty-eight codices ; and the fable was spread that Guarino's hair turned suddenly white through his having lost in a shipwreck many codices that

---

[1] Poggii, " Opera," Basle edition, pp. 301–305.
[2] L. Aretini, " Epist." bk. iv. ep. 5.

he was bringing to Italy from the East.[1] But no one equalled Bracciolini in diligence and good fortune.

In England, however, while with Cardinal Beaufort, he found himself isolated, in the company of wealthy uncultured nobles, who passed the chief part of their life in eating and drinking.[2] During those dinners, which sometimes lasted four hours, he was obliged to rise from time to time and bathe his eyes with cold water, in order to keep himself awake.[3] Yet the country offered, by its novelty, a vast field of observation to Bracciolini, who had the acuteness to notice that even in those days it was a special characteristic of the English aristocracy readily to admit within its ranks men who had raised themselves from the middle classes.[4] But the novelty of the country and the variety of customs and characters, all of which he noticed and which occupied his mind, were not sufficient recompense for the slight account in which the learned were held there, and he, therefore, sighed for his native land.

And in a short time we find him established in Rome as secretary to the Roman Curia during the reign of Martin V. There at last he was in his true element. He used to spend the long winter evenings with his colleagues, in a room of the Cancelleria, which went by the name of *the place of lies* (*il bugiale, sive mendaciorum officina*), because there they amused each other with anecdotes, both true and false, and more or less indecent, in which they ridiculed the Pope, the Cardinals, and even the dogmas of the religion in defence of which they wrote Briefs. In the morning he attended to the slight duties of his office, and composed literary works, among others his dialogues on avarice and hypocrisy—vices which he declared to be peculiar to the clergy—and, therefore, severely scourged. But no serious motive is to be found in these satires; only the same biting and sceptical spirit shown by our comic writers and novelists, who, like Poggio, laughed at the faith which they professed. These latter sought to paint the manners of the day; Poggio and the other men of learning chiefly desired to show the ease with

---

[1] Tiraboschi, "Storia della Letteratura Italiana," vol. vi. p. 118; Rosmini, "Vita e disciplina di Guarino Veronese," Brescia, 1805-6.

[2] *Vide* his letter to Niccoli, dated 29th October, 1420, published in the translation of Shepherd's Work, vol. i. p. 111, Note C.

[3] Vespasiano, "Vita di Poggio Bracciolini," s. 1.

[4] Poggii, "Opera," p. 69.

which they could use the Latin tongue on all kinds of subjects, sacred or profane, serious, comic, or obscene. That was all.

In fact Bracciolini, notwithstanding his onslaughts on the corrupt manners of the clergy, led a very intemperate life. And when Cardinal St. Angelo reproved him for having children, which was unfitting to an ecclesiastic, and still more for having them by a mistress, which was unfitting to a layman; he replied without at all losing countenance : "I have children, and that is fitting to a layman; I have them by a mistress, and that is an old custom of the clergy." And farther on in the letter he tells the story of an Abbé who presented a son of his to Martin V., and receiving a reproof, answered, amid the laughter of the Curia, that he had four others also ready and willing to take up arms for His Holiness.[1]

Coming to Florence with Pope Eugene IV., he was thrown among the learned men gathered together there, and drawn into very violent disputes with the restless Filelfo, who was then teaching in the University. This scholar, who had been to Constantinople and there married a Greek wife, was almost the only man in Italy who could then speak and write the language of Plato and Aristotle. He worried every one by his boundless vanity and restlessness of character ; at last he made attacks against the Medici, and was compelled to leave Florence. Then he began to write satires aimed at the learned who had been his friends and colleagues, and Bracciolini replied to him in his "Invettive." It was a warfare of indecent insults, in which the two scholars showed off their strength in rhetoric and their masterly Latinity. Filelfo had the advantage of writing in verse, and therefore his insults were easier to retain in the memory ; but Bracciolini, having greater talent and wit, was better able, by writing in prose, to express all that he wished to say. He repulsed the abuse which "Filelfo had vomited from the fetid sewer of his mouth," and attributed his adversary's foulness of language to the education he had received from his mother, " whose trade it was to clean the entrails of beasts ; it was her stench therefore that now emanated from her son."[2] He accused

---

[1] *Vide* Shepherd's Work, vol. i. pp. 184-85.

[2] " Verum nequaquam mirum videri debet, cum eius mater Arimini dudum in purgandis ventribus, et intestinis sordi deluendis quæstum fecerit, maternæ artis fœtorem redolere. Haesit naribus filii sagacis materni exercitii attractata putredo et continui stercoris fœteris halitus " (Poggii, " Opera," p. 165).

him of having seduced the daughter of his master, in order to
marry her and then make a traffic of her honour, and wound up
by offering him a crown worthy of so much foulness.[1] Not
content with all this, they even accused each other of vices which
modesty forbids us to mention in these days, but of which these
learned scholars were accustomed to speak without reserve and
almost in jest, after the manner of Greek and Roman writers.

Our minds shrink from dwelling on the frightful moral depravity
with which all these things saturated the Italian spirit. And
Poggio composed these much-praised invectives of his in a
delightful villa, full of statues, busts, and ancient coins of which
he made use to gain a closer knowledge of antiquity, thus
inaugurating the study of archæology, as he had already done in
Rome by describing its monuments and remains. He considered
this to be the fit paradise for a chosen spirit, for an encyclopædic
man of letters destined to immortality. At the age of fifty-five,
in order to marry a young lady of high birth, he abandoned the
woman with whom he had lived up to that time, and who had
made him the father of fourteen children, of whom four survivors,
legitimized by him, were left destitute by this marriage. But he
remedied this by writing a dialogue : *An seni sit uxor ducenda*,
in which he defended his own cause. An elegant Latin composition was all that was needed to solve the hardest problems of
existence, and soothe his own conscience. To a man of learning
words were of greater value than facts ; to be eloquent in the
praise of virtue was as good as being virtuous, and the greatest of
mankind owed their immortality solely to the eloquence with
which their lives had been narrated by first-rate writers. Where
would be the fame of Hannibal or Scipio, of Alexander or
Alcibiades, without Livy, without Plutarch ? He who could
write Latin with eloquence, was not only sure of his own
immortality, but could bestow it upon others at his own good
pleasure.

From Tuscany Poggio returned to Rome, and during the
pontificate of Nicholas V., profited by the wide liberty accorded
to the learned, to publish attacks on priests and friars and the

---

[1] " At stercorea corona ornabuntur fœtentes crines priapei vati " (Poggii,
" Opera," p. 167). It is impossible to give the most obscene fragments of Poggio's
" Invettive " and Filelfo's " Satire." Mons. Nisard in his " Gladiateurs," &c.,
attempted to give several in the appendices to his " Vita del Filelfo e di Poggio ; "
but he too found it impossible to continue.

"Liber Facetiarum, in which he collected all the satires and indecencies that used to be related in the *bugiale*. In the preface to this book, he plainly stated that his object was to show how the Latin tongue ought and might be made to express everything. In vain the more rigorous blamed this old man of seventy for thus contaminating his white hairs : since Panormita had published his "Hermaphroditus," the Italian ear was shocked by nothing, and Poggio tranquilly passed his time in writing obscenities and keeping up literary quarrels. About this time he had one with Trapezunzio that ended in blows ; another with Valla, and this gave rise to a new series of "Invectivæ" on his part, and on his opponent's to an "Antidotus in Poggium." The question turned on the worth of the Latinity and the grammatical rules asserted in·the "Elegantiæ," of Valla, who, possessed of a superior critical faculty, came off victor in the fight. And in this quarrel also the disputants rivalled each other in scandalous indecency. Accused of every vice that was most horrible, Valla gave as good as he got, without much concern for his own defence, and indeed often showing a remarkable amount of cynicism. Thus, when Poggio accused him of having seduced his own sister's maid, he replied merrily that he had wished to prove the falsity of his brother-in-law's assertion, namely, that his chastity did not proceed from virtue.[1] It would, however, be a great mistake to measure by the violence of these writers' insults the force of their passions. The "Invectivæ" were almost always simple exercises of rhetoric ; the two disputants came down into the arena in the spirit of performers about to give a display of their dexterity and nudity. But even if the passions were unreal, there was terrible reality in the moral harm resulting from these miserable shows.

We gladly turn aside from these foul places, for we have as yet by no means fully described the prodigious activity of Poggio Bracciolini. Next to epistles, orations were the compositions most in favour with the learned. They crowded into these all possible reminiscences of antiquity, all possible figures of rhetoric. A good memory was frequently the only faculty necessary to secure certain success—"he had an endless memory, he quoted every one of the ancient writers"—was the eulogium Vespasiano used to make on the most celebrated of these orators, who seemed to have

---

[1] "Volui itaque eis ostendere id quod facerem non vitium esse corporis, sed animi virtutem " ("Antidotus," p. 222).

some thesaurus from which to draw inspiration for their own eloquence. Were a general mentioned, instantly a list of great battles was given : a poet, and forth came a torrent of precepts from Horace or Quintilian. The real subject disappeared before the desire to turn everything into an opportunity of gaining greater familiarity with antiquity ; style was false, artifice continual, exaggerations innumerable, and all funeral orations became apotheoses. Once Filelfo, wishing to attack one of his persecutors, took the chair and began in Italian ; " Who is the cause of so many suspicions ? Who is the originator of so many insults ? Who is the author of so many outrages ? Who and what is this man ? Shall I name so great a monster ? Shall I designate such a Cerberus ? Shall I tell you who he is ? Certainly I must tell you, I say it, I will say it, were it at the cost of my life. He is the accursed, the monstrous, the detestable, the abominable. . . . Ah ! Filelfo, hold thy peace, for heaven's sake utter not his name ! He who is incapable of controlling himself, is ill-fitted to blame the intolerance and inconstancy of another."[1] This was what was then considered a model of eloquence ; hence Pius II. was right in saying that a skilful orator could only stir hearers of small intelligence.[2] A Frenchman of good taste, the Cardinal d'Estoutville, when listening to an eulogy on St. Thomas of Aquinas, delivered by Valla, could not refrain from exclaiming : " But this man is stark mad ! "[3] Yet these orations were then so much in vogue, that they were considered indispensable on all great occasions, whether a proclamation of peace, the presentation of an ambassador, or any other public or private solemnity. Every court, every government, sometimes even wealthy families, had their official orator. And precisely as now-a-days there are few *fêtes* without music, so in those times a Latin discourse in verse or prose was the choicest diversion of every cultured company. Numbers of these discourses were printed, but these were the minority ; Italian libraries contain hundreds still inedited. But in all this abundance no examples of real eloquence are to be found, with the exception of a few of the orations of Pius II., whose utterances were not always mere literary exercises, but who

[1] Rosmini, " Vita di Filelfo," vol. i. doc. ix. p. 125.
[2] Platina, " Vita di Pii II."
[3] Gasparo Veronese quoted by Voigt. *Vide* " Die Wiederbelebung," &c., p. 437.

often spoke with some definite aim, and did not then pour forth floods of rhetoric.

Poggio Bracciolini was held to be one of the first masters of oratory, and seldom lost an opportunity of making an oration, particularly in praise of deceased literary friends. The ease of his style, though often sinking into prolix verbosity, his vivacity, dash and good sense, render him more readable than the others, but never eloquent. The last years of his life were passed in Florence, where, on the death of Carlo Marsuppini (April 24, 1453), he was made secretary of the Republic, and wrote his last work, a " History of Florence" from 1350 to 1455. In this work, following the example of Leonardo Bruni, he forsakes the manner of the Florentine chroniclers, to the loss of the graphic power and vivacity of which they had given such splendid examples. There is not a single anecdote or narrative drawn from life, not a trace of a personal knowledge of events in the midst of which the author had really lived and in which he had taken his part. He seems to be narrating deeds of the Greeks and Romans ; he never deigns to speak of the internal affairs of the Republic ; we hear only of great battles, and listen to long and solemn Latin speeches recited by Florentines always in the Roman dress. In point of fact Poggio's great object was the imitation of Livy's epic narrative, and although this made him lose the spontaneous qualities of the old chroniclers, it at least compelled him to try and link facts together in a literary if not a scientific way. And thus began the transformation of the chronicle into history. He and Bruni were the precursors of Machiavelli and Guicciardini, although in every respect very inferior to them. Of the two, Bruni is the better critic, while Bracciolini has an easier style, that, however, is frequently verbose. Sannazzaro accused the latter of overweening partiality for his own country ; [1] but that consisted chiefly in the tone he assumed in always speaking of Florence as though it were the Republic of Rome.

Poggio Bracciolini, although the chief, was not the only representative of this second period of Italian learning ; he was one of a numerous band of other scholars, and of these the most celebrated was Leonardo Bruni, born in 1369, at Arezzo, and known

---

[1] Sannazzaro wrote :

" Dum patriam laudat, damnat dum Poggius hostem ;
   Nec malus est civis, nec bonus historicus."

therefore as the Aretino. We have already seen how, on the arrival of Crisolora in Florence, he threw aside his legal studies to devote himself entirely to Greek ; and so rapid was his progress that he was soon qualified to translate not only the principal historians and orators, but also the philosophers of Greece. He thereby rendered an immense service to literature, for his versions of the classic authors were the first from the original Greek, and were not only written in elegant Latin, but were faithful translations, and appeared at a moment when the need for them was great and universal. His versions of the "Apologia" of Socrates, the "Phaedo," "Krito," "Gorgias," and "Phaedrus" of Plato, and those of the Economical and Political Ethics of Aristotle, were one of the great literary events of the age. On the one hand it was a revelation of the Platonic philosophy, till then almost unknown in Italy ; on the other, it was the first appearance of what was called the true Aristotle, unknown in the Middle Ages. The learned could now admire the eloquence which Petrarch had vainly sought in the travestied and almost barbarous Aristotle of his time ; they were no longer compelled to study the Greek schoolman instead of the Greek philosopher.

Thus Bruni gave an immense impulse to philosophy and criticism. His, in fact, was a critical mind, as we see even by his Epistles, in which, for the first time, we find the opinion maintained that Italian was derived from the spoken Latin, which differed from the written tongue, and this opinion he enforced by arguments which show this scholar of the fifteenth century to have been in some respects a true precursor of modern philology.[1] These qualities are still more noticeable in his historical works, first of which is his "Storia di Firenze," from its origin down to 1401. Of this we may repeat what we have already said of Bracciolini's history, which is its continuation. Here also the internal conditions of the Republic are neglected to make room for descriptions of great battles, speeches, and dissertations. Here, too, local colouring is wanting, and Florentines appear in a Roman dress. Bruni, as we have before remarked, is inferior to Bracciolini in ease of style ; but he forestalled his friend in forsaking the track of the chroniclers, and as he did not write of contemporary

---

[1] This letter is addressed to Flavio Biondo of Forli, and is also to be found in the first number of a work now in course of publication, entitled, " I due primi secoli della Letteratura Italiana," by A. Bartoli : Milan, Vallardi. The author, like other men of learning, holds it in due consideration.

events, had a freer scope for the display of his critical faculty. In fact it does Aretino the greatest honour that he should have been the first who, rejecting at once all the fables current on the origin of Florence, sought out in the classical writers the primitive history of the Etruscans, and applied the same critical sagacity to that of the Middle Ages.[1] Elsewhere we shall have occasion to return to these historical works ; for the present it is enough to remark that criticism gradually became one of the principal occupations of this century, that was so eager in demolishing the past.

Leonardo Aretino was a man of very great personal weight in Florence, where he filled many important offices, among others, during a long period, that of secretary to the Republic.[2] Dying in 1444, he was succeeded by Carlo Marsuppini, of Arezzo, called therefore Carlo Aretino. This latter wrote little, and nothing of any importance ; he was, however, a renowned teacher, the fortunate rival of Filelfo in the Florentine Studio, and enjoyed great fame, chiefly owing to the strength of his memory, which enabled him to make a distinguished figure in public discourses. His first lecture was loudly applauded, because, as Vespasian tells us, " the Greeks and Latins had no writer left unquoted by Messer Carlo that morning."[3] He displayed a great contempt for Christianity, and a vast admiration for the Pagan religion.[4] To him, as to Bruni, solemn funeral honours were decreed by the Republic. Both bore the poet's laurels on their bier ; both repose in Santa Croce, the one opposite the other, beneath monuments equally elegant, with inscriptions equally pompous, despite the great distance between the talent of the one and the other. Marsuppini's funeral eulogy was read by one of his pupils, Matteo Palmieri ; that of Bruni, on the other hand, was read by another first-rate literary man, and was a solemn event. It was in the centre of the public square, standing beside the bier on which lay Bruni's body, with his volume of " Storia Fiorentina " on his

---

[1] An elegant edition of this History, with Donato Accinoli's translation, was published at Florence, 1856–60, 3 vols. 8vo. Signor Cirillo Monzani published an accurate " Discorso " on Bruni in the " Archivio Storico," new series, vol. v. part I, pp. 29–59 ; part 2, pp. 3–34. See also the remarks upon Bracciolini's and Bruni's histories made by Gervinus in his work, " Florentinische Historiographise," published in the vol. entitled, " Historische Schriften " : Frankfurt, à M., 1833.

[2] The first time in 1410 for a single year ; the second from 1427 to 1444.

[3] Vespasiano, " Vita di Carlo d'Arezzo."

[4] Ibid., Tiraboschi, " Storia della Letteratura Italiana."

breast, that Giannozzo Manetti, by many esteemed the first of living *literati*, pronounced his oration in the presence of the chief magistrates of the Republic.

Yet no one can now read this oration without experiencing great amazement that so *barocco* a composition should have aroused such universal applause in an age of so much culture and devotion to the classics. Manetti begins by declaring that had it been possible for the immortal muses (*immortales Musæ, divinæque Camœnæ*), to make a Latin discourse and weep in public, they would hardly have left the task to him on so solemn an occasion. Then narrating Bruni's life, he seizes the occasion of his nomination as secretary to the Republic, to run through the history of Florence. He touches on his works and then branches off into a dissertation on Greek and Latin authors, and particularly on Cicero and Livy, placing Bruni above both, for the important reason that the former not only translated from the Greek like the one, but also wrote history like the other, thus uniting in himself the merits of both. Then, the moment having arrived for placing the wreath on the head of his deceased friend, he speaks of the antiquity of this usage, and of the various wreaths, *civica, muralis, obsidionalis, castrensis, navalis*, and continues his descriptions through five large and closely written pages. He asserts that Bruni had earned the wreath by his true poetic gifts, and then digresses into a series of empty phrases, in explanation of the signification of the word poet, and the nature of poetry ; winding up with a pompous apostrophe, and crowning "the happy and immortal slumber of the marvellous star of the Latins." [1]

Manetti was born at Florence in 1396, and at the age of twenty-five, on his father's death, left his counter to give himself up to study with such exceeding ardour, that he only allowed himself five hours' sleep. His house had a door opening into the garden of Santo Spirito, where he used to study, and for nine years he never crossed the Arno into the centre of the town.[2] He acquired Latin, Greek, and Hebrew ; wrote with great ease, and had an "eternal, immortal" memory according to Vespasiano's usual phrase. But his chief excellence lay in his moral character. A practised man of business, religious, steadfast, and truly honest, the principal effect of his studies was to give him a lofty ideal of life,

---

[1] *Vide* this oration in the preface to Bruni's " Epistole."
[2] Vespasiano, " Vita di G. Manetti," sec. ii.

to which he was ever faithful in the various offices with which he was entrusted. Vicar and captain of the Republic in many cities distracted by hostile factions, he was able to inflict very severe sentences, and impose heavy taxes, without ever being accused of partiality. He refused to accept the customary donations, giving liberally from his own purse to all who were in need, and establishing peace and concord wherever he went. He passed his leisure hours in writing lives of Socrates and Seneca, *De dignitate et excellentia homines*, and the history of the cities which he successively inhabited. As a learned man he chiefly shone by his orations, delivered in the various ambassadorial missions on which he was sent in consequence of his celebrity as an orator. In Rome, Naples, Genoa, and Venice, he was received with the honours of royalty ; and so high was his reputation, that by means of a Latin letter, he succeeded in regaining from the Condottiere Piccinini eight horses that had been stolen by some soldiers of his band. Being sent to congratulate Nicholas V. on his election, in the name of the republic of Florence, people crowded from the neighbouring cities to hear him, and the Pope listened to him with such absorbed attention, that a prelate beside him nudged his elbow several times thinking that his Holiness had fallen asleep. "When the oration was over, everybody shook hands with the Florentines as though Pisa and its territory were won," [1] and the Venetian Cardinals wrote home to their government that they ought to send an orator equal to Manetti for the sake of the dignity of the State. At Naples King Alfonso sat like a statue on his throne all the time Manetti was speaking. Yet he was a speaker of no originality. His orations—of a false and inflated style—are mere medleys of facts, collections of Latin phrases, which was exactly what pleased best in those days, and gave free scope for the display of his vast reading, powerful memory, and prodigious facility for stringing together sonorous periods. He was the author of many histories and biographies, which had neither the vivacity of the old chroniclers, nor even the merits of Aretino and Bracciolini. His treatises on philosophy are empty dissertations ; his numerous translations from the Greek and Latin are inferior to those of his predecessor Aretino. His versions of the Psalter from the Hebrew and of the New Testament from the Greek prove his dissatisfaction with the Vulgate, but do not support the theory of those who tried to attribute to

[1] Vespasiano, "Vita di G. Manetti," sec. xv.

him a religious daring of which he was incapable. The last years of his life were embittered by the envy that drove him from Florence ; but he found protection at Rome and Naples, and died in the latter city, where he was a pensioner of Alfonso of Aragon, on the 26th October, 1459.

Although Manetti's great reputation has not survived, he merits an important place in the history of the fifteenth century, precisely because his life is a proof that no profession or age, however corrupt, need prevent a man from preserving true nobility of mind. The same Pagan learning that was to entail so great moral ruin on Italy was used by him for the elevation of his whole nature. Indeed it is plainly an error, though a very common one, to condemn in one sweeping sentence the general character of the learned men. We have already found ourselves forced to admire Coluccio Salutati and Palla Strozzi ; many other worthy characters are to be found among the less known men. This is sufficiently proved by the biographies of Vespasiano whose excessive ingenuousness may excite our blame, but can leave no doubt of the sincerity of his admiration for virtue. He tells us of Messer Zembrino da Pistoia, who taught "not only letters, but morals," and abandoning every other employment to devote himself to philosophy, "lived a frugal and temperate life, giving all he had to the poor, and contenting himself with hermit's fare. Also he was of "thoroughly sincere mind, generous, without fraud or malice, as all men ought to be." Speaking of Maestro Paolo, a Florentine, learned in Greek, Latin, the seven liberal arts, and also given to astronomy, he adds, that he never held intercourse with woman ; slept in his clothes upon a board beside his writing table ; lived on vegetables and fruit ; "was devoted to virtue, and had placed therein his every hope. . . . When not at study, he would go and take care of some friend." [1] All this notwithstanding, it cannot be denied that the greater number of these *eruditi* had no force of character, although ardently devoted to learning. The continued exercise of the intelligence on questions that were frequently of mere form ; the wandering life of courtiers compelled to gain their bread by the sale of eulogiums ; the perpetual rivalries ; the absence of all spirit of brotherhood or caste in the exercise of their common work or office, and their moral destructiveness did not help to ennoble their characters. If, too, it be added, that all this was going on at a moment in which liberty was

[1] See in Vespasiano the two " Vite di Zembrino Pistolese e di Maestro Pagolo."

already extinguished, society decayed, religion scandalously profaned by the Popes ; it will be easily understood what profound
moral corruption must have been rife in Italy, when the learned
were the expositors of virtue, the apportioners of glory, the representatives of public opinion.   But still we must not refuse to
acknowledge the handful of righteous men who escaped from
the general wreck.   If we do not impartially take into account
all the elements of culture and of the diverse natures of men, we
stand in danger of never being able to understand how the Italian
genius then contrived, amid so many dangers, to find sufficient
strength in itself to promote an extraordinary intellectual advance,
and avoid the total moral destruction, to which perhaps another
nation might have succumbed under similar conditions.

3. LEARNED MEN IN ROME.

After Florence, Rome is certainly the city of highest standing
in letters.   From the days of Petrarch, the Popes began to feel
the need of having their Briefs composed by men of learning.
And during the Pontificate of Martin, the learned members of the
Curia already asserted the right of taking precedence at all public
ceremonies over the consistorial advocates, of whom they spoke
with much contempt.[1]   P. Bracciolini was then the principal
personage among them, and with him were others of lesser fame,
such as Antonio Lusco, a writer of rhymed epistles and epigrams,
who had extracted the rules of rhetoric from Cicero's orations,
and composed a formulary for transacting the business of the Curia
in classical language.[2]   But while in Florence men of learning
enjoyed an important social standing and great independence, in
Rome they merely formed a small clique, and were subordinate
employés who, though generally well remunerated, could only
aspire to the condition of favoured courtiers.   Still they daily increased in number, obtaining posts in the *Abbreviatura*, where
there were as many as a hundred writers of Briefs, or in the Pope's
private secretary's office, where the clerical dress had to be assumed without the obligation of taking orders.   The post of *Ab-
breviatore* or Brief writer was a permanent one ; that of secretary

---

[1] Voigt, "Die Wiederbelebung," &c., p. 279, note 3.
[2] " Scripsit item exempla quædam et veluti formulas, quibus Romana Curia in
scribendo uteretur, quæ etiam ab eruditissimis viris in usum recepta sunt " (Facius,
" De Viris illustribus," p. 3).

generally lasted only for the Pope's lifetime, but as besides many perquisites, it implied hopes of possible favour and promotion : with these offices it fetched a high price (everything could be bought in Rome), although the first was the more sought after and the dearer of the two.[1]

The golden age for men of letters in Rome was the reign of Nicholas V., who, had it been possible, would have collected, within the walls of the Eternal City, all the manuscripts in the world, all the men of learning and all the monuments of Florence. The savings he made, and the sums received at the jubilee in 1450, gave him the means to set to work upon his project. The Curia and the Segreteria were quickly filled with learned men, whom the Pope, who knew little or no Greek, employed in making translations, for which he paid them largely. Valla was entrusted with the translation of Thucydides, and on its completion received five hundred crowns and a commission for the translation of Herodotus ; Bracciolini was charged with that of Diodorus Siculus ; Guarino Veronese, who was at Ferrara, with that of Strabo and the promise of five hundred crowns for each part of the work : others received similar commissions. But Nicholas V. could find no one able to undertake a rendering of Homer into Latin verse, although he had sought everywhere, and made most generous offers to Filelfo.

Theodore Gaza, George Trapezunzio, Bessarion, and many other Greek exiles, also found their way to Rome, many of them receiving similar offices and similar commissions. The majority of them, however, were restless adventurers who had changed their religion in the hope of gain. Bessarion, one of the converts, was certainly a man of weight, learned, and a better Latin scholar than most of his compatriots ; he became a Cardinal, was wealthy, and a diligent collector of manuscripts.[2] He posed as a a Mæcenas, and Nicholas V. gave him the post of Legate at Bologna, probably in order not to have him as almost his own rival in Rome.

All this great company of translators and refugees, gathered

---

[1] Voigt, " Enea Silvio dei Piccolomini, als Papst Pius der Zweite," vol. iii. p. 548 fol.

[2] His library, in thirty cases, containing six hundred volumes, was left to Venice, and formed the first nucleus of the Library of St. Mark. Vespasiano, "Vita de Card. Niceno ; " Voigt, " Die Wiederbelebung," &c., Tiraboschi, " Storia della Letteratura Italiana."

together at the Pope's expense, may be called a medley of hetero-
geneous elements.   They were undoubtedly useful in the diffusion
of the results of labour begun in Florence, but they were incapable of any really original work ; they doubtless produced many
useful translations, but we may observe that whereas those of
Bruni, at Florence, had opened a new road to research, and were
made by a man who had undertaken them of his own free choice,
those purchased by Nicholas V. were, on the contrary, commissioned works, often executed by learned men, such as Poggio
and Valla, whose principal merit scarcely consisted in knowledge of Greek, or by Greek refugees who knew very little Latin.
The most notable productions of this Roman company of scholars
were works like the " Facezie " and the " Invettive " of Bracciolini
or the " Antidoto " of Valla, in which, as we have seen, they hurled
vile insults at each other's heads.   The Pope might easily have imposed a check on this unedifying spectacle, but, on the contrary,
he seemed to take pleasure in it.   But it is necessary to observe
that, under his pontificate, the learned men whom he protected
also published works on serious subjects and of high importance ;
these, however, were either not written in Rome, or written, as
we shall see, without his encouragement.

It was natural that one who had formed so great a workshop
of translators should also found a great library.   And, in fact,
although before his time Martin V. had begun to collect
manuscripts, and later on Sixtus IV. opened to the public the
famous Vatican library, its true founder, as we have elsewhere
remarked, was Nicholas V.   Enoch of Ascoli went all over the
world ransacking monasteries for manuscripts, furnished with
Briefs authorising him to transcribe or buy them.[1]   Giovanni
Tortello, author of a manual of orthography for copyists,[2] was
the librarian of this Pope, who, according to Vespasiano, collected
five thousand volumes, had them sumptuously bound, and spent
forty thousand crowns on them.[3]   He also began the restoration

---

[1] Tortellii, " Commentariorum grammaticorum de Ortographia dictionum e
Graecis tractarum Opus," Vicentiæ, 1479.

[2] Vespasiano, " Vite di Enoche d'Ascoli, di Niccolo V., di Giovanni Tortello."

[3] So he says in his "Vita di Niccolo V. ; " in that of " Tortello," s. 1. he says
instead : " Aveva fatto inventario di tutti i libri che aveva in quella libreria, e fu
mirabile cosa la quantità ch 'egli diceva avere, ch 'erano da volumi novemila."
Others give other numbers ; it is difficult to ascertain the exact number.   Voigt,
" Die Wiederbelebung," &c., p. 364.

of the streets, bridges, and walls of Rome ; he laid the foundations of a new Vatican ; he fortified the Capitol and the castle of St. Angelo ; restored or rebuilt from the foundations a great many churches in Rome, Viterbo, Assisi, &c., and constructed new fortresses in many cities of the State. In short, under Alberti's advice, and with the help of Bernardo and Antonio Rosselli, Nicholas V. was enabled to transform Rome into a great monumental city, thus rivalling not only the Medici, but even the greatest of the ancient emperors.[1] From all this it is easy to understand how, without having any special talent, Nicholas has succeeded in sending his name down to posterity. It must also be added that his reign was made illustrious by the presence of three men of singular ability, two of whom were in his employ. And although, as we have already noticed, their principal works were either written away from Rome or without exciting any attention on the part of the Pope ; yet they indirectly conferred on him an honour that was quite undeserved. The first of the learned trio was Lorenzo Valla, whom we have seen among the Papal secretaries and translators, but who had previously led a very adventurous life. Of a Piacenza family, but born in Rome (1406), he boasted of his Roman birth. Up to the age of twenty-four he remained in Rome, where he was the pupil of Leonardo Bruni, and also, it would seem, of Giovanni Aurispa.[1] He then went as professor to Pavia, where his restlessness of character and originality of mind soon made him conspicuous. In that great centre of legal studies, he fiercely attacked the doctrine of the celebrated Bartolo, on account of his barbarous and scholastic style. How, said he, could Bartolo, who was ignorant of the classic language of antiquity, in which Roman jurisprudence was and ought still to be written, and even ignorant of history, either understand the real significance of Roman law, or properly comment upon it. This audacity was considered rank heresy, and made so much noise among the law students, that poor Valla had to fly from Pavia and go to teach in other cities.[3]

[1] Vespasiano, "Vita di Niccolo V." G. Manetti, in his "Vita Nicolai V.," gives minute details of this Pope's designs. See too Voigt, "Die Weiderbelebung," &c. ; Gregorovius and Reumont in their histories of Rome.

[2] The former was then a member of the Curia ; but of the latter, who is supposed to have instructed Valla in Greek, it is not certain that he came to Rome before 1440. It is difficult, therefore, to determine the dates. *Vide* Tiraboschi, "Storia della Letteratura Italiana," vol. vi. p. 1029 and fol.

[3] Poggio and Fazio even accuse him of having given a false bond, and attribute

Yet, it was amid these agitations that he brought out his first work, " De Voluptate et Vero Bono," [1] in which we find manifestations of original thought, and perceive that learning had already given birth to the new spirit of the Renaissance. Comparing the doctrines of the Stoics with those of the Epicureans, Valla exalts the triumph of the senses, and protests against all mortification of the flesh. Life's objects, he says frankly, are pleasure and happiness, and these we ought to pursue according to nature's command. Virtue itself, being derived from the will, not from the intellect, is a means for attaining beatitude, namely, true happiness, which is ever incomplete on this earth. It is impossible to explain all things by reason ; the dogmas of religion often remain a mystery, and philosophy only seeks, as far as may be, to expound them rationally ; it is not even possible to conciliate free will with divine prescience. Science is founded on reason,—which is in harmony with the reality of things, on nature,—which is God. Truth manifests itself in a true, precise, simple form ; logic and rhetoric are almost one and the same thing ; a confused and incorrect style is a sign of badly understood truths, of a false or incomplete science.—And for these reasons Valla fiercely attacked scholastic philosophy, Aristotle, and Boetius, continually appealing from authority to the healthy use of reason, to reality, to nature, which he exalted in a thousand ways. This need of reality, this redemption of the senses, and of nature, forms the new spirit that animates the whole book, constitutes the special characteristic of Valla's writings, is, in short, the actual spirit of the Renaissance of which he was the incarnation. There is here no question of a new system of philosophy ; but one sees the triumph of nature and of good sense, and the independence of reason presents itself to us as a logical consequence of the revival of antiquity.

This work would have been much more successful if Valla, in his restless, quarrelsome spirit, and frequent love of paradox, had not allowed himself to be too much carried away by his own pen. In taking up the defence of the senses, he declares that virginity is in opposition to nature, and makes Panormita declare, that if nature's laws are to be respected, courtesans are

to that his flight. They were, however, his enemies, and not, therefore, credible witnesses against him.

[1] It is divided into three parts. *Vide* the edition of Valla's " Opere," published at Basle, 1543.

of more use than nuns to the human race. In expounding and defending the Epicurean doctrines against the Stoics, in condemning and despising everything that implies contempt of the world, he lets slip many expressions contrary to the letter and spirit of Catholic doctrines. And while protesting his intention of respecting the authority of the Church, his attacks against the clergy were exceedingly violent, and far more formidable than those of Poggio and other learned men. Sarcasm was their principal weapon ; that of Valla criticism, which had a far deadlier effect. Therefore he had many bitter enemies, and was soon accused of being a heretic, an epicurean, and a blasphemer of everything that was sacred. Nor was his assertion that for him divine beatitude consisted in true pleasure, true happiness, considered a valid defence, for the most insolent and daring phrases in his own work were cast in his teeth, and the most immoral actions of his life—which was certainly open to attack—were brought up against him.

After teaching in various cities, Valla is found at the Court of Alfonso of Aragon, between the years 1435 and 1442, was appointed his secretary in 1437, and accompanied him in the military enterprises which afterwards established that prince on the Neapolitan throne.[1] In '43 he was in Rome, but had to fly that city, and once more take refuge in Naples, because of the persecution that threatened him on account of his as then unpublished work, " De falso credita et ementita Constantini donatione." [2] Valla maintained that the donation of Constantine was never made, could not be made, and that the original of the pretended document had never been seen. Then by a critical examination of the terms of the document, he proved its falsity. After this he fiercely attacked the simony of the clergy, openly declaring that the Pope had no right to govern either the world or Rome ; that the temporal power had ruined the Church, and deprived the Roman people of liberty. He even incited them to rise against the tyranny of Eugene IV., and against all Popes, who from shepherds had become robbers and wolves. "Even were the donation authentic," he said, in conclusion, "it would be

---

[1] He says of this period : "Tot praelia vidi, in quibus de salute quoque mea agebatur." "Opera," Basle edition, 1543, p. 273. The learned men, however, were fond of boasting of the perils they encountered, whenever they accompanied a prince on any warlike expedition.

[2] See his "Opera."

null and void, for Constantine could have no power to make it, and in any case the crimes of the Papacy would have already annulled it." He hoped to live long enough to see the popes constrained to be mere pastors, with only spiritual power. It is true that already during the Council of Basle, Cusano and Piccolomini had maintained the falsity of the donation by means of arguments which are also found in Valla.[1] But to him we owe the thorough demolition of the false document, accomplished by pungent criticism, and with all the impetus of his Ciceronian eloquence. Besides, he did not confine himself to a literary and theoretical examination, but sought to totally overthrow the temporal power, by threatening to excite the population to revolt against the reigning pontiff. It was no longer a matter of a simple theological or historical dispute, but this was the first time that an already celebrated scholar, after having exhausted the critical view of the case, rendered it popular, and gave it a practical application.[2]

At that time Alfonso of Aragon was at war with Eugene IV., and Valla, in taking up the cause of his protector, was able to give full vent to his eloquence. Attacked by priests and friars, he, safe in his vantage ground, returned to the charge in other writings. In these he maintained that the letter of Abgarus to Jesus Christ, published by Eusebius, was false ; that it was false that the Creed had been composed by the apostles, that in reality it was the work of the Nicene Council. Even before this he had already discovered many errors in the Vulgate, and collected them in a book of annotations, which Erasmus of Rotterdam afterwards republished with an eulogistic letter of defence.[3] These writings and these disputes procured him a summons before the Inquisition in Naples, but, assured of the king's support, he defended himself partly by satires, and partly by declaring that he respected the dogmas of the Church, which had nothing to do with history, philosophy, or philology. As to the donation of

---

[1] Voigt, "Enea Silvio di Piccolomini, als Pabst Pius der Zweite," vol. ii. p. 313 ; "Die Wiederbelebung," &c., p. 224. See also an article by Professor Ferri on Cusano in the " Nuova Antologia," year 7, vol. xx., May, 1872, p. 109, and fol.

[2] "Lorenzo Valla, ein Vortrag," von Z. Vahlen. Berlin, F. Vahlen, 1870, p. 26, and fol.

[3] *In Novum Testamentum e diversorum utriusque linguæ codicum collatione annotationes,* &c., in Valla's " Opera."

Constantine, nothing was said about it, in order not to re-open so thorny a question.

Freed from this danger, he continued his lessons at the university, and prosecuted literary disputes with Bartolommeo Fazio and Antonia Panormita, against whom he wrote four books of invectives.[1] But besides these works he published others, historical, philosophical, and philological, always dictated by the same critical and independent spirit, and of these the "Elegantiæ" and the "Dialectica" are the most noteworthy. The first[2] speedily achieved great popularity, for in its pages Valla displayed his mastery of classical Latin, which he wrote with as much elegance as vigour. He also showed a—for those times—very profound knowledge of grammatical theory, and, what is more surprising, slipped insensibly from philological to philosophical questions. Language, he said, was formed in accordance with the laws of thought, and for this reason grammar and rhetoric were based upon dialectics of which they are the complement and the application. Erasmus also occupied himself with this work, and prepared and published an abbreviation of it.[3] In this, as well as in the "De Voluptate et Vero Bono," we see all the author's originality and the movement of learning towards criticism and philosophy. His "Dialectica," an exclusively philosophical work, is of very inferior merit ; but this, too, strikes the same chord, namely, that the true study of thought must be prosecuted by study of language.[4]

---

[1] "In Bartholomeum Facium ligurem, Invectivarum sive Recriminationum, libri iv." The cause of this dispute was a criticism by Fazio on Valla's "Life of the Father of King Alfonso."—L. Vallae, "Historiarum Ferdinandi regis Aragonia, libri iii." Parisiis per Robertum Stephanum. In replying to Fazio, Valla also attacked Panormita.

[2] "Elegantiarum, libri vi.," in Valla's "Opere."

[3] "Paraphrasis, seu potius Epitome in Elegantiarum libros Laur. Vallae." Parisiis, 1548.—"Paraphrasis luculenta et brevis in Elegantias Vallae." Venetiis, 1535.

[4] Ritter, "Geschichte der neuern Philosophie," part 1, p. 252, notes in fact the superiority attributed by Valla to "Rhetoric" over "Dialectics" : "Noch viel reicher is die Redekunst, welche ein unerschöpfliches Gedächtniss, Kenntniss der Sachen und der Menschen voraussetz, alle Arten der Schlüsse gebraucht, nicht allein in ihrer einfachen Natur, wie sie die Dialektik lehrt, sondern in den mannig-faltigsten Anwendungen auf die verschiedensten Verhältnisse der öffentlichen Geschäfte nach der Lage der Sachen, nach der Verschiedenheit der Hörenden abgeändert. Dieser reichen Wissenschaft solle die philosophische Dialektik dienen (' Dial.,' diop. 11, praefatio). Das meint Valla, wenn er die Philosophie

Amid so many battles and so much literary activity, enjoying the protection of so magnificent a monarch as Alfonso, and resident in a city that had always shown a singular aptitude for philosophical studies, Valla might have been content. Yet he always yearned for Rome, since that was the great literary centre, and his present position was far from secure. The king might be reconciled with the Pope, might be succeeded by his son, and all things be suddenly changed. In fact, before long the Aragonese were once more in agreement with the Holy See, and Valla had to take care of himself. With the lightness that was special to the learned men, he then decided to retract all the perilous doctrines which he had hitherto maintained, especially those touching the donation of Constantine, which, in the judgment of his adversaries, were all the more dangerous, the less they were talked of. He began by writing letters to several Cardinals, stating that he had been moved by no hatred for the Papacy, but by love of truth, religion, and glory. If his work was of man, it would fall of itself, if of God, no one could overthrow it. Furthermore—and this was the most important point —if it were true that with a pamphlet he had wrought great harm to the Church, they ought to recognize that he was able to work it equal good. But all this did not suffice to pacify Eugene IV., and Valla, who went to Rome in 1445, soon returned to Naples, whence he wrote an apology addressed to the Pope, to whom he promised a complete retractation.[1] In this he repelled the accusations of heresy, brought against him by the malice of his enemies, and ended by saying : "If I sinned not, restore my good fame to its pristine purity ; if I sinned, pardon me."

But not even this submission obtained the wished-for result. Only on the election of Nicholas V. (1447), Valla was immediately sent for and employed in making translations from the Greek, of which he had no great knowledge. There in Rome, he spent his days amid lessons, translations, and literary quarrels with Trapezunzio and Poggio, without at all concerning himself with religious

unter der Oberbefehl der Rede stellen will." This is the idea he expounds in the "Dialectica," but in the "Eleganze" he goes still farther, and seeks to discover philosophy and logic in language.

[1] "Ut si quid retractatione opus est, et quasi ablutione, en tibi me nudum offero." "Ad Eugenium IV., Pont. Apologia : Vallae Opp." The letters to Cardinals Scarampo and Landriani are to be found in the "Epistolæ Regum et Principum," Argentinæ per Lazar. Zetzenerum A. 1595, pp. 336 and 341.

questions. He was secretary to the Curia and even Canon of St. John Lateran, which was afterwards the burial-place of this pretended religious innovator, who had been a man of little principle, of immoral habits, and of very great literary, critical, and philosophical talent. He ceased to live on the 1st of August, 1457.[1]

At this time there was another scholar of great ability in Rome, and this was Flavio Biondo, or Biondo Flavio, as some call him ; born at Forlì in 1388 ; he was secretary to Eugene IV., Nicholas V., Calixtus III., and Pius II., was used by all and neglected by all to such an extent that from time to time he attempted to better his fortune elsewhere. Yet he had served Eugene IV. through good and evil fortune with unshaken fidelity, and had dedicated some of his principal works to him ; he had done the same to Nicholas V., the Mæcenas of all learned men, and to Pius II., who made use of his works, and even epitomized one of them, to give it the elegance of style that it lacked. This in fact was Biondo's great defect, and that helped to keep him almost unknown amongst the Humanists, many of whom were not worthy of comparison with him. He did not know Greek, was not an elegant Latinist, was neither a flatterer, nor a writer of invectives ; he had but one dispute with Bruni, and that was wholly literary and scientific, on the origin of the Italian language, and was free from personalities. His epistles contain neither *bon mots* nor elegant phrases, therefore they were never collected, and no one wrote his biography. Yet his was one of the purest characters and noblest minds of that century, and his works have a keenness of historic criticism to be found in none of his contemporaries.

Biondo's first work, dedicated to Eugene IV., and entitled "Roma Instaurata," is a description of Pagan and Christian Rome and its monuments. It is the first serious attempt we have of a complete topography of the Eternal City ; the author opens the way towards a scientific restoration of the monuments, and refers to classic authors with singular critical power. Also,

[1] Tiraboschi, "S. L. I.," vol. vi. p. 1029 and fol. ; Voigt, "Die Wiederbelebung," &c., p. 294 and fol. ; Voigt, "Pius II., und seine Zeit," vol. i. p. 237 ; Zumpt, "Leben und Verdienste des L. Valla," in vol. iv. of "Zeitschrift für Geschichtswissenschaft," von A. Schmidt ; Ritter, "Geschichte der neuern Philosophie," part i. Invernizzi, "Il Risorgimento" (fifteenth and sixteenth centuries), chap. iii. ; this work forms part of the "Storia d'Italia" in course of publication at Milan : Vallardi and Co.

it is still more worthy of notice that antiquity by no means makes him forgetful of Christian times : "I am not," he says, "of those who forget the Rome of St. Peter for the Rome of the Consuls." Thus his learning gained a wider and deeper basis, for it comprised the Middle Ages and his own time. His second work was the "Italia Illustrata," written at the instance of Alfonso of Aragon, and dedicated to Nicholas V. In this he gave a description of ancient Italy, defined its different regions and enumerating its principal cities, investigated their monuments, their ancient and modern history, and their celebrated men. His third work, dedicated to Pius II., was "Roma Triumphans," in which he undertook to examine the constitution, customs, and religion of the ancient Romans, thus making the first manual of antiquity. Finally, not to mention his book " De Origine et Gestis Venetorum ; " he wrote a history of the decline of the Roman Empire, "Historiarum ab inclinatione Romanorum," &c., a work of vast bulk, of which, however, we have only the three first decades and the beginning of the fourth. The author's intention was to bring it down to his own times ; but even in its unfinished state, it is the first universal history of the Middle Ages worthy of the name. And Biondo has an admirable method of seeking out the fountain heads and distinguishing contemporaneous from posterior or anterior narrators, by carefully comparing them with each other. It was first in this work that history began to be a science, and historic criticism came into existence. We shall have occasion to refer to it again, when the moment comes for observing that Machiavelli made great use of it in the famous first book of his " Istorie," sometimes translating literally from it. And even Pius II. recognized the great importance of the work, by making a compendium of it in order to give it a classic mould. He also made frequent use of other of Biondo's works, while leaving the author to pass his last days in poverty and almost unknown (1463).[1]

The third learned man whom it is requisite to mention is Enea Silvio dei Piccolomini, the same who succeeded Nicholas V. as Pius

---

[1] Voigt, "Die Wiederbelebung," &c. ; Gregorovius, "Geschichte der Stadt Rom.," vol. vii. p. 577 (2nd edition) ; Tiraboschi, "S. L. I.," vol. vi. p. 635 and fol. The "Roma Instaurata" and "Italia Illustrata" were printed for the first time "Romæ in domo nob, v. Johannis de Lignamine, 1474," and reprinted with all Biondo's other works at Basle in 1559. They were afterwards translated into Italian.

II. (1458–64). We have already had a glimpse of him at the Council of Basle, where he supported the election of the Anti-Pope Felix V., to whom he was secretary ; later, we saw him in the Imperial Chancery, where he remained many years and changed his opinions, becoming a supporter of the Papal authority in opposition to the ideas of the Council, which he had previously upheld. In his youth he had given free play to his natural frivolity and versatility of talent, and had written verses, comedies, coarse tales, and letters, in which he spoke with sarcastic cynicism of the dissolute life that he led. As a scholar he was wanting in knowledge of Greek and the Grecian authors, of whom he had only read a few translations sent to him from Italy ; of the Latin authors, however, especially Cicero, he had made very prolonged study ; he aimed at ease and simplicity of style, and Poggio Bracciolini was his *beau idéal.* His writings had a spontaneous dash, chiefly resulting from the practical nature of his intellect, from his knowledge of mankind, and of the world. He differed from all the other learned men in this, that in his writings he always tried to go straight to the practical and real point, without indulging in too many classic reminiscences. Even in his obscene works, instead of trying effects of style and citing examples from the ancients, he narrated real facts from his own life or that of his friends. His " Orations in Council " were certainly no specimens of great eloquence, but they had a clear intention, and sought to reach a definite end. In the " Epistole " he either treated of affairs or described the places he lived in ; and thus we often find the poor secretary of the Imperial Chancery in despair at being among Germans who drink beer from morning to night. The students (as now) swallowed enormous quantities of it ; a father awakened his children in the night in order to make them drink wine.

But meanwhile Piccolomini was certainly the first to propagate Italian humanism in Germany, and for many years his letters formed the connecting link between the two countries, and hence have much historical importance. Piccolomini had neither the weight of an independent thinker, the erudition of a true Humanist, nor the patience of the collector ; but in him the vivacity, readiness, and spontaneity of the man of letters, who is at the same time a man of the world, reached so high a pitch that he may justly be called an original writer. He was no philosopher ; indeed, in this respect he was so imbued with antiquity as to wish to confound the Greek and Roman with the Christian philosophy. In such matters he was out of his real element ; this is plainly seen when he turns to subjects relating to philosophy, but of more practical tendency, as, for instance, education. Then he makes few quotations from Aristotle and Plato, but notes instead observations derived from his own experience. He never succeeded in composing any really scientific treatises, and their most attractive parts are always his descriptions of scenery and manners. Thus when writing " De curialium miseriis," [1] the best part of his book is that in which he relates the unhappy life which he himself led with the subordinates of the Imperial Chancery ; their travels, their life in common, the badness of the inns, the vile cookery, the absence of quiet.[2] In other works of his we find descriptions of the countries through which he had travelled, of natural scenery, customs, institutions. These things in short are those that he saw most clearly and describes to us most graphically. Although no traveller in search of unknown regions, nature is ever fresh, ever admirable to him ; he can always hear its voice. Even after he was Pope, and was old and infirm, he would have himself carried over the hills and valleys to Tivoli, Albano, and Tusculo, to enjoy the beauty of the scenery, which he so graphically describes in his " Commentarii," that to this day they would make a good guide for visitors to those places. The character and the variety of the vegetation, the mountain and river systems, the philological derivation of their names, the different local customs ; nothing escapes him ; everything is harmoniously arranged. He also wrote descriptions of Genoa, Basle, London, and Scotland, noting the extent of the latter country, its climate, customs, food, manner of living, construction of the houses, and the political opinions of the inhabitants. There is a description by him of Vienna which is so vivid that to this day fragments of it are given in the most recent guides to that city.[3] Its extent, the number of its inhabitants, the life led by its professors and students, its political and administrative constitution, its mode of life and street scandals, the condition of the nobles and burgesses, its justice, its police,

---

[1] It is a treatise, in the form of a letter, to Giovanni Aich, dated 30th November, 1444.

[2] " Opera."   Basle : Hupper, 1551, vol. i. pp. 91–93.

[3] " Wiener Baedeker, Führer durch Wien und Umgebungen," von. B. Bucher und K. Weiss.   Zweite Auflage : Wien, Faesy und Frich, 1870, pp. 43, 44.

everything seems to bear the same stamp as the Vienna of to-day.[1]
He does not write as a learned man ; he is a simple traveller
impelled by his own curiosity to observe and describe all that he
sees. Piccolomini is a man of his time, his qualities are in the
very atmosphere he breathes, and his want of individual originality makes him show them all the plainer. He lived, it is true,
in the age of the men of learning, but that was also the age which
gave birth to Christopher Columbus and moulded his genius.

It is for these reasons that Piccolomini's historical and geogra-
phical writings were his most important works, and that their
principal merit lies in the author's descriptions of things and men
actually seen by him, and when History, Geography, and Ethno-
graphy presented themselves to him as one science. He had only
a fragmentary knowledge of Greek and Roman history ; he treated
but slightly of that of the Middle Ages, taking much from Biondo
and others. Still he examined the writers of whom he made use,
the epoch, value, and credibility of their works, for criticism ran
in the blood of the men of that time. But he never arrived at
any true scientific severity or method ; he strung together his
information in a confused way, from memory and from memoranda
in which he had noted down what he saw, read, or heard. This
mode of composition, joined to the mobility and mutability of his
character, made him at different times express very different judgments upon the same subject ; for he always wrote under the
impression of the moment. This, however, increases the spontaneity of his writings, and allows us to read in the mutability of
his opinions the history of his mind.

He long meditated a species of " Cosmos," in which he intended
to write of the geography of all then known countries, and their
history from the beginning of the century to his own day. His
" Europa " is a fragment of this colossal work, that was never
completed, and in it he makes geography the substratum of
history. He treated of the different nations without order, without proportion, often writing from memory, according to his
custom. Later, he wrote the geography of Asia, making use of
the traditions of the Grecian geographers, and of the travels of
Conti, the Venetian, who had been twenty-five years in Persia,
and of which Poggio's works contained a very minute narrative,
taken from the traveller's own lips.[2] Piccolomini's last and most

---

[1] " Epist." 165, Basle edition, 1571.

[2] Poggii, " De varietate fortunæ," Parisiis, 1723. This work begins with a

important work is the autobiography, written when he was already Pope, and which, in imitation of Julius Cæsar, he styles his " Commentaries." These he was accustomed to dictate in intervals of leisure ; they are therefore made up of fragments loosely strung together, but perhaps for that very reason give a just idea of the author's intellectual qualities, and show the many and versatile merits which are scattered through his other works. In this, we see him in his varied aspects, as the scholar, the poet, the describer of foreign countries, the enthusiast for nature, the *genre* painter, and the mind imbued with a spirit of thoroughly modern realism.[1] Here are those descriptions of the Roman Campagna, Tivoli, the valley of the Anio, Ostia, Monte Amiata, the Alban Hills, which may still serve as travellers' guides, and almost make you feel the rush of mountain breezes ; here, too, if with little order, is the image of a whole century, faithfully reflected in the mind of the writer, who just because he lacks individual character and personality, never gives a subjective tint to the things and men he describes. These " Commentaries " extend from the year 1405 to 1463, and were carried on by another hand down to 1464.[2]

All that we have related of Valla, Biondo, and Piccolomini will clearly show that, although the learned men of Rome had neither the importance nor special character of those of Florence, still the Eternal City was always a great centre, to which the learned thronged from all parts of Italy, and soon from all parts of Europe.

long introduction, in which the author speaks of the ruined condition of the monuments of Rome. The first book describes the ruins, and then goes on to narrate the deeds of Tamerlane, and the misfortunes of Bajazet. In the second book, Antonio Lusco speaks of the vicissitudes of Europe, from 1377 to the death of Martin V. The third contains a compendium of the history of Italy under Eugene IV. The fourth, which is like a separate work, and has been frequently translated, contains an account of India and Persia, which Poggio derived from Conti, who had been beyond the Ganges. It is certainly one of the most important works Poggio has left, and in it one finds a little of everything ; philosophy, descriptions of Italian policy in the fifteenth century, Eastern travels, &c.

[1] Paolo Cortese says : " In eo primum apparuit sæculi mutati signum " (" De Cardinalatu," p. 39, edition of 1510).

[2] The "Commentarii" were revised and partly retouched by Giannantonio Campano, Bishop of Teramo. Giovanni Gobellino (Gobel or Göbel) continued them from April '63 to April '64. See Gregorovius, "Geschichte," &c., vol. vii. p. 599, and fol. (second edition). Voigt has given a complete biography of this Pope in his work, "Enea Silvio dei Piccolomini als Papst Pius der Zweite und Seine Zeitalter." Berlin : G. Meyner, 1856–63, in 3 vols. See vol. i. chap. 12 *e passim*, vol. ii. book iii. chap. 6–11.

After the death of the three scholars mentioned above, we find flourishing there Pomponio Leto, Platina, and the Roman Academy. The first of these was better known for eccentricity than for talent, and was generally believed to be a natural son of Prince Sanseverino of Salerno. A pupil of Valla, whom he succeeded as teacher, he left his family in order to come to Rome ; and it is said that when they summoned him home, he replied with his celebrated letter—"*Pomponius Lætus cognatis et propinquis suis salutem. Quod petitis, fieri non potest. Valete.*" Inflamed with an enthusiastic ardour for Roman antiquity, he led the life of a hermit, cultivating a vineyard he possessed, according to the precepts of Varro and Columella ; going before daybreak to the University, where an immense audience awaited him ; reading the classics, and passing long hours in contemplation of the monuments of old Rome, which often moved him to tears. He arranged representations of the comedies of Plautus and Terence, and became the head of a large group of learned men, whom he gathered into the Roman Academy, of which he was the founder. Every member of this Academy was rebaptized with a Pagan name, and on the recurrence of the Roman *fasti*, especially on the anniversary of the foundation of Rome, they all met at a dinner, during which compositions in verse and prose were read aloud.[1] At these meetings republics and paganism were discussed ; and it was here that Platina, and many other learned men, whom Paul II. had dismissed from the secretaries office, came to vent their rage against the Pope. He was an energetic and impatient man and soon dissolved this academy ; many of its members were imprisoned, a few even put to torture, others sought safety in flight (1468). Pomponio Leto was in Venice, and was sent back to Rome, where he saved himself by making his submission and asking pardon.[2] He was thus enabled to reopen his academy under Sixtus IV., and it lasted until the sack of Rome in 1527. He died in 1498 at the age of seventy, and was buried with great pomp. He published several editions of the classics, and some works on Roman antiquities ; but his

[1] Jovii, " Elogia doctorum virorum," Tiraboschi, " S. L. I.," vol. vi. pp. 107, 210, 644–49 ; Burckhardt ; Gregorovius, " Geschichte," &c., vol. vii.

[2] " Fateor et me errasse, peccasse et ideo penas mereri. . . . Rursus petor, veniam, ad pedes me Pauli Pont. clementissimi esse credatis, qui solita pietate et misericordia omnibus parcit," &c. So runs the confession, of which Gregorovius could not find the original, but only a copy in the Vatican ; " Geschichte de Stadt Rom." (second edition), p. 587, and fol.

chief importance consisted in his teaching, in the Pagan enthusiasm that he had the power of communicating to others, and
in his simple and exclusively studious life.

Another member of the Academy, and one of greater ability,
was Bartolommeo Sacchi, of Piadena, in the Cremonese territory,
surnamed Platina. First imprisoned for protesting against the
loss of his office, he was again shut up in St. Angelo, when the
Academy was dissolved ; being put to torture, he not only yielded,
but made a most abject submission to the Pope, promising to
obey him in all things, to celebrate him with highest praise,[1] to
denounce to him whoever should speak ill of him. And all this
he said while nourishing an intense desire for revenge. Freed
from prison, and named Vatican librarian by Sixtus IV., with the
obligation of collecting documents on the history of the temporal
power, he revenged himself in his "Vite dei Papi," by describing
Paul II. as the most cruel of tyrants, whose delight it was to
torment and torture the learned in the castle of St. Angelo, of
which he had made a true tower of Phalaris. As Platina's
biographies achieved great popularity, Paul II. descended to
posterity as a monster, and the scholar attained his end. The
book's principal merit, and the cause of its success, lay in the
style, the author's historic criticism being poor enough. Yet he
attempted a most difficult undertaking, for which, in these days,
the powers of no one man, however learned and gifted, would
suffice, and he was the first to succeed in extracting from the
fabulous chronicles of the Middle Ages, a manual of history of
great clearness, comprising many specimens of the learned biography of the fifteenth century, the which are pleasant reading,
because the author sincerely sought for historic truth, if he did
not always succeed in finding it. As he approached his own
times, the value and importance of his biographies increase,
always excepting when he is blinded by passion. His remaining
historical works have less merit. He died in the year 1481 at the
age of sixty-one.[2]

---

[1] "Tibi polliceor, etiam si a praetervolantibus avibus aliquid contra nomen
salutemque tuam sit, audiero, id statim literis aut nunciis Sanctitati tuae indica-
turum. Celebrabimus et prosa et carmine Pauli nomen, et auream hanc ætatem,
quam tuus felicissimus pontificatus efficit." This letter, by Platina, to be found
in Vairani, "Monum. Cremonensium," vol. i. p. 30 is quoted by Gregorovius,
"Geschichte," &c., vol. vii. p. 588 (second edition).

[2] Gregorovius, "Geschichte," &c., vol. vii. p. 603, and fol. (second edition);
Tiraboschi, "S. L. I.," vol. vi. p. 317, and fol.

As we have already noted, Rome was the resort, not only of Italians, but also of foreigners, particularly Germans, and among these latter are three youths deserving special mention. Conrad Schweinheim, Arnold Pannartz, and Ulrich Hahn, came from the workshops of Faust and Schöffer, and were the men who introduced the art of printing into Italy about the year 1464. They had to fight against starvation, and overcome immense difficulties, for in Italy so great was the passion for ancient manuscripts, that many—among others the Duke of Urbino—preferred written to printed volumes. Yet the new industry rapidly spread, and before the year 1490 printing presses were already at work in more than thirty of our cities. In 1469 the famous Cardinal Niccola di Cusa, also called the Cusano, died, and was buried in St. Piero in Vincoli : he was the son of a fisherman of the Moselle, had studied at Padua, and became one of the most illustrious thinkers of the age. He preceded Piccolomini and Valla in doubting the authenticity of the donation of Constantine, but he did not combat the temporal power of the Holy See. He afterwards somewhat modified his opinions, and was raised to the cardinalate, always, however, preserving great integrity of character. Opposed to the authority of Aristotle, he had a philosophic intellect of very great originality ; a pantheist and the true precursor of Giordano Bruno, he was a deep thinker as well as scholar.[1] In 1461 another foreigner made his first appearance in Rome, Johann Müller, better known as the famous Regiomontanus, a learned Greek scholar of highest eminence in the mathematics and astronomy of the time. Sixtus IV. entrusted him with the improvement of the calendar, and he died at Rome in 1475. In 1482 came Johann Reuchlin, who afterwards caused Argiropulos, then professor in the Roman University, to exclaim that the

[1] Ritter, "Geschichte der neuern Philosophie"; Gregorovius, "Geschichte," &c., vol. vii. p. 592 (second edition); Ferri, "Il Card Niccolo di Cusa e la Filosofia della Religione" ("Nuova Antologia," vol. xx., seventh year, May, 1872, p. 100 and fol.). In this article the author examines the philosophical system of Cusano : "Its ruling idea," he says, "is the Absolute, conceivable, but incomprehensible in its infinitude; minimum and maximum, beginning and end of all existence ; from it arise the contradictions that it brings into harmony. The idea of Cusano is not the identity of thought and being, but is only an image of the absolute truth. The human intellect remains distinct from the divine, but Creation is a development of the world from God, not a Creation *ex nihilo*. The Dialectic of Cusano does not reach like Hegel's to the identity of thought and being, his system is not yet pure Pantheism, for it admits of two orders of existence, the finite and the infinite." Bruno went a step farther upon this road.

Grecian Muses passed the Alps in order to emigrate to Germany.[1]
There in fact learning had been widely propagated and had already
borne fruit. The sun of the new Italian culture, risen high above
the horizon, now illumined the whole of Europe ; but its light
still proceeded from Italy, the ancient cradle of knowledge.

From the death of Paul II. to that of Alexander VI., matters in
Rome went from bad to worse, and the Popes had other things to
think of than scholars, learning, or the fine arts. However, Sixtus
IV. opened the Vatican to the public, and completed many impor-
tant constructions in the city. Neither, for a long time, did the
Roman people lose their admiration for all that was ancient, as an
incident that happened during that period serves to show. In
April, 1485, a rumour spread that some workmen, digging in the
Appian Way, near the tomb of Cecilia Metella, had discovered a
Roman sarcophagus, containing the remains of a beautiful and
well-formed maiden, according to the epitaph, JULIA FILIA CLAUDI:
" whose blond tresses were adorned with many and very rich precious stones, and tied with gold and a ribbon of green silk." [2] The
workmen carried off the jewels ; but an indescribable enthusiasm
reigned throughout the city. It was said that this corpse had the
colour and freshness of life, that its eyes and mouth were still open.
It was carried to the Capitol, and forthwith a sort of religious
pilgrimage began of people coming to admire, describe, and
delineate it with pencil and brush. It may perhaps have had a
waxen mask, like those found at Cumae and elsewhere ; but every
one then believed that an ancient beauty must be infinitely
superior to any living one. This was the idea and illusion of the
age, yet already it began to seem like the echo of a world on the
point of change. Harsh reality was preparing new and very bitter
experiences ; under Innocent VIII. and Alexander VI. all things
went to ruin in Italy.

4. MILAN AND FRANCESCO FILELFO.

The other cities of Italy are of much less importance than
Florence and Rome in the history of letters. In Republics such as

---

[1] Gregorovius, "Geschichte," &c., p. 596.

[2] Matarazzo, "Cronaca di Perugia" in the "Archivio Storico," vol. xvi. part ii.
p. 180. The MS. has a gap which prevented its editors from seeing the date of
the year. See Nantiporto in Muratori's "Scriptores," vol. ii. part 2, col. 109 ;
see Infessura in Eccard, "Scriptores," vol. ii. col. 1951 ; Burckhardt, "Die
Renaissance," p. 183 (1st edition).

Genoa and Venice they began to flourish much later than in Tuscany. Naples had been too long in a state bordering upon
anarchy, and at Milan there was little to be hoped under the rule
of a monster such as Filippo Maria Visconti, a Condottiere such
as Francesco Sforza, or of so dissolute and cruel a youth as his son,
Galeazzo Maria. Yet such was then the state of the national
spirit, that no one could or might keep entirely aloof from
studious pursuits ; Visconti himself felt the need of reading
Dante and Petrarch, and tried to collect a few learned men round
him. It was, however, difficult to find any one willing to stay
long with him. Panormita, though by no means a scrupulous
man, could not be induced to remain, even by a salary of eight
hundred zecchins, and departed to seek his fortunes elsewhere.
The only man fitted for that Court was Francesco Filelfo of
Tolentino, who there found a secure asylum whence to insult his
enemies with impunity, and live by adulation and the traffic of his
pen. This man believed himself and was generally believed to be
one of the greatest intellects of the age : but on the contrary he
was totally wanting in originality, and his acquirements were very
confused and open to dispute. Having been sent by the Venetian
Republic as ambassador to Constantinople, where he married the
daughter of his Greek master, Emmanuele Crisolora, he came
back to Italy in 1427, at the age of twenty-nine. He brought a
good store of manuscripts, spoke and wrote Greek, had a great
facility for the composition of Latin verses, and that was quite
sufficient in those times to establish his reputation as an extraordinary man. His enormous vanity and restless temperament
did the rest. Sent for to teach in the Florentine Studio, he speedily
wrote to all of his great success ; "Even noble matrons," said he,
"give way to me in the streets." However, he was soon at war
with everybody. He was a bitter enemy of the Medici, and
advised the execution of Cosimo, at that time a prisoner in the
Palazzo Vecchio ;"[1] at last he had to take refuge in Sienna, where

---

[1] One of the Satires he wrote at this time, concluded thus :

" . . . Vobis res coram publica sese
Offert in medium, referens stragesque necesque
Venturas, ubi forte minus pro lege vel æquo
Supplicium fuerit de sonte nefando ;
Aut etiam officium collatum munere civis
Namque relegatus, si culpæ nomine mulctam
Pendent, officiet magnis vos cladibus omnes."
(Philelphi, *Satiræ* quartæ decadis hecatostica prima.)

he ran the danger of being killed by one whom he believed to be
an assassin in the pay of the Medici in that place. And meanwhile
in Florence he was tried and condemned as a conspirator against
the lives of Cosimo, Carlo Marsuppini, and others.

At Sienna he wrote his obscene " Satire " against Poggio ; later
we find him at Milan, where he received a stipend of seven hundred zecchins per year, and a house to live in, and wrote in
exalted terms of the virtue, and particularly the liberality of
his "divine prince," Filippo Maria Visconti, that tyrant almost
unrivalled for perfidiousness and cruelty. On the death of Visconti
and the proclamation of the Ambrosian Republic at Milan, he
lauded the new Conscript Fathers, and then formed part of the
deputation that bore the keys of Milan to Francesco Sforza, in
whose honour he wrote his great poem, " The Sforziad."

A fertile composer of biographies, satires, and epistles, his
eloquence, as Giovio expressed it, resembled a river which overflowed and muddied everything. Yet he looked upon himself as
a dispenser of immortality, of fame or infamy, to whom he chose.
When he had to write an Italian commentary on Petrarch, he
deplored the degradation to which this reduced his epic muse ;
nevertheless, he was always ready to sell his Latin verses and com-
mendations to the highest bidder, without being troubled with any
sense of shame.

His principal works, besides the "Satires," were only two, and
have remained unpublished, without much loss to letters. The
first, entitled " De Jocis et Seriis," is a collection of epigrams,
divided into ten books, each of a thousand verses, according to
the author's always artificial rhetoric. Full of jests, and indecent
and very prosaic insults, its only object seems to be an exhibition
of the author's facility in verse-making, and gaining money by
unworthy adulation, or still more unworthy abuse. Now, it is his
daughter who has no dower, and whose clothes are in tatters ;
now the muse of Filelfo is silent for want of money, and he sup-
plicates half threateningly, half humbly, that some may be granted
to him.[1]

[1] Rosmini in his " Vita di **F.** Filelfo " (Milan, Mussi, 1808, 3 vols.), has published some 6f these verses.

Of Francesco Sforza, Filelfo says :

> " Nam quia magnifici data non est copia nummi
> Cogitur hinc uti carmine rancidule.
> Quod neque mireris, vocem pretiosa canoram
> Esca dat, et potus excibat ingenium.

On the 18th of June, 1459, precisely while he was engaged on this work, he wrote to Cardinal Bessarion : "Being now free from fever, I can fulfil my duty towards yourself and the Holy Father Pius II., namely, that of writing verses in exchange for coin." [1]

Nor was his conduct different while writing his other work— also unpublished—"The Sforziad," divided into twenty-four cantos, of which only ten are to be found in the libraries. It is an attempt at an epic poem, relating Sforza's enterprises, and starting from the death of Filippo Maria Visconti. In easy verses, sometimes in the Virgilian, but oftener in the Ovidian style, the author lauds to the sky every action of his hero, even the most perfidious. The gods of Olympus, occasionally even St. Ambrose and other Christian saints, are the real actors in this drama ; but they are never more than mere abstractions, and their sole effect is to deprive the hero of the poem of all personality. There is no atom of true poetry in it, and Filelfo was more in the right than he imagined, when declaring that gold was the only muse that gave him inspiration. Whenever he had to bring some fresh personage on to the stage, he immediately began to bargain. Woe to him who did not pay him ! And in this way he managed

> Ingenium spurco suevit languescere vino,
> Humida mugitum reddere rapa solet."
> ROSMINI, vol. ii. p. 283, doc. vi.

To Gentile Simonetta :
> " Filia nam dotem petit altera et altera vestes
> Filiolique petunt illud et illud item."
> Vol. ii. p. 287, doc. vi.

To Bianca Maria Sforza :
> " Blanca, dies natalis adest qui munera pacis
> Adtulit eternæ regibus et populis,
> Dona mihi quæ, Blanca, tuo das debita vati,
> Cui bellum indixit horrida pauperies ?
> Fœnore mi pereunt vestes, pereuntque libelli,
> Hinc metuunt Musæ, Phæbus et ipse timet.
> . . : .
> Non ingratus ero : nam me tua vate per omne
> Cognita venturis gloria tempus erit."
> Vol. ii. p. 288, doc. vi.

To Francesco Sforza :
> " Si, Francisce, meis rebus prospexeris unus,
> Unus ero, qui te semper ad astra feram."
> Vol. ii. p. 290, doc. vi.

[1] C. de Rosmini, " Vita di F. Filelfo," vol. ii. p. 317, doc. xx.

to obtain money, food, horses, clothes, everything. He feigned to be poor and starving, while living in luxury with six servants and six horses. He deplored the misery to which, according to his own account, his immortal muse was reduced ; he was ashamed of needing money, but never of begging for it. And all paid court to him, because they stood in fear of his verses. Even Mahomet II. freed Filelfo's mother-in-law and sister-in-law from prison, on the poet's sending him a Greek ode and a letter, in which he said : " I am one of those whose eloquence celebrates illustrious deeds, and confers immortality on those who are by nature mortal, and I have undertaken to narrate your glorious feats, which by the fault of the Latins and the will of God, have given victory to your arms." [2] He maintained the same behaviour in writing the " Satires," of which there were one hundred, divided into ten decades ; and each satire containing one hundred verses was called by him a *Hecatostica.*

Filelfo did not consider himself well treated by Rome. It is true that Nicholas V., after hearing him read his " Satires," awarded him a gift of five hundred golden ducats ; he was overwhelmed with courtesies, was commissioned to make a translation of Homer, with the offer of a generous stipend, gratuities, a house, and other things besides if he accepted. But having other views he refused all this. After the death of his first, and then of his second wife, he signified that he might be persuaded to settle in Rome, if a Cardinal's hat were bestowed upon him either at once or later. This request being neglected, he took a third wife, and declined every future invitation. But at Sforza's death his fortunes changed ; he fell into poverty, and had to supplicate the patronage of the hated Medici, who recalled him to the Florence University. He arrived there at the age of eighty-three, in 1481, with worn-out strength and exhausted means, and died shortly afterwards. Filelfo was an example of what could be done in those days by a man of good memory, great facility for writing and speaking various languages, inordinate vanity and pride, no principles, no morality, and no originality.[2]

<hr />

[1] C. de Rosmini, "Vita di F. Filelfo," vol. ii. p. 90, and pp. 305 and 308, doc. x.

[2] On Filelfo, one can consult, besides his own works, the three vols. of biography published by Rosmini (who is, however, much too laudatory), with many documents, among which are fragments of Filelfo's unpublished writings. Mr. Shepherd, in his " Vita di P. Bracciolini," speaks at length of Filelfo. See

He was not certainly the only learned man in Milan. As before noticed, we find there in the times of Francesco Sforza, Cicco Simoneta, a very learned secretary ; his brother Giovanni, Court historian, who narrates the Duke's life and deeds from 1423 to 1466, in a history that is not without merit, for it describes matters of which the author was an eye-witness ; and Guiniforte Barsizza, preceptor to the Duke's children Galeazzo Maria and Ippolita, who was afterwards celebrated for her Latin discourses.[1] Battista Sforza, daughter of Alessandro, Lord of Pesaro, and Francesco's brother, also famous for her Latin compositions,[2] was likewise educated at this Court. Still this does not suffice to give Milan any real value of its own in the history of learning.

5. LEARNED MEN IN NAPLES.

Alfonso of Aragon, besides being a warrior, was also a man of no ordinary mind, and knew how to endow his Court with a higher importance. He laid aside his national characteristics with singular facility, and became thoroughly Italian, emulating our native princes as a patron of the fine arts, in the search for ancient manuscripts, in studying the classics, and in surrounding himself with literary men, on whom, according to Vespasiano, he spent some twenty thousand ducats annually.[3] Titus Livius was his idol, so much so, that it is related how Cosimo dei Medici, wishing to gain his friendship, sent him a precious manuscript of that historian's works. He wrote to beg the Venetians to obtain for him from Padua one of Livy's arm bones, as though it had been a sacred relic. On a march with his army one day, Sulmona, the birthplace of Ovid, was pointed out to him, whereupon he immediately made a halt, to give vent to exclamations of joy. He effected his state entry into Naples through a breach in the walls, carefully imitating all the ceremonial of a Roman triumph.

also Nisard's " Gladiateurs," &c., vol. i. ; Guillaume Favre, "Mélanges d'Histoire Littéraire," Tome i., Genève, 1856 ; Tiraboschi, Vespasiano, and Voigt in their previously quoted works.

[1] In 1465 she became the wife of Alfonso of Aragon, Duke of Calabria.

[2] Afterwards wife of Frederigo, Duke of Urbino.

[3] Vespasiano, "Vita d'Alfonso d'Aragona," vi. and xiv. Voigt, "Die Wiederbelebung," &c., p. 235, says one hundred and twenty thousand ducats ; but this is certainly a mistake, perhaps an error of the press.

Trapezunzio, Valla, Fazio, Beccadelli, and Porcellio dei Pandoni, resided long at his Court, and for a short time Filelfo, Gaza, Manetti, and Piccolomini were also there. All were treated with munificence and kindness. When Fazio had completed his "Historia Alphonsi," the king, who already paid him five hundred ducats a-year, made him a present of fifteen hundred more, saying, " This is not intended as payment for your work, which is above price." [1] When he sent an invitation to Manetti, who was flying from his Florence, he said to him, " With you I will divide my last loaf."

A man of unprejudiced mind, continually at war with the Papacy, he gave shelter and protection to all men of learning, whatever their opinions, and guaranteed them full freedom of speech, defending them against the Inquisition and every other danger. Thus Valla, who was the most important man of learning at the Neapolitan Court, was enabled to inveigh against Popes and priests, and freely expose his religious and philosophical opinions both in his writings and from his professorial chair. This bestowed on the learned society of Naples a distinct physiognomy and special importance. It was the same with Antonio Beccadelli, surnamed the Panormita. Born at Palermo in 1394, he, after studying at Padua, had suddenly achieved a noisy celebrity by writing a book, that excited great scandal by an indecency that was not as yet very usual in learned writings. This work, bearing the title " Hermaphroditus," is a collection of epigrams, that for shameless pungency and indecent flippancy surpasses anything before written in imitation of the Roman satirists. Not only vice in general, but obscenity and viciousness of every description, were the continual subject of his verses, which, possessing some elegance and mastery of many difficult points of style and language, obtained an extensive success. But very fierce attacks were also made upon the author. He, however, was in no wise disconcerted by them, and gloried in his book, because he had written it in imitation of the ancients, and proved that anything and everything could be expressed in Latin. He defended himself by quoting Tibullus, Catullus, Propertius, Juvenal, and even Greek and Roman philosophers and politicians, who, although virtuous men, had written similar obscenities. He added that if his poems were open to the same

---

[1] Vespasiano, " Vita d'Alfonso," § vii.

reproach, his life was without stain.[1] Nevertheless, there was great uproar. Poggio—certainly a man of few scruples—decidedly blamed him ; the Minorite friars hurled their thunders on him from the pulpit, and according to Valla, went the length of burning him in effigy. But Guarino Veronese, a very celebrated scholar, an old man of sixty-three, the father of many children, of the purest character, and quite incapable of imitating him, yet defended him energetically, deriding his detractors, who, said he, " are ignorant that life has one scope, poetry another." And such were, in point of fact, the ideas of the age. Sigismondo, king of the Romans, crowned Panormita poet laureate in Sienna, and the " Hermaphroditus " created a school : for from that time forward it was considered almost a merit for an Italian scholar to write Latin indecencies.

Alfonso, being quite indifferent to the accusations launched against the poet, and firm in his wish to give refuge to all those who were persecuted by others, always held Panormita in great esteem. So the poet wrote the " Dicta et facta Alphonsi," for which he received a reward of a thousand ducats ; afterwards " Alphonsi regis triumphus," and numerous works in the shape of letters, orations, and Latin verses, which prove him to be a facile writer of no especial merit. He read aloud, and commented to the king, Livy, Virgil, and Seneca ; he was made a noble, and presented with a villa and large sums of money. Bartolommeo Fazio and others were men of even less weight. The only really original mind, therefore, at the Court of Naples was Valla, who contributed in no small degree to foster the critical and philosophical spirit for which Neapolitans have a natural aptitude. Another eminent man, Giovanni Gioviano Pontano, was also there, but he flourished later, and belongs to a subsequent period in the history of our letters.

6. THE MINOR ITALIAN STATES.

On turning our attention to the smaller cities and lesser States of Italy, we shall find society exposed to such continual and violent shocks, and torn by so many bloody crimes, that it is

---

[1] " Crede velim nostra vitam distare papyro,
    Si mea charta procax, mens sine labe mea est."
(Antonii Panormitæ, " Hermaphroditus." Primus in Germania edidit et Apophoreta adjicit F. C. Forbergius : Coburgi, 1824. *Vide* " Epig.," ii. 1.)

impossible to conceive how arts and letters should ever have flourished at all in them. The petty tyrants were continually exposed to the attacks of their neighbours, or to conspiracies daily breaking out in their own States. Where a city like Ferrara or Bologna was in question, the strategical position of the former, and the territorial importance of the latter, afforded certain help in their continual vicissitudes. Where two princes were concerned as powerful as Alessandro Sforza of Pesaro,—who had the support of his brother of Milan—or as Federico d'Urbino—who was also a captain of adventurers—with an army at his back, then, even if dangers were unavoidable, it was at least comparatively easy to save the States. But where all such assistance was lacking, we find nothing but bloody chronicles such as those of the Baglioni in Perugia. These never succeeded in establishing an undisputed lordship over the city ; they were, it is true, the dominant family, but their chief was not always recognized by its members, and there was a strong adverse party, headed by the Oddi. The town was always filled with armed men and bravos, and violent tumults would break out at a moment's notice.

Towards the end of the fifteenth century, bloody fights within and without Perugia were so frequent and so furious, that the houses in the country round were all knocked to pieces, the fields devastated, the peasants converted into assassins, the citizens enlisted in the free companies ; while wolves prowled about feeding on " Christian flesh." [1] Yet it was precisely at this period that the noblest, most ideal and delicate painting of the Umbrian school flourished at Perugia : another of the same strange contrasts then to be observed throughout the length and breadth of Italy.

Sigismondo Pandolfo Malatesta of Rimini was another of the petty tyrants, and one of the most remarkable of them. A renowned captain of adventurers, without ever having held the command of large armies, he frequently showed himself a true monster of cruelty. He repudiated his first wife, after receiving her dowry ; out of jealousy or revenge he murdered his second and third ; but ardently loved his mistress Isotta to the end of his life. Stained by a thousand crimes, he was extremely cynical

---

[1] " Archivio Storico," vol. xvi. parts 1 and 2. The Chronicles of Graziani and Matarazzo.

and irreligious. On his tomb he desired the following inscription to be placed :—

> " Porto le corna ch'ogn'uno le vede,
>   E tal le porta che non se lo crede."

He denied God, denied the immortality of the soul, and when the Pope pronounced sentence of excommunication against him, he inquired if the excommunicated still continued to enjoy the flavour of good wine and good dinners. On the occasion of some great festival of the Church, he had the holy water pyx filled with ink, in order to enjoy seeing the faithful stain themselves with it unawares.[1] Yet even this coarse tyrant was surrounded by literary men, to some of whom he gave estates, to others assigned salaries ; and in his castle, *Arx Sismundea*, they sang the praises of the prince, and extolled his passion for the beautiful Isotta, to whom a monument, *Divae Isottae sacrum*, was erected in the church of St. Francesco beside that of her lover. The church itself, upon which Leon Battista Alberti worked from 1445 to 1450, and one of the most elegant and purest edifices of the Renaissance bears on its façade the name of Sigismund, and the initials S. and I. are introduced into the ornaments. In the two outer sides are niches intended for the tombs of the Court soldiers and men of learning. And there was no affectation in all this ; it was the expression of a real need of the cultured and artistic side of his character. Pius II., who was at fierce war with him, and burnt him in effigy, wrote that he (Malatesta) " was learned in history ; had great knowledge of philosophy, and seemed born for everything that he undertook." [2]

At Ferrara, Mantova, Urbino, the capital cities of small but nevertheless important States, things wore a very different aspect. Without being great centres like Rome and Florence, they had a character and distinct importance of their own in the history of letters. Ferrara was the more celebrated. Its strategical position rendered it independent, since none of the great Italian States could allow another to take possession of it. The Lords of Este, who ruled and fortified it, were men of ability and also often of great military power. Yet the interior of the Ducal

[1] G. Voigt, " Enea Silvio dei Piccolomini," &c., vol. iii. p. 123.

[2] Pii II. " Comm.," Romæ, 1584, lib. ii. p. 92. Burckhardt, pp. 223, 224, observes that the word *historia* is here used to indicate a knowledge of antiquity.

Palace witnessed many scenes of bloodshed. Parisina, wife of the bastard Niccolò III., being enamoured of a natural son of her husband, both she and her lover were beheaded (1425). And the same duke had afterwards to consolidate his power, combating the hostile nobility with every stratagem of war and all manner of treachery. This bastard was succeeded by two natural sons, Lionello and Borso. In after years Ercole, legitimate son of Niccolò III., seized the dukedom by force of arms from the hands of Lionello's son, and did bloody execution on his enemies. And so matters went on even in the sixteenth century, when Cardinal Ippolito d'Este put out the eyes of his brother Giulio, another bastard, because they were praised by a lady whom both loved, and who alleged to the cardinal as the reason why she preferred his brother to himself, the irresistible beauty of the former's eyes. The operation was imperfectly performed, thereby causing fresh tragedies at the unhappy Court, for Giulio, to whom the sight of one eye remained, conspired with Don Ferrante against their common brother, Duke Alfonso I.,[1] husband of Lucrezia Borgia. The cardinal betrayed the plot (1506), and the two brothers were condemned to a perpetual imprisonment, in which Don Ferrante died, and from which Giulio was only liberated on the accession of Alfonso II. (1559).

Yet this was the Court so celebrated for its artistic and literary splendour, even to the days of Bojardo, Ariosto, and Tasso, who shed over it the lustre of their names and of their immortal works. Having been, in the Middle Ages, a Lombard, feudal, and knightly city, it had not shared the great literary movement that showed itself in Florence in the thirteenth and fourteenth centuries. But in the fifteenth century it was one of the most flourishing cities of Italy, and the disorders of the Court seldom seemed to spread beyond the walls of the Ducal Palace. Ferrara had been built after a pre-arranged design, was governed in an orderly way, and exiles from Florence and other Italian cities took refuge there and erected palaces. The houses and streets, which are now so deserted, barely sufficed for the needs of the population. Its dukes looked after everything, and invited learned men to settle in the city. Among these, the first place must be given to Guarino Veronese, who, in bringing learning to Ferrara where feudal and knightly traditions were in full force, promoted

---

[1] The brothers were four: Alfonso I., Cardinal Ippolito, Don Ferrante, and Giulio the bastard, all sons of Ercole I.

the revival of letters that afterwards gave us the " Orlando Inamorato," the " Orlando Furioso," and so many other works of imperishable fame.[1]

Guarino, born in 1370, studied Greek at Constantinople, whence he returned to Italy with a rich store of manuscripts, and so tenderly did he value these, that there was a generally received fable of his hair having suddenly turned white on the loss by shipwreck of a large portion of his treasure.[2] He taught first in Florence, then at Venice, where one of his pupils was Vittorino da Feltre, to whom he imparted his learning and theories of education. Called to Ferrara in 1424 by Niccolo III., he became the instructor of Lionello and professor at the university, devoting himself with feverish ardour to his double office, besides writing a great number of works : translations of Plutarch, Plato, Strabo, and Lucian ; biographies, grammars, and more than fifty orations. But above all else, his principal merit consists in the nobility of his character and his method of instruction, in which there was great originality, and that produced very remarkable results. An excellent father of his family, of temperate and sober life, speaking ill of no man, he lived in the midst of his scholars, of whom he had always a houseful. It was said that more learned men issued from his school than Greeks from the Trojan horse. And certainly more than thirty of his pupils were celebrated for their learning,[3] although Vittorino da Feltre was the only one who achieved a lasting reputation. But Guarino's labours may best be measured by the impulse he gave to letters in Ferrara, which, by his teachings and under the rule of his pupils Lionello and Borso d'Este, was transformed into a small Italian Athens. He continued his work with unremitting zeal to the last day of his life, when, on the 4th of December, 1460, in the ninetieth year of his age, he expired in the bosom of his family, beloved and venerated by all.

The Gonzaga of Mantova, some of whom were leaders of mighty armies, never committed any of the crimes which so deeply stained the history of the Estes. Their Court, it is true, had no splendour until the sixteenth century, in the times of

---

[1] Giosnè Carducci, "Delle poesie latine edite ed inedite di Ludovico Ariosto." Bologna, Zanichelli, 1875, p. 21 and fol.

[2] C. de Rosmini, " Vita e disciplina di Guarino Veronese ; " Brescia, 1805-6, vol. i. p. 6 ; Tiraboschi, " S. L. I.," vol. vi. p. 118.

[3] Rosmini in his " Life of Guarino " gives us ample details of all these pupils.

Bembo, Bandello, Ariosto, and Tasso, and especially during the life of the good Marchioness Isabella. But in the fifteenth century Mantova was honoured by being the place of residence of Vittorino Rambaldoni da Feltre (born 1378, died 1446), the first of modern pedagogues, and who, as we have already seen, was Guarino's most illustrious pupil. Summoned to Mantova by Giovanni Francesco Gonzaga, he received a munificent stipend and a dwelling in which he founded his celebrated school, soon to be known by the name of *Casa Gioiosa*, from the constant gaiety that prevailed among his well-cared-for pupils. His method of teaching was excellent, and he taught the classics with the aid of renowned Greeks, such as Gaza and Trapezunzio. To these and to other studies usual in schools of that time, were added music, dancing, drawing, gymnastics, and riding. The fundamental principle of Vittorino's school was : that for the formation of character, the education of the body should be coupled with that of the mind. And Vittorino's success in so immoral an age, was entirely owing to the nobility and elevation of his mind, and the generosity with which he spent all his salary in pedagogic education of the poor, who thus pursued their studies side by side with the Marquis of Mantua's sons and the young Federico da Montefeltro, afterwards the celebrated Duke of Urbino. And this community and equality in school of all orders of citizens, formed part of Vittorino's giving system, for he was the first to conduct instruction and education upon scientific principles.[1] The excellent results of the *Casa Gioiosa* were plainly visible in Mantua and elsewhere, since for a long time Vittorino's pupils were distinguished by a loyalty of character that was in strong contrast with the general corruption.

It was mainly owing to this system of education that Urbino became the model Court of Italy, and that the Duke Federico was good, loyal, and faithful in spite of being a Condottiere Captain. Universally renowned for his strategy, for the discipline maintained by his soldiers, and for being the only leader of his time who never betrayed his word nor his oath, he was acquainted with Latin, philosophy, and history ; he read the classics, and had a pronounced taste for theological controversy. These acquirements, united to those gained in the camp and the council chamber, gave him possession, or at least comprehension, of

[1] C. de Rosmini, " Idea dell' ottimo precettore nella Vita e disciplina di Vittorino da Feltre e dei suoi discepoli." Bassano, " Remondiniana " Press, 1801.

nearly all the knowledge of his day. His life was ordered with the regularity of a time-piece, and all his leisure moments were devoted to discussion and study. When riding to Tivoli with Pope Pius II., beneath a burning sun, amid the dust raised by the hoofs of the cavalry, the glitter of helmets and swords, he chatted with the Pope on the arms of the ancients, on the Trojan war, and could not quite agree with him on the subject of the confines of Asia Minor.[1] The money earned by the rich pay of a free-captain he spent during peace in beautifying the city and Court of Urbino. It almost seemed as though he wished to make his State a work of art. The palace built by him was one of the most celebrated in Italy, not for its richness, but for its exquisite taste. It housed many hundreds of persons, to each of whom a definite office was entrusted, with a fixed time-table and written instructions. It resembled a great military school, to which many nobles sent their sons, in order that they might be trained in soldierly discipline, and exercises, and in elegance of manners. His greatest treasure was the extensive library, on which he spent 30,000 ducats,[2] and gave employment for fourteen years to thirty or forty copyists in Urbino, Florence, and other places.[3] He had it arranged with the nicest order, following in part the system of Parentucelli,[4] but trying to embrace the whole circle of ancient

---

[1] Pii II., "Comm.," p. 131.

[2] Professor E. Piccolomini, in his work " Sulla libreria privata dei Medici," before quoted by us, gives, at p. 25, the instructions given to the librarian, which clearly prove the great precision and order exacted by the Duke.

[3] This library, afterwards stolen by Duke Valentino, and later bought by Pope Alexander VIII., is now to be found in the Vatican. Castiglioni, in his " Cortegiano," mentions it briefly, but Vespasiano speaks of it at length, and describes it with ecstasy. " This Duke alone has had a mind to do that which no one has undertaken for more than a thousand years, and to collect a library, the worthiest ever made in all these ages. . . . And he has taken the road that needs must be taken by whomsoever wishes to make a worthy and famous library such as this is. . . . What letters ! what books! what goodly books ! collected without regard for expense." (" Vita di Federico, Duca d'Urbino," sec. xxviii.) . . . " In that library all the books are superlatively beautiful, all written with the pen, and not a single printed one, for the Duke would have taken shame to himself for it ; all most elegantly illuminated, and none that is not written upon kid. But its principal merit was the order with which it was arranged, containing the principal ancient and modern authors in every branch of knowledge, and not many specimens of the same author, one copy of each, neither is there a single sheet of their works that is not complete" (Ibidem, sec. xxxi.).

[4] Professor Piccolomini, at p. 111 and fol. of his above-quoted work, gives the bibliographical canon composed by Parentucelli, afterwards Pope Nicholas V., and one can see how incomplete it is, and therefore how exaggerated the praises which it obtained.

and modern lore.[1] Thus he succeeded in obtaining something unique in the world. Surrounded by Italian and foreign artists, and also by soldiers, he had few learned men at his Court, but many were in correspondence with him, and dedicated to him their works. He went about unarmed among his people, dined frugally in the open air, listening to readings from Livy or other ancient authors. Towards evening he attended the military and gymnastic exercises performed by his youths and pages in the field of St. Francesco. The people loved their duke, and his successors followed in his footsteps.[2] It would be too much to assert that Urbino gave any extraordinary impulse to literary culture in Italy ; but we may say that it was like a shining jewel amid the Apennines ; a model city, the birth-place of many great men, the greatest of whom was Raphael.

7. THE PLATONIC ACADEMY.

The writers hitherto noticed lived, as we have already said, amid a multitude of others, whose names, though famous in their own day, gradually fell into oblivion. No century in fact has contributed to history so great a hecatomb of supposed celebrities as the fifteenth century. And this is easily explained by the double work that age carried on. In its efforts to revive antiquity, it set in motion, on the one hand, an often mechanical imitation and reproduction of the past, in which those who have since been forgotten took part ; on the other, new and unexpected results were obtained, which were the work of a much smaller number of scholars, whose names deserve historical mention. And this double order of facts and individuals is to be met with in nearly all the culture of the Renaissance—in philosophy no less than in letters. Philosophy had apparently a great and general importance among the learned ; but the greater number of these merely extracted from the ancient writers a dictionary of phrases on glory, friendship, contempt of death, the *summum bonum*, happiness and virtue, which they continually repeated, without conforming to them either their deeds or their convic-

[1] Vespasiano, " Vita di Federico, Duca d'Urbino," sec. xxxi.
[2] Ibid., " Vita di Federico, Duca d'Urbino " ; Ugolini, " Storia dei Conti e Duchi d'Urbino," two vols. : Firenze, 1859 ; Dennistoun, " Memoirs of the Dukes of Urbino" : London, Longmans and Co., 1851 ; Burckhardt, " Die Cultur der Renaissance," pp. 44–46 ; Voigt, " Die Wiederbelebung," &c., p. 263.

tions. We constantly find in these phrases a strange mixture of Paganism and Christianity, in odd contradiction one with the other ; a point which was quite indifferent to the writer. Soon, however, the need was felt of finding some unrevealed but rational basis of human life to explain at once Pagan and Christian virtue, and to harmonize their too apparent contradiction. Then, work that was more or less original began, first started by the Neo-Platonists and the Academy, they had founded in Florence.

The Greek exiles did not contribute much to the diffusion among us of their language (which had already begun to be studied in Italy), and still less to the learning which already flourished before their arrival, but they greatly helped to direct learning itself to the study of the ancient philosophers. The first origin of Platonism, or rather of Neo-Platonism, in Italy, is in fact owed to Giorgio Gemistos, surnamed Plethon on account of his professed admiration for Plato. Born in the Peloponnesus according to some, only a refugee there from Constantinople according to others, he was the most learned and influential of the many Greeks gathered together at the Council of Florence. And so earnest and enthusiastic was his devotion to Platonism, that he even hoped from it a revival of religion. This caused his detractors to assert that he desired the revival of Paganism ; but judging by his writings, by those of his followers, and the positive results of his doctrines, we may safely affirm that he was convinced that Christianity would derive fresh confirmation from the Platonic philosophy, and might therefore be revived under another, and in his opinion, more rational form. In a pamphlet, that became very celebrated,[1] he examined the points of diversity between the Platonic and Aristotelian philosophies, and giving preference, of course, to the former system, reduced everything to a single question. The two great philosophers, said he, admit that nature works, not by chance, but for a given purpose. Aristotle, however, maintains that this purpose is achieved unconsciously *non consulto ;* Plato, on the contrary, asserts with more justice that nature is rational, is conscious, *consulto agit ;* its art is divine, since it is God Himself who works in it.[2] A most burning dispute arose upon this question, which, unimportant as it may seem to us, was of immense consequence at that time. For it opened the

---

[1] " De Platonicæ atque Aristotelicæ philosophicæ differentia." Basileæ, 1574.
[2] In my " Storia di G. Savonarola," &c., I have gone into this subject more minutely. See vol. i. book 1, chap. iv.

way to Pantheism ; and the conception of the personal God, of the Omnipotent Jehovah of the Jews, of the Father Almighty of the Christians, was here transformed into the conception of the philosophical absolute.[1] The Greek and Italian men of learning, though with no clear understanding of what they were doing, still foresaw the great importance of the question at issue, and therefore dwelt upon it with insistency.

Giorgio Scolarius and Thedore Gaza, both Greeks and both Aristotelians, fiercely attacked Plethon in the gross language customary to learned men in those days. Cardinal Bessarion, in endeavouring to make peace, allowed it to escape him that he considered Thedore Gaza more learned than Giorgio Trapezuntios, whereupon the latter attacked every one, including Plato himself, with greater fury than before. Then Bessarion published a voluminous work, " In Calumniatorem Platonis," in which, while repulsing Trapezuntios' assaults, he tried with an easy and most diffuse Latin eloquence, barren of all literary or philosophical originality, to conciliate all opposing opinions. According to him, Aristotle and Plato both said in substance the same things. This contest waged among the Greeks, had no genuine philosophical importance, and remained where it was left by G. G. Plethon ; but it served to attract Italian minds to a branch of erudition, which they had hitherto neglected, their study of the Greek philosophers having been chiefly literary. Meanwhile G. G. Plethon, without wasting time in replying to abuse, succeeded, before returning to his own country, in infusing so much admiration for the Platonic doctrines in Cosimo dei Medici's mind, that he left him decided to use every

---

[1] " Unser heutiger monotheistischer Gottesbegriff hat zwei seiten, die der Absolutheit und die der Personlichkeit, die zwar in ihm vereinigt sind, doch so, wie bisweilen in einem Menschen zwei Eigenschaften, davon die eine ihm nachweislich von den väterlichen die andre von den mütterlichen Seite kommt ; das eine Moment ist die judisch-christliche, das andre die griechisch-philosophische Mitgift unseres Gottesbegriffs. Das alte Testament können wir sagen hat uns den Herrn-Gott, das neue den Gott-Vater, die griechische Philosophie aber hat uns die Gottheit oder das Absolute vererbt " (Strauss, " Der alte und der neue Glaube," Bonn, 1873, fifth edition, p. 107). The same author observes in the preceding page : " In Alexandria war es, wo der jüdische Stamm-und National-gott mit dem Welt-und Menschheitsgotte zusammenfloss und bald zusammen wuchs den die griechische Philosophie aus der olympischen Göttermenge ihrer Volksreligion heraus entwickelt hatte " (p. 106). From Alexandria these ideas came to Italy, spread throughout Europe, and became the bone and substance of modern culture.

means for their propagation in Italy, and to re-establish the old academy.

To attain this object, Cosimo's practical common sense, showed him that first of all he must find a suitable man. And such an one he believed that he had found in a young man of Figline, a doctor's son, aged eighteen, who was devoting himself with much ardour to his father's profession. "Thy son," said Cosimo, "is born to minister to minds, not bodies;" and he took him to live in his own palace, intending him to be the future champion of Platonism. This youth was Marsilio Ficino (born 1433), who, setting to work with fervent zeal, produced after five years' study a work on the Platonic philosophy, that was based, however, solely on translations. And from that time to his life's end, Ficino studied nothing but Plato and the Neoplatonists, writing a great number of translations and original tractates, besides giving instruction to the sons and grandsons of Cosimo, and afterwards to a large class in the Florentine Studio.

To describe Ficino's works is to give the history of Platonism in Italy; to narrate his life is to give the history of the Platonic academy. His followers contented themselves with repeating their master's ideas, and the academy was born and died with him. It was in reality a mere assembly of friends and disciples who gathered round him, under the protection of the Medici, for the discussion of Platonic philosophy. It resembled the reunions formerly held in the cell of Marsigli or of Traversari; excepting that the Medici, especially Lorenzo, oftener joined in these, promoted them with more ardour, and the philosophical matters discussed in them had a much louder echo throughout Italy. During the summer some of these meetings were held in the forest of Camaldoli; others more solemn were held every year in Florence, and in the Medici villa at Careggi on the 7th November, which, according to the Alexandrine tradition, was the anniversary of Plato's birth and death.[1] The custom of solemnly celebrating it, observed down to the times of Plotinus and Porphirius, was, after twelve hundred years, according to Ficino, now resumed.[2] The festival began with a banquet, followed by a philosophical discussion, generally ending with an apotheosis, which was almost

---

[1] A similar tradition was also current respecting Pythagoras and Apollonius, arising perhaps from the old custom of the primitive Christians, who often styled the day on which martyrs passed to a better life their birthday.

[2] Ficino states this in his Commentary on Plato's "Symposium."

a sacred hymn to the great Master. Less solemn meetings and discussions were held on many different occasions, but always in the same easy and friendly manner.

The title of Academy was only taken from the doctrines entertained by its members, since as far as we can ascertain, it had no peculiar statutes or regulations. It was held together by Ficino's teachings and personality, and by the fervour of his friends and disciples.[1] And if, on the one hand, this reduces it to insignificance as an institution, on the other, it increases its historical importance, since it proves it to be a natural and spontaneous outcome of the social conditions which gave it birth. In fact, no sooner were these social and intellectual conditions changed, than it became impossible to keep it alive. It went on very regularly down to 1478 ; when the bloody conspiracy of the Pazzi having broken out, and persecution commenced, men's minds were disturbed ; there was an end to the tranquillity requisite for philosophic contemplation, and the meetings, already sadly thinned, ceased altogether with Ficino's death. Those afterwards held in the Oricellarii Gardens, and at which Machiavelli was often present, had very little to do with Platonism, as is clearly seen by Machiavelli's dialogues, " Delle Arte della Guerra," and by the plots that were hatched there. We might almost say that the title of Platonic still given to these meetings was sometimes a mask to hide their real purport. The attempts made by Leopoldo dei Medici in the seventeenth century to bring the Academy to life again, belong to another age, have another signification, and are of very slight importance in the history of science.[2]

Almost all those who have written on the Platonic Academy and on Ficino have contented themselves with carefully collecting biographical and literary anecdotes, which are things of very secondary value.[3] What chiefly concerns us is to know the intrinsic

[1] Ficino in his letters divides his Platonists into disciples and friends, saying, that from the latter he often learned much. One of them was Poliziano, who wrote to him : " Thou seekest the truth and I seek the beautiful in the writings of the ancients ; our works complete each other, being like two halves of one and the same whole."

[2] Respecting these attempts, one may refer to the notices collected by Professor A. Alfani, in his work, "Della Vita a degli Scritti di O. R. Ruccellai," Firenze, Barbera, 1372. This author, however, endeavours to give Ruccellai a philosophic importance, which, in our opinion, he does not possess.

[3] We must make one exception in favour of a very brief but learned work by K. Sieveking, "Die Geschichte der Platonischen Akademie zu Florenz," Hamburg, Druck und Lithographie des Rauhen Hauses zu Horn, 1844. This fine mono-

merit of these doctrines, the reason of their immense popularity in the fifteenth century, and what was the talent of those who dis-covered and propagated them. Certainly when we consider the numerous group of Platonists collected round Ficino, it astonishes us to find that two only merit some respect as writers of philo-sophical works. One of these is Cristoforo Landino, the cele-brated commentator of Dante and of Petrarch, an Hellenist of good repute, professor at the Studio and author of the "Dispu-tationes Camaldulenses,"[1] in which he gives long and minute reports of the Platonic discussions. The other is Leon Battista Alberti, a first-rate artist, poet, prose writer, scholar, scientist, a universal man, and a precursor of Leonardo da Vinci in the pro-digious variety of his intellectual gifts. To these two were added the lesser lights: Donato Acciajoli, Antonio Carrigiani, Naldo Naldi, Peregrino Agli, Alamanno-Rinuccini, Giovanni Cavalcanti, Ficino's most intimate friend, and many others. Yet among all these, without excepting even Landino and Alberti, not a single true philosopher is to be found ; they all repeat the same ideas, and these ideas are Ficino's. It may certainly be remembered that Angelo Poliziano and Lorenzo dei Medici, both intellects of undoubted eminence, were also members of the Platonic Academy ;

graph was published without the author's name, as an appendix to a valuable short history of Florence by the same writer. Most of his information regarding the Platonic Academy and Ficino is drawn from Ficino's own works. Of the Academy he makes special mention in his Epistles, and the Introduction or Commentary to his version of Plato's "Symposium." Many notices are also to be found in Tiraboschi, in the "Life of M. Ficino," written in Latin by Corsi ; and in that of Lorenzo dei Medici, written by Roscoe and by Reumont : in A. M. Bandini's "Specimen Litteraturæ Florentinæ," sec. xv. &c. : Florentia, 1747. This work is chiefly a biography of Cristoforo Landino, a follower of Ficino, and member of the Academy. Many notices too were collected by Leopoldo Galetti, in his "Saggio intorno alta Vita ed agli Scritti di Marsilio Ficino," published in the "Archivio Storico Italiano," new series, tome ix. second issue, and tome x. first issue. For an exposition of Ficino's doctrines, see Ritter's "Geschichte der neuern Philo-sophie," part 1, book 2, chap. iv., and for the philosophy of those times in general, see also F. Schultze's "Geschichte der Philosophie der Renaissance" (Jena, 1874).

[1] Of a Pratovecchio family, but born in Florence in 1424, learned in Greek and Latin, he was appointed teacher in the Studio in 1427. He was chancellor to the Guelph party ; afterwards one of the secretaries of the Republic, an office which he held until 1497. Then on account of his age he retired to Pratovecchio, continu-ing to enjoy his stipend of one hundred florins per annum until 1504, when he died at the age of eighty, in a villa bestowed upon him by the Republic in recompense or his "Comento su Dante," Tiraboschi, "S. L. I.," vol. vi. p. 1065 ; Bandini, "Specimen," &c.

but their writings all show them to be men of letters and not philosophers. Pico della Mirandola only appeared later as a propagator of Ficino's ideas, and neither had he any philosophical originality. But, few or many, of what matters did they speak, what and of what value were these doctrines which found so many and so ardent champions ?

And the nearer we approach to them the more does our astonishment increase. In the summer of 1468[1] we find them in the pleasant convent of Camaldoli, whither they had gone to enjoy the country air, and hold the famous Camaldolensian disputes. There were Lorenzo dei Medici, Giuliano dei Medici, Cristoforo Landino and his brother, Alamanno Rinuccini, Leon Battista Alberti—then just come from Rome—and Marsilio Ficino. After hearing mass they went to sit in the shade of the forest trees, and there passed the first day in disputing on the contemplative and the active life. Alberti declared in favour of the former, supporting his preference by very common-place arguments ; while Lorenzo dei Medici held that both kinds of life were equally necessary. On the second day they spoke of the " Summum Bonum," and we have a series of empty phrases and classical quotations. On the third and fourth days Alberti demonstrated his Platonic wisdom by a long commentary upon Virgil, endeavouring by means of the strangest allegories to prove that in the Æneid are to be found concealed the whole Platonic doctrine, and the whole Christian doctrine, which, in his opinion, are at bottom one and the same thing. And these allegories, which moved Angelo Maria Bandini to say in reporting them that the Platonists often seemed to have lost their wits,[2] are exactly what they lay most stress upon, almost as though these formed a sub-stantial part of their philosophy.

We will now glance at the speeches pronounced at one of the grandest banquets of the Academy, given by order of Lorenzo il Magnifico in the villa at Careggi, under the presidency of Messer Francesco Bandini. Here it is no less a personage than Ficino

---

[1] Bandini says that these meetings were held in 1460 : but Roscoe observes that Lorenzo dei Medici was only twelve years old at that time, and gives instead the date of 1468. " The Life of Lorenzo dei Medici," &c., chap. 11.

[2] " Hoc pronunciare liberi possum, opiniones eorum tenebricosis allegoriarum involucris et dicendi, genere plusquam poetico, qui omnium fere academicorum mos erat, fuisse absconditas." After which he goes on to quote expressions which, as he justly observes, no man of sound mind would think of using.—" Specimen," vol. xi. page 58.

himself who gives a minute report of the proceedings.[1] The
number of the guests was nine, in honour of the nine muses.
Francesco Bandini, Antonio Agli, Bishop of Fiesole, Marsilio
Ficino and his father, C. Landino, Bernardo Nuzzi, Giovanni
Calvacanti, Carlo and Cristoforo Marsuppini. The dinner over,
Plato's " Symposium " was read aloud, and the discourses held in
the house of Agathon were strangely expounded by the guests at
Careggi. Phaedrus says in the " Symposium," that love inspires
heroism, was born directly after Chaos, and before the other gods,
and is admired by all admirers of beauty. And this is Cavalcanti's
commentary upon that passage : God, beginning and end of all
the worlds, creates the angels, who in their turn, form the third
essences out of the universal soul created by God. These essences
are the souls of all things, and therefore also of the different
worlds to which they give life, because the body is formed from
the soul. When Chaos begins to assume shape, it feels a desire
for beauty, which is love ; and it is for this reason, according to
Plato, that love precedes the other gods, who are· identical with
the angels. And hereupon Cavalcanti begins to show how the
angels are identical with the ancient deities, and how the third

[1] See the " Commentarium Marsilii Ficini, in Convivium Platonis de Amore,"
which is added to his Latin translation of Plato. The banquets of the Platonic
Academy seem to have been held in the villa at Careggi, generally presided over
by Lorenzo the Magnificent, and in Florence under the presidency of Francesco
Bandini. So says Ang. Maria Bandini (" Specimen," vol. i. pp. 60–61), and so
Ficino himself says in a letter to Jacopo Bracciolini, published in Bandini's
" Specimen," vol. i. pp. 62–63. "Platonici veteres urbana Platonis natalitia
quotannis instaurabant; novi autem Platonici, Braccioline, et urbana et suburbana
nostris temporibus celebrarunt; suburbana quidem apud Mag. Laurentium Medicem
in agro Caregio. Cuncta in libro nostro de amore narrantur. Urbana vero
Florentiae sumtu regio celebravit Franc. Bandinus vir ingenio, magnificentia
excellens. . . ." At the town meeting, of which he here makes mention, the subject of discussion was the immortality of the soul. But the Careggi banquet of
which Ficino gives such very minute details in his " Commentarium," was by order
of Lorenzo, who was then in Florence, presided over by Franc. Bandini. In fact,
at the beginning of the first chapter he says : " Plato philosophorum pater, annos
unum et octoginta aetatis, natus septimo, novembris die, quo ortus fuerat, discum-
bens in convivio, remotis dapibus, expiravit. Hoc autem convivium, quo et
natalitia et anniversaria Platonis pariter continentur, prisci omnes Platonici usque
ad Plotini et Porphyrii tempora quotannis instaurabant. Post vero Porphyrium
mille ac ducentos annos, solennes hae dapes praetermissae fuerunt. Tandem
nostris temporibus, vir clarissimus Laurentius Medices platonicum convivium inno-
vaturus, Franciscum Bandinum Architriclinum constituit. Cum igitur septimum
Novembris diem colere Bandinus instituisset, regis apparatu in agro Caregio·
novem platonicos accepit convivas."

essences are at the same time the ideas of Plato and the forms of Aristotle. But not content with this, he further asserts that the third essences, created by the angels, become in their turn identical with the ancient gods ; nor is this sufficient, for such a confusion of ideas follows that we can no longer follow the author. Jove is heaven, Saturn and Venus are the two planets thus named ; but they are likewise the third essences, or the souls of heaven, and of the two planets ; they are the three divinities of the ancients, and also three angels ; they are finally the soul of the world, inasmuch as it informs, moves, and generates.[1] What is chiefly clear in all this confusion is, that in the opinion of the Academicians, Christianity and Paganism ought to form one and the same thing with Platonism. Allegory is the key-stone of this edifice, or rather artifice, in which things do not mean what they are, but become symbols and emblems of other things, and as all this is arbitrary, so they can be twisted to any signification one chooses to give them.

Aristophanes, one of the speakers in the " Symposium," says that, in the beginning, there were three sexes, male, female, and promiscuous, that is to say, individuals who were men and women, at the same time, with two heads, four hands, &c. These beings tried to struggle against the gods, and were therefore divided into two halves, one of which is always seeking the other, hence it is only when united that lovers can be happy. If mortals, however, persist in their pride, they will be punished by a new division ; it will then be curious, adds Aristophanes, to see them going about the world with only half a head, one eye, one hand, one foot. Landino, who had to comment upon this strange discourse, seeks neither the origin of the legend, nor its mythological explanation. The soul, he says, was created whole by God, furnished with divine light with which to look upon the higher things, with natural light, inborn, with which to look upon the lower. But man sinned by pride, wished to make himself equal with God, thinking that his natural, inborn light was sufficient for him ; whereupon his thoughts were directed to corporeal things alone, and the original unity was broken. If he persists in his pride, trusting entirely to his natural light, he will be punished anew by losing that also.[2] This was the easy explanation of everything.

The last to speak is Cristoforo Marsuppini, who concludes by

---

[1] See Cavalcanti's two speeches in the " Commentarium."

[2] " Commentarium," Oratio iv.

commenting on the very beautiful speech of Alcibiades, and the words which he, at the end of the "Symposium," addresses to Socrates. The orator makes his commentary by expounding the ideas of Guido Cavalcanti upon love, and speaking of the *divine fury*, by means of which man, rising above his own nature, *in Deum transit*. By this God draws the soul, sunk in inferior things, once more upwards to the higher. And all terminates with an eulogium of Socratic love, and a hymn to the divine love or Holy Spirit, that has inspired the discussion, and illumined the Platonic orators.[1]

These philosophers, in trying to reconcile Paganism with Christianity, spirit with matter, the divine with the human, God with the world, and unable to discover the rational unity of all those things, reduced everything to symbols. Yet the great popularity and immense influence of this philosophy upon the literature and culture of the age, cannot be placed in doubt by any one ; and it is impossible to deny its great historical importance. This philosophy, in fact, was the result of a new way of regarding the world, that emerges clearly enough, even from amid the clouds of the wildest allegories. For the Platonists the world had become the great physical and moral cosmos, created by divine love, in the image of the God who dwells therein, and whom they regarded no longer as a living personality, but as the supreme unity of all, the universal spirit, the absolute. And owing to their labours this conception penetrates and permeates the literature of the second half of the fifteenth century, and serves to determine its character. Hence it is plain that Italian Platonism, without having much scientific value, is yet a highly important element of modern culture.

But fully to understand this, we must also fix our attention upon the works of the man who best knew how to formulate and teach it. Marsilio Ficino had a boundless admiration for all the philosophy of the ancients ; he studied and tried to assimilate Plato, Aristotle, the Neo-Platonists, and every fragment he could find of quotations from Confucius, Zoroaster, &c. All that which they say is sacred to him, merely because it is ancient ; and thus his writings become a huge congeries of different elements, without his ever discovering a true dominant and organic principle, upon

---

[1] "Commentarium," &c., Oratio vii. chap. xvii. "Quomodo agendae sunt gratiae Spiritu Sancto, qui nos ad hanc disputationem illuminavit atque accendit."

which to build up a system, and earn a right to the title of an original philosopher.

The Neoplatonic allegories imported among us by G. Plethon and other Greeks formed the only means by which he could harmonize the different elements. Yet Ficino's proposed aim was a highly remarkable one, and affords us a glimpse of his philosophic importance. Amid the triumph of Pagan antiquity, he sees that Christianity cannot fall ; but he also sees that the mere authority of the prophets, of the Bible, and of revelation, no longer suffices to maintain it and keep it alive in men's minds. Hence it was necessary to have recourse to reason, to true philosophy, *i.e.*, to ancient philosophy ; and among the diverse systems, that which best lent itself to his object, was certainly the Platonian. Thus, as he himself declares, arose in his mind the notion of founding Christianity upon the Platonic doctrine, and even of proving that they were one and the same thing, that the one was the logical consequence of the other. At that time this appeared to be a new revelation, and therefore he burnt candles before Plato, and adored him as a saint. In fact, in his book, "Della Religione Cristiana," the most solid arguments that he can find in its favour are the answers of the Sibyls and the prophecies of the coming of Jesus Christ, to be found in Virgil, Plato, Plotinus, and Porphyrius.

To him the life of Socrates is a continual symbol of the life of Jesus, the doctrines of the one are identical with those of the other. Thus antiquity received the benediction of Christianity, which in its turn was proved to be true by antiquity. What fact could be of higher concern to the learned of the fifteenth century ? Ficino was so full of these ideas, so enthusiastic about them, that he sometimes seemed to look upon himself as the founder of a new religion rather than the inventor of a new system.

He wrote a large number of epistles, translations, and tractates in Latin ; but the greatest and most solid monument to his fame was the first and, for a long time, the only good translation of Plato's works. At this he laboured unremittingly for a great part of his life, while meditating another work which was to be a systematic summary of the mass of his doctrines. Touching this, he tells us that he was long in uncertainty as to whether this work should be a philosophical exposition of the ancient Pagan religion, or a demonstration of Christianity, made with the assistance of ancient philosophy. The latter idea prevailed : nevertheless his new book was entitled " Platonic Theology," which plainly shows the author's groove of thought. It is a vast and ill-arranged encyclopedia of learning, written in a confused and colourless style, a defect observable in all his works, since, although he had consumed his whole life over the classics, the uncertainty of his ideas made it impossible for him to acquire any real originality or vigour of style. After careful examination of the "Theologia Platonica," we might almost say that the materials accumulated in it are, as it were, beginning to ferment, and that consequently certain assimilations take place, of which the author is unaware. In fact, there is something in it that may be called a result of the thought of the age, an impersonal progress in science, of which Ficino himself appears to be rather the instrument than the author. The question of the *consulto* or *non-consulto agit* in nature is, that around which from the commencement all the others are grouped, and it is solved in the same manner as by Gemistos Plethon. He finds in the world two different categories of souls. The first consists of intellectual, universal souls ; the other of sensitive, mortal, but also reasoning souls. These, which he calls the *third essences* of things, are to be found throughout nature, which they animate. The earth, light, air, the planets, have each their third essence, and that explains why the earth produces plants, the water fish, &c. The third essences are also divided into twelve orders, according to the twelve constellations of the zodiac ; but these are united, and are mingled together to form souls or third essences of a more general character. Thus in our own planet, water, earth, and air has each its own third essence ; but this planet has also its special, more general, third essence which embraces all the others.

Then, too, man has two souls, one rational and sensitive, the third essence of the body, which dies ; the other intellectual, immortal, emanating directly from God. By means of this, the creature finds himself in relation with the Creator and with the possibility of coming into contact with Him ; in this are mirrored all the others, which breathe life into the universe. Thus man is a microcosm ; he can descend to the animals, to inanimate nature, and rise to the angels, to God who speaks to him and guides him. Then, too, stars, planets, and even the stones have, by their third essences, direct influence over man's passions, man's destiny. And thus is demonstrated the truth of the occult sciences, in which Ficino had an almost childish belief. His continual melancholy was attributed by him to the influence of Saturn ; and every day he was careful to change the amulets which he always wore upon his person. He wrote a treatise on all these things, entitled : " De vita cœlitus comparenda," [1] which must be read in order to understand the point reached by the superstitious prejudices of a very learned man, and of a very advanced age. The faith in occult sciences cherished by the most remarkable men of the Renaissance, is another of the numerous contradictions we find in that period. Yet, on carefully considering the question, we perceive that this faith was fed by the need of replacing supernatural by natural explanations, even when science was impotent to find them. If we now glance at this philosophy of Ficino's in its entirety, there clearly stands out an irresistible tendency to such an universal and rational soul, which, in his writings, seems in fact to be confounded with the world and with God Himself. His third essences are identical with the ideas of Plato in an Aristotelian shape, which are afterwards united in more general souls, and how was it possible that they should not all be united in one soul ? Is not the world, according to Ficino's own words, a great living animal ? Has not nature a rational soul that *consulto agit ?* Only in presence of these natural, inevitable consequences of his own premises, our author stops himself, as it were, in affright, because he *must* accept and explain creation from the void, and cannot renounce the personal God of Christianity.

When, however, he begins to give a philosophical explanation of creation, he always recurs to the same ideas, and again approaches the consequences from which he rebels. God conceives (and in the Divine mind conception is equivalent to creation) the sensitive soul of things, and the angelic immortal soul. With this He forms the angels, and by their means creates the third essences which are too far beneath Him for Him to condescend to directly create them. But in man, besides the third essences, or soul of the body, there is also an immortal one directly infused by God, and by means of which the creature comes in contact with the Creator. In short, Ficino's creation is an emanation ; his God is the soul and the unity of the world, indeed, the only definition he can give of it is the absolute unity of all things. Pantheism, the logical consequence of this system,

[1] Lugduni, 1567.

was, in the very atmosphere of the fifteenth century, which found no other way of reconciling God and nature, the Divine and the human. Already scientifically sketched out by Cusano, and rendered popular by Ficino, it was afterwards lucidly formulated and maintained by Bruno. Cusano and Bruno, however, were real thinkers and philosophers, while Ficino was merely a learned man who wrote on philosophy without much originality. The Pantheistic idea showed itself in his works in an indistinct, confused, almost unconscious manner ; but it was precisely this that proved it to be an outcome of the general need of the time, caused its instant popularity, and made it penetrate deeply into literature. In the verses of Lorenzo the Magnificent, of Poliziano, of Alberti, in many even of the contemporaneous prose writers, we see the personal God changed into the absolute, the world is the great cosmos which it inhabits and animates ; nature herself, no longer despised, becomes almost divine. And this transformation, as we have already said, was the work of Ficino and the Platonic Academy. Both vanished without establishing a new system, but they left instead a new method of looking upon the world, and a new conception of the Deity.

Ficino's enthusiastic ardour in expounding the new doctrines found a wide echo both in Italy and abroad. Students came from all parts of the world to attend the lectures he gave at the Studio. Many Englishmen carried Italian Hellenism to their own country ; Reuchlin himself, in passing through Florence, was more than ever converted to the new ideas, which met with great favour in Germany, where Reformation began with the individual interpretation of the Holy Scriptures, and by placing the believer in direct communication with his Creator, without the need of any mediator. In Italy, on the contrary, the results of learning always remained merely literary and scientific.

Giovanni Pico della Mirandola, so celebrated throughout Europe, was known among us by the name of the intellectual Phœnix, on account of the knowledge attributed to him of twenty-two languages, of his great learning and extraordinary memory. To these gifts he united much goodness of character and an amiable and attractive appearance, and although of princely family, he had abandoned everything for his studies. Excited by the praises showered upon him, and by a philosophy which pretended to embrace the whole universe in its allegories, he proposed a strange species of scientific tournament, that was to be held in Rome. He had summed up all knowledge in nine hundred conclusions, on each of which he declared himself prepared to make a reply to scholars from all parts, whom he invited to discuss with him, promising to pay the travelling expenses of all those who were poor. The experiment was prevented from taking place by the difficulties raised by the Pope, to whose authority Giovanni Pico was always most submissive. But notwithstanding his great reputation, this scholar's intellect was substantially but little different from that of Ficino's other followers. His acquirements, though extensive, were superficial, his judgments dictated rather by enthusiasm than critical faculty. He considered the poems of Lorenzo dei Medici superior to those of Dante and Petrarch. Of the majority of the twenty-two languages he was supposed to have studied, he knew little more than the alphabet and the elements of grammar. He was, however, one of the first promoters of Oriental studies, as well as one among the best of Greek and Latin scholars. But neither his Italian and Latin writings, much less his philosophy, show any marks of originality. He tried to reconcile Averhoes and Avicenna, Scotus and St. Thomas, Plato and Aristotle, in order to combat the enemies of the Church. This, of necessity, brought about his union with Ficino, who desired to fight "the religion of ignorance and the philosophy of unbelief." At first a friend of the Medici, he ended by becoming an enthusiastic admirer of Savonarola, and was buried in the Church of St. Mark, shrouded, according to his last wish, in the frock of the Dominican friars.[1] He ceased to live in 1494, a memorable year in the history of Italy, and of all Europe. Platonists and the learned men now disappeared very rapidly from the scene, and the national literature, so long in course of preparation, began to shine forth in all its new brilliancy.

8. REVIVAL OF ITALIAN LITERATURE.

In the fifteenth century our vulgar tongue had much decayed, chiefly by fault of the men of learning, who either wrote in Latin or twisted Italian into an artificial imitation of that tongue. In the year 1441, on the occasion of the stay of Pope Eugene IV. in Florence, a grand literary meeting took place in the Cathedral under the name of *Academia Coronaria*, because a silver crown

---

[1] See my "Storia di G. Savonarola," &c., book i. chap. v.

was offered to him who should recite the best Italian verses upon friendship. And after all the prize could not be adjudged to any of the competitors, and so wretched were these verses that to this day no one can read them without amazement at their corrupt taste and puerile artifice. Still it would be a mistake to suppose that all had given up writing in the vulgar tongue. Italian songs composed by writers of little note, but many in number, were sung by the people both in town and country, and many familiar letters, tales, romances, and chronicles were also written in Italian. It was a literature chiefly made for the people, and in which the people took part in many ways, although it cannot be called popular in the strict sense of the word. And throughout the fifteenth century it continued to increase in importance, until the men of learning also forsook Latin, and recurring to Italian, thus initiated a second epoch in the history of our letters. The Platonists may be included among those who first returned to the vulgar tongue. Cristoforo Landino had materially assisted in this, promoting by his commentaries the study of Dante and Petrarch. But to Leon Battista Alberti must be awarded a still more honourable post. Born in 1404 at Venice, whither his family had been exiled, he soon proved himself a most remarkable man. Of very rare strength and beauty, he succeeded no less admirably in all bodily exercises than in mental labour. Accomplished in music, singing, and the arts of design, he was versed in letters and had studied the moral, as well as the mathematical or natural sciences, in which many discoveries are attributed to him.[1] Landino, Poliziano,[2] and others exalt not only the universality of his genius, but also, which is more noteworthy, his singular merit in promoting the study and use of Italian. This, too, is plainly shown in his works, although many disputes have arisen concerning them. Some of Alberti's verses have certainly

[1] See the "Commentario alla Vita di L. B. Alberti," in the fourth volume of Vassari, Le Monnier edition, Tiraboschi, "S. L. I.," vol. vi. p. 414 and fol.; the edition of L. B. Alberti's "Opere," edited by Bonucci and published in Florence (Tip. Galileiana) in 1843 and following years. This edition includes a Life of Alberti by an anonymous author. See also the "Elogi di L. B. Alberti" in the works of G. B. Nicolini, Le Monnier edition, 1843, vol. iii. p. 401 and fol.; the "Elogio" written by Pozzetti, published in Florence in 1789, and finally "Gli Alberti di Firenze, Genealogia," &c., recently brought out by Cav. L. Passerini in two large and elegant volumes, by commission of the Duc de Lugnes. Florence, Cellini, 1870.

[2] See Bandini's "Specimen," vol. i. p. 164; Tiraboschi's "S. L. I.," vol. vi. p. 420, in which a letter by Poliziano is given.

a singular freshness and spontaneity [1] which would excite surprise, had not Poliziano and Lorenzo dei Medici already warned us that the Italian muse was now awaking, animated by a new spirit, and almost born again to a second youth. His prose is still very artificial in its imitation of Latin ; yet one work entitled "La cura della famiglia" merits special mention, particularly its third book, "L'Economico" or "Il Padre di famiglia," in which a good father of a family and the best way of ruling a household is carefully described. This is almost a separate work, and in a preface to it, Alberti takes the defence of the Italian language which he declares to be in no wise inferior to the Latin,[2] and promises to try and make use of a "bare and simple style" ("stile nudo e semplice.") Certainly, in this book his prose is far more spontaneous and familiar than usual ; the author seems to wish to return to the golden simplicity of the Trecento.

"L'Economico" is generally known in the much freer and more popular form given to it by Agnolo Pandolfini under the title of "Del Governo della famiglia," and in this form it is one of the finest monuments of our national literature. It is maintained by some that Pandolfini copied and improved on Alberti, but this is denied by others. What is certain is that the former writes in familiar Italian, in a rich and graphic style, not always free from grammatical errors, while Alberti in correcting these errors, obscures the golden simplicity of him who appears to be his precursor. In his language one perceives the mixture of the popular and learned styles, but the two elements are not always well combined. If Alberti decided on imitating and almost copying the work of another, this is only additional proof that the book expressed the feelings and opinions of the period, and this gives it importance not only in the history of our language and literature, but also in that of Italian society.[3]

---

[1] See the "Opere" of Alberti and Trucchi's "Poesie Italiane inedite." Prato, 1846–47, vol. ii. p. 335.

[2] Alberti, "Opere," vol. ii. p. 221 and fol.

[3] This book, generally held to be the work of Pandolfini, was afterwards attributed to Alberti, especially by Signor F. Palermo, who took up the question so hotly and exaggerated so much in his "Prolegomini" added to the "Padre di famiglia" (Florence, tipografia Cenniniana scientifica, 1872) as to entirely forget the method and limits of scientific criticism. Pandolfini died before Alberti, and it is hard to imagine that he would have copied from learned prose and not only turned it into familiar spoken Italian, but introduced idioms and ungrammatical expressions where none existed before. Alberti, however, ex-

The "Governo della famiglia" is the work of a man who lived between the end of the fourteenth and beginning of the fifteenth century, and, after taking part in political struggles, had retired disgusted to the country to devote himself to composition. Thus we have a faithful description of the social, moral, and intellectual condition of Italians in the fifteenth century, such as we search for in vain in the pages of history. In particular, we find a profound disgust of political life, "that life of insults, envy, passions, and suspicions."[1] The Italian spirit already feels condemned to fall back upon itself, without finding in its own conscience the comfort of religious life. Virtue seems to be nothing but the result of an almost artistic well being, "it is all gaiety and grace."[2] All that is desired is to have the mind undisturbed by any cupidity, repentance, or grief ;[3] honesty is woman's finest *ornament ;* vice makes her vulgar and ugly.[4] In this book the new tendencies infused by Platonism in the Italian mind are very apparent. Virtue, in fact, proceeds from a necessary law of our nature, not from the command of any superior authority. When the head of the family marries, he leads his wife before the household shrine of the Madonna, and there kneeling down together, they pray, not to the virgin nor the saints, but to the Most High. Neither do they supplicate for happiness in the other world, but only that it may be given to them to enjoy the goods of this life. The wife must know how to govern her household with tact and gentleness, in order to maintain general harmony, and ensure general well being. Reading these things is like looking upon one of Masaccio's or Lippi's pictures. There is no effort towards the Infinite, there is a quiet, self-contented harmony, resembling the universal principle of life as it was then understood by Italians. Every little detail of the picture brings before our eyes the democracy of Florence, with its refinement and civil equality. Whereas in almost all the rest of Europe the peasant was still the slave of the soil, here he had already become his master's torment. He wants an ox, a cow, or sheep to be bought for him ; wants to have his debts paid ; asks for a dowry for his daughter ; to have a house built and the furniture provided ; and withal, is never contented.[5]

---

pressly declared himself to be the author. The question has been recently discussed by Cortesi, Scipioni, and Pellegrini. The first sustains the priority of Pandolfini, the other two with some strong arguments take a contrary view.

[1] Pandolfini, "Trattato del governo della famiglia," p. 21 ; Venice, Gondoliere Printing Press, 1841.   [2] Ibid., p. 5.   [3] Ibid., p. 14.   [4] Ibid., p. 262.
[5] Ibid., p. 42.

But the founts of the new literature are many in number ; and while speaking only of prose, we must mention the political and diplomatic correspondences which became, in this century, one of the most notable branches of our literature. These were no displays of rhetoric, but written for the purpose of conducting affairs to a given end ; therefore they soon attained remarkable simplicity, spontaneity, and lucidity.

In the recently published " Commissioni " of Rinaldo degli Albizzi,[1] we notice the writer's efforts to graft the uncultivated language of the people upon the Latin periods of the learned. But in the letters of Lorenzo dei Medici, these efforts are at an end, and the new political prose has triumphed over every difficulty without however concealing its two original elements. Of these letters, Guicciardini himself speaks in the highest praise.[2] They show on the one hand the admirable prudence with which Lorenzo sought to maintain the political balance of Italy, the great authority exercised by him over all the States of the Peninsula, and on the other, the popular ease with which this disciple of Ficino and Poliziano knew how to write. When Ferdinand of Naples wished to form a special alliance with the Pope, Lorenzo immediately sets to work to prevent " this spark of change in Italy," [3] and a general peace is concluded instead. When his daughter Maddalena marries Francesco Cibo, the Pope's natural son, he instantly gives notice that he does not intend to form any compacts to the hurt of the general peace of Italy, nor to make far-stretching plans for the future, since it is better " to think day by day, and dance in time to the music that one hears." [4] When the Pope wished to call the Duke of Lorraine into Italy, Lorenzo uses every effort to prevent it, alleging the many dangers it would bring about, and reminding his Holiness " that human hands cannot hold the reins of fortune." The Duke of Milan, Lodovico il Moro, always uncertain, changeable, and ambitious, who hourly caused fresh complications, must be treated, says Lorenzo, as suits

---

[1] These have been published in three vols. by the Società di Storia Patria : Florence, Cellini, 1867–69, and go from the year 1399 down to 1433.

[2] In his " Storia Fiorentina."

[3] A. Desjardins, "Négociations diplomatiques de la France avec la Toscane" (3 vols. 4to) : Paris, 1859–65, Imprimerie Impériale, vol. i. p. 214. It is only just to mention that the chief part of these documents were discovered by an Italian, G. Canestrini.

[4] Fabroni, " Vita Laurentii Medicis," Pisis, 1784, vol. ii. p. 312, note 179.

[5] Ibid., vol. ii. p. 359, note 206.

his nature, namely, by giving way to him as long as is possible without danger ; but in such a way "as to remain in the saddle even if he should try to fling out." Therefore is it all the more necessary to keep on friendly terms with the Venetians, "so as always to have some anchors in the sea." [1]

And when his son Giovanni, who at the age of seventeen years had been for some time a Cardinal, is starting for Rome, Lorenzo warns him of the dangers to which he will be exposed in that very corrupt city, and reminds him that union with the Church is useful to Florence, and that "the interest of our family goes with that of the city, so that you ought to be a good link in the matter ; and at all events there should not fail you the means of saving both the goat and the cabbages, as the saying goes." [2] This easy, familiar, vigorous style of prose soon became very general in Tuscany, and Lorenzo dei Medici was one of the first to make use of it, as he was also one of the first to write verses in the vulgar tongue. In the fourteenth century, two different styles of poetry had been grafted one upon the other, which to this day can be easily distinguished in the sonnets and canzonets of that time, and even in the "Divina Commedia" itself.

The one was simple, clear, natural—an inspiration which, if not wholly popular, was certainly much nearer to the people than the other poetry, which was artificial, allegorical, scholastic, courtly, of the French or Provençal school. Out of this union of different elements, the national genius, even then assisted by classical studies, had extracted a new literature. And this easily penetrated among the people, who, fascinated and carried away by an art beyond their own power, and yet entirely to their taste, and fitted to their comprehension, had little longer need of other songs, and other tales. But towards the end of the fourteenth century, literary men wrote in Latin, and the people, who, amid their struggles for liberty, had made much progress in civilization, had once more to provide for themselves. Throughout the Tuscan land were then heard new songs, new *rispetti*, new roundelays, [3]

---

[1] Fabroni, "Vita Laurentii Medicis," Pisis, 1784, vol. ii. p. 363.

[2] Fabroni calls this letter the song of the swan, *tanquam cycnea fuit*, because Lorenzo died soon afterwards (vol. ii. p. 308, note 178).

[3] We have already seen in Pandolfini, that the Italian peasantry, and more especially the Tuscan, who are here in question, were in the fifteenth century superior in culture and prosperity to those of the rest of Europe. The novel writers, like Sacchetti, for instance (see Novelle 88 and 202), frequently speak of shrewd, well-to-do peasants. In the "Beca di Dicomano," in which the author,

while in the towns there was a prodigious crop of novels, tales, and knightly adventures, which had travelled to us from France, besides sacred representations or mysteries. And all these were naturally in the vulgar tongue.

A few Rispetti, a few Strambotti, and a certain number of songs really issued from the heart of the people. To this day they are still to be heard in the villages of Tuscany, where, as D'Ancona observes, they seem echoes of the last creative efforts of a nation on the point of losing its liberty.[1] But there are many others, besides tales of chivalry, and sacred and profane plays, which cannot be called popular creations, since they were generally the compositions of public storytellers, who, although belonging to the class for which they wrote, possessed a certain amount of rough and imperfect culture. In these, many classical reminiscences and tricks of rhetoric are to be found, but very seldom the true impulsiveness of the popular vein. Still these works have a certain simplicity, and even a certain ingenious delicacy of feeling, which attest their semi-popular origin, and recall the fact that in those times the higher classes and men of cultivation were much more corrupt than the people. While the learned men were employed upon works like the "Ermafrodito,"[2] the "Invettive," and obscenities of every description, the story-tellers narrated the fantastic feats of knights-errant, the unhappy loves of Hippolitus and Dianora, and their heroic self-devotion ;[3] the sorrows of Ginevra degli Almieri, who, coming out of the tomb in which she has been buried alive, is not recognized either by her husband or her own mother, who both refuse her shelter. Her first lover, from whom she had been forcibly torn, is the only one who sees that she is really flesh and blood, and who now joyfully gives her refuge.

" Mischiando la letizia col dolore."[4]

Pulci, describes peasant life, a peasant says to his sweetheart :—" Thou knowest that I am ignorant and worthy—and I have cattle, and houses, and land. If thou wouldst take me, I would take thee."—See also Burckhardt, " Die Cultur der Renaissance," first edition, p. 356.

[1] A. D'Ancona, " La Poesie Popolare Fiorentina nel Secolo," xv.

[2] This work was published in the " Rivista Contemporanea " of Turin, vol. xxx. No. 106, September, 1862. See also Carducci's remarks in his preface to the volume, " Le Rime, le Stanze e l'Orfeo " of A. Poliziano : Florence, Barbèra, 1863. These two writers are those who have gone most thoroughly into the subject of ancient popular Italian poetry.

[3] This legend is also to be found in the works of Leon Battista Alberti.

[4] Republished by A. D'Ancona (Pisa, Nistri, 1863). See, too, the three

Italian poetry of the fifteenth century was chiefly based by the *literati* on what was generally, if somewhat incorrectly known as popular poetry. Among us undoubtedly the songs of men of letters and those of the people are so much intermingled, and exercise so much reciprocal influence, that even for the most acute and intelligent critics it is often extremely difficult to disentangle the one from the other. But in any case, one of the first, not merely to protect, but to promote and cultivate the new poetry, was Lorenzo dei Medici. To one who founded a tyranny by leaning on the people in opposition to the nobility, it was highly convenient to make himself also a popular poet, particularly in a city like Florence, where intellectual dominion was the firmest basis of political power. In fact the woodcuts of the period represent Lorenzo singing verses to the populace.

In order to do justice to Lorenzo's literary merit, it is by no means necessary to join in the extravagant flights of Roscoe and Ruth, who try to prove him a genius.[1] In his poetry, as in everything else, he displayed great knowledge of human nature and a fine taste, without, however, having sufficient elevation of mind to reach the heights of art. This too is shown by his own account of his earliest inspirations. On the death of the beautiful Simonetta, the beloved of Giuliano dei Medici, many poets, among them Poliziano,[2] wrote verses in her honour. Lorenzo, in order to do something of the same kind, feigned to have lost his lady love, but then sought for a living one, whom he found in Lucrezia Donati,[3] a beautiful and spirited young girl, and immediately applied himself to the composition of love songs. But this did not prevent him from making arrangements in Rome for his marriage with Clarice Orsini. His mother Lucrezia Tornabuoni, writing at this time to her husband, Piero dei Medici, speaks of the

volumes of "Sacre Rappresentazioni dei Secoli," xiv., xv., and xvi., by the same author : Florence, Le Monnier, 1872.

[1] Far juster is the judgment of Gino Capponi in his "Storia della Repubblica Fiorentina," and of Baron de Reaumont in his work, "Lorenzo dei Medici," Leipsic, 1873. Carducci has frequently written with great originality of Lorenzo's poetic faculty and temperament, but in our opinion he praises him rather too highly.

[2] "Dum pulchra effertur nigro Simonetta feretro Blandus et examini spirat in ore lepos," &c.

[3] "Comento di Lorenzo di Medici sopra alcuni dei suoi Sonetti, nel fine delle sue poesie volgari" (edition of 1554). See also Roscoe, "Life of Lorenzo dei Medici," chap. 11.

bride in the following terms : "She is of seemly stature and of fair complexion, and has sweet manners, if less gracious than ours ; she has great modesty, and so will soon fall in with our customs. Her hair is not fair, for there is no such thing here ; her tresses incline to red, and she has great abundance of them. Her visage inclines to be rather round, but it does not displease me. Her throat is well turned, but seems to me somewhat thin. Her bosom we cannot see, for it is here the fashion to wear it covered up, but it appears to be of good quality. Her hand is long and slender, and altogether we rate the maiden much above the common." [1] But after this minute description of the bride's physique, she has not a word to say of her mind, talents, or character. Lorenzo, who became betrothed to this young girl at the age of twenty-one, wrote these words in his Ricordi,[2] June 4, 1469 : "I have taken a wife, or rather she was given to me" (Tolsi donna . . . ovvero mi fu data), and his verses show him to be the true son of his mother. At the age of seventeen, he described the lips, eyes, and hair of his mistress, praised the mountains, the flowery meadow, the river, the rustic solitudes, in which he could gaze upon her image far from the noise of towns. Even at that time we find fine taste and ease in his verses, which are written in a spontaneous, and sometimes too familiar a manner : he describes nature and the actual world with the graphic power of a keen observer. These qualities were afterwards still more conspicuous in Lorenzo's various compositions, for he had a genuine admiration for the beautiful, loved country life, and was a true artist and painter of the outer world. To his descriptive power he unites in his "Beoni" a mordant and satiric spirit ; but the special characteristics of his poetry are chiefly apparent in his "Canzoni a ballo" taken from popular sources and given in their real form, and in his "Canti Carnascialeschi" of which barely the germ existed, and to which he gave a place in literature, thus becoming the creator of that description of verse.

The ruling idea in these poems is : enjoy your life to-day, give yourselves up to pleasure, and take no thought for the morrow. Young men, be not timid with women, and as for you ladies— :

---

[1] "Tre lettere di Lucrezia Tornabuoni a Piero dei Medici, ed altre lettere di vari concernenti al matrimonio di Lorenzo il Magnifico con Clarici Orsini." Marriage album collected by Cesare Guasti. Florence : Le Monnier, 1859.

[2] Reprinted by Roscoe, in the Appendix to his "Life of Lorenzo," Doc. xii.

> " Arrendetevi, belle,
> A'vostri innamorati,
> Rendete e' cuor furati,
> Non fate guerra a l maggio." [1]

The crafty politician who sought to stupefy his people in the gross sensuality in which he himself indulged, here shows his nature openly, with great impulsiveness of style and freshness of form. But here, too, we see that his is an art of corruption carrying its own condemnation on its face. If in his " Canzoni a ballo" (songs for dancing), he contents himself with the pleasures of idleness and of a life of sensuality, in the " Canti Carnascialeschi," he goes much further. Some of these bring before us with much gaiety, mythological figures that are full of life ; others again describe indecencies too horrible to be mentioned in these days, and which were then openly sung in the public thoroughfares, the acknowledged works of a prince who had gained the admiration of the whole civilized world. He was accustomed to direct the carnival festivities and masquerades, calling sculptors and painters [2] to his assistance to enhance their brilliancy, and using elegance of taste as an engine for the corruption of manners. He had music composed on purpose to accompany his obscene songs. He associated with the *literati*, artists, and populace, and was the soul and leader of the bacchanalian revels. Still it must be confessed that Lorenzo, by taking up the different kinds of poetry he found diffused among the people, and endowing them with artistic dignity, made himself the promoter of a literary revolution, in which, although surpassed by some of his contemporaries, he nevertheless took a very high place. [3]

But the principal reviver of Italian poetry in the fifteenth century was Angelo Ambrogini of Monte Pulciano, called Poliziano. Born the 14th of July, 1454, he was, up to 1474, a student in the Florentine Studio, where he followed the teachings of

---

[1] The Canzone begins thus:—

> " Ben venga maggio
> E 'l gonfalon selvaggio."

[2] Vasari, in his " Vita di Piero di Cosimo," tells us of the care with which these fêtes, which long continued in Florence, were arranged, and declares them to be *things to sharpen men's wits.* " Canti Carnascialeschi " by different authors were afterwards collected in two volumes by Lasca : Fiorenza, 1559.

[3] See the remarks of Carducci in his fine " Prefazione alle Poesie di Lozenzo." Florence : Barbèra.

Ficino, Andronicus, Argiropulos, and Landino. At the age of sixteen he had already begun a translation of Homer, which made Ficino accord him the title of the Homeric child, and secured to him the lasting protection of Lorenzo, who receiving the youth in his own palace, made him tutor to his son Piero.[1] At twenty-nine years he was professor of Greek and Latin eloquence in the Studio, and his lessons were attended not only by Italians like Pico della Mirandola and the Medici themselves, but by foreigners of all nations. Soon after, in 1486, he was named canon of the cathedral. In a short time his fame filled all Italy, and even crossed the Alps. He showed very great critical acumen in his " Miscellanea," particularly in his collations of old texts. Afterwards, too, in collating the edition of the " Pandects," published at Venice in 1450, with the Laurentian Codex known as the " Pandects of Amalfi," he made certain observations which, although overpraised, showed the great aid philosophy could render to jurisprudence.[2] Poliziano's best productions are undoubtedly his poems, and often the finest introductory addresses which he delivered in the chair were nothing but Latin verses, in the composition of which he was unrivalled, even during early youth. At the age of eighteen he had earned praise by his Greek verses ; but had taken the world by storm with his Latin elegy on the death of Albiera degli Albizzi. In this the pagan feeling for beauty of form, and the ethereal grace of the painters of the Quattrocento seem to be blended together ; the Italian language fused with the Latin, which, in spite of being a dead tongue, has here the freshness of a living and spoken language. It would seem as though the breath of popular Italian song inspired new life into the man of learning, and enabled him to endow his Latin with the primitive spontaneity of the Greek. In this elegy we find the same unapproachable elegance, the same wealth of description, the same somewhat artificial diction as in his immortal Italian stanzas. Very beautiful are the last words of the dying woman to her husband, who, with terror-stricken eyes is watching

---

[1] Isidoro del Lungo, " Uno scolare dello Studio Fiorentino," a memoir published in the " Nuova Antologia of Florence," vol. x. p. 215, and fol. By the same author see " La Patria e gli antenati di Angelo Poliziano " in the " Archivio Storico Italiano," Series III., vol. xi. p. 9 and fol.

[2] Professor Bonamici of Pisa has examined the notes on the Pandects of his work " Il Poliziano Giureconsulto" (Pisa), Nistri, 1863, and has endeavoured to reduce the author's merit within its just limits.

the ever-increasing pallor stealing over the countenance of the loved one who

> "Illius aspectu morientia lumina pascit,"

and already feels herself being borne away to another life :

> ". . . . Heu ! nostro torpet in ore sonus ;
> Heu rapior !   Tu vive mihi, tibi mortua vivam.
> Caligant oculi iam mihi morte graves."

These gifts, which Poliziano possessed from the first, grew ever riper, as may be seen by many of his later poems, especially in that on the death of the fair Simonetta, and the very fine one upon violets.[1]   In reading these lines, more classical than any before written by the men of learning, the reader, sometimes almost carried away, may fancy he sees the Latin transforming itself into the new and lovely flower of Italian poetry, which in truth is budding to life again before his eyes.   For now, in fact, the Italian chrysalis breaks though the Latin shell in which it had so long been hidden, and at last comes forth into the sunlight.

Poliziano has earned immortality in the history of our literature, by the "Stanze" written by him for the Joust of Giuliano dei Medici, and which signalize the commencement of the second and no less splendid period of Italian poetry.   They form the beginning of a poem that breaks off at the forty-sixth octave of the second book, interrupted, very probably, by the murder of Giuliano in the Pazzi plot.[2]   The work, however, is not of a nature to lose

---

[1]   "Molles o violae, Veneris munuscula nostrae,
    Dulce quibus tanti pignus amoris inest ;
    Quae vos, quae genuit tellus ? quo nectare odoras
    Sparserunt Zephyri mollis et aura comas ?
    Vos ne in acidaliis aluit Venus aurea campis ?
    Vos ne sub Idalio pavit Amor nemore ?
    His ego crediderim citharas ornare corollis,
    Permessi in roseo margine Pieridas.
    Hoc flore ambrosios incingitur Hora capillos,
    Hoc tegit indociles Gratia blanda sinus,
    Hoc Aurora suae nectit redimicula fronti,
    Cum roseum verno pandit ab axe diem," &c.

[2]   It is generally believed that these "Stanze" were written in 1469, that is, when Poliziano was only fifteen years of age.   The mistake arose through confounding the Joust of Lorenzo with that of Giuliano.   The former was really given in 1469,

much by being left unfinished, as it is totally wanting in unity and epic matter, so that it is very hard to divine how the poet would have continued or finished it. Its great merit consists in its limpid, elegant style, which has an incomparable freshness. Carducci justly observes that the octave verse, that was diffuse in Boccaccio, diluted in Pulci, harsh and unequal in Lorenzo dei Medici, acquires in Poliziano's poetry the unity, harmony, colour, variety, and character which it has ever since preserved. Placed between the original primitive literature of the Trecento, and the more varied, refined, yet still imitative literature that flourished in the Cinquecento, it unites the vigour of the one with the grace of the other, thus resembling those masters of the Quattrocento, who improved upon the painting of Giotto, and perfected the technicalities of their art without falling into the conventionalities which so quickly arose in the Cinquecento. But we must remember that all this is only true as regards form, since, as to substance, Poliziano certainly has neither the elevation nor vigour of Dante, nor the imagination of Ariosto. But it is a form which may be called poetry itself, since it always depicts nature with unapproachable eloquence. Poliziano's women are neither so mystic and ethereal as Dante's, nor so sensuous as Ariosto's ; they have, however, a delicious delicacy and sweetness ; they recall the pictured forms of Lippi and Ghirlandaio. The fair Simonetta stands out in the " Stanze " a real and visible woman, yet she does not lack ideal beauty ;

> " Ridegli attorno tutta la foresta,
>
> .   .   .   .
>
> L'aer d'intorno si fa tutto ameno,
> Ovunque gira le luci amorose." [1]

The poet only seeks reality, but it is always an elegant and

and was described by Luca Pulci, say some, by his brother Luigi, say others. In any case, it is a work of little merit and very artificial. The poet says to Lorenzo : " Thy victory (in the tilting match) has naught to envy of the victories of Æmilius, Marcellus, Scipio ; thou hast well earned the honour :

" ' Di riportar te stesso in su la chioma,'

i.e., laurels upon Lauro's head." The Joust of Giuliano was instead given January 28, 1475, and was described by Poliziano, who was then twenty-one. It is, indeed, possible that the " Otta ve " were written in 1478, and that they described another Joust, which took place in the early part of that year. All this has been brought to light by Professor Del Lungo. See his own words given in Carducci's preface to Poliziano's Poems, p. xxix.

[1] " Stanze," book i. pp. 43, 44.

gracious reality. His images, freed from mediæval mysticism, seem to make use of the mythological garb in which they are often enfolded, to cover without hiding the forms of the body from which they are never separated. Their nudity appears from time to time adorned with classic enamel of a Pagan freshness that is specially characteristic of the Renaissance.

Who, after reading in the "Vita Nuova" or the "Divina Commedia," the descriptions of Beatrice, ever on the point of transformation into theology, turns to the ballad written by Olimpio of Sassoferrato and notes these lines :

> " La brunettina mia
>   Con l'acqua della fonte
>   Si lava il dì la fronte
>   E il seren petto," &c.,

will immediately perceive the distance traversed, and appreciate the change that has taken place.

Poliziano raised the popular Rispetti and Strambotti to a new dignity, and with so much taste and elegance, " that for the first time perhaps in poetry," says Carducci, " he gave an Attic stamp to Florentine idioms, and artistic finish to familiar expressions." [1] The ballad, too, which already in the Trecento had received a literary form, and thus embellished retained popularity, serving as a model for the many sacred Laudi composed during the fifteenth century, and even for the songs of Lorenzo dei Medici who endowed them with a new literary garb, was now raised by Poliziano almost to the dignity of the Ode, without losing any of its primitive simplicity.[2] Although in these lyrics we meet with sensual allusions which remind us of Lorenzo's companion, the poet never forsakes decency in the same fashion as his Mæcenas.

In his " Orfeo " he also made an attempt at drama ; but his dialogue is sometimes lyric, without ever rising to a true display of the passions. Dramatic poetry is born late in the life of a nation, that is, only when the national spirit and national tongue have reached a healthy and vigorous maturity. Italy had barely

---

[1] See the Prefazione to Poliziano's poems, p. cxvii. D'Ancona is of opinion that the " Rispetti " still sung among the hills in Tuscany are, at least in their general characteristics, the same that the Medician school took from the people, in order to give them back dressed in a more literary shape. And thus by force of custom the people have gone on singing them to this day.—" Rivista Contemporanea " quoted above.

[2] Carducci, " Prefazione," &c., p. cxxv.

touched this point when she fell a prey to foreign invaders, who destroyed her institutions and prevented her from finding, in this essentially national kind of poetry, a way of escape from the Latin travesty, whose fetters she had so often before shaken off.

And Poliziano, in spite of a fineness of taste, that was almost Greek, could never have had the power to attain to real dramatic elevation, or create the theatre required by us. We have only to remember his career as a courtier, to understand why his genius could take no lofty flights. Often our indignation is excited by seeing the author of so many beautiful verses condescending to write others full of the most fawning adulation. This it is impossible to pardon him, even when we remember the depth and sincerity of his affection for his patron. He was standing by Lorenzo's side when the conspiracy of the Pazzi broke out ; he was the first to close the door of the sacristy as soon as his master was safely within it ; on Lorenzo's return from his perilous Neapolitan journey, he welcomed him with very beautiful Latin verses, such as might be addressed by a lover to his mistress ; and on Lorenzo's death he lamented him in words of intense grief, and quickly followed him to the tomb. But all this cannot prevent us from feeling deep and contemptuous compassion for a poet who humiliates himself to his patron, even to the extent of begging for his old clothes, and it is easy to understand that the summit of art can never be reached in that way.

The literature of the Trecento may be considered as exclusively Tuscan ; that of the Renaissance quickly became national. In fact, as we have seen, men of learning flourished in all parts of the Peninsula, and now writers in the vulgar tongue began to spring up contemporaneously and with the same characteristics in different provinces. Thus from Poliziano and Florence, we may travel towards the south where we shall find Giovanni Gioviano Pontano. Born at Cerreto in Umbria (1426), he soon made his way to Naples, and became the minister and ambassador of Ferdinand of Aragon ; he accompanied him everywhere ; advised him in the weightiest affairs of the State, in which he always took a prominent part, and was tutor to Alfonso II. Little by little he became a thorough Neapolitan, and we may say that he was the best representative of the state of culture of that Court and of that time. A man of business, an acute diplomatist, and one of the most celebrated of the learned men, he instituted the *Academia Pontaniana* by the reorganization of that already founded by

Antonio Panormita under the name of the *Porticus Antoniana*. He wrote—always in Latin—an infinite number of philosophical, scientific, astrological, political, and historical works. But in all these works the approaching decline of learning was already fore-shadowed. His tractates " Della Fortezza," " Della Liberalità," " Della Beneficenza," &c., as also that " Del Principe," are mere dissertations without any originality, diffuse collections of moral sentences. His various astrological works include all the prejudices of the time, without any attempt to build them upon any pretended philosophical theory, after the manner of Ficino. The sun, the heart of heaven and of the universe, is the generative principle of all things. The constellation of Cancer, which influences cold bodies, is called the house of the moon, because when that planet, by nature damp and cold, is in this constellation, it acquires greater efficacy. Even his history of the *Guerra Napolitana* between Giovanni d'Anjou and Ferdinand of Aragon, although of some interest as the work of a contemporary writer, is full of useless digressions, wanders into astrological considerations, and lacks all critical power.[1] To really know Pontano and under-stand the value of his writings, a purely literary value, we must read his " Dialoghi " and Latin poems, especially those that are lyrical.

These are marked by the same qualities found in Poliziano : an extremely fine classical taste, and a lucid, graphic style, as vigorous as that of one using a living language, for in this case also, the freshness of the Latin springs from its intermixture with the language spoken by the author, which, however, is not Floren-tine but Neapolitan Italian. Hence, notwithstanding Pontano's great poetical talent, his works show an undeniable inferiority of form compared with those of Poliziano ; Tuscan atticism lends to the Latinity of the latter a Grecian elegance that does not exist to the same extent in that of Pontano. Nevertheless he certainly succeeds admirably in binding the Latin to modern ideas, and where it fails him, he Latinizes Italian or Neapolitan words, and

---

[1] For Pontano's Life see Tiraboschi, "S. L. I.," vol. vi. p. 950 ; Professor C. M. Tallarigo, " Giovanni Pontano e i suoi tempi," 2 vols. (Naples, Morano, 1874). This monograph contains many chosen specimens of Pontano's best Latin poems, with translations by Professor Ardito, and the whole of the Latin dialogue (Charon). Settembrini, in his " Storia della Letteratura Italiana " (Naples, 1866–72, 3 vols.), speaks of Pontano with a truth and eloquence (vol. i. pp. 281–83), which incited Professor Tallarigo to the composition of the above-quoted monograph. See also the Basle edition of Pontano's works.

rushes onwards with the speed of one speaking a language learnt from the cradle. In his dialogues " Charonte," " Antonio," " Asino," which are all works of imagination in elegant Latin prose, and intermingled with beautiful poems, there are pictures of Neapolitan manners, popular festivals, rustic love scenes, and a series of anecdotes so full of *verve* as to remind the reader of Boccaccio's finest pages. The fète of the *Porcello* at Naples, the temper of Italian cities, the corruption of the Roman priesthood, the ridiculous disputes of the pedants, and the fury with which they fall upon those who dare to use some particle or ablative in a manner opposed to their own, often, fallacious rules, all these things are given with a descriptive power, a freshness and *vis comica* sufficing to place Pontano among men of true literary genius. He writes in Latin, it is true, but his spirit and his intellect are modern, and his works are therefore real gems of Italian literature. In his *Antonius*, we see Neapolitans sitting in the shade and cutting jokes on passers-by ; Pontano himself alive and speaking ; his son, who recounts family quarrels ; a poet who, preceded by a trumpeter, according to the Neapolitan custom of the day, mounts a hill to recite the description of a battle, and halts from time to time to take a pull at his wine flask. Then we read the Ode of Galatea pursued by Polyphemus, which is one of his best poems :—

> " Dulce dum ludit Galatea in unda,
>   Et movet nudos agilis lacertos,
>   Dum latus versat, fluitantque nudae
>   Aequore mammea," &c.

and in all we find an exquisite taste, a spirit that even in old age was intoxicated with sensual and artistic pleasure, and a profound scepticism that turns everything into ridicule.

In the lyrics, the author's literary genius rises to its highest pitch, and shows us even better than those of Poliziano the image of the Renaissance. His women, says Carducci, laughingly bare all their charms to the sun and to love. " And with his tranquil sense of voluptuousness and genuine enjoyment of life, Pontano, though writing in Latin, is the most modern and truest poet of his age and of his country." [1] Assuredly, in reading his Odes, it is admirable to see the ease and agility of his movements in Latin attire ; he resembles a swimmer floating down with

---

[1] Carducci, " Studi letterarii," Livorno, 1874, p. 97.

the current. His Neapolitan Italian seems to infuse new life into the old idiom, even when it changes it too much :—

> " Amabo mea·chara Fanniella,
> Ocellus Veneris, decusque amoris,
> Jube isthaec tibi basiem labella
> Succiplena, tenella, mollicella,
> Amabo, mea vita, suaviumque,
> Face istam mihi gratiam petenti." [1]

He laughs and jests, sings lullabies, steeps himself in voluptuous beauty, between the soft arms of the nymphs who, surrounded by flowers, await him on the seashore, in the presence of nature. This is his world, the world of the Renaissance. All the cities, villas, and islands in the neighbourhood of Naples, the streets, and the fountains, personified in fantastic beings, move and dance around the poet. The nymphs Posilipo, Mergellina, Afragola, Acura, *Panicocolis studiosa lupini*, and Marianella, who sings in accompanying Capodimonte,

> " et cognita bucellatis
> Ulmia, et intortis tantum laudata torallis," [2]

are all moving and living beings in his " Lepidina." [3] Vesuvius, in the form of an old man, descends the mountain on an ass to come to the fête, and the women all crowd round him. To one he gives a thimble, to another a spindle, to a third a jest, and all push to get nearer to him and his donkey, greeting both with loud and joyous cries,

> " Plebs plaudit, varioque asinum clamore salutant,
> Brasiculisque apioque ferum nucibusque coronant."

The same merits are to be observed in the two books of his " Amori," in his " Endecasillabi," in his " Buccolica," and in his dydaschylic poem " L'Urania," in which there are admirable descriptions of nature. And we always find a strange mixture of two languages, one living, the other dead, in which both seem to acquire fresh life ; and this rich and varied medley of classical imagery, fantastic whimsies, splendid descriptions of scenery, and modern feeling, all mingled and all fermenting in the fancy of this

---

[1] Among the verses reprinted by Tallarigo, *op. cit.*, vol. ii. p. 627.
[2] *Taralli* are cakes very common in Naples to this day.
[3] See Tallarigo, *op. cit.*, vol. ii. p. 619 and fol.

man of learning changed into a poet, show us how the new literature was born of the ancient, and how, in the midst of the classical world so carefully conjured up, it was possible for the chivalric poem, apparently so unsuited to the age of learning, to spring into existence.

At this point we ought perhaps to mention the political letters of Ferrante d'Aragona, which also bear the signature of his prime minister Pontano, who certainly had no small part in their compilation. But, besides the difficulty of precisely determining what this part was, we shall have occasion to return to the subject at a more fitting moment. For the present it is enough to say that these letters are of rare merit, so perspicuous and eloquent, that they might bear comparison with some of our best prose, were not their Italian style too often adulterated with Neapolitan dialect, which, although it may add strength and spontaneity, naturally detracts from the unity and elegance of the language.

Besides Pontano, there was another Neapolitan writer, who died in the second half of the fifteenth century, and left a volume of tales, which are worthy of notice, especially if we remember, that after Sacchetti, that style of composition was almost entirely forsaken. A man of the world and destitute of learning, though living in the company of the learned, Masuccio Salernitano tells us, that it was his endeavour to imitate " the ancient satirist Juvenal, and the much esteemed idiom and style of the well-famed poet Boccaccio." [1] He frequently invokes the immortal Deities, and the most eloquent god Mercury speaks to him of the deceits practised by women " upon our great father Jove, the radiant Apollo, ourselves and other gods." [2] He, like Sacchetti, declares that he will narrate tales " approved as authentic histories, and certain modern, and other not very ancient facts." [3] His language is very artificial, from his imitation of Latin and of the Decameron ; and a great admixture of the Neapolitan and

---

[1] " Il Novellino di Masuccio Salernitano, restituito alla sua antica lezione," by Luigi Settembrini : Naples, Morano, 1874. See the prologue to the third part. There are fifty tales divided into five parts. Each part begins with a prologue, and the first of them is addressed to Ippolita d'Aragona, to whom the book is dedicated. Each tale has an Exordium, dedicating it to some illustrious Neapolitan personage ; the tale itself follows, and then comes a conclusion always entitled " Masuccio," because in it the author sets forth his reflections. The little we know of Masuccio is to be found in the Discourse, with which Settembrini has prefaced the volume.

[2] Prologue to the third part.   [3] First prologue.

Salernitan dialects, while lending much vivacity to Masuccio's style, impairs both his Italian and his grammar. His freshness and graphic power are so considerable, that were his style less incorrect, he would be one of our standard authors. Even as it is, the " Novellino " gives us a faithful representation of the times and of the Neapolitan Court. With a wide knowledge of men and things, with an intelligence that appears to be keen and good, the author knows how to give life to his characters, and can narrate with the ease and cheerful ingenuity of a true writer of the Renaissance. His dominant feeling is a profound hatred for the immorality of the priesthood, whom he scourges pitilessly, without, however, showing any hostility to religion. In the Exordium to the third tale dedicated to Pontano, he lauds his virtues, while lamenting that they should be contaminated by his constant intercourse with priests, friars, and nuns, " since with such persons only usurers, fornicators, and men of bad life are seen to converse." All this is not very surprising in a writer resident at the Aragonese Court, which was in continual warfare with the papacy, and had taken under its protection Antonio Panormita and Lorenzo Valla. But it is a surprising sign of the times, to find dedicated to Ippolita, the daughter of Francesco Sforza, and the youthful bride of Alfonso II. of Aragon, a book of tales, many of which are very obscene, and certain of which bear special dedications to this or that noble lady.

From the Dialogues of Pontano and the Tales of Masuccio, no great leap is required to pass on to the poems of knight-errantry, another species of literature peculiar to the age. Truly these had their birth in France, and may appear totally opposed to the national genius of Italy. Chivalry, in fact, was hardly at all diffused among us ; feudalism had been opposed and in a great measure destroyed ; in the Crusades we had only played a secondary part ; Charlemagne, the national hero of France, was for us merely a foreign prince and a conqueror. Yet these subjects were substantial elements of the poems of chivalry. The religious scepticism, that early arose in Italy, was also opposed to the temper of poems chiefly founded on the wars of the Christians against the infidels. Neither was the marvellous, which is the very essence of these poems, adapted to the temper of Italians, with their constant admiration for classical beauty. Having passed at one stride from a state of decay to a new form of civilization, they had never known the savage and robust youth, in which had been created that world of heroes, with their impossible adventures and fantastic, ever-changing natures. Nevertheless, these French poems so rapidly diffused throughout all feudal Europe, found their way to us also, and were much more widely propagated than might have been expected.

Even before the rise of our literature, and when in the north of Italy many wrote in Provençal or French, we had a series of knightly poems, compiled by Italians, in an Italianized French, or Frenchified Italian. In the South these tales were brought to us by the Normans, and in the centre of the Peninsula were spread by means of Italian writings and wandering minstrels. But those knightly heroes, the growth of a mist of fantasy, that was thoroughly outlandish, fell upon barren soil here, particularly in Central Italy, and had almost vanished from our literature to take refuge in mountain cottages and the hovels of the poor, when the sun of Dante's verse rose above the horizon. In many of Boccaccio's works, in Petrarch's " Trionfi," even in the " Divina Commedia," we often meet with reminiscences showing that the romances of chivalry had been always well known among the people. Paolo and Francesca in the " Inferno " remind each other how, in happy times, they had read together of the loves of Launcelot ; and Sacchetti telling of the smith who spoilt Dante's verses in reciting them, and the harshness with which the poet reproved him, adds that the smith would have done better to keep to the songs of Tristan and Launcelot ; an evident sign that even in Florence these songs were considered more adapted to the popular fancy. Then, when the learned began to write in Latin, the romances of chivalry seemed to awake from a temporary trance, and together with the " Rispetti," " Strambotti," " Laudi," and " Mysteries," formed part of what, as we have seen, was the literature of the people. In fact, so widely and deeply were they diffused, that, to this day, the Neapolitan story-teller (*cantastorie*) relates the feats of Orlando and Rinaldo to an enchanted audience, and in the rural districts of Tuscany the *Maggi*, or May plays, performed among the peasantry in the spring, take their subjects from the same poems. Some of these *Maggi* and romantic tales are of recent composition, but not a few of them date from the fifteenth century. At that time they were produced in enormous numbers, and read with the same avidity as novels are now-a-days. The Italians neither created new poems nor exactly reproduced the old, but made compilations in verse or prose, generally the latter, in which they often fused many into one, thus forming a huge repertory of fantastic tales. These, the story-tellers, who were generally authors themselves, went about reading to the people in town and country, and were everywhere listened to with the most eager attention. The so-called Chronicle of Turpin, and the cycle of Charlemagne in general furnish the groundwork of the Italian fables ; but the cycle of King Arthur and the Round Table have also great part in them. The chief of these compilers, and who will suffice to give us an idea of the rest, lived in the second half of the four-teenth and beginning of the fifteenth century. This was Andrea dei Mangabotti of Barberino in the Val d' Elsa, who calls Florence *my city*, because he lived and was educated there. Of unrivalled industry, he not only wrote the famous " Reali di Francia " in six books, but also " Aspromonte," in three books, " Storia di Rinaldo," in seven, " Spagna," in one, the " Seconda Spagna," in one, the " Storie Narbonesi," in seven, " Aiolfo," in one very stout book, " Ugone d'Avernia," in three, and, finally, " Guerino il Meschino," which although a continuation of the events nar-rated in the " Aspromonte," forms a separate work, the popularity of which, little inferior to that of the " Reali," endures to the present day. All these works are in prose, excepting certain por-tions of " Ugone d'Avernia."

The object proposed by the author was the collection and arrangement of the great multitude of tales forming part of the cycle of Charlemagne. And thus in the " Reali," his principal work, he compiled the history of the great emperor's race, without, however, making either a true history or a genuine romance of chivalry. He tries to introduce connection and precision in the midst of a deplorable chaos ; he makes geo-graphical corrections ; arranges genealogies ; but in so doing, sacrifices ingenuousness and poetic originality. It seems as though the Italian realism, so much admired in those stories, which are the most characteristic and national outcome of our literature, predominates even here, and spoils the romance, making it, despite certain merits, a hybrid work.

It is, in truth, neither popular nor literary poetry ; but rather epic matter in course of transformation, seeking a new shape which it has not yet found. The spoken language is inter-mingled with classical reminiscences, then familiar to all Italians ; narrative has a quiet solemnity, almost in the style of Livy, and

the author tries to fuse together within the limits of an idea
and well defined machinery, a myriad of tales which had
originally sprouted up with the exuberant and disorderly fertility
of a virgin forest.[1] These qualities of Mangabotti's writings are
common to those of numerous other compilers of prose and verse.

From all that we have said, it is plain that when our men of
letters began once more to write in Italian, and drew nearer to
the people, sated with the pompous rhetoric of poems like the
Sforziade and the Berseide, they found together with the
"Rispetti" and the "Ballate," many diffuse narratives like the
"Reali di Francia," in verse and in prose. Upon these they
exercised their powers, endeavouring to convert them into true
works of art. They left intact the general machinery of the tale,
the division into cantos, the recapitulations at the beginning of
each, addressed to "friends and good people," by the popular
poet, who was, as it were obliged to make an independent work
of every canto. And these new writers also were accustomed
to read their tales in fragments, not, it is true, in the public
squares, but at Court, at the dinners of the nobility, to cultivated
persons, who, however, desired entertainment, and were weary
of the empty solemnity of the learned men. Frequently the
changes made in rewriting these popular poems, as we may now
call them, were confined to a few touches, the addition of new
episodes, fresh descriptions, sometimes of entire cantos. But the
art of infusing life where none was before, consisted precisely in
these re-touches, which opened the way to new and original
creation.

The personages of these tales and poems began to stand out
from the still fantastic and nebulous background with which they

[1] Among the works giving precise details of this part of our literary history, we
should first quote the memoir read in the Berlin Academy of L. Ranke, " Zur
Geschichte der italienischen Poesie," Berlin, 1837. This short composition is one
of those that first opened a new path in the history of the Romance of chivalry ;
although it is no longer on a level with the present state of our knowledge.
More ample and with many new investigations in the history of literature,
particularly that of France, but in some degree also that of Italy, is the work of
Mons. G. Paris, " Histoire Poétique di Charles Magne," Paris, A. Franck, 1865.
As regards our literature, the most recent and complete work is that of Professor
P. Raina, " Ricerche intorno ai Reali di Francia," Bologna, Romagnoli, 1872
(in the collection published by the Commission for *testi di lingua*). In this book
and in other writings published in the " Propugnatore," Professor Raina shows a
profound knowledge of his subject, often obtained from fresh sources discovered
by himself. See also Carducci's "Scritti letterarii," Leghorn, 1874.

had hitherto been confused, and to assume life and consistency ;
the descriptions of nature were fragrant as it were with the
breath of spring, and that which still remained of their primitive
form, helped to enhance the truth, and we might say, the youth-
fulness of all that was now presented in a new shape. It was
almost an improvised rebellion against all conventional rhetoric,
all artificial trammels ; the Italian spirit was as a man who
again breathes the fresh air of fields and mountains after long
confinement in an unwholesome atmosphere. To seek for depth
of feeling, logical development of character, or a general and
philosophic design in these poems, would be to expect the improbable and impossible. On the contrary, the author of those
days often purposely disarranges the monotonous narration of the
romances which he finds already compiled, mingles and re-orders
at his own caprice the intricate threads of the vast woof, in order
the better to keep alive the curiosity of his readers. The
important point for him is to be the master of his heroes, so that
they may always stand out vividly at the moment when he summons them on the stage. The ideal he pursues is different from
ours, he has no desire to sound the depths of the human heart ;
his object is to depict the changeful reality of all passing events
and things.

If again and again he dismisses his personages into the obscurity
of the fantastic background he has given to his picture, it is only
to complete our illusion, and make us better appreciate truth and
reality when once more he brings them near to us, presenting
them almost like those baby boys of Correggio, who thrust forth
their heads between flower-laden branches, or like those on the
walls of the Vatican who seem to move amid a labyrinth of
graceful arabesques. Thus, although the author is continually
telling us of monsters, fairies, enchantments, and magic philters,
his narrative has so much life, that we seem to be reading a
history of real events. Still, as is very natural, a perpetual smile
plays round the author's lips, for he is himself exhilarated by the
spell of illusion under which he holds his readers, and appears to
laugh at them, the better to dominate and stir their hearts. It
is a great mistake to imagine that any satire or profound
irony exists in these romances. But as the poet himself cannot
believe seriously in his personages, he is content to make his tale
a vehicle for expressing all the various turns of life, all the contradictions existing in his own mind, in an age so full of different

and antagonistic elements, content to delight and be delighted by his own creations. Still it needs an artistic temperament thoroughly to appreciate the value of these poems, which are most enjoyable when read in bits, as the story-tellers used to read them to the people, as Pulci, Boiardo, and Ariosto read them to an audience of friends and patrons.

The first of these poems, worthy to be called a work of art, is the "Morgante Maggiore" of Luigi Pulci (born at Florence in 1431). This work is a compound of other older ones. The first twenty-three cantos reproduce, with more or less fidelity, one of these poems which the story-tellers used to read to the people, narrating the adventures of Orlando. The last five tell the tale of the rout of Roncesvalle instead, and are made up of two other popular compilations, entitled "La Spagna." An interval of twenty-five or thirty years passes between one part of the Morgante and the other ; so that the characters who were young in the first are old in the second, a circumstance of little weight with the author.[1] Nor does he hesitate, specially in the first part, to follow his model so closely—merely correcting or modifying some of the stanzas—as to appear a positive plagiarist.[2]

---

[1] See Professor P. Rajna's two very important works upon this subject : " La materia del Morgante Maggiore in un ignoto poema cavalleresco del secolo," xv. (" Propugnatore," iii. year, 5th and 6th Nos. ; iv. year, 1st, 2nd, 3rd, 4th and 5th Nos.)

[2] I quote at hazard a few stanzas of the many given by Rajna (" Propugnatore," ii. year, 1st. No., pp. 31-33) :

> " Quando più fiso la notte dormia
> Una brigata s' armò di pagani,
> E un di quegli la camera apria,
> E poi entraron ne' luoghi lontani,
> E un di lor ch'è pien di gagliardia
> Al conte Orlando legava le mani
> Con buon legami per tanta virtute,
> Ch'atar non si può dalle genti argute."
> ("Orlando," foglio 92.)

> " Quando più fiso la notte dormia
> Una brigata s'armar di pagani,
> E un di questi la camera apria :
> Corsongli addosso come lupi o cani ;
> Orlando a tempo non si risentia,
> Che finalmente gli legâr le mani ;
> E fu menato subito in prigione,
> Senza ascoltarlo o dirgli la cagione."
> ("Morgante," xii. 88.)

Yet it is these slight and simple touches of a master hand, which change a vulgar work into a work of art, give life and relief to the characters, and lead us away from tricks of rhetoric into the presence of nature. Now and then, however, the poet forgets his original, and then we have, for instance, the 275 stanzas narrating the episode of Morgante and Margutte, resplendent with all the careless scepticism, rich fancy, and pungent irony for which Pulci [1] was renowned. This poem, which at every step breaks the leading thread of the narrative, seems only to acquire unity from the clear, definite, and graphic precision of its ever-changing and inexhaustible string of episodes. It is a strange hurly-burly of incidents : of pathetic, ridiculous, marvellous and jovial scenes. The elements constituting the culture of that age, Paganism and Christianity, scepticism and superstition, irony and artistic enthusiasm for the beauties of nature, here co-exist, and without the need of any effort at agreement seem to harmonize with one another, exactly because the poet's sole object is to reproduce the restless changes of natural events and the realities of life. Pulci is an unrivalled tale-teller ; his irony is directed, like that of the novelists, against priests and friars, occasionally against religion itself,[2] but always in a manner to imply that he intends

> " Tu sei colei che tutte l' altra avanza,
> Tu se' d' ogni beltà ricco tesoro ;
> Tu se' colei che mi togli baldanza,
> Tu se' la luce e specchio del mio cuore," &c.
>
>   ("Orlando," foglio 114.)

> " Tu se' colei ch 'ogni altra bella avanza,
> Tu se' di nobiltà ricco tesoro,
> Tu se' colei che mi dài tal baldanza,
> Tu se' la luce dello eterno coro," &c.
>
>   ("Morgante," xiv. 47.)

[1] This episode was afterwards printed separately with the title of "Morgante Minore," whence the addition of "Maggiore" to the title of the entire poem which the author had simply styled "Il Morgante."

[2] The following well-known verses give a good idea of Pulci's pungent, laughable and sceptical style :

> " Rispose allor Margutte : A dirtel tosto,
> Io non credo più al nero che all' azzurro,
> Ma nel cappone, o lesso, o vuogli arrosto,
> E credo alcuna volta anche nel burro ;
> Nella cervogia, e quando io n' ho, nel mosto,
> E molto più nell' aspro che il mangurro ;
> Ma sopra tutto nel buon vino ho fede,
> E credo che sia salvo chi gli crede.

no disrespect. He is familiar with antiquity, and his work is impregnated with its spirit, although there is nothing of it in the writer whom he takes as his model ; nevertheless his muse is essentially popular :

> " Infino a qui l' aiuto del Parnaso
> Non ho chiesto nè chieggo . . . .
> Io mi starò tra faggi e tra bifulci,
> Che non dispregin le muse del Pulci."

So popular in fact is his style, that it frequently lacks finish, and when weak is rather vulgar than rhetorical. More than all else it is this quality of spontaneousness that established the success of the "Morgante," composed at the request of Lucrezia Tornabuoni, Lorenzo dei Medici's mother, at whose table it was read aloud, during the flying hours of festive banquets.

Yet the ever-laughing Pulci was condemned to many days of sadness by the failure of his brother Luca, in which he also was involved. Nor was the friendship of Lorenzo, with whom he was a great favourite, of much use to him, since, although upon terms of the greatest familiarity, he was never more than a favoured courtier. His best help lay in the unconquerable gaiety of his temperament. Obliged to fly far from Florence to escape falling into the hands of creditors to whom he owed nothing personally, he complains in his letters to Lorenzo of the unlucky star that made it his fate to be always the prey of others. "Yet in my time many rebels, thieves, assassins, I have seen come here, obtain a hearing, and gain some reprieve from death. To me alone is all denied, nothing conceded. If they continue to harass me in this wise, without hearkening to my reasons, I will come there (to Florence) to be unbaptised in the very font in which, in a cursed hour, was I unworthily baptised, since it is certain that I was better fitted for the turban than the cowl." [1] And he promised that on reaching Mecca, he would send Lorenzo verses in the Moorish

> E credo nella torta e nel tortello,
> L' uno è la madre, e l'altro è sil suo figliuolo ;
> Il vero paternostro è il fegatello,
> E possono esser tre, e due, ed un solo,
> E diriva dal fegato almen quello."
>
> ("Morgante Maggiore," xviii. 115, 116.)

[1] Letter iv. in the "Lettere di Luigi Pulci a Lorenzo il Magnifico." Lucca, Guioti, 1868. For this fine publication we are indebted to Cavaliere Salvatore Bongi of the Lucca Archives.

tongue, and many others from hell itself by means of some familiar spirit.[1] Then he goes on to say, "Do not, in the height of your felicity, allow your friends to be driven and worried like dogs. Much I fear that when I do not send thee verses, all I write to thee in prose is unwillingly read, and hastily cast aside.[2] Lorenzo was always the same, he patronized all, but had no real affection for any one, not even for those who like Pulci had been the companions of his childhood, and loved him as a brother. Later, however, the author of the Morgante was commissioned by him to arrange affairs of some gravity at various Italian Courts, and even in these circumstances his letters always show the bent of his genius, often appearing like fragments of his poem turned into prose.

The 20th of May, 1472, he wrote from Fuligno that he had been to Rome, "to visit the daughter of the despot of the Maremma, that is to say of the Morea. . . . I will therefore briefly describe this mountain of grease that we visited, the like of which I did not think could have existed in all Germany, much less in Sardinia. We came to a room where this pudding (*berlingaccio*), was set up in a chair, and she had wherewithal to sit, that I can tell you. Two Turkish kettledrums for her bosom, a double chin, a broad, shining face, a pair of hog's chaps, a throat sunk between the drums. Two eyes, big enough for four, with so much flesh, and fat, and grease around, that the Po itself has smaller banks."[3] In Pulci's poems this extremely familiar style becomes much more elegant, without losing its spontaneity, as is also to be seen by his sonnets, which correct the too common, often low, manner of the poor barber Burchiello, in whose shop according to his own phrase—

"Poetry with the razor fights."

Pulci at that time wrote in emulation of Matteo Franco, with whom he exchanged all kinds of pleasantries, obscenities, and insolence, as a simple pastime, turning his sonnets into a species of rhymed dialogue, full of the spontaneous simplicity, which was now the chief aim of the new literature.[4]

One year earlier than Luigi Pulci, Matteo Maria Boiardo was

---

[1] Letter iii.   [2] Letter iv.   [3] Letter xxi.

[4] "Sonetti" of Matteo Franco and Luigi Pulci published in 1759. Franco has much dash and spontaneousness; but Pulci is the better poet and has more

born, and three cities contested the honour of being his birth-place.   Probably this dispute arose from his being of a Reggio family, born at Scandiano, educated at Ferrara.[1]   A learned writer of Latin eclogues, and translations from the Greek, he was both of noble birth and noble character ; he lived in the society of the Este family, but had no liking for Court life, inasmuch as he wrote :

> " Ogni servir di cortigiano
>   La sera è grato e la mattina è vano."

He was first Governor of Modena, and then of Reggio—Emilia ; he also filled other important offices ; but while honourably fulfil-ling every duty, his mind turned more willingly to meditation upon heroes and romances of chivalry than to political and administra-tive details.   It is related of him, that one day as he wandered in the fields, racking his brains to find a name for one of his heroes, it suddenly occurred to him to call him Rodomonte, and so great was his delight, that he ran back to Scandiano as fast as he could, and ordered all the bells to be set ringing.   He had a sincere belief in chivalry, and hoped to see it revived in Italy.   For the framework of his poem he made use of tales belonging to different cycles.   A fervent admirer of the Round Table, he mingled Arthur's heroes

gaiety.   Among the former's Sonnets is one giving a good idea of its author, beginning :

> " Costor, che fan si gran disputazione
>   Dell' anima, ond' ell' entri o ond 'ell 'esca,
>   O come il nocciol si stia nella pesca,
>   Hanno studiato in su n' un gran mellone," &c.
>   (Sonetto cxlv. p. 145.)

The viii. Sonnet—

> " Ah, ah, ah, ah sa' di quel ch' io rido ; "

The lv.—

> " Don, don, che diavol fia ?   A parlamento ; "

The lxi.—

> " Chiarissimo maggior dite su presto,"

and many others are by Franco, and afford good proof how he strove to rival Pulci in the attainment of ease and skill.   In the same volume at p. 151 we have Luigi Pulci's " Confessione a Maria Vergine."   In this the *ungrateful sinner* con-fesses his sins, and acknowledges past errors—

> " Però qui le mie colpe scrivo e 'ncarno
>   Con le lacrime miste con l' inchiostro ; "

naturally this was no obstacle to his committing still worse sins the following day.

[1] This is likewise the opinion of Professor Ulisse Poggi in his short " Elogio di Matteo Maria Boiardo," published in the Supplement to No. 35 of the " Italia Centrale " of Reggio (Emilia), March 23, 1871.

with those of Charlemagne, for in his opinion the former monarch
was the grander of the two, since, unlike Charles, his heart was not
closed to that source of all greatness, the passion of love. In fact
his Orlando is a hero whose virtue finds in love its first origin and
its final reward. Many episodes are from beginning to end of
Boiardo's own creation, for he lived and breathed in the world
evolved from his own fancy, with an ingenuousness which is at
once his chief merit and his chief fault. It renders him more
touching, more sincere ; but naturally the fact of his relating impossible adventures in all seriousness, and without any shade of
irony, renders him far less modern than Pulci. The latter brings
out better the individuality of his personages ; while Boiardo is
more successful is describing the general tumult of fantastic events,
in which, however, his heroes are often involved to a degree that
clouds the precision of their outline. Too often is love renewed
or extinguished by enchanted beverages ; victory or death given
by enchanted weapons. Pulci seeks psychological truth even amid
the spells of magic ; Boiardo even amidst reality invokes the
fantastic and the supernatural. But to recompense us for this,
there is always something noble and generous in his heroes, and
throughout his poem, that is lacking in other authors. He
praises and sincerely admires virtue, exalting the consolations
which friendship affords to noble minds :

> " Potendo palesar l' un l' altro il core,
> E ogni dubbio che accada raro o spesso
> Poterlo ad altrui dir come a se stesso." [1]

It is true that there is some amount of coarseness and indecent
jesting in the " Orlando " ; but these things are to be found in the
poem, because we find them in life. And there is always a background of moral seriousness, which gives singular elevation to
Boiardo's noble diction, especially when compared with that continual ridicule of all things which predominates in the other writers
of the time. Here we have a world full of variety, of imagination,
of affection, and it is in this world that the poet lives wrapt in
illusion. But this illusion was destined to be of short duration.
It is in vain that he tells us :—

> " E torna il mondo di virtù fiorito ; "

while all things were hastening to ruin. Too soon he himself is

---

[1] Boiardo, " Orlando Inamorato," book iii. canto vii.

driven to acknowledge it ; and at the end of the second book his melancholy breaks out :—

> " Sentendo Italia di lamenti piena,
>   Non che ora canti, ma sospiro appena."

He again took up his work, and reached the point, in which, by the arrival of Orlando, the French prevent the Saracens from entering Paris. Then shortly before his death, which took place on the night of the December 20, 1494, he beheld the French pass the Alps, and his pen dropped from his hand for ever, leaving the thread of his poem interrupted by that celebrated stanza beginning :—

> " Mentre ch' io canto, oh Dio redentore !
>   Vedo la Italia tutta, a fiamma, a foco,
>   Per questi Galli che con gran furore
>   Vengon per disertar non so che loco . . ."

Although the merits of the " Orlando Inamorato " are so many and so great, that Berni set to work to re-cast it in another shape, and Ariosto continued it in his "Orlando Furioso ;" yet its want of polish, and the incorrectness of its diction, often degraded into the Ferrarese dialect, prevented it from becoming really popular, or acquiring the fame so well deserved by the intellect and character of its author, notwithstanding his lack of Tuscan atticism. He too was a classic scholar, but so thoroughly immersed in his fantastic world, that whenever the images and heroes of antiquity presented themselves to his mind, he always compared them to those of chivalry, with which he was more familiar.

Ariosto, also a native of Ferrara, was the first who was able to conquer the obstacle of a non-Tuscan birth, and it was in his writings that our tongue finally became Italian. Gifted with the true genius of style and the faculty of the patient labour of the file ; by means of art he attained to a marvellous spontaneity, and opened the way for future followers. Much less learned than Boiardo, and ignorant of Greek, he had nevertheless a far more lively sense of classic beauty. Contrary to his precedessor's custom, he prefers to compare his heroes of chivalry with the personages of the Pagan world. His knights-errant have the wisdom of Nestor, the cunning of Ulysses, the courage of Achilles ; his women are as beautiful as though chiselled by Phidias, they have the seductions of Venus combined with the wisdom of Minerva. Ariosto is always returning to his Virgil and his Ovid ; but as Ranke has observed, he seems to recur to them in order by force of imagination to lead them back to the primitive Homer. And with more resemblance to Pulci than to Boiardo, he gives little attention to plot, *ensemble* or unity of incident ; but rather seeks to depict the fugitive moments of changeful reality, and describe individual passions. The events of his own life and times are introduced into the poem in a sufficiently transparent fashion, and they sometimes seem to exist even where they are not, so great is the poet's graphic power. Therefore, although the "Orlando Furioso" continues the history of "Orlando Inamorato," it has more literary connection with the "Morgante" of Pulci, who, much as he availed himself of preceding writers, may be called the creator of this description of poem. But Ariosto extends beyond the period to which we have hitherto dedicated our attention, so we can say no more. Nevertheless we may observe in conclusion, that even from the days of the "Divine Comedy" and the "Decameron," Italian literature had begun to arouse the human mind from the mists of the Middle Ages, and lead it back towards reality. Alike in poetry and prose, it had always sought for nature and mankind. Arrested in its course by the political disorder and social decay which subverted all things in the middle of the fourteenth century, it sought the aid of antiquity, in order to continue the same path. And thus after the middle of the fifteenth century we behold the same realism come still more clearly to the surface, not only in letters, but in science, in society, in mankind. It was indeed the impulse to study and know the world, free from all bonds of authority or prejudice, which created the new literature, the new science, initiated the experimental method, spurred men to the most daring voyages, and reanimated, as with a second life, the whole mind of Italy. And what renders this marvellous is the fact that it happened during a thorough upheaval of society, which, in the midst of corruption and decay, gave birth to the grand elements of modern culture.

At that time all distinctions of caste, of class, nay even of sex, seemed to have utterly vanished. Mæcenas and his *protégés*, in conversing on letters or science, treated one another on terms of equality, and addressed one another with the familiar thee and thou ; women studied Latin, Greek and philosophy, sometimes governed states, and clad in armour, followed Condottieri to the field. To us it causes an astonishment almost amounting to disgust and horror to hear indecent talk carried on in the presence, not only of refined matrons, but of innocent girls ; to hear politics treated as though no such thing as conscience were known. The man of the Renaissance considered that all that he dared to do might be freely talked of, discussed and described without the slightest scruple. And this was a necessity of his observant and inquiring mind, not always in consequence of his corruption, often, on the contrary, in consequence of his realism. He appeared to live in an Olympian calm, always master of himself, always wearing an ironical smile ; but it was a deceptive calm. He suffered from the want of harmony and balance between the emptiness of his heart and the feverish activity of his brain, which often raved as in an unconscious delirium. The ruins of the mediæval world that he had destroyed, and those of the antiquity which he had exhumed, were falling around him on all sides, before he could discover the generative principle of a new world, or could convert into genuine organic material all the remains of the past.

Whether it be that the Italians, after having created the grand entities of Pagan Rome and Catholic Rome, had lost all capacity for forming a new order of society, founded solely on the free modern individualism, for which they had not only opened the way, but which they had even initiated by their labours ; whether it be that foreign invasions had arrested their progress on this road, certain it is that they often appear as if bewildered and uncertain of themselves. While daringly denying God, they believe in fate and fortune ;[1] while despising all religion, they study the occult sciences with ardour. Almost every republic, every prince, every Condottiere owned an astrologer, without whose counsel no treaty was signed, no war commenced. Cristoforo Landino and Battista Mantovano drew the horoscopes of religions ; Guicciardini and Machiavelli believed in spirits of the air ; Lodovico il Moro, notwithstanding his unbounded belief in his own sagacity, took no step without previous consultation with his astrologer. Reason, in trying to explain all things, found itself confronted by its own impotence.

The feeling for the beautiful seemed to be the only and surest guide of human life which sought to identify itself with art. In

---

[1] This faith in fortune is sometimes shown in a singular manner. In the books of the " Provvisioni " of the Florentine Republic, there is one dated February 20th (Old Style) beginning with the usual formula : *In Dei nomine : Amen*, and within the large capital I are written the following words : *Fortuna in omni re dominat.* Florentine Archives, " Consigli Maggiori, Provvisioni," Register 190, sheet 122t.

Castiglione's " Cortegiano " we are shown to how high a point of refinement and culture the gentleman of the sixteenth century could attain ; but we are also shown the weak foundation of his moral conscience. Virtue, if not the natural result of a happy temperament, is only to be prized because it is in itself pleasant, gracious and elegant, to use the phrase of Pandolfini. Great indeed must have been the intellectual and even the moral qualities of Italians, if in so tremendous a confusion they not only escaped total ruin, but gave a powerful impulse to art, science and the social conditions of life. Besides, this was a period of transition and restless mutability, of which it is hard to form an accurate judgment, unless we consider it as a consequence of the past, and a necessary preparation for the future. Suddenly foreign invasions strangled our whole political life, and thus the Italian Renaissance, with all its uncertainties, all its contradictions, is, as it were, instantaneously turned into stone before our eyes. And possibly this is exactly the reason of its eminent instructiveness. In it we see the anatomy of the past bared before us, we behold the origin of modern society, and even discover the earliest germs of many of our national defects.

IV.

POLITICAL CONDITION OF ITALY AT THE END OF THE FIFTEENTH
CENTURY.

1. THE ELECTION OF POPE ALEXANDER VI.

THE nearer the fifteenth century approached to
its end, the more inevitable became the catastrophe already foreseen for many years.
When Galeazzo Maria Visconti was assassinated at Milan (1476), his son, Giovan
Galeazzo, was only eight years of age, and
his mother, Bona di Savoia, therefore assumed
the regency. But the brothers of her deceased husband conspired
against her, and finally Lodovico il Moro, Duke of Bari, the most
able and ambitious one among them, took possession of the
government. His first act was to separate the Duchess from her
faithful counsellor, Cicco Simonetta, who was put to death ;[1] he
then separated her from her child, at that time only twelve years
of age, and persuaded the latter to sign a deed, choosing himself,
the usurper, for his guardian (1480). The Duchess left the Court,
and Lodovico remained *de facto* lord of Milan, but, having no
legal right to his position, was continually environed by a thousand dangers. In 1485 he had a narrow escape from a conspiracy.
In 1489 Giovan Galeazzo, then twenty-one years old, married

---

[1] He was then seventy years of age, and the following verses were inscribed to
him :—

> " Dum fidus servare volo patriamque Ducemque,
>   Multorum insidiis proditus interii.
> Ille sed immensa celebrari laude meretur
>   Qui mavult vita quam caruisse fide."

Isabella of Aragon, daughter of Alfonso, Duke of Calabria, and thus, partly in consequence of his manhood, partly from the impatience of his wife, who sought and hoped for the aid of her grandfather in Naples, the state of affairs became dangerous.

In 1491 Lodovico il Moro married Beatrice d'Este, and feminine impatience and jealousies still further embittered men's minds, and fostered discontent. Tormented by continual fears, the restless spirit of the man, who was ever ready to turn all Italy upside down, rather than renounce his ill-acquired power, was always brooding over new schemes. At present his favourite design was that of calling the French to aid him against the Neapolitan king, since, by this means, he hoped to stir up a general war, in the midst of which his subtlety, in which he had unlimited trust, would enable him to arrange his own concerns at the expense of both friends and enemies. It was very doubtful whether he would be successful in this ; but it was easy enough to bring about a general war, and a foreign invasion. In fact, it was only the great sagacity and tenaciousness of Lorenzo dei Medici that could preserve the general equilibrium and prevent the sudden outbreak of the catastrophe. For these reasons the year 1492 was fatal for Italy. Lorenzo died on the 8th of April, and was succeeded by his son Piero, a man of vain, presumptuous, frivolous character, who passed his time playing at football and the game of pallone, and was totally incapable of governing Tuscany, much less of exercising any influence over Italy. Nor did this misfortune come alone, for on the 25th of July, Innocent VIII. died, and was succeeded by the worst Pontiff who ever filled the chair of St. Peter— a man whose crimes were sufficient to convulse any human society.

No sooner did the Conclave meet on the 6th of August than one might have imagined it assembled for a game of speculation rather than for the election of a Pope, so plain was the corruption exercised on the voters. From all parts of Europe money poured into the hands of Roman bankers, in favour of this man or that of the three candidates engaged in the race. France supported Giuliano della Rovere, Lodovico il Moro his brother Ascanio, and these two seemed to have the best chances of success. But Roderigo Borgia, by means of his great wealth and lavish promises, was enabled to add to the votes he had already won, all those promised to Ascanio, as soon as the chances began to turn against the latter ; and in this way he gained his election. On the night of the 10th of August he exclaimed in a frenzy of joy :—"I am Pope, Pontiff, Vicar of Christ!" and Cardinal Giovanni dei Medici whispered in the ear of his neighbour, Cardinal Cibo :—"We are in the jaws of the wolf, and he will devour us if we do not escape in time." The day after the election, all Rome repeated that four mules laden with gold had been seen carrying to the house of Ascanio Sforza the price of his vote. At all events it is certain that on the very day of his consecration (26th of August), under the name of Alexander VI., the new Pope nominated Sforza Vice-Chancellor of the Church— a very lucrative office—and also gave him his own palace, now the Sforza Cesarini, with all that it contained. Estates, offices, and generous incomes were lavished upon the other Cardinals ; since, with five exceptions, every vote in the Conclave had been obtained by purchase.

Alexander VI. is so prominent a figure in Italian history, the name of Borgia arouses so much horror, recalls so many tragedies, and is so often involved with the main subject of these volumes, that it is necessary to speak both of the Pope and of his children. At this period the offspring of a Pope were no longer styled his nephews. Roderigo Borgia, born the 1st of January, 1431, at Xativa near Valencia, was the nephew of Calixtus III. who had raised him to the rank of bishop, cardinal and Vice-Chancellor of the Church, with an allowance of 8,000 florins per annum. He had studied law at Bologna, was well-practised in affairs, and although not always able to keep his passions under control, and apt to let people see what he thought, could become, on emergencies, a perfect dissembler. He was neither a man of much energy, nor of determined will ; both by nature and habit he was doubled-faced and double-minded, and the ambassadors of the Italian States frequently allude to him as "of a mean nature," " *di natura vile.*"[1]

The firmness and energy wanting to his character were, however, often replaced by the constancy of his evil passions, by which he was almost blinded. Always smiling and tranquil, with an air of ingenuous expansiveness, he liked to lead a merry

---

[1] Guidantonio Vespucci and Piero Capponi wrote from Lyons the 6th of June, 1494, to Piero dei Medici who had sent them on an embassy to France : " Our Lord, His Holiness, who has a vile nature and is *conscius criminis sui*," &c., Desjardins, " Négociations diplomatiques de la France avec la Toscane," vol. i. p. 399. Ferrante d'Aragona, in a letter of the 17th January, 1494, which will be quoted farther on, speaks of the Pope as a man of " acute and timid nature."

life, was temperate, even frugal at table, and perhaps for that reason, remained very fresh and robust even in his old age. Extremely covetous of gold, he sought to obtain it by every means, and spent it with lavish profusion. His ruling passion was lust for women ; he ardently loved the children he had by them, and neglected no means for augmenting their wealth and position. And this was the chief cause of his crimes, all of which he committed with a quiet conscience, without scruple, without remorse, almost indeed boasting of them, and never for an hour losing his equanimity or the power of enjoying life. He was, though very young, already a cardinal, living at Sienna, when Pius II. thought it necessary to send him a very severe letter, reproving him for passing his nights in festivity and dancing with ladies as though he were a layman or worse. But this had no effect, for he neither could nor would alter his way of life.[1]

Among the Cardinal's many passions, one of the most lasting was his love for a certain Giovanna or Vannozza dei Cattani (*de Cataneis*), who, born in 1442, became his mistress in 1470, and bore him many children. To cover this scandal, Borgia gave her several husbands, and to the husbands gave offices and coin. The last of those was a learned man, Carlo Canale, of Mantua, to whom Poliziano dedicated his "Orfeo."[2] Yet Borgia made no mystery of the parentage of these children, and openly acknowledged them as his own. There is no doubt that Giovanni, afterwards Duke of Gandia (born 1474) ; Cesare, afterwards Duke of Valentino (born 1476) ; Lucrezia (born 1480) ; Goffredo or Giuffré (born 1481 or 82)[3] were all his children by this Vannozza.

[1] All this portion of Alexander's life is minutely related by F. Gregorovius and by A. di Reumont in their Histories of Rome. Gregorovius is specially distinguished for his researches regarding the Borgias.

[2] Gregorovius, "Lucrezia Borgia nach Urkunden und Correspondenzen ihrer eigenen Zeit": Stuttgart, Cotta, 1874, vol. i. pp. 21, 22. This work of the illustrious author contains many important documents. It has been translated into Italian by Sig. R. Mariano, and has gone through three editions in Germany.

[3] The latest and most precise notices on the genealogy of the Borgias are to be found in the "Lucrezia Borgia" of F. Gregorovius. But the reader may also consult the two above-mentioned Histories of Rome, the "Saggio di Albero genealogico e di memorie sulla famiglia Borgia" of L. N. Cittadella : Turin, 1872 ; the "Rassegna bibliografica" upon this work of Cittadella's (not free from errors), published by Baron A. di Reumont in the "Archivio Storico," series iii. vol. xvii. 2nd No. of 1873, p. 318 and fol.; and "La Genealogia dei Borgia,

Besides these he had also three elder children, Girolamo, Isabella, and Pier Luigi, of whom but little is known, and all that can be said is that very probably the last of these was also by Vannozza. However that may be, after the birth of Giuffrè, namely shortly before Borgia's elevation to the Papacy, his passion for Vannozza, who was now over forty years of age, sensibly slackened, although he showed her consideration as the mother of his children, upon whom he heaped enormous sums of money and every kind of benefit. Thus Vannozza remained in the background, and had no share in the tragic events so soon to take place. Borgia had entrusted his favourite daughter Lucrezia to the care of a relation, Adriana De Mila,[1] who was also the closest confidant of his scandalous intrigues. The widow of Lodovico Orsini since 1489, she had about the same time married her son, Orsino Orsini, to the famous Giulia Farnese, who, fair as Lucrezia, was by reason of her great beauty known as the beautiful Giulia. This young lady was barely fifteen years old when she had already attracted the admiration of the Cardinal, who became her declared lover, on his desertion of Vannozza. Even in this intrigue he was assisted by Adriana.

Such was the state of things when Borgia became Pope. His consecration was celebrated with unusual festivities on the 26th of August, and the Eternal City overflowed with flowers, draperies and triumphal arches, allegorical and mythological statues, and inscriptions, one of which ran as follows :

> " Caesare magna fuit, nunc Roma est maxima, Sextus
> Regnat Alexander, ille vir, iste Deus." [2]

This election aroused no alarm in any one excepting those who knew Borgia well, like Cardinal Medici and Ferrante d'Aragona, a keen-witted prince, who remembered the ingratitude of Calixtus III. towards the house of Aragon ; [3] the rest of the

Nota," by Reumont to his own article, 3rd No. p. 509. Mr. Yriarte has thrown some fresh light on the subject in his book, " César Borgia, sa vie, sa captivité, sa mort," vol. ii. (Paris, Rothschild, 1889).

[1] His second cousin.

[2] Gregorovius, " Lucrezia Borgia," vol. i. pp. 22, 23, 36, 37.

[3] Guicciardini, who was a bitter enemy of the Borgias, tells us in his " Storia d'Italia," that Ferrante's alarm at this election, caused him to shed tears, in him a most unusual demonstration. Gregorovius, on the contrary, asserts that the official letters of congratulation prove that none of the Italian states was at first

world was disposed to hope rather than fear. The scandalous life of the new Pope was not unknown ; but what prelates were then without mistresses and children ? At first all went smoothly ; salaries were regularly paid, administration was carried on in an orderly fashion, necessities of life diminished in price ; even justice was administered with a rigour of which there was the greatest need, for in the short interval between the fatal illness of Innocent VIII., and the coronation of Alexander VI., two hundred and twenty murders had taken place.

Very soon, however, the tiger began to unsheath his claws. The Pope's passion for aggrandizing his relations, especially his children, some of whom he loved to distraction, grew to a blind frenzy, capable of leading him to every excess. At the first consistory held by him (1st September), his nephew Giovanni Borgia, bishop of Monreale, was made Cardinal of Santa Susanna. His favourite son Cæsar, a youth of sixteen, who was studying at Pisa, and had already appeared in Rome, was on the same day consecrated Archbishop of Valencia. As for Giovanni, Duke of Gandia, and Giuffré, the youngest of all, the Pope had conceived vast schemes for their benefit in the kingdom of Naples, and wished to bestow upon the former the fiefs of Cervetri and Anguillara. But this brought about serious complications which greatly exasperated Alexander VI.

No sooner had Innocent VIII. breathed his last, than his son Franceschetto Cibo, conscious of his altered position, had fled to Florence to seek the protection of his brother-in-law Piero dei Medici, and had sold for the sum of 40,000 ducats these same fiefs of Cervetri and Anguillara to Gentil Virginio Orsini, head of that family, who, arrogant as he was powerful, had once threatened to throw Innocent VIII. into the Tiber. It was asserted at the time that Ferrante d' Aragona had advanced the money for the purchase. Hence the fierce and inextinguishable hatred of the Pope towards Ferrante, and even more towards

displeased with the election. But perhaps in this, as in many other cases, there is some truth in either theory, and Reumont is of the same opinion (*vide* his article on the "Codice Aragonese," in the "Archivio Storico," 3rd series, vol. xiv. pp. 375-421). It is undoubted that the king of Naples opposed the election of Alexander VI. In the November of 92, the Florentine Ambassador, Piero Alamanni, wrote to Piero dei Medici from Naples, that the Pope was aware how much the king had tried to prevent his election; "and the Pope being the man he is, the king does not persuade himself that this will be easily forgotten by him." *Vide* Desjardins, "Négociations," vol. i.

Orsini. In the midst of these disorders, Lodovico the Moor, the better to distinguish his friends from his enemies, proposed that his ambassadors should go to congratulate the new Pontiff, together with those of Naples, Florence, and Venice. The proposal was not accepted, since Piero dei Medici, in order to enjoy the honour of sending an embassy in his own name, induced Ferrante to invent some pretext for refusal. Thereupon Lodovico, believing himself isolated in Italy, took the desperate resolution of appealing to the French.

While the already gloomy horizon was becoming darker and darker, the Holy Father took no decided part, but wavered between this side and that, waiting to see which would be most advantageous to himself and his children. And meanwhile, old as he was, he profited by the interval to plunge into dissipation. The Vannozza was kept away from the Vatican, and he abandoned himself more and more to his intrigue, first begun in 1491, with Giulia Bella, who was then seventeen years old. His daughter Lucrezia, some four years younger, continued to live with Adriana, and received her first education in this atmosphere of corruption. It may easily be imagined, that it was impossible for her to have the culture attributed to her by some writers on the strength of her fluency in many languages.[1] It is true that besides Italian, French, and Spanish, which latter was the family language of the Borgia, she also understood Latin and had some superficial knowledge of Greek, probably learnt from the

---

[1] In describing the character of Lucrezia Borgia, many writers have been led away by illusions, and often for very futile reasons. They have drawn singular conclusions from the expressions used by contemporary historians, such as "Lucrezia was wise and learned," &c. But these same expressions are used regarding Giulia Bella and even Valentino. It was a phrase in general use, especially with reference to those who had good manners and managed matters so as to avoid much open scandal. Burckhardt, in relating in his diary, one of Valentino's orgies, the notorious courtezans' supper, begins thus: "In sero fecerunt cœnam cum Duce Valentinense in camera sua, in Palatio Apostolico, quinquaginta meretrices *honestae* cortesanæ nuncupatæ," &c. Less unreasonably, Lucrezia Borgia's general conduct at Ferrara, and the praises showered upon her by Ariosto and others, have been alleged in her defence. We cannot go into the matter here, but will content ourselves with remarking, that even in the biography by F. Gregorovius, there are certain particulars touching her life at Ferrara, much resembling other particulars of her Roman life. Certainly they are few, but Lucrezia had now to do with a husband who bade her remember the fate of Parisina ; nor had she any longer the protection of her father. As to Ariosto's praises, he was accustomed to lavish them on many who were undeserving of them.

Greek exiles who frequented the Vatican. But among those of her letters which have been preserved, very few are of any importance, and these give no evidence of her boasted culture. As to the mystery of her character, it is better to wait and judge it from known facts. So far the air she breathed was as poisonous as the blood that ran in her veins.

In 1491, when only eleven years old, she was officially betrothed to a Spaniard, and soon after, that contract being dissolved, was engaged at the same time to two other Spaniards, to one of whom, Don Gasparo, Count of Aversa, she was regularly married. But when Alexander ascended the throne of St. Peter, the Pope's daughter could not be satisfied with a similar alliance, the husband was bought off, the bond dissolved, and on the 2nd of February, 1493, Lucrezia Borgia, *virgo incorrupta œtatis jam nubilis existens*, was married to Giovanni Sforza, Lord of Pesaro.[1] The wedding was celebrated in the Vatican ; the bride, who had a dowry of 31,000 ducats, received many rich gifts ; there was a splendid festival, to which one hundred and fifty ladies were invited, and the Pope gave a supper to the bridal couple, at which Ascanio Sforza, many other Cardinals, and a few ladies were present. The ambassador of Ferrara tells us that among them, " Madonna Giulia Farnese *de qua est tantus sermo*,[2] . . . and Madonna Adriana Ursina, who is the mother-in-law of the said Madonna Giulia," were the most prominent. They passed the whole night in dancing, acting plays with songs and instrumental music, and all received rich presents. The Pope, concludes the ambassador, took part in everything, and it would take too long to describe all that passed." *Totam noctem consumpsimus, iudicet modo Exc. Dominatio Vestra si bene o male.*[3]

The Duke of Gandia was preparing to go to Spain to contract a wealthy marriage. The Pope's other son, Cæsar, who, young as he was, held a bishopric with a yearly revenue of 16,000 ducats, was nevertheless very impatient of ecclesiastical life ; he went out

---

[1] Natural son of Costanzo, who was the son of Alexander, brother of Francesco Sforza.

[2] Infessura, who also gives a description of this marriage, speaks of Giulia openly as the Pope's mistress, *ejus concubina*, and adds that he will not repeat all that was related of that supper, "because it was either not true, or if true, incredible."

[3] This letter, dated 13th of June, 1493, addressed to the Duke of Ferrara by his ambassador, Giov. Andrea Boccaccio, *ep mutinensis*, is to be found in the " Lucrezia Borgia " of Gregorovius, Document x.

shooting in the dress of a layman, was violent and unbridled in his passions, and exercised an extraordinary ascendency over his father's mind. As to Giuffré, new marriage schemes were always being formed for him.[1] Meanwhile Rome swarmed with assassins, priests, Spaniards, and light women ; crimes of all kinds abounded. Each day witnessed the arrival of Mussulmans and Jews driven from Spain, and who found here an easy welcome, since the Pope, by the imposition of heavy taxes, made them pay freely for his Christian tolerance. He himself appeared at the chase and the promenade surrounded by armed men, with Djem on one side, and the Duke of Gandia on the other, both clad in Turkish costume. Sometimes he was even seen among his women in Spanish dress, with high boots, a dagger, and an elegant velvet cap.[2]

The Popes of the Renaissance had long led a worldly life, and given themselves up to vice ; but Borgia was the only one to cast aside all show of decency and display his vices with open cynicism. Neither before nor after was religion ever so publicly profaned by derisive mirth and the most shameless debauchery.

2. The Arrival of Charles VIII. in Italy.

Charles VIII., educated in the study of romance, of chivalry, and histories of the Crusades, his head crammed with fantastic schemes, and without any steadiness of character, was entirely under the influence of two ambitious men, who were always at his side. The first of these, Etienne dei Vesc, had been raised from the position of gentleman-in-waiting to that of Chamberlain and Seneschal of Beaucaire, and thus enriched, was ever greedy for fresh gains ; the other, Guillaume Briçonnet, a rich gentleman of Touraine, having lost his wife, had been nominated Bishop of St. Malo in 1493 ; he aspired to a cardinal's hat, and meanwhile controlled the chief affairs of the State. By means of promises and gold, Lodovico il Moro had gained over both these men. After the marriage of Lucrezia Borgia to the Lord of Pesaro, one of the Sforza family, the Duke knew that his power in Rome was increased by the presence there of his brother, Cardinal Ascanio. He was now treating simultaneously with all the Italian poten-

---

[1] Gregorovius, "Geschichte," vol. viii. p. 327, second edition.
[2] Despatch of Giacomo Trotti, Milan, 21st of December, 1494, quoted by Gregorovius in his "Lucrezia Borgia," vol. i. p. 83.

tates, for his secret intention was—after having called the French
into Italy—to form a league for their expulsion, hoping by that
means to become the sole arbiter of the destinies of all. The
Italian exiles, and in particular the Neapolitans, seconded him in
this design, using all their efforts to induce King Charles to set
out ; but the chief statesmen and most reputed military leaders in
France highly disapproved of the enterprise. No one was sure of
what the next day might bring forth, and all men's minds were
stirred by strange fears.

During this stage of affairs, the ambassadors of all the Italian
States were travelling about the Peninsula and the whole of
Europe. So great an activity had never yet been seen in the
world : all Italy's literary labour was suspended to make way for
diplomatic work, and the infinite number of despatches penned at
that time have become a literary and historical monument of
capital importance, which brings clearly before us the true state
of things in those fatal years. Now, as ever, the Venetian ambassadors took the lead for practical good sense and political prudence ;
the Florentine for strength of psychological analysis, study of
character and the passions, power of description, incomparable
elegance and ease of style. These same gifts were to be found
more or less in all, and this was the moment that gave birth to
the new political education of the Italian people, and created the
modern science of statesmanship.

Since the year 1492 the Venetian ambassador, Zaccaria Con-
tarini, had supplied his government with very minute reports of
the commercial, political, and administrative condition of France.
In his opinion it was impossible that the country should ever
decide upon an expedition to Italy, encompassed as it was by
dangers and enemies, and with a monarch who, according to him,
was fit for little either mental or bodily.[1] But in that same year
the king pacified England by gold, Spain by the surrender of
Roussillon and other lands on the Pyrenean frontier, and
Maximilian by a treaty guaranteeing other important cessions.[2]
Lodovico il Moro bound himself to give arms and money, and free

---

[1] Albéri, " Relazioni degli Ambasciatori Veneti." Series i. vol. iv. p. 16 and
fol.

[2] C. de Cherrier, "Histoire de Charles VIII. roi de France," 2 vols., Paris,
Didier, 1868, vol. i. p. 235. This valuable work must be read with caution,
since it is not free from mistakes ; and the author has not availed himself of all
the materials within his reach, neither has he always consulted the best authorities.

passage to the Italian army.   Also, at the same time he continued
his secret negotiations with several Italian States, and promised
the hand of his daughter Bianca and a rich dowry to Maximilian,
in exchange for the investiture of Milan.[1]   Nevertheless matters
had not yet reached a definite conclusion.   The Florentine ambassador wrote from Naples : " The Duke of Bari " (thus to his great
annoyance Lodovico il Moro was always entitled) " has much
delight in keeping things unsettled, and forms a thousand projects
at present only successful in his own imagination.   Therefore it is
necessary to be upon our guard." [2]

Casa, the Florentine orator, at the French Court, in June, 1493,
still considered the enterprise impossible, on account of the general
disorder and the weakness of the king, who allowed himself to be
pulled this side and that, and was so incapable as to be ashamed
to give his own opinion.[3]   But later, seeing that the king had
decided against the judgment of the most influential men, and
that preparations went on in spite of every opposition, he became
almost doubtful of his own judgment, and wrote : " To understand
things here, it were needful to be a magician or prophet ; to be
prudent does not suffice.   This affair may turn out any way." [4]
And Gentile Becchi, another orator who arrived in September,
wrote to Piero dei Medici, " that matters had gone so far that it
was impossible to hope that those bronze-headed Frenchmen
could be turned aside from their purpose." [5]   " This snake has its
tail in Italy.   The Italians are urging things on with all their
might ; Lodovico would like to overthrow Naples only, and
remain winner of the game ; but his rage has led him into the
trap prepared for others." [6]   " The best plan therefore was to swing
at anchor between Naples and Milan ; let those scratch themselves
who have the itch." [7]   " To stop all this it would be necessary to
spend more money than Lodovico ; so now the expedition will be
undertaken, and if the king wins, *actum est de omne Italia*, everything will be topsy-turvy ; if he loses he will revenge himself

---

[1] C. de Cherrier, " Histoire de Charles VIII. roi de France," vol. i. p. 242.

[2] Letter from Piero Alamanni to Piero dei Medici, written from Naples the 2nd
of January, 1493.   *Vide* Desjardins, " Négociations diplomatiques de la France
avec la Toscane," vol. i. p. 442.

[3] Desjardins, same work, vol. i. p. 227.

[4] Ibid. vol. i. p. 256 : letter of 18th of September, 1493.

[5] Ibid. vol. i. p. 237 : letter of 20th of September, 1493.

[6] Ibid. vol. i. pp. 330, 331 : letters of 28th and 29th of September, 1493.

[7] Ibid. vol. i. p. 350 : letter of 21st of November, 1493.

upon the Italian merchants in France, especially upon yours." [1]
Piero dei Medici still hoped to win over Lodovico, and Becchi,
who had known him from the cradle, almost scolded him, writing:
" Attend to your own affairs, for you have a world of trouble
before you. Do you think that Lodovico does not know the peril
to which he is exposing himself and others ? With your counsels
you will only make him more obstinate." [2] New ambassadors
were sent, among them Piero Capponi, who at that time appeared
to be a friend of Piero dei Medici ; and all wrote decidedly that
nothing could be done but prepare for defence.

Meanwhile the Florentine ambassadors at Milan could get very
little information from Lodovico. Agnolo Pandolfini, who was
there in 1492 and 1493, found him employed in weaving plots and
consulting astrologers, in whom he had the profoundest faith. He
said that he wished to bridle the mouth of Ferrante, who was too
fond of novelty. In 1494 the die was cast, but even then the
Ambassador Piero Alamanni could learn nothing from him. " You
always speak to me of this Italy, whose countenance I have never
beheld. No man has ever given thought to my affairs, therefore
I have had to assure them as best I might." [3] And when the
ambassador pointed out to him the danger in which he had placed
himself, he replied that he saw it clearly ; but that the worst
danger was " to be held a fool." Then, almost laughing at him,
he added : " Speak then ; what would the Florentines suggest ?
Be not enraged, but help me to think." [4] Nor could anything
more be extracted from him. From Venice the ambassadors
wrote that the Venetians maintained an extreme reserve, and
changed the conversation whenever the French were mentioned.
" They believe that it will best serve their turn to remain at peace
themselves, and let the other Italian powers spend and suffer." [5]
" They distrust all the world, and are persuaded that they are rich
enough to hire at any moment as many men at arms as they may
need, and thus always have it in their power to make things go
the way they will." [6]

---

[1] Desjardins, same work, vol. i. p. 358 : letter of 17th of January, 1494. See
also at pp. 350 and 352 the letters of the 29th of November and 9th of December,
1493.

[2] Ibid. vol. i. p. 359 : letter of 22nd and 23rd of January, 1494.

[3] Letter of 31st of March, 1494. See Appendix, Doc. p. 1.

[4] Desjardins, vol. i. p. 555 : letter of 7th of June, 1494.

[5] Ibid. vol. i. p. 504 : letter of 12th of August, 1494.

[6] Ibid. vol. i. p. 514 : letter of 20th of September, 1494. These letters are

The King of Naples, meanwhile, was a prey to the utmost agitation, and with the aid of Pontano, wrote letters that were sometimes almost prophetic of the evils about to overwhelm Naples and the whole of Italy. The Pope could not forgive him for having opposed his election, and for having seconded the sale of Cervetri and Anguillara to the Orsini. His niece, Isabella, the wife of Galeazzo Sforza, was kept as a prisoner by Lodovico, who was convulsing all Italy by his dark designs; his daughter, Eleonora, wife of Ercole d'Este, and the only person who had any soothing influence over the Moor, had died in 1493; his other daughter, Beatrice, had been repudiated by the King of Hungary, and the Pope favoured the dissolution of the marriage.[1] Meanwhile, all men spoke of the speedy arrival of the French! At one moment there was a glimmer of hope when the Pope proposed to marry one of his sons to a natural daughter of the king; but his Holiness afterwards drew back as though he had only been mocking him. Ferrante then wrote to his ambassador in Rome, with bitter complaints of the Pope's conduct at the moment when they were about to mingle their blood. "Keep in mind," he

nearly all from Paolo Antonio Soderini to Piero dei Medici. When shortly afterwards the latter was driven to take refuge in Venice, Soderini, who had already declared for the new Government, hardly looked at him. Speaking of this, De Commines, who had changed his flag so many times, says that Soderini "estoit des saiges hommes qui fussent en Italie." Ph. de Commines, "Memoires," vol. xi. p. 359, Dupont edition. See also: "Lettres et Négociations de Ph. de Commines," by Baron Kervyn de Lettenhove (3 vols.) Brussels, 1867–74. This is a very valuable work. Piero Capponi, who tore the contract in Charles VIII.'s face, and so greatly contributed to the expulsion of the Medici, had been, while in Paris, the confidant of Piero. Commines, however, is scandalized this time, and styles him a traitor ("Memoires," vol. xi. p. 340); but he had personal motives for disapproving Capponi. When together with Etienne de Vesc and Briçonnet he tried to hatch intrigues in Piero dei Medici's favour, it was Capponi who replied to him "*comme par mocquerie.*" Lettenhove, vol. xi. pp. 98, 144. It must, however, be remembered that when Capponi received from the bishop of St. Malo proposals adverse to the Medici, he wrote to Piero on the subject saying, "I am sure that you have no one who treats your affairs with more zeal than myself." Desjardins, "Négociations," &c., vol. i. p. 393 and fol. It is true that his conduct was not very open; but we cannot rely upon De Commines' judgment of him, for he was then intriguing on his own account. In his opinion Lodovico had given too little money to the king's ministers: "Si argent ils devoient prendre, ils en devoient demander plus." (Commines as quoted by Lettenhove, vol. xi. p. 97.)

[1] Beatrice had married Mathias Corvinus, King of Hungary, on the 25th of June, 1475. After his death, she espoused Ludovic, King of Hungary, the 23rd of July, 1493. This marriage being dissolved, she returned to Naples in 1501, and died in 1508.

said in conclusion, " that we are no longer young, nor mean to let him lead us by the nose." [1]

Alexander VI. cared little for all this, and continued his negotiations with Venice and Milan ; whereupon the king wrote : " From whom does he wish to defend himself, when no one is attacking him ? It seems to be our fate that the popes should leave no one in peace, but try to ruin all Italy. We are now forced to take arms ; but the Duke of Bari should think of what may be the consequences of the tumult he is fomenting. He who arouses this storm will not be able to quell it at his own pleasure. Let him think well of the past, and he will see that whenever internal dissensions have brought foreign powers into Italy, they have oppressed and tyrannized over the land in a way that has left its traces to the present day." [2] And shortly afterwards he wrote to his ambassador in Spain, in the tone of a man driven to desperation : " This Pope plainly intends to overturn all Italy. In order to gain money, he is about to create at one stroke thirteen cardinals, from whom he will extract no less than 300,000 ducats. He found all tranquil, and immediately began to make plots and create tumults." " He leads a life that is the abomination of all men, without respect for the chair which he occupies, nor care of aught but of exalting his children by hook or by crook, and this is his sole desire ; and it seems to him a thousand years before he can go to war, for, from the beginning of his pontificate, nothing else has he done, save troubling himself and molesting all men, now in one way, now in another. . . . And Rome is more full of soldiers than of priests ; and when he goes about Rome, it is with squadrons of men-at-arms before him, with helmets on their heads and lances by their sides, for all his mind is given to war, and to our harm, nor does he omit anything that he can machinate against us, not only stirring up in France the Prince of Salerno, and some other of our rebels, but in Italy encouraging every desperate character whom he deems adverse to us : and in all things he proceeds with fraud and dissimulation, according to his nature, and to make money, he sells every smallest office and benefice." [3]

---

[1] " Codice Aragonese," published by Commendatore Trinchera, head director of the Neapolitan Archives, in 3 vols. Naples, 1866–74. The letter we quote is dated 11th of April, 1493, and is in vol. xi. part i. p. 355.

[2] Ibid., vol. xi. part i. p. 394 : Letter of 24th April, 1493.

[3] Ibid., vol. xi. part xi. p. 41 and fol. ; Letter of 7th June, 1493.

Yet, in August, Virginio Orsini bound himself to pay to the Pope, in return for free possession of the disputed estates, the sum of 25,000 ducats, under the guarantee of Ferrante and Piero dei Medici ;[1] and on the same day, a contract of marriage was finally signed between Giuffrè Borgia, aged twelve, the Pope's son, and Doña Sancia, daughter of Alfonso of Aragon. She was represented by Don Federigo,[2] her uncle, who, as her proxy, received the nuptial ring amid the laughter of the guests, and especially of the Pope, who took him to his arms.[3] Ferrante was beside himself with joy at this marriage, which was to be kept secret until Christmas. He was now so full of hope, that on the 5th of December he proposed an Italian league to the Pope.[4] But before Christmas, Alexander had already changed his mind, and had allied himself to Lodovico. "We and our father," now wrote the king to his ambassador, "have always obeyed the popes, yet there has not been one who has not sought to work us the greatest ill in his power. And with this pope, albeit he be of our own country, it has been impossible to have a single day's peace. Truly we know not why he tries to trouble us in this wise, unless it be by the influence of the heavens, and to follow the example of the others, for it seems our fate that all popes should torment us." "He seeks to keep us in continual suspense, while we have

---

[1] Piero dei Medici always gave his support to Ferrante. See the letters written by him to his ambassador at Naples, in July, 1493. They are to be found in the Archives at Florence, cl. x. dist. 1, No. 1, doc. 6.

[2] Prince of Altamura, Alfonso's brother, and King Ferrante's second son.

[3] Gregorovius, "Geschichte," &c., vol. vii. p. 332 (2nd edition). See also in the "Codice Aragonese," the letters of 3rd August, and 29th August, 1493, pp. 198, 200, and 223. But in these letters apparently some of the dates are misprinted. The Florentine ambassador, A. Guidotti, in a letter of 17th August, 1493, directed to the Eight (Archivio Fiorentino, cl. x. dist. 2, No. 18, doc. 21), gives minute details of the agreement with the Orsini and of the marriage contract, in which was inscribed, how "the Pope came into affinity with the most serene King Ferdinand, and how in the stead and name of their excellent Majesties, Don Federigo promised to give to wife to the most illustrious Don Geffré, *His Holiness's son*, Madonna Xances, daughter of the Duke of Calabria. . . . Such contract being stipulated and consented to by the parties, then *per verba de presenti*, Don Geffré contracted matrimony with Madonna Xances in the person of Don Federigo, her proxy, to whom *in signum matrimonii*, he gave and his Excellency received the ring, nor did this act of standing in the place of a woman, and as a woman receiving the ring, pass without much laughter and merriment, and lastly with great gaiety Don Federigo was embraced as a relative by the Pope, and by all the relations of His Holiness."

[4] "Codice Aragonese," vol. ii. part ii. p. 322 : letter of 5th December, 1493.

not a hair upon us that has ever thought of giving him the least cause for it." [1]

The king now saw that the inevitable catastrophe was at hand, he felt that his strength was failing, that death was near, and that his kingdom would be shattered to pieces. His anguish was apparent in every line of the letters in which he continually harped upon the same theme, now with bursts of hot wrath, now with forebodings of humiliation. On the 17th of January, 1494, he wrote what may be considered his last letter. "Lodovico counsels the Pope to keep up appearances with us, so that if the French should not come, he may still be able to come to an arrangement with us, although as Lodovico says, we do not desire him for our chaplain, much less for our relative. If after all the French come, then he will be freed from all fear of us, or of the Orsini and the other barons, whose lands he may then bestow upon his children ; and thus the Pontiffs will in future be able to rule their States, rod in hand. In this way Lodovico continues to set Italy ablaze, as he himself allows ; but he adds that the Pope must not think too much of the ills of Italy, because to avoid perpetual fever, one must put up with tertian ague. And the Pope being both keen and timid, lets himself be entirely dominated by Ascanio and guided by Lodovico ; so that in vain we seek to persuade him to enjoy his papacy in peace, without mixing himself up in party intrigues like some mercenary leader, as the Duke of Bari would have him do. The latter asserts that we only make a show of warlike preparations, and that in any great emergency we would even have recourse to Turkish aid. But we are prepared to defend ourselves, and we shall be ready for the most desperate resolves, if others will respect neither faith, country, nor religion. We remember that Pope Innocent himself wrote :—

"Flectere si nequeo Superos, Acheronta movebo."

Finally, as though he already beheld the dreaded enemy before him, he concluded with these almost prophetic words : "Never did Frenchmen come into Italy, without bringing it to ruin, and this coming of theirs is of a sort, if one well considers it, that must bring universal ruin, although they threaten us alone." [2]

[1] "Codice Aragonese," vol. i. part ii. p. 348 and fol. : letter of 18th December, 1493.

[2] Ibid., vol. ii. part ii. p. 421. After this come only a few very brief letters of Ferrante.

And Ferrante, his mind distracted by these tormenting thoughts, finally ceased to breathe after a three days' illness, on the 25th of January, 1494.[1] He was succeeded by Alfonso, who, more impetuous, more cruel, and of less capacity than his father, now perceived the desperate condition of his kingdom, and sought for aid from the Pope, from Lodovico, from the Turk, and from all in vain, for now the coming of the French was inevitable—inevitable, therefore, the fall of the Aragonese in Naples.

Meanwhile, Piero dei Medici in Florence was indifferent to everything : his inclinations were in favour of the Aragonese, but his chief occupation lay in tilting matches ;[2] the Venetians looked on quietly ; Ferrara declared herself friendly to France ; Bologna made an alliance with Lodovico ; the Pope, always true to his character, alarmed by the threat of a council that Charles VIII. talked of assembling, declared that he should give him a friendly reception in Rome,[3] while at the same time he despatched one of his nephews to Naples to place the crown on King Alfonso's head. Confusion was at its height, and the Italian exiles pushed on the French expedition with greater urgency than ever, each one hoping in this way to revenge his own particular wrongs upon existing governments.

On the 1st of March, Charles VIII. made his state entry into Lyons, to assume the command of the expedition ; an advanced guard under the Scotchman d'Aubigny, was already pushing towards the Neapolitan frontier, and the Duke of Orleans was at Genoa. The Neapolitans on their side sent the Prince of Altamura with thirty galleys towards Genoa, while the Duke of Calabria, an inexperienced youth, entered the Pontifical States, under the guidance of tried generals, among whom was G. G. Trivulzio, a valiant Milanese exile. The Pope seemed to have lost his head, and no longer knew what course to adopt. Yet,

---

[1] "Cronaca di Notar Giacomo," Naples, 1845, p. 178. Guicciardini and Machiavelli pretend that King Ferrante at the last wished to throw himself into Lodovico's hands, and Machiavelli adds that he desired to take his daughter from Gian Galeazzo and give her to the Moor, evidently forgetting that she was the mother of three children and that Lodovico had a wife.

[2] *Vide* his letters dated 5th and 23rd of January, 1494, among the documents published by A. Cappelli, under the title : "Fra Girolamo Savonarola and Notices of his Times," Modena, 1869.

[3] Brief of the 1st of February, 1494, in the "Archivio Storico" ("Annali" by Malipiero), vol. vii. p. 404.

taking advantage of the emergency, he asked the Sultan to anticipate the yearly payment of the 40,000 ducats due to him for the custody of Djem, and in order to frighten the Turk, he added that the French were coming to liberate that prince, in order with his help to carry the war into the East. And the Pope would have obtained this money, had not the ambassador who brought it, been seized and robbed at Sinigaglia, in the month of September by the Prefect Giovanni della Rovere, brother of the Cardinal of San Piero in Vincoli.[1]

Charles the VIII. having passed the Monginevra, entered Asti in the first days of September. He soon received intelligence that Don Federico and the Neapolitan fleet had been repulsed with heavy losses before Porto Venere, and that the Duke of Orleans and his Swiss had entered Rapallo, sacked the place, and put all the inhabitants, even the sick in the hospital, to the sword, thereby striking terror into the Italians, who were un-accustomed to carry on war in so sanguinary a fashion. On reaching Piacenza, the king learnt that Gio. Galeazzo, whom he had recently seen at Pavia, had just died there, poisoned, as all men said, by the Moor, who after celebrating his obsequies at Milan, had entered St. Ambrogio, at the hour indicated by his astrologer, to consecrate the investiture already granted to him by Maximilian, King of the Romans. All this filled the minds of the French with suspicion, almost with terror ; they were beginning to understand the nature of their closest ally's good faith. In fact, while Lodovico with one hand collected men and money for their cause, with the other he wove the threads of a league intended to drive them from Italy, when the moment should arrive. In 1493, Perrone dei Baschi, a man of Italian origin,

---

[1] On the person of the Ambassador Bozardo, besides the 40,000 ducats, a letter from the Sultan to the Pope was found, offering 300,000 ducats more for Djem's dead body, and concluding thus : " In this way, the worthy father of the Catholic Church could purchase states for his children and our brother Djem would find repose in the other life." Both the letter and that of the Pope to the Sultan are to be found in Burckhardt's Diary and in Sanudo's "De adventu Karoli regis Francorum in Italiam," a work still in great part unpublished, and of which the original MS. is in the National Library in Paris. A copy which I caused to be made of it, with the assistance of our Ministry of Public Instruction, is in the library of St. Mark at Venice, and Professor Fulin has commenced its publication in the "Archivio Veneto." It may be considered as the 1st vol. of the "Diarii," by the same author, since they begin where this leaves off. See Cherrier, *op. cit.*, vol. i. p. 415 ; Gregorovius, "Geschichte," &c. (2nd edition), vol. vii. p. 350, note (1).

had come to visit the Courts of the Peninsula, *carrying back wind for his pains*, as Piero dei Medici wrote.[1] Next came Philip de Commines, a man of much acuteness and talent, though of no integrity of character, and well acquainted with Italy, where he had already been several times before, but he found at no Court any hope of assured friendship, much less of material assistance, although many looked forward to the arrival of the French as a means of promoting their own designs. He who in his "Memoirs" said of the men of his own time : "Nous sommes affoiblis de toute foy et loyaulté, les uns envers les aultres, et ne sçauroye dire par quel lieu on se pouisse asseurer les uns des aultres,"[2] experienced in Italy, the truth of his observations, and discovered that he was among a people still keener and more cunning than himself.[3]

Nevertheless the fortunes of the French prospered rapidly. The Duke of Calabria, having entered Romagna, withdrew across the Neapolitan frontier at the first glimpse of D'Aubigny's forces ; and the bulk of the French army, commanded by the King in person, marched through the Lunigiana without encountering obstacles of any kind. After taking Fivizzano, sacking it, and putting to the sword the hundred soldiers who defended it, and part of the inhabitants, they pushed on towards Sarzana, through a barren district, between the mountains and the sea, where the slightest resistance might have proved fatal to them. But the small castles, intended for the defence of these valleys, yielded one after the other, without any attempt to resist the invaders ; and hardly had the siege of Sarzana commenced than Piero dei Medici arrived, frightened out of his senses, surrendered at discretion, and even promised to pay 200,000 ducats.

But on Piero's return to Florence on the 8th of November, he found that the city had risen in revolt, and sent ambassadors to the French King on its own account to offer him an honourable reception ; but that at the same time it was making preparations for defence in case of need. So great was the public indignation that Piero took flight to Venice, where his own ambassador, Soderini, hardly deigned to look at him, having meanwhile declared for the republican government just proclaimed in Florence, where everything had been rapidly changed. The

---

[1] See the previously quoted inedited letters of Piero dei Medici, and those published by Desjardins. [2] "Mémoires," vol. i. p. 156.

[3] Lettenhove, *op. cit.*, vol. i. p. 194 ; vol. ii. pp. 108 and 123.

houses of the Medici, and their garden at St. Mark had been pillaged, exiles had been recalled and acquitted ; a price put on Piero's head and that of his brother, the Cardinal. At the same time, however, Pisa had risen in rebellion under the eyes of King Charles, and cast the Marzocco [1] into the sea : Arezzo and Montepulciano, too, had followed Pisa's example. The fabric, so long and so carefully built up by the Medici, was now suddenly crumbling into dust.

On the 17th of November, Charles VIII., at the head of his formidable army, rode into Florence with his lance in rest, believing that that fact sufficed to make him master of the city. But the Florentines were armed, they had collected six thousand soldiers within the walls, and they knew perfectly well that from the vantage posts of towers and houses, they could easily worst an army scattered through the streets. They therefore repulsed the King's insolent proposals, and when he threatened to sound his trumpets, Piero Capponi, tearing up the offered treaty, replied that the Florentines were more ready to ring their bells. Through this firmness equitable terms were arranged. The Republic was to pay 120,000 florins in three quotas ; the fortresses, however, were to be speedily restored to her. On the 28th of November the French left the city, but not without stealing all that remained of the collection of antiquities in the Medici Palace. Commines tells us that all did the best they could for themselves, and that the highest officers stole most. Nevertheless the citizens were thankful to be finally delivered alike from old tyrants and new invaders.

Having reached Rome, Charles VIII., in order to have done with the Pope,[2] who now seemed inclined for resistance, pointed his guns against the Castle of St. Angelo, and thus matters were soon settled. On the 17th of June, 1495, Briçonnet was nominated Cardinal of St. Malò, and the King attended a grand mass celebrated by the Pope in person, who was so little accustomed to perform any religious ceremonies, that he was only enabled to go through it by the help of Cardinal di Napoli, who filled the office of prompter.

---

[1] The lion with the lily, ensign of the Florentine Republic.

[2] At this juncture a circumstance occurred which caused much mirth to all Italy. The Beautiful Giulia, her sister, and Madonna Adriana had fallen into the hands of the French. At this the Pope was in despair, and knew no peace until his Giulia and her companions were liberated on payment of the sum of 3,000 ducats. Gregorovius, "Lucrezia Borgia," vol. i. p. 81.

In accordance with the treaty signed in Rome, Charles VIII. continued his journey towards Naples, accompanied by the Cardinal of Valencia as hostage, together with the Prince Djem. On their arrival at Velletri, however, the Cardinal had vanished ; his plate-chests had already stopped half-way ; the trunks containing his baggage, with which seventeen mules were loaded, were discovered to be empty ; Djem fell so gravely ill upon the way that he died directly he reached Naples. Everybody said that he had been poisoned by the Borgias ; but the Venetians, who always had accurate intelligence from their ambassadors, asserted on the contrary that he had died a natural death.[1] The King was highly indignant at the Cardinal's escape, and exclaimed : " Perfidious Lombard, and more perfidious Pope ! "[2] His attempts to recapture the Cardinal were all in vain. Scarcely encountering any obstacles, Charles led his army on to Naples. Alfonso of Aragon renounced the throne, and fled to Sicily ; Ferdinand II., or Ferrandino, as he was called, after vainly seeking aid from all, even from the Turk, made a fruitless stand at Monte San Giovanni, which was taken, destroyed, and all its population put to the sword.[3] Gian Giacomo Trivulzio deserted the Aragonese, and passed over to the enemy ; Virginio Orsini prepared to do the same ; Naples rebelled in favour of the French, who marched in on the 22nd of February. The following day Ferrandino fled to Ischia, then to Messina. And shortly the ambassadors of the Italian States appeared to offer congratulations to the conqueror.

Now at last the Venetians were aroused, and having sent their

---

[1] Cherrier, *op. cit.*, vol. ii. p. 137, gives a translation of the letter, in which the Ten mention this event. And in fact the Borgia, by Djem's decease, lost the annual payment of 40,000 ducats, without obtaining the 300,000 promised to them on receipt of his corpse. Sañudo recounts the rise and progress of Djem's malady. It was a feverish cold, which the doctors treated with bloodletting and other energetic remedies. At Aversa he was already so much worse, that he had to be carried on *a bier* (" De adventu Karoli regis," p. 212 of the copy in the Library of St. Mark). This author, according to his wont, refers to the letters of the Venetian ambassador who was present, and who observes that Djem's death had been hurtful to Italy, "and especially to the Pope, who was thus deprived of the 40,000 golden ducats, yearly paid to him by his brother (the Sultan) for keeping Djem in safe custody." Following the Venetian orthography, we write Sanudo ; some authors call him Sanuto.

[2] Sanudo, "De adventu," &c., p. 230.

[3] " Il ne sembloit point aux nôtres, que les Italiens fussent hommes," wrote de Commines *à propos* of French cruelties.

envoys to Milan to know if Lodovico were disposed to take up
arms to drive out the French, they found him not only ready to
do so, but full of indignation. "The king has no head," he said,
"he is in the hands of persons who only think of getting money,
and would not make half a wise man." He recalled the haughti-
ness with which he had been treated by the French, and declared
himself resolved to join in any league in order to drive them from
the country. He advised that money should be sent to Spain
and to Maximilian, to induce them to attack France; but added
that care must be taken not to call them into Italy, "since having
already one fever here, we should then have two."[1]

A league was in fact concluded between the Venetians,
Lodovico, the Pope, Spain and Maximilian. And Philip de
Commines, who was ambassador to Venice, and who at the news
of his king's entry into Naples had beheld the Senators so cast
down, that, as he says, the Romans after the defeat at Cannae
could not have been "plus esbahis ne plus espouvantés,"[2] now
found them full of courage and indignation. The Neapolitans,
soon wearied of bad government, had risen in revolt, and Charles
VIII. after a stay of only fifty days in Naples had to make his
departure with excessive haste, before every avenue of retreat
should be cut off, leaving hardly more than 6,000 men in the
kingdom, and taking with him a numerous army, which however
only numbered 10,000 real combatants. On the 6th of July a
pitched battle took place at Fornuovo near the river Taro. The
allies had assembled about 30,000 men, three-fourths of whom
were Venetians, the rest composed of Lodovico's soldiers and a
few Germans sent by Maximilian. At the moment of attack they
had in fighting array double the number of the French force;
but half of them remained unused owing to a blunder of Rodolfo
Gonzaga, while the enemy were in good order, with their vanguard under the command of G. G. Trivulzio, who, notwithstanding that he was in arms against his own countrymen, displayed
great valour and military genius. The battle was bloody, and
it was a disputed question which side obtained the victory; but
although the Italians were not repulsed, remaining indeed masters
of the field, the French succeeded in cutting their way through,
which was the chief object they had in view. The King made

---

[1] This letter is to be found in Romanin, "Storia documentata di Venezia,"
vol. v. p. 50. See also Cherrier, "Histoire de Charles VIII.," vol. ii. p. 97.

[2] Commines, *op. cit.*, vol. ii. p. 168; Cherrier, *op. cit.*, vol. ii. p. 151.

a halt at Asti and received the Florentine ambassadors, to whom he again promised to deliver up the strongholds held by his forces—the city of Pisa included—and received 30,000 ducats in lieu of the 120,000 promised in Florence, but gave in pledge jewels of an equal value, to be restored to him as soon as the fortresses should be given up. Besides this the Florentines promised 250 men-at-arms to help the King's cause in Naples, as well as a loan of 70,000 ducats, which, however, they never gave, as they did not receive the fortresses.[1] Lodovico, taking advantage of the situation, soon made an agreement with the French on his own account, without concerning himself about the Venetians ; he believed that in this wise he had freed himself from both, but in reality he had earned the hatred of both, as he was soon driven to confess.

The fortunes of the French now declined rapidly in Italy, and all the more speedily owing to their bad government in the Neapolitan kingdom, and most abominable behaviour towards the new friends who had remained faithful to them. In fact, Captain d'Entrangues, in direct violation of all his sovereign's promises, gave up the citadel of Pisa, on receipt of a bribe, to the inhabitants of that city, who took possession of it on the 1st of January, 1496, to the bitter mortification of the Florentines. Later, for more money, he surrendered Pietrasanta to the Lucchesi ; other captains in imitation of his example, yielded Sarzana and Sarzanello.[2] Meanwhile Ferdinand II., with the aid of the Spaniards under Consalvo di Cordova, advanced triumphantly through Calabria and entered Naples on the 7th of July, 1496. In a short time all the Neapolitan fortresses capitulated, and the French who had held them returned to their own country, more than decimated and in an altogether deplorable condition. On the 6th of October Ferdinand II. breathed his last, worn out by the agitation and fatigues of the war, and was succeeded by his uncle Don Federico,[3] the fifth king who had ascended the Neapolitan throne within the last five years. He was crowned by the Cardinal of Valencia.

Once more Italy beheld herself freed from foreigners. It is true that the same year witnessed a brief invasion by Maximilian, who at Lodovico's instigation, came to help Pisa and prevent her

---

[1] This treaty is to be found in Desjardins, *op. cit.*, vol. i. p. 630. See also Cherrier, *op. cit.*, vol. ii. p. 293.   [2] Cherrier, *op. cit.*, vol. ii. p. 338.

[3] Ferdinand I., Alfonso II., Charles VIII., Ferdinand II., Federico.

from falling into the hands of either the Florentines or Venetians ; but he came with a small following, found no supporters, and went away without having accomplished anything. In fact, Naples was now in the absolute power of the Spaniards, who were already maturing their iniquitous designs upon the kingdom ; these, however, were only discovered at a later period. Charles VIII. declared himself a penitent man, talked of changing his mode of life, of punishing the Pope, and renewing the Italian expedition ; but meanwhile he remained in France and abandoned himself to excesses. Thus, at least in appearance, all was tranquil. But on the 7th of April, 1498, the King died of apoplexy ; with his death the line of the Valois became extinct, and he was succeeded by the Duke of Orleans under the title of Louis XII. In consequence of his relationship with the Visconti, this potentate had always asserted rights upon the Duchy of Milan. Now in assuming the French crown, he could lay claim to other rights in Italy, and had also the power to assert them openly. And in fact, his reign initiated the long series of fresh invasions which heaped so many calamities upon our land.

3. THE BORGIA.

While, however, the apparent peace lasted, general attention was fixed upon the events occurring in Rome and the Roman territory. Alexander VI. had profited by the ill-fortune of the French, to confiscate the possession of the Orsini, who had deserted the Aragonese to go over to Charles VIII., and after abandoning him, as soon as they saw his luck beginning to turn, had joined his party once more. In this way, Virginio Orsini had been taken prisoner by the Spaniards when they came to replace Ferdinand II. on the Neapolitan throne. According to the terms of the treaty, they ought to have sent him across the frontier, but the Pope opposed the idea fiercely, even with threats of excommunication, for his object was the extermination of the Orsini family. Upon this Virginio was shut up in the Castel dell Uovo at Naples, and there died. His followers were in the meantime stripped of everything in the Abruzzi ; where also Alviano and Giovan Giordano Orsini were made prisoners. This was the moment chosen by the Pope to declare war against these, his perpetual enemies, who were still both numerous and power-

ful. On the 27th of October, his troops under the command of
the Duke of Urbino and Fabrizio Colonna, took the field against
the Orsini who had withdrawn to Bracciano. Although the
principal members of the family were in captivity, and many
cruel blows had been that year inflicted upon all their race ; yet
they were still strong enough to measure their forces with his.
Their hopes rose high, when Bartolommeo d'Alviano,[1] having
escaped from prison, arrived at Bracciano with a handful of his
men. Very shortly the conflict began in earnest, and not only
Alviano, but also his wife, the sister of Virginio Orsini, distinguished themselves by their valour. In the first skirmishes the
Papal troops were continually worsted. Afterwards, Carlo
Orsini and Vitellozzo Vitelli arrived from France ; but the
Pope's army receiving reinforcements at the same time, on the
23rd of January, 1497, a real battle took place, which terminated
in a signal victory for the Orsini. In the previous encounters,
the Cardinal of Valencia had been hotly pursued up to the
very walls of Rome ; now the Duke of Gandia was wounded,
the Duke of Urbino a prisoner, and the flight of Cardinal Lunate
was so headlong, that he died from its effects. The enemies of
the Borgia were in a state of exultation, and the Orsini were once
more masters of the Campagna. The Pope, beside himself with
rage, made fresh preparations for war, and had even appealed for
aid to Consalvo de Cordova, when the Venetians came forward
as mediators, and peace was made. The Orsini paid a sum of
50,000 ducats, but were reinstated in their own lands, and all
those who were still prisoners in the Neapolitan kingdom, were
liberated, excepting Virginio, who had expired before the news of
the victory arrived. The Duke of Urbino, for whom they
demanded a ransom of 40,000 ducats, was handed over to the
Pope on account of the sum they owed him, and the Holy
Father refused to set him at liberty, although his own Captain,
until he paid the sum imposed by his enemies. The Duke, who
was the son of the celebrated Federico, had no family, and the
Borgia made use of him as their defender, first despoiling him
of his wealth and then, still more shamelessly, of his state.

Notwithstanding the hard terms of the peace, the Orsini were
possessed of immense power ; the Pope, detested by all men,
could depend upon none excepting his 3,000 Spaniards, and on the
friendship shown to him by Consalvo de Cordova, who recaptured

---

[1] Bartolommeo d'Alviano di Todi, husband of Bartolommea Orsini.

the Castle of Ostia for his benefit. As the Borgia could no longer undertake fresh warlike enterprises, some demoniac impulse seemed to compel them to turn their weapons against themselves, and exterminate their own relations, under circumstances of incredible iniquity. On the night of the 14th of June, 1497, the Duke of Gandia never returned to his house. The day after, his groom was found wounded, without being able to give any account of his master ; the mule ridden by the Duke was caught running about the streets with only one stirrup left, the other having been cut off. The mystery thickened. It appeared that on the preceding evening, the Duke had supped with his brother the Cardinal of Valencia, at the house of their mother Vannozza. They rode away together, but presently separated, the Duke being followed by a man in a mask, who for a long time had gone everywhere with him, and by the groom whom he left in the Piazza dei Giudei. This was all that could be ascertained. At first, the Pope took the matter lightly, thinking that his son was probably in hiding with some woman.[1] But when on the following night he was still missing, the Pope became violently alarmed, and showed the greatest agitation. Suddenly—no one knew how—a rumour spread through the city, that the Duke had been thrown into the Tiber.

One of the Sclavonian charcoal-mongers on the Ripetta, being summoned and interrogated, replied that while resting in his boat on the night of the 14th, he had seen a gentleman ride up, carrying a corpse behind him, and accompanied by two men on foot ; and that all three disappeared as soon as they had thrown the body into the river. Being asked why he had not mentioned this fact sooner, he replied that he had seen the same sort of thing occur at the same place hundreds of times, night after night, without any one making any stir about it.[2] Numerous sailors were sent to drag the river, and the Pope's son was found with his boots, spurs, and mantle still on. His hands were tied ; he had nine wounds about the head, arms, and body,—one, and that mortal, in his

---

[1] " Ipsum ducem alicubi cum puella intendere luxui sibi persuadens, et ob eam causam puellæ domum exire ipsi duci non licere " (Burchardi, " Diarium," in the National Library of Florence, cod. ii. 150, fol. 21).

[2] " Respondit ille ; se vidisse suis diebus centum in diversis noctibus in flumen proiici per locum prædictum, et nunquam aliqua eorum ratio est habita ; propterea de casu huiusmodi existimationem aliquam non fecisse " (Burchardi, " Diarium," cod. ii. fol. 43. National Library, Florence).

throat ; there were thirty ducats in his purse,[1] an evident proof that robbery was not the object of the murder.[2] The corpse was solemnly interred in the church of Sta Maria del Popolo. Most people rejoiced at this assassination, though the Spaniards uttered curses and lamentations ; and the Pope, when he learnt that his son had been cast into the Tiber like other rubbish from the Ripetta, abandoned himself to a grief of which no one had deemed him capable.[3] He shut himself up in the castle of St. Angelo, haunted, said many, by the Duke's spectre, and wept bitterly. For many days he refused food, and his cries could be heard from afar. On the 19th of June, he held a consistory, at which he declared that never had he experienced so heavy a sorrow : " If we had seven Papacies, we would give them all to bring the Duke to life." [4] He showed an apparently sincere repentance for his past life, and announced to all the potentates that he had entrusted the reform of the Church to six cardinals : that this henceforward would be the sole aim of his existence.

These pious designs, however, speedily evaporated. Who was the author of the assassination ? What had been his motives ? The Orsini [5] were suspected ; Cardinal Ascanio Sforza, who had recently had some differences with the Duke, was also accused, and the suspicions against him were so strong, that the Cardinal, even after receiving an explicit declaration from the Pope that he had never given credence to such rumours, thought fit to present himself to his Holiness, with an escort of faithful friends carrying

---

[1] Burchardi, Malipiero, Sanudo, &c.

[2] The Duke of Gandia was twenty-four years of age, and through his descendants the line of the Borgia was carried down to the eighteenth century. A nephew of his was the third general of the Jesuits.

[3] " Pontifex, intellecto ducem interfectum, in flumen ut stercus proiectum, computum esse, commota sunt omnia viscera eius " (Burchardi, " Diarium," cod. ii. fol. 23t).

[4] This speech of the Pope, reported by the Venetian ambassador, is to be found in Sanudo, and is quoted by Reumont, " Geschichte der Stadt Rom," vol. iii. part ii. p. 338.

[5] Sanudo in his " Diarii," of which the original is in the Library of St. Mark, cites various letters in proof that the Orsini were among the suspected. Manfredi, the Duke of Ferrara's ambassador to Florence, in the letters published by A. Cappelli, from which we have before quoted, gives one of the 12th of August, and another of the 22nd of December, 1497, in the first of which it is mentioned that suspicion had fallen upon the Orsini, and in the second, upon Bartolommeo d'Alviano. Cappelli, " Fra Girolamo Savonarola e notizie intorno al suo tempo," &c.

hidden weapons.[1] Numberless researches were begun and then
suddenly suspended ;[2] and a generally credited rumour was spread
that the Duke's assassin was no other than his own brother, Cardinal Cæsar Borgia. "And certainly," wrote the Florentine
ambassador from the beginning, "whoever arranged the deed had
both plenty of wits and courage ; and however one may look at
it, 'twas a master's stroke."[3] Gradually rumours ceased as to the
author of the assassination ; and people only made surmises as to
his probable reasons for so abominable a crime.

Men spoke of the jealousy existing between the Cardinal and
the Duke regarding Donna Sancia, Don Giuffrè's wife, who led a
notoriously scandalous life. Worse things still were said, and
people publicly talked of rivalry between the two brothers, saying
that they disputed with their father the favours of their sister
Lucrezia.[4] And these revolting rumours were noted and believed
by grave historians ; recalled by illustrious poets. Yet although
every one repeated these things in public, and all looked upon
Cardinal Cæsar Borgia as the author of the assassination ; pre-

[1] The Florentine ambassador, Alessandro Bracci, gives details of this affair in
his letters, which are to be found in MS. in the Florentine Archives, and are of
considerable importance. That, however, of the 16th of June, giving an account
of the murder of the Duke of Gandia, is unfortunately missing from the file.
Archivio Fiorentino, "Lettre dei Dieci di Balia da Maggio a Dicembre, 1497,"
cl. x. dist. 4, No. 54, sheet 53.

[2] Letter of A. Bracci, dated the 4th of July, 1497, MS. above quoted, sheet 78.

[3] Ibid., dated the 17th of June, 1497. See Appendix, doc. 11.

[4] The death of the Duke of Gandia is related in detail by all contemporary historians. Gregorovius, in his "Storia di Roma," cites many original documents,
among them a very remarkable letter from Ascanio Sforza to Lodovico the Moor,
dated the 16th of June, 1497 (vol. vii. p. 399, note 1). Burchardi gives in his
"Diario" a minute and tragic report of the event ; Matarazzo, Malipiero, all contemporary writers, and the letters of private individuals and of the ambassadors
resident in Rome, make mention of it. Sanudo quotes much from all these, and
we perceive the extraordinary impression the deed had made in Rome, where men's
imaginations were greatly excited. In a letter of the 16th of June (Sanudo, vol.
i. sheet 310), he says : "Maxima demonum caterva in basilica beati Petri audita
e visa fuit per plures, et ibidem tot et tanta luminaria, ut ipsa basilica penitus a
fundamentis supra ardere et comburi videretur : ecce quanta prodigia !" Letters
of the 17th of December, 1497 (vol. i. sheet 391), and other later ones quoted by
the same (vol. i. sheet 408), repeat things of the same kind. We have still the
letters in which the Pope announces the deed and his grief to the different powers,
but from these nothing new is to be learnt. In a speech made at a Consistory, the
Pope explicitly scouted the suspicions weighing upon Ascanio Sforza, the Prince of
Squillace, and the Lord of Pesaro, which proves that such suspicions had been
entertained. *Viae* Reumont, "Geschichte," &c., and Sanudo, "Ragguagli storici,"
published by Rawdon Brown (Venice, 1837-38, vol. i. p. 74).

cisely for that reason he became the most powerful man in Rome, and likewise the most dreaded, for even the Pope seemed to cower beneath the mysterious fascination of his own son. Cæsar had now decided on forsaking the ecclesiastical career, and already there was some talk of making his brother, Don Giuffrè, Cardinal in his stead, who, for that end, was to be separated from his wife, so that she might marry Cæsar as soon as he should have become a layman.[1]

Meanwhile Alexander VI. continued his intrigues with the beautiful Giulia and several Spanish women. According to public rumour, he had had another son by a Roman woman, whose husband revenged himself by killing her father, for having sold her to the Pope.[2] Lucrezia, who in the June of 1497, namely, at the time that the Duke of Gandia was murdered by his brother, had been shut up in a convent, without any one knowing for what reason, was, in December, by command of her father, separated from her husband Giovanni Sforza, now declared to be impotent.[3] In March, 1498, according to accounts reported even by the ambassadors, she gave birth to an illegitimate child, whose parentage was involved in much mystery. On the one hand, we find no further mention of him ; on the other, some years afterwards a Giovanni Borgia appears, who by his age must have been born somewhere about 1498.[4] By a Brief of September 1, 1501, the Pope legitimatized him as one of Cæsar's natural sons, calling him about three years old.[5] By a second Brief, dated the same

[1] Sanudo mentions this at length in his "Diarii," vol. i. sheet 556 and 559. Rawdon Brown gives some fragments of these in his before-quoted work, vol. i. p. 212. [2] Gregorovius, "Lucrezia Borgia," vol. i. p. 48.

[3] On the 19th of July, the Florentine ambassador, A. Bracci, wrote that a divorce was being arranged between the Lord of Pesaro and Donna Lucrezia, " whom his Holiness recalled to the palace three days after the Duke of Gandia's death, and who still remains there." In separating from the Lord of Pesaro, Lucrezia declared herself prepared to take her oath that she had never had any relation with her husband, and was therefore still a virgin. On this head, adds Matarazzo, at p. 72 : " Etiam advenga ad dio che fusse stata e fusse allor la piu gran p—— che fusse in Roma."

[4] Reumont in his " Storia di Roma " first believed him to be a son of Lucrezia ; then a son of the Pope by an unknown mother (" Archivio Storico," Series iii. vol. vii. dispensa 2nd, 1873, p. 329). The documents published by Gregorovius in his " Lucrezia Borgia " (vol. i. p. 159 and fol.) throw a sinister light upon this event.

[5] " De dilecto filio nobili viro Cesare Borgia . . . et soluta (muliere)." The Brief also states that Giovanni was three years old, *vel circa*. Gregorovius, " Lucrezia Borgia." doc. 27.

day, he recognized him for his own son instead, with the proviso
that, notwithstanding this,[1] the preceding act of legitimacy must
be held good. And in fact this was done in order that the
mysterious child might be able to legally inherit property. All
the documents relating to this matter are to be found among
Lucrezia's private archives at Modena. Also at one period we find
that she had with her in Ferrara this very Giovanni, of whom we
can only say, that most certainly it was the fact of his existence
that gave rise to all the disgusting rumours regarding the relations of the Pope with his own daughter. These rumours were
chiefly propagated by her husband, Sforza, who at Milan plainly
said that this was the reason why the Pope had insisted on
separating him from his own wife.[2]

In the July of 1497, Cæsar Borgia went to Naples to the
coronation of King Federico, and petitioned for money, privileges,
and land, with so great an importunity that the Florentine ambassador wrote : " It would not be astonishing if the poor king
had recourse to the Turk in his despair, were it only to free himself from these annoyances."[3] On the 4th of September he was
again in Rome, where it was remarked that when he kissed the
Pope neither of them uttered a syllable : Cæsar in those days
spoke but little, and put all men in fear.[4] He was in want of
money to replace the revenues he lost in resigning his cardinal's
hat, and to carry out his new and extended designs. Therefore
the Pope who yielded to him in all things, set about finding new
victims. His secretary Florido was accused of the composition of
false Briefs, and instantly his house was pillaged, and all the
money, hangings and plate it contained, conveyed to the Vatican.
The unhappy prelate was condemned to perpetual imprisonment,

---

[1] " Cum autem tu defectum predictum (natalium) non de prefato duce *sed de nobis* et de dicta muliere soluta patiaris, quod *bono respectu* in letteris predictis specifice exprimere noluimus," &c. And it concludes saying that the preceding legitimization holds good, and the power to inherit. And according to Gregorovius Alexander did all this, because, although unable to legitimatize the child as his own, he wished to prevent Valentino from being able to annul the act of legitimacy, on the score of false grounds. Gregorovius, " Lucrezia Borgia," doc. 28.

[2] See the despatch of the ambassador of Ferrara quoted by Gregorovius, " Lucrezia Borgia," vol. i. p. 101.

[3] Letter of the Florentine ambassador A. Bracci (of the 19th July, 1497), who says that he has these details from a person who is " a worthy prelate an inmate of the Vatican" (Archivio Florentino).

[4] " Et bene non dixit verbum Papae Valentinus, nec Papa sibi, sed eo deosculato descendit de solio " (Burchardi, " Diarium," *cod. cit.*, sheet 39).

and shut up in a dungeon with some bread and water and a lantern. From time to time the Pope sent other prelates to visit him, in order that while playing at chess with him they might extract confessions that would implicate fresh victims. This went on till July, 1498, when the wretched man ceased to live.[1]

Meanwhile negotiations were being carried on with the King of Naples for the marriage of his daughter Carlotta with Cæsar who was still a cardinal. The king was sorely harassed by many vexations, and was heard to declare that he would rather lose his kingdom than bestow his legitimate daughter upon " a priest, the bastard of a priest."[2] Nevertheless to save himself from the Pope's heavy threats, and notwithstanding the abominable rumours referred to above, and which were already in circulation, he was compelled to compromise matters by consenting to the marriage of Lucrezia Borgia with Don Alfonso,[3] Duke of Bisceglie, a youth barely seventeen, and a natural son of Alfonso II. The wedding was celebrated on the 20th of June, 1498, " and the Pope," wrote the Venetian ambassador, " sat up till morning at the feast, *adeo* behaving like a young man."[4]

On the 13th of August, 1498, Cæsar made a declaration in the Consistory, to the effect that he had only accepted the Cardinalate to please the Pope ; but that the ecclesiastical life did not suit him, and that he wished to forsake it. The Cardinals gave their consent, Alexander VI. cynically declared that he also consented for the good of Cæsar's soul, *pro salute animæ suæ ;*[5] and the latter, as soon as he had thrown aside his frock, was sent as envoy to France, bearer of a Bull of divorce to Louis XII., who wished

[1] Burchardi, " Diarium," fol. 39. See also a letter of the ambassador A. Bracci, dated 27th September, 1497, *cod. cit.*, fol. 144.

[2] According to Sanudo, the King had said : " Mi para el fiol del papa, ch'è Cardinal, non sia in grado di darli mia fia per moglie, *licet* sia fio del papa." " Diarii," vol. i. part ii. p. 75. (See note 1 to following page.) The King wrote to his ambassador in France : " The unbearable anxiety we have suffered in order to prevent the marriage . . . . between our legitimate daughter and the Cardinal of Valencia, a thing most unsuitable and contrary to all reason, is already well known to you. Rather would we have consented to lose our kingdom, our children and our life " (" Archivio Storico," vol. xv. p. 235).

[3] " Not to exasperate the Pope, who plainly threatened him " (" Archivio Storico," vol. xv. p. 235).

[4] Sanudo, " Diarii," vol. i., part ii. p. 164. This second part of the 1st vol. is missing in the original MS. at St. Mark's Library, and is only to be found in the copy at the Imperial Library of Vienna.

[5] Brief of 3rd September, 1498, in Gregorovius, " Geschichte," &c., vol. vii. p. 423.

to be separated from his wife, and married to the widow of Charles VIII., bringing him Brittany as her dower. The King had already promised Cæsar the Duchy of Valentinois and a certain number of soldiers, who, under the French flag, would be of great assistance to him in his enterprise on Romagna. In order to procure the large sums of money necessary for this French journey, which was to be on the most magnificent scale, many offices were sold, and no less than three hundred individuals accused of infidelity, and then allowed to purchase their pardon. On the same pretext the Pope's Maggiordomo was thrown into prison, and robbed of 20,000 ducats, which he had in his own house and in different banks.[1] The 1st of October, 1498, Cæsar started for France with the Bull of divorce, a Cardinal's hat for Monseigneur d'Amboise, and a letter, in which the Pope told the King: "destinamus Maiestati tuæ *cor nostrum*, videlicet dilectum *filium* ducem Valentinensem quo nihil carius habemus."[2]

The ostentatious splendour of Cæsar and his train certainly dazzled the French ; the costume of the new Duke of Valentinois was studded with jewels, and he scattered money broadcast in the streets. Yet he was unsuccessful in the fresh attempts he now made to obtain the hand of Carlotta d'Aragona, who was then at the French Court. It was in vain that the Cardinal of San Pietro in Vincoli—at one time the Pope's enemy—used his best efforts in his favour.[3] The Duke ardently desired this marriage, in the hope that it might one day be the means of giving him possession of the kingdom of Naples ; but the Princess, fully sharing her father's feelings, had a positive loathing for him.

Therefore Cæsar, having gained the Duchy of Valentinois and a hundred French spearmen, was obliged to content himself with espousing Carlotta, sister of Jean d'Albret, King of Navarre, and related to Louis XII. The latter monarch promised the Duke

---

[1] In Sanudo's "Diarii," vol. i. part ii. p. 44, there is a letter dated August, 1498, ending with these words, "In conclusion, he is a very bad Pope, and shrinks from no evil to swell his children's substance."

[2] This letter is in Molini's "Documenti di Storia Italiana," Florence, 1836-37, vol. i. p. 28.

[3] Sanudo frequently mentions the reconciliation which had taken place between the Pope and Cardinal Della Rovere. The Prefect of Rome, often called Prefect of Sinigaglia, his place of abode, was the Cardinal's brother, and was not included in the reconciliation, for having (as before related) shared in the robbery of the Turkish ambassador ; but he was afterwards pardoned by a Brief of the 18th November, 1499. See Gregorovius, "Geschichte," &c., vol. vii. pp. 425-29.

further aid, as soon as France should have conquered Milan, for which purpose he was gathering an army, and had already made an alliance with Venice (15th April, 1499), to which the Pope, always ready to change sides, had also given his adherence. On that account a most lively altercation arose between the Pontiff and the Spanish ambassador. The latter threatened to prove that Alexander was not the true Pope, and Alexander in his turn threatened to have the ambassador cast into the Tiber, and to proclaim that the Queen Isabella was not, after all, "so chaste a woman as the world believed."[1] Nevertheless the Holy Father was considerably frightened, for although he had gone over to France, he still cherished many hopes concerning the kingdom of Naples, which could only be realized with the help of Spain. It is true that he was now fond of saying and repeating, that he wished to make Italy "all of one piece;"[2] but the Venetian ambassadors, who clearly saw through him, always maintained that this false and dissimulating man—still at the age of sixty-nine, of most robust health, and always given up to dissipation—daily changed his policy, and got up discussions with the sole intent of obtaining the kingdom of Naples for his son; having meanwhile "converted Rome into the *cloaca* of the world."[3]

On the 6th October, 1499, Louis XII. entered Milan at the head of his army, which was under the command of G. G. Trivulzio; and Lodovico the Moor, who had prepared for defence, now seeing that he had both French and Venetians against him, and that his own people were forsaking him, thought it best to make his escape and go to Germany in search of aid. Meanwhile the ambassadors of the Italian States hastened to Milan to present their respects to the King, and with them also came Valentinois in person, with a small suite, and bearing the French flag. He assured himself of the friendliness of the victorious monarch, earned the promise of fresh help in the conduct of his sanguinary enterprises, contracted in Milan a debt of 45,000 ducats, and he then went back again to Rome, where the Pope was collecting money for the same purpose in any and every way, honest or dishonest, and even by fresh assassinations. The Protonotary,

[1] Sanudo, "Diarii," vol. ii. fol. 156.
[2] Ibid., vol. ii. fol. 274. Further on in folio 393 there is a description of the Pope's changeable nature.
[3] Ibid., vol. ii. folio 326: the ambassador says that the Pope "wants the kingdom (of Naples) for his son."

Caetani, was thrown into prison, died, and his goods were confiscated ; his nephew, Bernardino, was murdered by Valentinois's bravos near Sermoneta, of which estate the Borgia immediately took possession.[1] Meanwhile Valentinois was nominated Gonfalonier of the Church, and he set out for Imola, after proclaiming the ejectment of the Lords of Romagna and the Marches, under the pretence of their having failed to pay the sums they owed to the Popes. To that place he had already forwarded his own men, who, together with his thousand Swiss, under the command of the *Bailli* of Dijon, made up an army of about 8,000 men. On the 1st of December Imola was taken, and afterwards Forlì, where, however, Caterina Sforza, who commanded the defence, held the fortress with determined valour up to the 12th January, 1500, only yielding to the onslaught of the French. These, in admiration of her manly courage, saved her both from Valentinois' soldiery, and from the revenge of the Pope, who desired her immediate murder, because, in his opinion, " the Sforza family were the spawn of hell serpents."[2] Thus Caterina was allowed to finish her days in Florence, in the convent of the Murate.

After Forlì, Cæsar captured Cesena, where he was obliged to pause. Louis XII. had returned to France, and General Trivulzio, whom he had left behind as governor, so greatly exasperated Milan and Lombardy by his tyrannous rule, that Lodovico, backed by a Swiss army, and favoured by the population, was able to repossess himself of his State, and entered his capital in triumph on the 5th of February. For this reason, Duke Valentinois's French troops were hastily recalled to join their companions already on the retreat, and he was compelled to suspend the war. He then determined to go to Rome, where the jubilee had begun to bring in large pecuniary supplies, which were as usual greedily seized and applied to the usual ends. Robed in black velvet, with a gold chain round his neck, and wearing a solemn and tragic aspect, Cæsar made a grand, triumphal entry at the head of his army into the Eternal City, where he was received by the Cardinals bareheaded. Proceeding a little further, he threw himself at the feet of the Pope, who, after exchanging a few words in Spanish with him *lacrimavit et rixit*

---

[1] Afterwards this estate was restored to the Caetani by Julius II., who declared that they had been unjustly despoiled of it.

[2] Sanudo, "Diarii," vol. ii. folio 329.

a un trato.[1] And now, as it was carnival time, great festivities were arranged. A figure representing *Victoria Julii Cesaris,* mounted upon a car constructed for the purpose, made the round of Piazza Navona, where *servatæ sunt fatuitates Romanorum more solito.*[2] And the festivities multiplied, when news arrived of the return of Louis XII. into Italy at the head of a fresh army ; and that Lodovico, betrayed and abandoned by his Swiss, had, on the 10th of April, fallen into the hands of the French, together with his brother Ascanio. The latter was confined in the tower of Bourges in Berry, and was afterwards liberated ; but Lodovico died in the castle of Loches, after ten years' imprisonment.

At the first announcement of this fortunate news, the Duke of Valentinois, certain of now being able to pursue his bloody enterprise in Romagna, found it impossible to restrain his joy. Close to St. Peter's, a grand bull fight was given, in which Cæsar, " mounted on his Spanish jennet, distinguished himself by killing six fierce bulls, cutting off the head of one of them at a single stroke, which appeared a mighty feat to all Rome."[3]

Meanwhile, pilgrims to the Jubilee continued to arrive in great numbers ; there were more religious ceremonies than ever, and indulgences and receipts were proportionately swelled. The corpses of persons murdered during the night were found every morning in the streets of Rome, and not seldom the victims were prelates. One day (27th of May) eighteen bodies were to be seen strung up on the Bridge of St. Angelo. These were thieves executed by order of the Pope, among them the doctor to the hospital of St. John Lateran, who was accustomed to spend his early mornings in robberies and assassinations.[4] No sooner did the confessor of the sick learn that any one of them had money, than he revealed it to the doctor, *qui dabat ei recipe,* and they then divided the booty between them.[5] This example of prompt and severe justice was only given because thirteen of

---

[1] The Ambassador V. Capello, in Sanudo, quoted by Gregorovius, "Geschichte," &c., vol. viii. p. 441.

[2] Burchardi, " Diarium," *cod. cit.,* folio 185.

[3] The narrative of P. Cappello, Venetian ambassador, published by Albéri in his " Relazioni," &c., Series II. vol. ii. p. 10.

[4] " Singulis diebus bono mane exibat in habitu brevi hospitale cum balista, et interficiebat quos poterat commode, et pecunias corum auferebat " (Burchardi, " Diarium," *cod. cit.,* folio 209).   [5] Burchardi, " Diarium," ibid.

CÆSAR BORGIA, CAPTAIN GENERAL OF THE PONTIFICIAL TROOPS.

(*After an engraving by Paul Jove.*)

the men hung had robbed the French ambassador, with whom the Pope wished to keep upon friendly terms.[1]

In the July of the same year another of the tragedies peculiar to the Borgia occurred. The Duke of Bisceglie, Lucrezia's husband, noticing that the friendship of the French had suddenly deprived him of the good-will both of the Pope and of Valentinois, no longer considered himself in safety. In 1499 he had witnessed the exile of his sister Donna Sancia, and seen how the Holy Father had threatened to drive her from her house by force, if she would not go quietly.[2] These and other signs awakened his suspicions, and after some hesitation, he suddenly fled to the Colonna at Gennazzano, intending afterwards to cross the Neapolitan border, and leaving his wife Lucrezia, who was in delicate health, in real or feigned sorrow. But in August he returned at her entreaty, and joined her at Spoleto, of which town she had been nominated regent. Thence they returned together to Rome.[3]

On the evening of the 15th of July, 1500, the Duke of Bisceglie coming down the steps of St. Peter's was suddenly attacked by assassins, who wounded him about the head and arms, and then took flight. He ran into the Vatican, and related how and by whom he had been wounded to the Pope, who, as usual, was sitting with Lucrezia. She first fainted away, and then led her husband to a chamber in the Vatican and attended to his wounds. For fear of poison, doctors were sent for from Naples. The sick man was nursed by his wife and his sister Donna Sancia, who " cooked for him in a pipkin," since there was no one to be trusted. But Valentinois said, "that which could not be done at dinner shall be done at supper;" and he kept his word. In fact, finding that the unhappy Duke was likely to recover in spite of the very severe wound in his head, he came suddenly into the room one evening, and having sent away the two ladies, who

---

[1] Sanudo, "Diarii," vol. iii. folio 141. The letters here given, dated 4th of June, 1500, speak of the pleasure of the King of France at this execution, and add that further, within ten days, all the Corsicans were driven away, who had been some of the worst assassins in Rome.

[2] She returned, however, after a short absence.

[3] About this time, and before the affair of the Duke of Bisceglie, the Pope had been in danger through the fall of a roof in the Vatican. The Venetian Ambassador, paying him a visit on the 3rd of July, found with His Holiness "Madonna Lucrezia, the princess, and her husband, and one of Madonna Lucrezia's damozels, who is a favourite with the Pope" (Sanudo, "Diarii," vol. iii. folio 172).

unresistingly obeyed, he had the Duke strangled in his bed by
Don Micheletto.[1]   Nor this time was much mystery made of the
business.   The Pope himself, after the first attempt, quietly
remarked to the Venetian ambassador, Paolo Cappello—"The
Duke (Valentinois) says that he did not strike him ; but if he
had struck him it was only what he deserved."   Valentinois, on
the contrary, merely excused himself by saying that he had
committed the crime because the Duke of Bisceglie meant to
kill him.

Cæsar was now twenty-seven years of age, in the flower of his
health and strength ; he felt himself master of Rome, and of the
Pope himself, who had so great a fear of him, that he did not
dare to utter a syllable the day on which his confidential servant,
Pietro Caldes, or Pierotto, was murdered in his arms, and the
man's blood spurted in his face.   But Alexander was little
disturbed by all this, and suffered no loss of rest.[2]   "He is
seventy years of age," wrote the ambassador Cappello ; "he

---

[1] "Cum non vellet ex huiusmodi vulneribus sibi datis mori, in lecto suo fuit
strangolatus circa horam 19*m*, et in sero circa primam horam noctis portatum fuit
cadaver ad basilicam Sancti Petri."   Burchardi, "Diarium."   This is another of
the facts related by nearly all contemporary historians and ambassadors, among
whom we must specially mention the Venetian ambassador Paolo Cappello, then
in Rome, and who, in his above-quoted "Relazione," minutely accounts all the
particulars which we have given.   His narrative agrees with that of Burchardi and
of Sanudo, the latter nearly always transcribing Cappello's Roman despatches
either in full or in abridgement.   After relating the deed, Sanudo ("Diarii,"
vol. iii. folio 201) adds that the author of the crime was the same who had caused
the murder of the Duke of Gandia.   Further on (folio 263 retro), he gives the
orator's letters of the 18th and 20th of July, stating that the Duke of Bisceglie
had been murdered "because he had been trying to kill the Duke (Valentinois),
and the Duke has had it done by some bowmen, and has had him cut to pieces in
his own room."   In the "Relazione," written afterwards, when perhaps he had
closer information, Cappello says instead, that Caesar had had him strangled by
Don Micheletto.   Further on, Sanudo (folio 273) quotes letters of the 23rd and
24th of August, in which it is narrated how the Pope made excuses for Cæsar,
alleging that the Duke of Bisceglie wished to kill him.

[2] P. Cappello, the before-quoted "Relazione."   Sanudo, on the contrary, quotes
letters from Rome, dated 20th of February, 1498, in which it is related that
Pierotto, the waiting man, was found drowned in the Tiber with a *faithful
girl, a creature* of the Pope !   "And the reason of this is not known."   The
following are Cappello's words in his "Relazione" : "And another time he
(Valentinois) killed Messer Pierotto with his own hand, and under the Pope's
own mantle, so that the blood splashed in the Pope's face."   The letter of Silvio
Savelli, quoted by Gregorovius ("Geschichte," &c., vol. vii. p. 447), says : "Ponti-
ficis cubicularius Perottus in ejus gremis trucidatus."   Burchardi says that he was
drowned in the Tiber.   Possibly he was thrown in already murdered.

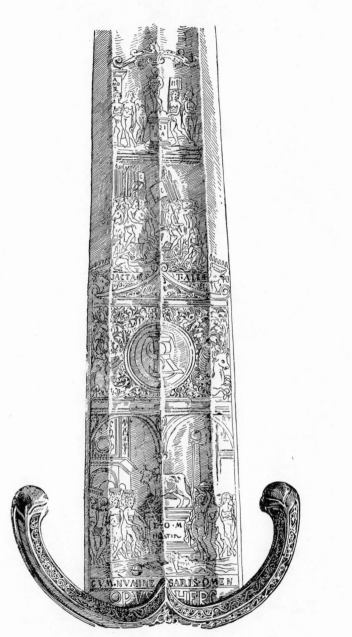

CÆSAR BORGIA'S SWORD.

grows younger every day.; his anxieties never last through a night ; he has a cheerful nature and does whatever is most useful to him."

On the 28th of September, as a means of obtaining money, he made twelve fresh cardinals at once, six of whom were Spaniards, thus gaining 120,000 ducats, which were at once given to Valentinois. With this money, the receipts of the jubilee, and the aid given by the French in addition to his own forces under the Orsini, Savelli, Baglioni, and Vitelli, he made himself master of Pesaro, driving out (October, 1500) his former brother-in-law, Giovanni Sforza ; he next dispossessed Pandolfo Malatesta of Rimini ; and finally, laid siege to Faenza, whose lord, Astorre Manfredi, a boy of sixteen, was so much beloved by his people, that the town stood out valiantly, until at last driven by famine to capitulate on the 25th of April, 1501. It did not surrender until Cæsar Borgia had sworn to spare the townsfolk and save Manfredi's life ; as usual, he broke his word, imprisoned Manfredi in the castle of St. Angelo ; and after subjecting him to the most loathsome outrages, caused him to be strangled and thrown into the Tiber on the 9th of June, 1502.[1]

The Pope next gave Cæsar the title of Duke of Romagna,— Imola, Faenza, Forlì, Rimini, Pesaro, and Fano were already included in his dominions, of which Bologna was to be the capital, and which was afterwards to be extended towards Sinigaglia and Urbino, in the hope of later annexing Tuscany as well. But for the present, France placed her veto upon any attempt against Bologna or Tuscany, which, on their side, were actively preparing for defence. Meanwhile, secret negotiations were going on between Spain and France, for the division of the kingdom of Naples between them, and the Pope entered into the arrangements, hoping, with his accustomed greed, to be able to extend his son's power in that direction likewise.

---

[1] At the time of his death, Manfredi was eighteen years of age. Nardi, always a temperate writer, speaks of this deed with the utmost horror. ("Storia di Firenze": Firenze, 1842, vol. i. pp. 237-38.) Guicciardini and many others also mention it. Burchardi's "Diario" tells us that in June the body of Astorre Manfredi was found in the Tiber with those of two youths, a woman, and several others. There is a notice of Manfredi's death in a despatch of 6th June, 1502, from the Venetian ambassador, Antonio Giustinian. ("Dispacci di Antonio Giustinian," published by P. Villari: Florence, successors Le Monnier, 1876, in 3 vols.)

4. Savonarola and the Republic of Florence.

While these events were happening in Rome, the Borgia had
planned another tragedy in Florence, where very grave changes.
had taken place, of which it is now needful to speak.[1]

From the time of Charles VIII.'s Italian expedition, a Dominican friar, prior of St. Mark's convent, and a very remarkable man,.
had become almost master of the city. Everything indeed that
was now done was dictated by the counsels he gave from the
pulpit. A native of Ferrara, and coming to Florence during the
rule of the Medici, he had preached against the general depravity of manners, and the corruption of the Church, always
attacking Pope Alexander more or less covertly, and proving
himself to be the champion of liberty. In many respects, he
neither was nor seemed to be a man of his time. Having no
true classical culture, he detested the Pagan spirit with which all
things were then impregnated. Learned in the Bible, the Holy
Fathers, and scholastic philosophy, he was animated by the
liveliest religious enthusiasm. Steeped in doctrines, at that time
held in slight esteem, he wrote verses which, if not particularly
well turned, at least were full of Christian ardour. Endowed with
great independence of mind and character, and much good sense,.
yet he often spoke as one who was inspired, for he really believed
himself a prophet, sent by God Almighty to reform the Church
and redeem Italy. The mere fact of being so different from other
men, and of not having the qualities and gifts then universal in
men who lacked precisely those which he possessed, gave this friar
a prodigious ascendency not only over the crowd, but even over
the most cultured minds. Lorenzo dei Medici summoned him to
his death-bed, beseeching for absolution from his sins ; and this
absolution Savonarola refused to grant to his country's tyrant.
Angelo Poliziano, and Pico della Mirandola, both followers of
that Pagan learning which Savonarola condemned, desired to be
buried in St. Mark's church, shrouded in the Dominican habit.
Many other literary men, and numerous artists, listened spell-
bound to the friar's utterances.

Carried away by his imagination, and also by a singular
presentiment, that often seemed to endow him with the gift of

[1] See my "Storia di Girolamo Savonarola e dei suoi tempi," in 2 vols. :.
Florence, F. le Monnier, 1859-61. Having already treated this subject at length,.
I may be allowed to make but brief mention of it here.

reading the future, not only did he predict the future evils of Italy in general terms, but he positively prophesied the coming of foreign armies, led by a new Cyrus. And this prophecy appeared to be miraculously fulfilled in 1494, by the descent of Charles. VIII. ; whereupon the friar became altogether the chief man in Florence, all citizens relying upon him in the most critical moments. Thus with Piero Capponi, and others, he was sent as ambassador to the king, after Piero dei Medici had vilely yielded up èverything ; and the king, who had shown great roughness to all others, humbled himself before him who threatened him with the divine wrath. When, too, all the terms of the agreement had been signed in Florence, and the army lodged within the walls remained stationary, to the great danger of the city, Savonarola was the only man who dared to present himself before the king, sternly bidding him depart. And his order was obeyed. Therefore it is not surprising if, when he set to work to form a new government, all men turned to the friar, and nothing was any longer done in Florence, save by the counsel of one, who had not only given signal proofs of disinterested love for the public welfare, but, fortunately, also of marvellous political common sense.

On the 2nd of December the bell of the Palazzo Vecchio rang out the summons to a general parliament, and the people hastened to its call in regular order, led by the Gonfaloniers of the different Companies. Twenty Accoppiatori were instantly elected for the nomination of Magistrates, and the arrangement of necessary proposals of reform. Thus, in a short time, the Republic was established upon a new basis, bringing to life old institutions, not, however, without considerably modifying them. The Gonfalonier, with the eight Priori forming the Signory, to be renewed every two months, were preserved ; and so also the Magistracy of the Eight, which charged with the maintenance of order within the city, was a tribunal for common offences, and more especially for those against the State. The old Magistracy of the Ten for war affairs was likewise preserved. The Gonfaloniers of the Companies and the twelve Worthies, a remnant of old institutions composing the so-called Colleges which gave their assistance to the Signory, without having any real importance, were also maintained. But serious disputes arose regarding the Councils or assemblies of the Republic. The Council of Seventy, organ of the Medicean despotism, was promptly abolished ; but it was found.

impossible to reconstitute those of the people and the Commune, because, under the old Republic, these answered to a state of things, to a division of the citizens which no longer existed, and which it was impossible to renew. Discussions therefore began. A few persons, at whose head was Paolo Antonio Soderini, just returned from Venice, positively proposed a Great Council, open to every citizen, and a less numerous council of *Ottimati*, precisely after the pattern of the Great Council, and of the *Pregadi* of Venice. But this proposal was combated by those who, headed by Guidantonio Vespucci, desired a more restricted form of government ; they opposed the institution of the Great Council, which they said might be useful in Venice, where there was an aristocracy which alone composed it, but would be most dangerous to Florence, where, failing the aristocracy, it would be necessary to admit citizens of all ranks. Even, according to Guicciardini, the danger of this great divergence of opinion consisted in this, that should a narrow form of government prevail instead of a moderately liberal one, there would ensue, as a necessary reaction, a government of too democratic a form, which would endanger the Republic. And it was for that reason that this great historian and acute politician took the part of Savonarola,[1] who, precisely at that time, took up the question and rescued everything, by preaching in favour of a *universal government*, with a Great Council on the Venetian plan, but adapted to Florentine needs and customs. The weight of his words speedily brought about the victory of Soderini's proposal, and the friar in consequence obtained so great an ascendency over the people, that from that moment the discussions in the palace and the laws passed frequently seem to be mere copies of his sermons.

On the 22nd and 23rd December a decree was issued for the Consiglio Maggiore, to which all citizens were bidden who were twenty-nine years of age, and were *beneficiati*, that is to say, who enjoyed *the benefit of the State*, or, according to the old laws of the Republic, had the right to govern. Should these exceed the number of 1,500, then a third of them only, in alternation with the other thirds, would form a council from six months to six months.[2] The city had at that time about 90,000 inhabitants ;

[1] As much in his " Storia Fiorentina," as in his treatise, " Del Reggimento di Firenze," published in the " Opera Inedite."

[2] All this is much more minutely detailed in my " Storia di Girolamo Savonarola," to which I must again refer the reader.

the *beneficed* (*beneficiati*) citizens of the age of twenty-nine numbered 3,200 ; so that the Great Council was in fact composed of little more than a thousand members.[1]   Also every three years sixty *non-beneficed* citizens and twenty-four young men aged twenty-four, were chosen to take part in the Council, " in order to give encouragement to the young and incite them to virtue." The chief function of the Council was the election of magistrates —in which the best guarantee of liberty then consisted—and in voting laws, though without discussing them.   Besides this, it was to elect immediately eighty citizens of at least forty years of age, to form the Council of Eighty, a species of Senate to be renewed every six months, and of which the membership belonged of right to some of the principal magistrates.   This sat once a week to deliberate, in conjunction with the Signory, on all grave and delicate questions which could not be communicated to the larger assembly.   The *Collegi* joined these sittings whenever it was a question of nominating ambassadors and captains, or making arrangements with mercenary leaders.

It was in this manner that the new Republic was constituted. Division of power being then unknown, the attributes of the magistrates were considerably confused.   Nevertheless, when a new law required sanction, the following was the usual mode of procedure : the proposal was made by the Signoria, who could—if the matter required it—first call together a so-called *Pratica*, composed of the colleges, the principal magistrates and the *Arroti*, *i.e.*, citizens selected for that special purpose.   When this measure was considered unnecessary, application was made at once to the Eighty, and then to the Great Council without farther delay.   In the Pratica some discussion of questions took place, but at the Councils members gave their votes without preliminary debate.   The same course was pursued with regard to matters of weightier import than the passing of laws—declarations of war, for instance, or the conclusion of some treaty pregnant with the gravest results.

This novel machinery of government soon began to work regularly, and Savonarola, as one of its principal authors, powerfully promoted other important reforms by means of his

---

[1] According to the law, the minimum was fixed at 500, so that if the *beneficiati* amounted to fewer than 1,500, they were not divided into thirds, but formed the Council altogether.   For this reason the Council Hall, then built by Cronaca in the palace of the Signoria, was named the Hall of the Five Hundred.

preachings from the pulpit. The irregular and arbitrary taxes upon real property were replaced by tithes (Decima). Parliament was abolished, for that assembly, having always approved every measure proposed by the Signoria, had frequently been made the docile tool of tyranny and change. The Monte di Pietà was established. A new law was also passed, granting—in State trials —a right of appeal from the Eight to the Great Council ; this was, it must be confessed, a highly imprudent act, inasmuch as it entrusted the administration of justice to popular feeling. Savonarola himself was in favour of a more restricted right of appeal, but on this point he was powerless to restrain the people, urged on as they were by his personal enemies. These latter hoped, by means of excesses, to put the Republic in danger, or at least—as they phrased it—to deliver it from the hands of the Friar. After-events proved the inexpediency of the law.

Nevertheless at first public business was carried on with sufficient regularity, nor did other disturbances arise, save those brought about by the war with Pisa, which indeed, not having as yet assumed a very serious character, served to keep the Florentines from quarrelling among themselves. It is true that the allies summoned Maximilian, King of the Romans, to the aid of the Pisans ; but when they beheld him arrive without an army, they would give him neither money nor men ; so that he had to return the way he came, without having achieved anything. But Florence already held the seeds of a very grave danger, destined to be the cause of fatal results. With ever-increasing fervour, Savonarola was urging reformation of manners, and the defence of freedom ; he suggested many useful measures, and painted the evils of tyranny in the liveliest colours. But he did not stop here.

He also urged the necessity of reforming the Church, which, as all men knew and saw, had lapsed into the most abject corruption. Dogma and even the principle of Papal authority he left untouched, for in fact he never ceased to be a Roman Catholic ; but at last he pointed out the need of a Council, and made allusions to Pope Alexander's scandalous mode of life. Thereupon the Pope began to feel serious disquietude at a state of things so novel for Italy, and dangerous for himself, who, as Piero Capponi had previously described him, was of a cowardly nature and *conscius criminis sui.*[1] First of all he sent Savonarola a very graciously

---

[1] *Vide* letters before quoted from Capponi to Piero dei Medici, published by Desjardins, "Négociations," &c., vol. i. p. 393, and fol.

worded invitation to Rome, which the Friar declined to accept.
On this the Pope interdicted him from preaching ; but the Ten
wrote so urgently in his defence, that—for fear of worse consequences—the brief was revoked. Once more the Pope resorted
to flattery, and even the possibility of a Cardinal's hat was suggested ; but again the Prior of San Marco refused, and during the
Lent of 1496 thundered louder than ever from his pulpit. He
predicted future calamities, recurred to the question of church
reform, and insisted that Florence must firmly consolidate her
popular government, in order to promote both at home and
abroad the renovation and triumph of religion cleansed of all
corruption.

The matter by this time had assumed such grave proportions,
that, stirred by conflicting psssions, the eyes of all Italy were
turned upon the courageous Friar. All men were convinced of
the frightful corruption of the Church, and all understood that
notwithstanding the universal and radical religious scepticism of
the Italians, things could not long go on as they were. The precur-
sory symptoms of reform already manifest at Constance, at Basle,
and elsewhere, were too significant to be forgotten. The enthusiastic, earnest attention with which flippant, sceptical Florence was
now listening to Savonarola, inspired in many a confused alarm,
and aroused the fierce rage of Alexander VI. He, who had so
easily dismissed prelates and cardinals from the world, now saw
himself personally attacked by a simple friar, without having the
power to punish him.

Still the Pope did not despair of turning aside the threatened
danger. Savonarola, it is true, was a powerful if rough orator ;
he was a man of prodigious activity ; he wrote an immense number of works, of pamphlets, of letters ; he gave himself no rest ;
daily and several times a-day, he delivered sermons in different
churches ; his zeal for good was great, his religious enthusiasm
most ardent, his power immense. Yet, as we have already remarked, he was not altogether a man of his day ; his culture was
in part scholastic, his enthusiasm frequently verged upon fanati-
cism ; he beheld visions and believed himself a prophet ; sometimes he imagined that the Almighty would make use of him to
perform miracles. He was an ardent lover of liberty ; but with
the true monastic spirit, he yearned for it as a means of promoting religious reform. At times, indeed, he seemed determined to
turn all Florence into a conventual establishment, which to many

must have appeared an almost childish illusion. He was surrounded by artists and men of learning, over whom, as over both people and politicians, he exercised an extraordinary ascendency. But while loving culture and encouraging the arts, he was a most bitter enemy of the pagan spirit that then impregnated and corrupted all things. Among his friars, as among his followers outside the convent, were men of lofty character and commanding energy ; but there were also not a few weak and superstitious spirits, to exaggerate the ideas of their master, who was not entirely free from exaggeration himself. The immense power which he had acquired in Florence through the wisdom of his political advice, the nobility of his mind, his irresistible eloquence, were more strengthened by the wonder awakened by the singularity of his character, than by his success in arousing in Florence a veritable religious fervour. And it was upon this point that Savonarola greatly deceived himself, and failed therefore to see that he was in fact building upon sand ; he desired a free government to promote religious reform, and the Florentines accepted religious reform, only for the better consolidation of a free government. Hence the base of his power was less solid than it seemed, and the Pope could not fail to find ways to create new parties and foment strife.

A considerable number of young men, lovers of the gay living so much in favour under the Medici, and now held in such bitter reprobation, banded together under the name of the Compagnacci (Bad Fellows) for the purpose of ridiculing the Friar and his friends whom they styled Piagnoni (Snivellers), Frateschi, &c., and of combating them by every means in their power. So in 1497, it came about that while this party made an attempt to revive the old Medicean carnival with its bacchanalian revels and indecencies, on the other hand the exhortations of Savonarola and his followers inspired bands of children to scour the streets and houses of Florence in search of *vanities*, namely, books, writings, drawings, and sculpture of a licentious character ; all carnival dresses and masks. The 7th of February and last day of carnival, was celebrated by a solemn procession, that terminated with the famous *burning of the vanities*, which were collected together in the Piazza of the Signoria, and heaped up on the stages of a great wooden pyramid constructed for the purpose. As was very natural, this affair gave rise to numerous accusations and much ridicule on the part of the Compagnacci, although this singular solemnity not only had the sanction of the chief authorities, but was almost directed by them, in order that it might be conducted with dignity and decorum. Indeed the Campagnacci loudly blamed the government for taking part in monkish shows. With this party sided the Arrabbiati, who desired a more restricted form of government, that is, one restricted to Ottimati and the Bigi (Greys), so called, because they did not venture to show their secret object, which was no less than the pure and simple restoration of the Medici.

As yet none of these intrigues endangered either the Republic or Savonarola. The Compagnacci were not a political party ; the Ottimati had few followers in Florence, which had always been a democratic city ; the Bigi, though with powerful adherents both at home and abroad, had in Piero dei Medici a leader at once too hated and despised, to be desired by many. The first attempt he made to re-enter Florence, where he expected a most favourable reception, ended in his having the city gate contemptuously closed in his face. A conspiracy for the same object got up by Bernardo del Nero and others, ended in their death. All this, however, produced a state of things, in which it was easy for Alexander VI. to find an opportunity for the revenge, that he had so long and so ardently sought.

Savonarola daily hurled fresh bolts against Roman licence, daily he insisted more openly on the necessity of calling together a council, and daily made allusions from the pulpit to the crimes and vices of the Pope. Frequently ordered to be silent, he raised his voice louder and louder. Finally sentence of excommunication was pronounced against him, and this he declared to be null and void, adding that he spoke in the name of the Almighty, and was ready to maintain his own innocence against the whole world ; that, however, he despaired of convincing Alexander VI., who, having been elected simoniacally, and stained with so many crimes and scandals, could not be considered as the true Pope. This was at the time of the murder of the Duke of Gandia, of the rumour of the Pope's incest with his daughter Lucrezia ; and Savonarola was worked up to a frenzy which he neither would nor could moderate. He addressed letters to the powers of Europe, urging them to assemble a Council for the salvation of the Church, which, as he would publicly demonstrate, had no true and legitimate head. One of these letters unfortunately fell into the hands of Alexander VI. Still more unfortunately, Charles VIII., who seemed to have repented of his sins and decided to put his hand to the reforms urged by Savonarola, by whom he was regarded as his strongest support, died suddenly in the early part of 1498. And although all this was not known in Italy, still it was already plain that all things were conspiring to the hurt of the poor friar. It was at this moment that an unexpected opportunity occurred which the Pope unhesitatingly seized.

The Signory then in office was hostile to Savonarola ; continued encouragement from abroad had increased the audacity of the Arrabbiati and the Compagnacci, the Bigi were always ready for anything that meant harm to the Republic, some even of the Piagnoni were disturbed by the fierceness of the conflict with the Pope, when a singular occurrence took place, of which no one could foresee the tremendous results. Francesco di Puglia, a Franciscan monk, in the course of a furious sermon against Savonarola in the Church of Santa Croce, declared himself ready to go through the ordeal of fire with him and thereby prove the falsity of the Friar's doctrines.

To Savonarola the affair appeared so strange and unseemly, that he disregarded it ; but not so his disciple Brother Domenico Buonvicini of Pescia. This friar, a man of small wits, but earnest, energetic and possessed with a burning zeal, accepted the challenge and unhesitatingly declared his readiness to go through the trial by fire in order to prove the truth of his master's doctrines. Francesco di Puglia replied that he had challenged Savonarola, and with him alone would he enter the fire ; Frà Domenico must be content to make the trial with Giuliano Rondinelli another Franciscan. The matter unfortunately went on notwithstanding Savonarola's attempts to put a stop to it ; Frà Domenico had fallen readily into the trap set for him, and Savonarola himself was not entirely disinclined to believe in the success of the experiment, convinced as he was of holding a mission from God and of being inspired by him to preach the doctrines which were now disputed. The Arrabbiati and the Compagnacci pushed the matter on with all their might, for they hoped to crush the Piagnoni by ridicule, and to accomplish the murder of Savonarola in the tumult for which they were making preparations. They were helped in this by the Signoria, now in secret agreement with Rome.

Accordingly this extraordinary experiment or ordeal—an evident anachronism in the fifteenth century—was fixed for the 7th of

April, 1498. At the hour arranged, the monks came in procession to the Piazza in front of the Palace, where everything had been ordered by the Signoria, and where an immense crowd had gathered, impatient to witness a spectacle that recalled the Middle Ages. Savonarola, finally persuaded that Frà Domenico's fiery zeal, against which he had vainly combated, was a veritable inspiration from on high, had consented to lead his brethren. However, when all was ready on their side, and Frà Domenico of Pescia awaited the signal to enter the fire, the Franciscans, whose only object was to lay a trap for their adversaries, began to hesitate, and it was plain that Rondinelli had no wish to face the ordeal. They did everything in their power to excite the wished-for disturbance, but without success, for Frà Domenico stood boldly forward, eager for the proof, and his attitude discomfited every adversary. But with their numberless objections and disputes the Franciscans contrived to waste the whole day, and at last a violent thunder-shower furnished the Signoria with an excuse for declaring that the ordeal could no longer take place.

According to all reason this should have completed the defeat of Savonarola's enemies ; but instead it had the contrary effect. The crowd was weary and furious at the loss of the longed-for spectacle ; and many laid the blame on Savonarola, saying that had he really been convinced of his divine mission, he would, without arguments, have entered the fire alone, and thus have silenced his adversaries for ever. His followers consisted chiefly either of devoted fanatics, or politicians who only regarded him as the champion of free government. The first regretted that the trial had not been made, the second deplored Savonarola's consent to it ; thus there was universal discontent. In this way it became possible for the Arrabbiati and the Compagnacci, seconded by the Bigi and favoured by the Signoria, to excite the people against the Piagnoni, some of whom were killed or wounded in the streets, and others insulted on all sides. And now the reaction had set in. A furious mob attacked the convent of St Mark, which in spite of the valiant resistance of some of the brethren, assisted by a small band of friends, was stormed and taken. Savonarola, his faithful companion Frà Domenico, and Frà Salvestro Maruffi, one of his most noted followers, but a mere visionary of the feeblest character, were carried to prison to await their trial.

The Pope would have paid any price to get the Friar into his hands, and made the most liberal offers ; but the Signoria, although composed of Arrabbiati most ready to agree to his death, could not reconcile it with the dignity of the Republic that the trial should take place elsewhere. In Florence, however, it was carried on in obedience to the orders and instructions received from Rome torture was repeatedly employed, and confessions extorted from the delirium of pain. While on the rack Savonarola could no longer command his nerves, and had not the strength to maintain that his doctrines and his works had been inspired by God, yet he steadfastly denied ever having been moved by any personal motives or of acting in bad faith ; on the contrary, he maintained that all that he had done had been solely and wholly for the public good To this we may add that although the weak, unstable Frà Silvestro gave way at once, denied his master, and said everything that his judges wished him to say, Frà Domenico, on the contrary, unconquered either by threats or torture, remained nobly consistent, unshrinkingly proclaiming his steadfast faith in his beloved master. Recourse was accordingly had to the common and easy expedient of altering as much as possible the very confessions extorted in the torture chamber, without however being able even in this way to find reasonable grounds for condemnation.

Meanwhile the Pope was sending furious letters demanding either that the Friars should be sent to Rome where he would know how to deal with them, or that they should be put to death without further delay. In fact the Signoria had neither will nor power to abandon its cruel purpose. As, however, two months had already passed, and it was time, according to the Florentine laws, for a new Signoria to come into office, the present one employed itself solely in providing that the new elections should be favourable to the Arrabbiati ; and this was easily contrived. The freshly elected magistrates speedily agreed with the Pope, that he should send two Apostolic Commissioners to Florence to bring the trial to a satisfactory conclusion ; finding grounds that is, for capital punishment, more especially as regarded the accusal of heresy. Savonarola in the meantime, during this interval of quiet in his prison, had written several religious pamphlets, in which, while re-asserting all his doctrines he once more declared himself to be in all things, as he had ever been, a most faithful and unshaken believer in the Roman Catholic faith. But that mattered nothing ; his death had been resolved upon.

On the 19th of May the Apostolic Commissioners arrived with the order that *were he another St. John the Baptist* he must be condemned to death. They began the mock trial again, torturing Savonarola even more cruelly than at first. And although, notwithstanding his bodily weakness, he now endured the agony better than before, and no good reason could be found for condemning him, yet without delay the Commissioners sentenced him and his companions to death, and handed them over to the secular arm, showing no mercy even to Maruffi, who had vilely slandered and denied his master, making every admission that was suggested to him. A friar more or less mattered little, they said. And certainly there would have been little prudence in sparing the life of so weak and shallow a man, who later might have revealed, even unwittingly, the shameless falsification of the trials. Accordingly, on the 23rd of May, 1498, a great platform was erected in the piazza of the Signoria, with a cross at one end on which the three friars were hung ; Savonarola in the middle, between the other two. The instant they had breathed their last, their corpses were burnt, and their ashes thrown into the Arno, in the presence of an applauding rabble of boys.

Throughout this drama there was a strange mixture of elements ; of the really heroic with the merely ephemeral. The faith of Savonarola, his zeal for the general good, his self-abnegation, were simply heroic ; mighty was his eloquence, wonderful his political wisdom ; merely ephemeral, on the other hand, the religious ardour which he believed that he had aroused in the Florentine people. In point of fact they had only been stirred to a love of liberty, and had listened with enthusiasm to the religious teachings of the Friar as long as these continued to give strength to the popular government. But as soon as they beheld in him a source of danger to the Republic, they had little hesitation in giving him up to the Pope. And certainly, no sooner had the unhappy Friar ceased to breathe, than all the dangers which had from all sides recently threatened the government which he had founded, seemed suddenly to melt away. The allies spoke no more of re-instating Piero dei Medici ; the Pope, in high good humour, sent praises and held out hopes ; Valentinois seemed to have renounced all idea of invading Tuscany, and Florence hoped to be able to turn all her attention to the war against Pisa, without having to think of other matters.

It was not long before she saw the vanity of these hopes, and that much more was needed to satiate the unquenchable avidity of the Borgia. But there was no longer any remedy. She could only repent having stifled the one voice that was ever raised in defence of her liberty ; of having unjustly, iniquitously destroyed a man who had done so much good, and would have done so much more to the cause of Florence, of liberty, of religion. To many his death rendered him a saint and a martyr, and for more than a century his memory was admired and worshipped by numbers in Florence, who, during subsequent perils of their country, showed themselves worthy followers of their master, and shed the glow of their heroism over the last moments of the Republic. However, that was in the future ; in the May of 1498 the Arrabbiati were triumphant, although they did not dare to change the form of government planned by Savonarola. On the contrary, it was consolidated. Still the Piagnoni continued to be persecuted, and many of them were driven out of whatever offices they held to make room for their declared adversaries and new men. At this moment a personage appeared upon the scene, and obtained official employ, who was certainly greater than Savonarola, if of a very different order of greatness. To him we must now turn our undivided attention.

BOOK THE FIRST.

FROM THE BIRTH OF NICCOLÒ MACHIAVELLI TO HIS DISMISSAL
FROM THE OFFICE OF SECRETARY OF THE TEN.

(1469–1512.)

CHAPTER I.

(1469–1498.)

NICCOLÒ MACHIAVELLI makes his first appearance in history in the year 1498, the twenty-ninth of his age. At that period the storm was already gathering which a few months later brought Savonarola to the scaffold. The Signoria was hostile to the Friar; the sentence of excommunication against him had already reached Florence. For the prevention of scandal, he had ordered his faithful disciple, Frà Domenico of Pescia, to preach in San Lorenzo to the women, while he himself had left the Duomo, and retired to San Marco, where he delivered his sermons to male hearers only. It was there that Machiavelli came to hear two sermons, of which he sent details to a friend in Rome, in a letter dated the 8th of March of the same year. In this we already find certain noteworthy characteristics of an intellect not merely different from, but opposed to, that of Savonarola. He could not understand that there was anything great or noble in the Friar. He listened with a smile of irony and scorn to the strange words of the man whom he afterwards described as the *weaponless prophet*. He heard him slashing at "your books, oh priests, and treating you in a way that even dogs would not submit to;" he heard him say of the Pope "everything that can be said of any great villain;" as it appeared to him "this Friar is

colouring his lies to suit the times ; " [1] but he failed to comprehend how he had gained so great a power in Florence, nor how the affair would end, wherefore he besought his friend to enlighten him upon the subject if possible. What manner of man, then, was this who remained a cold inquirer in the midst of these seething popular passions ? Remembering the no inconsiderable part that he played in after-years in the affairs of his Republic, and his very considerable part in the history of modern thought, the smallest particulars of his youth and his studies would be very precious. But the early years of Machiavelli remain, perhaps always will remain, involved in obscurity. He is seldom mentioned by his contemporaries, and after his death none of his friends or acquaintances thought of writing his life. And he, continually occupied in the observation of contemporary men and events, never refers to himself, never alludes to his own past. As a man, as an individual character, he does not appear to have exercised much influence upon those about him ; his actions were either of little importance or excited little remark. Even his prodigious business activity was chiefly of the pen ; it may be said that his life was nearly all in his writings, although he went through many and varied experiences. In this he is very different from Guicciardini, whom he resembles in many other respects. The latter, in fact, having attained to an elevated office, made his power and personal authority very clearly felt. Assailed by many contemporaries, he defended himself in his " Apologia," in his " Ricordi Biografici," and in other writings, in which he often speaks at length of himself. However, we shall now try to put together all the information we have been able to collect relating to Machiavelli's family and early life. Unfortunately it is extremely scanty.

Machiavelli came of a very old Tuscan family, originally of Montespertoli, a small commune, situated between the Val d'Elsa and the Val di Pesa, at a short distance from Florence. In their family records—" Quaderno di ricordanze," some of which are still to be found in the libraries of Florence—we read that the Machia-

---

[1] This letter, the second in every edition of Machiavelli's Works, bears the date of the 8th of March, 1497. It is, however, well known that, down to the middle of the last century, the Florentines dated the year *ab incarnatione*, that is, beginning it on the 25th of March. The first letter, to which we shall refer later, is followed in the " Opere " by a Latin fragment, not generally numbered. In all quotations from the " Opere," the reader will understand that we refer to the Italian edition of 1813, unless another be specially indicated.

velli were allies of the lords of Montespertoli, and positively descended from the same stock. According to these *ricordanze*, about the year 1120 a certain Buoninsegna, son of Dono dei Machiavelli, was the father of two sons, Castellano and Dono. From the former were descended the Castellani, lords of Monte-spertoli ; from the latter those who bore the name of Machiavelli. A spread eagle, field azure, was the arms of the first ; that of the second a cross azure, field argent, with four nails, likewise azure, at the four corners of the cross. In 1393 Ciango dei Castellani of Montespertoli bequeathed to Buoninsegna and Lorenzo, children of Filippo Machiavelli, the celebrated author's great-great-grand-father, the castle of Montespertoli, with rights of patronage over many churches. This inheritance, though of little value—feudal rights being then abolished—brought the Machiavelli certain privileges, as, for instance, the monopoly of the public scales and measures, a yearly offering of wax candles, and the permission to affix their arms to the well on the market-place which now bears their name. The property itself was of no great value, and was divided among the many branches of the numerous family. Very little, therefore, came into the hands of Niccolò Machiavelli's father, whose own lands were in the neighbouring commune of San Casciano. But he still preserved certain barren rights upon the castle, and rights of patronage over various churches, belong-ing in part to the Montespertoli inheritance.[1] The Machiavelli also possessed houses in the quarter of Sto. Spirito, near Santa Felicità and the Ponte Vecchio in Florence, where they had long been established, and were among the most notable of the *popo-lani*.[2] Indeed, we find them among those who had to go into

[1] The house in which Machiavelli lived and died is the present No. 16, Via Guicciardini, Florence.

[2] In the Marucelliana Library in Florence (Cod. 229, A. 10), is the "Qua-derno," or Book of Records of Ristoro, son of Lorenzo, who was the son of Niccolò Machiavelli. This Niccolò, who was the son of Alessandro, was several times member of the Signoria and of the Ten, and was a contemporary of the great writer, but of another branch of the family. The two have occasionally been confused with each other, and thereby many mistakes have arisen. Ristoro's Book of Records begins on the 1st of September, 1538, and contains, besides family accounts, several important notices, part of which are copied from the most ancient of the family records. Thus, there are notes written by Lorenzo Machia-velli, and others still older, extracted from a "Record" by Bernardo, son of Niccolò Machiavelli, written in the year 1460. And it is in this Record that the father of our Machiavelli, nine years before the birth of his son, notes down the family genealogy. Part of these records are corroborated by Giuliano dei Ricci in his "Priorista," a manuscript in which he frequently speaks of the Machiavelli

exile in 1260,[1] after the defeat at Montaperto. But they soon returned to Florence with the other Guelphs, and are frequently mentioned in the history of the Republic, in whose government they shared, being able to boast of a large number of priors and gonfaloniers.[2]

Bernardo, son of Niccolò Machiavelli, born in 1428, was a juris-consult, and filled for some time the office of treasurer in the Marca,[3] in 1450 he inherited the property of his uncle Totto, son of Buoninsegna Machiavelli.[4]   In 1458 he married Bartolommea,

family, to whom he was related. (*Vide* in the National Library of Florence the "Priorista," by Giuliano dei Ricci: Quartiere Santo Spirito, Sesto d'Oltrarno, Machiavelli.)

The branch to which our Machiavelli belonged was extinguished in the beginning of the seventeenth century by the death of Ippolita, daughter of Alessandro, who was the son of Bernardo, Niccolò's third son.   Married in 1608 to Pier Francesco dei Ricci, she died in 1613.   Bacchia, the daughter of Niccolò Machiavelli, had married Giovanni dei Ricci, and thus was mother of Giuliano dei Ricci, author of the " Priorista," and collector of many memorials and papers concerning his illustrious ancestor. (*Vide* Baldelli, "Elogio di Niccolò Machiavelli," London, 1794, pp. 86, 87.)   Another branch of the Machiavelli was extinguished in Florence, in the year 1727, by the death of Francesco Maria dei Machiavelli. The inheritance passed to the Rangoni of Modena, who for that reason bore the name of Rangoni-Machiavelli.

Count Passerini, first in his notes to Ademollo's romance, "Marietta dei Ricci," and then in the essay prefixed to the new edition of Machiavelli's " Opere " (vol. i. : Florence, Cenniniana Press, 1873), asserts that Machiavelli's consanguinity with the lords of Montespertoli was a fable invented in the days of the Principality, in order to flatter the ambition of the Machiavelli, who were then powerful.   But, as is clear, the circumstance is of much older origin.

See also the " Monografia storica e statistica del Commune di Montespertoli, compilata dall Avv. Marcello Nardi-Dei," Florence, Co-operative Press, 1873. Among other notices, at p. 21, a document is quoted proving that on the extinction, towards the end of the fourteenth century, of the seigneurial family of the lords of Montespertoli, by the decease of Ciango d'Agnolo, he named as his heirs *pro indiviso* Lorenzo and Buoninsegna, children of Filippo Machiavelli.

[1] Giovanni Villani (" Cronica," vol. i. book viii. chap. 80, Florence, Coen, 1847), in giving the list of those then sent into exile, places the Machiavelli " among the *popolani* of the said Sesto (Oltrarno), notable houses."   The same notice is to be found in Ammirato, " Delle famiglie nobili fiorentine " (Florence, 1615), at p. 12, " Famiglia Soderini."

[2] G. Baldelli, " Elogio," &c., in note 6, at pp. 86, 87, tells us that the Machiavelli had twelve gonfaloniers and fifty priors.   Ricci, in his " Priorista," enumerates fifty-seven priors; but it must be observed that here several names are found repeated over and over again, even in the same year.

[3] *Vide* Baldelli, " Elogio," &c., and the " Life " prefixed to Machiavelli's Works in the Florence edition of 1782.

[4] *Vide* the " Libro di Ricordanze," by Ristoro Machiavelli, from which we have already quoted.

widow of Niccolò Bennizzi, and daughter of Stefano dei Nelli, of old Florentine family. It cannot be supposed that this marriage increased his personal property, for in those days women brought very scanty dowers. However that may be, in the Catasto of 1498, his income—all of which, as we shall see later, passed to his son Niccolò in 1511, according to a stipulated agreement—was valued at 110 broad florins and 14 pence,[1] so that, if not a wealthy, neither was he a poor man. It is impossible to make a perfectly exact calculation ; but considering the much higher value of gold in those days, we may venture, without being far from the truth, to estimate this income as about equal to four or five thousand francs[2] of our present currency. Bernardo was a studious man, and Bartolommea a pious woman, evidently of some culture, since she composed certain religious verses and hymns to the Blessed Virgin, dedicated, as we find it asserted, to her son Niccolò.[3] Four children were the issue of this marriage : Totto, Niccolò, Primerana, and Ginevra. The elder daughter was married to Messer Francesco Vernacci, the second to Messer Bernardo Minerbetti. It is not known if the elder son Totto, born in 1463, ever married, and he soon fell into obscurity. Niccolò, on the contrary, born the 3rd of May, 1469, speedily, as we shall see, became the most influential member of the family, by reason of his acquirements, as well as of his natural ability. The death of Machiavelli's mother took place on the 11th of October, 1496, yet, not even touching this—one of the most serious events in a man's life—do we find a single word to enlighten us as to what he

---

[1] Equal to 132 *sealed* florins, 16 soldi, and 10 denari, the which sum paid a tax or decima of 11 florins, 1 soldo, 5 denari. *Vide* the two documents published by Passerini in the first volume of the " Opere di M. Machiavelli," quoted above, pp. lviii and lx. This edition was commenced by Sigri. Passerini and Fanfani in 1863. Signor Fanfani having withdrawn, Signor Gaetano Milanesi replaced him, and with Passerini's collaboration has already brought out five volumes. Henceforth, for the sake of brevity, we shall quote this edition as follows— " Opere " (P. M.).

[2] The florin of ordinary gold, somewhat smaller than the broad florin, had the same value and same amount of alloy as the more modern zecchin. Estimating this at 12 Italian livres, and admitting that gold at that time had four times its present value, a much higher figure would be reached. This, however, is almost a chance calculation, since it is well known how much even the most careful writers differ as to the relative value of gold in our time and in the fifteenth century.

[3] " Discorso del Senatore G. B. Nelli, con la vita del medesimo," Florence, Paperini and Co., 1753, p. 8. The Nelli library seems to have been divided among the heirs.

felt on the occasion. All is entirely hidden from us. At that time he was already twenty-six years of age, yet up to that period we have not a single line from his pen, nor a single word from other writers, giving any information about him.[1]

The very first words we have from his pen consist of one letter in Italian, and a fragment of another in Latin, both written in the December of 1497,[2] both upon the same subject. From the days of Pope John XXIII., the Machiavelli had had in their gift the living of Santa Maria della Fagna, in the Mugello. The Pazzi were now trying to usurp this right, and therefore the Machiavelli family, although Bernardo was still living, commissioned his son Niccolò to petition for their common rights. Thus we have the two letters " *to a Roman prelate*," who was probably Cardinal of Perugia, since it was to him that the Republican Government wrote urgently upon the same subject.[3] In these letters, Machiavelli, with much acumen, much flattery, and many promises to the prelate, asserts in grandiloquent language the just rights which the *Maciavellorum familia* had charged him to defend, and which, in fact, were ultimately triumphant.

In this way two things are clearly proved to us—1st, that Niccolò then knew and wrote the Latin tongue, a fact which some had considered doubtful ; 2nd, that all the Machiavelli held him in high esteem since they chose him for their representative and defender. Among the scanty and often contradictory notices which have come down to us, it is quite necessary to dwell upon

---

[1] There is a small fragment from Machiavelli's pen of a very free translation of the " Historia persecutionis vandalicae " of Vittore Vitense. Passerini, without giving any proofs, states that it was written before 1494 ; but nothing being known about it, it may be attributed to any year, and, from its style, may be believed to be a youthful production. The Ricci manuscript, to which we shall refer later, and which comprises many writings by, and relating to, Machiavelli, contains a " Risposta fatta ad uno ambasciatore pel re di Francia," dated 1495, and by some attributed, with no reason, to Machiavelli. Machiavelli was in the habit of collecting documents of all kinds for his studies, especially for his " Storie," and Ricci copied and preserved them. Hence one must be cautious of attributing all these to Machiavelli.

[2] They are the first of Machiavelli's published letters. Among the " Machiavelli Papers," preserved in the Florence National Library in six cases, there is a letter speaking of another *patronato* of the family, but unsigned, and, although in Niccolò's hand, speaking of him as of a third person. *Vide* Appendix, document i.

[3] This is proved by a document quoted by Nitti, " Machiavelli nella vita e nelle opere " : Naples, 1876, vol. i. p. 39. This Cardinal of Perugia must have been Giovanni Lopez, a Spaniard.

those which are undoubtedly authentic. It is certainly no matter for astonishment that a man, so singularly gifted by nature, should have already possessed a satisfactory amount of literary instruction ; especially, too, when we remember that he came of a family deficient neither in means nor in culture ; that he had passed his youth under the rule of Lorenzo the Magnificent, when schools and public university lectures abounded, when Italian and Latin literature could be learnt almost unconsciously, even in daily conversation, and reminiscences of antiquity were in the very air which men breathed. It would have been strange indeed if, as some have pretended, on the faith of Giovio's little trustworthy assertions, Machiavelli had been at that time utterly wanting in culture, only acquiring later from Marcello Virgilio Adriani all that he introduced into his works of Greek or Latin authors.[1] But, on the other hand, although Machiavelli was already a fair scholar in his youth, and, as time went on, made much progress in the classics, and gained not a little by his intimacy with Marcello Virgilio, we cannot believe the assertions of those who credit him with profound learning and Grecian scholarship.[2] Whether he knew or did not know the elements of Greek, can neither be affirmed nor denied, and it is a point of no importance. It is certain that he diligently studied translations of Greek authors, and made use of them in his writings ; but of his ability to read them in the original—a point which it would certainly be very desirable to know—we have no satisfactory proofs whatever. Amid his numerous Latin quotations, we never meet with one in Greek ; we have some translations of his from the Latin, but not a single page purporting to be translated from the Greek, nor does he ever mention having read a single author in that tongue. Besides, it is certain that his contemporaries did not rank him

---

[1] Giovio's brief " Elogio " begins thus—" Quis non miretur in hoc Macciavello tantum valuisse naturam, *ut in nulla vel certe mediocri latinarum literarum cognitione*, ad justam recte scribendi facultatem pervenire potuerit . . .? " And further on—" Constat eum, sicuti ipse nobis fatebatur, a Marcello Virgilio, cuius et notarius et assecla publici muneris fuit, graecae atque latinae linguæ flores accepisse quos scriptis suis insereret." (" Elogia doctorum virorum," auctore Paulo Jovio : Antuerpiae, 1557, pp. 192–93.) These very inexact assertions, too common in Giovio, were the origin of those afterwards repeated by many other writers.

[2] " He knew Greek and Latin perfectly," says Passerini at p. xi of the "Discorso," prefixed to the " Opere " (P. M.) ; but he makes the assertion without proving it, and without alluding to the disputes of noted authors on the subject.

among the men of learning ; Varchi indeed speaks of him as one
" rather not without letters, than lettered." [1]   Giuliano dei Ricci
a descendant of Niccolò on his mother's side, and who collected all
obtainable information about him, combated Giovio's assertion by
proving that his illustrious ancestor was really acquainted with
Latin, without, however, saying a word as to Greek.[2]   In short,
from all that we know with certainty, it may be concluded that
Niccolò Machiavelli received in his youth the ordinary literary
education of his day, by no means that of a man of learning, and
that his wide knowledge of Greek authors was gained from translations ; neither would it appear that he had gone very far in the
study of law, of which, however, he had evidently some knowledge.[3]

[1] " Storia di Firenze " : Florence, Pazzi, 1851, vol. i. p. 266.

[2] Giuliano dei Ricci, in the manuscript already quoted (and of which there are
two copies in the Florence National Library), observes that there is no foundation
for Giovio's remarks ; that Machiavelli was never the notary of Marcello Virgilio,
but secretary to the Ten ; that the fragment of the Latin letter written by him in
December, 1497, proves his knowledge of Latin.   That fragment, Ricci tells us,
is only the eighth part of the whole, the rest having been lost through the tearing
of the sheet.   At that period Niccolò Machiavelli " had hardly begun to know,
much less to be intimate with Virgilio."   *Vide* the MS. marked No. 692, among
the Palatine MSS., pp. 8–10.   Both copies of this MS. seem to be by the same
hand.   At the end of one of them is written, " The present volume has been
copied by me, Marco Martini, in this year 1726, from the copy of the Abbe Corso
dei Ricci.   The whole copy was made by Giuliano dei Ricci from the original
papers of Niccolò Machiavelli, and this copy by Rosso Antonio Martini has been
collated with the above-mentioned copy of Giuliano dei Ricci."   The same words
are to be seen in the other copy, but partially scratched out.

[3] Thus much at least may be presumed from his relations having entrusted him
with the defence of their rights concerning Santa Maria della Fagna, and from
some other business of a similar nature which he took in hand long afterwards.
His father might have early initiated him in these studies, concerning which, however, no mention is to be found in Machiavelli's works.

Gervinus, in his work, " Florentinische Historiographie," before quoted by us,
indulges in long and somewhat exaggerated reflections on the injury to Machiavelli's studies and even to his genius, resulting, in his opinion, from the great writer's
ignorance of the Greek language and literature.   On the other hand, Professor
Triantafillis, first in his work entitled " Niccolò Machiavelli and the Greek Authors "
(Venice, 1875), and shortly after in another on Machiavelli's " Vita di Castruccio
Castracani," published in the " Archivio Veneto," believes to have triumphantly
proved that Machiavelli understood Greek, and studied Greek authors in the
original.   These two works certainly show that the Florentine Secretary made
great use of those writers ; but, in our opinion, are not sufficient proof that his
Greek studies were carried on in the original language instead of in translations.
The error of Professor Triantafillis lay in believing it sufficient to consult Hoff-
mann's " Lexicon Bibliographicum," and when in this he finds no mention of a

He acquired all else later in life by private reading, by meditation, and above all by practical experience and knowledge of mankind. His comparatively restricted culture must doubtless have been a drawback to him ; but it also had the inestimable advantage of preserving the spontaneous originality of his genius and his style, and preventing them from being suffocated, as frequently happened at that period, beneath a dead weight of erudition.

And even his ardent enthusiasm for the ancients, and especially for the Romans, rather reminds us of that of Cola di Rienzo and Stefano Porcaro, than of that of a man of learning, pure and simple. Living too in that age of letters, fine arts, conspiracies, papal scandals, and foreign invasions, he did not dwell alone with his books, but in continual conversation and meditation on the events going on so swiftly around him. And among these events, it is certain that the coming of the French in 1494 must have made a very deep and painful impression upon him, an impression mitigated only partially by the expulsion of the Medici, and the proclamation of the Republic in Florence. For, with his pagan

translation of some author known to have existed in Machiavelli's time, and of which the latter availed himself, he takes it for granted that no such translation existed, and that the author was studied in the original. It is clear that no certain results can be obtained by this method, since in that century numerous translations were made, which were unpublished and even unknown. In fact, of some of the authors of which Triantafillis believes no translations to have been made at that period, several exist in the Florence libraries, and nothing forbids us to think that Machiavelli may have made use of these and of others unknown to us. Professor Triantafillis also endeavours to prove at length that the dialogue "Dell'ira o dei modi di curarla " is almost a translation from Plutarch, without at all endeavouring to ascertain if there be any foundation for the opinion of those writers who affirmed that the work was not by Machiavelli. Neither does he seem to be aware that there is in the Laurentian Library an ancient translation of this very pamphlet of Plutarch's, attributed to Colluccio Salutati, and of which Machiavelli might have availed himself.

Therefore, Professor Triantafillis' two works, however praiseworthy in other respects, in nowise alter the state of the question, and do not change our own opinion, which is also that most generally approved. We may add that Ricci in his "Priorista " tells us that Machiavelli composed a treatise in the form of a comedy entitled "Le Maschere," which was afterwards lost. In this, continues Ricci, the author, incited by M. Virgilio, imitated " The Clouds" and other comedies of Aristophanes, and made it a vehicle for bitter satire on many of his contemporaries. This fact might be adduced in favour of the opposite argument to that maintained by us ; but even this would be a very weak argument, since it would refer to a generical imitation, which might have been grounded on the spoken or written commentaries of M. Virgilio himself or some other professor of the university.

reminiscences and sympathies, and his most profound aversion for everything savouring of priesthood or monkery, he could not reconcile himself to the circumstance of the Republic being ruled by the eloquence of a friar, and his inclinations bent towards the friar's executioners. Later in his writings we meet with some expressions of admiration for Savonarola, but these expressions are not entirely free from irony. When the friar's ashes were cast into the Arno, and the Piagnoni were objects of persecution, matters were more congenial to his ideas. Then, as was natural, many changes took place in the public offices, and Machiavelli, who at twenty-nine was still without a profession and without an income of his own, set about seeking for an occupation that would bring him fair remuneration for his work. He cannot have had much difficulty, since his views were not too ambitious, and the Republic had long been accustomed to employ men of letters in salaried posts, especially as secretaries.

The chief secretary's office was that of the Signory, at the head of which was the official properly known as the Secretary, or Chancellor of the Republic. This was a very honourable office, entrusted to men like Poggio Bracciolini, Leonardo Aretino, and so on. Then came the second Chancery, that of the Ten, which although having an importance of its own, was dependent to a certain extent upon the first. The Ten combined the functions of a War Office, and in part of Ministry for Home affairs, and consequently had an enormous amount of business to transact. It was also their duty to despatch ambassadors to foreign countries, and to keep up a correspondence with them ; but in these matters they worked in conjunction with or rather subordinated to the Signory. Thus the second Chancery was often at the orders of the first, and when, as frequently happened, the Ten were not elected, then the two chanceries were almost fused together under the direction of the first secretary.[1]

[1] This much is ascertained from the examination of the registers of the Republic in the Florentine Archives. The missions and instructions to ambassadors from 1499 to 1512 are sometimes in the name of the Signory, sometimes of the Ten, or even occasionally of both (Florence Archives, class x. department i. No. 105). The Ten were often delegated to reply to letters addressed to the Signoria. According to the statute of 1415 (printed in 1781, and dated from Fribourg, vol. ii. p. 25, and fol.), the Ten have the power of nominating syndics, procurators, ambassadors, secretaries, &c. They have, however, no power to appoint ambassadors to the Pope or emperor, or to a king or queen, without the consent of the priors and colleges.

Towards the end of 1497 the death occurred of Bartolommeo Scala, a celebrated man of learning, long secretary of the Republic, and Marcello Virgilio Adriani was nominated in his stead in the February of 1498, with a yearly stipend of 330 florins.[1] Shortly afterwards, Alessandro Braccesi, another secretary of the Signoria, but placed in the second Chancery, was dismissed from office, and it was then that four names were put to the vote, first in the Council of Eighty, and four days later—that is on the 19th June—in the great Council. Among these names we find that of Niccolò, son of Bernardo Machiavelli ; he it was who gained the greater number of votes, and was elected with the yearly stipend of 192 florins.[2] On the 14th of July in the same year, his nomination was confirmed by the Signory, and he was transferred to the second Chancery, at the head of which he remained until the downfall of the Republican Government in 1512. This promotion must have increased his stipend to 200

---

[1] " Bartolomei Scalæ Collensis, Vita," auctore Dominico Maria Mannio : Florentiæ, 1768.

Passerini in his " Discorso " at page xii, " Opere " (P. M.), affirms that Machiavelli, " desiring of entering into his country's service, placed himself, about 1494, under the direction of Marcello Virgilio Adriani, in the second Chancery of the Commune." But we do not know where he could have discovered that Machiavelli and Marcello Virgilio were already in office before 1498, and neither does he quote any authority.

It is true that by a deliberation of 28th December, 1494 (" Deliberazione dei Signori," reg. 86, a. c., 120), it would seem that then, on the formation of a new government, Bartolommeo Scala and others received their dismissal. But on the 31st December the priors " *attenta* capsatione facta perdictos Dominos de domino Bart. Sch., et *attenta* necessitate Palatii et negotiis eiusdem," re-elect him chancellor of the first Chancery, together with Pietro Beccanugi, who had replaced him. And thus he remained in office until 1497, as Manni too affirms in his " Life " of him. And in the reforms of the Chancery, passed in the Great Council on the 13th February, 1498 (new style), it is decreed that the first chancellor, the post held by Bartolommeo Schale, " should have a salary of 330 florins, and a little further on the decree mentions the secretaries of the Signoria, and alludes to the secretaryship," in which Alessandro Braccesi has served. " Braccesi in fact had just then been dismissed." (" Provvisioni," reg. 187, sheets 56–58.)

[2] The act of Machiavelli's nomination has frequently been published, but always with some omissions. Recently it has been republished by Passerini, in the volume before quoted, page lix ; but here two documents have been turned into one, through the omission, at the beginning of the second paragraph, of the date, Die xviiii. *mensis junii*, by which it appears that the deliberation of the Great Council was taken four days after that of the Council of Eighty. (Florentine Archives, cl. ii. No. 154, sheet 104.) The two decrees are written on the margin of the sheet indicated. This *filza*, or file, also bears the more modern indication of " Signori e Collegi, Deliberazioni," reg. duplicate 169.

florins, that being the fixed salary of the second Chancellor.[1] But it is necessary to remark that, according to the law, these florins were only worth four livres each, and not seven like the ordinary florins of that time ; there was furthermore a deduction of nine *denari* from every livre ; so that Machiavelli's stipend did not really amount to much more than one hundred gold florins.[2] Machiavelli was about thirty years of age when established as secretary in the company of Marcello Virgilio, who, although he may have been his very learned friend, was certainly not his preceptor.

Marcello Virgilio, born in 1464, was only five years older than Machiavelli. He had been the pupil of Landino and Poliziano ; he knew Greek and Latin, medicine, and the natural sciences ; he had a great facility for improvisation, even in Latin. These oratorical gifts were assisted by the nobility of his appearance ; he was tall, had a dignified bearing, a spacious forehead, and an open countenance. Being nominated Professor of Letters at the Studio in 1497, he continued to give lessons until the year 1502. His literary remains consist of many Latin orations, of which the greater number are still unpublished ; a translation of Dioscorides, which, although neither the first nor a very correct version, gained him the title of the Tuscan Dioscorides. In short he was a learned man of what might then have been called the old school, and notwithstanding the duties of his office, never abandoned the classical studies which were the constant theme of his conversation and correspondence with his friends.[3]

---

[1] This deliberation also has been frequently published. In none of the decrees of nomination is the salary mentioned. But in the reform of the chanceries carried out in 1498 before quoted, it is settled that the post which had been held by Alessandro Braccesi should have the yearly stipend of 192 florins, and that of Chancellor to the Second Chancery, namely that held by Antonio di Maria Nuti, should be of 200 florins per year. Machiavelli was really first secretary or Chancellor of the Second Chancery.

[2] These facts are extracted from the before-quoted Reform of the 28th December, 1494, and are further confirmed by the orders of payment, one of which can be seen in the Florence Archives, cl. xiii. dist. 2, No. 69, a. c. 142.

[3] Angelo Maria Bandini, " Collectio veterum aliquot monumentorum : " Aretii, 1752. In the preface he speaks of Marcello Virgilio, of whom a eulogium also may be found in vol. iii. of the " Elogi storici degli Uomini illustri Toscani : " Florence, 1766-73.

In the above-mentioned preface Bandini says : " Id vero in Marcello mirum fuit quod etsi publici florentinam iuventutem humanioribus literis erudiret, nomine

Very different was Machiavelli. Of middle height, slender figure, with sparkling eyes, dark hair, rather a small head, a slightly aquiline nose, a tightly closed mouth : all about him bore the impress of a very acute observer and thinker, but not that of one able to wield much influence over others.[1] He could

tamen reipublicae literas scribendi munus nunquam intermiserit." This preface is followed by letters addressed to Marcello by Calcondila (1496), and by Roberto Acciaioli, by Aldo Manuzio (1499), and by Cardinal Soderini (1508), all on the subject of classical research, discoveries of ancient monuments, &c. *Vide* too Prezziner's "Storia del pubblico Studio," &c., vol. i. pp. 181, 187, and 190 ; Fabroni's "Historia Academiæ Pisanæ," vol. i. pp. 95, 375, and 377. By an unpublished letter from Marcello Virgilio to Machiavelli, to be quoted further on, it is plainly to be seen that even in 1502 when the latter was with Cæsar Borgia, the former was at the head of the first secretary's office, and was continuing to give lectures.

In 1515 Adriani had a fall from his horse, and suffered much in consequence, not only his eyes, but his speech also remaining affected to the end of his life. This is mentioned by Valeriani, "De literatorum infelicitate ;" Venetiis, 1630, p. 71, and by Bandini at p. xix of his before-quoted preface. Regarding this scholar's works, see the printed catalogue of the Laurentian Library in Florence, compiled and illustrated by Bandini and Moreni, "Bibliografia toscana."

Marcello died in 1521 at the age of 56 years, and was buried in the family tomb at the Franciscan church at San Miniato al Monte, which Michael Angelo styled *La Bella villanella.* Here is his monument and bust beneath which is written :

> " Suprema nomen hoc solo
> Tantum voluntas iusserat
> Poni, sed hanc statuam prius
> Erexit hæres, nescius
> Famæ futurum et gloriæ
> Aut nomen aut nihil satis."

It is possible that the concluding words may have suggested the beautiful inscription afterwards placed on Machiavelli's tomb in the church of Santa Croce. Marcello Virgilio's son, Gio. Battista, the historian, and his grandson filled the same chair as their father and grandfather. So little is generally known about Marcello Virgilio, that I have tried here to put together a few notices concerning him.

[1] In the gallery of the Uffizi there is preserved a plaster cast, which is said to have been executed on Machiavelli's corpse, solely on the ground of its having been discovered during the present century, in the house of Machiavelli, in Via Guicciardini. It is also asserted that Bartolini made use of this cast, whilst engaged at his statue of Machiavelli, which is erected under the Uffizi. We, however, found in Bartolini's studio the cast (of which we have a reproduction) of another bust, and this bears much more resemblance to the statue. It is almost identical with a bust in stucco, probably of the times, which belonged to the Ricci family, the heirs of Machiavelli, and afterwards passed to Marchese Bentivaglio d'Aragona. An ancient portrait bust in terra cotta, apparently taken from the corpse, was once to be seen in Florence, but its owner, Baron Seymour Kirkupp, took it with him to Leghorn, and we do not know where it is now.

not easily rid himself of the sarcastic expression continually playing round his mouth and flashing from his eyes, which gave him the air of a cold and impassable calculator ; while nevertheless he was frequently ruled by his powerful imagination ; sometimes suddenly led away by it to an extent befitting the most fantastic of visionaries. He applied himself to the faithful service of the Republic, with all the ardour of an ancient Republican, inspired by reminiscences of Rome, pagan, and republican. If not altogether satisfied with the present form of government, he was well content that the Medicean tyranny and the dominion of a monk were both at an end. Doubtless his intercourse with Marcello Virgilio was beneficial to his studies, and it is possible that he still attended some of the lectures given by his superior in office, but he could not have had many leisure hours, being occupied from morning to evening in writing official letters, of which to this day many thousands are preserved in the Florentine archives. Besides this employment he was continually sent by the Ten on state errands, throughout the territories of the Republic, and before long he was also entrusted with important missions beyond the frontiers. He entered zealously into all these affairs, for they suited his tastes and the feverish activity of his nature. His leisure was devoted to reading, conversation, and the usual pleasures of life. Being of a cheerful temper, he was on good terms with his colleagues in the Chancery, and if intimate with his superior, Marcello Virgilio, was far more so with Biagio Buonaccorsi, who, although in an inferior position and but a mediocre scholar, was a worthy man and a firm friend. He it was, who when Machiavelli was at a distance used to write him long and affectionate letters in a tone of real friendship, and from these we learn that the first secretary of the Ten was much given to gay living, and to various irregular love affairs, of which the two wrote to each other in a style that is far from edifying.

Bartolini and other sculptors who had seen it had high opinion of it. In conclusion we must mention the engraving, frontispiece of the old edition of Machiavelli's works, dated 1550, which is known as the "Testina," on account of this very portrait. There is a certain resemblance in all these different portraits, with the exception, perhaps, of the mask found in Machiavelli's house.

CHAPTER II.

Niccolò Machiavelli begins to exercise the office of Secretary to the Ten—His mission to Forlì—Condemnation and Death of Paolo Vitelli—Discourse upon Pisan Affairs.

(1498–1499.)

HE principal undertaking in which the Republic was now engaged was the war with Pisa, and it seemed as though at last she would be granted fair play without interference from any quarter, in this trial of strength with her old adversary. In fact the Pope and the allies declared themselves satisfied with Florence in consequence of the execution of Savonarola, and demanded no other concessions ; while the friendship which she had always kept up with France seemed sufficient to curb the other Italian potentates. It is true that Louis XII., on his accession to the French throne, had likewise assumed the titles of King of Jerusalem and Sicily, and Duke of Milan ; thus in addition to the old pretensions upon Naples, also asserting those which he boasted over Lombardy, in right of descent from his grandmother, Valentina Visconti ; it is true that this was prophetic of fresh troubles to Italy, and had indeed already spread general consternation in Milan and Naples ; but on the other hand all this procured the Florentines the friendship and secret assistance of the Moor, and encouraged their hopes. Still the Venetians continued openly to favour the Pisans ; the Lucchese, being weaker, limited themselves to giving secret help, and Pisa, with stern resolve and marvellous energy, was always upon the defensive. Not only did all the Pisan citizens carry arms, but even the inhabitants of the out-lying territory were rendered practised

combatants by the continually occurring skirmishes. Venice had sent them 300 Stradiote or Albanian cavalry, lightly armed and very effective in raids and skirmishes ; while a small number of French had remained in Pisa ever since the expedition of Charles VIII., and helped to defend the walls. It must also be noted that of late, in consequence of internal dissensions, the Florentines had greatly neglected military matters, and their Captain General Count Rinuccio da Marciano, together with their commissary Guglielmo dei Pazzi, had suffered so disastrous a defeat in an encounter of some importance, that they had barely escaped with life.[1] And this was the moment chosen by Venice to threaten an advance into the Casentino, in order to divert the besieging army in that direction. Fresh and more energetic measures were therefore pressingly required.

First of all urgent letters were sent to the French king, begging him to prevent his allies, the Venetians, from marching on the Casentino ; a considerable loan of money was asked and obtained from the Moor ; it was decided to recall from France, with the king's consent, Paolo and Vitellozzo Vitelli, and to Paolo, who had great military renown, the chief command of the army was offered.[2] His arrival in Florence, in the beginning of June, 1498, was the signal for a solemn festival. There was an assemblage of the people and of the magistrates of the Republic in front of the palace ; Marcello Virgilio read a Latin oration,[3] in which, lauding the prowess and excellences of the new Captain, then present, he compared them to those of the greatest men of antiquity. And while this was going on, the astrologer, whom Vitelli had brought with him, remained with those of the Signoria in the palace courtyard, taking observations and "awaiting the arrival of the fortunate moment." No sooner was the signal agreed upon made, than trumpets sounded, the oration was interrupted, and the Gonfalonier hastened to present the baton of command,

---

[1] Nardi, "Storia di Firenze," vol. i. p. 174.

[2] Nardi says that the engagement of Paolo and Vitellozzo, advised by the Moor, was made in agreement with the King of France, and at the joint expense of the said monarch and the Florentine people. "Storia di Firenze," vol. i. p. 173.

[3] This Oration is in the Laurentian Library, Plut. lxxxx., ood. xxix.: "Oratio pro eligendo imperatore exercitus Paullo Vitellio, et dandis illi militaribus imperatoriis signis." In it the orator alludes to perils which he had recently incurred, perhaps in the Savonarola riots : "Scitis enim omnes quantis vitæ periculis his diebus iactatus sim, quantoque metu coactus sim fugere presentem ubique mortem, quam nescius ipse mecum forte trahebam."

with wishes for success in the field. After which all went to hear mass in the cathedral, and on the 6th of June, 1498, the celebrated captain set out for the camp. Then the Ten began to push on the war with great activity, and made use of Machiavelli's services in numerous important affairs.

It is almost incredible what an immense amount of trouble, vexation, and danger this miniature war brought upon the Republic. First of all, the jealousy between the old captain and the new, made it necessary to give Count Rinuccio the same pay as Vitelli, and to allow him to retain the title of governor, while the new captain was entrusted with the chief direction of the war. The campaign began prosperously enough with the capture of several places, then news came of the Venetians being already on the march towards the Casentino. It was necessary, therefore, to hire fresh troops and new leaders, and to slacken the war in the Pisan territory, in order to bring a larger force against the Venetians, who, in September, passed the Val di Lamone, and captured Marradi. Here, however, they were checked by the Florentine troops, commanded by Count Rinuccio, and strengthened by a reinforcement from Duke Lodovico. Before these they retreated, but then marched towards the Casentino, taking the Abbey of Camaldoli on the way; after which they crossed Monte Alvernia, and took Bibbiena by surprise. These events compelled the Florentines to suspend altogether the war with Pisa, and, leaving a small force to defend the more important places in that territory, to despatch Vitelli with the whole army against the new enemy. In the meantime, Don Basilio, the Abbot of Camaldoli, was scouring the country, raising the peasantry of the mountain districts, with which he was so well acquainted, and by this means succeeded in arresting the march of the Venetians, and harassed them severely.[1] At this juncture the Duke of Urbino, who commanded in the enemies' camp, chancing to fall ill, asked a safe conduct from Vitelli for himself and his troops, which was immediately granted to him. This roused the anger and suspicions of the Florentines, especially when they learnt at the same time that their general had been speaking in public with Piero and Giuliano dei Medici, who were following the hostile army.

---

[1] Speaking of this Don Basilio, Abbot of San Felice in Piazza, and afterwards Vicar General of Camaldoli, Machiavelli says in his "Historical Fragments": "Cuius fuit summa manus in bello, et amor et fides in patriam" ("Opere," vol. ii. p. 366).

Winter had now set in, and although neither side was willing to retire, it was becoming difficult to carry on the war among the mountains, when Duke Ercole of Ferrara offered to arrange a peace between Florence, Pisa, and Venice. His arbitration being accepted, he pronounced his verdict at the beginning of 1499. By the 24th April the Venetians were to withdraw from the Casentino, and from Pisan territory; the Florentines were to pay them the sum of 100,000 ducats within twelve years; the Pisans, while remaining masters of their fortress, and preserving their trade rights, were again to be subject to Florence. All parties were dissatisfied with these terms; yet the Florentines accepted them, and the Venetians withdrew their troops, but the Pisans, on the other hand, made preparations for war with greater fury than ever.[1] The secret of all this was, that new and startling events were expected elsewhere, Louis XII. having pledged himself to the Pope and Venetians that he would come to Italy to attack the Moor. Every one therefore withdrew his troops from Tuscany, and Florence and Pisa were at last left to face each other alone.

During these events Machiavelli had had a great deal to do, for all the work of the Chancery of the Ten was transacted by him. He wrote an immense number of letters, despatched orders, forwarded money and arms, and sometimes had to go to confer in person with the captains. Thus on the 24th of March, 1499, he was sent to Pontedera on a mission to Jacopo IV. of Appiano, lord of Piombino, who being in the service of the Republic, demanded a larger number of men, and pay equal to that received by Count Rinuccio. He succeeded in persuading him to be content with increased forces;[2] but the other captains were more pertinacious, and there was no end to their claims and complaints. Paolo Vitelli, disliking to be on an equality with Count Rinuccio,

---

[1] See the "Storie di Firenze" of Nardi and Guicciardini. Regarding the sum which the Florentines were to pay to the Venetians, Nardi tells us that it was 100,000 ducats in twelve years, Guicciardini, 150,000 in fifteen years. There is a break in Buonaccorsi's Diary at this point, and the original manuscript in the Riccardiana Library contains a note stating that the author had to interrupt his work, owing to a six months' absence from Florence. We may observe that that is in itself sufficient to disprove the opinion of some who wished to attribute the Diary to Machiavelli, who certainly was not absent for six months at that period. But of this more will be said later.

[2] The letter of the Ten giving the commission to Machiavelli in date of the 24th March, 1498 (Florentine style), is to be found among the "Legazioni," and in the published "Opere," is generally preceded, erroneously, by another of November, 1498, delegating not Niccolò Machiavelli, but Niccolò Mannelli.

demanded and obtained increased pay, and this instantly aroused
the jealousy of the Count, who in his turn began to make complaints. All these things had augmented the expenses of the war,
and consequently the taxes, to such an extent, that the latter
had become unbearable. The books of the decrees issued by the
Republic during these years exhibit nothing but a series of new
and ingenious contrivances for extorting money from the citizens.
The popular discontent was increased on seeing that the Ten, for
that reason nick-named the "ten expenders," had squandered
large sums, not merely from carelessness, but in granting unlawful
favours to personal friends, giving them useless commissions and
commanderships ;[1] and there was a threatening of almost open
rebellion. Thus when in May the time came for the new
elections, there was a popular cry of—Down with the Ten and
the taxes (*nè Dieci nè danari non fanno pei nostri pari*), and the
people unanimously refrained from voting.[2] The Signoria there-

---

[1] According to the Reform of the 2nd December, 1494, the Ten were to hold
office for six months (Florentine Archives, " Provvisioni, reg. 186, sheet 4). By
the decision of the Council of Eighty (11th May, 1495) the elections were to be
made in the Great Council.

By the Reform of the 27th of April, 1496 (" Provvisioni," reg. 188, sheet 16 and
fol.), it was decided that " both general and special Commissioners throughout the
dominions were to be elected by the Council of Eighty at the instance of the Ten
who were to give ten names to be balloted for." The Ten, however, had the power
of extending the term of office of those elected, to six months. Also, in emergencies, they had the right of sending a commissioner to the camp for fifteen days
upon their own authority, and afterwards proceed to a regular election, which confirmed the powers of the delegate of the Ten. This was the origin of many abuses,
since, to oblige friends, they appointed commissioners *d'urgenza*, when no urgency
existed, they kept them on from fortnight to fortnight, and finally sought to have
them elected. Besides nominations of " commissarii e rettori dei luoghi," the Ten
engaged the military leaders, and had the control of the war expenses ; all things
which opened the door to many abuses.

[2] See Guicciardini's " Storia Fiorentina," p. 202 and fol., and Nardi's *op. cit.*, vol.
i. pp. 189-91. This latter writer at p. 184, in speaking of the straits to which
the Republic was reduced, mentions a certain Lorenzo Catucci, who offered a free
gift of a thousand florins and a loan of five thousand for five years, on condition
" of having the *benefit* (*beneficio*) of the state for the lesser trades." His offer was
refused, but on the day on which the *beneficio* could be legally granted, Catucci's
name was put to the vote by the major trades, and he thus obtained gratis more than
that which he had asked in return for his money. This shows us that some
Republican virtues still remained in Florence at this date.

A measure of the 31st May 1499 (Florentine Archives, " Consigli Maggiori,
Provvisioni," reg. 191, a. c. 10) established new rules for the election of magistrates,
since it often being necessary at that time to call repeated meetings of the Great
Council, in order to obtain the legal majority of votes, many wearied of it all and

fore had to condescend to assume the direction of the war, with the aid of certain of the more influential citizens. The accusations brought against the Ten had no reference either direct or indirect to Machiavelli, their secretary, who indeed had already gained considerable authority and renown. The second Chancery of which he was at the head, was now attached to the Signoria as well as the first ; but this made little or no change in his position, and only brought him some additional occupation.

On the 12th of July, 1499, he received his first important commission, being sent with a despatch from the Signory, signed by Marcello Virgilio, to Caterina Sforza, Countess of Imola and Forlì. The friendship of this small State was carefully cultivated by the Republic, for not only was it situated on the high road from Upper to Lower Italy, but also on that leading into Tuscany by the Val di Lamone. From this side the Venetians had advanced, from this side the Duke of Valentinois had made threatening demonstrations. That part of the country too was warlike, and furnished mercenaries to all who asked them of the Countess, who made almost a trade of it. Her first-born son, Ottaviano Riario, though a mere youth, was always ready to earn money by taking a command (*condotta*). In 1498, he had obtained one worth fifteen thousand ducats, from the Florentines, who were anxious to keep upon friendly terms with his mother. His engagement was to expire at the end of June, but might be renewed at the pleasure of the Signori for another year. But at the end of the first period Riario was very discontented. He said that the Florentines had not observed their part of the bargain, and that he objected to renew it. The Countess, however, being a much more prudent person, seeing that the Florentines desired her friendship, and knowing that Valentinois still had designs upon Romagna, showed herself disposed to ratify the *beneplacito*, adding that her uncle the Moor had sent her a request for men-at-arms, and that she would therefore be glad of a speedy reply in order to know what she should do. For this reason Machiavelli was sent as Envoy to her Court.

The Countess Caterina was an extraordinary woman, and quite

left off attending the meetings. It was therefore decided that all names obtaining the half of the beans and one extra, should be entitled to be put to the ballot. As regarded the Ten, however, all decisions were suspended until the Eighty should declare, by a majority of two-thirds of the votes, whether they desired that magistrature to be continued or not.

CATERINA SFORZA, WIDOW OF COUNT GIROLAMO RIARIO.
(*From a medal attributed to Nicolo Florentino*)

capable of holding her own against the secretary. Born in 1462, an illegitimate daughter of Galeazzo Maria Sforza,[1] by Lucrezia, wife of a certain Sandriani of Milan, she was a woman of handsome, regular features, of great bodily strength, and of more than masculine intellect. She had gone through many and singular adventures. At a very early age she was married to the dissolute son of Sixtus IV., Girolamo Riario, who, owing to the violent tyranny of his rule, was in continual danger of assassination by conspirators. In 1487 when far advanced in pregnancy, she was nursing her husband in an illness at Imola, when news arrived that the Castle of Forlì had been seized by Codronchi, master of the palace, who had murdered the governor. Whereupon Caterina started the same night, entered the castle, and leaving Tommaso Feo in charge of it, brought Codronchi back with her to Imola, where she gave birth to a child on the following day. On the 14th of April, 1848, a conspiracy broke out in Forlì, Girolamo Riario was stabbed, and she, left a widow at the age of twenty-six, and with six children, found herself a prisoner in the hands of the Orsi, ringleaders of the revolt. But not even then did her courage fail her. The castle still held out for her, and she was allowed to enter it, in the hope that she would order its surrender to the people, in whose hands she had left her children as hostages. But she had already sent messengers to ask for aid from Milan, and now that she was in safety, she prepared to defend the castle until succour should arrive. To those who sought to subdue her, by threatening the murder of her children, she replied that she was able to give birth to more. The city was recaptured, and the rebellion put down with bloodshed. Afterwards the faithful Castellan who had saved her life, was suddenly disarmed and dismissed, and his post given to his brother, Giacomo Feo, a handsome youth whom the Countess soon married.

This second husband also died by assassination in 1495, while driving home with the Countess from the chase. She instantly mounted a horse and galloped into Forlì, where she took a sanguinary revenge. Forty persons were put to death, and fifty imprisoned or otherwise persecuted. Yet it was asserted by many that she herself had hired the assassins of her husband, and was

---

[1] It is an odd fact that Nardi, the contemporary and usually faithful historian (*op. cit.*, vol. i. p. 34), speaks of her as the sister of Lodovico, when she herself in her letters to the Florentines calls him *il nostro barba*, our Uncle.

now making his death a pretext for ridding herself of her enemies. She answered the accusation by saying, that thanks to the Lord, neither she, nor any other member of the Sforza house had ever found it necessary to make use of common assassins, when they wished to get rid of any man. In 1497 she married for the third time, and became the wife of Giovanni, son of Pier Francesco, one of the younger branch of the Medici, who had come to her Court as ambassador of the Florentine Republic.[1] On this occasion she was made citizen of Florence, partly because it was wished to flatter and keep on good terms with her ; partly because the old laws prohibiting the marriage of citizens, particularly of powerful citizens, with foreigners, had been revived since the intermarriage of the Medici with the Orsini of Rome had so greatly swelled the pride of that family. In the April of 1498 Caterina gave birth to another son, afterwards renowned as Giovanni delle Bande Nere, father to Cosimo, first Grand Duke of Tuscany ; and towards the end of the same year her third husband also breathed his last. She was therefore at thirty-six years of age, a widow for the third time, the mother of many children, absolute mistress of her little State, and noted as a woman of excellent prudence and courage, when Niccolò Machiavelli presented himself at her Court.[2]

The Florentines were disposed to confirm their *beneplacito* to Count Ottaviano, but not to grant him a command exceeding the value of ten thousand ducats, their only object being that of gaining the Countess's good-will. They also commissioned Machiavelli to purchase of her as much powder, saltpetre, and ammunition as she could spare, since perpetual supplies were needed for the camp before Pisa.[3] After a necessary halt at Castrocaro, whence he sent information to the Signory of the factions which divided that place, he reached Forlì on the 16th

[1] This Giovanni dei Medici (1467–98) was, as we have said, son of Pier Francesco, who was the son of Lorenzo, second brother of Cosimo, *pater patriæ*. As all know, the father of Cosimo and Lorenzo was Giovanni dei Medici, the real founder of the family. The elder branch, namely that directly descended from Cosimo, was extinguished in 1537 by the death of Alessandro, murdered by Lorenzino dei Medici. The Grand Dukes of Tuscany were descended from the second branch.

[2] See the " Vita di Caterina Sforza," by Abate Antonio Burriel, 3 vols. in 4to ; Bologna, 1795. See also, "A Decade of Italian Women," by T. A. Trollope ; London, 1859, 2 vols.

[3] See the " Istruzione " given to Machiavelli, decreed on the 12th of July, 1499, in vol. vi. p. 7, of the " Opere."

·day of July, and presented himself straightway to the Countess.
He found with her the agent of Lodovico, and in his presence set
forth the object of his mission, the intentions of his Republic,
and its desire to be on friendly terms with her. The Countess
listened to him with great attention, said that the words of the
Florentines "had always satisfied her, whereas their deeds had
always much displeased her,"[1] and that she must have time for
reflection.

She afterwards let him know that she had been offered better
terms by Milan, and then negotiations began. She had neither
powder nor ammunition for sale, not having sufficient for her own
needs. On the other hand she had an abundance of soldiers whom
she passed daily in review and sent on to Milan. Machiavelli, at
the instance of Marcello Virgilio, tried to obtain some of these to
send to Pisa, but could not come to terms with the Countess
·either for the price to be paid, or as to when he could have them.[2]
On the 22nd of July he thought that he had concluded the
bargain, having raised his offer to twelve thousand ducats ; yet
he added that he was not certain, because the Countess "had
always stood upon her dignity," so that he could never clearly
determine whether she inclined towards Florence or Milan. "I
see on the one hand," he wrote, "that the Court is crowded with
Florentines, who appear to manage all the concerns of the State ;
also, and what is still more important, the Countess beholds the
Duke of Milan attacked, without knowing whether she may rely
upon his aid or not ; but on the other hand the Moor's agent
seems to have authority, and foot soldiers are continually leaving
for Milan."

In fact, although by the 23rd of July everything appeared to
be concluded, and it was settled that the agreement should be
signed the following day, when Machiavelli presented himself to
ask for her signature, the Countess received him as usual in the
presence of the Milanese agent, and told him that, "having
thought the matter over in the night, it seemed to her better not
to fulfil the terms, unless the Florentines would pledge themselves

[1] Letter of the 17th of July, in the " Legazione a Caterina Sforza."

[2] The Florentines required them at once, " for the Captain begs, worries and
presses for them daily and hourly." Letter of the 18th of July, signed by Marcello
Virgilio. These and other letters from the same, which are however of little or
no importance, are in the National Library of Florence (" Carte del Machiavelli,"
case 11), and were published by Passerini, together with the " Legazione " to
Caterina Sforza of Forlì, in vol. iii. of the " Opere " (P. M.).

to defend her State. That although she had sent him a message of a different nature the previous day, he ought not to be surprised at the change, since the more things are talked over, the better they are understood."[1] But the Florentine Government had expressly told Machiavelli that it was decided not to undertake any such obligation, therefore there was nothing for him to do but return to Florence, which he accordingly did.[2]

The failure of this mission seems to show that the Countess was more cunning than Machiavelli, who allowed himself to be outwitted by a woman. Nor can that be very astonishing when we remember that Caterina Sforza was a woman of masculine intellect, long sole ruler of her State and of great business experience, whereas the Florentine secretary, notwithstanding his wonderful abilities, was only a man of letters making his first campaign in diplomacy. But at bottom the Florentines had no motive for discontent. Their real object was not the arrangement of the *condotta*, but rather that of winning the Countess's friendship without any expense ; and in this their success was complete, for the negotiations were not broken off, a confidential agent from Forlì being sent to continue them.[3] To Machiavelli himself the mission had been most useful, for his letters had been highly praised by all in the Palace. His ever-faithful friend and colleague, Biagio Buonaccorsi, a Republican admirer of Savonarola, of Benivieni, of Pico della Mirandola, wrote to him continually and kept him *au fait* of everything. He was a lover of learning, although but a mediocre writer, author of some poems and of a Diary which gives a very accurate account of Florentine events from 1498 to 1512. "In my opinion," he said in a letter of 19th of July, "you have acquitted yourself so far with much honour of the mission imposed upon you, in the which thing I have taken and am still taking great delight ; go on as you have begun, for hitherto you have done us much honour." He

---

[1] See the "Legazione" to Caterina Sforza, coming first in every edition. There are seven letters from Machiavelli. "Opere," vol. vi. pp. 11-31.

[2] For this mission Machiavelli received, in consequence of the decree of 31st of August, 1499, nineteen broad florins in gold, " to cover his expenses going, stopping and returning in nineteen days, counting from the 13th of July up to the 1st of the present month inclusive." This document is in the Florence Archives, "Signori, Stanziamenti del" 1499, sheet 11. It was published in the "Opere" (P. M.), vol. iii. p. 32, note 2.

[3] "The respectable Messrs. Joanni, my auditor." See the Countess's letter, dated 3rd of August 1499, in the "Opere," vol. vi. p. 31.

repeats the same in other letters, in one of which he asks for a portrait of the Countess, and begs that it may be forwarded " in a roll, to avoid its being spoiled by folding." And he also earnestly begs Machiavelli to return at once, because in his absence there was great disorder in the Chancery, and envy and jealousy were very rife ; wherefore " remaining away is not " good for you, and here there is a deluge of work such as never " was." [1]

---

[1] Three of the letters written by Buonaccorsi in July are to be found in the National Library of Florence, namely two dated the 19th, one the 27th, " Carte di Machiavelli," case 11, Nos. 1, 77, 78. Biagio Buonaccorsi was faithful to Machiavelli, even when the latter fell into misfortune, and was exposed to many attacks for the publication of the " Principe "; he was born in 1472, and married a niece of Marsilio Ficino, who was afterwards the friend of Machiavelli's wife. He was the author of several poems which still remain unpublished in the Florence libraries, and have not much literary merit. He also wrote the "Impresa fatta dai Signori Florentini l'anno 1500, con le genti Francesi, per espugnare la citta di Pisa, capitano Monsignor di Belmonte." This little work which is of slight literary value, but useful on account of its historical accuracy, was published by F. L. Polidori in the " Archivio Storico," vol. v. part 11. It consists of nineteen pages, to which Polidori added a preface of his own, giving many details regarding the author. During his life Buonaccorsi published nothing but a species of epistle dedicated to Girolamo Benivieni regarding Pico della Mirandola's commentary on Benivieni's own composition, " Canzone dell amor divino." See " Opere di Girolamo Benivieni " : Florence, Giunti, 1519. But Buonaccorsi's principal work is his " Diary " of events happening in Italy and especially in Florence, from 1498 to 1512, during which period Machiavelli and he were together in the second Chancery of the Republic, and quitted office at the same time, when the Government was changed. The " Diary " was published in Florence by Giunti in 1519 ; and though without much literary merit, has great historical importance, being based upon official letters. The style in which it is written forbids all comparison with the works of Machiavelli ; yet strange to say, it was frequently attributed to his pen.

Ammirato, in his " Famiglie nobili Italiane," at page 103, alludes to a *very small note book*, written by Machiavelli, " perhaps to put him in the way of the history which he never continued." And in the " Elogi di Uomini illustri Toscani " (Florence, 1766-73, vol. iv. p. 37) we find that a man of letters had discovered that the " Diary " was not by Buonaccorsi, but by Machiavelli, founding this theory on Ammirato's observation, and on the circumstance that the " Diary " begins almost at the point where the " Historical Fragments," the continuation of Machiavelli's " Histories," come to an end. Moreni, in his " Bibliografia della Toscana," repeated this assertion without disputing it. Yet it would have been easy to observe that Ammirato quotes a fragment of the *quadernuccio* alluded to, and this fragment is the description of Niccolò Valori, written by Machiavelli and published among his " Nature d' Uomini illustri fiorentini," which might have been comprised in a *quadernuccio* or quire, whereas the " Diary " is a volume of respectable bulk. Thus the strange assertion might easily have been refuted. All the old MSS. of the " Diary " bear Buonaccorsi's name, the auto-

Before setting out on his mission to Forlì, Machiavelli was en
gaged, as we have already noted, in penning letters to calm the
jealousies of the captains using every argument to inspire them with
a love for the Republic which none of them felt, and induce them
to prosecute the war on good terms with one other. Vitelli had
made a proposal to attack Cascina, and this being agreed to, he
took it by assault on the 26th of June, thereby raising the spirits
and hopes of the Florentines, who immediately conceived a high
opinion of his valour. But from that moment everything came
to a standstill, while all expenses increased enormously, so that
Machiavelli, on his return from Forlì, found the Signory in con-
sternation, the people irritated, and the captains demanding
remittances which were not to be had. Early in August he had
letters despatched to them in the name of the Signory, stating
that there were the greatest difficulties in the way of getting the
Councils to vote funds for fresh expenditure ; and that if matters
went on long in this fashion "it would be impossible for half
Italy to furnish supplies for all this artillery."[1]

graph one preserved in the Riccardiana Library of Florence (codex 1920) also has
a note, as we before mentioned, recording the author's absence from Florence
during six months, when Machiavelli was almost always in the Chancery. Some
have tried to maintain that the handwriting of the autograph "Diary" might be
confounded with that of Machiavelli ; but comparisons of the two is sufficient to
disprove the assertion. Hence it were useless to dwell too long upon these
unfounded doubts.

It is necessary to mention that almost the whole of this "Diary" has been incorporated in the "Storia di Firenze" by Jacopo Nardi, who has, however, made
many corrections in the style.

[1] Florentine Archives, "Lettere dei Dicci di Balia," 1499, cl. x. dist. 3, No. 91.
According to the new arrangement of the archives, the same *filza* or file is labelled
Signori, missive, No 21. Both labels are preserved, in order to facilitate research.
The letter quoted above is of the 5th of August, and is to be found at sheet 64.

We now begin to avail ourselves of Machiavelli's official letters, of which a large
number still remain inedited in the Florence Archives. Of original letters only
there are more than 4100. Among them, however, are included the 264 published
by Canestrini in his volume, "Scritti Inediti" of Niccolò Machiavelli, and also
some of the legations. To these we shall refer later on.

These letters were written by Machiavelli himself in the minutes or protocols,
and then copied into the registers by the clerks of the Chancery. Naturally all
the minutes are not in his hand, but his autograph is easily distinguished. We
have not been able to find the minutes of the letters he wrote in August, but only
the register or the copies ; therefore the few letters we quote as having been
written by him in that month, are judged to be his on the strength of their style.
Of all the letters which we quote, dating from the 1st September, 1499, we have
seen the autograph originals, excepting when the contrary is stated.

And a little later he added "that having expended up to this date about 64,000 ducats for this expedition, everybody has been drained ; and to make up the present sum which we now send (2,000 ducats), every strong box has been emptied. . . ." If you do not act quickly, "we shall surely be stranded, for were other 6,000 ducats required, we should have to renounce all hope of victory." [1]

After this, however, came a moment of joyful encouragement : news arrived that the tower of Stampace had been captured and a wide breach effected in the walls of Pisa, so that hour by hour the Florentines expected to hear that their troops had entered the city. They learnt instead that on the 10th there had been a pitched battle ; that the Church of San Paolo had been reached, but that just when the whole army, and especially the youthful Florentines who had joined the camp as volunteers, were carrying all before them by their indomitable ardour, they were suddenly ordered to retreat. And Paolo Vitelli, seeing the unwillingness of the soldiers to obey, rushed among them with his brother Vitellozzo and drove them back with blows. [2]

This news raised to the highest pitch the indignation of the Florentines, and awakened grave suspicions of treachery on the part of Vitelli. All remembered the safe conduct granted by him in Casentino to the Duke of Urbino, at the time when he had also allowed himself to be seen in conversation with Piero and Giuliano dei Medici. Shortly before the capture of Cascina he had taken a certain Ranieri della Sassetta prisoner, who, after having been in the pay of the Florentines, had gone over to the Pisans, and taken part in numberless intrigues against the Republic. The Signory had ordered that he should be instantly sent to Florence for trial, but Vitelli allowed him to escape, saying that "he would not become the jailor of a valiant and worthy soldier." [3] And now he checked his army exactly when victory was assured and Pisa itself on the point of being taken, saying that he was sure of getting it to surrender on conditions. All this was more than enough to make the Florentines lose patience. The Signory openly declared that they would no longer be "led in the dark ; " [4] and on the 20th of August Machiavelli was

---

[1] Letter on the 7th August, at sheet 68 of the before-quoted Register.

[2] Nardi, "Storia di Firenze," vol. i. p. 196 and fol.

[3] Guicciardini, "Storia Fiorentina," p. 204.

Letter of the 14th August, at sheet 74 of the Register before mentioned.

ordered to write as follows to the Commissaries at the camp :—
"We have granted the captain all that which he desired, yet we
behold" "all our trouble put to nought through his various
shufflings and deceit." ¹ For the which reason, had our laws
permitted of it, two of our number would have come in person
to try and discover the cause of this double dealing, "since it
appears that you either will not write to us of the matter or are
ignorant of it." ² But all was in vain. Fever was making great
havoc in the army, which daily diminished, whereas the Pisans
were receiving reinforcements. The two Commissaries were
seized with fever, and one of them died. In writing to the new
ones who quickly replaced them, Machiavelli said, in the name of
the Signory : "We should have preferred defeat to inaction at so
decisive a moment." "We neither know what to say, nor with
what reasons to excuse ourselves before all this people, who will
deem that we have fed them with lies, in holding out to them
day by day vain promises of certain victory." ³

Some decision had to be taken, and no money being available,
the only thing now to be done, after Vitelli's strange conduct and
the serious suspicions to which it had given rise, was to send him
immediate orders to break up the camp, leaving only a few of the
more important places in a state of defence. But even then all
went badly ; since, among other things, ten boats loaded with
ammunition and artillery were sunk in the Arno, and some of
these fell into the hands of the Pisans, who fished them up.⁴ But

---

¹ At this point, we find on the margin of the Register, the following note, in
the writing of the period : "Quantus moeror."

² We give in the Appendix this letter of the 20th August together with another
of the 15th, Documents ii. and iii.

³ This letter also of the 25th August is given in the Appendix, Document iv.

⁴ See in the "Scritti inediti di Niccolò Machiavelli," illustrated by G.
Canestrini (Florence, Barbéra, Bianchi & Co., 1857), the letters dated the 8th,
10th, and 13th September, and that of the 27th October, 1499, at pp. 81, 82, 85,
and 118.

In this volume Canestrini has reprinted the letters written by Machiavelli, when
he had the ordering of the militia in Florence, and which he had already published
in the "Archivio Storico." He has also added many other inedited letters. They
are 264 in all, and all treat of the affairs of the Republic. Excepting those concerning the militia, they may be said to be chosen haphazard, without a purpose,
without any proper chronological arrangement or distribution of subjects. He
jumps from one letter to another, leaves out portions longer than those which he
gives, without assigning any reason, and even without warning the reader. Evidently, too, he was ignorant of the greater part of Machiavelli's official letters,
since he publishes many of no value and leaves out a large number of those of
importance.

Vitelli could not extricate himself from the consequences of this affair. Besides what had already occurred, and when every one in Florence believed him to be a traitor, a rumour was also spread that, in the flight of Lodovico from Milan, papers had fallen into the hands of the French, proving beyond doubt that he (Vitelli) had made secret arrangements for prolonging the war.[1] Braccio Martelli and Antonio Canigiani had already been despatched as war commissioners, apparently for the purpose of furnishing the necessary funds for breaking up the camp, but in reality to seize the persons of Paolo and Vitellozzo Vitelli, the latter of whom had made an attempt to escape, by asking for a leave of absence, that was refused him.

Letters written by Machiavelli at this period show that the secret of the business was in his hands, and that, convinced of Vitelli's bad faith and treachery, he laboured with exceeding zeal and ardour to achieve the desired object. On the 27th of September the *dénouement* of the drama was close at hand, and he urged the commissioners to proceed with energy against "rebels and enemies of the Republic," since it was a question of saving the Florentine honour, and also of showing France that Florence had the courage to provide for her own safety, and claimed equal respect with all other Italian potentates. In conclusion, he recommended that to vigorous action should be joined so much circumspection and prudence, "that you may not be misled, by over-zeal or over-caution, to accelerate matters more than is necessary on the one hand, or more than opportunity permits on the other." [2]

The two commissaries fulfilled their orders with prudence. Vitelli was quartered about a mile beyond Cascina, to which place the field artillery was being withdrawn. They invited him to come thither on the 28th under colour of wishing to consult with him on the conduct of the war ; but, after dining together, they led him into a secret chamber, and kept him confined there. At the same time they had sent in search of Vitellozzo, who was ill in bed ; he, however, suspecting a trap, asked for time to dress himself, and contrived to make his escape towards Pisa.[3] Paolo,

[1] Nardi, "Storia di Firenze," vol. i. pp. 199, 200.

[2] "Scritti Inediti," as before at p. 95. See also the letter of the 29th September at p. 96, and those following on the same subject.

[3] Nardi, "Storie di Firenze," vol. i. pp. 201 and 202. That same day, the 28th September, Paolo Vitelli wrote from Cascina, after being made a prisoner, a letter to a certain Cerbone da Castello, which is to be found among the "Carte de

being conveyed to Florence, was examined on the last day of September, and, although he had confessed to nothing, was beheaded within four-and-twenty hours. This event made much noise both in the city and abroad, Vitelli being a renowned leader, and one who also enjoyed the friendship of France. Guicciardini considers that he was innocent of treachery, attributing his inexplicable conduct to the nature and habits of mercenary captains ; Nardi, on the contrary, declares that he was guilty and well deserved his fate ; Buonaccorsi, who was in the Chancery, relates the matter without comment, concluding with these words : " and this was the end of Pagolo Vitegli, a very excellent man." As to Machiavelli, although he had no opportunity of mentioning the affair in his " Storie " or in the " Frammenti," which do not go beyond the middle of '99, yet his opinion is manifested in the " Decennali," [1] by the letters which he wrote, and the ardour he displayed in the conduct of the affair.

We do not know that any decisive proof of Vitelli's treason was discovered at the time, but from the deliberations of the Venetian Council of Ten, it is clearly shown that Vitelli was really a traitor ; that he had promised to reinstate Piero dei Medici in Florence ; and that negotiations to that effect had gone so far that the Venetians had promised to reward him with a Condotta of the value of forty thousand ducats, or of an even larger sum, should he insist upon it.[2] At any rate, it was known to the Florentines that Vitelli did not intend to conquer Pisa before seeing the result of the war between the French and Lodovico the Moor, with whom the Republic had never come to an open rupture.[3]

Machiavelli," case II, No. 75. Nardi in fact tells us (*op. cit.*, vol. i. p. 204) that this Cerbone was seized and questioned, and that letters and papers concerning Vitelli were found on his person.

[1] " Opere," vol. v. p. 364.

[2] Archivio dei Frari, " Misti," c. x. vol. n 275, carte 213t. Herr M. Brosch was the first to call attention to these documents in the pages of Sybil's " Historische Zeitschrift."

[3] From the information sent by Machiavelli between April and July, 1499, to Francesco Tosinghi, commissary at the camp before Pisa, it is very clear that the Florentines pressed on the one side by the French, on the other by the Moor, would not declare themselves openly, " and temporizing with one party and the other, were making a benefit of delay." See the " Opere," vol. viii. letter v., in date of the 6th July, 1499, and the two preceding. In the letter of the 27th September, edited by Canestrini, and quoted by us above, the Florentines, while urging the immediate seizure of Vitelli, said that they desired to act with severity, to make it

The victory of the French being assured, it seems that he had changed his mind and decided,[1] so at least Nardi tells us—to do his part in earnest ; but he had then lost his reputation, and it was too late.[2]

Another proof, were any necessary, of the prominent part taken by Machiavelli in all affairs relating to the war, and of the esteem in which his labours were held, is to be found in his short " Discorso fatto al Magistrato de' Dieci sopra le cose di Pisa," which, though undated, bears internal evidence of having been written in this year.[3] It was one of the many compositions

understood, "especially by His Most Christian Majèsty, that they knew how to take care of themselves, and meant to be respected." This serves to confirm the suspicion that Vitelli, as a friend of France, was dragging out the campaign in order to wait for the result of the war in Lombardy.

[1] Nardi, " Storia di Firenze," vol. i. p. 210.

[2] Many were the reports spread about this Vitelli affair. Signor Nitti (*op. cit.* vol. i. pp. 67 and fol.) publishes a letter found among the " Carte del Machiavelli " (case 1, No. 49) without address, date or signature, which likewise mentions these reports, and this he gives as a letter by Machiavelli, on account of the hand-writing ; but the hand is certainly not that of Machiavelli, nor does the style appear to be his. For greater certainty, we have also submitted the manuscript to the examination of competent friends.

In the June of 1501, a certain Piero Gambacorti, who had been in the service of the Pisans, was seized and questioned. An account of his trial, written in Machiavelli's own hand, exists in the Florentine Archives. Being interrogated as to the affair of Stampace, he said that the Pisans thought that all was lost : "all abandoned the idea of resistance, and throughout Saturday and half Sunday Pisa was yours." He had gone away thinking the town was lost ; many soldiers and constables prepared to depart ; " but seeing that your troops did not follow up their victory, they returned to the bastions and the wall." Being asked if he considered that Paolo Vitelli was a traitor, he replied that, without being positive of his treachery, he could affirm that for a day and a half Pisa was in his hands. That he had said as much to Vitellozzo at Faenza, who had answered that, at that time they were ignorant to what condition the Pisans were reduced ; that they thought to have done enough in taking Stampace, and that they meant to fortify in order to take the city afterwards ; also that it was Paolo's nature " to spare his men, and avoid exposing them to peril." This almost insignificant trial was published by Passerini in the " Opere " (P. M.), vol. iii. p. 78. We certainly should not give it a place in the " Opere " of Machiavelli, since little or nothing of his could be in it, besides, it is well to remember, that owing to the duties of his office, and to collect necessary materials for his " Storie," he copied and preserved many writings which were not his own.

[3] " Opere," vol. ii. p. 380. As to the year in which this "Discorso" was written, some doubts may arise from its being addressed to the Dieci, who in 1499 were not elected. Yet, on reading it, it is very difficult to assign it to another year, since it alludes to the *recent example* of the Venetians who had abandoned the Pisans, who indeed found themselves "not accepted by Milan, and repulsed by Genoa." Now, the Venetian event happened at the end of 1498, and towards the

which his office made it necessary for him to write, and in it, after proving by a series of just arguments the folly of hoping to reduce Pisa otherwise than by force, he gives details of the various opinions expressed by the captains about the method of dividing the Florentine troops into two or three camps, and the war operations that were proposed. He narrated and expounded these opinions and proposals with an exactness and precision clearly proving that, even at that period, his intellect and his studies were not only dedicated to State affairs, but likewise to military matters. Or, to put it more plainly still, it is evident that he already recognized that a knowledge of the art of war was an essential element of statesmanship.

end of 1499 the French had already entered Milan. Still the title may have been written at a latter date, and may not have been written by Machiavelli. Besides which, although the Ten were not elected in 1499, their office was not suppressed, their Chancery remained, carried on the affairs of the war, and the series of their protocols and registers went on as before.

CHAPTER III.

Louis XII. in Italy—Defeat and imprisonment of the Moor—Niccolò Machiavelli at the camp before Pisa—First embassy to France.

(1499-1500.)

NE of the Florentines' special reasons for the hurried trial of Vitelli, was their fear lest the new and important successes of the French in Lombardy should prevent the execution of the sentence. These events, in fact, caused no slight changes in the affairs of Tuscany, and therefore it is necessary to speak of them.

After the battle of Fornuovo, Lodovico seemed actually to have realized his old desire of holding complete sway over Italian affairs. In the streets of Florence, people sang :

> " Cristo in cielo e il Moro in terra
> Solo sa il fine di questa guerra." [1]

He himself had caused a silver medal to be coined, with a vessel of water on the obverse, and fire on the reverse, symbolic of his power as master of peace and war. Also, upon one of the inner walls of his palace, he had had the map of Italy painted with a number of cocks, hens, and chickens and a Moor, broom in hand, sweeping them all away. When, however, he asked the Florentine Ambassador, Francesco Gualterotti, for his opinion of the picture, the latter replied that it was a pretty fancy, but that it

[1] Which may be rendered in English doggerel :

> " The Lord above and the Moor below
> Alone can tell how the war will go."

appeared to him that the Moor, in trying to sweep the cocks out of Italy, was being smothered by the dust ; [1] and such was in reality the case.

Louis XII., who had always claimed a right to the Duchy of Milan, no sooner ascended the throne of France, than he began to provide for the internal security of the State. He reduced the taxes ; arranged the administration of justice, and nominated as chief minister, Georges d' Amboise, archbishop of Rouen. He respected the constituted authorities, and took no deliberations without their advice ; he maintained the independence of the courts of justice ; he encouraged Gallican liberties ; he was economical. When, by means of these wise provisions, he had assured the order of the State, and gained much favour with his people, he turned his attention to the Italian war, which was no longer unpopular in France, by reason of the increased confidence in the sovereign, and the general desire to revenge past humiliations. On the 9th of February, 1499, Louis concluded with the Venetians a treaty offensive and defensive for the conquest of the Duchy of Milan, pledging himself to yield a portion of it to them. Thus the Moor found himself between two fires, with no one to look to for help ; since the Florentines had always been the friends of France, and the Pope, after the promises of aid to the Valentinois, also gave his approval. The French army, under the command of the Milanese G. G. Trivulzio—who, since the battle of Fornuovo, had become very famous—of other captains of renown, and strengthened by a large body of Swiss, advanced with singular rapidity. Some of Lodovico's captains were treacherous, others incapable, and the people rose against him ; so that he had to arrange for his flight before he had recovered from his first reverses. He first sent away his two sons in the care of his brother, Cardinal Ascanio, to whom he entrusted the sum of 240,000 ducats. On the 2nd of September he followed them himself into Germany.

On the 11th of that month the French army marched into Milan, where, shortly afterwards, Louis XII. made his solemn entry. When the ambassadors of the different Italian States presented themselves before him, those of Florence were the most favourably received, for, notwithstanding some occasional vacillation, that Republic had ever remained faithful to France alike in prosperity and ill fortune.

[1] Nardi, "Storia di Firenze," vol. i. pp. 209, 210.

The Florentines, nevertheless, had many reasons for discontent with the French captains who had remained behind in Tuscany, to whom they attributed the resistance of the Pisans, and, in part, the unfortunate result of the siege that had just compelled them to raise the camp and put to death Paolo Vitelli. But, instead of venting their anger in useless complaints, they concluded a fresh treaty with the king in Milan (19th October, 1499). By this he was bound to assist them by every means in the conquest of Pisa ; they, on their side,. were to be prepared to send 400 men-at-arms and 3,000 foot-soldiers to Milan, and were to aid the Neapolitan expedition with 500 men-at-arms and 50,000 crowns. The surrender of Pisa was to take place before the French went to Naples, and the Florentines meanwhile were to restore to the king the sums of money lent them by the Moor, according to an estimate to be made by G. G. Trivulzio, after examination of the papers found at Milan.[1] And likewise they were to take into their pay the Prefect Giovanni della Rovere, brother of the Cardinal of San Piero in Vincoli, whom the French wished to oblige.[2]

All these proceedings were suspended by new events. The French, and more especially their general Trivulzio, who had been made governor of Milan, had so greatly excited the discontent of the people, that when the Moor presented himself at the head of 8,000 recently-hired Swiss, and 500 men-at-arms, he was joyfully received by the very men, who, a short time before, had expelled him, and on the 5th of February he re-entered Milan. Trivulzio had already quitted the city, but leaving a strong body of men to guard the fortress ; he stationed 400 more at Novara, and then advanced towards Mortara, where he stayed to wait for reinforcements, while many even of his Swiss deserted to the Moor, who gave higher pay. However, in April, 10,000 Swiss mercenaries, under the command of La Trémouille, marched into Italy to assist the French expedition. The hostile armies were already facing each other in order of battle, when Lodovico's Swiss troops declared that, having been hired as individuals they could not fight

---

[1] In the Florence Archives are certain letters sending Niccolò Machiavelli to Trivulzio, in order to fix these sums. But afterwards this idea was abandoned, the letters were not despatched, and he did not go.

[2] Molini, "Documenti di Storia Italiana," Firenze, 1836–37, vol. i. pp. 32–36. Desjardins gives a summary of the convention, extracted from the Florence Archives. See "Négociations," &c., vol. ii. p. 26, note 1.

against the Helvetian flag borne by their compatriots whom Louis XII. had taken into his employ by special agreement with the Confederation itself. Thus they betrayed him in presence of the enemy, and, under various pretexts, demanded their arrears of pay upon the spot, without even waiting till he could receive Italian reinforcements. All that the wretched duke could obtain from them was permission to hide himself in their ranks, disguised as a monk. But, whether by his own fear, or some fresh treachery of the soldiers, he was recognized and taken prisoner on the 10th of April, 1500. The same fate befell several of his captains, and his brother Ascanio, who, having fled from Milan, was betrayed by a friend to the Venetians, who in their turn gave him up to the French. Thus, as Gualterotti had prophesied, the Moor was indeed "smothered by his own sweepings," and his fortunate career was for ever at an end. When brought into Lyons as a prisoner, so great a multitude thronged to gaze upon him, that force was required for his protection. Confined in the Castle of Loches in Touraine, he died there after ten years of severe imprisonment. Cardinal Ascanio was placed in the tower of Bourges; but regained his liberty after a time.

The king, whose past experience had taught him caution, sent Georges d'Amboise—now a Cardinal—as governor to Milan, and Cardinal de Rouen was summoned into Italy. He, thinking it was "better to fine than to sack," condemned Milan to contribute 300,000 ducats towards the expenses of the war, and levied proportionate fines on the other cities, in this way exciting far less discontent than Trivulzio. After this he made his entry into the Lombard capital. The king soon followed, and was speedily joined by the Florentine Ambassador, Tommaso Soderini, who came to offer his congratulations, and to arrange about the number of soldiers to be sent to Pisa according to the terms already agreed upon. The number considered sufficient was 500 spearmen, 4,000 Swiss, and 2,000 Gascons, the former at the expense of the French, the others with the artillery and waggons to be paid for by the Florentines, at the rate of 24,000 ducats the month.[1] These terms were extremely onerous to the Republic, which had already assumed so many other obligations towards France; yet it submitted to everything in the hope that, with the

[1] Buonaccorsi ("Diario," p. 30) is very confused in fixing this sum, but we believe that we have interpreted him accurately; Nardi ("Storia di Firenze," vol. i. p. 223) copies Buonaccorsi's account word for word.

aid of a strong army, it might be able to bring the enterprise to a successful termination, at the cost of only two or three months' pay.

But now the Florentines were to gain cruel experience from their dealings with the French. The Cardinal de Rouen, who was at the head of all things, tried to keep up the French army at others' expense, and accordingly demanded that payment should commence in May, that is long before the troops were in Tuscany, and also that their return journey should be paid. And to this it was necessary to consent. It was only on the 22nd of June that the Swiss and Gascons set out from Piacenza with twenty-two falconets and six guns, commanded, at the request of the Florentines, by Beaumont, instead of by Ives d'Alègre, whom the king wished to appoint. This Beaumont, or Belmonte as he was called, was the only one of the French leaders left in Tuscany, who had kept faith. When governor of Leghorn, he had, according to the stipulated terms, given it up to the Florentines, who, for that reason, had confidence in him alone. The new Swiss and Gascon mercenaries advanced very slowly, fining and pillaging all the places upon the road, for their own benefit, or that of their king, although they had already received their pay. When the roll-call was counted at Piacenza, it was found that there were twelve hundred more than had been agreed for, and these extra troops also had to be paid.[1] The conduct of these people would be inexplicable, did we not know what mercenaries were in those days, and if we had not already stated that Cardinal de Rouen, in order to spare the purse of his economical sovereign, tried all means of extorting money both from friends and enemies. They halted at Bologna to levy a requisition upon Bentivoglio; in Lunigiana—to the entire disapproval of the Florentines—they despoiled Alberigo Malaspina of part of his own state, at the instigation of his brother Gabriello, to whom they surrendered it. They took Pietrasanta, but did not fulfil their contract of handing it over to the Florentines. Besides this, the riots, tumults, and threatening demonstrations got up by them, in order to obtain

---

[1] Buonaccorsi, in his " Diario," tells us that the number of the Swiss was fixed at 5,000, but that there were 2,000 more to whom it was necessary to give two months' pay. In the " Impresa contro Pisa, *ec* " (" Archivio Storico," vol. iv. part ii. p. 404), it is stated instead that 4,000 Swiss and 2,000 Gascons was the stipulated number ; but that, there being 1,200 more, it was necessary to give them a month's pay, in order to make them go back to their own country.

provisions, with which, however, they were never content, were something incredible.

The Republic had sent Giovanni Battista Bartolini as Commissary to the Camp, with orders to prepare everything, bu warned of the violent insolence of foreign troops, it also sent two special commissioners, Luca degli Albizzi and Giovan Battista Ridolfi, with Niccolò Machiavelli as their secretary. The mission entrusted to them was extremely arduous, for they had to accompany the army on the march, and satisfy the insatiable appetite of these famished hordes, who, at the end of a meal, were hungrier than at the beginning. Their route was to Pistoia and Pescia, and with brief despatches they kept the Signory informed of their movements. On the 18th of June they met the army at Camaiore, and accompanied it to Cascina where they arrived on the 23rd. Here threatening complaints were soon heard respecting a pretended scarcity of provisions, and especially of wine.[1] Giovan Battista Ridolfi, who had always been opposed to asking or accepting aid of the French, from whom no good was to be expected, hurried away from the camp at the first outbreak of disorder, with the pretext of laying before the Signory the true state of the matter and procuring speedy remedies. But Luca degli Albizzi, a man of almost foolhardy courage, remained behind with Machiavelli among the mutinous troops without once losing his presence of mind. To some one who advised him to lodge at a little distance from the camp, he replied—"He who is afraid may go back to Florence," [2] and marched on with the army.

[1] One of Albizzi's letters, written on the 24th of June, was dated : "*Ex terribilibus Gallorum castris*," which shows that then the disorder was very great. This letter, which has never been published, is in the Florence Archives, and like the greater part of those sent by the Commissioners, is in Machiavelli's handwriting. It is of little interest.

[2] Among the "Carte del Machiavelli" (case 1, No. 83) is a narrative of the events occurring at this time, written by Biagio Buonaccorsi and Agostino Vespucci, who were both in the Chancery, and compiled for the uses of their office. At one point Buonaccorsi states, that Albizzi was unwilling to allow Ridolfi to go, not wishing to remain alone in the camp, and on the margin we find this note in another hand, *Mentiris Blasi*. And when the writer says that Albizzi's presence of mind was shown in all his actions, the same hand has written on the margin, *Immo temerarie*. And Buonaccorsi, in his "Impresa contro Pisa," has rendered the amplest testimony of praise to Albizzi's well-known courage. We cannot agree with Passerini in attributing to Machiavelli the two marginal notes. Moved by that idea, he has published a fragment of the narrative in the 3rd volume of the "Opere" (P. M.).

When envoys from Pisa arrived, offering to give up the city to the French, provided they would hold it twenty-five or thirty days before surrendering it to the Florentines, Beaumont wished to accept ; but Albizzi refused in the name of the Signoria, saying, that in a month many changes might take place, and that now, being prepared for war, warlike means must be employed.[1]

At last on the 29th of June the army arrived before the walls of Pisa, numbering 8,000 men, who were still threatening mutiny because of the scarcity of provisions ; nevertheless they planted their tents at night, and placed their guns in position. Albizzi, who was always among them, did all that he could to see that everything necessary was furnished, and did not lose heart, although seeing very clearly that from one moment to another he might find himself in the greatest peril. "If it be possible to send us some bread, you will restore our soul to our body," wrote he on the 30th of June to the Commissary Bartolini, who was then in Cascina.[2] That same day they began to fire on the town, and continued firing till late in the afternoon, by which time some thirty yards of wall had been thrown down. This was the moment to give the assault and finish the affair, but it was then seen that the Pisans had dug a trench behind the wall, and thrown up works on the other side, from whence they returned the fire ; so that it was impossible to proceed further. And thus once more, at the very moment when the city seemed on the point of being taken, the enterprise ended in smoke. The besieging army lost courage, and began to retire again, rioting about the scarcity or bad quality of the rations ; and so great was the confusion in the ranks, that Beaumont informed Albizzi that he could no longer answer for the success of the campaign, and threw the blame of everything on the bad arrangements of the Florentines. And no protestations nor assurances sufficed to change his opinion.[3]

[1] At a later period Machiavelli in his "Discorsi sopra la prima Deca di Tito Livio" (bk. i. chap. xxxviii.), blamed this proceeding of the Florentines ; but this is not the place to turn our attention to that point. We will merely observe that in those that may be called his theoretical writings, he often quotes historical facts in his own way, and for some special reason or aim, as we shall see hereafter.

[2] This letter, to be mentioned hereafter, is in the Florence Archives.

[3] Buonaccorsi, "Diario," p. 32 and fol. See also the "Impresa contro Pisa," by the same, p. 413 and fol. Jacopo Nardi, who copies from the "Diario," adds that the French went so far as to hide the bread and wine, in order to have pretexts for complaint. Nardi, "Storia di Firenze," vol. i. p. 227.

On the 7th of July the Gascon soldiers deserted *en masse*, upon which Albizzi wrote to Bartolini that they were to be treated as enemies. And on the following day he wrote to the Signory, that the Swiss had forced their way into his room, clamouring for money and threatening to pay themselves with his blood. "The French appear frightened, they make excuses and calm themselves with cold water ; the Commander Beaumont himself has lost his head, but always insists upon having his pay. I have refrained hitherto from worrying your Excellences in vain ; but now it is absolutely necessary to decide what is to be done with these people and take measures accordingly. It might also be well to think whether it is desired that my life should be saved." "Let not your Excellences think that cowardice moves me in this, since by no means would I flee from any peril, that should be deemed indispensable by my city." [1]

Albizzi's presentiments were realized on the following day. Machiavelli, by whose pen the greater part of these letters were written, wrote from the camp in his own name, that towards three o'clock a hundred Swiss had presented themselves to demand money, and being unable to obtain it, had seized upon Albizzi as their prisoner.[2] They dragged him upon foot to the quarters of the Baily of Dijon, and from thence he wrote the same day to say that he was disputing for his life from hour to hour, in the midst of soldiery brandishing their halberds threateningly in his face. They also insisted that he should give pay to a company of about five hundred Swiss who had come from Rome, and to this most unreasonable request he had energetically refused to consent. But even in these critical moments he remained calm, and gave some useful advice in the same letter ; he could not, however, refrain from bitter complaints of having been abandoned "like a lost and rejected person. If with nought else, let God at least console me by death." [3] But he could not obtain his liberation

[1] This letter signed by Albizzi, and written in his own hand, is the first of those printed in the " Commissione in campo contro i Pisani." Machiavelli, " Opere," vol. vi. p. 32.

[2] Dated : *Ex castris apud Pisas, die nona julii, hora* 14, is the second of those that are printed, and is to be found with the others in the Florence Archives. It is addressed to the Signory ; and bears the inscription :

C{ito.
ito.
ito.

[3] This is the fourth of the published letters.

until he had signed a paper, with his personal security for the payment of 1,300 ducats to the Swiss who had come from Rome.[1] The army then dispersed, the men-at-arms being the last to depart. Thus, after heavy expenses and heavy sacrifices, the Florentines were left with a deserted camp, and with their enemies the Pisans more audacious than before.[2] New commissioners, however, Piero Vespucci and Francesco della Casa, were speedily sent to ascertain what it was possible to do, both as regarded the payment and gathering of fresh troops from the country round. The king wrote various letters, regretting what had happened, reproving the captains, threatening the soldiers, and promising to reduce Pisa at any price.[3] But these were empty words quite

[1] Historians differ slightly as to the exact sum. It is, however, fixed in a letter of the Signoria to Courçon. "Carte del Machiavelli," case i. *inserto* 83, p. 6.

[2] See Nardi's "Storia di Firenze," the "Diario," and Buonaccorsi's previously quoted "Impresa contro Pisa," &c.

[3] See the printed edition of the "Commissione." This, besides other documents, contains in all four letters. The first and fourth are by Albizzi, the second by Machiavelli, the third by Bartolini. Only that signed by Machiavelli is in his handwriting. Passerini and Milanesi in their new edition of the "Opere," reprint these letters only, and at p. 51, vol. iii. tell us that: "It is necessary to explain that we have not been able to fulfil our wish of enlarging this series, because the registers of the Signoria's correspondence, as well as of that of the Dieci, are both missing." So without adding to the Commissioner's letters they give other documents. But the Florence Archives contain many more unpublished letters of this commission in the file or *filza* marked: Class x. dist. 2, No. 44, or according to the new classification: *Signori, Carteggio, Responsive*, reg. 17. A few others are also to be found in the 3rd file of the Strozzi Papers in the Archives.

These inedited letters are of no importance, but many are in Machiavelli's handwriting, and signed first by Albizzi and Ridolfi, then, after the latter's departure, by the former alone. In his hand are those of the 10th June, from Pistoia; 11th June, from Pescia; 18th June, from Camaiore; 23rd June, from Cascina; 24th June, from near Cascina; 24th June, from Cascina; 27th June, from near Campi. Also in his hand and of some interest, are those of 26th June, near Campi: 29th June, *ex Gallorum castris ;* 30th June, from this camp (this is at sheet 159 of the 3rd file of the Strozzi Papers) ; 2nd July ; *ex Gallorum castris.* Of no importance whatever are the letters dated : 4th July, from the camp ; 6th July, from the camp (in this there is only a short portion written by Machiavelli) ; 7th July, from the camp (Strozzi Papers, 3rd file, sheet 160); from the camp without date (Strozzi Papers, 3rd file, sheet 161) ; 11th July, from Cascina (signed by the Commissioner Vespucci) ; 12th July, from Empoli (with a postscript in Machiavelli's hand). In the Archives there are also other letters belonging to this Commission, but not in Machiavelli's hand. We give none of these in the Appendix, not wishing to swell needlessly the number of the letters printed.

For this commissionership to the camp before Pisa, Machiavelli received six broad gold florins, " the which florins are bestowed upon you in remuneration for

unsupported by deeds. He merely sent Duplessis, lord of Courçon, styled by the Florentines *Carcon* or *Corco*, to inquire into
what had happened upon the spot, and to send in a Report.

But while this was going on, the Pisans made a sally from
behind their walls, captured Librafatta and soon after the *Ventura*
bastion, which had been constructed at so great an expense by
Vitelli. And in this manner they opened communications with
Lucca, whence they received continual reinforcements. Courçon,
it is true, offered more soldiers to the Florentines in the King's
name, saying that with their assistance, Florence might harass the
Pisans by constant skirmishes during the winter, and thus reduce
them with greater ease as soon as the spring set in. But the
Republic would have nothing more to do with either French or
Swiss, much to the irritation of the King, who, disgusted with the
result of the campaign, in which his troops had reaped nothing but
dishonour, tried to throw the entire blame upon the Florentines.
They had, he said, insisted on taking Beaumont as their captain
instead of Ives d'Alègre whom he had proposed, and likewise
had neglected to victual the army or to give it regular pay. But
the real reason of his disgust was his inability to any longer
saddle Florence with the maintenance of part of his army. Indeed
so heavy were his threats as well as his complaints, and so diligently did the enemies of the Republic blow upon the flame, that
it was thought necessary to send Messrs. Francesco della Casa and
Niccolò Machiavelli as envoys to the French Court, since having
both followed the camp, they were in a position to give exact
information to the King and contradict all unjust and calumnious
accusations, while, at the same time, they could announce the
speedy arrival of new ambassadors to make terms of agreement.[1]

Up to the year 1498, Niccolò Machiavelli had had little
experience of mankind or of the world ; his intellect had been
principally devoted to books, especially to the Latin authors and
the history of Rome. But during the two following years he had
gained much and rapid experience of real life and State affairs.
The Legation to Forlì had given him his first initiation in the

the fatigues which you supported, and the perils which you incurred." The document relating to the gift was published by Passerini, "Opere" (P. M.), vol. i.
p. lx.

[1] Buonaccorsi, "Diario" and "Impresa," &c. ; Nardi, "Storia de Firenze ;"
Guicciardini, "Storia d'Italia," Pisa, Capurro, vol. iii. book v. p. 11.

intrigues of diplomacy, the Vitelli affair and the engagement of the Swiss soldiery had inspired him with a contempt almost amounting to hatred for all mercenary troops. His father's death, which took place on the 19th of May, 1500, four years after that of his mother, and only a few months before the loss of a sister, made him as it were the head of his family—although he was not the eldest son—and increased his cares and responsibilities. His journey to France opened up a new field of observation, and enlarged his mental horizon, the more too, since, in consequence of the illness of his colleague, the whole weight of the unpretending, but not unimportant mission devolved upon him.[1]

On the 18th of July, 1500, the decision or decree was passed for sending Della Casa and Machiavelli to the King. Written instructions were supplied charging them to convince the monarch that all the disorders at the camp had been solely caused by the fault of his own troops, and to try to persuade him to reduce his unjust and exorbitant claims for sums of money, in anticipation of the conquest of Pisa. Their first efforts were to be made upon the Cardinal de Rouen, and they were carefully to avoid all injurious mention of his *protégé* the Captain Beaumont. "If, however," so wrote the Signory, "you should notice any disposition to listen to things to his prejudice, you may attack him with energy and accuse him of cowardice and corruption." [2]

Lorenzo Lenzi, already established for some time with Francesco Gualterotti, the Florentine ambassador in France,[3] re-

---

[1] On the first sheet of one of the Registers of the Ten (Florence Archives, "Lettere de' Dieci di Balia dal 1500 al 1501," class x. dist. 3, No. 93), is the following inscription :—"This book is of the Commune and relates to war matters infra dominium, scripto, for the second chancery, cuius caput est Nicolaus Machiavellus, qui hodie mittitur ad regem Francorum a dominatione Franciscus Della Casa ibidem, XVIII. Julii 1500, die Sabb," &c. In the same way when he was at the camp before Pisa, we find written at the head of another register : " Hic erunt literae de rebus bellicis scriptae per magnificum dominum Marcellum ad commissarios in castris quo tempore Nicolaus Maclavellus fuit apud commissarios." See vol. vi. of the " Opere," p. 32, note 1.

[2] See the commission and the instructions at the commencement of the legation, " Opere," vol. vi. pp. 48 and fol.

[3] The Florentines, after having sent three ambassadors in June, 1498, to congratulate the King upon his ascension to the throne, elected Francesco Gualterotti and Lorenzo Lenzi on the 18th of September, 1499. Salviati was also sent with them as far as Milan to congratulate the King upon his victory, and if the terms for the Pisan affair were not yet signed, to obtain the royal signature. The two ambassadors then went to France in the suite of the King, who left Milan on the 22nd of November, 1499. See Desjardins, " Négociations," &c.

peated almost the same advice. They were at liberty to speak ill of the Italians at the camp, but only " as by a slip of the tongue," could they be permitted to accuse the real criminals.[1] Therefore to avoid arousing the insolence of the French, it was necessary to steer cautiously between Scylla and Charybdis. And to these difficulties was added that of the very modest social[2] position of the two envoys, who were neither wealthy nor well paid. To Francesco della Casa a stipend of eight *lire* per day was assigned, and Machiavelli, having a post of inferior rank, only succeeded in obtaining an equal sum, after much difficulty and many complaints of incurring[3] enormous expenses no lighter than those of his colleague.[4] Even then he had to disburse a great deal more than he received. His forty ducats very speedily vanished, and he had to commission his brother to obtain seventy more for him on loan. Being compelled to follow the monarch from city to city, it was requisite to provide himself with servants and horses, and although on starting, the envoys had eighty florins each, they soon got through one hundred ducats, since it proved impossible to find decent board and lodging for less than a crown and a half a day, a larger sum than that which they received. Therefore both grumbled sorely,[5] especially Machiavelli, who was not rich, and yet had no talent for economy.

Meanwhile, the two envoys on reaching Lyons on the 28th of July, found that the King had already started. They caught him up at Nevers, and after having spoken with the Cardinal de Rouen, both were granted an audience on the 7th of August, in the presence of the Cardinal, of Rubertet, Trivulzio and others. A third of the Court consisted of Italians who were all very discontented and desirous that the French army should speedily cross

---

[1] Machiavelli, " Opere," vol. vi. p. 54.

[2] In this letter of the 30th of July, Machiavelli says, " We being men of no money and no credit.

[3] On the 27th of August, 1500, Totto writes to his brother Niccolò Machiavelli, that after a fortnight of continued efforts, the Signori had consented to equalize the salaries. He adds that he had spent eleven florins for him in the spring, and afterwards sent him fifty more. This letter is among the " Carte del Machiavelli," case 1, No. 8, and has been published by Nitti, in his work, " Machiavelli nella vita e nelle dottrine," vol. i. p. 89. The increase of stipend alluded to, only began from the 28th of August, as may be seen by the accounts in the archives (class xiii. dist. 6, No. 64, a. c. 90).

[4] Letter of the 12th of August, signed by Machiavelli only.

[5] See letters of the 29th of August and 3rd of September.

MEDAL OF POPE ALEXANDER VI.

(Reverse showing Castle of St. Angelo.)

the Alps again.[1] The facts having been related, no sooner was an attempt made to blame the French soldiery, than the King and his supporters "quickly changed the conversation."[2] All was to be laid to the charge of the Florentines. Louis XII., for the sake of his own dignity, wished to conclude the Pisan expedition, and therefore the necessary funds must be supplied. The reply of the orators was, that the resources of the Republic being exhausted, and the people displeased by recent events, it would be impossible to procure those funds. It might however be possible to obtain them at the end of the campaign, after the surrender of Pisa. But thereupon all cried aloud with one voice that this was a most unseemly proposal, for the King could not pay the expenses of the Florentines. And from day to day matters went on after the same fashion. Louis wished to send soldiers whom the Florentines refused to take ; he complained that the Swiss did not receive the amount fixed, and would not listen when it was replied that neither did they give the services promised. The Cardinal[3] irritably insisted on his view of the case,[4] and Courçon, who had just returned from Tuscany, so aggravated matters, that their aspect became threatening. "The French," wrote the two orators, "are blinded by their own power, and only think those who are armed or ready to give money worthy of their esteem. They see that these two qualities are wanting in you, so they look upon you as Sir Nihil, ascribing the impossibility to your disunion, and the dishonesty of their own army to your bad government. The ambassadors resident here have gone away, nor do we hear

[1] There is a description of the Royal Court in the second letter of the 12th of August.

[2] Letter of the 7th of August.

[3] It is evident from the letter of the 11th of August that the Cardinal de Rouen did not know Italian, for the two orators were obliged to translate an Italian letter into French for him. Neither did the King know Italian, but Rubertet spoke it.

[4] According to a letter of the Signory, dated 30th of July, 1500, addressed to Gualterotti and Lenzi, Courçon had only passed one evening in the camp, " so that we do not perceive how after so short a stay he can be able to satisfy his Majesty the King about the investigation of the causes and the authors of the disorders which had there occurred " ("Carte del Machiavelli," case 1, *inserto*, 83, No. 4). Passerini gives it in the "Opere" (P. M.), vol. iii. p. 111, as a letter of the Ten ; but the Ten had not as yet been re-nominated. It is also stated in this letter, that when the Florentines explained to Courçon their reasons for not believing themselves obliged to pay the Germans, he had answered that "it was brain-splitting work to try and reason with Germans." The Germans alluded to were the German Swiss.

that new ones are coming. Our degree and quality, on an unwelcome errand, do not suffice to bring sinking things to the surface.[1] The King therefore is highly displeased, always lamenting having had to pay the Swiss 38,000 francs, which according to the Convention of Milan, you ought to have paid, and he threatens to erect Pisa and the neighbouring territory into an independent State." [2] Then, as a piece of good advice, they suggested that the Republic " should try to obtain by bribery some friends in France who would be stirred by more than natural affection, since that is what has to be done by all who have affairs at this Court. And he who refuses to do it is like one who would win a suit without feeing his attorney." [3]

Up to the 14th of September the letters were always signed by both envoys, though nearly all were written by Machiavelli. But on that day the King left Melun, and Della Casa, being ill, went to Paris for advice ; so that Machiavelli was left alone to continue the journey, and pursue the mission, which, after the 26th of September, increased in its importance, and extended over a wider field. He did not confine himself to the one affair, with which he was encharged, but investigated the various questions bearing upon Italian policy, and sent precise details of everything, first to the Signory, and then to the Ten, who were re-elected during this period ; and he showed so much zeal, so much ardour in all these matters, that occasionally he almost seemed to lose sight of the special and very limited object of his mission. By the use, now of Latin and now of French—for neither King nor Cardinal could speak Italian—he conversed with both and questioned every one. And now for the first time the penetration and originality of his intellect, the power and marvellous vigour of his style, began to be manifest. While travelling with the Cardinal de Rouen, and finding him still inflexible regarding the money, he turned the conversation upon the army which the Pope was forming, with the help of France, to forward the designs of Valentinois. And he was able to discover, " that if the King had conceded everything for the expedition in Romagna, it was rather because he knew not how to withstand the unbridled desires of the Pope, than from any real desire for his success." [4]

" Yet," continued Machiavelli, " the more does he fear Germany, so much the more he favours Rome, because there is the well-armed

---

[1] Letter of the 27th of August.   [2] Letter of the 29th of August, from Melun.
[3] Letter of the 14th of September.   [4] Letters of the 2nd and 8th of October.

head of Religion, and also because he is urged in that direction
by the Cardinal, who, knowing himself to have many enemies
here, the direction of all things being in his hands, hopes to
receive efficacious protection from that quarter." But whenever
he touched upon money matters, the Cardinal fell into fresh fury,
and threateningly said, " that the Florentines knew how to reason
finely, but would repent of their obstinacy in the end." [1]

After this, fortunately, the aspect of affairs began to greatly
improve, owing to the election of a new ambassador, Pier Francesco Losinghi, with much wider powers, and the permission
obtained by the Signory from the Councils for granting a fresh
sum of money ; thus Machiavelli had less difficulty in calming the
French wrath and continuing his discourses upon general politics.
He even obtained an explicit assurance that Valentinois would not
be allowed to injure Tuscany.[2] But on the 21st of November he
learnt from a friend that the Pope was doing his best to make
mischief, asserting that he should be able, with the expected aid
of the Venetians, to replace Piero dei Medici in Florence, and
that Piero would speedily pay any amount of money the King
wished. His Holiness also promised to deprive Bentivoglio of his
state, while as to Ferrara and Mantova, who showed so much
liking for Florence, he would " bring their necks under the yoke."

Upon hearing this, Machiavelli instantly went to seek the
Cardinal, and finding him at leisure, was able to speak with him
at length. To combat the Pope's calumnies of the Florentines,
he dwelt " not upon their good faith, but upon its being their
interest to side with the French. The Pope tries by all means
to compass the destruction of the King's friends, to wrest Italy
from his hands with greater ease." " But His Majesty should
follow the method of those who have before wished to possess a
foreign province, which is, to abase the powerful, caress their
subjects, maintain friends, and beware of comrades, that is, of
those who desire equal authority in such a place." "And certainly
it is not the Florentines, neither is it Bologna nor Ferrara, who
desire to mate with the King ; but rather those who have always
pretended to the domination of Italy, namely, the Venetians, and
above all, the Pope." The Cardinal gave affable attention to these

---

[1] Letters of the 11th of October, from Blois. By this letter it is shown that
Machiavelli was accustomed to speak Latin with the Cardinal de Rouen.

[2] Letter of the 4th of November from Nantes. It seems that this conversation
was held in French.

theories which the modest secretary, warming as he went on, expounded almost in the accents of a master, and replied that the King "had long ears and short belief; that he listened to all, but believed in nothing but that which he could touch with his hand."[1] And this may have been the occasion when, the Cardinal having said that the Italians knew nothing about war, Machiavelli made the reply that the French knew nothing of statesmanship, "for understanding that, they would never have allowed the Church to attain to so much greatness."[2]

On the 24th of November he wrote the two final despatches of this Legation. By that time the progress of Valentinois had become very threatening, and the Florentines, in their keen anxiety on that head, had not only hastened the departure of the new ambassador, but promised the representatives of France that they would shortly send money to the king. The latter therefore waited more patiently, and sent special orders to Valentinois, forbidding him to attack either Bologna or Florence. Having given this news in his first letter, Machiavelli wrote the second on the same day, to recommend the suit of a certain Giulio de Scruciatis,[3] a Neapolitan, against the heirs of the Bandini family in Florence. "De Scruciatis had rendered and might again render useful services to the Republic. I know nothing," he continued, "of this lawsuit of his; but I do know that while your standing with his French Majesty is so airy and precarious, few can help you, and all can injure you. Wherefore it is necessary to soothe him with smooth words, otherwise at the first letter of yours that comes here, he will be like a thunderbolt in this court;" "and the evil he may say will be believed more easily than any good that he may have said; furthermore, he is a

---

[1] Letter of the 21st of November. This is addressed to the Ten who had already been re-elected, on which matter Machiavelli had congratulated them in his letter of the 2nd of October.   [2] "Principe," at the end of chap. iii.

[3] In Florence he was known as Scurcigliato, Scorciato, or Scruciato, and so even Machiavelli calls him in his letters. He belonged to the De Scruciatis family of Castelluccio, Neapolitan nobles; he was a judge of the Vicaria, counsellor of Santa Chiara, fiscal advocate, and was one of those who had passed judgment on Antonello Petrucci, and the other members of the conspiracy of the barons. Ferdinand of Naples held him for one of his most faithful instruments, and made frequent use of him in the commission of his principal iniquities. Later, however, on the decline of the Aragonese fortunes, De Scruciatis forsook them in favour of the French, who, in 1499, named him a Roman senator. He afterwards followed the French camp, held many posts and filled missions even in Tuscany, committed rascalities of many descriptions, and ended in Rome as an inquisitor of the Holy Office.

man of some credit, very daring, loquacious, persistent, terrible, and being without measure in his passions, is capable of effecting somewhat in all that he undertakes." And having written these things Machiavelli made ready to leave France.

The reader will have perceived how in certain portions of these despatches, a foreshadowing—if as yet misty—of the author of the "Discorsi" and the "Principi" is already apparent. Those maxims, afterwards expounded by Machiavelli in a scientific shape, are here hurriedly sketched with an uncertain touch, and as it were by chance ; in succeeding despatches we shall see them gradually assuming a firmer outline, and clearer development. Even his style now began to acquire the vigour, that was soon to enable him to paint true and living men with a few strokes of his pen, to express his thoughts with truly wonderful lucidity, and hence to deserve his universally acknowledged title of the first of Italian prose writers. It will therefore surprise no one to learn that this mission to France brought great honour to Machiavelli in Florence, and that Buonaccorsi, as far back as the 23rd of August, wrote to tell him with unfeigned joy, that his despatches had been highly commended by the most influential citizens.[1] Yet in August he was still with Della Casa, who, as chief envoy, placed his signature first. We may therefore well imagine that the Republic was increasingly satisfied with its secretary.

On his return home, Machiavelli applied himself with his usual ardour to his office work, and the registers of the chancery were again filled day by day with his letters. Business was soon carried on with greater regularity, either because he exercised much authority over his subordinates, or because the Ten now re-elected,—who had been chosen among those most experienced in military matters,—were less distracted by other cares, and remained in office six months, instead of two only, like the Signory. Also, by the decree of the 18th of September, 1500, which replaced them in office, their attributes were better defined and restricted ; they could no longer, of their own authority, make peace, form a league or engage troops for more than one week, and in all important matters, required the sanction of the Eighty before pronouncing their decision.[2]

[1] This letter of Buonaccorsi is included, like his others, among the " Carte del Machiavelli " (case 1, No. 7).

[2] Florence Archives : " Consigli Maggiori, Provvisioni," register 191, at sheet 26.

CHAPTER IV.

(1501–1502.)

HERE was certainly no lack of public business, although the hostilities with Pisa were somewhat slackened. At Pistoia the bloody conflicts between the Cancellieri and the Panciatichi had assumed the gravest proportions ; the Panciatichi having been driven from the city, which was still subject to Florence, but ever on the eve of rebellion. To restore order therefore it was necessary to send special commissioners, men and arms. Machiavelli not only conducted the correspondence, gave orders, was applied to for advice by the Signory and the Ten ; but had frequently to go in person to Pistoia. And it is there that we find him in February and June, in order to see for himself and report upon the state of things.

Many members of both factions were confined in Florence, all the others requested to return to Pistoia ; that commune binding itself to defend them and indemnify them for all fresh injury, by the payment of a large sum of money for which the offenders would be liable, according to a decree of the Signory and the

Ten, in date of the 28th of April, 1501.[1] The Pistoians wished to banish the Panciatichi, on account of their known hostility to Florence ; but, on the 4th of May, Machiavelli wrote to them in the name of the Signory, that it would be highly dangerous to keep the Cancellieri within the town and the Panciatichi without, since thus they might suddenly " lose all the city or all its territory, and perhaps both together, the one being full of malcontents, the other full of suspicion." In conclusion, he insisted on the immediate execution of the orders of the government, and bade them employ the forces sent there, to compel the Panciatichi to re-enter the town unarmed and ensure their being kept under surveillance.[2]

Heavier anxieties soon assailed Florence from another quarter. Valentinois, prevented from attacking Bologna by the French prohibition, now turned towards Tuscany, and having seized upon Bersighella, the key of the Val di Lamone, and gained the assistance of Dionigi Naldi,[3] a military man with influential connections in those parts, had the whole district at his mercy. In threatening terms he next requested free passage through the territories of the Republic, alleging that he wished to lead his troops back to Rome. And the Florentines, knowing with whom they had to deal, sent to him a certain Piero Del Bene, one of his own personal friends, sent a commissary of war to Castrocaro on the frontier, and despatched a special envoy to Rome to inform the French ambassador of all that had happened : at the same time they prepared 20,000 ducats [4] to be forwarded to Louis XII.,

---

[1] Published by Passerini in the " Opere " (P. M.), vol. iii. p. 279. The sum was 500 florins, half of which went to the injured parties, a fourth to the magistrate who exacted it, the other fourth for the repairs of the Pistoia fortresses. See also the " Sommario della Città " and the " Sommario del Contado," included among the " Carte del Machiavelli " (case 1, No. 12), and published by Passerini, " Opere " (P.M.), vol. iii. p. 355. They consist of the measures decreed and the rules to be followed for the restoration of order in the city and its territory. They are official documents of no literary value, and should not be included among Machiavelli's Works, not being even written by his pen.

[2] " Opere " (P. M.), vol. iii. p. 299. The letter also contains other orders and details not in Machiavelli's hand. His signature is appended to this and other letters published by Passerini. It must, however, be observed that Machiavelli's signature, which very often is in another's handwriting, is merely used in these cases to indicate the head of the office, and thus is appended to letters written by his coadjutors, as well as to those written by himself. It is therefore necessary to examine the handwriting.

[3] Called indifferently *Dionigi Naldi*, *Naldo*, and *di Naldo*.

[4] See the letter of the Ten dated the 3rd of May, " Opere " (P. M.), vol. iii. p. 298.

to make him—as in fact it did make him—more decidedly favourable to their cause.   Meanwhile a thousand different rumours were afloat : the Siennese and Lucchese were sending continual reinforcements to Pisa, where Oliverotto, one of Valentinois's officers, had marched in with a few horsemen ; the Vitelli were helping the Panciatichi to revenge themselves upon their enemies, and so on, and so on.   All these matters had to be attended to, and Machiavelli did the work of several men, writing letters and issuing orders to captains, commissaries and magistrates.[1] Fortunately, however, news arrived from France, with promises of certain aid, and thus the Republic had a respite from its worst anxieties during the month of May.

But Valentinois continued his attempts.   News reached Florence that the Orsini and the Vitelli were already menacing the frontiers ; that a certain Ramazzotto, an old adherent of the Medici, had presented himself in Firenzuola, demanding the State in the name of the Duke, and of Piero dei Medici.[2]   And men's minds were so stirred in Florence by these events, that there was even a talk of creating a Balìa with extraordinary powers, and,[3] although this was not done, necessary measures were taken to defend the city from any sudden attack.   Irregular native troops who had been summoned from the Mugello and the Casentino and were commanded by the abbot Don Basilio, were stationed all round Florence ; others arrived from Romagna ; and more men were collected within the walls.   Machiavelli was the life and soul of these military movements, and devoted himself to them with a zeal that was most singular in a literary man of his stamp. But in fact—contrary to the prevailing opinion of the time—he had lost all faith in mercenary troops, and these irregulars seeming to him the germ of a national militia, destined to defend their country, after the manner of the ancient Romans, this was enough to inflame his enthusiasm.

When all these arrangements were concluded, ambassadors were sent to the Duke, giving him permission to pass through the territories if he chose ; but with small bodies of men at the

---

[1] An enormous number of letters were written by Machiavelli during these months, and they exist in his handwriting in the Florence Archives.   We only quote from a few of those in the file which is countersigned : class x. dist. 3, No. 95, at sheets 12, 18, 30, 92, 103, 163, 183, &c.

[2] Nardi, " Storia di Firenze," vol. i. p. 239 ; Buonaccorsi, " Diario."

[3] Guicciardini, " Storia Fiorentina," chap. xxii. p. 237.

time, and without the Orsini or the Vitelli. Upon this he angrily advanced through the Mugello, his soldiers pillaging as they went, and insulting every one ; for which reason the popular irritation rose to a high pitch both in town and country, and there was universal outcry against the " asinine patience " of the magistrates who had the greatest trouble to prevent a general rising against that army of freebooters.[1] At last the Duke, seeing how dangerous a turn matters were taking and knowing that the Florentines were really under the protection of the French, declared that he wished to be on terms of sincere friendship with them, and would accept an engagement as their captain. He added, however, that they must grant him free passage to continue his expedition against Piombino, and must also change their form of government and recall Piero dei Medici, as a guarantee that they would carry out their promises.

In order to combat these pretensions, the Florentines first of all armed another thousand men within the city, insisting on greater zeal and watchfulness on all sides ; then they sent Cæsar their reply. As regarded the Piombino expedition, he was, they told him, at liberty to continue his march, but as for changing their government, he might hold his tongue about it, for that was no business of his, and no one in Florence would have aught to do with the Medici. Whereupon Valentinois, on his arrival at Campi, without alluding to other subjects, let it be known that he would be satisfied with a condotta, or engagement, of 36,000 ducats annually for three years, without obligation of active service, but always in readiness to supply 300 men-at-arms in case of emergency. In short, after the usual fashion of the Borgia, other things failing, he determined at least to have money. The Florentines, in order to be rid of him, signed a convention on the 15th of May, 1501, granting the condotta and concluding a perpetual alliance with him.[2] They hoped to avoid paying him

[1] Nardi, " Storia di Firenze," vol. i. p. 242.

[2] " Archivio Storico," vol. xv. p. 269. According to this convention the Duke was to be ready to bring 300 men-at arms for the defence of the Republic, on any emergency ; for other enterprises he was to receive three months' notice, and was not bound to come in person ; he might, however, be obliged to accompany the French on the expedition to Naples. This last clause suited the Duke's purpose, since he knew that he must go with the French in any case, and he would thus receive his money without added obligations ; it also suited the Florentines, since, being pledged to assist the king with men-at-arms, they might, when necessary, fulfil both compacts with the same sum of money.

a farthing, and the Duke, although aware of this, accepted the terms, because, were the money not forthcoming, he would have a good excuse for further aggressions at the first convenient opportunity. Meanwhile he went on his way sacking and pillaging, and reached Piombino on the 4th of June. There he could do nothing but seize a few neighbouring domains and the island of Pianosa ; he then crossed over to Elba with some ships sent by the Pope.[1] But he was speedily recalled to the mainland to join the French who were returning from the Neapolitan war ; and then, leaving the few places he had conquered well garrisoned, he hurried to Rome, entering it as a conqueror, although his campaigns had been rather those of a freebooter than of a military chief.

But if the Neapolitan war freed the Republic of the Duke's presence, it entailed evils and anxieties of another kind. The French army was composed of 1,000 lances and 10,000 infantry, 4,000 of whom were Swiss, exclusive of a force of 6,000 men, who were coming by sea ; they advanced in two bodies, one of which, with the larger portion of the artillery, marched by Pontremoli and Pisa, while the other, coming down by Castrocaro, was to traverse nearly the whole of Tuscany. Besides these, small bodies of the Duke's men under Oliverotto di Fermo, Vitellozzo Vitelli and other captains, came straggling in the rear, either pillaging as they passed, or going to Pisa to help the rebels. It was therefore necessary to write to the various Commissaries and Podestas, instructing them to furnish provisions for the army, and defend themselves from the roving soldiery ; it was also necessary to find 12,000 ducats to satisfy the French who were always demanding money on the pretext of arrears owing to the Swiss who had served the Republic so badly.[2] Machiavelli entered into all

[1] Buonaccorsi in his "Diario" (pp. 44 and 45) does not speak of the journey to Elba ; Nardi, however, mentions it, and also Guicciardini in his "Storia d' Italia." But the latter, in his "Storia Fiorentina" (chap. iii. p. 244), says that it was then that Valentinois drove away the Lord of Piombino, an event which took place later.

[2] In the Florence Archives are many letters of this period, also written by Machiavelli, which are still inedited. We call attention to a few only. On the 18th of May he announces the Condotta concluded with Valentinois (Cl. x. dist. 3, No. 96, sheet 23). On the 28th of the same month (at sheet 41) he says that Valentinois has come, and "with his innumerable turpitudes has ravaged and reduced to famine half our land." On the 2nd of June orders are given to send all women and children away from Cascina, on account of the passage of the army. An undated letter (at sheet 57 of the same file) orders that all those of Valentinois' men who had been captured should be set at liberty, with the exception of Dionigi Naldi. One of the 16th July (sheet 77 retro) is addressed to Luigi Della Stufa,

these affairs with the utmost zeal, and finally, at heaven's pleasure, the army left Tuscany and passed into the States of the Church. Only then was the Pope informed of the secret treaty concluded at Granada between the kings of Spain and France, and, with his accustomed cynicism, he promised investiture to both sovereigns.

On the arrival of the French at the Neapolitan frontier, the unhappy Frederic gathered together his scanty forces, having already placed his sole hope in the help of Spain, whose army was commanded by the valiant Gonsalvo of Cordova. But at this moment the latter announced that he must give up his estates in the Neapolitan kingdom, since his duties as Frederic's vassal were no longer compatible with those of a Spanish captain. Thus the miserable monarch was left utterly forsaken, and shortly the whole of his kingdom was occupied by foreigners. Capua only held out against the French, but in July it was taken by assault, cruelly sacked, and cost the lives of seven thousand persons. Guicciardini asserts that not even cloistered virgins were respected by the soldiery, that many women in their despair cast themselves into the Volturno, and others took refuge in a tower. According to the same writer, Valentinois, who had followed the army with his guards, but without a command, and had plunged during the sack into every excess, went to inspect these women in order to choose for himself forty of the loveliest among them.

On the 19th of August the French entered Naples, and shortly after Frederic surrendered entirely to the king, who gave him the Duchy of Anjou in France, with a revenue of 30,000 ducats. There

who is directed to pacify the factions in Scarperia, and keep an eye upon Vitellozzo's men, who have appeared in that neighbourhood.

Many others are to be found in the following file, marked No. 97. In a letter of 7th July (same file, 97) Piero Vespucci is told : We command thee *not* to give a safe conduct to Oliverotto di Fermo. If it be already given, withdraw it, and give orders "that he should be seized, stripped of everything, treated as an enemy" (file 97 a.c. 73). On the 8th of July to the same : We are content with the orders given against Oliverotto. Forty of Don Michele's horse are expected in Pisa. If they come, "do thy best to plunder them and treat them as enemies." Do not, however, seek to pick quarrels, for we do not want a new war, unless they provoke us to it, as if, for instance, they were to send troops to Pisa (folio 74). On the 13th to the commissaries of Leghorn and Rosignano : "The Lord of Piombino advises us that a Turkish fleet of sixty sail has appeared near Pianosa, seemingly bound for Genoa. Should they disembark in search of victuals, allow them to do so, telling them that we are good friends of their Lord. But if they attempt to march inland, you must try to stop them, and gain time by waiting for instructions" (at sheet 77). And thus many more of the same kind.

he died on the 9th September, 1504; his sons, one after the other
followed him to the grave, and with them was extinguished th
Neapolitan House of Aragon. Gonsalvo, in the meantime, ha
seized, without meeting any resistance, the portion of the kingdor
belonging to Spain. The treaty of Granada, however, had bee
drawn up—not perhaps altogether by chance—in a manne
which allowed of different interpretations of the due division
Soon indeed it was plain, that one or the other of the tw
potentates must remain master of the whole kingdom, and th
final decision be made by arms. Nevertheless a temporary agree
ment was patched up between the two armies, who jointly governe
the disputed provinces.

On the 3rd of September the troops of Duke Cæsar marche
into Piombino; Appiani fled for his life, and in February th
Pope in person came with his son to examine the plans of th
fortresses which the latter was having built there.[1] Thus th
Florentines again saw the dreaded enemy at their gates, while a
the same time the Lucchese and Pisans were becoming mor
daring, and France once more slackening in her friendship
although the Republic, after having already given her 30,00
ducats for the Swiss, was now negotiating to pay her from 12
to 150,000 within three or four years, for the sake of the usua
promise of the conquest of Pisa.[2]

And while these things were keeping the Republic in eve
increasing difficulties, and making the Ten more and mor
unpopular, urgent demands for aid arrived from Pistoia, for tha
city was again a prey to the fury of the two factions, and n
manner of government was possible there. Machiavelli, who in
July had already gone there for the second time, was again sen
twice in the month of October, to take instructions, and to
consult, on his return, with the Ten and the Signoria,[3] as to what
was necessary to be done.

According to instructions received, he wrote that the sole
remedy to be thought of at present was to reform the govern-

[1] Buonaccorsi, "Diario," p. 53.

[2] See in Desjardins ("Négociations," &c., vol. ii. pp. 43–69), the various instructions sent to the ambassadors in France.

[3] Machiavelli, "Opere" (P. M.), vol. iii. pp. 330, 332. In the August of that
year he had also been sent to Sienna, to Pandolfo Petrucci, to Pistoia, and to
Cascina. See the documents at p. 358 of the same volume. Another document
would seem to show that in May he had been sent to Bologna to confer with
Giovanni Bentivoglio, but there is no proof that he really went there.

ment and administration of the city, by immediately recalling the
Panciatichi, and then afterwards take measures about the territory,
where still greater evils were rife.[1] During these months, besides
all these letters, orders, and instructions, Machiavelli also indited,
as secretary, an official report of the events at Pistoia, to give the
magistrates a clearer idea of the whole.[2] Many such reports or
narratives of what happened in the territories of the Republic were
compiled in the chanceries of the Ten and the Signoria, and this
by Machiavelli was likewise a strictly official work of no particular
interest.

Hardly had the Pistoian disturbances been put down, than
news came in May, 1502, that Vitellozzo and the Orsini were
advancing on the Val di Chiana, followed at a short distance by
the Duke of Valentinois. And the Emperor Maximilian, desiring
to come to Italy to be crowned, asked of the Florentines—under
the usual pretext of making war on the Turks—the sum of 100,000
ducats, of which 60,000 were to be paid down on the nail. This
money Florence refused to pay, but she found herself compelled
to promise France the sum of 120,000 ducats payable within three
years, for a treaty of alliance concluded on the 12th April, 1502,
by which the king was bound to protect the Republic, and supply
it on demand with 400 lances.[3] All these things, while insufficient
to frighten away Valentinois, who was marching slowly forward,
had utterly exhausted the treasury of the Republic, which knew
not what fresh tax to invent, after levying even the *Decima scalata*
or graduated tithe, a species of progressive tax.[4] On this account
the war with Pisa was almost suspended, and restricted to raids
on Pisan territory. The Florentines, extremely dissatisfied with
the Ten, declined to re-elect them, and placed the conduct of the
war in the hands of a Commission chosen by the Signoria, whereupon all things went from bad to worse.[5] The Pisans, in fact,
assumed the offensive, advanced on Vico Pisano, took possession of

[1] See in the "Opere" (vol. vi. p. 166) a letter of the Signoria, dated 26th
October, 1501, almost entirely in Machiavelli's hand. Guicciardini speaks of
these disorders on Pistoian territory in his "Storia Fiorentina," pp. 269–70.

[2] "Opere" (P. M.), p. 352.

[3] Buonaccorsi, "Diario," pp. 49–53 ; Guicciardini, "Storia Fiorentina," chap.
xxiii.

[4] Guicciardini, "Storia Fiorentina," chap. xxi. This tax was very heavy,
although part of it was placed to the credit of the contributor and considered as a
loan, as Canestrini tells us in his work, "La Scienza e l'Arte di Stato," Florence,
Le Monnier, 1862.   [5] Ibid., chap. xxiii.

it, and continued the negotiations begun in the preceding December with the Pope and Valentinois, for the formation of an independent State stretching to the coast, including the inland territory occupied by the Florentines, with whom neither peace nor truce was ever to be made. Valentinois was to have the title of Duke of Pisa, and the Duchy was to be hereditary ; the time-honoured magistrature of the Anziani (elders) was to be preserved, and one of the Borgia was to be named Archbishop of Pisa.[1] These designs were never carried out, but they sufficed to cause anxiety to the Florentines, against whom the Borgia tried to stir up enemies on every side, for the purpose, as they now pretended, of uniting all Italy in a league against foreigners in general and the French in particular.

Meanwhile Vitellozzo was already close upon Arezzo with the manifest purpose of exciting a rebellion there, and Valentinois was at a short distance, feigning to take no part in the proceedings of one of his own captains.[2] The Republic, having at this moment no troops at its command, hurriedly despatched as war commissary, Gugliemo de Pazzi, father of the Bishop of Arezzo, who was already on the spot. But the commissary had barely arrived when the people broke into rebellion (4th June), and both father and son had to take refuge with the captain in the fortress. Vitellozzo then entered the town with 120 men-at-arms and a good number of foot soldiers, soon followed by Giovan Paolo Baglioni, another of the Duke's captains, with fifty men-at-arms and five hundred infantry. To face these dangers, France was requested to send the promised contingent of four hundred lances, and also Piero Soderini was sent to Milan to ensure their departure. The troops encamped before Pisa received orders to advance by the Val di Chiana, where Antonio Giacomini Tebalducci, was sent as commissary, and likewise to fill the post of captain. This man had dedicated himself to military studies for some time, and already had given proofs of the immense superiority of patriot captains over mercenaries.[3] Machiavelli, who was in

[1] Desjardins, " Négociations," &c., vol. ii. pp. 69–70.

[2] The Venetian ambassador wrote from Rome on the 7th June, 1502, that the Arezzo business was " an old scheme of the Duke," and on the 20th June he added, that the Pope, " ever intent on his own private passions," in spite of the vigorous French protest regarding the affair of Arezzo, spoke of nothing but this and the other enterprises of his Duke. See the " Dispacci " of A. Giustinian.

[3] Nardi, " Vita di Antonio Giacomini." Napier, in his " Florentine History " (vol. iv. p. 105), tells us on the authority of Jacopo Pitti (book i. p. 77), that Giacomini's appointment caused the re-election of the Ten.

constant correspondence with him, and followed his career step by step, now renewed his observations and matured his ideas on the subject of a national militia.

Meanwhile events were hurrying on, for the citadel of Arezzo, after holding out for a fortnight, had to surrender without being able to receive succour from the troops on the march from the camp before Pisa. The latter therefore received orders to retire on Montevarchi, while the enemies, with their Arezzo reinforcements, occupied the whole of the Val di Chiana, and had been already joined by Piero dei Medici and his brother.[1] The Florentines, as may easily be imagined, awaited most anxiously the French contingent which was to rescue them from their imminent danger, and while in this suspense, a message came from Valentinois demanding that some one should be sent to confer with him. Francesco Soderini, Bishop of Volterra, was chosen for this mission, and was accompanied by Niccolò Machiavelli. The Duke was at that time at Urbino, which he had seized by treachery, and the unhappy Guidobaldo di Montefeltro had barely saved his life by hurried flight to the mountains, although he had always considered himself the friend of the Borgia, and assisted them with the very troops, whom they had roused against him to strip him of his State.

Machiavelli only remained a few days with Soderini, having then to return to Florence to give *viva voce* details to the Signory. Therefore only the two first despatches of this legation are written by him, and both bear the signature of Bishop Soderini. In the second dated from Urbino the 26th of June, *ante lucem*, we find a description of Borgia, clearly showing how profound an impression he had already produced upon the mind of the Florentine secretary. They gained audience on the evening of the 24th at two o'clock of the night,[2] in the palace inhabited by the Duke and a few of his men, who kept the doors well locked and guarded. Borgia told the envoys that he wished to be on a clear footing with the Florentines, their firm friend or declared enemy. Should they decline his friendship, he would be justified, before both God and man, in seeking by every means to ensure the safety of his own dominions which bordered upon theirs along so extended a frontier. " I desire to have explicit surety since too

---

[1] Buonaccorsi, " Diario," p. 54 and fol.

[2] *I.e.*, two hours after sunset, according to the old style.

well I know that your city is not well minded towards me, but would abandon me like an assassin, and has already sought to plunge me in heavy embroilments with the Pope and King of France. This government of yours does not please me, and you must change it, otherwise if you refuse me for a friend, you shall know me for an enemy." The envoys replied that Florence had the government which she desired, and that none throughout Italy could boast of keeping better faith. That if the Duke's intentions were really friendly he could easily prove it by compelling Vitellozzo, who was in fact his subordinate, to withdraw at once. Upon this the Duke asserted that Vitellozzo and the others were acting on their own account, although he was by no means ill-pleased that the Florentines should, without any fault of his, receive a severe and merited lesson. Nor was it possible to get anything else out of him, whereupon the ambassadors hurried to write their despatches, feeling that it was most necessary to acquaint the government with the Duke's motives in sending for them, the more so "as these people's mode of action is to sneak into others' houses before they are aware of it, as was the case of the last Lord of this place, whose death was heard of before his illness." [1]

The Duke had also asserted that he was sure of France, and caused the same to be repeated to them by the Orsini, who not only gave it to be understood that Vitellozzo's expedition had been undertaken by agreement with that country, but added that all was in readiness for a speedy invasion of Tuscany with twenty or twenty-five thousand men, which force however the orators reckoned at sixteen thousand only. " This Duke," said the letter in conclusion, " is so enterprising that nothing is too great to seem small to him, and for the sake of glory and the extension of his dominions, he deprives himself of rest, yielding to no fatigue, no danger. He arrives at this place before one hears that he has left the other, he gains the goodwill of his soldiers, he has got hold of the best men in Italy and has constant good luck ; all which things make him victorious and formidable." But the fact was, that he knew that the French were coming to the aid of the Florentines, and therefore wished to bind the latter at any price. Accordingly, at three o'clock of the night of the 25th, after the orators had already spoken with Orsini, he sent for

---

[1] This was Guidobaldo di Montefeltro, Duke of Urbino.

·them again to signify that he wished an instant reply from the Signoria, nor would he grant them a longer delay than of four days. So the letter,[1] finished at dawn, was instantly sent off by a special courier, followed closely by Machiavelli himself, who had nothing more to do at Urbino. He went away filled with a strange intellectual admiration of this enemy of his country, which admiration was probably increased by that already inspired by Borgia in Bishop Soderini.[2] The latter remained with the Duke, who daily increased both his demands and his threats. The Florentines, however, paid slight attention to these, for they knew that the French contingent was already on the road. For the same reason, when Giacomini—who on this occasion had shown marvellous courage and activity—now wrote to say that if they sent him three thousand foot soldiers and a thousand irregulars he would be able to attack the enemy, they replied in the first week in July, that he need only stand on the defence, for that the artillery and four thousand Swiss sent by France were already on their way. They added that it would be necessary to pay these troops at once, and it would therefore be imprudent to involve the Republic in fresh expenses, especially as Valentinois himself seemed already folding his wings.[3] And they wrote to the same effect at later dates.[4]

On the 24th of July the King wrote that horse and foot would speedily arrive, together with a sufficient supply of artillery under the command of La Trémoille. The Florentines therefore must have pay and provisions ready for them.[5] And very soon the Captain Imbault appeared with a small troop before Arezzo, and speedily brought Vitellozzo to terms. The latter was to surrender all the places he had taken excepting the city he was then occupying, and where he was to be allowed to remain with Piero dei Medici until the return of Cardinal Orsini, who had gone to treat with the King in person. But even this concession

---

[1] The greater part of this letter, with a few by Soderini, was published by us at the end of vol. i. of the "Dispacci" of A. Giustinian. Passerini has published all the documents of the legation, which, as we have already said, only include two by Machiavelli. "Opere" (P. M.), vol. iv.

[2] Machiavelli himself says this, as we shall shortly see.

[3] Letters of the 1st and 12th July, in the Florence Archives, class x. dist. 3, No. 101, sheets 2 and 24. See Appendix, document v.

[4] Letters of the 2nd, 4th, and 15th July, in the "Scritti Inediti" published by Canestrini, pp. 3, 5, and 8.

[5] Desjardins, "Négociations," &c., vol. ii. p. 70.

—which the Florentines rightly considered unseemly,[1]—was afterwards withdrawn, because the Pope and the Duke—throwing the blame of everything on Vitellozzo and the Orsini whom they mortally hated—abandoned them altogether ; neither in fact did they care much about the Medici, precisely for the reason that these were friends and relatives of the Orsini.[2] On the contrary they pledged themselves to assist France in the Neapolitan expedition.[3] And the Florentines having previously settled that Captain Imbault, who had not satisfied them, should be superseded by De Langres,[4] soon recovered all their territory, a circumstance which was made known in an epistle of the 28th of August, together with orders for public festivals to be held in commemoration of the event.[5]

Towards the middle of August Machiavelli was sent to the French camp, to accompany De Langres and collect information prejudicial to Imbault, but he was not long absent from his post. Piero Soderini and Luca degli Albizzi, both men of great influence, had been sent to Arezzo for the purpose of restoring order as soon as the rebellion should be quelled, and preventing De Langres from going away too soon, since the Florentine forces were all engaged in keeping back the Pisans, who were advancing in the opposite quarter.[6] Meanwhile he wrote from his Chancery, praying Soderini to hasten at all events to send to Florence, before the departure of the French, all such Aretini, " as may seem to you likely ; either by their brains, courage, pugnacity, or wealth, to draw other men after them, and it were better rather to send twenty too many than one too few, without troubling yourself as

---

[1] *Vide* letter of the 30th July in Canestrini's " Scritti Inediti," p. 19.

[2] The Venetian ambassador in Rome plainly stated in a letter of July, 1502, that the Pope had been compelled by orders from France, to insist on the withdrawal of Vitellozzo and the Orsini from Arezzo ; but that he had no real desire to reinstate the Medici in Florence, for they were friends of the Orsini whom he wished to root out. See the " Dispacci " of A. Giustinian, especially those dated 1st and 7th July. Then Buonaccorsi at page 54 of his " Diario," tells us that Valentinois would have willingly joined the Florentines in injuring the Orsini and Vitelli, but did not dare to speak his mind for fear of meeting with a refusal.

[3] Buonaccorsi, " Diario," p. 62.

[4] Buonaccorsi, " Diario," p. 63 ; Canestrini, " Scritti Inediti," p. 21. Worthy too of note are the letters of 4th August and following in the Florence Archives, class x. dist. 3, No. 100, at sheets 68 and fol.

[5] Florence Archives, class x. dist. 3, No. 101, at sheet 104.

[6] Letters of the 3rd, 4th, and 6th September, 1502, in the Florence Archives, cl. x. dist. 3, No. 100, folio 107, 109, and 111.

to their number, or about leaving the town empty." [1]   He quitted his post again on the 11th and 17th September to make two journeys to Arezzo, in order to look into the state of things, and provide for the departure of the French, who had now decided on going away.[2]

Fortunately everything turned out fairly well, and Machiavelli, having long begun to think seriously on political matters, not from the official point of view, but from that of a student and man of science, in whose mind particular facts were marshalled according to general principles and rules, composed, after his Arezzo experiences, a short treatise entitled : "Del modo di trattare i popoli della Val di Chiana ribellati." [3]

The author is supposed to pronounce this discourse before the magistrates of the Republic, but it is not one of those compiled in the usual routine of office work : on the contrary, it was a first attempt to soar above his daily work to the highest scientific level. And in this treatise we can already perceive the germs of all the signal merits and defects, which we shall see displayed later in the secretary's principal writings. That which first arrests our attention is the singular manner in which we find, grafted the one upon the other in the author's mind, experience of actual facts, judgments formed of the actions of men personally known to him—among whom Cæsar Borgia is not the last—together with an extraordinary admiration for Roman antiquity, which seems to have been the only link of connection between the results of his daily observations and the general principles of his, as yet, uncertain science. By comparing, he says, that which happens under our own eyes with that which in similar circumstances occurred in Rome, we may succeed in understanding what we should do, since, in point of fact, men are always the same, and have the same passions ; thus when circumstances are identical, the same causes lead to the same effects, and therefore the same facts ought to suggest the same rules of conduct. Certainly in those days it was a daringly original idea to have recourse to antiquity and history, in order—by comparison

---

[1] Letter of the 8th of September, written *nomine Priorum, loc. cit.*, at sheet 116. A similar letter in the name of the Ten is in the "Scritti Inediti," pp. 28 and 29.

[2] See in Machiavelli, "Opere," vol vi. pp. 182–84, several letters referring to these journeys.

[3] "Opere," vol. ii. p. 385.

with recent experiences—to discover the principles regulating the movements of human actions, and bound to regulate those of governments. But if history teaches us the successive order of human affairs, it also shows the continual mutations of mankind and society, and the difficulty of discovering absolute and unchangeable rules. In truth, on close examination, although history is the original model to which Machiavelli constantly refers, we shall frequently find that it only serves to give greater weight to, or furnish the demonstration of those maxims which were, in fact, the fruits of his own experience. And this is the primary source of his chief merits and defects. Having as yet no accurate vision of the process, by which an ever different present results from the past ; being as yet too uncertain of his method to deduce with scientific precision general principles from concrete facts, he placed antiquity between the two, and antiquity proved to be an artificial link, whenever it was only called upon to demonstrate foregone conclusions. Nevertheless this first attempt shows us plainly, that Machiavelli used it—one may say as a ladder—in order to climb to a higher world far above the wearying routine of daily labour amidst a policy of petty subterfuge. Urged on by genius, great powers of analysis, and a restless fancy, he attempted to create a new science, not without occasionally falling into exaggerations, which never entirely disappeared from his works, and which later brought upon him the blame of Guicciardini, who accused him of over-preference "for extraordinary deeds and ways."

This is the manner in which his discourse opens : "Lucius Furius Camillus entered the Senate, after having conquered the rebellious peoples of Latium, and said—'I have done all that war can do ; now it is your concern, O Conscript Fathers, to assure your future safety as regards the rebels.' And the Senate generously pardoned the rebels, excepting only the cities of Veliterno and Anzio. The first was demolished, and its inhabitants sent to Rome ; the second, after its ships had been destroyed, and it had been forbidden to build others, was colonized by new and loyal inhabitants. This was because the Romans knew that half measures were to be avoided, and that peoples must either be conquered by kindness or reduced to impotence." "I have heard that history is the teacher of our actions, and especially of our rulers ;[1] the world has always been inhabited by men with

[1] That is—Statesmen.

the same passions as our own, and there have always been rulers and ruled, and good subjects and bad subjects, and those who rebel and are punished." "One can therefore approve your general course of conduct towards the inhabitants of the Val di Chiana ; but not your particular conduct towards the Aretini, who have always been rebellious, and whom you have neither known how to win by kindness nor utterly subdue, after the manner of the Romans. In fact, you have not benefited the Aretini, but on the contrary have harassed them by summoning them to Florence, stripping them of honours, selling their possessions ; neither are you in safety from them, for you have left their walls standing, and allowed five-sixths of the inhabitants to remain in the city, without sending others to keep them in subjection. And thus Arezzo will ever be ready to break into fresh rebellion, which is a thing of no slight importance, with Cæsar Borgia at hand, seeking to form a strong state by getting Tuscany itself into his power. And the Borgia neither use half measures nor halt half way in their undertakings. Cardinal Soderini, who knows them well, has often told me that, among other qualities of greatness possessed by the Pope and the Pope's son, they likewise have that of knowing how to seize and profit by opportunities, the which is well confirmed by our experience of what they have already done." At this point the unfinished discourse suddenly breaks off.

Machiavelli who had shown so much zeal in prosecuting the business of the capture and condemnation of Vitelli, and, on the 8th of September, had written to the Florentine commissaries that in order to clear Arezzo of dangerous men, they should rather send twenty too many than one too few, without caring if the city were even depopulated, had no need to demonstrate that he disapproved of half measures in politics, trusted solely to prompt and resolute conduct, and was by no means satisfied with the perpetual petty tergiversation of his fellow citizens. But neither must we believe that in these theoretical discourses he intended positively to condemn the conduct of the magistrates. They naturally had to consider the passions and character of the men over whom they ruled ; his object in writing was to inquire into what should be the true policy of a people such as he imagined after meditating on the history of Rome.

Certainly the affairs of the Republic at this juncture were carried on with a weakness and timidity making all men feel the necessity of some active reform. In the April of this year

a new law had been passed for the abolishment of the Podestà and
the Captain of the people, ancient offices which had originally
been political and judicial posts; but having long lost the
former of their attributes, now fulfilled the second very indifferently notwithstanding its great importance. Therefore, according to one of Savonarola's old suggestions, a *ruota* was instituted
of five doctors of the law, each of whom presided in turn for six
months, and filled for that period the place of the Podestà. The
Ruota had to sit in judgment on civil and criminal suits, and by
a provision of the 15th of April, 1502, was instituted for three
years only, a term that was afterwards extended.[1] By another
of the 21st of April, the Court of Commerce was remodelled,
and compelled to restrict its operations to commercial affairs
only.[2] But similar alterations, as may easily be understood,
brought no improvement to the general course of affairs under
a government, the primary cause of whose weakness lay in
changing the Gonfaloniere and the Signoria every two months.[3]
Thus no traditions of office were formed; no State secrets were
possible; all was carried on in public, and only the head chancellor
or secretary, Marcello Virgilio, managed, in virtue of his own zeal
and influence, to maintain a certain degree of uniformity in the
conduct of affairs.[4] All measures were slow and uncertain;
money was squandered; the citizens, weighed down by excessive
taxation, were full of discontent, and had no one to appeal to,
since the magistrates disappeared from the stage almost as soon as
they had taken office. At last necessary grants of money ceased to
be voted, the soldiery received no pay, and influential citizens
refused to accept embassies or other -high offices, which were
consequently bestowed on obscure and insignificant men, who—
as Guicciardini phrased it—"had more tongue than presence,"
and were merely chosen because they pushed themselves forward.[5]

For these reasons it was proposed to make some radical change
in the form of government. The first idea was to create a Senate

---

[1] "Consigli Maggiori, Provvisioni," reg. 194, at sheet 1. Guicciardini, "Storia
Fiorentina," pp. 250–51; Giovanni Cambi, "Delizie degli Eruditi Toscani," vol.
xxi. p. 172.   [2] Ibid., reg. 194, at sheet 11.

[3] Guicciardini, "Storia Fiorentina," chap. xxv.

[4] Nardi, "Storia di Firenze," vol. i. p. 276. He makes no mention of
Machiavelli.

[5] Guicciardini, "Storia Fiorentina," chap. xxiv., at pp. 257-58, and chap.
xxv. p. 274.

for life, like the Pregadi of Venice, but it was feared that this might throw the State into the hands of a few individuals ; then it was proposed instead to create a Gonfaloniere for life like the Doge,[1] and on the 26th of August, 1502, that measure was carried.[2] The legal position of the new Gonfaloniere differed little from what it had formerly been ; he was at the head of the Signoria and nothing more. But at all its sittings, he had the right of initiative in proposing laws ; also that of taking part in and voting with the judges in criminal trials, which was in itself an increase of power. Then the fact of being elected for life, among political magistrates with so brief a tenure of authority, greatly increased both his influence and his strength. It was necessary that he should be at least fifty years of age, and should hold no other office ; his brothers, sons, and nephews were excluded from the Signoria, and both himself and his sons were forbidden to trade. His salary was 1,200 florins a year. The number of eligible candidates was large, even the citizens belonging to the lesser trades being admissible. The election was to be made by the Great Council, for, on that day, all who had a right to sit there were to have the power to vote. Every counsellor was called upon to give the name of the citizen whom he wished to elect, and all those obtaining half the votes *plus* one, were again balloted thrice. At the third time whoever obtained the majority, among those having more than half the whole number of votes, was the successful candidate. The Signory, the Colleges, the Ten, the Captains of the Guelph party, and the Right in conjunction could deprive him of office by a majority of three-fourths, in the event of his violating the law.[3] This pro-

---

[1] Guicciardini, " Storia Fiorentina," chap. xxv. p. 278.

[2] This provision (" Consigli Maggiori, Provvisioni," reg. 194, at sheet 150) has been published by L. Banchi, Director of the Siennese Archives, in a "Raccolta di scritture varie," made for the Riccomanni-Fineschi marriage. Turin, Vercellino, 1865. See also the documents published by Razzi in his " Vita di Piero Soderini," Padua, 1737.

[3] Guicciardini (" Storia Fiorentina," pp. 280–82) gives a very minute and exact report of the Provvisioni. Careful comparison with the original documents enables us to see the marvellous accuracy of Guicciardini on this subject, as indeed on all others, in his " Storia Fiorentina." Frequently he gives *verbatim* the laws and documents which he has occasion to mention. This proves that the illustrious historian Ranke was mistaken in his over severe judgment respecting the studies, acquirements, and historic fidelity of Guicciardini. However it is true that when the illustrious German expressed that opinion in his "Zur Kritik neuerer Geschichtschreiber " (Berlin, 1824), he could not have read Guicciardini's " Opere Inedite," which, even in Italy, exhibited him in an entirely new light.

vision, twice discussed by the Eighty and twice by the Great Council, was finally carried—after a hard struggle—by sixty-eight votes against thirty-one in the Council of Eighty, and by eight hundred and eighteen against three hundred and seventy-two in the Great Council.

On the the 20th of September, Piero Soderini, the Bishop's brother, was elected Gonfaloniere by a large majority. He had already officiated as Gonfaloniere eighteen months before, had filled many other posts, and although of ancient and wealthy family, was a good friend of the people and the Liberal Government. Likewise he was a facile speaker, a good citizen, and had none of the large energies or lofty gifts exciting too much hatred or too much affection, and this was by no means the least cause of his success.[1] On the 23rd of the same month Machiavelli despatched to him at Arezzo the official announcement of his election, expressing at the same time the hope that he might succeed in conferring on the Republic that prosperity for the sake of which the new office had been created.[2] This election was a very notable event, not only in the history of Florence, but also in the life of Machiavelli ; for he was an old acquaintance of the Soderini family, and speedily gained the full confidence of the new Gonfaloniere, who entrusted him, as we shall see, with very important State affairs.

[1] Guicciardini, "Storia Fiorentina," p. 200; Buonaccorsi, "Diario," p. 64.
[2] Florence Archives, class x. dist. 3, No. 101, at sheet 134. The letter was not written by Machiavelli, only corrected by him.

CHAPTER V.

Legation to the Duke of Valentinois in Romagna—The doings of the Pope in Rome at the same period—Machiavelli composes his "Descrizione" of events in Romagna.

(1502–1503.)

NCE more it is the turn of the Borgia to claim the attention of all Italy. Lucrezia had now, to her own advantage, disappeared from the Roman stage, after having been the chief personage of the most scandalous and nefarious tales. But she seemed heedless of reproach, since she was often to be seen with her father and brother merrily taking part in masquerades and balls which were nothing better than orgies too indecent for description.[1] At last, in the January of 1502, she set out for Ferrara with an immense suite, and travelling with an excessive pomp and luxury of which contemporary chroniclers give minute and tedious accounts repeated *ad nauseam*. In Ferrara she became the bride of Duke Alfonso d'Este, and splendid festivities were held there during many days.[2] But from that time her

---

[1] Burchardi and Matarazzo give particulars of them.

[2] Marchioness Isabella Gonzaga, a lady whose elevated mode of thought is strikingly contrasted with the prevailing tone of the times, went to Ferrara to join in these festivities, and wrote to her husband that she found them very wearisome, and that it seemed *a thousand years* before she could return to Mantova, "not only for the sake of coming back to your lordship and my little son, but also to get away from this place where one has no pleasure in life." (Letter of the 5th February, 1502.) "And were they veritable pleasures," she wrote, "they could not satisfy me without the presence of your lordship and our little boy." Isabella Gonzaga was not deceived by the show of official gaiety, for she remarked: "to say the truth this wedding is a very cold one." (Letter of the 3rd of February.) *Vide* the collection of her very interesting letters published by Signor Carlo d'Arco in the "Archivio Storico," Appendix xi.

life entered into a quieter and more decorous phase, for she now had to deal with a husband capable of sending her out of the world with little hesitation after the Borgia's favourite style. For this reason, although some of her actions were in accordance with her past career, they have always been enveloped in the deepest mystery.[1] She surrounded herself with *litterati* who flattered her, even applied herself to works of piety and charity, thus gaining the improved reputation that she ever after enjoyed, and almost complete exculpation at the hands of many writers.

But in Rome with the Pope, and in Romagna with the Duke of Valentinois, the scene only shifted from one tragedy to another, from bloodshed to more bloodshed. Insulting pamphlets, atrocious epigrams, were continually appearing in the Eternal City ; but the Pope was too full of other matters to pay any attention to them. From time to time, some cardinal, after accumulating great riches, would fall ill and die suddenly, or be unexpectedly impeached and sentenced to confinement in the castle of St. Angelo, from which he never issued alive. All his possessions—plate, money, even furniture and tapestry—speedily found their way to the Vatican. His vacant benefices were conferred upon other prelates, often destined to come to the same end as soon as they were rich enough. "Our Lord," wrote the Venetian ambassador, "generally fattens them up, before feasting on them." And, in the July of that year, this was the fate of the Datario, Battista Ferrari, cardinal of Modena, who had been his most faithful instrument in squeezing money from everybody and everything. Having amassed great riches he was suddenly seized with a mortal sickness ; the Pope gave him spiritual assistance at the last hour, and then, as usual, stripped his palace and took all his property. The greater part of his benefices were conferred upon Sebastiano Pinzon who had been his private secretary, and, as it was generally rumoured, had poisoned his master by the Holy Father's own command.[2]

The city was illuminated during these days ; the Governor of Rome and the Pope's guards, followed by a great crowd, went about the streets shouting—*The Duke, the Duke.*[3] Cæsar Borgia

---

[1] Gregorovius, "Lucrezia Borgia."

[2] And it is publicly said that he had them *in premium sanguinis,* "since by many evident signs all hold that the cardinal died *ex veneno,* and that this Sebastian was the murderer. . . . The pope has received him *inter familiares.*" Antonio Giustinian, "Dispacci": Despatch of the 20th July, 1502.

[3] Despatch of the 24th of July, 1502.

had entered Camerino and captured its Lord, Giulio Cesare da
Varano, and his sons. The Pope therefore was so excited with joy,
as to be unable to keep it concealed. Having called a Consistory
to announce a victory of the Hungarians over the Turks, he
spoke only of Camerino and the Duke. Reminded by the cardinal
of Santa Prassede of the object of the meeting, he at once ordered
the letter to be fetched ; but then, pursuing his other subject,
forgot to have it read.[1] While speaking with the Venetian
and Spanish ambassadors, he walked about the room too restless
to sit still ; had the Duke's letter read, which after relating
all that occurred concluded as follows : " May this do good to your
Holiness ; " and then exalted the Duke's prudence and magnanimity, " praising him *ab omni parte*."[2] He predicted his son's
future conquests, and in his mind's eye already beheld him master
of all central Italy. He was however uncertain of what might be
the attitude of Venice with regard to changes so rapid. Therefore
calling to him the Venetian ambassador, he immediately began to
make great protestations of friendship, in order to see how he
would reply. But Antonio Giustinian was a wary politician, and
wrote to his Doge : " In answer to what I have just related,
Principe Serenissimo, *ambulavi super generalissimis* while the
Pope went *super generalibus*."[3]

Meanwhile Valentinois had assumed the titles of Cæsar Borgia
of France, by the grace of God, Duke of Romagna, Valencia and
Urbino, Prince of Andria, Lord of Piombino, Gonfalonier and
Captain-General of the Church, and he advanced upon Bologna
without delay. But at this moment France put her *veto* upon any
farther proceedings, giving it to be understood that she could not
permit the Borgia to extend their conquests in Italy : that they
must renounce all idea of Bologna and Tuscany.[4] At the same

---

[1] Despatch of the 29th July.   [2] Despatch of the 27th July.

[3] Despatch of the 22nd July, 1502.

[4] The good Isabella Gonzaga wrote to her husband on this subject : It is said
that the king of France means to make you march against the Duke, but it seems
to me that we must be very cautious, "for now one knows not whom to trust,"
and soon we might see the King once more in agreement with the Duke. (Letter of
the 23rd July, 1502.) She was not mistaken in this. But it was no sympathy
for Valentinois that made her express this opinion. For at the time when the
people of Faenza were valiantly defending their lord, she had written to her husband : " I am pleased that the Faentini are so faithful and constant in the defence of
their lord, for they restore the honour of the Italians. Thus may God grant them
grace to persevere, not to wish ill to the Duke of Valentinois, but because neither
that lord, nor his faithful people, deserve so heavy a ruin." (Letter of the 20th

time the Duke's principal captains, who were nearly all of them petty tyrants from central Italy, perceived how he was destroying one by one all their companions, and understood that before long their own turn would come. And, on learning that he had already resolved to take possession of Perugia and Castello, and then fall upon the Orsini, they all met together " in order not to be devoured by the dragon one after another," [1] and decided to raise the standard of rebellion against the Duke and seize the present opportunity for attacking him, now that he was deserted by France. The first result of this agreement was, that on the 8th of October some of the conspirators carried by surprise the fortress of San Leo in the Duchy of Urbino, the which made an extraordinary impression, as the signal and forerunner of fresh events. In fact, on the 9th day of October,[2] the conspirators all assembled at La Magione near Perugia, for the formal arrange-ment of the terms of the league. There were several of the Orsini, namely, the cardinal, the Duke of Gravina, Paolo and Frangiotto, besides Ermes, son of Giovanni Bentivoglio, with full powers as representative of his father, Antonio da Venafio, with full powers from Pandolfo Petrucci, Messer Gentile and Giovan Paolo Baglioni, and Vitellozzo Vitelli who, being ill, was carried in on a couch.[3] They pledged themselves to the common defence, to make no attack without the general consent, and to collect an army of 700 men-at-arms in blank (*in bianco*),[4] 100 light horse, 9,000 foot soldiers, and more if necessary ; and all who should fail to observe these legally stipulated terms, were to be fined 50,000 ducats, and be stigmatized as traitors. Florentine assistance was

April, 1501.) And on the 3rd of July of the same year she wrote, that for the anni-versary of the battle of Fornuovo she had ordered " that mass should be cele-brated for the souls of those valiant men of ours, who lost their lives to save Italy, according to your excellency's prudent and pious advice." Language such as this is very rare, and therefore all the more worthy of note in the age of the Borgia and Lodovico the Moor.

[1] This expression is to be found in a letter of the 11th October, written by Giovan Paolo Baglioni, one of the conspirators, to Messer Vincenzo Count of Montevibiano, the last who filled the office of Podestà in Florence. It is included in the correspondence published by Passerini, " Opere " (P.M.), vol. iv. p. 94 and fol.

[2] The date is extracted from the before-quoted letters. Several preparatory meetings had however been previously held, as we learn from the historians and from the documents of Machiavelli's own Legation to Borgia in Romagna.

[3] Letters of Baglioni quoted above.

[4] That is to say, they were bound to engage 700 men, but had not already got them in readiness. As we shall see, Cæsar Borgia mocked this expression of theirs.

soon asked, but they took to arms at once, and Paolo Vitelli, having carried the citadel of Urbino by assault on the 15th of October, now stirred the whole Duchy to revolt, so that only a few of the numerous fortresses remained in Borgia's hands.

Cæsar perfectly understood the gravity of this revolt. But without losing his presence of mind, he sent against the enemy the portion of his army still remaining faithful to him, under the command of one of his captains, Don Michele Coriglia, a Spaniard of notorious cruelty,[1] and his strangler, better known as Don Michelotto. This man established his quarters in the citadel of Pergola, which still held out for the Duke, making sorties thence into the surrounding territory, and laying it all waste. We are told that it was then that he murdered Giulio da Varano, his wife, and two of his sons, who were in prison, while another of them, after being first tortured at Pesaro, was dragged half dead into a church, and there butchered by a Spanish priest, who was afterwards, in his turn, cut to pieces in a popular riot at Cagli. From Pergola the army went to Fossombrone, where many women, to escape the ferocity of the soldiery, threw themselves and their children into the river.[2]

Meanwhile the rebel army, being now joined by Baglioni and his troops, had increased to 12,000 men, and three miles from Fossombrone, gave battle to Borgia's army, under the joint command of Don Michelotto and Don Ugo di Moncada, another Spaniard. The Duke's forces were utterly routed ; Don Ugo was taken prisoner, Don Michelotto barely escaped, and the exultation of the rebels was at its height. The fugitive Guidobaldo di Montefeltro re-entered his dominions, and had a triumphant re-ception at Urbino ; Giovan Maria da Varano, the only survivor of his unhappy family, returned to Camerino. Thus the laborious and sanguinary work of the Borgia seemed all crumbled to dust in one moment. Yet skirmishes on a large scale still went on ; Don Michelotto continued to hold out at Pesaro ; the Duke was at

---

[1] A note in the edition of Machiavelli's works (vol. vi. p. 485), also repeated in the Passerini and Milanesi edition, styles him a Venetian, and quotes a letter from the commissary in Arezzo, which we have searched for in vain in the Florence Archives. All other writers call him a Spaniard, and when he was engaged by the Florentines as Captain of the Guard, the decree of the 27th of February, 1507, runs as follows : "Dicti Domini, they decided, &c., that Michele Coriglia, *the Spaniard*, should be engaged as Captain . . . ." Cl. xiii. dist. 2, No. 70 ("Delibe-razioni dei ix d'ordinanza "), at sheet 9*t.*

[2] Ugolini, " Storia dei Conti e Duchi d'Urbino," vol. ii. p. 98 and fol.

Imola with a considerable force that he tried to augment. The rebels had asked aid from Venice, who remained a passive spectator ; from Florence, who mindful of the doings of the Orsini and Vitelli in Tuscany, and unwilling to go to war with the Borgia, first temporized and then refused outright. The Duke on the other hand applied to the French, who instantly sent him a small body of spearmen under the command of Charles d'Amboise, Lord of Chaumont. This dishonourable action brought about an instant change in the aspect of affairs, and struck terror into Borgia's enemies, who, having neglected to take advantage of the favourable moment, now beheld in the banner of France his salvation and their own ruin.

From the first moment of the open rupture with the Orsini, the Duke and the Pope had pressed Florence to send ambassadors to both courts, in the desire to assure themselves of the friendship of a State which, by reason of its extended frontier towards Romagna, would be a very useful ally, a very formidable enemy. As to the Pope, the Florentines quickly decided to send Gian Vittorio Soderini, but he being too ill to start before the 7th December, Alessandro Bracci went as his substitute in the meantime. They could not, however, come to so speedy a decision respecting the Duke, for without wanting to make him their enemy, neither did they wish to contract a friendly alliance that might compel them to assist him. They had certainly no interest in irritating him, but it was undesirable to attract the hostility of the rebels who were in arms and in great force ; neither were they able nor willing to come to a decision without previous consultation with France. So that after much dispute it was impossible to get a majority for the nomination of an ambassador, and it was finally arranged that the Ten should despatch a special envoy.[1] The choice fell upon Niccolò Machiavelli, who, though not yet raised to the rank and renown required in an ambassador, had proved his ability on previous missions, and, as Cerretani observes, was "a man to gain the favour of the few,"[2] *id est,* to obtain the con-

---

[1] It was generally the office of the Signory not the Ten to send ambassadors to Kings, Emperor, Pope, or other potentates. This dispute about the election is mentioned by Parenti, in his " Storia di Firenzi" (National Library of Florence, room 11, shelf 11, Cod. 133, at sheet 62), and by Cerretani in his " Storia di Firenze" (same place, room 11, shelf 111, Cod. 74, at sheet 301*t*). See also the " Dispacci " of A. Giustinian, vol. i. p. 181, note 1.

[2] Cerretani, *loc. cit.*

fidence of those with whom he was in direct communication, as afterwards with the Gonfaloniere Soderini.[1]

As secretary of the Ten, he could not refuse so honourable a charge ; yet he appears to have accepted it with much regret, and set out most unwillingly. Every one of these missions drove him into debt, for he was always ill paid, and yet felt obliged to spend money and keep up his official dignity. Besides he was conscious of lacking both the rank and influence demanded for treating with Valentinois upon honourable terms. And in addition to all this he had recently married Marietta, daughter of Lodovico Corsini, who was warmly attached to him, and much afflicted by so speedy a separation.[2] In reality we know very little of this undoubtedly important event in Machiavelli's private life. But we know that all that has been written to the injury of this poor Marietta, asserting that her husband made allusion to her in his famous story "Belphagor," has not a shadow of foundation. On the contrary, a few of her letters and others written to Machiavelli by friends, prove her to have been an affectionate wife and a good mother.[3] Nevertheless it is certain that Machiavelli seldom spoke of his wife, nor does he appear to have often written to her, generally contenting himself with sending messages by others. Neither did his marriage put a stop to his dissipated mode of life, concerning which he spoke freely and wrote jestingly to many, among others to his friend Buonaccorsi, through whom he received news of Marietta and sent her his own. Without attempting to endow him with an ideal delicacy of feeling, which was certainly unknown to him, nothing justifies us in concluding that he felt no affection for his wife and family. We see instead in his conduct and mode of conversation the results of the scant respect, if not positive contempt for women

[1] Although elected in September, Soderini did not come to Florence before the beginning of October, and entered upon his office towards the end of that month. Cerretani, *cod. cit.*, at sheets 301*t* and 302; Parenti, *cod. cit.*, at sheet 65.

[2] We are unable to determine the precise date of the marriage; but it certainly took place in the year 1502. In 1503 a son was born to him as we learn from several of Buonaccorsi's letters. Buonaccorsi, who never before mentioned Marietta, speaks of her, as we shall see, during Machiavelli's mission to Valentinois, in a way that leaves no doubt of her being already married. On the 27th of October, 1502, the Florentine ambassadors in France make allusion, in a letter to Machiavelli, which we shall quote later, to his having left his wife alone in Florence.

[3] The first to prove this by authentic documents was Signor Inocenzio Giampieri, in an article upon Machiavelli, published in the "Monumenti del Giardino Puccini : ' Pistoia, Cino, 1846.

that began in Italy on the decay of national morality, and of the cynicism with regard to manners, introduced among us by men of learning, that was habitual even among the best and most affectionate of men. For instance, by all that we know of Buonaccorsi, he must have had an excellent character in every respect ; yet his letters to Machiavelli are noteworthy proofs of what we have just stated, and in preparing them for the press it is often necessary to expunge many words and even entire sentences, to avoid arousing the disgust of the modern reader.

However this may be, Machiavelli, unable to decline the proffered mission, and with every reason to hope that his absence would be short, made his wife believe that it would be still shorter, and set about his preparations for the journey.

On the 4th of October the safe-conduct was signed, and on the following day the commission. This instructed him to start without delay to present himself to the Duke, to make large protestations of friendship, and assure him that the Republic had positively refused all assistance to the conspirators, who had already applied for it. "And on this head you can enlarge as may seem best to you ; but if His Excellency should question you upon other points, you will defer answering till after communicating with us and receiving our reply." He was also charged to ask a safe-conduct for Florentine merchants, having to pass through the Duke's dominions, on their way to and from the East, and told to strongly urge that request, since "the matter was of vital importance to the city." [1] All will understand how weighty an undertaking it must have been for the modest Florentine secretary to bandy words with a man like Cæsar Borgia, who used few words, desired less, and was at this moment thirsting for revenge. Yet it was this mission, so unwillingly accepted by Machiavelli, that first showed the extent of his genius as a political writer.

Still unversed in practical affairs, and by nature and temperament more inclined to thoughtful scrutiny than to action, he now had to face a man who acted without speaking ; one who never discussed a point, but signified his ideas by a gesture or movement, indicating that his resolution was already taken or carried out.

---

[1] "Tal cosa è lo stomaco di questa città. Commisione a Niccolò Machiavelli, deliberato a di 5 Ottobre 1502 : Opere," vol. vi. p. 185. It is made out in the name of the Signoria, although Machiavelli carried on his correspondence with the Ten by whom he was sent.

While conscious that, intellectually, he was the Duke's superior, he acknowledged himself inferior as a man of action, and saw the small use, amid the clash of warring passions and the realities of life, of subtle pondering and lengthened reflection. All this tended to increase in him that admiration of which the first signs were displayed during his journey to Urbino with Cardinal Soderini. Borgia, as we have already noted, was neither a great statesman nor a great captain, but a species of brigand-chief, whose strength principally lay in the support of France and the Vatican. He had had, however, the ability to create a State out of nothing, intimidating all men, including the Pope himself ; and when taken by surprise by a large number of powerful enemies, had contrived to free himself, and get rid of them by means of boundless audacity and devilish craft. His audacity and craft were the qualities which so many then admired, and Machiavelli even more than the rest. Considering these qualities in themselves, and scruples apart, the question with him was : what might they not achieve could they only be directed towards a different and nobler purpose ? And in this way his imagination began to take fire.

The Duke, on the other hand, finding himself confronted by a man trained in learning and in the office work of the Florence Chancery, was conscious of his own practical superiority, and plainly showed this consciousness in his conversation. The man, however, was Niccolò Machiavelli, whose keen vision pierced far beneath the surface of things, and who, if sometimes deficient in the instinct suggesting quick repartee and immediate action, had an incomparable power of analysing the actions of others after the event. He had neither ability nor inclination to take part in what happened before his eyes ; but now for the first time his mind began to formulate with clearness and precision the idea of giving to politics an assured and scientific basis, treating them as having a proper and distinct value of their own, entirely apart from their moral worth ; as the art, in short, of finding the means to the end, whatever that end might be. And although the Republic he served was by no means overburdened with moral scruples, in Cæsar Borgia he first beheld the personification of this art, living and breathing before his eyes ; he therefore chose him for its representative type, and at last came to admire him almost as a creation of his own intellect. But we shall recur to this subject later on.

Meanwhile Machiavelli began his journey upon horseback, and reaching Scarperia travelled on by post to Imola, where he arrived on the 7th October ; and at the eighteenth hour of the day presented himself to the Duke without even changing his clothes, "*cavalchereccio* "—horseman like as he was—to make use of his own expression. At that period the rebellion had barely commenced, and the gravity of it was not yet understood. The Duke listened without reply to the protestations of friendship offered by Machiavelli in the name of the Republic, evidently receiving them as conventional forms of speech. Then he said that he desired to confide to the envoy secrets which he had told to no living man ; and began to relate how the Orsini had at one time supplicated him, almost on their knees, to proceed to attack Florence, and how he had always refused his consent. He had had no hand in their expedition on Arezzo, but had not regretted it, since the Florentines had broken faith with him. However, on the receipt of missives from France and the Pope, he had been obliged to order them to withdraw. Hence the rancours leading them (the Orsini) to this " Diet of bankrupts ; "[1] but they were fools for their pains, because the Pope being alive, and the King of France in Italy, " the ground was burning under their feet, and it needed more water to put it out than such men as those could throw." The conclusion of the whole discourse was, that this was the moment for the Florentines to conclude a firm alliance with him. If they waited till he had " patched up matters with the Orsini," there would be as many difficulties and hesitations as before. They must declare themselves and come at once to terms. Machiavelli was obliged to answer that he must write to Florence, which so much vexed the Duke, that he would add nothing more, when pressed to say something definite, as to what kind of agreement he wished, &c. " And notwithstanding that I pressed him, to extract something definite, he always kept wide of the point."[2] On the 9th, the day on which the rebels signed their league at La Magione, the Duke summoned Machiavelli, and showed him so much courtesy, that the latter wrote that he knew not how to describe it. He made him listen to some favourable letters from France, showing him their well-known signature, and again insisted on the necessity of a speedy agreement. "One can plainly see," concluded Machiavelli, after giving many details, "that the Duke is now ready for any bargain ; but it would be advisable to send an ambassador empowered to offer definite terms."[1] The secretary and agents of the Duke all repeated the same things, pressing him on every side. Then came the news of the defeat of Don Ugo and Don Micheletto by the Orsini and Vitelli, and Machiavelli had the greatest difficulty to learn the particulars, "for at this Court all is arranged with admirable secrecy, and matters that are to be hidden are never alluded to." With his usual impenetrability the Duke affected the utmost contempt for his adversaries and the number of men-at-arms which they pretended to have, saying that it was well to call them "men-at-arms in blank, which means in nothing." Among the rest Vitellozzo had never been seen to do anything "beseeming a man of courage, always excusing himself on account of having the French sickness. He is fit for nought else than pillaging defenceless places, robbing those who run away from him, and committing treachery such as this." And the Duke enlarged a good deal on this subject, speaking quite gently without any show of anger.[2] In these days danger had made him more tractable, and Machiavelli was able to obtain the safe-conduct for the Florentine merchants, which he instantly forwarded to the Ten,[3] to whom he was continually sending all the intelligence it was possible to collect.

On the 23rd of October he had another long conference with the Duke, who read to him a very encouraging letter from the King of France, adding that the French lances would soon arrive, and also the foreign infantry. Then he spoke with great indignation of the treachery of the Orsini, who were already trying to come to terms with him. "Now," said he, "they are playing the part of friends, and write me kind letters." "To-day Signor Paolo is to come to see me, to-morrow the Cardinal, and thus they think to bamboozle me at their pleasure. But I, on the other hand, am only dallying with them, I listen to everything, and take my own time." He again repeated that the Florentines ought to conclude a strict friendship with him.[4]

All his conversation hinged upon this point, to which as yet the

[1] Letter of the 7th October, 1502.   [2] First letter of the 20th October.
[3] See the "Legazioni : Opere," vol. vi. p. 225.
[4] Letter of the 23rd October, 1502.

orator could give no reply.   And what greatly added to Machiavelli's perplexity was his inability to discover what would be
the probable result of the agreement.   On the 27th of October,
Paolo Orsini, in the disguise of a messenger, came to treat in
person, " but what is now the Duke's mind I cannot tell : I do
not see how he can pardon this offence, nor how the Orsini can
cease to dread him." [1]   The Secretary Agapito informed him that
nothing was yet concluded, because the Duke wished to add a
certain clause to the terms, " that, if accepted, opens him a
window, and, if refused, a door by which to escape from these
stipulations, at which even babes might laugh." [2]   Other agents
continued to repeat to him that this was the moment to conclude
a friendly alliance with Florence, who ought to give the promised
Condotta, without loss of time.   " As to the agreement with the
rebels it was not even settled, and in any case he need not trouble
about it, since *where there are men there are ways of managing
them.   A* few only of the Orsini will be spared ; for as to
Vitellozzo, who is the real enemy of Florence, the Duke will
not hear a word, knowing him to be a venomous snake, the brand
of Tuscany and Italy."

At last the terms of the agreement were concluded, dating from
the 28th of October, signed by the Duke and Paolo Orsini,
and Machiavelli sent the Ten a secretly obtained copy of them
with his despatch of the 10th of November.[3]   Peace was sworn,
and a league for offence and defence between the Duke and the
rebels, with the obligation of reducing Urbino and Camerino to
obedience.   The Duke promised to continue the previous stipends
to the Orsini and Vitelli, without obliging both to be in
camp at the same time, and the cardinal was only to stay in
Rome when it pleased him to be there.   As to Bentivoglio,
he was left out of the agreement, since, being under French
protection, the Borgia dared not break any pledges made to
him.   The mutual distrust with which both parties drew up
terms was so plainly evident, that it is hard to understand
how the Orsini and Vitelli could let themselves be so miserably entrapped, unless indeed they were frightened by the Duke's
French reinforcements, while want of money made it impossible
for them to continue to struggle against a powerful foe with
France and the Pope at his back.   They hoped to gain time

---

[1] Letter of the 27th October.   [2] Letter of the 8th November, 1502.
[3] This agreement is in the " Opere," vol. iv. p. 264.

in order to begin over again ; but the Duke was on the alert, and in spite of being surrounded by many enemies, it was easy for him to lop off some, and thus weaken the rest—a course impossible for his foes who had only a single individual to contend with.[1]

Very graphically and regularly Machiavelli described the march of all these events to the Ten, and when on the 11th of November those magistrates complained of having had no letters from him for eight days,[2] he answered : " Your excellencies must hold me excused, remembering that matters cannot be guessed, and that we have to do with a prince who governs for himself, and that he who would not write dreams and vagaries, has to make sure of things, and in making sure of them time goes, and I try to use time and not throw it away." [3] In fact, he threw into the observation of the drama then unrolled before his eyes, all the ardour of one seeking for truth in a scientific spirit and method. At times he seemed to be an anatomist dissecting a corpse, and feeling sure of discovering in it the germ of an unknown disease. He had an unequalled gift of faithful and graphic narrative, and his style attains to a vigour and originality, of which modern prose had as yet given no example. In these letters we see Machiavelli's political doctrines growing into shape under our eyes, we note his rigourness of method, and also find the greatest eloquence of which he was capable.

Yet, strange to say, he was thoroughly discontented, and daily begged for his recall with increasing insistence. We have already noted some of the motives of this discontent. Naturally restless, he disliked staying long in one place ; [4] and on this, as on all his

---

[1] Thus wrote Machiavelli in his letter of the 13th November, and in that of the 20th he related how he had said to the Duke, that for that reason he had always judged that he (the Duke) would be victorious, and that had he written what he thought from the first, he should have proved himself a prophet. Later he built up a theory upon this observation, giving it as a general rule, that one who is surrounded by many enemies, can easily weaken and conquer them exactly because he can divide them, which is not possible for his adversaries.

[2] Letter of the Ten, signed by Marcello, dated 11th November, 1502. See " Opere " (P.M.), vol. iv. p. 168. Buonaccorsi repeated the same complaint in his letters.

[3] Letter of the 13th November.

[4] In a letter of the 18th November, Buonaccorsi tells him : " Having so much firmness, that you cannot keep in the same mind for an hour." " Carte del Machiavelli," case iii., No. 16. Ser Agostino Vespucci da Terranuova wrote to him on the 14th of October : " Vides igitur quo nos inducat animus iste tuus equitandi, evagandi ac cursitandi tam avidus." Idem, cassetta iii., No. 38.

legations, could not pay his way with the scanty sum allowed him by the Republic ; and neither wishing to follow the example of those who lived at court at the Duke's expense, nor to compromise the dignity of his position, he was obliged to spend freely and contract debts. His wife, finding herself forsaken almost as soon as married, for her husband, after having promised to come back to her in a week, seldom wrote to her, and left her to struggle through domestic embarrassments, was daily at the Chancery asking news of him, making complaints, and worrying Buonaccorsi and other friends who in their turn continually wrote to him upon the subject.[1]

To these reasons may be added others of even greater importance to him. It was certainly a most troublesome mission to have to temporize with the Duke without the power to settle anything, to find him daily more impatient, and be derisively told by his agents that : " he who waits for time and has it, seeks better bread than wheaten bread." [2]   At any rate, matters could only be concluded by an ambassador charged with clear and exact proposals. In his opinion it had been an error to send one to Rome instead of Imola, because it was the Duke that was to be satisfied by the agreement, not the Pope, who could never undo what was done by the Duke, whereas the contrary might easily occur.[3] But although Machiavelli complained that these anxieties and worries were injuring his health, his laments led to nothing,[4] for the

[1] On the 18th October, 1502, Buonaccorsi wrote to him at Imola, that Marietta asked about him and complained of his remaining absent so long when he had promised to come back to her in a week. She would not write to him herself, and she does thousands of mad things, . . . so in the devil's name pray come back." "Carte del Machiavelli," case iii. No. 5. And in another of the 21st December, 1502, he says to him : "Monna Marietta blasphemes God, and thinks that she has thrown away both herself and her property. For goodness' sake give orders that she may have her own dower, like others of her position, otherwise she will lose all patience with you. . . . I now sit in your place at certain little suppers given by the Ten. . . . &c." Idem, case iii. No. 17.

[2] Letter of the 13th November, 1502.

[3] Letter of the 14th December. On the 27th June, 1502, Bishop Soderini had written to the Signoria from Urbino, that the duke had told him, that as regarded war matters, it was he who ruled Rome, not Rome him." "Opere" (P.M.), vol. iv. p. 19.

[4] On the 22nd November he wrote from Imola : "Besides perceiving that I can do no useful thing in this city, I am in a bad state of body, and two days ago I had a great fever, and still feel ailing. Likewise there is no one to look after my affairs at home, and I lose in many ways." And from many of his friends' letters it was evident that he was compelled to borrow money at this time. And in his

Florentines had excellent reasons for wishing to temporize. The Republic could place no faith either in the Borgia or the Orsini and Vitelli, for alliances made with them were only observed as long as suited their own purposes. The basis of the Republic's policy in Italy was the French alliance, which if not altogether safe, afforded better security than one with the Borgia. To the latter words alone were to be given, and although an ambassador might be sent to the Pope in token of respect, none must be despatched to the Duke who wanted to bring matters to the point. Besides, before sending one to him it was requisite to wait for intelligence and instructions from France. This was the continual purport of the letters of the Ten to Machiavelli, no little to his discontent, since his condition still remained unchanged.

Then too it was most necessary for Florence to have exact information regarding the intentions as well as the movements of the Duke, and on that account the importance of Machiavelli's despatches being now universally recognized, no one would hear of his recall, particularly as no satisfactory person could be found to replace him. Niccolò Valori wrote to him on the 21st of October : "And truly there is so much force in the two last letters you have sent, and they so well show the excellence of your judgment, that they could not have been better approved. And I spoke at length of them with Piero Soderini, who does not think it possible to recall you from your post." [1] Later he was addressed by Buonaccorsi, Marcello Virgilio and the Gonfalonier himself, who all repeated that it was impossible to recall him, since it was necessary to have some one at the Duke's court, and none fitter than himself could be found. [2] At the same time the

first letter of the 6th December, he wrote as usual, asking to be recalled, " to relieve the government of this expense, and me of this inconvenience, since for the last twelve days I have been feeling very ill, and if I go on like this, I fear I may have to come back in a basket."

[1] " Carte del Machiavelli," case iii. No. 30. On the 11th of October he had written to the same : "Your discourse and the portrait could not have been more approved, and all recognize what I have particularly noticed in you, a clear, proper and sincere mode of narration, upon which one can rely." Idem, case iii. No. 12. The Ten, Soderini, many friends wrote to the same effect. See among others the letters of Soderini, dated 14th and 28th November, " Opere " (P. M.), vol. iv. pp. 169 and 201.

[2] M. Virgilio's letter is dated 7th of November, 1502, and is among the " Carte del Machiavelli," case iii. No. 32. In it he says that he gives him this now very unwillingly, for, " I find myself with my own affairs, thine, and thy lectures all on my hands at once." Which is a proof of what we have elsewhere remarked, that the First Secretary still continued to teach at the University.

Gonfalonier and the Ten sent him twenty-five gold ducats and sixteen *braccia* (eleven yards) of damask, the first towards his own expenses, the cloth to be given away in presents.[1]

And there is still another reason to be added to those already mentioned. It is true that Machiavelli found the amplest materials for study in observing the actions of Valentinois and those around him ;[2] it is true that he regarded politics as abstract from morality ; equally true that he was troubled by few scruples of conscience where State affairs were concerned ; yet notwithstanding all this it was intolerable to one of his disposition, to be continually involved in so dense a tangle of infamy ; to live among men steeped in crime, ever ready for treachery and bloodshed, amenable to nothing but brute force, without having the slightest power to prevent ·or modify their misdeeds. No opinion can be more erroneous than that held by those supposing that the actions of Valentinois at this period were counselled and directed by Machiavelli.[3]   On the contrary, all his letters tend to prove the great difficulty he experienced in discovering the intentions and secret designs of the Duke, and how often he failed in this being kept altogether in the dark. The Duke did not heed the advice of the Florentine secretary, whom he sometimes seemed almost to ridicule. Machiavelli was neither bloodthirsty nor cruel, indeed the gentleness of his disposition made all contact with evil most repugnant to him. Frequently, during this legation, expressions fell from his pen, betraying a certain agonized terror

---

[1] The letter of the Gonfaloniere Soderini, written on the 21st December, is also included among the " Carte del Machiavelli," and was published in the " Opere " (P. M.), vol. iv. p. 243. See too the letters of the Ten published in the same volume, at pp. 239–41.

[2] On the 27th October, 1502, the Florentine ambassadors in France, Luigi Della Stufa and Ugolino Martelli, wrote to him : " We should have some compassion on you, who, like ourselves, have had to leave your wife and your home, were it not that you must have been already wearied out by the grave nature of your business in Florence, and that you must willingly relax your mind and repose your body ; that change of air and seeing other faces, especially when of such a sort, generally sharpens the wits ; and therefore we congratulate you, and we pray you, when you have time, to write us some news."   "Opere " (P. M.), vol. iv. pp. 132–34.

[3] Passerini, in his notes to Ademollo's romance Marietta dei Ricci, said outright, that Machiavelli believing to have found in Borgia " the fitting instrument to carry out his cherished idea of the liberty and union of Italy, *instigated him to his famous treachery at Sinigaglia.*"   (Note 10 to chap. iv.) He repeats this in the " Opere " (P. M.). This opinion, maintained before and after, by other writers also, found in Gervinus one of its first and most energetic opponents.

beneath a veil of cynicism. Then, to banish the memory of horrible sights, he wrote ribald and facetious letters to his official colleagues, which made them burst with laughter,[1] as they told him in their replies, and, in their turn, they related to him all the gossip and scandal of the Chancery—where, in his absence, there was always great disorder—or else their own excesses and indecencies.

At other times, weary of such themes, he withdrew to meditate on the writers of antiquity. We find him writing to Buonaccorsi with feverish insistence for " Plutarch's Lives," and he was continually applying to this kind and obliging friend for books, money, and help of all kinds. In a letter of the 21st of October, Buonaccorsi wrote to him : " We have been searching for ' Plutarch's Lives,' but it is not to be bought in Florence. Have patience, for we must write to Venice for it ; and to tell you the truth, you are a worry to ask for so many things."[2] A strange spectacle to see Machiavelli, while divided between contemplation of the heroes of Plutarch and of the deeds of Valentinois, beginning to create a science of politics founded on the history of the past and experience of the present. Scholastic writers had sought the first origin and basis of human society, starting from the conception of God and the Supreme Good, and digressing into reflections having no weight on the practical affairs of life. Even Dante had been unable in his " Monarchia " to free himself from theories that were too abstract and artificial. For similar theories Machiavelli had neither time, opportunity, nor liking. Face to face with the realities of life, he investigated the ruling laws of human actions, in order to formulate useful precepts for the government of men. He sought to know the sources from which the statesman derives his strength, and how that strength should be employed to attain the desired end.

Meanwhile it became increasingly difficult to obtain audience of

[1] A letter of Bartolommeo Ruffini, dated the 23rd October, 1502, said : " Your letters to Biagio and the others are most grateful to all, and the jests and merry saws contained in them make all crack their jaws with laughter. Your wife desires you, and often sends here to ask of you and of your return."

[2] " Carte del Machiavelli," case iii. No. 6. His affection for Machiavelli was so great, that on the 18th of October 1502, after writing to him concerning it, he added : " For the which I do not desire you to be grateful, since even if I wished not to love you and be all yours, I could not help myself, being as it were forced by nature to love you." Idem, case iii. No. 5.

the Duke, who always harped on the necessity of concluding an alliance, confirming the already stipulated *Condotta*, and, whenever forced to listen to fresh protestations of friendship, without any definite proposals, broke out indignantly : " *Ecco !* nothing can be settled " with these Florentines ! [1] Yet from time to time he summoned Machiavelli, and under colour of making fresh confidences, tried to see how the land lay. One day he told him that in past times Giovan Paolo Baglioni had begged for a letter empowering him to follow Vitellozzo and assist him in the restoration of the Medici in Florence, and that he had written the letter. " Now I know not," he continued, looking at Machiavelli, " whether he may have boasted of this to lay the blame at my door." And the Secretary replied that he had heard nothing of the matter.[2] Another day he confided to him with much gravity how Paolo Orsini declared that the Florentines had just offered him a *Condotta* for the army before Pisa, and that he had refused it. Thereupon Machiavelli asked whether Orsini had given the name of the person bearing the offer, or had shown the letters, and if he was in the habit of telling lies. The Duke, perceiving that the secretary would not fall into the trap, replied that Orsini had neither mentioned names, nor shown letters ; but had told plenty of lies. "And thus this matter passed off in laughter, although at first he had spoken of it with disquiet, pretending to believe it and be vexed by it." [3] He then spoke of a secret agreement made by the Venetians in Rimini, by means of a compatriot who dwelt there, adding that he—the Duke—had caused him to be hung to save their honour." After uttering this warning, as it were by chance, he went on to talk of the conquest of Pisa, remarking that " it would be one of the most glorious any captain could make." " Then he referred to Lucca, saying that it was the richest of States, and a mouthful for a *gour-*

---

[1] Letter of the 20th November.

[2] Letter of the 20th November. In a despatch of the 7th August, 1502, Giustinian wrote, that the Pope confessed that he had been dragged into seconding Vitellozzo and the Orsini in the affair of Arezzo. The ambassador, with his usual keenness, drew the conclusion that he spoke in this way, as a measure of precaution, having probably written compromising letters to Orsini and Vitellozzo.

[3] In the despatch of the 13th November, Giustinian writes that the Pope had told him how the Orsini were continually tempting the Florentines with the offer of giving them Pisa, " and these fools believe them ; . . . for to get Pisa they would sell their souls to the devil, would abandon the king of France, ourselves, and all the rest of the world."

mand. He afterwards added that if he, Florence and Ferrara were allied, they need be afraid of nothing."[1] It was the old story of the cat and the mouse, only in this case the mouse with whom he tried to play was Niccolò Machiavelli.

Meanwhile the negotiations with the rebels were still being continued, in order to drag as many as possible into them. Vitellozzo was still restive and hesitated, so that he was spoken of with much indignation at court. "This traitor has given us a dagger-thrust, and now thinks to heal it with words."[2] Yet he too was at last caught in the noose. When all was concluded, the Duke of Urbino again found himself alone and abandoned ; wherefore he had to immediately provide for his own safety, and, after demolishing some of his fortresses, leaving others in the care of trusty adherents, he took flight upon a mule, bemoaning his sad fate, and hotly pursued by the Pope and Valentinois. At Castel Durante he fell into a swoon from fatigue and suffering. Yet after all he succeeded in his escape.[3] Antonio da San Savino was sent as governor over his dominions, and ruled with tolerable moderation ; but in Romagna a certain Messer Ramiro showed the most unheard of cruelty in a similar post.[4] At the same time the Duke set out with his army for Forlì, accompanied by Machiavelli, who on the 14th of December wrote from Cesena that all was uncertainty and suspense, for that not one lance had been dismissed ; and in spite of the treaty one naturally judged of the future by the past, which compelled one to believe that the Duke now meant to make sure of his enemies. He harped upon the necessity of coming to an agreement by means of an ambassador and again begged to be recalled.[5] But the Republic was less than ever inclined to listen to him now that matters were drawing to a conclusion, and France allowed it to be seen that she would no longer leave the Borgia unbridled.

In fact, the four hundred and fifty French Lances who had so much added to the Duke's prestige, were suddenly recalled, and took their departure thereby, wrote Machiavelli, " driving this

---

[1] First letter of the 6th December.   [2] Letter of the 28th of November, 1502.

[3] " Lettero di Piero Ardinghelli, Commissario Fiorentino," published by C. Guasti. " Archivio Storico," Series iii. vol. xix. No. 1st, p. 21 and fol.

[4] Known indifferently as Messer Rimino or Messer Ramiro d' Orco ; his real name was Remigius de Lorqua. See the " Dispacci " of A. Giustinian, vol. i. p. 226, note.

[5] Letter of the 14th of December, 1502, from Cesena.

court out of its wits ... ; and every one is building castles in
the air." The reason of this sudden change was not then
understood, and none could foresee its possible consequences.[1]
It is certain however that this fact, that of all the strongholds of Urbino being either dismantled or still held in Guidobaldo's name, and the impossibility of placing any confidence in
the recently concluded agreement, "had already deprived the
Duke of half his forces and two-thirds of his reputation."[2] Yet
his artillery continued its march as though nothing had happened;
1,000 Swiss had arrived at Faenza, and, between Swiss and
Gascons, he had already a force of about 1,500 men. No one
could guess the object of his movements; all was mystery, for
"this lord never reveals anything excepting when doing it, and
he does it under pressure of necessity, on the moment and not
otherwise; wherefore I pray your Excellencies to excuse me and
not charge me with negligence, when I cannot satisfy your
Excellencies with news, for at most times I fail to satisfy even
myself."[3] And the mystery was farther increased by a strange
circumstance that took place at this time. Messer Rimino or
Ramiro, the duke's trusted instrument in Romagna, where he
had committed most atrocious cruelties to bring the country into
subjection, and excited universal hatred, came from Pesaro to
Cesena and, to the astonishment of all, was arrested on the 22nd
of December and thrown into a dungeon.[4] Four days later
Machiavelli wrote to the Ten: "This morning Messer Rimino
has been found cut into two pieces, on the Piazza where he still
lies, and all the people have been able to see him; the cause of
his death is not well known, excepting that such was the pleasure
of the prince, who shows us that he can make and unmake men
according to their deserts."[5]

---

[1] Letters of the 20th and 23rd of December.

[2] Giustinian, despatch of the 29th of December, and note to the same.

[3] Letter of the 26th of December, last of those written from Cesena.

[4] Letter of the 23rd of December, 1502.

[5] Letter of the 26th of December. In chap. vii. of the "Principe," Machiavelli says in allusion to this fact, that the Duke wished to clear himself from the
charges of cruelty brought against him on account of Messer Rimino's misdeeds
as soon as the latter had freed him of his enemies. See also the "Dispacci" of
A. Giustinian, vol. i. p. 293.

In the same letter Machiavelli thanked the Ten for having sent him the twenty-
five gold ducats and the black damask of which we have already spoken. And
à propos to this Buonaccorsi wrote to him on the 22nd of the same month: "You
will crib a coat of this cloth, rascal that you are." See the "Opere," note to
p. 332 of vol. vi.

But now things were hurrying to their end; all was in train for the taking of Sinigaglia. From the days of Sixtus IV. this city had belonged to Giovanni Della Rovere, the husband of Giovanna, sister of Guidobaldo d'Urbino, and now, by the death of that nobleman, had passed in 1501 to his son Francesco Maria, a boy of eleven years, whom Alexander VI. had nominated Prefect of Rome, like his father before him. The first time Guidobaldo had taken flight, his little nephew had accompanied him, but was now again at Sinigaglia with his mother, who governed for her son, aided by the counsels of his guardian, the celebrated Andrea Doria, and was styled the Prefettessa. Doria, perceiving the hasty advance of the Duke's army, and being already confronted by the troops of Vitellozzo and the Orsini, who were disposed to attack the city, first placed in safety the mother and child entrusted to his care, and then ordering his men to defend the citadel to the utmost, hurried in person to Florence.[1]

On the 29th of December, Machiavelli wrote a letter from Pesaro that was lost on the way, giving a very minute narration of what he afterwards summarized in other letters; namely, how Vitellozzo and the Orsini had entered Sinigaglia, and how the Duke on hearing this ordered them to station their men in the suburb outside the walls, and instantly marched his army towards the city, which he entered on the morning of the 31st of December. The first to seek his presence was Vitellozzo, who having resisted reconciliation more stoutly than the others, knew himself to be the most hated. This captain came humbly forward, cap in hand, mounted on a mule, and unarmed. He was followed by the Duke of Gravina, Paolo Orsini, Oliverotto da Fermo, and all four accompanied the Duke through the streets of the city, to the house prepared for his reception. The Duke, who had already given the signal to those who were to seize them, made them prisoners as soon as they entered the house, ordered their foot soldiers in the suburb to be stripped and disarmed, and sent half his army to perform the same office on the men-at-arms quartered in the neighbouring castles at six or seven miles from Sinigaglia. And on the same day Machiavelli immediately reported the event, adding : "The sack is still going on, although it is now 23 o'clock" (an hour before sunset). "I am much troubled in my mind ; I know not if I can send this letter,

[1] Ugolini, "Storia dei Conti e Duchi d'Urbino," vol. ii. pp. 106–115.

having no one to carry it. I will write at length in another ; and it is my opinion that they (the prisoners) will not be alive to-morrow morning." [1]

Another letter, much longer and of more importance, written at the same date, was lost. We have, however, that of the 1st of January, 1503, in which he relates how towards one o'clock of the night, he had been summoned by the Duke, "who, with the brightest face in the world, expressed his satisfaction at this triumph, adding wise words and expressions of exceeding affection towards our Florence. He said that this was the service which he had promised to render you at the fitting moment. And as he had declared that he would offer you his friendship all the more pressingly, the surer he was of himself, so now he kept that promise ; then he expounded all the reasons inducing him to desire this friendship, in words which excited my admiration. He also begged me to write to you, that having destroyed his capital enemies, who were also those of Florence and France, and uprooted the tares which threatened to overrun Italy, you should now give him a manifest token of friendship, by sending troops towards Perugia, to arrest the flight of Duke Guidobaldo who had gone in that direction, and to take him prisoner should he enter Tuscany. It has likewise happened that, at ten o'clock last night, the Duke had Vitellozzo and Messer Oliverotto da Fermo both strangled ;" [2] "the other two have been left living, in order, as

---

[1] Letter of the 31st of December, 1502.

[2] The letter only states that they were put to death, but it is known that they were strangled, and Machiavelli himself mentions it elsewhere. At chap. viii. of the " Principe," he relates that Oliverotto da Fermo, brought up by his uncle, Giovanni Fogliani, and sent to fight under Paolo and then under Vitellozzo Vitelli, had become the chief leader of the latter's troops. Longing to make himself master of Fermo, where many were discontented with his uncle's rule, he first made an agreement with a few of the citizens, and then wrote to his uncle that he wished to come and see him and his native city. He arrived with a hundred horsemen, was, by orders of his uncle, most honourably received ; gave a grand dinner to him and the principal men of Fermo, and then had them all put to death.

Niccolò Vitelli had five sons, four of whom died a violent death. The elder, Giovanni, by a cannon shot at the siege of Osimo ; the second, Camillo, by a stone at Circello in the kingdom of Naples, in fighting for the French ; Paolo was beheaded ; Vitellozzo strangled.

Gregorovius in a note to p. 483 of vol. vii. of his " Geschichte," &c., remarks, how *à propos* to these murders, Giovio wrote in his " Life of Cæsar Borgia," that "he had assassinated the Orsini by means of a splendid deception ; and the King of France had said—according to the orator of Ferrara—that it was 'an action

it is thought, to see whether the Pope has seized the Cardinal[1] and the others who were in Rome, and it is surmised that he has seized them; that they may all be cheerfully got rid of at the same time." The citadel had already surrendered; the army had that same day begun its march towards Perugia, before going on to Sienna; Machiavelli followed on its track, and it being now the winter season, the soldiery and all following the camp were exposed to many hardships.[2]

Turmoil and disorder everywhere prevailed, and all the petty tyrants of the land fled in dismay on the Duke's approach, as though pursued by a dragon.[3] It can easily be believed that amid so great a confusion few letter-carriers could be found, and still fewer who were trustworthy, and for this reason many of Machiavelli's despatches were lost. On the 4th of January, 1503, he gave notice that the soldiery of the Vitelli and Orsini had managed to escape. Meanwhile the march was continued, and the Baglioni fled from Perugia, which surrendered on the 6th. Their sisters, on reaching the frontier where, in consequence of superior orders, the Florentine commissary, Piero Ardinghelli, had repulsed all the refugees, disguised their young daughters as boys, preferring to trust them to the commissary's compassion, rather than see them fall into the hands of the enemy. And Ardinghelli wrote to the Gonfalonier Soderini on the 19th of January, saying: "Now, I cannot avoid being stirred to pity by the spectacle of so much youth and misfortune. . . . I have preferred to write to your Excellency in person, to know if I may give shelter to these four women, or at least to the two damsels. . . . Should this not be contrary to the government's intentions, having a natural compassion for the afflicted,

---

worthy of a Roman.'" The Venetians had disapproved of the deed because of its great cruelty; but the Ferrara orator there had declared that they ought to bend their heads, when he proved to them that the Pope and Duke had been quite right "*etiam* to quarter these men, and utterly root out their family." It is singular too that on this occasion Isabella Gonzaga, with a letter of the 15th of January, 1503, sent the Duke 100 masks from Mantua, and he warmly thanked her for them in a letter of the 1st of February. See documents xliv. and xlv. in the "Lucrezia Borgia" of Gregorovius.

[1] Cardinal Orsini.

[2] Letter of the 1st of January, 1503.

[3] " Sentì Perugia e Siena ancor la vampa
 Dell' Idra, e ciaschedun di quei tiranni
 Fuggendo innanzi alla sua furia scampa."
 Machiavelli, "Decennale," dec. 1.

I should be greatly obliged to you."[1] And the request was granted.

On the 8th Niccolò Machiavelli wrote from Assisi that all were wondering why no one had yet come from Florence to congratulate the Duke, who repeated that by his after-achievements he had rendered signal service to the Republic, for " it would have cost your Excellencies two hundred thousand ducats to put an end to Vitellozzo and the Orsini, and even then you could not have done it so neatly." And meanwhile he pursued his march, always " proceeding with unheard-of good fortune, and more than human energy and hope,"[2] resolved to expel the tyrant Pandolfo Petrucci from Sienna, and, if possible, take him captive, to which end the Pope tried to " lull him to sleep with Briefs," for it was well, said the Duke, " to deceive those who have been masters of treachery." He did not attempt to take the city, for that was forbidden by France ; but he was determined to get rid of Pandolfo, who had been " the brain " of the conspiracy.[3]

On the 13th of January they were at Castello della Pieve, and as the new Florentine ambassador, Jacopo Salviati, was at last on the point of arriving, Machiavelli prepared for his own departure, which occurred in fact on the 20th. First, by way of replacing the many letters which had been lost, he wrote one containing a summary of all the events that had happened, but unfortunately the first sheet is all remaining to us of it. In this, with great zeal and care, he begins to give a general sketch of the expedition which, in his opening lines, he pronounces truly " rare and memorable." He does not attribute any premeditated treachery to the Duke, but rather a stern resolve on speedy revenge, when aware that his captains meant to betray him on account of the departure of the French lances. He describes the exceeding caution shown by him in concealing from the Orsini and Vitelli the amount of the forces still at his disposal, making them pass for fewer than they were. And with equal admiration, Machiavelli minutely describes the orders given for dividing the whole army into small corps, and then marching them altogether upon Sinigaglia, so as to arrive there unexpectedly with an overwhelming force, while the enemy's troops were dispersed at

---

[1] " Lettere di Piero Ardinghelli," as before quoted.
[2] Letter of the 8th of January, 1503.   [3] Letter of the 10th of January.

a distance from the city, and could not disobey him, without prematurely revealing their treachery. But just as we are at the point of the entry into Sinigaglia we come to the end of this fragment,[1] in which the writer, while endeavouring to remain faithful to historic truth, seems almost to have persuaded himself that he was depicting a hero ; indeed some reproofs to that effect had already reached him from Florence, as we learn by Buonaccorsi's letters.[2]

Machiavelli was still at Castello della Pieve on the 18th of January, when the Duke, having received the long-expected news that the Pope had imprisoned Cardinal Orsini and the others in Rome, strangled Paolo and the Duke of Gravina Orsini, whom he had brought with him under strong escort from Sinigaglia. The Duke then continued to lay waste the Siennese territory, and threatened to attack the city itself if Petrucci were not immediately expelled, but was appeased when the latter begged to be allowed to depart with a safe-conduct, for the French forbade any attack upon Sienna, and the Pope had summoned him suddenly to Rome. But although he granted Petrucci a safe-conduct and a letter recommending him to the care of the Lucchesi, this did not prevent him from despatching fifty armed men on his track with orders to capture him dead or alive. And truly on this occasion the tyrant of Sienna had a miraculous escape from death. He had left his city on the 28th of January, and accompanied by Giovan Paolo Baglioni taken flight towards Lucca with headlong speed, for although ignorant that he was pursued, no one put any trust in the promises of a Borgia. The assassins were on the point of overtaking him, when they were arrested by the Florentine commissary, who, as the war between Florence and Pisa was still going on, would not allow armed men to rove freely about the field of war. Being ignorant of what had passed, he kept them prisoners till he could receive instructions from Florence. This gave the fugitives time to escape from the poisoned claws of the Duke. The latter was now obliged to hurry to Rome where his presence was anxiously desired by the

---

[1] " Carte del Machiavelli," case 1, No. 19, autograph. This fragment was published in the " Opere " (P. M.), vol. iv. p. 254. Passerini asserts that it was written on the 31st of December, 1502 ; but it mentions the arrival of the new ambassador, who was still being waited for on the 13th of January, 1503.

[2] Buonaccorsi often tells him that he is accused of too much admiration for Valentinois.

Pope, who felt by no means secure with the Campagna full of armed men hostile to his authority. On the other hand France had again issued a severe prohibition of all farther conquests.

While in Romagna and Central Italy we behold the Duke, and have Niccolò Machiavelli to give us so graphic a picture of all that occurred there ; in Rome we may look upon the equally tragic reverse of the medal. Here we see the Pope possessed of far less self-control than his son, confronted by Antonio Giustinian, who without having the genius or culture of Machiavelli, had much greater influence, larger experience of the world, and extraordinary knowledge of mankind, and who, as Venetian ambassador, had many means lacking to the Florentine secretary, of penetrating to the root of affairs. From the 6th of August he had written to the Doge, that Vitellozzo was "fighting shy" of the Duke, and that he foresaw that both the latter and the Pope were decided to "clip the wings" of the Orsini. When the news of the rebellion arrived, and then that of the defeat of Don Ugo and Don Micheletto, the Pope broke out in expressions of mad rage against the Orsini in Consistory, but immediately afterwards lowered his tone, and showed himself almost humble and downcast. At the first intelligence of French encouragement, his joy was so overpowering that the Cardinals sneered among themselves at the Holy Father's want of self-command.[1] Then began the preliminaries towards a reconciliation, and the ambassador, without being troubled by the doubts and uncertainties of the Florentine, instantly noticed that they were being carried on so as to omit powerful personages who might afterwards prove obstacles to any violation of the terms or any sanguinary solution.[2] Meanwhile no time was lost. The Pope acknowledged having sent the Duke within a few days the sum of 36,000 ducats.[3] He collected artillery, made warlike preparations as though the enemies were thundering at the gates, and took money " as much from friends as from enemies, not caring whether from Orsini or Colonnesi, and behaves like a drowning man clutching hold of straws."[4]

Without at all endeavouring to discover the principles of a new science of politics, Giustinian was no less intent than Machiavelli on giving a graphic picture of all that he beheld ; and from the early part of November, observing that the monstrous ill faith

[1] Giustinian, despatches of the 1st, 7th, and 18th of October, 1502.
[2] Despatch of the 22nd of October.   [3] Despatch of the 23rd of October.
[4] Despatch of the 24th of October.

with which the negotiations were pursued, was evident from the Pope's own words, he transcribed these to the Doge *de verbo ad verbum*, adding : " And were it possible, I would fain paint the thing before your eyes, for often the manner of speech teaches men more of the intrinsic meaning than the words themselves ; " and every one is persuaded that this is a mock reconciliation.[1] In fact, on reading over the names of the Orsini who had signed it, the Pope said, laughing, to the Venetian ambassador, " Does it not seem to you that this is a company of scoundrels and bankrupts ? Do you not see by the terms, how fearful they are, and how they confess themselves traitors, not excepting the Cardinal himself, who feigns to be our friend, and yet insists on the condition of only staying in Rome when it may suit him to do so ? " And Giustinian then remarked that, " The Orsini might be very sure that they had now cut their own throats." [2] In fact, they showed incomprehensible blindness, especially the Cardinal, who was always in attendance on the Pope, as though he wished to fall into the trap of his own accord.

Alexander's endeavours to gain the friendship of the Venetian Republic coincided with his belief in the near approach and certainty of the Duke's new triumphs in Romagna. He called the ambassador aside, and with his arms crossed and pressed to his breast, deplored to him that the jealousy of Italian potentates should have delivered the land into the hands of foreigners who had their mouths open to swallow it. " So far our only safety has lain in the jealousy between France and Spain, otherwise we should already be ruined. But do not fancy that you (Venetians) are the children of the white goose (privileged people). Your turn would have come also. We are old, and must think of our posterity, wherefore our only hope is in your *Serenissima Republica*, which is everlasting. For the love of God, let us unite together to provide for the salvation of Italy. Do you know what is said of you ? That you try to be over wise. Be content with being wise enough. And in saying these things (adds the ambassador) his breast seemed as though it would burst, and as though the words came from his heart instead of his mouth." [3]

[1] Giustinian, despatch of the 4th of November.

[2] The original expression in Venetian dialect is : " that the Orsini had taken *tossego a termene*," *i.e.*, poison that would act in a given time. Giustinian, despatch of the 6th of November, and note to p. 195 of vol. i.

[3] Giustinian, despatches of the 7th and 15th of November, and 2nd of December, 1502.

But who could put faith in the Borgia ?   Therefore he said very
few words in reply to the Pope ; "and *solum* I thanked his
Holiness for his good intentions towards your Most Excellent
Lordship."   Besides even Venice was not capable at that period of
pursuing a really national policy, nor of profiting by the just
notions, such as were now in his own interest and for badly disguised ends expressed by the Pope, while ready the following day
to act in direct contradiction of all that he so passionately urged.

On the 24th of November, while Machiavelli in Romagna was
still in the dark respecting the Duke's designs and torturing his
wits to divine them, Giustinian wrote from Rome : " The first
blow will be struck at Sinigaglia to prevent the Prefettessa from
helping the Duke of Urbino, whom the Pope madly desires to get
into his hands." [1]   The latter was continually collecting money for
his son, who spent about 1000 ducats a day [2] besides all that he
got by robbery and pillage.   So extraordinary was his impatience
for news of the Duke's progress that when the latter halted for
some time at Cesena, he repeatedly shouted, beside himself with
vexation : " We don't know what the devil he is staying there
for ; we have written to him to make the best of this good time—
' al fio de putta bastardo ! ' and such like oaths and words in
Spanish." [3]   To distract his mind from these thoughts and the
public attention from his secret manœuvres, he got up popular
festivals and masquerades, which marched in procession through
the streets of Rome and became most indecent in front of the
windows, whence he looked down upon them, his old frame
shaking with libertine laughter. [4]   He passed his evenings in the
Vatican, often keeping up his "customary diversions," till dawn,
for certain fair ladies never failed him, and indeed, " without
them there was no feast worth having ; " and also hundreds of
ducats were staked at his Holiness's gambling tables.   In these
amusements the Cardinal Orsini often shared, to the astonishment of the whole Court, who could not understand why he
should so weakly "entangle himself in the net" of his own accord. [5]

---

[1] Giustinian, despatch of the 15th of November, 1502.   It is the second written
on that day, and is marked No. 168.

[2] Despatch of the 17th of December.   [3] Despatch of the 23rd of December.

[4] Burchard speaks in his " Diario " (25th November) of a masquerade of thirty
persons in the Piazza of St. Peter *habentes nasos longos et grossos in formam
priaporum sive membrorum virilium, in magna quantitate, precedente valigia
cardinalari.*   The Pope looked on at his window.

[5] Despatch of the 30th of December.

On the 31st of December the Pope wandered about the halls of the Vatican, saying that he could not imagine what the Duke was doing spending a thousand ducats a-day for nothing ; but then, unable to restrain his good humour, would laughingly add : " He always wants to do something fresh, his mind is too great." And the cardinals begged him to be easy, for the Duke knew how to turn his money to account. " We are all awaiting his return to get up a fine carnival. We know well, we know well," said the Pope, still laughing, " that you all think of nothing else." This was the very day upon which Niccolò Machiavelli announced the capture of Sinigaglia and of the Duke's enemies. After mass the following day, the Holy Father summoned the ambassadors there present, and told them the great news, affecting to have been surprised by it ; and he added that the Duke never forgave any who had injured him, and did not leave his vengeance to others, and he threatened those who had offended him, especially Oliverotto, " whom the Duke had sworn to hang with his own hands." The cardinals stood round him and tickled his ears [1] " with their various congratulations, while he freely descanted on the virtues and magnanimity of the Duke." Then they glanced at each other, and shrugging their shoulders, began to speculate upon what would happen next.[2]

In fact, on the 3rd of January, 1503, the Pope having received the positive intelligence — still unknown to the rest of the world—of the strangling of Oliverotto and Vitellozzo, called Cardinal Orsini in great haste to the Vatican. The victim presented himself with the Governor and Jacopo da Santa Croce, who, it seems, had received orders to accompany him, although pretending to do so by chance. As soon as the Cardinal arrived he was seized and—as all had foreseen—thrown into the castle of St. Angelo, never to leave it alive. His house was immediately stripped, and his mother and two young maidens who were with her were driven forth and allowed to take nothing but the clothes they wore at the time. These poor women wandered about Rome without finding any one to give them shelter, for all were trembling for their own safety. Numerous other arrests speedily followed. The auditor of the Chamber, bishop of Cesena, was torn from his bed, while suffering from

---

[1] An expression used by Giustinian to signify that they praised and flattered him.

[2] Giustinian, despatch of the 1st of January, 1503.

fever, and his house pillaged ; the same fate befell the Protonotary Andrea *de Spiritibus,*[1] and many others besides. Whoever had money trembled for his life, for now " the Pontiff seems to think of nothing but obtaining gold, and says that what he has already done, is nothing to that which he shall do."[2] Even the Medici in Rome were terror-stricken ; the bishop of Chiusi died of fear, and so many took flight that the Pope thought it necessary to summon the Conservators of the city, to inform them that, all guilty persons having now been seized, the others might set about preparing a grand carnival.[3] And he himself, while continuing his work of extermination, passed the months of January and February in carnival pleasures. The Venetian ambassador, going to confer with him upon business, found him laughing in the balcony, watching the tricks of the masks beneath his windows ;[4] and afterwards being invited to a supper party, found the Pope— who had passed the day attending races—enjoying the per- formance of plays, for which he had always much liking, in the midst of his cardinals, " some in their cardinal's dress, and a few in masquerade, together with several companions of the kind most pleasing to the Pontiff, some of whom lay stretched at his Holi- ness's feet."[5]

On the day succeeding this festival, Cardinal Orsini expired in the prison of St. Angelo—by poison—as all men said. In vain his fellow cardinals had petitioned for his life, in vain had his relations offered 25,000 ducats as its ransom. His mother after being at first allowed to send food to her son, and then forbidden to do so, sent a woman beloved of the Cardinal to the Pope, to offer him a large pearl that he was known to covet. He accepted the pearl, but did not grant the pardon. However at that period the Cardinal was showing " signs of frenzy," and according to the " general opinion had already drunk of the cup poisoned for him by the Pope, who then ordered the physicians to give him their best care."[6] The 15th, he was found, they said, in high fever ; the 22nd he was dead ; the 24th they were called on to depone that he had died a natural death.   Then, by

---

[1] Giustinian, despatch of the 5th of January, 1503, at 20 of the clock.
[2] Despatch of the 6th of January.
[3] Despatch of the 8th of January, 19 of the clock.
[4] Despatch of the 7th of January.
[5] Despatch of the 8th of January, hora 2 noctis.
[6] Despatch of the 21st February, 1503.

order of his Holiness, public obsequies were performed in his honour.[1]

The Duke was now expected. The Cardinal d'Este had fled from Rome at this announcement, in terror of his life. Among the thousand different rumours afloat, it was even said that he loved Donna Sancia, the Duke's sister-in-law and the Duke's mistress.[2]

Such of the Orsini as had escaped slaughter, the Savelli, and the Colonna, had taken arms, and having entrenched themselves at Ceri, Bracciano, and other points, attacked the bridge of Nomentano on the 23rd of January. And although they were repulsed, the Pope had the palace placed in a state of defence ; became maddened with rage and alarm ; went about shrieking that he would root out the Orsini family, and begged his Duke to come to him without loss of time. The latter was now on the road, to the very last spreading devastation by the way. At San Quirico, finding that all the inhabitants had fled upon his approach excepting two old men and nine old women, he had them strung up by their arms, with a slow fire under their feet, to make them reveal where treasure was hidden ; and, as they could not tell him this, they had to die. He committed similar atrocities at Montefiascone, Acquapendente, Viterbo, &c.[3]

Although everything gave way before him, and many of his foes had retreated, yet Ceri and Bracciano held out against the insufficient artillery of the Pope, whom the Duke did not dare to assist openly, on account of the orders received from France, to which however the Holy Father paid no attention. In this way matters proceeded slowly, and on the 26th of February, leaving the fifty armed men who had accompanied him in a neighbouring villa, the Duke entered Rome with Cardinal Borgia, Cardinal d'Alibret and three servants, all masked. In the evening he was present at the representation of one of the usual comedies at the Vatican and retained his disguise, although recognized by every one.[4]

Machiavelli meanwhile, his imagination fired, his mind full of

---

[1] Despatches of 22nd, 23rd, and 24th February.

[2] " Quia idem Cardinalibus diligebat et cognescebat principissam, uxorem fratris dicti Ducis, quam et ipse Dux cognoscebat carnaliter." Burchardi, as quoted by Gregorovius, " Geschichte," &c., vol. vii. p. 486, note 4.

[3] This is the account given by Burchardi in his " Diary," at the date of the 23rd January, 1503.

[4] Giustinian, despatches of the 26th and 27th of February.

all he had seen and heard of the Duke Cæsar and the Borgia in general, had returned to his Florence chancery, where he continued to read and write letters relating to those personages. But any one inclined to think him thoroughly deceived in his judgment of the true character of the Pope and the Pope's son, need only look through the first "Legazione" to Rome and the first "Decennale," to be convinced of the contrary. In the latter he styles the Duke "a man without compassion, rebellious to Christ, the Hydra, the basilisk, deserving of the most wretched end, and speaks of the Pope in almost identical terms." [1]

Yet, as we have related, it was in associating with Valentinois, that his mind first conceived and shaped out the idea—which was henceforth to occupy his whole life—of a science of Statecraft separate from, and independent of, every moral consideration. In such separation he saw the sole means of clearly formulating this science, and founding it on a new basis. He was going through a process of thought almost resembling that of a man attempting for the first time to investigate the laws of the rise and decline of the wealth of nations, and studying the economic problem no less in the merchant, manufacturer, or agriculturist who are producers, than in the soldier who is a pillager, or the brigand and pirate who are robbers. It was from this more or less abstract and forced separation of a single social phenomenon from all the rest, that political economy in fact arose, and to this the rapidity of its growth was due as well as some of the errors which it afterwards tried to eliminate. Machiavelli, in studying the actions of Cæsar Borgia made a

---

[1] When the Duke hoodwinks the Orsini, he calls him the *basilisk* ; when the Duke goes towards Perugia, he calls him the *hydra;* when the Duke hopes in Julius II., he remarks :—

> " E quel Duca in altrui trovar credette
> Quella pietà che non conobbe mai."

When the Duke is treacherously seized, and imprisoned by Consalvo di Cordova, Machiavelli says :—

> " gli pose la soma
> Che meritava un ribellante a Cristo."

And lastly, after narrating the death of Alexander VI., he adds :—

> " Del qual seguirno le sante pedate
> Tre sue familiari e care ancelle,
> Lussuria, Simonia e Crudeltate."

We shall see what he says later in the first " Legazione " to Rome.

distinction of somewhat the same nature, for this distinction appeared to him in the light of a real fact rather than as an hypothesis or abstraction. At that time he only succeeded in formulating a few general maxims, without rising to a theoretic conception of principles, neither had he sufficient grasp of his method to attempt to enrol his principles in a body of doctrines. Almost unconsciously, his ideas assumed the form of an ideal personage, representing the acute, able, and audacious statesman restrained by no scruples of conscience, no moral influence, from trying to achieve his fixed purpose, no matter what obstacles stood in the path, no matter what acts of treachery and bloodshed had to be performed. In short, in examining the actions of Valentinois, his mind had created an imaginary Valentinois, to which later he continually recurred. It is the well-known figure so often making its appearance amid the maxims of the " Discorsi " and the " Principe," as though to recall their primary origin, and to once more testify that the author had laid the foundations of his policy solely in the realities of life, without going back to the Supreme good, or running aground on any metaphysical abstraction. At a later period he obeyed a similar impulse in writing his " Vita di Castruccio Castracani," which, as all know, is no history, but rather an effort to glean from history his own political ideal. This explains to us the great praise coupled with severe blame accorded by him to Valentinois. His praise is generally bestowed on the ideal personage, his blame on the historical. The one however is not so different from the other as to prevent us from sometimes confusing them, especially as the author himself occasionally does so, when carried away by his imagination, which seems especially to dominate him when he is apparently reasoning in cold blood. Nor is it an uncommon case to find that men of the most reflective and cautious temperament may at times fall a sudden and complete prey to their own imaginations.

But at this period of his life, whatever the state of his mind and ideas may have been, Machiavelli had no time for scientific meditations, nor for the composition of elaborate works. He therefore contented himself with writing a brief narrative of all that he had witnessed in Romagna, not for the purpose of giving exact historic details—for those existed in the numerous despatches of the Legation, in spite of several having been lost—but rather to establish more clearly the prudence and, in his opinion, the marvellous talent of the Duke. And he composed the well-known "Descrizione,"[1] in which the Duke's crafty fashion of killing his enemies is painted in the manner most suitable to the object that the author had in view. Otherwise it would be impossible to account for the diverse manner in which Machiavelli now narrates the very facts which he had described in the "Legazione," at the time when he was upon the spot, and it was his duty to supply the Ten with correct information.

The "Descrizione" begins with a picture of the Duke on his return from Lombardy, whither he had gone to exculpate himself to the King of France "from the many calumnies concerning him spread by the Florentines in consequence of the Arezzo rebellion." This is positively untrue, since the Florentines had not calumniated him, and this should in any case suffice to change the opinion of all those who considered the "Descrizione" to be no more than one of Machiavelli's usual letters. Certainly the secretary could not have spoken to the Ten or the Signoria of the *calumnies* of the Florentines. In continuation he gives a very brief account of the conspiracy at "La Magione," and the reconciliation afterwards concluded between the rebels and the Duke, whose astuteness he brings out in high relief. In this work the Duke is made to leave Imola when "November is going out," and in the "Legazione" on the 10th of December ; he sets forth from Cesena "about the middle of December," whereas in the "Legazione" he was still "about to start" on the 26th of December.

The "Descrizione" then goes on to relate how, after the taking of Sinigaglia by the Vitelli and Orsini, the fortress refused to surrender, the governor having declared that he would yield it to none "but the Duke in person," who, on that account, was invited to come. And, observes Machiavelli, he considered the occasion a good one and unlikely to arouse suspicion, and to give a still better colour to the affair, dismissed the French.[2] In the "Legazione," on the contrary, he had said—what too is clearly proved by all contemporary historians and ambassadors—that the French suddenly went away on the 22nd of December, because

---

[1] " Descrizione del modo tenuto dal Duca Valentino nello ammazzare Vitellozzo Vitelli, Oliverotto da Fermo, il Signor Pagolo e il duca di Gravina Orsini."

[2] All the editions say—"*and for greater security*, he dismissed the French soldiery ; " but the original autograph preserved in the Florence Archives (Carte Strozziane, file 139, sheets 208 and fol.) says—"*e per piu assicurargli,*" *i.e.*, to better deceive the conspirators.

they had been recalled without any reasons being given, and certainly much to the Duke's peril and chagrin.[1]   Indeed, on the 20th of December Machiavelli wrote that this matter " had turned this Court's brains topsy-turvy," and on the 23rd, that thus the Duke " had lost more than half his strength and two-thirds of his reputation."   Now in the " Descrizione " all this is changed into a stroke of cunning on the part of the Duke.   Even the road from Fano to Sinigaglia is here described very differently from the minute description given in the fragment remaining to us of the letter from which we quote, and which gives a summary of recent events.

And to the end the " Descrizione " goes on in the same strain The Duke communicates his design to eight of his trusty adherents, some of whose names are even given, yet in the " Legazione " there is no mention of anything of the sort.   There is also a very different account of the seizure of the four captains, and the dying utterances of Oliverotto and Vitellozzo are given verbatim, although of such words none can confirm nor deny the historic truth, the author having made no mention of them elsewhere, nor it being at all likely that he had any certain knowledge of them.   How can patent contradictions such as these be accounted for, without admitting that this " Descrizione " is something different from exact history ?   The Duke, whom Machiavelli here depicts as calumniated by the Florentines, and far more able and acute than the personage described in the " Legazione," is in fact the precursor of his " Principe," in which we shall behold later, put in a theoretic form, that which we now see only in an individual and concrete shape.   The scientific conception, though not as yet very clear, is however already contained in the ideal personage evoked before us.

[1] On the 28th December, 1502, the Ten wrote to the Commissary Giovanni Ridolfi, in consequence of news received from Machiavelli and others, that they could not understand the cause of this sudden withdrawal, no danger having arisen in Lombardy.   " Whence it may be concluded that it has been in order to check this sinister career and all these designs of aggrandisement."   At all events it was certainly no trick of the Duke.   Archivio Florentino, cl. x. dist. 3, No. 104, sheet 59.   See also A. Giustinian, " Dispacci," vol. i. p. 293, and document iii. at the end of that volume.

CHAPTER VI.

Necessity for new taxes—"Dicorso sulla provvisione del denaro"—Defensive measures against the Borgia—War with Pisa—New misdeeds of the Pope—Predominance of the Spaniards in the Neapolitan kingdom—Death of Alexander VI.—Election of Pius III. and of Julius II.

(1503.)

HE Florentines were now in great straits from the difficulty of finding the funds urgently required for hiring fresh troops: since not only were they threatened by the Borgia on the one hand, and the Pisans on the other, but a new French army was on the march towards Naples, and all dreaded the complications and dangers of which this might prove the source. Yet this was the moment at which the Gonfaloniere Soderini, whose rule hitherto had been very popular, for the first time encountered the strong opposition of the citizens. Seven different proposals were brought before the Great Council during February and March, for the purpose of obtaining the necessary funds, but none could be carried. Nor was it easy to decide what measures to adopt, for were a heavy tax proposed, it could not be accepted by a people already so overburdened, while a slight one would fail in its object. Besides, there were additional motives of discontent to increase the present opposition. The wealthier citizens had not only paid the usual imposts, but had been obliged to lend very considerable sums of money to the Commune, which was therefore their debtor to the extent of four hundred thousand florins, eighteen thousand of which were due to Soderini and his nephews. Accordingly, the rich declined to hear of any special measures, but demanded a general tax of the usual kind, which, weighing equally upon all, might enable the Republic to pay at least a portion of her debt

to those upon whom she had pressed most heavily. In fact, the
various proposals supported by the Gonfaloniere had been drawn
up in conformity with this rule, but all these were rejected by the
Council, where the majority, composed of poorer men, complained
that Soderini, the people's choice, showed undue favour to the
powerful. He sought, they added, to regain the sums which
he had lent to the State, although in receipt of so generous a
stipend. Then, too, there were the outcries of those who were
impoverished by the numerous economies introduced into the new
administration ; and there was even much grumbling, because the
Gonfaloniere's wife, one of the Malaspini family, " very handsome,
though middle-aged, and a good woman of royal manners," to use
Cerretani's expression, had in these days taken up her abode in
the palace, so that ladies were continually seen going up and down
its stairs, an unheard-of thing in Florence.

As the natural consequence of all this, the credit of the
Republic, which had rapidly increased through the election of the
new Gonfaloniere, and the regularity of his administration, now
sank with equal rapidity, and the shares of the Monte Comune
and the Monte delle Fanciulle [1] were negotiated in the market
at the same low figure as before. Accordingly Soderini, being
weary of temporizing measures, assembled the Great Council and
made a notable speech, in which, after dwelling on the dangers
now imminent, he charged the citizens themselves to determine
the nature of the new tax in any way that pleased them, provided
it fulfilled the object of furnishing the requisite funds for the
preservation and defence of the Republic. So finally a *decima*—
or tithe—was voted on all landed property, including that of the
Church, if permission could be obtained from Rome ; and even
a small "*arbitrio*" was agreed upon. This so-called *arbitrio* was
a tax upon professions, and probably derived its name from the
fact of being imposed without any fixed rules, especially in the
present emergency, when it was left entirely to the discretion of
the magistrates. Matters then speedily returned to their normal
condition, all difficulties having been overcome far more easily
than was anticipated.[2]

[1] Monte Comune—the Public Debt—Monte delle Fanciulle—a State Insurance
Office, which gave marriage portions to girls in return for small yearly payments.
—*Translator's note.*

[2] Parenti, "Storie Fiorentine," MS. in the Florence National Library, Cl. ii.
cod. 133, vol. v. at sheet 87 and fol.

Machiavelli now applied himself to the composition of a discourse, that, in his opinion, should have been made upon the occasion. We cannot ascertain whether it was written by command of Soderini, or was veritably the speech read or recited by the latter in the Council. It was certainly composed as though destined for that purpose. Written in a way to allow of certain points being more freely developed in delivery, it has singular strength and concision of style, and contains many of those maxims, general reflections, and historical reminiscences, which were still, as it were, floating in the secretary's mind, and, if not as yet thoroughly arranged, were always expressed with incomparable lucidity.[1]

He begins by remarking that all States find it necessary to unite strength with prudence. The Florentines had testified their prudence by giving unity and a head to the government; but they failed in their duty, in refusing to furnish supplies, when,

---

[1] "Parole da dirle sopra la provvisione del danaio, fatto prima un poco di proemio e di scusa." It was first published in the Florence "Antologia" (July, 1822, vol. vii. pp. 3–10), from one of Machiavelli's autograph manuscripts; it was afterwards reprinted in Milan by the Rusconi Press, 1823, in the "Opere Minori" of Machiavelli: Florence, Le Monnier, 1852, and the more recent but little known edition of the entire works, issued in Florence by A. Usigli, 1857. Some believed it to have been recited by Machiavelli himself in the Great Council; but he, as a salaried official of the Government, had no power either to vote or join in the discussion, nor could any citizen, with the solitary exception of the Gonfaloniere, have held the language contained in this discourse. In the Great Council members either voted for the government proposals, or spoke in favour of them, previous to voting. Members did not, however, vote in their own names, but in that of the different benches (*pancate*) into which the citizens divided in order to consult on the decision to be taken; and all this with infinite care and precaution. Parenti tells us of a certain individual who, on this very occasion, was subjected to imprisonment and then exile, for having spoken too violently against past taxes. (See too my "Storia di Girolamo Savonarola," Book II. chap. v., in which I have given a minute description of the mode of procedure then in force in the Council.) In the "Pratiche" (answering to the Committees of the English Parliament), which were less public, greater freedom of language was employed; but setting aside the improbability of Machiavelli taking part in these "Pratiche," the "Discorse" here in question is addressed to the citizens in general, and has the gravity of tone suitable to a large assembly. And still less can we admit the other hypothesis of its having been addressed to the Dieci di Balìa, who were Machiavelli's superiors. It is written for delivery in the Great Council, where Soderini alone could hold similar language. In fact, Parenti tells us that the Gonfaloniere made a great speech then, and certainly Machiavelli composed it on this occasion, either by command, or as a literary exercise. Guicciardini has left us many discourses of the same description which are simply exercises in composition.

but a few months before, they had been on the verge of total
destruction at the hands of Valentinois. Nor did it avail them
to say that the Duke had now no pretext for attacking them,
because all are to be considered as enemies who can deprive us
of our own, without our being able to defend ourselves. "And
at present you are incapable of defending your subjects, and
you stand between two or three cities, desiring your ruin rather
than your preservation. And looking beyond Tuscany, you will
see that all Italy is subject to the Venetians, or to the Pope,
or the King of France. The former hate you, and seek to
extort money from you for the purpose of attacking you; it
were better you should spend it in making war upon them. All
know what small confidence may be placed in the Pope and the
Duke, with whom it has been impossible as yet to conclude any
alliance; and even did you succeed in forming one, I repeat that
these latter will only be your friends, while unable to attack
you, for whereas laws, agreements, and contracts bind private
individuals to keep faith, arms alone avail with potentates.
Regarding the King of France, it is necessary that some one
should tell you the truth, and I will be that person. Either he
will find you the only obstacle to his designs upon Italy, in which
case you are lost, or he will find an obstacle in others, and then
your salvation will depend upon your making yourselves respected
in such wise that none may dare to leave you at his mercy, and
that he may not dare to set you aside among those of no account.
Remember, at all events, that one cannot always use another's
sword, and therefore it were well to keep your own in readiness
and girded on, even when the enemy be far off. Many of you
might remember that when Constantinople was about to be taken
by the Turks, the Emperor foresaw the coming destruction, and
his own resources being insufficient to ward it off, he called the
citizens together, and explained to them their danger and the
remedies required. They all laughed him to scorn. "The siege
took place. The very citizens who had jeered at the forebodings
of their master, no sooner heard the cannon thundering against
the walls and the shouts of the enemies' host, than they ran
weeping to the Emperor with heaps of gold; but he drove them
all away, saying—'go, die with your gold, since ye would not
live without it. . . . If, however, others learn wisdom from their
neighbours' perils, you do not learn it even from your own. . . .
For I tell you that fortune will not help those who will not help

themselves ; nor will heaven itself sustain a thing that is determined to fall. But beholding you free Florentines, with your liberty in your own hands, I will not believe that you desire to fall. For surely I must believe that men born free, and wishing to remain free, will have due respect for liberty ! ' "

Here we must call attention to the tendency, more and more observable in Machiavelli, to build up maxims of general policy, even in speaking of so simple a matter as the suggestion of a new tax.

Meanwhile the negotiations set on foot by the Borgia towards an alliance with the Florentines, still dragged on without hope of any definite result, for now the latter did nothing without the consent of France, who at this period was alienated from the Pope on account of the favour shown by him to the Spaniards. France was endeavouring to arrange a league between Sienna, Florence, Lucca and Bologna, of which, so far, the only effect had been to assist the return of Petrucci to Sienna. Thither in April the Florentines despatched Machiavelli to communicate to Petrucci the Pope's wishes and designs ; and this was done rather in proof of friendship, than from any hope or desire of arriving at a practical conclusion.[1] As soon as the necessary supplies were voted, they gave serious attention to preparations of defence against any sudden attack from the Borgia, and Machiavelli again returned to his desk to write letters. He advised one commissary to keep an eye upon the enemy, another to provision the fortress, a third was severely reproved for negligence and laziness. In May he gave notice that Valentinois was disbanding his troops, who might possibly hazard some *coup de main* on their own account, or even attempt, under like false pretences—to do good service to the Duke, whose soldiers were near Perugia, and threatening the confines. " Wherefore, although the prohibition of France prevents our believing an attack possible, nor allows us the faintest suspicion that His Majesty would consent to one, still we must not slumber, but be as much upon the alert as though we expected one, seeing the way in which things now go on, almost always turning out as no one could have imagined. The more then you see affairs darkening, and know them to be menacing, so much the more does it behove you to keep your eyes open ! "[2]

[1] See the *Commissione* entrusted to him by the Ten, " Opere," vol. vi. p. 261.
[2] *Loc. cit.*, at sheet 163.

It is true, the Ten had little fear of open attack, but they dreaded thefts, rapine, pillage, and incitements to rebellion, in some parts of their territory, since the responsibility of such deeds could be easily disavowed. " If our fears of open attack are as of twelve *soldi* in the *lira*, our fears of robbery are as of eighteen to twenty." [1] It may have been that the sole object of all these threatening signs, was to prevent the usual raids on the Pisans, by diverting elsewhere the strength and vigilance of the Republic. But, as regarded Pisa, Florence was determined to take advantage of the favourable season.

In fact two commissaries of war had already been sent to the camp, Antonio Giacomini—who filled the office of Captain with ever-increasing zeal—and Tommaso Tosinghi. In April a circular of the Ten decreed the enrolment within the territory of several thousand pioneers and delvers to lay waste the country, and in May, beams, mortars, carpenters, and so large a number of foot soldiers, men-at-arms and foragers were made ready, that the Pisans were alarmed and showed signs of wishing to come to terms. But neither Giacomini nor Tosinghi were to be deceived by their devices, and declared that only deeds availed, not words ; and for this they received much praise from the Ten, in whose name Niccolò Machiavelli addressed a letter to them on the 22nd of May, exhorting them " to pursue the same course in all your actions, ever flourishing the sword in one hand, and salve in the other, so that they may know they have the option of choosing which they will." [2] And on the 23rd of this month 300 men-at-arms, 200 light horse, 3000 infantry, and 2000 pioneers took the field, and thanks to the energy of Giacomini, in two days did such tremendous havoc in the valley of the Arno, that the Ten were astounded as well as gratified, and wished the work of devastation to be carried on into the Valley of the Serchio. [3] In writing all these letters Machiavelli did not always confine himself to transmitting superior orders ; but sometimes digressed into advice, directions, suggestions, entering into the minutest particulars, as though he were a military leader upon the spot,

[1] The *Lira* being of 20 soldi, the first chance was as of 12 to 20, the second of 18 to 20. Letter of the 14th of May, 1503, cl. x. dist. 3, No. 103, at sheet 172. See the Appendix, document vi. Files 103 and 104 contain numerous other letters by Machiavelli on the same argument.

[2] Archives Fiorentino, cl. x. diet 3, No. 108, at sheet 7t.

[3] Letter of the 25th of May, 1503, in the Florence Archives, cl. x. dist. 3, No. 108, at sheet 18.

while all the time repeating that he left everything to the commissaries and captains.[1]

By the first week in June the Valley of the Serchio had been entirely laid waste, and the army had been joined by the Baily of Caen, who though bringing with him little else than the French flag and a few men-at-arms, immediately began the usual complaints, the usual pretensions. Yet his presence and that of his followers, though almost ineffectual either for good or evil, depressed the courage of the Pisans and raised that of the Florentines, who soon captured Vico Pisano and La Verruca, much to the content of the Ten,[2] and on the 18th of June they ordered an attack upon Librafatta and Torre di Foce.[3] But news of the French advance towards Naples under La Trémoille, brought all these operations to a standstill, since it was now necessary to keep the army in readiness for any unforeseen emergency ; and therefore orders were issued only to take Torre di Foce, "so as to deprive the Pisans of that refuge, and prevent them from rebuilding a nest there."[4] After this the war was suspended in that quarter, and Giacomini was recalled to be sent to guard the frontiers.

In the kingdom of Naples matters had taken a most discouraging turn for France, whom the Borgia accordingly now began to hold in slight account ; and the Florentines felt less assured of safety than ever. Some of Cæsar's men were already scouring the Siennese territory, a matter which gave great anxiety to the Commissary Giovanni Ridolfi, so that in a letter of the 4th of August, Machiavelli sought to encourage him, saying : Gaeta has not yet received the sacrament *in extremis* as you suppose ; the Spaniards are beginning to retreat, the French are advancing. And you also err in thinking that their army remains in Lombardy, through fear of the Venetians ; "who are no firmer in their stirrups, than they have been all this year, nor do we hear that they have changed a single horse, nor moved a single man-at-arms, so that—to return to the point—we do not perceive how the Duke in this state of affairs, could be likely to begin a

[1] See letter of the 27th May in Appendix, document vii. cl. x. dist. 3, No. 107, at sheet 24.

[2] Letter of the 14th of June, cl. x. dist. 5, No. 107, at sheet 47*t*.

[3] Cl. x. dist. 3, No. 108, at sheet 54.

[4] Letter of the 22nd of June, 1503, Florence Archives, cl. x. dist. 3, No. 108, at sheet 58.

war and openly disturb the affairs of Tuscany, since with the half of the favours at our command, we should have a thousand ways of burning his house about his ears."[1] But notwithstanding these encouraging words, orders were given to prepare for defence, and two hundred and fifty French lancers were despatched. The greater part of the year passed amid these uncertainties, and then fresh events in Rome changed the entire aspect of Italian politics.

In that city, after Ceri had at last been captured by the Duke's adherents, some dissension seemed to have arisen between him and the Pope, Cæsar being reluctant—from respect to France —to proceed energetically against Bracciano and the Orsini, whereupon the latter became so enraged as to threaten his son with excommunication, and it was even rumoured that one evening they had come to blows.[2] However, in the opinion of the Venetian ambassador, all this was a mere farce. In the actual uncertainty as to pending events in Naples, the Pope showed a leaning towards Spain, the Duke towards France, and thus "each blaming the other, both pursued their common designs."[3] Indeed they had greater hopes than ever of carrying out their plans, amid the inevitable coming confusion, and they left no means unturned of collecting money. On the 29th of March the Venetian ambassador wrote that a Bull had been issued, creating eighty new offices in the Curia, which were immediately sold at seven hundred and sixty ducats apiece. "If your Sublimity will cast up the sum, you will see how much money the Pontiff has gained."[4] And in May he added that nine men of the worst description had been made cardinals, on payment by each of a round sum of money, and by some of more than 20,000 ducats, so that altogether between 120 and 130 thousand ducats had been got together; and Alexander had shown the world that a Pope's revenues might be swelled *ad libitum.*[5]

All this did not suffice, and resort was had to other means. On the night of the 10th of April, Cardinal Michiel expired after two days of violent sickness, and before dawn his house had been stripped by the order of the Pope, who, according to Giustinian,[6] obtained

---

[1] Florence Archives, cl. x. dist. 3, No. 108, at sheet 111.

[2] Giustinian, despatches of 1st and 28th of February, of 1st, 4th, 8th, and 11th of March, 1503.

[3] Despatch 304, the first dated 3rd of March. See also that of the 19th of March.   [4] Despatch of the 29th of March.

[5] Despatch of the 31st of May.

[6] Giustinian, despatch of the 13th of April, 1503.

more than 150,000 ducats in gold, plate, and precious stuffs. In fact, on going to the Vatican the ambassador found all the doors closed, and could not be received because the money was being counted over. This was still going on in the hall to which he was admitted on the morning of the 13th, on a summons from the Pope. His Holiness said to him : " See, there are only 23,832 ducats, yet all the land rings with the news that we have had between 80 and 100,000 ducats in cash." And he appealed to the testimony of those who were present, " as though," observes the ambassador, " 'twould be a great matter for them to serve him by a lie." Nevertheless the Pope earnestly begged him to institute inquiries in the Venetian territories where there was more of the Cardinal's money ; the sum he had found seeming very small to him. Before long Jacopo da Santa Croce—he who had assisted the Pope to seize Cardinal Orsini, by conducting him to the Vatican —was also made prisoner, and after treating with him for the purchase of his life for a good sum of money, lost his head on the 8th of June. His corpse was left stretched on the bridge of St. Angelo until evening, his possessions both in land and in gold were confiscated, and his wife and child made homeless wanderers.[1]

Meanwhile, on the 19th of May Troches [2] or Troccio, one of the Borgia's most trusted assassins, suddenly fled from Rome, and was hotly pursued by his late masters. Valentinois, in a letter of that date, ordered " all our vassals," under pain of being considered rebels, to stop the fugitive, and prayed all his friends to assist them, since the motive of his flight was a matter " against the honour of the King of France." [3] Others however affirmed

[1] Despatch of the 8th of June.

[2] Despatch 387, the first dated May, 1503, and despatch 390 the second dated 20th of May.

[3] This letter is among the " Carte del Machiavelli, " case 1, No. 1, and was published by Passerini, " Opere " (P. M.), vol. iv. p. 298. But he did not correctly interpret the name of the individual in question, having read it Noch instead of Troche, and therefore mistaking him for some unknown soldier. Nor did he perceive that the sheet only contains a copy made by Machiavelli of the original letter. Deceived perhaps by the circumstance that Machiavelli had somewhat imitated the conventional signature specially used by Valentinois in official letters, he took it for granted that this letter had been written by Machiavelli and signed by Valentinois. This obliged him to imagine that the Florentine secretary had made an unknown journey to Rome, and caused him to recur to his other hypothesis, that Machiavelli had been the counsellor of Borgia's policy and assassinations. An examination of the document destroys all these theories.

that the reason of this assassin's flight was rage at not being included in the list of new cardinals, that he had manifested his anger to the Pope, who bade him hold his tongue unless he wished to be killed by the Duke ; and that upon this Troccio had revealed to France the secret manœuvres with Spain. Hence the fury of the Borgia, and their ardent desire to get him into their hands.

However this may be, Troccio was seized on board a vessel bound for Corsica, and being instantly brought back to Rome, was confined in a tower in the Trastevere quarter. There, after a few hours, the Duke made his appearance, and after a short colloquy with the prisoner, withdrew to a spot from whence he could secretly spy into the cell, and sent Don Micheletto in to strangle him. An inventory had already been made of his effects, which were distributed according to the orders of the Pope. And thus, observed Giustinian, of all the Borgia's trusted and most faithful tools two only survived, Don Micheletto and Romolino, for whom the same fate as had befallen the others was probably in store.[1] It really appeared as if there would never be an end to

Cæsar's signature is not an autograph, but an imitation of one ; the signature of Agapito is wanting, though found on all Cæsar's decrees ; there is no seal nor stamp of any sort, and the letter bears no address ; but on the back of it there is written in Machiavelli's hand and with some abbreviations : 1503, concerning Messer Troche. Signor Nitti, *op. cit.* vol. i. pp. 223-24, note (1), in noticing that Machiavelli wrote a letter from Florence dated the 16th May, doubts the pretended journey to Rome, and brings forward another equally impossible hypothesis, *i.e.*, that Valentinois had sent Machiavelli a blank decree already signed. When he formed that theory Signor Nitti must have forgotten for a moment who the Borgia were, and what manner of man was Valentinois. For it is not intelligible that a blank decree should have been sent to Machiavelli, when only a simple circular had to be written ; and in no case would Valentinois have committed himself to such a proceeding, even with Agapito, Don Micheletto, or any other of his trustiest adherents, among whom Machiavelli cannot certainly be included. And in conclusion we must remark that not only did Machiavelli write letters from Florence on the 16th, but also on the 17th, 18th, 19th, and 21st of May, as is shown by the Registers of the Ten in the Florence Archives (class x. dist. 3, No. 108, from sheet 2 to sheet 12). The Roman journey therefore becomes not only improbable but impossible. Troccio fled from Rome on the 19th of May (Giustinian, despatch of 19th of May), and the order for his arrest is dated from Rome the same day. Machiavelli therefore could not possibly have written it.

[1] Giustinian, despatch of the 8th of June, 1503. It may seem strange that a man like Troccio should have occupied himself with poetry ; yet that would seem to have been the case from two letters of his, in which he earnestly begs the Marchioness of Mantova to send him certain sonnets. See the " Lucrezia Borgia " of Gregorovius, documents 42 and 43. Similar facts are by no means uncommon

persecution and murder. Many were imprisoned as Jews, a still larger number as heretics. These pretexts sufficed for forcibly entering their houses, and stripping them of all their contents ; then bargains were made to sell the prisoners their lives for sums of money varying in amount. " All these (arrests) are tricks to make money," wrote the Florentine ambassador Vittorio Soderini, and Giustinian said much the same thing.[1] The latter reported later that on the 1st of August, towards the Ave Maria, after only two days' illness, died Giovanni Borgia, Cardinal of Monreale " at whose death the Pontiff wore a very cheerful aspect, although Monreale was his own nephew." On going to the Vatican the ambassador was refused admittance on the score of the Pope's trouble at the death of his nephew the Cardinal, " and this trouble must have consisted in counting gold and fingering jewels." In fact, every one calculated that the property in cash and other effects amounted to 100,000 ducats, and it was generally asserted, " that he (the Cardinal) had also been sent the same way that all the other well fattened ones have gone, and the blame of this affair is laid upon the Duke "[2] Things had now reached such a point, that all who possessed or were supposed to possess money, trembled for their lives, " every moment thinking to see the executioner standing behind them." [3]

The Borgia made every effort to make ready for new expeditions, amidst the general confusion expected from the rapid changes now sweeping over the kingdom of Naples. In Calabria, D'Aubigny had been defeated by the Spaniards who had crossed over from Sicily at Cerignola, Nemours by Gonsalvo de Cordova, who, having issued from Barletta, and achieved a brilliant victory, entered Naples as a conqueror in May. In short, the French had lost everything but the fortress of Gaeta—where a great part of the defeated survivors took refuge, and Venosa, occupied by Louis d'Ars and Santa Severina, where the Prince of Rossano was besieged. Louis XII. had to make a fresh beginning by openly attacking Spain, and sending another army into Italy under Louis La Trémoille and Francesco Gonzaga, an army to be increased by the

in the period of the Italian Renaissance. The Captain G. G. Trivulzio among other things lost in the taking of Milan, especially deplored the loss of a Quintus Curtius, and offered a large reward for its restitution.
[1] Giustinian, despatch of 19 of June and note.
[2] Ibid., despatch of 2nd of August, 1503.
[3] Ibid., despatch of the 8th of June.

promised contingents from Florence, Sienna, Mantova, Bologna and Ferrara. This expedition however proceeded with incredible slowness, on account of the suspected neutrality of Venice, and the more and more fickle and incomprehensible policy of the Pope. His Holiness openly leaned towards Spain, who was allowed by him to enlist men publicly in Rome ; but he gave the French to understand that he would help them in their enterprise, and even pay two-thirds of the expenses, provided they gave Naples or Sicily to Valentinois, indemnifying themselves for the gift, by taking what they pleased in North Italy.[1] At the same time he made the largest offers of friendship and alliance to the Venetians, to induce them to join with him against France and against Spain, for the general preservation of Italy from foreigners.[2] On the other hand, he pressingly demanded from Maximilian King of the Romans—who was still thinking of coming to Italy to possess himself of the imperial crown—the investiture of Pisa for the Duke, saying that otherwise he would be compelled to throw himself into the arms of France, who promised him the kingdom of Naples in exchange for Romagna.[3]

What successful result was to be expected from conduct so foolish, we leave to the judgment of those who have exalted the acumen and political insight of the Borgia. Treating with all against all, the Pope found himself, after. so many exertions, condemned to inaction and unable to count on the friendship of any power. And the Duke, who was preparing to march on Sienna to unite with Pisa, and, once in possession of the latter city, to push on to the attack of Florence, was also prevented from stirring a step ; since he would have met the French army on his road, and would have been forced to declare himself openly for or against it—that is, either to attack it, or join in the march towards Naples. Wishing to be prepared for every eventuality, neither of these courses was open to him, and thus all his efforts, displays of craft and numerous assassinations, resulted in nothing but forced inaction and uncertainty.

This state of things was suddenly altered by a most unlooked-for event. On the evening of the 5th of August the Pope went with the Duke to a supper in the vineyard of Cardinal Adriano behind the Vatican, and remained there till after nightfall. The

---

[1] Giustinian, despatches of the 7th and 8th of June, 1503.
[2] Despatch of the 29th of May.
[3] Despatches of the 7th of June and 31st of July.

Roman fever, always prevalent in the month of August, was rag-ing more severely than usual that year. Some of the ambassadors, many members of the Curia—especially those resident in the palace—had fallen ill ; and therefore all who attended this supper, suffered more or less from fever in consequence. On the 7th, Giustinian found the Pope in his room covered with wraps, and he told the ambassador that he was taking care of himself, being alarmed by the many fever cases and deaths then happening in Rome.[1] On the 11th, Cardinal Adriano was in bed with the fever ; on the 12th, the Pope was seized by an attack of fever and sickness ; and the Duke also fell ill of the same complaint.[2] The Pope was now seventy-three years of age, and the danger of his condition was evident. In fact, symptoms of cerebral conges-tion soon set in ; to reduce them copious blood-letting was resorted to, which, by weakening the patient, heightened the malady. An alarming stupor—almost like that of death—came on ; on the 17th, the fever, which the Ferrarese ambassador styles " the well-known tertian," [3] returned with such violent paroxysms, that the physician declared the case to be hopeless. The greatest disorder instantly ensued in, the Vatican, and many began to provide for the safety of their property. The Pope, who during all these days had neither asked for the Duke, nor Lucrezia,[4] on the 18th confessed and received the last sacraments. Towards six o'clock he had a fainting fit which resembled death, and only revived from it to draw his last breath immediately afterwards, about the vesper hour, in the presence of the Bishop of Carinola, the Datary and a few serving-men.[5]

The confusion was at the highest pitch. The Duke, although still so sick that his life was considered in danger, caused a large portion of his effects to be carried to‾ the castle of St. Angelo, and his soldiers to be summoned to Rome. Don Michele, with some armed men, entered the Pope's apartments, and closing the doors, held a dagger to the throat of Cardinal Casanuova, threatening to kill him and throw him out of the window if he

[1] Giustinian, despatch of the   of August, 1503, note 1, p. 99 of vol. ii.

[2] Despatch of the 13th of August.

[3] Also Burchardi speaks of it in his diary as *febris tertiana.*

[4] " Dux nunquam venit ad Papam in tota eius infirmitate nec in morte, nec papa fuit unquam memor sui vel Lucretiae in aliquo minimo verbo, etiam in tota sua infirmitate." Burchardi, " Diarium," MS. of the National Library of Florence, vol. iv. at sheet 1.

[5] Giustinian, despatches 484–87, dated 18th of August, 1503.

did not immediately give up the Pope's keys and money. In this way more than 100,000 ducats in gold, besides plate and jewels, amounting altogether to the value of above 300,000 ducats[1] came into the hands of the Duke. But Don Michele forgot to search a room adjoining that in which Alexander had died, in which were precious mitres, jewelled rings, and silver vases enough to fill many chests.[2] The servants took everything else they could find in the rooms already pillaged. At last the doors were thrown open, and the death of the Pope was announced.

Up to the moment of the funeral, everything wore a lugubrious and sinister aspect. The corpse, after being washed and dressed, was left alone, with only two lighted candles. The Cardinals did not come, although summoned, nor even the *Penitenzieri* whose duty it was to recite prayers for the dead. On the following day the body was so much changed by corruption as to have lost all semblance of humanity. It was very black, swelled almost as broad as it was long, and the tongue so large that it filled the whole mouth and kept it agape.[3] At midday on the 19th of August, it was, according to custom, exhibited in St. Peter's church ; "*tamen* being the ugliest, most monstrous and horrible dead body that was ever seen, without any form or likeness of humanity ; for shame's sake they kept it covered with a cloth, and then before sunset they buried it, *adstantibus duobus cardinalibus* of those resident in the palace."[4]

In St. Peter's the breviary, from which the prayers were to be read, had been mislaid, and then a riot ensued between the priests and soldiers, whereupon the clergy broke off their chants, and fled towards the sacristy, leaving the dead Pope almost alone. But, having deposited the corpse on the high altar, they feared it might be outraged by the indignant people, and

[1] Sanuto gives details increasing this sum to 500,000 ducats. We have fixed it at the sum mentioned by the majority of writers.

[2] Burchardi, " Diarium," vol. v. at sheet 1, and fol.

[3] " Et continuo crevit turpido et negredo faciei, adeoque hora vigesima tertia qua eum vidi factus erat sicut pannus vel morus nigerrimus ; facies livoris tota plena ; nasus plenus ; os amplissimum ; lingua duplex in ore, quae labia tota implebat ; os apertum et adeo horribile, quod nemo viderit unquam, vel esse tale dicerit." (Burchardi, " Diarium," MS. in the National Library of Florence, tom iv. at sheet 6.) And it went on growing more and more horrible, as declare also all the ambassadors, Costabili, Giustinian, &c.

[4] Giustinian, despatch of the 19th of August, 1503, *hora* 24.

therefore placed it with four lighted tapers behind a locked grating, and left it there all day. After four - and - twenty hours, it was carried into the chapel *de febribus*, where six workmen were joking and insulting the Pope's memory while digging the Pope's grave. Here the carpenters, having made the coffin too short and too narrow, pulled off the mitre, and covering the body with an old cloth, thrust it into the coffin by main force.[1] The mode of burial was such that the Marquis of Mantova—who was then in the neighbourhood of Rome with the French army—remarked in a letter to the Marchesa Isabella : " so mean was the tomb, that the deformed wife of the cripple at Mantova has a better one." [2]

The rapid decomposition of the body, owing to the corrupt state of the blood, and the circumstance of the Pope, Valentinois, and Cardinal Adriano all falling ill at the same time, gained universal credit for the rumour that all had been poisoned, for poison seemed inseparably connected with the name of the Borgia. It was asserted that the Pope and the Duke had intended ridding themselves of the Cardinal ; but that through the blunder of the cup-bearer, they themselves had drunk of the poisoned wine. But even could it be conceived that the Borgia should have been clumsy enough in their own special calling to allow such blunders to occur, the fact of the Cardinal's illness would still require explanation.[3] Others declared that the Cardinal was saved, because, foreseeing the attempt, he had given the cup-bearer a bribe of 10,000 ducats to poison the Borgia instead. But these rumours lose all value when confronted with the ambassadors' despatches, especially those of Giustinian, who,

---

[1] " Et cum pugnis pestarunt eum ut capsam intraret, sine intorticiis vel lumine aliquo, et sine aliquo presbitero vel persona una vel lumine." (Burchardi, " Diarium," *loc. cit.*)

[2] Letter of the 22nd of September, 1503, quoted by Gregorovius, " Lucrezia Borgia," doc. 49. Afterwards the remains of Alexander VI. were transferred from the Crypt of the Vatican to San Giacomo degli Spagnuoli, and then to Santa Maria di Monserrato, where they repose with those of Calixtus III., behind the high altar, with no inscription over them. And even the memorial slab, placed in Santa Maria del Popolo over the burial-place of Vannozza and her children, was also removed.

[3] Giovio declares that the Cardinal told him that he believed his illness to have been caused by poison given to him by the Borgia. Still Giovio's assertions are not always to be credited, and besides, when all were suggesting poison, the Cardinal may easily have attributed his illness to that cause, without any foundation for his belief.

day by day, details the origin and progress of the malady ; and, being in continual intercourse with the Pope's physician, knew that cerebral congestion supervening on the fever was the real cause of the death. Even the Ferrarese ambassador, Beltrando Constabili, who, on the 19th, after the rapid change of the body, mentioned the generally credited rumour of poison, had explicitly declared on the 14th that the Pope's illness was tertian fever, and that there was no cause for wonder in it, since nearly the whole Court was suffering from the same malady, then very prevalent in Rome, " owing to the bad condition of the atmosphere." In any case, it would have been strange, to say the least, if poison administered at that supper, had only begun to show its effects after the interval of a whole week, when the fever was first manifested.

We will spare our readers other tales then spread about, of devils seen by the Pope's bedside, of how he had sold his soul to them at the very beginning of his reign, and similar fables, all the more readily believed, because of the incredulity of the age. On the 19th of August the Duke seemed on the point of death ; all shops were closed, the Spaniards concealed themselves, and a rumour spread that Fabio Orsini had entered Rome, with Alviano and the other members of his family, full of the most furious schemes of revenge. Cæsar Borgia knew this ; but he had thought of everything, as Machiavelli afterwards said, excepting the chance of being himself dying when the Pope was dead, and was now in the greatest perplexity.[1] His soldiers were riotous and set fire to the Orsini's houses, some of which were burnt down. At last, with the intervention of the ambassadors, the conclave succeeded in persuading all to make a kind of truce. The Orsini and the Colonna withdrew ; the Duke, somewhat better, sent forward his artillery, and on the 2nd of September left Rome in a litter and went to the castle of Nepi, that was still in his possession. Here he was in the vicinity of the French army, actually on its way to Naples, and on which he relied for assistance ; for he had suddenly declared for France, although still placing his entire confidence in the Spanish cardinals, by whom he was surrounded and supported.

Many cardinals were now arriving in Rome ; among them Giuliano della Rovere, after ten years of exile, and Cardinal

---

[1] " Et nescit quo se vertit, nec ubi reclinet caput." Giustinian, despatch, 489, the second of the 19th of August, 1503.

Ascanio Sforza, released from prison by the good offices of Cardinal de Rouen, one of the aspirants to the Papacy. On the 3rd of September a solemn funeral service was performed in honour of the dead Pope; and on the 22nd, Francesco Todeschini dei Piccolomini, nephew of Pius II., was finally elected; and assumed the name of Pius III. He was sixty-four years of age, and so hopeless an invalid, that his pontificate resembled that of a passing shadow, only serving as it were for the continuance of the intrigues going on on all sides, and to give the various parties already at work time to measure their strength for the next election. The French army, which had halted, pursued its march immediately the new Pope was proclaimed; and the Duke, afraid to stay alone with his followers at Nepi, which, Alviano, thirsting for blood and vengeance, was preparing to attack, immediately returned to Rome. There he learnt that the cities once his, were recalling their former lords and welcoming them with open arms. Romagna, however, having been better governed, still remained faithful, and the strongholds under Spanish commandants, still held out for him. Yet he never thought of placing himself at the head of his little army, and cutting his way through his enemies, to reconquer and defend his own state by force of arms. He hoped always and only in the intrigues which were to render the next Papal election favourable to his views; and the present Pope, a man of very gentle temper, showed him compassion for the time. But meanwhile the Orsini, hearing that he had gone over to the French, and had been accepted by them, were greatly enraged, and instantly concluded an alliance with the Colonna, Gonsalvo, and Spain. Some of them attacked the Borgo, and set fire to the Torrione gate, in order to enter the Vatican and seize Borgia, whom they pursued with great fury. He barely escaped by the aid of certain of the Cardinals, who hurried him away down the narrow passage communicating with the castle of St. Angelo. Thus in the very place where so many of his own and his father's victims had expired in the agonies of poison, Valentinois now found himself almost a captive. While here he learnt that Pius III., who could not stand upright on the 8th of October, the day of his coronation, had breathed his last ten days later.[1]

---

[1] In a letter dated 8th of November, 1503, signed *Sigismundus doctor et clericus senensis,* and addressed to Alessandro Piccolomini, nephew of Pius III., the writer, after lauding the Pope's goodness, says, that " he could not have died at

There could be no longer any doubt as to the result of the new election, for all had been arranged by bribes, promises, intrigues of every kind, even with Spanish Cardinals, on the part of Valentinois, who had thus secured himself valid protection. On the 31st of October thirty-five cardinals took their seats in conclave, and hardly were they assembled, hardly indeed had the doors been closed according to custom, than the new Pope was already chosen in the person of Giuliano delle Rovere, who took the name of Julius II. This bitterest enemy of the Borgia—whom, however, he had favoured when finding it expedient—was a native of Savona, of low origin, and now of sixty years of age ; but he came of the robust race of Pope Sixtus IV., who was his uncle ; he had been a Cardinal since 1471, was the holder of many fat bishoprics, and possessed an iron constitution. Although his youth had been passed much as that of other prelates of those times, and although a man of few scruples, he showed a zeal and daring marvellous for one of his years, in forwarding the power and political grandeur of the Church. Without neglecting his own family, he never subordinated to their interests the needs of Church or State, and therefore indulged in no excess of nepotism. His views, his ambitions, his violent impetuosity of character, were all totally contrary to those of the Borgia. Yet, when necessary, he was able to feign and dissimulate, and had had no scruples in bargaining for his election with Valentinois, by promising him the post of Gonfaloniere of the Church and government of Romagna, as well as to give his daughter in marriage to Francesco Maria della Rovere, Prefect of Rome : but although not deliberately determined to violate these promises, he had but little intention of keeping them. All depended upon his seeing whether the Duke might or might not be—at least for a time—a useful instrument in forwarding the Pope's design of driving the Venetians from Romagna, whither they were advancing. Sooner

---

a better moment than now when just exalted to that felicity, and before anything had occurred to mar it ; for such could not have failed to happen. . . . He has committed no simony ; he has made no war against Christians ; he has done no murders, nor hangings, nor executions ; he has not squandered the patrimony of St. Peter in warfare, nor on bastards, nor other people." Such was the credit then enjoyed by the Pontiffs. This Sigismondo, a native of Castiglione Aretino, made citizen of Sienna in 1842, was the author of various histories written in Latin, and still unpublished. This letter has been published in Sienna by the Ancora Printing Press, 1877, on the occasion of the marriage of Professor Enea Piccolomini, by Signor Giuseppe Palmieri Nuti.

or later the Duke would have to give up the fortresses still holding out for him—notwithstanding all promises and hopes—since
the general interest of the Church must not yield to any human
consideration. On these points the resolutions of Julius II. were
already taken, and, with his obstinacy of character, nothing could
now induce him to change them. Hence the position of affairs
was becoming more and more involved ; indeed with this pontificate, a new epoch began, not for Italy only, but for all Europe.
On that account, the new legation of Machiavelli—who was at
this juncture despatched to Rome—possesses great additional
importance.

CHAPTER VII.

(1503–1504.)

HILE the events just related were going on in
Rome, the attention of Florence was directed
to what was occurring in the States which
had belonged to Valentinois and touched the
frontiers of the Republic. It was especially
necessary to prevent the advance of the
Venetians, who still aspired to the *Monarchy
of Italy*. Therefore Machiavelli, by command and in the name
of the Ten, wrote to the Commissaries and Podestàs, bidding
them second the designs of the Church, and either the return of
former rulers, or even that of the Duke himself—according to the
way events turned, whichever best served to close the door against
Venice.[1] Nor did the Ten neglect to take into consideration,
whether it might not be possible to profit by the general turmoil
to seize some neighbouring territory on their own account : this,
however, was only to be done with extreme caution, and without
exposing the Republic to dangerous consequences.   Written
instructions to this effect were sent to the Commissary Ridolfi
regarding Citerna, Faenza, Forlì, with the declaration that to

---

[1] Circular of the 20th August, 1503, in the Florence Archives, cl. x. dist. 3,
No. 108, at sheet 129.   Many more of Machiavelli's letters are to be found in the
same file.   We only quote those at sheets 136, 139, and 148.

obtain the latter State, Florence would be willing to expend as much as 10,000 ducats. But they added as usual that, the Republic not being strong enough for daring enterprises, it would to necessary to favour whichever party—excepting the Venetians— had the best probability of success.[1] While they were discussing the propriety of taking possession of Forlì, Signor Antonio Orde- laffi entered that city, was well received by the inhabitants, and immediately declared that he relied upon the protection of the Florentines. The latter were now puzzled what course to adopt. They had no fitting excuse for refusing him their protection ; but did not feel sufficiently powerful to defend him against the Church and Valentinois, who might both probably attack him. At the same time Machiavelli wrote to the Commissary at Castro- caro : " This arrival will raise the spirits of the men of Forlì, and the suspicions of the Duke's people. You must tell the former that we made him (Ordelaffi) come, the better to help him : the latter on the contrary must be told, that we summoned him for the Duke's advantage, to shut that door which was open to the Venetians, and to deprive them of a tool. And in this way you must trim matters, so that we may gain time. You must, how- ever, manage this affair with dexterity and secrecy, colouring it in such wise that neither party may perceive that it is being tricked or circumvented."[2] It was this perpetual petty tergiver- sation that chiefly disgusted Machiavelli, and inspired him with an exaggerated admiration for the conduct of men like Valentinois, who, untroubled by scruples, either human or divine, went straight to the end they had in view.

By good fortune he was soon relieved from this torment, for on the 24th of October he received orders to go to Rome, with special instructions and letters of recommendation to many cardinals whom it was necessary that he should see, especially the Cardinal Soderini, then managing the principal affairs of the Republic, and by whose advice he was to be guided.[3]

He was the bearer of condolences on the death of Pius III. ;

---

[1] Letter of the 25th August, *loc. cit.*, file 107, at sheet 136, and letter of the 12th September, at sheet 156.

[2] Letter of the 5th October to Americo Antinori, file 107 at sheet 171.

[3] From the 28th August it had been determined that he should be sent to Rome, as is shown by the Registers of the Ten. But he did not set out at that time ; and afterwards his mission was decided upon afresh. The instructions given him and the letter to Cardinal Soderini are in the " Legazione " contained in vol. vi. of the " Opere," p. 364 and fol.

he was to collect as much intelligence as possible during the conclave, and—by means of the Cardinal de Rouen—conclude a Condotta with G. P. Baglioni. This Condotta was arranged in the
name of Florence, but altogether in the interest and service of
France, to counterbalance the injury done to that power by the
desertion of the Orsini, who, together with the Colonna, had joined
Gonsalvo of Cordova immediately the French had accepted the
friendship of Valentinois. As was natural, the Condotta was
speedily arranged, and Baglioni prepared to start for Florence without delay to receive his money, for the Republic had pledged itself
to pay to him the 60,000 ducats owing to France " in return for her
protection." [1] And on this head, Machiavelli wrote of Baglioni,
that " he was like the other pillagers of Rome, who are thieves
rather than soldiers, and whose services are sought for the sake of
their names and influence, rather than for their valour, or the
number of men at their command. Moved as they are by personal interests, the alliances they make only last till it suits their
purpose to break them, and therefore all understanding these
leaders only seek to prevent them from doing harm." [2] Fresh
events soon occurred to change the aims and nature of this
legation. Machiavelli arrived in Rome towards the close of the
scandalous manœuvres, by which—according to the Venetian
ambassador—votes were bought and sold, not for thousands, but
for tens of thousands of ducats ; " there is no longer any difference between the Papacy and the *Soldanate*, since *plus offerenti
dabitur.*" [3] Cardinal Giuliano delle Rovere had gained ground so
rapidly, succeeding so well—as we have already noted—in winning the Spanish Cardinals, by means of promises held out to
Valentinois, that he was now certain of success. But men's minds
were still greatly agitated, and the city in so anarchical a condition,
that on the evening of the 31st of October, one of the Cardinal's
attendants was accompanied to Machiavelli's dwelling by an escort
of twenty armed men. Nevertheless on that same evening the
Secretary wrote that the election was now assured. In fact, on
the following day, the Conclave met, the new Pope was proclaimed,
immediately took the name of Julius II., and without hesitation
seized the reins of government with a firm hand. Thus it was
no longer a question of collecting and transmitting intelligence

[1] Buonaccorsi, " Diario," p. 83 and fol.
[2] Letter of the 29th October, 1503.
[3] Giustinian, despatch of the 19th October.

regarding the Conclave; but two questions of much higher importance now arose. What did the Pope intend to do with Valentinois, to whom he had promised so much? What would be his attitude towards Venice, who already manifested her intention of marching into Romagna?

Two men were employed in studying these questions with the utmost diligence and penetration: Machiavelli and Giustinian. Naturally, however, the latter concerned himself much less than the former with the affair of Valentinois, whom his Republic had little occasion to fear. As soon as he had heard of the promises made to him by Delle Rovere, he had set about ascertaining the latter's intentions with great acuteness. And he had been told in reply: "See that the election be successful, and have no doubts. You behold the miserable state to which we have been reduced by the carrion Pope Alexander has left behind him, with this great crowd of cardinals. Necessity compels men to do that which they would not, so long as they are dependent upon others; but once freed, they then act in a different fashion."[1] After that, Giustinian required no more explanations, nor occupied himself any more with Valentinois, indeed, when repeatedly invited to visit him, he refused to go, in order, as he said, to avoid swelling the Duke's importance. On the other hand, he showed marvellous discretion and perseverance in scrutinizing the most secret ideas of the Pope touching the advance of the Venetians, and reported them to his government with a diligence surpassing description. He speedily discovered that the first symptoms of benevolence and the first waverings were mere illusions; that the Pope was resolved to risk his tiara and the peace of Europe in order to win back the territories which, in his opinion, appertained to the Church. Thus, before they were manifest to any other human eye, we may discern the germs of the League of Cambray in the despatches of the Venetian ambassador,[2] who in vain counselled prudence to his government, and in vain sought to calm the haughty and irritable spirit of the Pope. Very different, with regard to these affairs, was the position of Machiavelli. Above all else, the chief anxiety of the Florentines was to see Julius II. the declared enemy of the Venetians. The necessary reserve maintained by him on the first news of their advance, was not only interpreted by the Florentines as a sign of unpardonable coldness;

[1] Despatch of the 30th October, 1503.
[2] Despatch of the 6th November.

but almost as a proof that he rejoiced at the event, and was perhaps acting in concert with Venice, in order thus to prevent the
restoration of the Duke. Therefore the Ten urged Machiavelli to
use every art to arouse jealousy and hatred towards Venice ; but
he was soon compelled to acknowledge that this was the easiest of
matters, for the first symptoms of the Pope's passionate and
deliberate indignation were not slow in breaking out. But he
had to keep a vigilant eye upon Valentinois, who—had he gone
to Romagna—must have passed through Tuscany, a circumstance
of no small danger to the Republic. Besides, unlike Giustinian,
he enjoyed few opportunities of approaching the Pope, and therefore ignored his real intentions towards a man whom he had
greatly hated, but to whom he had promised much.

The importance of this Legation, so far as it touches the life of
Machiavelli, proceeds from its shortly bringing him once more in
contact with Valentinois, when fallen from the high estate in
which he had first known him. The secretary now writes and
speaks of him with an indifference and cold contempt which has
scandalized many, who looked upon this not only as a flagrant
contradiction of all that he had previously written of him ; but
also as a proof of a low nature, only capable of admiring successful
prosperity and good luck, and ready to trample upon his hero,
directly he saw him in the dust. This erroneous judgment, however, is nothing but the natural consequence of the previous
blunder of giving to Machiavelli's admiration for Valentinois
a significance and a value which it never possessed. Even if a
brigand chief had had the daring and dexterity to upset a country
and subject it to his rule, Machiavelli would have admired his
ability and courage without taking alarm at any sanguinary and
cruel action. Indeed the workings of his own fancy would have
converted the object of his admiration into a sort of imaginary
hero, while lauding Cæsar's prudence and *virtue*, in the sense in
which the latter word was employed during the Italian Renaissance. This all came from the nature of his genius, the character of the times, and—it may be—the coldness of his heart,
which, though certainly not bad, was not easily inflamed with any
very ardent enthusiasm for goodness. Naturally enough, therefore, had he afterwards encountered the same brigand, fallen from
his previous position into obscurity, and had beheld the *man* in all
his immoral and repulsive monstrousness, Machiavelli, in pursuance of his customary impassable examination of reality, would

have described and judged him in his true light, without any hesitation or fear of contradicting himself. And this was not very unlike his attitude with regard to Valentinois, therefore the contradiction lies, not in his judgment, but rather in that of individuals wishing to attribute to him opinions, virtues and vices which he never possessed.

Meanwhile many and various rumours were afloat as to the Pope's intentions respecting his given promises. He did not wish to keep them, but neither did he wish to pass for a perjurer— the very accusation so often hurled by him against the Borgia. And the Duke, on the other hand, wrote Machiavelli—"always transported by his daring confidence, believes that the words of others are more trustworthy than were his own, and that the promised marriage alliance must be maintained." [1]   On the 5th of November came letters from the Ten telling of the revolt of Imola against Valentinois, and the advance of the Venetians towards Faenza. Machiavelli conveyed this news to the Pope, who heard it unmoved, and then to several cardinals, to whom he remarked that if his Holiness followed this course, he would soon be no better than a Venetian chaplain. He then presented himself to the Duke, who was greatly agitated, and complained bitterly of the Florentines ; he said that they might, with a hundred men, have saved him those States, and yet had not done so. Since Imola is lost, and Faenza attacked, he declares that he will no longer collect soldiers, nor be fooled by you. He will place all that remains to him in the hands of the Venetians. In this way he believes that he shall soon witness the destruction of your State, and will exult over it, for the French have too much to do in the kingdom of Naples, to be able to assist you. " And he enlarged upon these points with poisoned and passionate words. I had no lack of things to say in reply, nor would my words have failed me ; yet I took the course of trying to pacify him, and took leave of him as quickly as possible, for it seemed a thousand years till I could quit his presence." [2]   The situation was now entirely changed ; the Duke had no longer the power to enforce his commands, and Machiavelli was conscious of his own superiority over his interlocutor, who in old times had seemed so much greater than he.

[1] Letter of the 4th of November.
[2] This letter has no date, and is the ix. of this Legation, " Opere," vol. vi. p. 388.

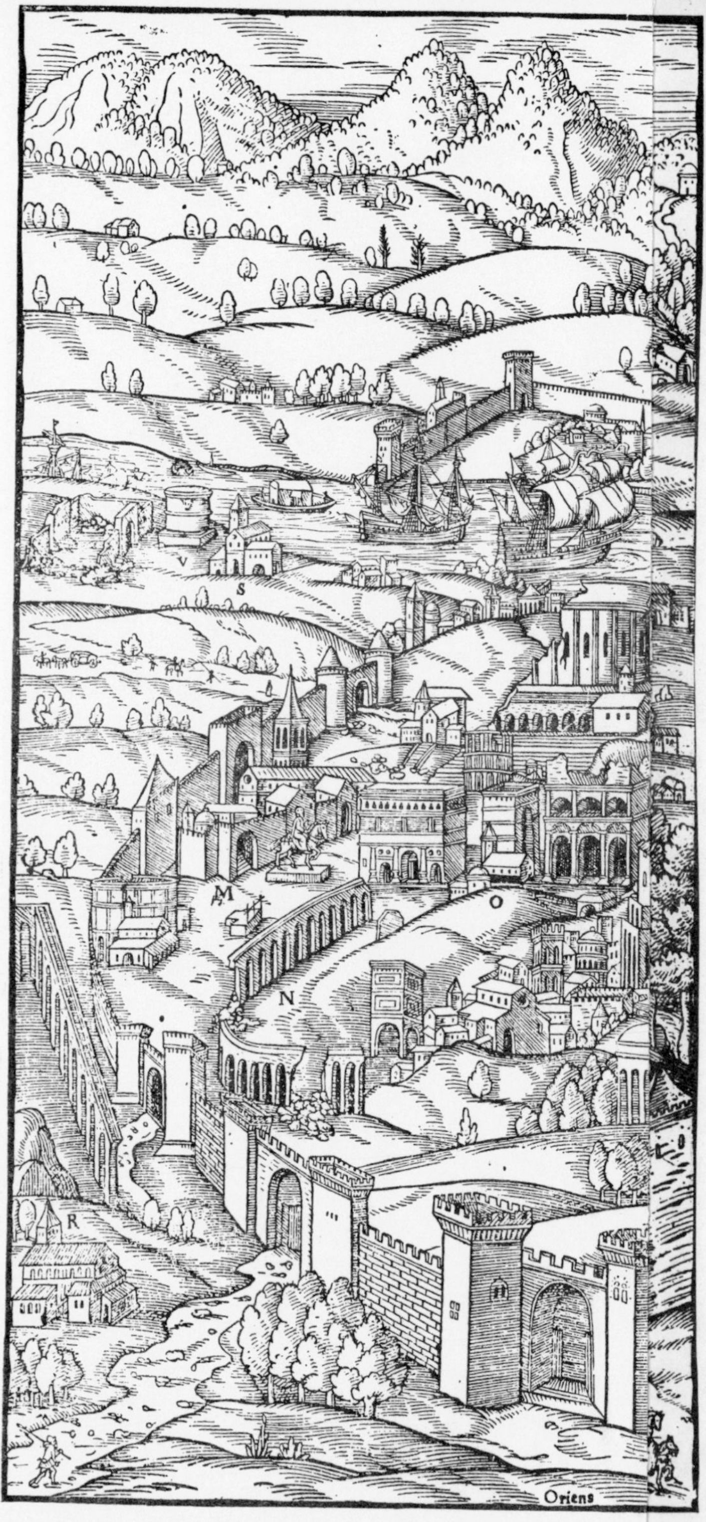

ROME AT T

We now see Rome the centre of the chief affairs of the world ;
of those between France and Spain, the most important of all ; the
concerns of Romagna ; the warfare of the barons. But the Pope,
equally indebted to all for his election, and not having as yet
collected either men or money cannot decide which to favour.
" He is of necessity compelled to veer with the wind until change
of times and circumstances force him to declare himself, or until
he be so firmly fixed in his seat, as to be able to favour or carry
out any undertaking that is to his mind." No one understands
what he means to do with Valentinois ; he presses him to depart,
he has written and caused others to write to your Excellencies, to
grant him a safe conduct, but he does not at all care that he
should really obtain it.[1] The Duke is preparing to take the road
by Porto Venere or Spezia, and thence by the Garfagnana and
Modena into Romagna. His troops consisting of three hundred
light horse and four hundred infantry, would pass through
Tuscany, if he has the safe conduct of your Excellencies, of whom
he now speaks with much affability. But who may count upon
his friendship, especially now, that he himself seems hardly to
know what he wishes ? The Cardinal of Volterra has found him
" changeable, irresolute, and suspicious, incapable of remaining
firm to any conclusion ; either because this be natural to him, or
because these blows of misfortune have stupified him, and travail
him inwardly as one unused to experience them." The Cardinal
d'Elna[2] has said that " he thought him out of his mind, for he
knew not himself what he desired to do, so involved and irresolute
did he seem." [3]

Besides, the name of Valentinois was so detested by the mass of
Florentine citizens, that, notwithstanding the recommendations—
somewhat lukewarm, we must admit—of Cardinals Soderini and
De Rouen,[4] when the proposal for the safe conduct was brought
before the Council of Eighty, out of a hundred and ten votes,
ninety were against it.[5] And on learning this, his Holiness
raised his head and told Machiavelli that it was best so, and that

[1] Letter of the 11th of November.

[2] Francesco Loris, bishop of Elna. Often mentioned as d'Euna, d'Herina,
d'Helna. For his true title see the " Dispacci " of A. Giustinian, vol. i. p. 247,
note (1). [3] Letter of the 14th of November.

[4] The two letters of recommendation are in the " Opere," P. M., vol. iv. p. 349.

[5] Letter of Buonaccorsi, dated 5th of November, 1503, " Carte del Machiavelli,"
case iii. No. 21. On this subject, see too the letter of the Ten, " Opere," P. M.,
vol. iv. p. 361.

he was content ; whereupon the latter wrote—one sees plainly that he wishes to be rid of him, without appearing to break faith with him, and therefore does not care in the least what others do against him.[1]   Very different, of course, was the impression this made upon the mind of the Duke, who, the moment he saw Machiavelli, burst into fury, saying, that he had already sent on his troops, was himself about to take ship, and could not possibly wait.   The orator tried to soothe him by promising to write to Florence, and suggested that the Duke should send one of his men there, which certainly would lead to some good arrangement. But what he really wrote to the Ten was, that he had said these things to pacify the Duke, and because the latter threatened to side with the Pisans, the Venetians, the devil himself, in order to injure Florence.   " When his messenger arrives, your Excellencies can neglect him and arrange about him as you will judge best. As to the troops which have already set out, namely, one hundred men-at-arms, and two hundred and fifty light horse, you can try to be informed of their movements, so as to have them disarmed and stripped at the first convenient opportunity." [2]

Valentinois started for Ostia with four or five hundred men, according to public rumour, which also swelled to seven hundred horse the cavalry on the road to Tuscany.[3]   These had been already preceded by the Bishop of Veroli, who had arrived in Florence with a letter of recommendation signed by Cardinal Soderini, and written by Machiavelli,[4] who instantly despatched another one to explain that the first was nothing but a *ruse* to soothe the Duke and send him quietly away.   They could act as they pleased with regard to the letter.[5]

Now, however, affairs were becoming complicated, for news arrived that the Venetians had taken Faenza, and soon after, that they had annexed Rimini by agreement with Malatesta.   Upon this, Machiavelli, in language that may truly be called prophetic, wrote that this expedition of the Venetians " will either be the

---

[1] Letter of the 18th of November. Giustinian wrote on the 17th of the same month—" The Pope is planning the Duke's destruction, but does not wish to appear in the matter."   And on the 13th he added, that the Pope himself had said to him—" This Duke is so changeable and incomprehensible, that certainly we do not know how to assert anything respecting his affairs . . . let him go if he chooses, for we think that he will be stripped of everything."

Letter of the 18th of November.   [3] Letter of the 19th of November.

[4] This is in vol. vi. of the " Opere," p. 430, note.

[5] Letter of the 20th of November.

gate opening all Italy to them, or prove to be their ruin." [1]   Here in fact was the germ of the future league of Cambray. The Cardinal de Rouen, terribly enraged, swore on his soul that if the Venetians threatened Florence, the king would put aside all else to help them ; the Pope declared that if the Venetians persevered in their present course of action, he would join with France, with the Emperor, with any one, to achieve their downfall, as in fact he afterwards did.[2]

Meanwhile the Pope was unable to restrain himself any longer, although he had permitted Valentinois to go to Ostia, without giving up the pass-words of the Cesena and Forlì citadels which were still holding out for him ; he now sent the Cardinals of Volterra and Sorrento after him to order him to give the pass-words and state that if he refused them, his Holiness would have him arrested and his adherents seized and disarmed.   In fact, when these messengers returned without having obtained anything from Valentinois, the Pope instantly sent orders to the naval commandant in Ostia for the Duke's arrest, and wrote to Sienna and Perugia that his people were to be stripped, and if possible their leader Don Michele made a prisoner.[3]   All this caused a rumour to arise that Cæsar Borgia had been thrown into the Tiber, and although Machiavelli did not give full credence to the report, he added, in writing of it—"I really believe that even if this have not already happened, it soon may. . . . This Pope begins to pay his debts honourably enough, but rubs them out with the tow of

[1] Letter of the 24th of November.

[2] Letter of the 21st of November.   In the following letter Machiavelli asks the Ten for money, and goes through his accounts.   On starting he had received thirty-three ducats.   He spent thirteen in travelling post, eighteen upon a mule, eighteen upon a velvet habit, eleven on a Catalan cloak, ten upon a loose robe, making a total of seventy ducats.   He was living at an inn with two men and a mule, spending ten *carlini* a-day.   Although the Ten had granted him the salary he had demanded, yet he was not then aware of the dearth of provisions in Rome.   Therefore he now asked to be reimbursed for his travelling expenses, according to the usual custom.   This request was granted.   In fact there exists in the Florentine Archives an order of payment dated 3rd of January, 1503 (1504), in which it is stated that, Machiavelli having been granted a salary of ten lire a-day— his usual stipend included, a sum of 300 lire was owing to him from the 23rd of November to the 22nd of December.   Deducting from this 164 lire, 3 soldi, 4 denari, as his usual salary, there remained 132 lire, soldi, 8 denari, still to be paid to him, and for which an order was given, as also for 25 broad yellow florins, and 6 lire, " which his accounts show him to have expended in going to Rome, and on his return journey by post."   " Opere " (P. M.), vol. i. p. 62.

[3] Letters of the 23rd and 24th November.

his inkstand ; and since he (the Duke) is taken, whether he be alive or dead, we need trouble ourselves no more about him.[1] One sees that his sins are gradually bringing him to punishment ; God grant that all may go well ! "[2]

This is a specimen of the language that so deeply scandalizes those who after having converted Machiavelli not only into a blind admirer, but almost into the counsellor and secret agent of Valentinois, are amazed to perceive that he now speaks of him with so much cold contempt, and make that a ground for fresh accusations against him. But Borgia's behaviour at this juncture appeared to all as it really was—vile, contemptible, and inconsistent. Instead of defending his badly acquired possessions sword in hand, he became humble and irresolute, trusting only to the basest intrigues. He is no longer the individual who excited Machiavelli's praise and admiration. And although the secretary's present tone of language may appear cynical to those either disposed to exalt him over much, or to blame him too severely, very different was the opinion entertained by his contemporaries. In Florence indeed he was blamed for always making too much account of the Duke, and to this accusation those least well disposed towards Machiavelli added derision and even calumny. Buonaccorsi, in one of his letters, tells him that—" In general you are laughed at for writing too earnestly of the Duke ; there are persons who even believe that you hope to get some benefit for yourself from him, but that you will not succeed."[3]

Meanwhile Cæsar Borgia, escorted by the Papal guards, was brought up the Tiber on board a galleon, as far as S. Paolo, on the 29th of November, and entered Rome the same evening. " Your Excellencies," so wrote Machiavelli, "need not trouble yourselves as to where he may land. The men who were with him have straggled back one by one, and those who went with Don Michele will not get on very well."[4]   In fact on the 1st of December came

---

[1] Letter of the 26th November.   It is almost unnecessary to add that many portions of these letters are written in cipher.

[2] First letter of the 28th November.

[3] Letter of the 15th November, 1503, from which we have before quoted.

[4] Letter of the 29th November. See too Giustinian's despatch of the same date. The two orators sometimes give the same news in almost identical words, as is by no means rare in the diplomatic correspondences of this period. This results in part from the faithfulness and precision of the Italian ambassadors, and in part, we believe, from their employment of the same secret agents to obtain news, or from having surreptitiously read the same documents, since we find the same

the news that this band pursued by the Baglioni and the Siennese, had been routed and disarmed, while Don Michele, seized by the people of Castiglion Fiorentino, had been sent a prisoner to Florence. The Pope was overjoyed at this, and wished to have him in his own hands, in order to "get to the bottom of all the cruel robberies, murders, sacrileges, and infinite other crimes committed in Rome against God and man during the past eleven years. He told me smilingly, that he wished to speak with him, that he might learn something from him, the better to govern the Church. He hopes that you will therefore surrender Don Michele to him, and the Cardinal of Volterra has encouraged him in this hope, and strongly urges your Excellencies to give him up as a criminal guilty of despoiling the Church." [1]

The Duke, as was natural, became more and more dejected, shut up in the apartments of the Cardinal of Sorrento. This, however, did not alter his mode of conduct. He had at last delivered the countersigns to Pietro d'Oviedo, who was to go with them to obtain the surrender of the fortresses ; but he asked the Pope to give him sureties for the Romagna territories, and required that the Cardinal of Rouen should guarantee these sureties in writing. "And while Valentinois," wrote Machiavelli in conclusion, "is making all these difficulties, and fighting over every point, the Pope, being quite easy as to the result, lets him run on and will not press matters to a conclusion. It is believed, however, that whether he have the sureties or not, D'Oviedo will set out to-morrow ; and thus it would seem that little by little this Duke is slipping into his grave." [2]

It is useless now to waste time in relating how D'Oviedo set out ; how he came to his death in Romagna, hanged by one of the commandants of the fortresses who would not surrender, because his master was in the power of the Pope ; how the Pope finally obtained the fortresses, and Valentinois, deserted by all, went to Naples where he was seized by Gonsalvo dei Cordova, and sent a prisoner to Spain. All these are things generally known, and besides would lead us too far astray from the subject of our narrative. Instead, it is only necessary to record one last circumstance, very typical of the Duke's behaviour at this period, and throwing a

phrases reproduced in the letters not of one or two, but of several orators. In the course of editing the Despatches of A. Giustinian we frequently had occasion to make this remark in collating them with those of other orators.

[1] Letter of the 1st December.   [2] Letter of the 3rd December.

new light upon his character. He had repeatedly implored as " a special grace " an interview with Duke Guidobaldo, who had then come to Rome from Urbino, and was on very good terms with the Pope. At first this nobleman—remembering how iniquitously he had been in former days driven from his dominions by the Borgia, and with what fury they had sought to hunt him down, refused the request ; but finally yielded to the intercessions of his Holiness. We are told by an eye-witness that Valentinois entered cap in hand, and twice bent his knees to the ground in advancing towards Duke Guidobaldo, who was sitting upon a species of couch in the pontifical ante-chamber. On seeing his old adversary in this attitude of humility, he left his seat, stirred by a sentiment of dignity and almost of self-respect, with his own hands assisted Borgia to rise, and made him sit down by his side. Thereupon Valentinois humbly besought forgiveness for the past, " laying the blame upon his youth, his evil counsellors, his bad companions, the abominable disposition of the Pope and of some others who had urged him to that undertaking, entering into many details concerning the Pope, and cursing his memory." He promised to restore all the stolen property, excepting a few brocaded robes, given to the Cardinal of Rouen, and certain other things which he no longer possessed. Guidobaldo replied with a few courteous words, but of such a nature that Borgia " remained much abased and understood his position." [1] Nevertheless he continued to bear himself towards all with the same abject servility, as may be seen from the continuation of the narrative we quote, and from the despatches of the various Italian ambassadors in Rome. Can we then be surprised that Machiavelli should now feel the utmost personal contempt for Valentinois, and almost endeavour to hide the present spectacle from his mind in order not to lose remembrance of the observations and ideas which had previously occurred to him ?

At this juncture the Legation may almost be said to be at an end. Machiavelli lingered in Rome a few days longer, prevented from starting by a cough then prevalent, and by the solicitations of Cardinal Soderini, who was very unwilling to part with him. During this interval he continued to forward the news that he collected day by day. He reported the arrest of the secretary who

---

[1] This most important letter was discovered and published by Ugolini in his " Storia dei Duchi d'Urbino," vol ii. p. 523. The date of the day is wanting, as it is only described : *Dat: Roma* v. . . . 1503.

had poisoned his employer, Cardinal Michiel, by order of Pope Alexander VI., and who would—it was said—be burnt alive in public.[1] He also continued as before to give the current news of the war in the kingdom of Naples, and having written some other particulars about Valentinois, who was now treated as a prisoner, he sent off his last letter in date of the 16th of December, and started for Florence, bearing one from the Cardinal Soderini, who praised him most highly to the Republic as a man of unrivalled good faith, diligence, and prudence.[2]

During his stay in Rome Machiavelli had always sent uncertain and contradictory news of the war then going on between the Spaniards and the French, who were encamped in the marshes on either side of the Garigliano and exposed to continual rains. In fact, up to the time of his departure, nothing very decisive had taken place, and the most contradictory rumours were afloat. But hardly had he reached Florence, than news came of what was called the rout of Garigliano, which took place at the end of December and was a downright catastrophe for the French. Their army was dispersed and destroyed ; their best captains either killed, taken, or put to flight ; the whole of the kingdom was now in the hands of the Spaniards. Among the many different news daily reaching Florence, there was one item that gladdened the whole city : Piero dei Medici, who was with the French army, had been drowned in the Garigliano, while trying to cross it in a boat. However, the knowledge that there was

---

[1] Letter of the 14th December. On the 17th Giustinian wrote the same intelligence.

[2] It is in the vol. vi. of the " Opere," in the note at p. 494. Among the other letters of this Legation, there is one in the " Opere," marked xlii., addressed to a Florentine citizen, in a private manner. In this Machiavelli writes that he can only repeat in homely fashion the things already written officially : " I will speak in the vulgar tongue, even if I have written to the Office grammatically ; though I doubt if I have done so." This is generally believed to have been addressed to Soderini, but as is justly remarked by Signor Nitti (*op. cit.*, vol. i. p. 261), the form is much too familiar for this to be probable. Nitti believes it to have been written to a Messer Tucci, one of the Signory, and who—according to a letter of Buonaccorsi, dated 4th December—had been much vexed that Machiavelli had not replied to him ; nor is this an improbable supposition, for in this letter the secretary makes excuses for his silence. Besides, this point is of no importance. We would merely observe that the phrase, *writing in the vulgate and not in grammar*, has not the angry meaning given to it by Signor Nitti, and that, in writing to one of the *Signoria*, the secretary would not, as he supposes, have made use of "sharp and cutting words." The letter of Buonaccorsi alluded to by Signor Nitti, is among the " Carte del Machiavelli," case iii. No. 26.

nothing more to be feared from this hated and despised tyrant, was but a slight compensation for the fresh perils now menacing the Republic, which had been the constant ally of France. Many already fancied that they beheld the great Captain Gonsalvo on the march towards Lombardy at the head of his victorious army, to drive the French altogether out of Italy. And what then would be the fate of Florence? Gonsalvo was known to be favourable to the Pisans, what therefore must be his sentiments towards France's most faithful ally throughout the Peninsula?

For these reasons, Machiavelli had hardly resumed his official duties in Florence, than he was despatched to France, where Niccolò Valori was already resident ambassador. His instructions, dated 14th of January, 1504, written in his own hand and signed by Marcello Virgilio, ran as follows: " You will go to Lyons, present yourself to Valori and the King, explain to them the position of affairs here, see for yourself the preparations being made by the French, and write to us quickly of all these things, giving your own judgment concerning them. And should the preparations seem insufficient to you, you will make it clearly to be understood that we are not in a position to gather troops sufficient for our defence, and that accordingly we should be obliged to turn for aid wherever it was to be found, since nought else is ours but this small liberty, that we must use every effort to preserve. Nor will you content yourself with great promises and designs, but also make it understood that immediate and effective aid is what is required." Besides this, Baglioni's Condotta having been broken off, he was to try to effect something towards settling that business likewise.

Machiavelli set out without delay, and on the 22nd of January, 1504, wrote from Milan that the Lord of Chaumont did not believe that Gonsalvo would advance, and declared that in every event the King would know how to defend his friends, that he would write to beg his Majesty to conclude Baglioni's Condotta and that meanwhile the Republic should exert itself to come to friendly terms with " the small coin of Italy ; " as to the Venetians, " they would be forced to attend to their fisheries." Others, on the contrary, assured Machiavelli that the King of France had exhausted his finances, had few troops, and those few scattered over many places, whereas " the enemies were in the saddle, fresh and ready for victory." [1] On the 26th he reached Lyons, and

---

[1] Letter of the 22nd January, 1450, from Milan.

on the 27th, together with Valori, he waited on the Cardinal of Rouen, and spoke very earnestly to him on the state of affairs and the necessity of prompt and energetic measures. The replies he received were too vague to be satisfactory ; but all of a sudden some of the clouds began to clear away from the gloomy horizon. Although Spain had obtained an extraordinary victory, she was not intoxicated by her good fortune, and sought rather to consolidate her recent conquests, than to engage in new and perilous enterprises. She therefore lent a willing ear to the proposals of truce made to her by the French, and as they could not exclude the Florentines from the agreement, the dangers threatening the Republic suddenly disappeared. In fact, a three years' truce was signed at Lyons on the 11th of February. The Spaniards were now masters of the Neapolitan kingdom, friendly relations were temporarily established between the two potentates, and the Florentines were included in the treaty as friends of France. Valori quickly informed the Ten of this, and Machiavelli was able to prepare for his departure. On the 25th of February he wrote that the moment news of the truce arrived he leapt into the saddle to return home. However, his departure was deferred for a few days owing to some small business that had to be done for Valori, who held him in the greatest esteem, commended to the Ten his zeal and intelligence, corresponded with and frequently made use of him. And as Valori thereafter pursued his diplomatic correspondence unaided, we only find three of Machiavelli's letters in this Legation, and of these the only noteworthy one is that written from Milan.[1]

Having returned to Florence, he was sent on the 2nd of April to Piombino to carry to the Lord of that place assurances of sin-

---

[1] Signor Gaspar Amico, at p. 182 of his work, "La vita di Niccolò Machiavelli" (Florence, Civelli, 1875), mentions a hitherto unknown journey of Machiavelli to France, in the January of 1502, and in confirmation of it quotes a letter, which he believes to be inedited, of Francesco Vettori, dated the 17th of January of that year, from Pulsano. This letter, however, which is at sheet 83, not 8, of the Codex quoted by him (Florence Archives, cl. x. dist. 4, No. 92), is written from Bulsano (Bolzano), and bears the date, not of the 17th January, 1502, but of the 17th January, 1507, when Vettori was ambassador to the Emperor. It has also escaped Signor Amico's notice, that the letter published by him is identical with the third letter of the *Legazione all' Imperatore*, which took place in 1507.

Another of Niccolò Valori's letters ("Carte del Machiavelli," case iii. No. 63) leads Signor Nitti to a series of conjectures (*op. cit.*, vol i. p. 220, note 1) which seem to us of but little probability. He considers it a proof that Machiavelli was

cere friendship on the part of the Republic, and to put him on his guard against the Siennese.[1]   And as usual he was instructed to study carefully the tendencies of the Lord of Piombino and all those about him, in order to bring full reports of these matters on his return, which he accordingly did.   And after this the business of the Chancery became brisker than ever, for the war with Pisa was resumed with fresh energy.

Meanwhile Soderini, now sure of his ground, began to rule in his own way, and Machiavelli, having great ascendency over him, seconded his efforts, the better to preserve his own influence. The office of Gonfaloniere for life, took all importance from others held for very brief terms, and these were therefore filled by men of little weight, who left more and more untrammelled the authority of chief magistrate of the State, whose economical administration—as contrasted with the former reckless squandering—had gained him the confidence even of the most prudent.   Therefore Soderini had all his own way in the Pratica, the Eighty, and even in the Great Council, although certain grave jealousies had arisen against him and also against Machiavelli, in whom he reposed the fullest confidence.[2]   Condotte were concluded with G. P. Baglioni, Marc Antonio Colonna, and other captains of more or less renown, for fifty, for one hundred or more men-at-arms a-piece.   Three thousand foot soldiers were hired to lay waste[3] the enemies' territory.

The commissary was Giacomini who quickly commenced operations.   In May he made a raid upon San Rossore, devastating it entirely in four days ; he did the same in the Val di Serchio,

---

working with Valori for the purpose of " reconstructing the former intimate union of the House of Borgia with the King of France."   Machiavelli would have been following a policy of his own, had he and Valori tried to reconstruct an alliance, without any authorization to do so.   But the Secretary of the Ten could not take similar liberties.   The mistake has arisen simply because it escaped observation that the date of the letter : Rouen, 7th of March, 1503, Florentine style, answers to the 7th of March, 1504, modern style.   At that time Alexander VI. was dead, Valentinois had been arrested at Ostia, and was no longer of any importance. The letter was written by Valori, while Machiavelli was on his way back to Florence from France, and it alludes to certain affairs, to which he was to apply himself on the journey for the benefit of the Republic, in the name of the Gonfaloniere.   There is no mystery in the letter, and there is nothing in it concerning the Borgia.

[1] " Opere," vol. vi. p. 564.

[2] Guicciardini, " Storia Fiorentina," chap. xxviii.

[3] Buonaccorsi, " Diario," pp. 88–89.

and instantly afterwards captured Librafatta. Three galleys were hired, which proved very useful in cutting off the enemy's supplies, and meanwhile he made several forays into the dominion of Lucca as a reprisal for the succour which that State was continually sending to the Pisans. On the 1st of July communications from the Ten were forwarded to him by Machiavelli, congratulating him on what he had already accomplished, and exhorting him to make the Lucchese clearly understand his resolve that for the future they should not help the Pisans with "so much as a glass of water; and that being aware that their (the Pisans') life is kept in their body by the Lucchese, you have firmly decided that this shall happen no more, even if you have to pursue them within the walls of Lucca." [1]

All this, however, was nothing unusual. But now Soderini had conceived a very unfortunate idea, that both he and Machiavelli followed with extravagant ardour, against the advice of all competent persons. This was nothing less than of altering the course of the Arno, and by turning it into a lake near Leghorn, leave Pisa without a river, and robbed of all communication with the sea. The engineers who were consulted stated that with two thousand workmen and a certain quantity of timber, it would be possible to construct a dam, which would stop the course of the river, and, by means of two trenches dug for the purpose, direct it into the lake, and thence to the sea. "Thirty or forty thousand days' work would suffice," *i.e.*, two thousand men might accomplish it in fifteen days. When the question was laid before the Ten in the Pratica, they refused to agree to it, considering it "little better than a fantasy." [2] But the Gonfaloniere used so many means to carry his project that at last he succeeded, and obtained the decree for its execution.

On the 20th of August Niccolò Machiavelli wrote a long letter to Giacomini, informing him of the resolution passed, and directing him to set about the necessary measures for carrying it out, in conjunction with Giuliano Lapi and Colombino, who were sent to him expressly for that purpose. [3] Neither Bentivoglio nor Giacomini believed in the feasibility of the project. The first demonstrated, pen in hand, that it being necessary to excavate

---

[1] Florence Archives, cl. x. dist. 3, No. 113, folio 32.
[2] Guicciardini, "Storia Fiorentina," chap. xxviii. p. 315.
[3] Florence Archives, cl. x. dist. 3, No. 112, folio 89*t*: Appendix, document viii.

800,000 *braccia* square of soil, two thousand workmen would have to be employed for at least two hundred days, and that even then nothing would be accomplished.[1]   Giacomini while declaring his readiness—as duty required to execute the orders received— added : " Your Excellencies will find that fresh difficulties will daily arise, and the work prove to be less easy than it now seems." [2]   He too saw nothing in the project but huge loss of time and money, and the necessity of guarding the workmen, without being able to perform any military operation.   And being a man of small patience, he very soon made the fever from which he was in reality suffering, a pretext for requesting his dismissal on the 15th of September.   It was granted to him on the following day, and the Ten chose Tommaso Tosinghi as his successor.[3]

Machiavelli meanwhile was employed in writing an interminable series of letters to direct the works.   All the Communes received orders to supply the camp with a quantity of sappers to dig the trenches ; soldiers were ordered to mount guard to defend the works ; master carpenters were sent to construct the dam ; engineers were summoned from Ferrara : the labour went on unceasingly.[4]   The excavation of the two canals which had to be seven *braccia* deep, and one of them twenty, the other thirty *braccia* wide, went forward rapidly ; but more rapidly still the expenditure, since with thousands of men employed night and day, not half the task was accomplished.   Worse still, grave doubts soon arose as to the success of the undertaking ; for, during a flood, the water being turned into the first trench, which was now completed, it all ran back into the Arno, the moment the

[1] Among the " Carte del Machiavelli," case vi. No. 78, there is a report of the whole of this affair drawn up by Buonaccorsi.   Bentivoglio declared the undertaking impossible, because, according to him, the gradient was slighter in the direction of the lake, than along the present course of the river.   " These reasons are all palpable and infallible," concludes Buonaccorsi, " yet they were not admitted.   Every man is enlightened by experience."

[2] Letter of Giacomini to the Ten, dated 25th of August, 1504.   " Archivio Storico," vol. xv. p. 296.   Nardi says in his " Vita di A. Giacomini " : " The which work was entrusted to Antonio, and he had it carried on with all diligence and solicitude, although approved neither by him nor Messer Ercole Bentivoglio, for they judged it a useless expense and labour."

[3] This letter too of Giacomini is published in the " Archivio Storico," vol. xv. p. 306 ; his permission to retire, and the announcement of Tosinghi's nomination are in the Florence Archives, cl. x. dist. 3, No. 113, at sheet 125*t*.

[4] See Florence Archives, cl. x. dist. 3, No. 112, at sheets 94, and 103*t*, and No. 113, at sheet 96*t*.   These two files are full of Machiavelli's letters on the deviation of the Arno.

flood subsided.[1] It was asserted that the dam, by arresting the course of the river, would raise the level of its bed ; but it was soon found, that, as it was built slowly, the narrowing of the bed increased the force of the current and again deepened the bed. Then it was thought that this inconvenience would cease as soon as the work was completed, and meanwhile the soldiers had to waste their time guarding the labourers. Nevertheless Soderini would not allow that he was beaten, and having carried the matter first before the Pratica, and then before the Council of Eighty, obtained a decree for the continuance of the work, and wrote to that effect to Tosinghi on the 28th and 29th of September.[2] Soon they had to be content with the hope that the seven thousand ducats already granted might not have been spent in vain, and that the trenches already dug might serve at least to check the advance of the Pisans, and lay the country under water.[3] A proclamation was issued, and read beneath the walls of Pisa, setting forth that the Signory had obtained from the Great Council the privilege of granting a free pardon to all who would leave that city and declare themselves obedient subjects of the Republic.[4] But this measure too failed in its purpose, for instead of reducing the strength of the enemy, its sole effect was to enable the Pisans to rid themselves of useless persons, while provisions were scarce. Some too, by leaving the city, regained possession of their lands, and then clandestinely returned. It was therefore necessary to publish fresh orders to prevent the benevolent clauses of the proclamation from defeating the main object of it.[5]

Disasters multiplied in these days. The ships hired to watch the coast had already been wrecked, with a loss of eighty lives ; the soldiery showed increasing discontent ; the labourers deserted as soon as the rainy season set in.[6] And although the new engineers from Ferrara, after consultation with those in the camp, did not altogether despair of the enterprise, yet on the 12th of October it was left to Tosinghi's decision whether it should be continued, or whether it would be best to pay off the army and

[1] Buonaccorsi, "Diario," p. 93 and fol.

[2] Florence Archives, cl. x. dist. 3, No. 113, at sheets 152 and 154. See in Appendix, document ix., the first of these two letters.

[3] *Loc. cit.*, No. 113, at sheet 147*t*.

[4] This proclamation is to be found in *loc. cit.*, No. 112, at sheet 156, Appendix, document x. See also Guicciardini, "Storia Fiorentina," chap. xxviii. pp. 314-15.

[5] Florence Archives, cl. x. dist. 3, No. 112, at sheet 160*t*.

[6] *Loc. cit.*, at sheet 157*t*.

suspend everything ; the which meant that Florence had lost all hope of being able to go on. Shortly afterwards, in fact, Tosinghi was recalled, and a successor sent to replace him ; the army was disbanded, and the trenches made at so enormous a labour and expense, were hastily filled up by the Pisans. And such was the end of this unlucky undertaking.[1]

It was precisely at this period that Machiavelli began to write the first verses that we have from his pen, the "Decennale Primo,"[2] which he composed in a fortnight, and dedicated to Alamanno Salviati in a letter of the 9th of November, 1504.[3] This work cannot be styled genuine poetry, for it consists of a simple historic account of events occurring in Italy during the decade commencing in the year 1494. The narrative flows on rapidly enough in simple and easy *terzine*, it dwells on none but the most important events, yet does not neglect anything worthy of note, especially with reference to the history of Florence. And from time to time some flash of bitter irony enlivens the poem with its pungent wit, and is in marked contrast with the expressions of real sorrow, escaping the author with equal frequency.

He invokes the aid of the muse in narrating the miseries which began for Italy when she once more allowed her soil to be trampled by barbaric hordes. The French, obeying the call of Italian internal discord, overrun the Peninsula, without encountering any resistance. At Florence alone they are withstood by the daring of Piero Capponi :—

> " Lo strepito dell' armi e de' cavalli
> Non potè far che non fosse sentita
> La voce d' un Cappon fra cento Galli." [4]

---

[1] On the 26th of October, 1504, Cardinal Soderini wrote to Machiavelli from Rome : " Much have we been grieved that this water plan should have proved so great a fallacy, for it seems impossible that it should not be the fault of those engineers who blundered so grossly. Perhaps too this may be the pleasure of the Almighty for some better end unknown to ourselves." " Carte del Machiavelli," case iii. No. 58.

[2] "Opere," vol. v. pp. 351-73. [3] Ibid. at p. 355.

[4] The sense of which may be roughly rendered—

> " For still amid the clang of arms, amid the clash of horse,
> Rose 'mid a hundred Gallic *crows* one Capon's stirring voice."
>
> *Translator.*

Yet when they are compelled to retreat from Italy, and pass the Taro, after repulsing the army of the League, Florence cannot bear to withdraw from her alliance with them, and " waits on with open beak till some one shall cross the Alps to bring her manna in the desert." But soon she found that she was deceived, for enemies encompassed her on all sides, and threatened her very existence ; especially when she allowed herself to be " dominated and divided by the doctrines of that great Savonarola, who, filled with divine virtue, fascinated her by his words." Nor could she ever again have been united,

> " Se non cresceva o se non era spento
> Il suo lume divin con maggior foco."

Then follow the misfortunes of the war in the Casentino and the war with Pisa, and here Machiavelli plainly alludes to the treachery of Paolo Vitelli, " cause of so much ill." And he goes on to recall the Lombard wars and the rebellion of Arezzo, *à propos* to which he praises somewhat too highly the prudence and virtue of Piero Soderini, who was then Gonfaloniere, though not for life. He next describes the events in Romagna, representing Valentinois and his captains as so many venomous serpents tearing each other to pieces tooth and nail. The Duke is the basilisk among them, who, by the sweetness of his whistling, entices them into his den and destroys them. And while once more the French descend into Italy to renew their Neapolitan expedition, " the glorified spirit of Pope Alexander is borne amid the souls of the blessed, closely followed by his three inseparable hand-maidens—lust, cruelty, and simony." Julius II. was then elected " doorkeeper to Paradise ; " the French were defeated and Borgia at last received from the Pope and Gonsalvo the merited chastisement of his iniquities.

Towards the conclusion of the Decennale Machiavelli again resuming his gravity says that—for ten years the sun has shone upon these horrible deeds which have stained the world with blood. " Now Phœbus redoubles his coursers' rations, for speedily other events will happen, compared with which all that has passed shall seem as nothing. Fortune is not yet content ; the end of the Italian wars not yet at hand. The Pope seeks to regain the dominions of the Church ; the Emperor wishes to be crowned ; France laments the blow she has received ; Spain spreads nets for her neighbours, in order to keep firm hold of that which she has seized ; Florence wants Pisa ; Venice oscillates between the dictates of her timidity and lust of fresh conquests ; so that it is easily to be seen that the new flame, once kindled, will soar to heaven itself.   My mind is divided betwixt hope and fear,

" ' Tanto che si consuma a dramma a dramma,'

for fain would I know into what port the tiny bark of our Republic will run.   My whole faith is in its dexterous steersman ; but the course would be far easier and shorter if the Florentines re-opened the temple of Mars."

Throughout this work we find a strange and continual contrast. Not only—as we have already observed—do we see a stinging, sometimes almost cynical irony joined to a profound sorrow for the miseries of Italy ; but likewise a very lively sèntiment of national unity, together with a still livelier affection for his native Florence.   The author begins by deploring the cruel wounds inflicted upon Italy by foreigners, and longs for power to heal them ; but his hatred for Venice, Pisa, and other neigh-bouring states speedily breaks forth.   He frequently recurs to his first grief ; but the closing idea of the canto is dedicated to Florence, not to Italy.   The last verse refers to the idea which he had long been turning over in his mind, *i.e.*, of saving the Republic, by arming it in its own defence.   This conflict between scepticism and political earnestness, between irony and genuine grief, between national and municipal feeling, is to be met with throughout the Italian Renaissance, and in no one is it better personified than in Machiavelli, especially during these years when—unable to devote himself to serious and prolonged study—he threw his ideas upon paper just as they occurred to him.

The "Primo Decennale" was only printed in the beginning of 1506 by means of one of Machiavelli's coadjutors in the Chancery,[1] and almost at the same time an illegal reprint of

---

[1] The first edition, prepared in February, 1506, by Agostino Vespucci, bore the following title :—"Nicolai Malciavelli florentini, compendium rerum decennio in Italiam gestarum ad viros florentinos, incipit feliciter."   It was counterfeited twenty days later, and Vespucci brought an action before the Eight, and speaks of it in a letter to Machiavelli, also adding that the magistrates, not knowing "your fable singer," he had gone out to have ten copies handsomely bound, so as to present one to each magistrate, and to two other citizens.   The letter is dated 14th March, 1506, and was published by Passerini, "Opere " (P. M.), vol. i. p. 63. This most rare edition, without date of time or place, was assigned by Libri to the year 1504 ; but Vespucci's letter, in our opinion, removes all doubt.

it was made without the author's knowledge ; it was quickly circulated among his friends and read with great avidity, but, nevertheless, did not much serve to the increase of his reputation. One noteworthy letter, however, was addressed to him on the 25th February, 1506, by Signor Ercole Bentivoglio, to whom he had sent a copy of his work, and who was then at Cascina on the service of the Republic. This correspondent, after thanking Machiavelli, exalts the art, with which all the principal events of the decade were gathered into so small a space, without any matter of importance being omitted. He urged him to continue the work, " for although these times have been, and still are, so full of wretchedness, that any record of them renews and increases our many sufferings, still it is grateful to us to know that a true written version of these things will go down to those who come after us, who, therefore, knowing our evil fate in these days, will not accuse us of wilfully neglecting to maintain the honour and reputation of Italy." " He who has not read the history of these times," says Bentivoglio, in conclusion, " could not believe how in so short a space of time Italy could have fallen from such a height of prosperity to such an abyss of ruin, towards which even the little that remains to us seems to rush as towards a desired end, unless he who saved the people of Israel from Pharaoh should unexpectedly come to our rescue." [1] This is certainly strange language from a free captain ; but such were the times, such the general anxiety felt in Italy.

It would seem that Machiavelli frequently amused himself at this period by mingling irony and satire with his official daily work and political meditations, for it was then that he must have composed a second literary work, which has unfortunately perished. This was an imitation of the Clouds and other comedies of Aristophanes, entitled " Le Maschere " (Masks). All that we know of it is that it was written at the instance of Marcello Virgilio, and, together with other papers and compositions of his, came into the hands of Giulian de Rìcci, who, though he had transcribed many other unpublished writings of his illustrious grandfather, declined to copy this, not only because it was reduced to barely legible fragments, but because the author had attacked in it, " under feigned names, many citizens who were still living in the year 1504." After which the same writer

---

[1] This letter was published by Nitti, vol. i. p. 301, note. It is included among the " Carte del Machiavelli," case iv. No. 99.

adds :—"In all his compositions Niccolò indulged in much license, as well in blaming great personages, lay and ecclesiastic, as in reducing all things to natural or fortuitous causes." Certainly this stinging satirical spirit of his procured him many enemies, and helped to embitter his life, but his persistency in reducing all facts to natural causes, although, as Ricci sadly remarks, it led to the interdiction of Machiavelli's works by Paul IV. and the Council of Trent, was likewise the source of his well-merited immortality.[1]

[1] See, in the Florence National Library, the "Priorista" of Ricci, Santo Spirito quarter, Machiavelli family, at sheet 161 and fol.

CHAPTER VIII.

Sad condition of Umbria—Legation to Perugia—War perils—New Legation to Sienna—Defeat of Alviano—The Florentines attack Pisa, and are repulsed—Legation to the Court of Julius II.—Institution of the Florentine Militia.

(1505–1507.)

OWARDS the end of 1504 the prospects of the Republic were exceedingly gloomy. Bartolommeo d'Alviano had parted from Gonsalvo dei Cordova in high discontent, and it was said that he intended to attempt some expedition on his own account in Central Italy. He was seconded by the Vitelli, the Orsini, the lords of Piombino and Sienna, and, what was still worse, it appeared that even G. P. Baglioni, although the paid Captain of the Florentines, was also in agreement with him. For this General remained at Perugia, without renewing the Condotta, which had now expired, and replied evasively, or not at all, to the official letters despatched to him.[1] Neither at Leghorn nor Pisa were things going on well,[2] and at the end of March, 1505, there was an encounter on the bridge of Cappellese, on the river Osole, between a considerable number of Pisans and Florentines, in which the latter were utterly routed, chiefly owing to the negligence of their commanders. Naturally, the Republic complained bitterly of this defeat,[3] and after sending supplies of money to refit the camp,

[1] Letter of the 9th December, in the Florence Archives, cl. x. dist. 3, No. 113, at sheet 211*t*. In files 114 and 116 there are many of Machiavelli's letters relating to events narrated in this chapter.

[2] Specially noteworthy is the letter to the Captain of Leghorn. Florence Archives, file 116, at sheet 23, Appendix, document xi.

[3] Florence Archives, cl. x. dist. 3, No. 116, at sheets 69 and 70.

began to take thought for the future. The first measure adopted was to send Niccolò Machiavelli to Perugia, in order to discover Baglioni's real intentions.

It is difficult to conceive an exact idea of the anarchy then reigning throughout Umbria, above all in Perugia, and of the manner in which the Baglioni ruled that city. It was in a state of perpetual warfare. The neighbouring cities were swarming with refugees, among whom the Oddi took the first rank, and these from time to time made sudden forays into Perugia, and turned the streets into bloody battle grounds. When Pope Alexander VI., driven by fear of Charles VIII., came to Perugia in 1495, he tried to profit by the opportunity, and proposed to the Baglioni that they should organize some great festival, when he secretly hoped to entrap them all together in the same net. But Guido Baglioni replied, that the best of all festivals would be to show His Holiness the people in arms under the command of his relations, who were their leaders. Upon this, says Matarazzo, the chronicler, " His Holiness understood that Guido had salt in his brains," and insisted no further. Hardly had the Pope taken his departure, than the Baglioni were fighting—some of them in their shirts—through the streets of Perugia, having been assailed by the Oddi, who suddenly forced their way into the town by night, burst into their enemies' houses, and even attacked them in their beds. More than a hundred corpses lay scattered about the streets, or dangling by their necks from windows ; blood ran in streams, and was—as the chronicler tells us—lapped up by dogs, and also by a tame bear that roamed freely about the city.[1] Yet at last the Baglioni were the victors.

Two years afterwards came Cardinal Borgia, commissioned by Rome to re-establish order in Umbria. All declared their obedience to the authority of the Pontiff, but added that they would rather raze their city to the ground than renounce their own vengeance. Wherefore the Cardinal wrote that it was impossible to come to any conclusion, unless men-at-arms were sent to him to combat " these demons who have no fear of holy water." [2] And when the Cardinal went away, without having

[1] Matarazzo, " Cronaca di Perugia, Archivio Storico Italiano," vol. xvi. part II, p. 59.

[2] His letters are in the Library of St. Mark at Venice. " Epistolæ Variorum," vol ii. cl. x. codex clxxvi. The Cardinal writes in Italian, adding a few words in Spanish, as for instance : *Y no obezen perque son vilans i mala gent que volen lo*

accomplished anything, war broke out between the Baglioni themselves, split into two factions by the fraternal hatred of Guido and Ridolfo.

The summer days of the year 1500, when fêtes were held in celebration of the marriage of Guido's son, Astorre, were chosen for the struggle. The Varano of Camerino were the first to begin the slaughter, by murdering many of the Baglioni in their beds. Giovan Paolo, who contrived to escape, after defending himself with his sword, was believed to be dead, and Grifone Baglioni triumphed in the bloodshed of his kinsmen. His mother cursed him, and drove him from the house to which she had retired with the children of Giovan Paolo. But soon after the latter reappeared at the head of some armed men, whom he had collected outside the city walls, and the shrieks of Grifone were heard as he fell beneath their daggers out in the Piazza. Hardly was there time for his bereaved mother and wife to reach his side before he drew his last breath. The assassins respectfully withdrew, and the son, pressing "the white hand of his youthful mother," as a token that he forgave his enemies in obedience to her wish, immediately expired. His corpse was placed on the same bier on which, the previous day, his victim, the bridegroom Astorre, had been stretched. Thus Giovan Paolo Baglioni became lord of Perugia by the destruction of his kinsmen, and passed in triumph beneath the arch erected for the wedding of his cousin Astorre, which bore an inscription shortly before composed by Matarazzo. This chronicler winds up his minute relation of all these events by saying that "Perugia must no more be called, *augusta* but *angusta, et quod peius est, combusta.*" Nevertheless, he goes into ecstasies when speaking of the Baglioni, especially when he describes the terror they inspired in all, and their reputation in the world. Whenever one of them appears, helmeted and sword in hand, Matarazzo speaks of him as though he were a new St. George, a new Mars, and as though the city should be proud of their deeds.[1]

Giovan Paolo Baglioni, however, was not content to live quietly at Perugia ; he went in search of warfare and military

---

basto, y que quyls ha da governar los puga manar, que altrament no sen pot aver overa (sic.)   And his usual mode of signature was : *De V. S. esclav y factura, qui los benerats pens li besa.*

el Cardinal de Boria.

[1] Matarazzo, pp. 130–144.

adventure, and left his few surviving relations to carry on the government at home. Together with Vitellozzo we find him engaged in pursuit of a certain Altobello da Todi, against whom the popular hatred was so inflamed, that many were wounded by their own weapons, in their eagerness to be the first to strike him down. The Perugians devoured bits of his flesh, so the chronicler tells us, and one man even died of a surfeit of the dainty ; others offered a very high price for a portion of it, and failing to obtain it, satisfied their vindictiveness by burning sticks of charcoal in the streets dipped in the victim's blood.[1]   At a later period Baglioni was one of the conspirators at La Magione ; but on this occasion, with worse fortune than before, he speedily had to fly before the advancing " Hydra," and became a Captain of Mercenaries in the service of France and the Florentines. Carlo Baglioni held Perugia for the Duke of Valentinois. On the decease of the Pope in August, 1503, Giovan Paolo quitted the Florentine service, and together with Gentile, cousin to Carlo Baglioni, hastened sword in hand to re-possess himself of his own State. The assault was given on the 8th of September ; the cousins Carlo and Gentile fought like two lions, " each showing the other his valour, and how mighty is the daring and strength granted by Mars to this magnificent house of the Baglioni with whose renown all Italy rings."[2] By the 9th of September Giovan Paolo was once more lord of Perugia ; and renewed his engagement with Florence ; but now under one pretext, now another, he lent no effective service. Receiving a more pressing summons in consequence of the suspicions he had aroused, he then proposed that his son should be given a Condotta, consisting of a few lances, in order thus to make Florence believe that he remained faithful to the Republic without compromising himself in the eyes of its enemies. On this point also the Florentines had yielded to him ; but now that Alviano was on the advance, and, above all, since their rout by the Pisans at the Cappellese bridge —they would no longer remain in so great an uncertainty. Accordingly, they forwarded to him part of the *prestanza* or advance of pay which it was customary to give to leaders about to take the field, and ordered him to immediately send the light horse in advance, and to follow them at once in person with his men-at-arms, upon which the remainder of the *prestanza* would be at his disposal. Finding that Baglioni neither took the money nor

[1] Matarazzo, p. 150.   [2] Ibid. p. 241.

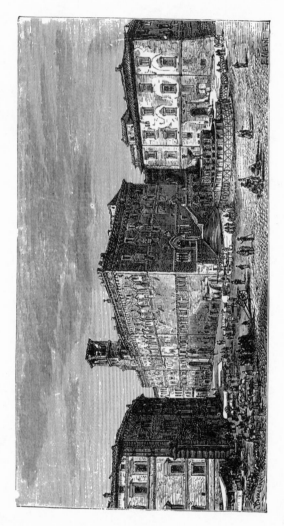

PERUGIA.

obeyed their summons, they resolved to send Machiavelli to clear the matter up, were it possible so to do.

The Secretary's instructions, dated the 8th of April, were to the effect that he was to feign to believe the excuses alleged by Baglioni ; but then " pricking him on various points," he was to try to ascertain the Perugian's real motives, and discover whether he acted in this way only to obtain higher terms, or because he was already in alliance with Alviano and the other enemies of Florence. On the 11th, Machiavelli wrote that Baglioni's pretended reason for refusing to stir was, because of the intrigues on foot against him in Perugia, and the fact that his capital enemies, the Colonna and the Savelli, were now in the service of the Republic, and that he added, that having had the terms of the Condotta examined by many learned doctors of Perugia, he was assured that the contract did not bind him to the service of the Florentines. I replied to him, writes Machiavelli, that, if so, worse might befall him than you, since if, by his fault, " you were now deprived of one hundred and thirty men-at-arms, there were so many unstalled horses in Italy, that you would certainly not need to remain on foot." But that for his ill there was no cure, because even if you did not complain of him, all who knew of his proceedings and of the Condotta granted to his son at his request, and of the *prestanza* brought to him to his own door, " will accuse him of ingratitude and bad faith, and he will be known as a stumbling horse whom no one will bestride, for fear lest he break his rider's neck ; and that these things are not to be judged by doctors, but by Signory, and that he who respects his armour and desires to wear it with honour, esteems no loss equal to that of men's faith in him ; and that this—as it seemed to me—he was now risking." Men should act in such fashion as to have no need to justify their deeds, but he on the contrary was obliged to justify himself much too often. " And thus I pricked him to the right and the left, telling him many things in a friendly way, and as though of my own accord ; and although I beheld him change countenance many times, he never showed by his speech that he had any hope of changing my opinion."

The end of all this was that Machiavelli became convinced that there was an agreement between Alviano, the Orsini and Baglioni to take Pisa from the Florentines, and do even worse, if possible ; that Petrucci of Sienna favoured the plot, and that while verbally professing friendship, all were in reality preparing for war

Therefore, after again repeating to Baglioni that he had better think well of what he was doing, for " that the matter was heavier than the weight of Perugia itself," Machiavelli went back to Florence. This legation is composed of a single letter, which however is written with great vigour, singular graphic power, and exhibits the intermixture of the homeliest and most familiar language with diplomatic dignity, that is one of the qualities of the Florentine Secretary's prose, and adds a lively colour to the originality of his style.[1] Meanwhile in Florence military preparations were being pushed forward with might and main, in order to be in readiness to face the threatened dangers. About this period a rumour was spread of the death of Louis XII., and it was instantly asserted that Alviano, with the assistance, not only of the Orsini and Vitelli, but also of the Venetians, of Gonsalvo dei Cordova himself, and of Cardinal Ascanio Sforza,[2] was about to advance on Tuscany in order to restore the Medici, and then drive the French from Milan, where he would re-establish the rule of the Sforza in the person of the Cardinal. All these rumours however were dispersed like smoke by the wind, when it was kown that the King of France was not dead, and Ascanio himself died in the month of May. This did not check Alviano, but his designs were restricted to Tuscany, as had at first been suspected, so that certain individuals in Florence even made the strange proposal to conclude the matter by giving him a Condotta. And although not a few tried to support this step, it could not be made acceptable to any man of prudence, for not only was it derogatory to the dignity of the Republic, but extremely perilous, inasmuch as all knew that Alviano and the Orsini desired the return of the Medici. Therefore at the next election of the Ten all

---

[1] See this " Legazione " in the " Opere," vol. vii.

[2] Buonaccorsi, "Diario," pp. 102, 103. Ascanio Sforza had long aspired to the government of Milan. As far back as the 10th of September, 1487, the ambassador at Rome, Lanfredini, had written to Lorenzo il Magnifico, that the Cardinal Ascanio had said to him : " I have advices from Milan, that the Lord Lodovico is seriously ill and without the grace of God, cannot be cured of his malady, and this the physicians say plainly. And should God not grant that grace, I should desire—as it also seems to be my duty—to enter upon that government, and no one thinks that there be any with a better right to it than I, nor any under whom that State and that Signore (his nephew Giovan Galeazzo, then still a minor) might live more quietly, both because I am his uncle, and because of my clerical garb." Afterwards, by means of the ambassador, he begged to be aided by Lorenzo in the matter. See the " Lettere dell' ambasciatore Lanfredini," Florence Archives, " Carte Medicee," file lvii.

intrigues failed, and a proposal was carried for the arrangement of
a Condotta with the Marquis of Mantova, as Captain-General,
with three hundred men-at-arms. But even in this quarter
negotiations proceeded very slowly, and although, on the 4th of
May, Machiavelli was sent to settle the matter, he did not
succeed in arranging anything, because the Marquis continually
brought forward fresh obstacles.[1]

Hence, instead of diminishing, the Republic's anxieties daily
increased. Even the Lord of Piombino appeared to be joining
the enemies of Florence, and it was said that one thousand
Spanish foot soldiers had arrived there, for which reason the
Commissary Pier Antonio Carnesecchi received orders to go and
see how affairs really stood.[2] After that, Ranieri della Sassetta,
another adventurer hostile to Florence, went to Piombino, and
Machiavelli, on the 28th of June, despatched another letter to
Carnesecchi—who seems to have been somewhat undecided and
presumptuous—bidding him keep in readiness on that side, and
come to an understanding with the governor Ercole Bentivoglio.

" And we urge you to this measure not because of any want of
confidence in you, nor because we deem your capacity not to be
fine enough and therefore desire you to lean upon that of
others ; but because Messer Ercole being a prudent man, with
all our forces at his command, it is necessary to arrange with
him on all points." [3] On the same day a letter was sent to
Bentivoglio, exposing the doubts of the Ten as to the conduct of
the lord of Piombino, who was always hesitating between Pandolfo
Petrucci and the Florentines, and equally distrustful of both. He
had applied to Gonsalvo, who was said to have sent him eight
hundred Spanish infantry in order not to have to pay them himself, and also that they might serve to alarm the Florentines. Even
if this news, concluded the letter, be not all true, there is no
doubt of the arrival of the Spaniards, hence it is in every way requisite to remain on the alert.[4] It was then proposed to despatch
an ambassador to Gonsalvo himself, and although Soderini wished

---

[1] See the " Commissione " in the " Opere," vol. vii. p. 13. In the " Opere "
(P. M.), vol. v. p. 103 and fol., the proposed terms of the " Condotta " are
published.

[2] Florence Archives, cl. x. dist. 3, No. 116, at sheet 151. See too Canestrini,
" Scritti Inediti," pp. 188, 190, 91.

[3] Letters of the 28th of June. Florence Archives, cl. x. dist. 3, No. 116, at
sheet 143.

[4] Ibidem, No. 116, at sheet 141t.

to send Niccolò Machiavelli, he met with so much opposition from the Councils, that Roberto Acciajoli was sent instead. Machiavelli had a much less important mission to Petrucci at Sienna who, although a declared adversary of the Florentines, now gave them warning of Alviano's hostile manœuvres, and proposed an alliance with them, offering one hundred men-at-arms for the expedition against Pisa, and fifty more the following year. This seemed a very extraordinary affair, and it was thought necessary to discover his true intentions.

While Baglioni was a tyrant of the Valentinois school, Petrucci was no warrior, but one of those who attained power, like the Medici, almost solely by acuteness and cunning, though not without some occasional bloodshed. His counsellor and secretary, Antonio da Venafro, a man of obscure parentage, was first known as a professor of the University of Sienna, and a judge of the *Riformagioni;* then, entering political life, he rose to fortune, and efficaciously assisted Petrucci to become tyrant of Sienna. The latter's power began to be consolidated in 1495, from the time when Charles VIII., in returning from Naples, left a few French lances in the city, and was more and more strengthened in the following years by the death of his most formidable rivals, who were all assassinated in some way or other, and by the aid of Venafro's counsels. Having sent Venafro, as the ablest man he had, to arrange all the plot of *La Magione*, he was driven from power by Valentinois who styled him *the brain* of that conspiracy, and afterwards returned to Sienna, backed by French assistance and the favour of the whole population. In fact the Siennese were attached to him, partly because his opponents were worse than himself, but chiefly because he was regarded as a man of talent, who, once sure of his position, did his best to rule with justice and lenity. Besides, in the universal hatred for Valentinois, popular sympathy was very naturally aroused in favour of one who had had an almost miraculous escape from his hands. Nevertheless Petrucci continued to have a share in all intrigues, and liked to be considered the prime mover in them. Amid the fresh complications now arising, he steered his way with wonderful dexterity, and while professing friendship to Florence, who had certainly the power to do him great harm, he tried to draw nearer to her enemies, perceiving that the bad fortune of the French was transferring strength to another quarter and continually increasing the power of the friends of Spain.

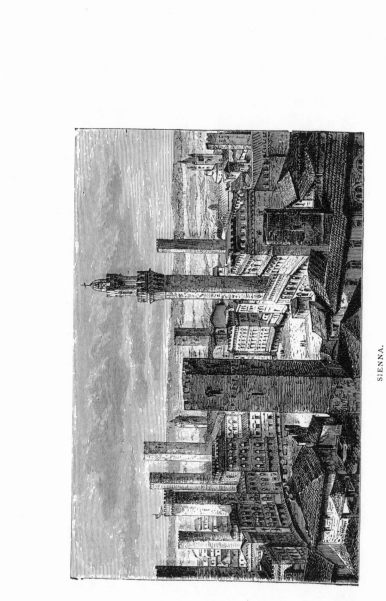

SIENNA.

The following is the gist of the instructions given to Machiavelli on the 16th of May, 1505. "You will ask his (Petrucci's) advice as to what should be done, and enlarging upon that topic, you will turn it about on all sides, using your own discretion and the prudence for which you have ever been noted, to ascertain, in course of conversation, that Lord's real mind." [1] And on the 17th Machiavelli wrote from Sienna, that Petrucci wished to form an alliance with Florence, without in any way engaging to check Alviano in his enterprise, proposing instead to try to weaken him by isolating him from the Vitelli, "for Alviano being of a haughty and unscrupulous nature, he might—now finding himself at the head of an armed force and without a State—attempt some desperate game ; and Italy is full of robbers, accustomed to live on other's property, wherefore many would be ready to follow his lead for the sake of plunder." [2] But from various quarters Machiavelli received warnings against Petrucci, and assurances that he was an enemy of Florence and the Gonfaloniere, that he was acting in concert with Gonsalvo and Alviano, was the author of all these movements, and "always had his foot in a thousand stirrups, so as to be able to withdraw it whenever he liked." [3] Accordingly, when Petrucci and Antonio da Venafro, "who is the apple of his eye and his chosen of men," renewed their proposal of first coming to an agreement, before thinking of isolating Alviano from the others, he, fearing that their only intention was to compromise the Republic still farther, demanded that something practical should be first done, "by stamping out those sparks." [4]

On the 21st of July they went deeper into the matter, Petrucci declaring with lengthy arguments that, notwithstanding his personal willingness, he was unable alone, and without previous concert with Florence, to oppose Alviano and check these movements. "It was not true that in this case it was he who held both reins and spurs ; for spurs he had never had, and was pulling the reins as hard as he could." In vain Machiavelli repeated all the arguments which his wit could suggest, for Petrucci, fixed in his resolve, tried to bewilder him by strange counsels and contradictory statements. Accordingly he wrote to the Ten—"To show him that I well understood his deceit, I said, ' that his conduct made me so confused, that I expected to lose

---

[1] See this "Legazione," in the "Opere," vol. vii. p. 16 and fol.
[2] Letter of the 17th July.   [3] Letter of the 18th July.
[4] Letter of the 20th July

my wits before I left Sienna.' First it was said that Bartolemmo d'Alviano was coming provided with Spanish money and Spanish infantry, then that Gonsalvo was opposed to him and would stop his advance ; now that he was ready to pass, then that he was begging for assistance ; now that he was agreed with the Pope, and now that they were enemies ; then that they were agreed with Sienna, and then again that his soldiers were pillaging the Siennese foragers. Therefore it was my wish that Sua Signoria should explain this tale to me."

Pandolfo, without any confusion, replied—" I will tell you that which King Frederic replied to an envoy of mine on a similar question, and this was 'that I should govern day by day, and should judge of things hour by hour, so to make fewer blunders, since these times were too confused for human wits,' and added that the confusion was heightened by Alviano, 'a man capable at any moment, while disposing of such a force, of inspiring his neighbours with hope and fear.'" [1] To the end Petrucci went on in this tone, "for he is a man," says Machiavelli, "whom it is little or no profit to look in the face." And on the evening of the 23rd Petrucci showed him a letter containing the intelligence that Gonsalvo had forbidden Alviano to make disturbances in Tuscany. "Reason suggests that Alviano should be obedient and remain quiet ; yet as men do not always listen to reason, despair may urge him on. And although of those spurred by despair, three out of four end badly, *tamen* it would be well that he should not be urged by despair, for the moving of one thing sets a thousand others in motion, and various are the chances of events." Therefore it would be well for the Florentines to take precautions.[2] Nor was it possible to extract anything more from him ; so after a conversation with Venafro, to whom he remarked that he had often seen " many who laughed in the summer and wept in the winter," [3] Machiavelli went back to Florence in greater uncertainty of mind than on his departure.

The only thing now to be done was to prepare for war, and the Ten recalled to office their distinguished Commissary Giacomini, sending him letters-patent on the 30th of July with injunctions to lose no time in concerting with the Governor on the steps to be taken ; and at the same time they raised the courage of the Commissary Carnesecchi in Maremma, by assuring him that there

---

[1] Letter of the 21st July, 19 of the clock.
[2] Letter of the 21st July.   [3] Letter of the 23rd July.

was no immediate danger.[1] Very soon, however, they had to change their tone and were lamenting to him that Alviano was already near Campiglia and beginning to assume the offensive "before our vanguard is formed, but we think that our plan is ordered in such fashion that, with the help of your prudence, all may be remedied." And they promised immediate reinforcements.[2]

Alviano was aware that he could accomplish nothing against the will of Gonsalvo, who, although not wishing the Florentines to take Pisa, would not allow them to be directly assailed, since they were included in the treaty with France, and whose only object in sending a few Spanish foot soldiers to Piombino, was to be prepared for every emergency. Therefore Alviano, notwithstanding the favour and secret assistance of Baglioni and Petrucci, had not yet been able to decide upon his plan of operations. He would have accepted a good Condotta from Florence in order to act as he chose afterwards ; but as there no longer seemed any possibility of that, he had remained till the 17th of July at Vignale, on the domains of the Lord of Piombino, and was now preparing to enter Pisa, from whence he could inflict much damage upon the Florentines. In fact, towards the middle of August, Giacomini gave intelligence of the enemies' advance, and his own determination to give them battle ; to which the Ten replied, that they left all to his judgment and that of the Governor, "begging them, however, to consider that however perilous Alviano's entry into Pisa might be, a decisive battle, in which all would be won or all lost, would be more perilous still." [3]

Florence had now in the field five hundred and fifty men-at-arms and three hundred and twenty light horse, beside a little artillery, and a few thousand foot. One hundred of their men-at-arms were at Cascina, the others at Campiglia and at Bibbona, the headquarters of the army. Alviano's forces were no less numerous, therefore the battle would be hardly contested and decisive. On the 14th Giacomini learnt that the enemy's troops were advancing, and at dawn, on the morning of the 17th, that they were close at hand and in battle array ; the Florentines came

[1] Florence Archives, cl. x. dist. 3, No. 114, at sheet 173, Ibid. No. 116, at sheet 171t.
[2] Ibid., cl. x. dist. 3, No. 116 at sheet 178t.
[3] *Loc. cit.*, at sheet 191t.

up with them at Torre di San Vincenzo, and the conflict immediately began.   The infantry, who were, it was said, in the pay of
Petrucci, were routed at the first onset, and then the squadrons
of Jacopo Savello and Marcantonio Colonna immediately sounding
the attack, the whole of the hostile army began to give way before
them.   Upon this Alviano himself pressed to the front with his
hundred men-at-arms and gained a little ground ; but being taken
in flank by Ercole Bentivoglio and the mass of the Florentine
army, the Republic won the day, and the artillery completed the
enemy's defeat.   From beginning to end the battle only lasted
two hours, after which time Alviano—who, though skilled, was
nearly always an unfortunate leader—seeing the total defeat of his
troops and bleeding from a wound in the face, escaped with some
difficulty over the Siennese border with eight or ten horsemen.
The Florentines captured about a thousand horses, a great number of waggons, many prisoners, and beheld the host that had
threatened them melt away as though by enchantment.[1]

But this victory was of very little service to the Florentines,
on account of the undue confidence it inspired in their own
strength.   Giacomini had sent a report of the enemy's defeat
without adding anything else ; but on the other hand, Bentivoglio,
who was generally esteemed to have more capacity for planning
campaigns than for carrying them out, proposed to make
the attack upon Pisa without loss of time, and likewise aim a
few blows at Sienna and Lucca.[2]   The Gonfaloniere was transported
by the idea of immediately assaulting and capturing Pisa, and thus
turning the heat of victory to account.   In vain the more prudent
citizens and the Ten opposed him with the argument that their
army was too small, and that with the Spaniards at Piombino,
they would be running an enormous risk.   It was true that these
Spaniards were few in number, but others might arrive at any
moment, and might perhaps be already on their way from Naples.
Some even spoke of a camp being already formed or forming at
Leghorn.   It was known for certain that the Great Captain had
flown into a fury, and sending for Acciaioli had burst into violent
threats against the Florentines, who had, he said, promised at

---

[1] Buonaccorsi, "Diario," p. 113.   The same evening Giacomini sent the Ten a
letter, in which he related the defeat of Alviano. " Carte del Machiavelli," case
iv. No. 11.

[2] Bentivoglio's letter also is dated the 17th August, and is among the "Carte
del Machiavelli," case iv. No. 10.

least to leave alone for the present the city of Pisa, which he was resolved to defend, if needful, with his own soldiery.[1] Soderini scoffed at this, declaring that within a week the campaign would be at an end. A very numerous Pratica was held by the Ten, and his proposal was rejected. Thereupon he carried the matter before the Eighty and the Great Council, where he was determined to have it passed ; and in fact on the 19th of August he succeeded in obtaining a grant of a hundred thousand florins to begin the assault without delay.

Machiavelli was sent to the camp as bearer of instructions to Giacomini and to Bentivoglio, who was nominated Captain-general.[2] On the 24th he was back in Florence, where he reported on all the requirements of the besiegers, and zealously set to work to forward the necessary preparations. Foot soldiers were levied throughout the dominions ; others were hired at Bologna, in Romagna, and even in Rome, where also pay was given to five hundred and seventy-five Spaniards who happened to be disengaged, not in order to make use of them, but to prevent their going to the help of the Pisans. Sappers were engaged, arms, ammunition, and all available artillery despatched.

On the 7th of September the army was at a few hours' distance from Pisa, and on the following day eleven guns were planted before the Calcesana gate. The fire began at sunrise, towards 22 o'clock (two hours before sunset), thirty-six braccia, that is, twenty-four yards, of wall had been demolished ; but an attempt to carry the breach by storm was instantly repulsed. Nevertheless, as only a third of the Florentine army was engaged in the attack, its failure was of no importance. But in the meantime three hundred Spanish foot, sent from Piombino by Gonsalvo, had entered the city by the Porta a Mare, and this boded ill for the Florentines. However, after changing the position of their guns, they resumed their fire and kept it up during the 10th, 11th, and part of the 12th. Then, as by 18 o'clock a hundred and thirty-six braccia of the walls had given way, a second and more general storming attack was made, with worse success than the first, for

---

[1] Buonaccorsi, 115–17 ; Canestrini, " Scritti Inediti," p. 205 and fol. ; Guicciardini, "Storia Fiorentina," chap. xxviii. pp. 321, 322; Nardi, "Vita di A. Giacomini;" Pitti, " Vita di A. Giacomini " in the " Archivio Storico Italiano," vol. iv. part ii.

[2] See the three letters of the Ten, not written by Machiavelli, published in the " Opere," vol. vii. pp. 48–55.

the Florentine infantry refused to fight, preferring death to storming the breach. And then arose the thousand different rumours which are always proofs of an army's disorder and demoralization. It was said that two thousand Spaniards had entered Pisa, that others were on their way from Naples to Leghorn, and it was asserted that at the latter place a camp had been formed, such as had never before been seen. And in Florence, where so many had been opposed to the enterprise, and where certain individuals had even been accused of secret practices with the enemy, with a view to its failure, the news of the army's second repulse and of the disorder in the camp, produced so great an effect, that it was instantly decided to abandon the undertaking. In short, at midnight on the 14th the guns were dismounted, on the 15th the camp was moved to Ripoli, and then to Cascina, from whence the men-at-arms were dispersed to their different quarters.

All this dealt a severe blow to Soderini's authority; but as all could not quarrel with him, popular rage turned, basely enough, against Giacomini, who had executed every order received with indomitable energy and admirable courage. He was so indignant at this ingratitude, that he sent in his resignation, which was immediately accepted, and a successor appointed. From that day—notwithstanding the eminent services which he had rendered to his country—his reputation was ruined for ever, and his military career may be said to have ended.[1] Machiavelli was one of the few always remaining faithful to him, and in the second "Decennale" exalts his merits, while blaming the ingratitude of the Florentines—who left their noble fellow-citizen to pass his last years in poverty and blindness, without doing anything for him—in language that is equally honourable both to author and object. Jacopo Nardi placed Giacomini on a level with Francesco Ferruccio, nor did Pitti award him scantier praise; but all this in nowise diminishes the shame of those who so unworthily forsook him during his lifetime. The deplorable result of the attack upon Pisa caused Machiavelli, in 1506, to turn his mind with greater ardour than ever to his old project of the institution of a special militia for the Florentine Republic. To this idea all his energies were now devoted for many years. But before speaking of it in detail, it is necessary for us to notice his mission to the Court

[1] See the "Vita di A. Giacomini" written by Nardi, and the other of which Pitti is the author.

POPE JULIUS II.

of Pope Julius II., which was an important episode in the history of 1506.

The new Pontiff, without neglecting his kinsmen, promptly provided for their wants, in order to dedicate himself heart and soul to the re-conquest of the provinces formerly appertaining to the Church. Now that Spain ruled in the kingdom of Naples, it was more necessary than ever to extend his dominions towards the north, so as not to be at the mercy of his southern neighbours. To drive the Venetians from Romagna, destroy the petty tyrants who had again risen to power on the downfall of the Borgia, and achieve all this for the benefit, not of his nephews, but of the Church, such was the object which this man of sixty-three years had in view and to which he devoted the rest of his life with a will of iron, the ardour of a youth, and the courage, not of a priest, but of a military leader. Already at the signing of the treaty of Blois between France and Spain, he had contrived to have it agreed that Louis XII., the Emperor and the Archduke Philip should attack Venice. This was not carried out ; but the peace definitively concluded in the same city on the 26th of October, 1505, between the French and the Spanish,—who had to submit to many sacrifices in order to retain possession of Naples—left Italy at rest, and the Pope then decided to undertake himself that which others would not do for him. Wishing to assure tranquillity in Rome, his first act was the reinstatement of many of the nobles in the possessions from which they had been ousted by Alexander VI., whom he stigmatized in his Bulls as a fraudulent deceiver and usurper. He also formed ties of relationship with the Orsini and the Colonna, giving one of his daughters in marriage to Giovan Giordano Orsini, and a niece to the youthful Marcantonio Colonna. On the 26th of August, with a retinue of twenty-four cardinals, at the head of four hundred men-at-arms, and his small Swiss guard, the Pope set out to attempt the conquest of Perugia and Bologna, both very strong and well-garrisoned cities. He expected one hundred Stradiotes from Naples ; other soldiery from the Gonzagas, the Este, the Montefeltro, from France and from the Florentines, for all these were friendly to him. The latter— from whom Julius had requested the loan of their Captain Marcantonio Colonna and his company—despatched Niccolò Machiavelli to him on the 25th of August, to signify their readiness to aid in his " holy work " ; but that they were unable for the moment to let him have Colonna, it being impossible to leave the army before

Pisa without a commander ; they promised however to give him all that he desired, as soon as the enterprise were "really begun." [1]

Machiavelli started at once, and on the 28th of August wrote from Civita Castellana, that he had found the Pope at Nepi already prepared to set out and full of hopefulness. His Holiness was satisfied with the Florentine promises, was expecting four or five hundred lances from the French, besides the hundred Stradiotes from Naples, "and had his pouch full of infantry." He was riding at the head of his troops, which were commanded by the Duke of Urbino. The Venetian ambassador promised him the assistance of his Republic on condition of its being allowed to retain Faenza and Rimini ; but the Pope laughed at this, and went on his way confident of success. [2]

Already on the 5th of September, Baglioni, terror-stricken by the unusual circumstance of beholding the Head of the Church marching in person against him, had come to Orvieto to negotiate a surrender. And on the 9th Machiavelli wrote from Castel della Pieve, that all was arranged : that the city gates and fortresses had already been given up. Baglioni was to take part in the expedition as one of the Captains of the Pope, who said that he was willing to forgive him the past ; but that if found sinning again, however venially, would certainly hang him. Julius II. had decided to have five hundred infantry drawn up in the Piazza of Perugia, and fifty at each gate, before making his entry, [3] but so great was his haste to go there, that on the 13th of September he entered the city with his Cardinals, without giving the Duke of Urbino time to execute the orders received. The Duke had marched his men to the vicinity of the gates, and Baglioni's forces were at a short distance, so that Pope and Cardinals were at the latter's mercy. "And if he works no evil," wrote Machiavelli, "against him who has come to strip him of his State, it will be because of his good nature and humanity. What will be the termination of this matter I know not, but we shall see, when the Pope has been here some six or eight days." [4]   Giovan Paolo said that he preferred saving his State by humility rather than force,

---

[1] See the instructions to Machiavelli, in vol. vii. of the " Opere," at p. 64.

[2] Letters of the 29th of August from Civita Castellana, and of the last day August from Viterbo.

[3] Letters of the 9th of September from Castel della Pieve, and of the 12th of September from Corciano.   [4] Letter of the 13th September.

and therefore trusted to the Duke of Urbino. But the Pope, without troubling himself about other things, occupied the city, and recalled the old exiles—not however the more recent, since that would have exposed the now deposed lord to too much danger ; meantime the hundred Stradiotes had arrived from Naples.[1]

It is well known how in the " Discorsi sulla Prima Deca di Tito Livio,"[2] Machiavelli blamed the conduct of Baglioni, accusing him of cowardice, for not having dared to seize the persons of the Pope and his cardinals, by which means he might have rid himself of them and been the first to prove to prelates " how little worthy of esteem be those who live and reign as they." But this is not the moment for us to enter upon an examination of works of so different a nature. This Legation, on the contrary, compels us to make another observation. Machiavelli had been enthusiastic about Valentinois, filled with admiration for his craft and dishonest actions, yet he showed little interest in Julius II., who, despite numerous defects and many crimes, was not without some of the qualities of true greatness. It is positive that the Secretary was much astonished, on seeing that Baglioni did not dare to resist, and made no use of the favourable moment ; but his indifference to the Pope was so great that this Legation is one of those of least importance, although it might have been expected to be of the highest. He confined himself strictly to his official work, without finding any special matter for study, and without indulging in any considerations of a general nature or foreign to the subject in hand.

In fact his thoughts were otherwise absorbed, namely in the institution of the Florentine militia, that he had already initiated, and was burning to carry on ; he was continually asking and receiving news on the subject from his friend Buonaccorsi. Then too he had always entertained a singular contempt—almost amounting to hatred—for the priesthood ; in his opinion Popes were, and had ever been, the ruin of Italy. Besides it seemed to him that the statesmen could derive but scanty profit from the study of ecclesiastical principalities, since their strength was derived from religion, and they were the sole States which—however governed—always remained permanent.[3]

If the authority of religion and the power of the Church were

[1] Letters of the 16th and 19th of September from Perugia.
[2] Book i. chap. xxvii.
[3] " Principe," chap. xi.

still so great that a perfidious, cunning daring man like Baglioni was awed by the mere presence of the Pope, Machiavelli did not believe that this fact could prove very instructive to one seeking to discover the secrets of statecraft, and wishing to investigate in the political phenomenon the *natural* causes, and *human* passions forming its basis. All that was or claimed to be divine, lay beyond the sphere of his chosen studies, and had no interest for him. Fate, the caprices even of fortune, might, he considered, be subjects of study, but not the will of God, which, in whatever light it be regarded, certainly transcends our intellect. The daring of Julius II., who, at sixty-three years of age, pursued his march, in the height of summer, without counting the danger of falling into his enemy's hands, did not appear to him a proof of true acumen. The foresight and demoniac cunning of Valentinois had been worthy of study as models of art ; but the blind foolhardiness of the Pope, if a personal merit, was no sign of political tact, and therefore he bestowed very slight attention upon it. In the same way that he had separated the political from the moral phenomenon, so also he mentally separated the art of the statesman from the individual or private character of him who exercised it, alone seeking in him the qualities useful or necessary to its due development.

At this time he did not even pause to describe the formation of the new government in Perugia. On the 25th of September he wrote from Urbino, that the Pope was more hotly bent than ever upon the accomplishment of his enterprise, of which it was very difficult to predict the conclusion, since—should French assistance fail him—the Pope might, in his furious haste, come to a bad end.[1] The Venetians were awaiting his first reverses, to bring him round to their wishes with the help of the king ; others asserted on the contrary that the Pope would know how to drive the king, " so powerful were the spurs he could plunge into his flanks . . . ; but what these spurs may be, I know not." [2] Certainly on the 3rd of October, Louis XII. had already declared for the Pope against Venice and Bologna, and six orators from the latter city were in Cesena to negotiate the surrender. When, however, they referred to terms agreed to by former Popes, Julius II. replied that he cared nothing for them, nor even desired to know anything of those signed by himself. His aim was to liberate that people from

---

[1] Letter of the 25th of September from Urbino.
[2] First letter of the 28th of September.

tyrants, and to bring into subjection to the Church all that rightfully belonged to the Church ; were he to neglect doing so, he would have no justification before God.

Being now assured of French assistance, and having passed in review at Cesena forces amounting to 600 men-at-arms, 1600 foot, and 300 Swiss, he begged the Florentines to send Colonna and his 100 men-at-arms without delay, as he was on the point of setting out for Bologna.[1] Giovanni Bentivoglio was already beginning to speak of surrender ; but on his proposal that the Pope should enter the city with his Swiss Guards alone, Julius in reply issued a Bull against him and his adherents, declaring them rebels to the Holy Church ; giving up their possessions to pillage ; and granting indulgence to any who would act against or kill them ; and he then continued his journey.[2] Not wishing to enter places occupied by the Venetians, his route from Forlì to Imola lay through the territory of the Florentines, who received no notice of his intentions, until he was actually crossing the border. Nevertheless the Republic did all in its power to show him friendship and respect : Marcantonio Colonna received orders to march to join him on the 17th ; Niccolò Machiavelli hurried on in advance, so that no necessaries might be wanting in so hasty and sudden a journey. Then the Ten wrote instantly to Piero Guicciardini, the Commissary in Mugello, to inform him of his Holiness's advance : " He was to send forward four or six mule-loads of Puliciano wine of the very best quality, a little Trebbiano wine, a few loads of good cream cheese, and one load at least of fine Camilla pears." [3]

The Pope passed rapidly through Marradi and Palazzuolo, where everything was in readiness ; and on the 21st he was at Imola which he made his head-quarters. On the same day Machiavelli wrote from thence that his Holiness demanded from Bentivoglio an unconditional surrender, and that, most probably, he would obtain it. He also said that now matters were becoming serious and the general state of Italy had to be considered, it was advisable that an ambassador should be sent to the camp. The Pope had requested this, so the Florentines despatched Francesco Pepi, and on his arrival at Imola on the 26th, Machiavelli took his

---

[1] Letters of the 3rd, 4th, and 5th of October.
[2] Letter of the 10th of October from Forlì.
[3] Letter of the 17th of October, 1506, published in the " Opere " (P. M.), vol. v. p. 231, note 1.

departure with the most anxious desire to resume the task of constituting the militia.

Bentivoglio could probably have repulsed the attack, had he not been hated by his people—who had already risen on the arrival of the Papal Bulls—and had he not been forsaken by France which sent eight thousand men to the Pope's assistance, under the command of Charles d'Amboise, who immediately made himself master of Castelfranco. The Bolognese, dreading a sack, drove out Bentivoglio on the 2nd of November, and i · n sent to Imola to make their submission to the Pope. When how ·ver the French tried to force an entrance, the people rose in revolt, overwhelmed the enemies' camp, showed themselves prepared for defence, and thus obliged the Pope to send away Amboise, on payment of a good sum of money, added to the promise of a cardinal's hat for his brother. Thus, on the 11th of November, Julius II. was able to enter Bologna in triumph like a Cæsar, surrounded by cardinals, bishops, prelates, and lords of the neighbouring cities. He changed the government, instituting a Senate of forty citizens, which lasted for a prolonged period ; he respected the municipal Statutes ; he caused a citadel to be built, and finally, on the 22nd of February, 1507, took his departure well content with having thus far succeeded in all that he wished. On the 27th of March, the Pope came by the Tiber to Ponte Molle, and then made his solemn entry into the Eternal City. This enterprise had rapidly raised him to a great height in the eyes of his contemporaries.

In the meantime Machiavelli was back in Florence working at his favourite scheme of the Militia. He had long been convinced that the ruin of the Italian States was caused by the want of native troops, and the necessity of always relying upon mercenaries. He had been farther confirmed in this idea every time that he had had to visit the camp, by being himself an eye-witness of the insubordination, insolence, and bad faith of the adventurers, to whom the magistrates were compelled to trust the safety of their country. He had seen the strength acquired by Valentinois, when the latter had made a levy throughout his possessions of "one man per household," [1] and thus formed a large nucleus of native soldiery. All the more powerful European States, such as Spain, Germany, France, were faithfully served by armies of their own ; even Switzerland, though so small a country, had succeeded,

---

[1] See the fragment of a document quoted by Canestrini in the " Scritti Inediti " of Machiavelli, Preface, p. xxxvi.

by means of free institutions, in forming the first infantry in the world ; why could not the Italians, the Florentines, do the same ? Had it not been accomplished by the Communes of the Middle Ages ; was not a feeble example of it now displayed in the obstinate defence of the Pisans, trained to arms by the force of necessity ; and, above all, was it not the method pursued by the Romans, the world's teachers alike in the arts of peace and of war ? Why could not their organization and that of the Swiss be imitated in Florence ; and what doubt could there be, but that here also identical results might be attained ?

This was the idea upon which Machiavelli's mind was so ardently bent. To give to Florence, and later perhaps to Italy, an army of her own and with it the strength which she now lacked, and the political dignity never possessed by weak States, was henceforward the dream of his life. And to this he devoted himself with so disinterested an ardour, with so youthful an enthusiasm, that, for the first time, his character awakes in us a sympathy and admiration which before it was impossible to feel. The cynical smile of the cold diplomatist disappears from his lips, and his physiognomy suddenly assumes, to our eyes, a serious and severe solemnity, revealing to us the flame of genuine patriotism, that is burning in his heart and ennobling his existence. If, as father, husband, and son, we have found little to blame in him, there has been equally little to admire. His habits are not exempt from the sins of his age. As a citizen, until now he has only faithfully served the Republic with the talents with which nature had so bounteously endowed him. We have seen, it is true, that in the many missions entrusted to him, he never thought of using his opportunities for the purpose of worldly advancement, but instead devoted himself to investigating the principles of a new science, with an ardour rendering him oblivious of his own personal interests, occasionally even of some of the smaller affairs daily recommended to his notice. But this was a scientific disinterestedness, of which we have numerous examples even in the midst of the corruption of the Italian Renaissance. When however Machiavelli endeavours to stimulate the Gonfaloniere to found the new Militia, and writes to Cardinal Soderini, to assist in influencing his brother, and travels throughout the dominions of the Republic ; distributing arms, enrolling infantry, writing thousands of letters, and begging to be allowed to continue his study of camps and garrisons, it is impossible not to acknowledge this to be a proof of deep and sincere self-abnegation in favour of the public good. In his quality of Secretary and as a man of letters, who had never followed a military career, he could expect no personal advantage from all this, not even one step of promotion in his own office. Therefore his sole motive was a pure patriotism, of which there were now but too few examples in Italy, and which on that account surrounds his image with a halo, such as no other of the most illustrious *literati* of his age can boast.

But, from all that we have just said, it by no means follows that our admiration should make us lose sight of Machiavelli's errors and defects, nor regard him, as some writers have tried, as a military genius. The grandeur and originality of his conception were what might have been expected from a patriot and a political man, having had the administration of war affairs in his hands, and who, at a time when war was a far simpler matter than at the present day, had often lived in camp, had held long conversations on military things with Giacomini and other contemporary leaders ; but who had never had the command of a single company. Even his book upon " L'Arte della guerra "— replete as it is with just observations and original ideas—contains much to remind us that he was not a military man. For instance, we need only cite his almost entire want of belief in the efficacy of fire-arms, which nevertheless destroyed the old and created the new system of tactics. Matteo Bandello, in one of the proems serving as preludes to his *Novelle*, relates that one day he found himself under the walls of Milan in the company of Giovanni dei Medici, the celebrated Captain—better known as Giovanni of the Black Bands—and of Machiavelli. The latter, wishing to give them an idea of a certain military manœuvre he had frequently described very well, kept three thousand men out in the sun for more than two hours without being able to effect the desired movement, until—dinner-time being long past— Giovanni lost patience, put him aside, and in an instant, with the aid of the drums, put them through several manœuvres in a masterly manner. After this, Machiavelli, in recompense for the time that he had caused them to waste, related a tale at table, which is included among those of Bandello.[1] And although history

---

[1] It is the fortieth tale in Part i. : " Imganno usato da una scaltrita donna al marito, con una subita astuzia." Machiavelli begins his narration as follows : " I hold the firm opinion, *Signor mio*, that if you had not got me out of the scrape this morning, we should still be broiling in the sun." See too the " Proemio "

makes no mention of this anecdote, there is nothing improbable in it ; and at all events it is additional evidence, that in his own day, the author of the "Art of War," so generally admired as a writer upon military subjects, was not recognized as a man of practical military knowledge.

The Republic had long thought of forming a militia of its own, but without any faith in the success of the plan ; Machiavelli, on the contrary, had entire faith in it. The nearly always unsatisfactory behaviour of the *comandati ;* the cowardice of the infantry who, during the last attack on the walls of Pisa, had refused to storm the breach, had convinced the majority that professional soldiers alone were to be trusted ; but Machiavelli had always struggled against this opinion, endeavouring to prove that the whole evil resulted from the lack of good instruction and discipline. First of all he tried to win over the Gonfaloniere, " and finding some chance of success, began to explain his method in detail." [1] But even when he had convinced him, a thousand difficulties opposed the execution of the scheme, and first of all the distrust of those who feared that Soderini might use it as a means of establishing himself as a tyrant. Recourse was therefore had to the prudent step of making experiments of the new method on a small scale, in the hope that the citizens would then recognize its utility, and vote the legislative measures acquired to give it permanence and stability. Such in fact was afterwards the result.

We have one of Machiavelli's reports containing all the details of the steps taken by him in this first attempt—steps which afterwards received legal recognition. These serve to show us how very different were the ideas of that period from our own, and how enormous and often insuperable the difficulties with which men had to contend. First of all he states, as a point beyond discussion, that if the Republic desires an army of its own, that army should be officered solely by Florentines, and its cavalry exclusively composed of them. And as the formation of

dedicated to Giovanni dei Medici, and in which the author, after relating the anecdote, goes on to say : " I beg you to well remember that Messer Niccolò is one of the finest and most copious and eloquent speakers of your Tuscany, and that I am a Lombard ; but when you recall that it is written by your Bandello, whom so much you love and favour, I venture to believe that it will not delight you less in reading it, than it delighted those who heard it narrated. Farewell to you."

[1] Guicciardini, " Storia Fiorentina," chap. xxix. p. 324.

cavalry was exactly the most difficult part of the new scheme, it was necessary for the present to begin with levying infantry outside the city. The territory, however, was divided into the *contado* (or territory proper), and into districts, that is to say those portions containing large cities, and formerly ruled by them, before becoming subject to the Republic either by conquest or of their own free will. These districts, it would be highly dangerous to arm, "for," writes Machiavelli, "of such sort are Tuscan humours, that he who once knew he might live independently, would never more seek a master."[1] Therefore, at least for the present, only the territory proper was to be armed. Nor was this the only precaution. So great was the general distrust, that it was even forbidden that any constables elected to the command of the companies formed under the different flags should be of the same birthplace as the common soldiers, or allowed to command the same troop for more than one year. The motive of this was to prevent the constables from becoming too much attached to their men, lest they should gain undue influence, and thereby become dangerous.[2]

All must perceive that the first and most essential elements of strength were wanting in a state where every town tended to separate itself from the dominant city, the which, by its monopoly of all political rights, was necessarily forced to regard with most distrust the very citizens to whom it wished to confide its defence. But the Florentine secretary was blind to some of these difficulties, since, according to the ideas of his time, there was nothing abnormal or unusual in them ; others, he hoped, would be overcome by degrees. Thus, for instance, he wrote that after arming the *contado*, it might perhaps be feasible—with certain precautions—to arm at least a portion of the *distretto*. He had unlimited faith in this new military organization, and in conclusion told his fellow-citizens : "You will learn, even in your own

---

[1] "Due scritture inedite di Niccolò Machiavelli," p. 11, Pisa, Nistri, 1872. They were published by Professor A. D'Ancona on the occasion of the Cavalieri-Zabron marriage. Only the first of these relates to the militia, and had already been published by Ghinassi for the Zambrini-Della Volpe marriage ; Faenza, Pietro Conti Press. These publications, made as wedding gifts, and for private circulation only, are often very difficult to obtain, and are little heard of, thus, as D'Ancona, so diligent in research, knew nothing of his predecessor's publication, so others may be unaware of his, or unable to find it. Therefore in Appendix, at document xii., we give the letter referring to the militia ordinance. [2] Ibid.

time, how great is the difference between fellow-citizens who are soldiers by choice, and not, as at present, from mercenary motives ; for now if any man has been a disobedient son and squandered his substance in dissipation, he it is who becomes a soldier, whereas, on the new system, well brought up men, educated in honest schools, will do honour to themselves and their country." [1]

Inspired by these ideas, he not only sought to directly infuse them in the mind of the Gonfaloniere, but also availed himself of the co-operation of those having influence over him. In the beginning of 1506 he wrote to Cardinal Soderini in Rome, begging him to persuade his brother that a severe and just *regimen* in the city and the *contado* would form a safe and solid basis for the new ordinance. And on the 4th of March the Cardinal replied to him—"I am more than ever convinced that facts confirm our hopes *pro salute et dignitate patriæ ;* there is no doubt but that other nations have become superior to ourselves solely through the maintenance of discipline, which has long been banished from Italy ; and great must be your content that your hand has begun so worthy a thing." In accordance with Machiavelli's request, he wrote the same day to the Gonfaloniere, congratulating him on the confidence universally reposed in the new militia, from which every one awaited the revival of past glories, and taking care to repeat that all depended upon good discipline, *quæ plurimum consistit in obedientia, maximaque fundatur in justitia,* concluded by proposing that, to maintain this justice, there should be nominated "some minister similar to Manlius and Torquatus (*sic*), very rigid and severe, who in urgent matters will know how to act with promptitude, but in lesser affairs will trust to his officers." [2]

The new militia being only in course of formation, did not as yet require a general-in-chief, and the recruits could be instructed by their so-called constables, some of whom were even foreigners ; but it was imperative to have a superior authority of some sort, if

---

[1] See Appendix, document xii.

[2] These two letters, and one quoted further on, also by Cardinal Soderini, are among the "Carte del Machiavelli," and were first published by Passerini in the "Periodico di Numismatica e Sfragistica," vi. year, No. vi. pp. 303–06 ; Florence, Ricci, 1874. These were afterwards republished, almost entire, by Nitti, *op. cit.*, vol. i. p. 340 and fol. From the "Machiavelli Papers" it is evident that as early as 1504 he wrote upon the subject of the militia to Cardinal Soderini, who, among other letters, replied to him in one dated the 29th of May of the same year. See case iii. No. 57.

only for the maintenance of discipline, and the punishment, when needed, of offenders. For this purpose it was decided, according to the suggestion given—or rather caused to be given—by the Cardinal to the Gonfaloniere, to elect a man of practical military knowledge and reputation. But who would have supposed that the Gonfaloniere and Machiavelli, both animated by so pure and noble a patriotism, so high an admiration for Manlius Torquatus, for Scipio and Camillus of ancient Rome, could have thought of nominating to such an office the Spaniard Don Micheletto, the assassin, the strangler, the confidant of Valentinois, the very man whom but a short time before the Republic had made prisoner and sent to Julius II. as a monster of iniquity, an enemy of God and of man ? Yet so it was. It is true that at first this choice aroused some jealousy in the magistrates and citizens, not, however, because of any moral repugnance, but only from dread lest Soderini should wish to use this man as a dangerous engine of tyranny. Machiavelli, who had been commissioned to dexterously probe the intentions of Francesco Gualterotti, G. B. Ridolfi, and Piero Guicciardini, and ascertain if the Ten would consent to nominate Don Michele, with a hundred men, as Bargello del Contado, found them little favourable to the idea ; but on this proposal being laid before the Eighty, it was finally carried after being thrice put to the vote.[1]

Both in Romagna and in Rome Machiavelli had had many opportunities of knowing what manner of man Don Michele was. He had seen him under Valentinois in command of men picked up in the country, and who, although neither mercenaries, nor soldiers by trade, acquitted themselves of their duties uncommonly well ; he therefore deemed the man adapted to maintain order and discipline among the raw Florentine militia. He was not ignorant of the many crimes and iniquities committed by him, for these were known to all the world, but considered that for the purpose in view the man's reputation for cruelty and bloodthirstiness would do more good than harm. He wished Don Michele to be feared and respected by his men, so that, in case of necessity, he might lead them against the enemy, and, by his own example, joined to the prestige of his cruel severity, render them hardy and formidable in the field. When in the June of that year, some of the new infantry, sent to the camp before Pisa, acquitted themselves but indifferently

[1] Guicciardini, "Storia Fiorentina," chap. xxix. p. 323.

of their duties, he wrote to the Commissary-general in Cascina, Giovanni Ridolfi, that he was sending him Don Michele with his company of one hundred men, to serve against the Pisans, for since these hold our infantry in slight esteem, we would willingly cause them to change their opinion. " And he (Don Michele) having been accustomed, while with the Duke, to the command and management of the same sort of men, we think that it would be a good plan, if possible, to quarter him there with them, so that he should get used to them first, and then in case of having to make any sudden expedition in any direction, he and his infantry could quickly effect a junction with them. And after having seen and handled the troops at the reviews, he will soon be able to turn them to account on active service." [1]

This then was Machiavelli's idea : Don Michele was to infuse the new military spirit into the young Florentine army. But why, it might be reasonably asked, did they not rather appeal to that valiant soldier and excellent patriot, Antonio Giacomini ? How could the rulers of Florence suppose an assassin capable of inculcating genuine discipline, that is, military honour ? Yet even if Giacomini had not been in disgrace just then, the Florentines would never have granted a fellow-citizen so much power over the new Florentine army. There would have been the usual alarm lest he might establish a tyranny. As in former times they had required their Podestà to be a foreigner, so now their Bargello del Contado.

The new militia, according to Machiavelli, was to be animated by a truly patriotic spirit, and must therefore be composed of honest and well-conducted men ; but the individual charged to command and instruct them need have nothing beyond a special capacity for that task, which would be in no way affected by his moral character. Often, indeed, goodness of heart might prove an obstacle to those acts of severity and cruelty, which the captain as well as the statesman is sometimes called upon to perform.

According to modern ideas there should be a bond of unity between leaders and their men ; they should be as one body with one conscience. This conscience should be personified in the commander, should render his conduct the higher and more intelligent manifestation, as it were, of the common thought ; should render his very severity an act of justice. But whether as regarded

[1] Letter of the 12th of June, 1506, in the Florence Archives, cl. x., dist. 3, No. 121, at sheet 1*t*.

armies or governments, Machiavelli had no perception of the need of any such unity. The people of his Republic should be virtuous ; but in his opinion the people had little individual conscience ; it was as softest clay in the hands of the statesman, who might mould it in any form he would, if he only knew his own intentions and how to carry them out unchecked by scruples of any kind. Machiavelli is either atrociously calumniated or misunderstood by those who pretend that he neither loved nor admired virtue. We often find him repeating that " no mortal man can fail to love it, to admire it," and his words in virtue's praise often rise to a degree of eloquence, which is evidently born of genuine conviction, rather than of rhetorical art. But for Machiavelli, as for his age in general, morality was an entirely individual and personal matter ; the art of governing, commanding, ruling, was not opposed to, but entirely independent of it. The idea of a public conscience and morality is intelligible only to one already having that conception of social unity and personality, which clearly teaches us that for nations as for individuals true government is self-government, with the inevitable accompaniment of responsibility. This idea was unknown to the fifteenth century, and never quite apparent even to the intellect of Machiavelli. To the mind of the Middle Ages all historical events, all social transformations were expressions of the Divine Will, which man could neither assist or prevent ; for Machiavelli, on the contrary, the social fact had become a human and a rational fact, of which he sought to discover the laws, but for him also the vicissitudes of history seemed almost always the exclusive work of princes or of generals. It is for this reason that the weight which he attributes to the arts of the statesman, to his determination and foresight, to the institutions and laws which he may create—given the required genius and energy—is almost unlimited.

Thus he had no difficulty in persuading himself that the new military system, planned by him on Swiss [1] and Roman models, must—if faithfully and severely followed — produce infallible results. No sooner had he convinced the Gonfaloniere of this, than at the end of December, 1505, he began to journey through Tuscany, furnished with letters patent, for the purpose of enrolling foot soldiers under the flag. In January and February his activity

---

[1] Guicciardini, at p. 324 of his " Storia Fiorentina," tells us that the infantry were drilled " after the Swiss fashion." Machiavelli had then had many opportunities of studying in Italy the Swiss and German militia.

must have been prodigious, for we find him in a different place every day.[1] He returned to Florence about the middle of March, and continued his work by means of a very extensive correspondence.[2] At the earliest date possible, namely in the February of the same year, a review was held of 400 men, who, dressed in gay uniforms and well-armed, were marched into the Piazza of the Signoria, and produced a most favourable impression upon the citizens ; this experiment being repeated from time to time, the popularity of the new militia continually increased.[3] As we have already seen, some of these foot soldiers were even sent to Pisa, but failing to acquit themselves particularly well, Don Michele received orders to unite them with his company.[4] And although even then no very great results were attained, still in August some skirmishes took place which were not altogether unsuccessful.[5]

In any case, the militia being now an accomplished fact, and already in favour with the people, it was necessary to give it definite legal sanction. It was for this reason that Machiavelli drew up the Report to which we have frequently referred. In this he stated that throughout the territories of the Republic, in all towns possessing a Podestà, a company had been levied, and a Constable nominated for every three, four, or five companies. There were altogether thirty companies (each with its own flag) and eleven Constables. More than five thousand men had been inscribed on the lists, but this number might be reduced by dismissing the less able-bodied among them ; twelve thousand had been already passed in review at Florence.[6] The Report then went on to prove the necessity of appointing a fresh magistrate entrusted with the regular enrolment of the militia. On 6th of December, 1506, a decree was passed in the Great Council, by a majority of 841 black beans against 317 white, for the creation of *Nove ufficiali dell' ordinanza e milizia fioren-*

---

[1] " Opere," vol. vii. pp. 56–58 ; " Opere " (P.M.), vol. v. p. 141.

[2] Canestrini, " Scritti Inediti," p. 284 and fol.

[3] Guicciardini, " Storia Fiorentina," pp. 324–25 ; " Opere " (P. M.), vol. v. p. 147, note 2.

[4] Florence Archives, cl. x. dist. 3, No. 121, at sheet 1*t* (already quoted).

[5] See numerous letters in the Florence Archives, cl. x. dist. 3, Nos. 120 and 121.

[6] At this passage of the Report there was the addition : *Et ne havete mandati 500 in campo.* These words were afterwards erased, perhaps in order to avoid recalling that the trials made of the militia had not always been successful.

tina, more generally known as *The Nine of the Militia ;* and this decree was in fact nothing more than the official sanction to all the proposals brought forward by Machiavelli. The Nine—who were selected from among the members of the Great Council—held office for eight months at a time, and were charged with the enlistment of the men, their armament, drill, and instruction in discipline, their punishments, the appointment of Constables, &c. ; but, on war being declared, the Militia would pass under the control of the Ten.[1] The same decree instituted a Captain of the Guard for the territory and district of Florence, with thirty mounted crossbow-men and fifty paid soldiers. This officer was to be subordinate to the Nine, and elected like other *condottieri*, with this difference, however, that " no native of Florence, of Florentine territory or district, nor of any place within forty miles of the Florentine border, could be nominated to the post."[2] The Nine were duly elected on the 10th of January, 1507, were sworn in on the 12th, and entered upon their duties on the 13th. This decree authorized them to have one or more chancellors, and, as was natural, they immediately fixed upon Machiavelli. By decrees of the 9th and 27th of February they then nominated Don Michele Captain of the Guard, both for the territory and district, with the thirty mounted archers and the fifty foot soldiers granted by law.[3]

Machiavelli's life now passes into a new phase, during which he was increasingly convinced that it was his special mission to restore the old military glories, the old virtues not of Florence alone but of all Italy. He had not been the first to conceive this hope,

[1] With regard to this arrangement, Machiavelli says in his Report : " And thus they would have no decided Chief of their own, and would recognize a public and not a private superior." Always the usual distrust.

[2] See the " Provvisione " in the " Qpere," vol. iv. p. 427 and fol. The words quoted above are at p. 444.

[3] The decision of the 27th of February is in the Florentine Archives, cl. xiii. dist. 2, No. 70 (" Deliberazioni dei IX di Ordinanza " at sheet 9ᵗ). The first Register of the " Deliberazioni dei Nove," from 1505 to 1511 (Florence Archives, cl. xiii. dist. 2, No. 70) is written throughout in Machiavelli's own hand. It was so certain beforehand, that he would, in any case, be nominated Chancellor of the Nine, that on the 28th December, 1506, Agostino Vespucci, one of his coadjutors, wrote to him to beg that he also might be transferred to the service of the Nine, who, besides the Chancellor, were to have one or more *employés :* " I pray you to kindly think of me on this occasion, and should you perceive that I might be more useful (under the Nine) than in this my present office, pray contrive matters in such wise, that I may become one of those coadjutors, cum pro certo habeam, fore ut tu sis Cancellarius illorum Novem, ni locum tuearis quo nunc frueris, quod Deus avertat." (" Carte del Machiavelli," case iv. No. 93.)

but he was now the only man who preserved it. Cardinal Soderini expressed a very general opinion when in writing to Machiavelli from Bologna on the 15th of December, 1506, he said : " We really believe that this Ordinance (of the Militia) *sit a Deo*, since it daily increases and flourishes, in spite of malignant opposition ;" and he added, in continuation, that it was long since the Republic had done so worthy a thing as this, which was all owing to Machiavelli.[1] And such being the opinion of the most influential citizens, it cannot surprise us, that he, the acknowledged author of this important reform, should look to the future with the strongest hopefulness. Certainly his hopes could not all be fulfilled, in part indeed could only prove to be noble and generous illusions ; nevertheless in after years they became the source of imperishable glory to the Republic. For when in 1527 Florence found herself beset and beleaguered by innumerable foes, the followers of Savonarola reawakened her ancient love of liberty, and the resuscitated Republic was heroically defended by the very Militia first proposed and instituted by Niccolò Machiavelli.

[1] " Periodico di Numismatica e Sfragistica," *loc. cit.*

CHAPTER IX.

The age of Julius II.—Fine Arts—Leonardo da Vinci—Michel Angelo—Raffaello—The new literature—Ariosto—The early writings of Francesco Guicciardini.

HE decade during which Pope Julius II. occupied the chair of St. Peter (1503-1513) was a memorable period in Italian history, and still more memorable in Italian culture. This sexagenarian Pontiff kept all Europe in a ferment by his indomitable energy, by his more than youthful ardour, by his fixed determination to reconquer the provinces which, as he thought, had been unjustly wrested from the Church, and to increase the extent and power of the Papal States.

Holding in his grasp the guiding threads of the world's policy, he twisted them this way and that, now to the advantage, now to the hurt, of Italy, which thus became the field of mighty conflicts, bringing irreparable calamities in their train. The gigantic proportions which these events almost instantaneously assumed, naturally made a deep impression on the minds of all men with eyes to discern what was going on around them. Hence the notable growth of culture and added splendour of all literary works, particularly on politics and history, in which the Italians gave proof of insuperable originality, and became the teachers of Europe.

When it is remembered that the writings of Machiavelli and Guicciardini were composed in the midst of the bloody cataclysm beginning with the battles of Agnadello, Ravenna, and Pavia, and ending with the sack of Rome and the siege of Florence, it is easy to recognize not only a relation, but a certain harmony between these two orders of facts. When, however, we find that during the same period, poems such as those of Ariosto and an infinite number of comedies, romances, satires, and sonnets were given to the world, we can discern a very singular contrast of opposing elements. In fact, it was now that the Italian Renaissance displayed the infinite variety of its brightest radiance. This was manifested, not only in a thousand fresh forms of national prose and verse, but reached its highest strength in those studies of the Beautiful determining the culture of this essentially artistic age,. and stamping it with their special mark.

It was as though a new spring had breathed fresh life into the soil and caused it to generate a multitude of flowers hitherto unseen of man—flowers which, opening their petals to the fertilizing rays of the sun shining down on them from above, gave forth an exquisite fragrance, a harmony of tints exciting the rapture of all beholders. While on the one side the furies of war and rapine were let loose on the world, on the other, celestial music seemed to announce that the Gods were again coming down to tread the earth with men.

The names of Leonardo, Raffaello, Michel Angelo are certainly enough for the glory of a single nation, the grandeur of a single age. Thanks to their immortal works, and especially to their paintings, Italy rose to a height attained by no other land. Beauty like unto this—even as that of Greek sculpture—cannot be twice born into the world, inasmuch as having become immortal it can neither be repeated nor reproduced. Florence was certainly the cradle and chief school of these masters, but as their most marvellous works were accomplished in Rome, the age had a Pope for its sponsor, and was called the age of Leo X. Yet,. although this Pontiff was one of the Medici house to whom the fine arts owed so much, and although he, too, was a great Mæcenas, he has usurped a fame far beyond his deserts. Raffaello and Michel Angelo received their chief commissions from Julius II., and it was during his reign that they completed the magnificent paintings and sculptures, making Rome a sanctuary of art, and a perennial goal of pilgrimage to all civilized peoples from every part of the globe. Julius II. not only ordered and recompensed these works, but yearned for them, and urged them on with an ardour special to himself, so that at last, and with good reason, modern writers are beginning to designate the age by his name rather than by that of Leo X.[1]

Up to this point we have had no occasion to speak of the fine arts, inasmuch as they had no visible influence on the character or intellect of Machiavelli. When in Rome he never made a single remark on the grandeur of the ancient or contemporary works before his eyes. Neither did those surrounding him in Florence ever seem to arouse his attention, for no word of his records the great artistic events taking place there in the century's first decade. Yet these events were mainly owed to the initiation of the Gonfalonier, Soderini, whose government gave a great impulse to the arts, and warmly fostered them after their long neglect under Piero dei Medici and during Savonarola's rule. It is now necessary to accord them a moment's attention, not only because, directly or indirectly, all citizens and magistrates of Florence took part in the new works in course of execution there, but because these works exercised so universal an influence upon Italian culture, so precisely determined its course and nature that they must have had at least some indirect action on the character and intellect of Machiavelli. For the spirit informing these works was part of the very air men breathed, and in no wise different from that contemporaneously producing a similar transformation in letters. And although in the fine arts this transformation assumed a more concrete, more plastic form, and one that was more patent and intelligible, yet our knowledge of it also opens the way to a better comprehension of the character and value of the new literature. Let us consider the subject for a few moments.

---

[1] Treating of this subject in one of his "Pensieri," Gino Capponi observed that America should have borne the name of Christopher Columbus, and was given that of Amerigo Vespucci; the sixteenth century should have borne the name of Julius II., and was given that of Leo X. "Those who deserved secondary honour, took the first; two Florentines snatched it from two Genoese." (Capponi, "Scritti Editi ed Inediti," Florence, Barbéra, 1877, vol. ii. p. 452.)

The same thought is thus expressed by another modern writer: "Als den Grunder der Kirchenstaates betrachtet ihn (Julius II.) der politische Geschicht-schreiber, als den wahren Papst der Renaissance preist ihn der Kunsthistoriker, und gibt ihm zugleich den Ruhmestitel zurück, welchen unbilliger Weise sein Nachfolger Leo X. an sich gerissen hatte. Das Zeitalter Julius II. ist das Heldenalter der Italienischen Kunst." (A. Springer, "Raffael und Michelangelo," p. 101. Leipzig, Seemann, 1877-78.)

This is one of the best of recent works on the two great masters and on Italian art in the sixteenth century.

During the Middle Ages painting and sculpture seemed to have become little more than a complement to architecture, with which they had joined hands, as though to form a single art, in the Gothic cathedral. Herein, not only the arts, but often the artists themselves, seemed to renounce all individuality by working together, without proclaiming their names. But at the same moment that the literature of Italy began to take shape, the individual genius of a Giotto, an Arnolfo, and a Niccolò Pisano, the personality of the artists, and the speciality of the three sister arts just setting forth on their glorious career, became clearly accentuated. Of this revolution the chief factors were the study of nature, and the study of antiquity now revived with as much potency in Italian art as in Italian letters. In the cathedral of Florence and in Giotto's bell-tower the observer will not find the Greek or the Roman style, but neither will he find the Gothic. It is as though a classical framework of greater solidity and symmetry, well hidden within these structures, were forcing them to essential diversity. The innumerable sculptures and carved decorations become transformed amid those layers and incrustations of marble which, as a modern writer expresses it,[1] are the mortal enemies of the Gothic. The horizontal line prevails to a far greater extent, forests of slender columns are bound in sheaves, fantastic curves are simplified, and the heavenward spring is arrested ; for here, the gaze of man seems again directed to earth. Out of these classic and Gothic elements, to which Oriental forms are now joined and admirably assimilated, a new and complex style is born, of which the only fitting name is the Italian style. Contemplating the Florence cathedral, and seeing it suddenly crowned by Brunelleschi's dome, the beholder marvels less at the diversity of the two styles than at the ease with which they are harmonized together. The classic cupola seems to be naturally evolved from the very heart of the wondrous temple, within which, hidden and invisible, lurked the germ of so strangely diverse an art.

This, in fact, was the art that triumphed when a new spirit, as it were, came to animate the Italian art of the fifteenth century,

---

[1] Jacob Burckhardt. Both in this author's work, " Geschichte der Renaissance in Italien " (Stuttgart, 1868), chiefly treating of architecture, and his other book, "Der Cicerone" (dritte Auflage. Leipzig, Seemann, 1874), an artistic Guide to Italy, there are many most weighty and original judgments and observations.

endowing it with a shape and physiognomy only apparently opposed to the preceding schools, and in reality evolved from them and following the same guides which had built them up : *i.e.*, nature and the antique. In literature we have noted the same facts, with this difference, that unlike the fine arts it had to pass through a period of apparent immobility, during which the influence of the Latin world almost suspended the development of the Italian. But the arts, on the contrary, though with altered direction, never abandoned their upward path. Painting in particular daily acquired greater force, originality, and independence, immensely aided by the use of the new medium, oil, brought to Italy by Flemish masters. In fact, painting now took the lead in art, not merely through the multiplicity and variety of its productions, nor because Italian genius found in painting its amplest and completest manifestation, but also because it communicated to the sister arts—and almost indeed imposed on them—its own special stamp.

By the genius of Brunelleschi, the student of Rome's ancient monuments, and the efforts of Leon Battista Alberti, no less a scholar than an artist, architecture was revived according to classical models. Like all edifices of the Italian Renaissance, the churches and palaces built by these men, however closely they may approach to the antique, are never servile reproductions of it. Lines and forms apparently identical with those of Greek and Roman art, acquired an expression and significance of a totally dissimilar kind. The ornate, by developing much variety and novelty of form, assumed great prominence now that, as we have noted, the picturesque was the predominant characteristic of all art, and had become the recognized aim even of architecture.

Florentine sculpture, led by Donatello, the Della Robbia, and Ghiberti, kept pace with the movement in study of nature and the antique. An expression of renewed youth, unusual energy, virgin freshness of form and movement, abounded in all things. While Brunelleschi manifested an iron strength of soul in the hardihood and austere simplicity of lines disdaining all Gothic ornamentation, Donatello succeeded in endowing his statues with so much force, originality, and *naïveté* of expression, that both artists may be said to be inspired by an identical spirit. And even in Donatello we discern, though less clearly than in the gracious prettiness, and varied, multi-coloured decorations of Luca della Robbia, the predominance of the picturesque, now the fundamental artistic idea both of the nation and the age. It was this idea that, by breathing new life into classic art, transformed and rejuvenated it. The bas-reliefs of Ghiberti's gates have often the effect of paintings ; those of Donatello occasionally condescend to the imitation of works drawn in outline. Certain of Mino da Fiesole's sculptured portraits resemble paintings by the Flemish masters who, thanks to the commercial intercourse between the two countries, contributed to the constituent elements of Italian art. In more than one instance we can plainly trace the effect produced on Florentine artists by the example of the immortal works of the brothers Van Eyck. The introduction of such diverse styles and elements, although marvellously absorbed and fused by the predominating national spirit, frequently deprived Italian art of the severe organic unity to be found in Greek, and sometimes even in Gothic art ; but undoubtedly it also gave birth to infinite variety and wider comprehensiveness.

The same results were effected in literature, and always through the same cause, namely, because the Italian national spirit imbibed at that time all the most diverse systems of literature, philosophy, art, and culture, and thus endued them with a new and more catholic unity. The creative genius of Italy seemed to have a power of assimilation capable of blending, under a new form, all that the East and the West, Paganism and Christianity, had been able to bring forth. But before all these elements could form a new organism, animated by a new spirit, there inevitably occurred a preparatory period, during which the dissimilar elements remained clearly distinguishable. Little by little they met and joined, and the first link to bind them closer together was, of necessity, plastic, exterior, essentially artistic, descriptive, and pictorial ; hence, painting became the chief art of the age. To Italian art, therefore, pertains the lasting glory of having possessed sufficient insight and width of sympathy to become the expression, the sentient and living personification of an intellectual microcosm. This new and plastic harmony then appeared to all men as a manifestation of the internal harmony already established in the spirit of mankind. The world seemed to be illuminated by an unwonted flood of light, shedding comfort on men in the midst of mortal disaster. It was the light of Italian literature and art, heralding the decease of the Middle Ages, the birth of a new era.

This art, however, never lost the memory of its first origin ;

never ceased to feel its effects. No sooner did the creative force of art slacken with the national decadence than the diversity of its primitive elements began to reappear, to fall at last into the abyss of the *barocco.* No similar fate befell either Greek or Gothic art. They instead died a natural death, the death of exhaustion, without ever experiencing a period of tumultuous anarchy, such as the Italian went through, especially in the last century, inasmuch as their primitive elements were simpler and less varied.

Florentine art clearly proves to us how these different elements were fused and blended together, and what enormous variety was thus engendered, particularly in painting. From the meeting and mixture of the deep religious fervour that we praise in the Trecento, with classic Grecian beauty and an accurate study of nature, was born a new and exquisite refinement of ideal, aerial form that might be styled supernatural, were it not visibly grounded upon nature. This hitherto unknown type of beauty seems almost the germ of the new art ; it is the creative power calling it to life. The first painter of this new school was Masaccio (1401–29), a glorious youth, whose life history is almost unknown to us. He disappeared from the world after completing a small number of works to show the path by which all were to follow him. Together with heads which seem photographed from life, we find majestic figures wrapped in noble, broad-folded draperies recalling the toga and chlamys of ancient statuary. Landscape, architecture, all nature enter into his pictures and help to constitute the new painting of the fifteenth century, in which everything finds a place. For a considerable time, however, Florentine artists continued to devote their attention, each to some special branch of art, almost each to the solution of some special problem. This one studied perspective ; that one anatomy ; another drew from life with realistic fidelity ; his neighbour studied the antique, or sought new types and new expressions ; while his friend gave infinite care to the composition of architectural or landscape subjects as backgrounds to his pictures. And all have a fineness, a grace and elegance, clearly proving the artistic genius of the whole nation. It was a strange and sudden flowering which, beginning in the valley of the Arno, spread round Florence and rapidly extended throughout Italy, breathing fresh life into all it touched, everywhere creating new forms and schools of art. Well may Gregorovius exclaim that had the

PORTRAIT OF LUCA SIGNORELLI
painted by Himself
after the original in the Forrigiani Gallery, Florence.

Printed by Chardon Wittmann Paris

Italy of the Renaissance produced nothing more than her painting, that alone would suffice to make her immortal.[1]

The universality and national unity of this great and varied labour daily became more evident. Artists obtained an ever-increasing freedom of touch and power of expression ; their ideas, nay, the men themselves, soared to higher levels. The solemn birth hour of art was at hand, and, as always happens at the turning-points of history, the men of genius, Titans of the immortal work that Italy was about to accomplish, were already prepared and eager for the task. All were either born or educated in Florence during Gonfalonier Soderini's term of office ; but it was their part to transform Florentine into Italian art, and make Rome the art-capital and scene of their greatest achievements. All things heralded their advent ; sometimes it almost seemed as though their presence was felt while as yet they were unborn. For instance, it cannot be said that Frà Bartolommeo Porta (1475–1517) was possessed of real genius. He has neither the intellectual force and fancy, nor the originality needed to establish that title. But his breadth of style, the grand and complex harmony of his compositions, his softness of expression, appear to the beholder to prelude the destined coming of Raffaello. In the same way the forcible draughtsmanship displayed by Luca Signorelli in the Orvieto Cathedral, his audacious grouping, his freely flying figures, foretold, if in shadowy fashion, Michel Angelo's Sistine Chapel. Art itself would seem now and then to begin the work of genius before the individual man of genius appears upon the stage. In fact, it is always the unconscious labour of many pioneers that prepares and smoothes the way for the one great man, who at last arises, equipped with complete power and full consciousness of his own might. The temple once finished, there only lacks the Divinity who is to inhabit its shrine and irradiate it by his presence, but the rustling of his pinions is always to be heard beforehand.

The great revolution was accomplished between the close of the fifteenth and the beginning of the sixteenth century. The first man to prove himself of genuinely superior genius, capable of giving organic unity to the work already accomplished by the national spirit, and leading it to a definite goal, was Leonardo da Vinci

---

[1] "So würde das allein hingereicht haben, ihm die geistige Unsterblichkeit zu sichern." Gregorovius, "Geschichte der Stadt Rom," vol. viii. p. 145. Stuttgart, 1872.

(1452–1519). His master, Andrea del Verrocchio, also possessed great versatility of talent. Painter, sculptor, most skilful goldsmith, a lover of music and of horses, he was also a scientific student, and had from his youth given much time to geometry and perspective. In some of the heads he painted, we note a singular grace and remarkable study of expression ; but these were the very qualities in which he was far outstripped by his pupil. All know the story relating how the master felt disheartened on seeing the angel painted by the young Leonardo in a corner of his picture.

In fact, Da Vinci at once stepped forward as one of Nature's privileged few, as one sent into the world to accomplish great deeds. His mental no less than his physical parts were admirably and harmoniously constituted. Strong and handsome in person, he vanquished all competitors in athletic exercises, and his universal intelligence enabled him to attain equal excellence in every branch of study. Engineer and naturalist, inventor of machines and mathematician, initiator of the experimental method, observer and discoverer of natural phenomena, writer on art and an excellent artist in every respect, he was, above all, supreme as a painter. The inventive restlessness of his mind urged him to perpetual research in newer and harder problems of art and science : to study these ardently so long as there was any difficulty to conquer, and then to throw them aside as soon as they were conquered.[1] For this reason he left a large number of unfinished works, and many scarcely begun ; while not a few of his conceptions and discoveries were merely jotted down in numerous note-books, some of which are still extant.

Yet his finished pictures and the map of designs he has left us, suffice for his enduring fame, suffice to prove his immense influence upon art and upon the most celebrated artists of his age. By anatomical research he gained exact knowledge of every movement of the human figure ; he applied himself with unflinching industry to the perception, invention, and reproduction of the most varied expressions—comic, tragic, severe, and serene—of the human countenance. Through his labours design became — especially in the Florentine school — the potent and independent means of expressing the most exalted thoughts, the most

[1] Burckhardt observes : " Man darf nicht sagen dass er sich zersplittert habe, deun die vielseitige Thätigkeit war ihm Natur." " Der Cicerone," Leipzig, 1874, p. 946.

subtle emotions of the soul. Leonardo reached so supreme an excellence in draughtsmanship and brush work, in faithfulness of portraiture, and in vivacity and novelty of expression, that his figures seem to be living, breathing creatures. The chief aim of his whole artistic career was to produce an ideal type of super-human loveliness, the exposition of a divine smile such as we find in many of his faces. This smile is especially noticeable in the Gioconda, and it is related that Da Vinci caused cheerful music to be played while he was painting, in order to give his model the expression that has immortalized her. Such is the life and truth-fulness of this work that the beholder almost expects the eyes to move, the lips to speak.

All who examine Leonardo's note-books can read in them the history of his most unique mind. Next to ideal countenances wearing, nearly all, that smile of the Gioconda, a smile never entirely free from a certain ironical subtlety, are grotesque, tragic, horribly monstrous heads. But even in his strangest, most fan-tastic freaks, natural laws are always observed. Given the idea, given the meaning of the first strokes, the rest of the figure follows as a logical sequence ; each type, whether divinely ideal or horribly grotesque, maintains an admirable unity and artistic truth. And beside these sketches we find now a design for an hydraulic machine, then some mathematical problem or anatomical study, investigations as to the flight of birds, philosophic maxims, new plans of fortification. So fervent was his zeal for universal research, that he conceived the most daring enterprises : as, for instance, of lifting by machinery the Baptistry of St. John in Florence, and of diverting the course of the Arno. There were moments when he no longer acknowledged any limits to the power of human inquiry and human science, as is proved by his remarkable and well-known letter to Lodovico the Moor. Even in his pictures he was always seeking new combinations of colour, some of which, blackening with age, have spoilt the most beau-tiful portions of his paintings. His Cenacolo is now completely ruined by the ravages of time. This work, finished in the closing years of the fifteenth century, still preserves some faintly visible traces of its more than human beauty ; and with the aid of existing prints we may see that the Cenacolo alone was sufficient for one man's fame, and to mark the inauguration of a new epoch in art. The effect of the Saviour's words—" One of you shall betray Me " —is so marvellously rendered in the facial expressions of the twelve apostles, that the work is a genuine psychologic poem. It is true that the composition, being divided into groups, two on either side of the Christ seated in the centre, with His air of unalterable calm, has something of the stiffness and uniformity of the *Quat-trocentisti*. But, as a modern writer has justly observed, the divine merit of this work consists in the fact that even its most studied and calculated effects seem spontaneous, necessary, and inevitable. In this composition a mighty genius displays its inexhaustible treasures, and brings into harmony the contrasts of expression it has created. Thus a subject, so long almost reduced to a conventionality became original, by force of the new spirit infused into it. With this masterpiece, sixteenth-century painting sprang into existence, and had little left to learn save some greater freedom of movement and variety of combination. These improvements were happily essayed by Leonardo himself in his Adoration of the Magi, in Florence, which he did not care to finish on seeing that he had succeeded in his purpose. He used the same treatment in another celebrated work executed immediately after his return from Milan, and that was almost entirely destroyed.

At Florence, in 1504, all seemed prepared for one of the greatest triumphs of art—a triumph, indeed, already begun, and that Leonardo could only hasten, by proving to the compeers now assembled on the banks of the Arno the might of his own genius. The youthful Raffaello had started from Urbino to come to Florence where Michel Angelo Buonarotti (1475–1564) had already completed some of the stupendous works that were such valuable factors in the special character of sixteenth-century art. This master, after studying painting under Ghirlandaio, and sculpture in the Medici gardens near St. Mark's, showed the power of his brush at the age of twenty-three by his Pietà group in St. Peter's at Rome. Completed during the period when Leonardo was engaged on his Cenacolo, this work also has something of the Quattrocento ; but only in so far as the new school now constituted still preserved certain reminiscences of that of the Della Robbia, Donatello, and Verrocchio, who had given it birth. And in this case such reminiscences were an advantage. The unity of grouping, the harmony of *ensemble*, the originality of conception, the forlornness of the dead Christ, joined with the noble reverence of the mother, whose expression of mournful austerity has a delicacy and grace which Michel Angelo never again achieved, any more than he could reproduce the same finish and

PIETÀ OF MICHEL ANGELO.

chasteness of design—all these things at once placed him among the first artists of the age. Dante's poems, Savonarola's sermons, his studies of the antique, the natural growth of art, and his own irrestrainable fancy impelled him farther and farther on the new path, beyond all remembrance of his first masters. His David, known to Florentines as "The Giant," marked his first step on this path.

On returning from Rome, in 1501, after serious contemplation of ancient art, he was pressed by the stewards of the cathedral works to attempt to carve a statue from an enormous block of marble which they had never been able to turn to account. Other artists had tried in vain to make use of it, but only succeeded in further injuring the block. Being eighteen feet in length and disproportionately narrow, it so nearly resembled a pillar that to give movement to any figure hewed from it seemed an impossibility. Michel Angelo consented, and willingly undertook the daring enterprise confided to him by the Republic in the August of the same year. In January, 1504, the statue was completed, only needing a few finishing strokes after being raised on its pedestal. At the close of a lengthy dispute among the first artists of Florence— and therefore of the age—as to its site, and the method of transporting the colossal mass, Michel Angelo's own idea carried the day. This was that the David should stand in front of the Palace of the Signoria, in place of Donatello's group of Judith and Holofernes. In 1495 the Florentines, having expelled the Medici, had removed this group from the Palace courtyard, and raised it on the terrace with the inscription : " Exemplum sal. pub. cives poserere MCCCCXCV.," as a symbol of liberty overcoming tyranny.[1] It was now moved to the Loggia dei Lanzi, where it stands to this day, and its place filled, as though for the guardianship of the palace, by the David with his sling. The difficulty of transport was overcome by the ingenuity of Giuliano and Antonio San Gallo, and so excellent was their method that when a few years ago it became necessary to protect the statue from further injuries from time and exposure, by removing it to a place of shelter, the progress of mechanics proved unable to suggest to the scientific and artistic committee charged with the task of removal any better plan than that formerly employed by the brothers San Gallo. Indeed, after much fruitless deliberation, it seemed almost like a happy and

[1] See my former work, "History of Girolamo Savonarola and his Times," vol. i. p. 281.

striking discovery none had thought of before.[1] Suspended in a
wooden cage, so that it might yield gently to the jar of movement, the Giant was mounted upon wheels and successfully set in
place. Then Michel Angelo gave it the finishing strokes under the
eyes of Soderini, who often came to admire the work, and sometimes proffered advice that greatly tried the patience of the immortal
artist.

The David stands proudly erect, his glance fixed on the enemy
he has just struck down. Concentrated purpose keeps him
motionless and apparently tranquil ; but he seems to pant for
breath, and the almost convulsive movement of his nostrils
testifies to his inward agitation. The right hand pendent by his
side holds a stone ; the left, with forearm bent, is raised to the
shoulder, grasping the sling ready to receive another missile.
Thus the whole figure was won from the long and shapeless block.
Wholly nude, this colossal youth presents himself to our gaze
with a vigorous simplicity, significant of a power hitherto unknown in art. It is true that Donatello's armour-clad St. George
has an austere loftiness that strikes awe in the beholder. But he
shrinks into insignificance beside the new Giant, in whose
grandiose form, almost too daring lines, and omnipotent calm,
patient observation finds the revelation of its creator's might.
This statue inaugurated a thorough revolution in art. Every
mediæval tradition was broken, every conventional form of the
Quattrocento surpassed. The antique, substantially changed, had
been born again in the new and spontaneous production of the
modern artist. On the 8th of September, 1504, the statue was at
last exhibited to the public, and the public applauded it with a
warmth never excited by any previous work of art. For all
things conduced to gain it the popular favour : its colossal proportions, the new impulse it gave to sculpture, the new school
it founded, and its position as guardian and defender of Florentine
liberty.

We may say that from this moment the colossal figure of
David led the march. In his other works Michel Angelo studied
the novel attitudes and artistic gestures of a people of Titans,
who, in a thousand different forms, seemed to leap forth from his

[1] On this subject reference can be made to the documents published by A. Gotti
in his " Vita di M. Buonarotti narrata con l'aiuto di nuovi documenti." Florence:
Printing Office of the *Gazzetta d'Italia*, 12th September, 1875, vol. ii. p. 35
and fol.

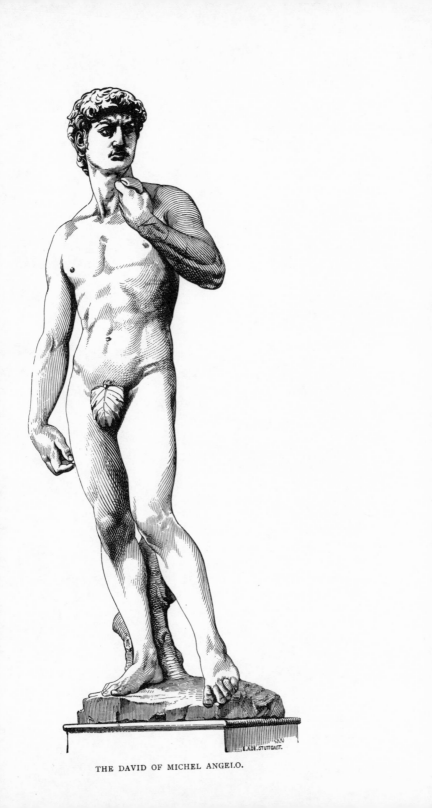

THE DAVID OF MICHEL ANGELO.

restless imagination. He sought the supernatural, no longer in mere expression and gesture, but in exuberance of life, vigour, and action, and to that end applied himself to prolonged ana-tomical study. In the same year, neglecting smaller commissions, he began another work that was to be the second event in his life, and the history of art. Soderini had entrusted him and Leonardo with the task of covering with frescoes the two principal walls of the hall of the Great Council. Leonardo was already at work on his cartoon, and had drawn the fight of Anghiari. This was the battle of the 29th of June, 1440, in which the Florentines routed the forces of the Duke of Milan, under Niccolò Piccinini, a victory they afterwards commemorated by yearly horse-races. Michel Angelo's chosen subject was an episode of the lengthy war with Pisa. In these two works both masters measured their strength as it were, both touched supreme excellence, but hardly anything remains to us of either compo-sition. Of Leonardo's we have only a bad copy by Rubens ; while during the revolution of 1511 Michel Angelo's cartoon was torn into fragments, which were afterwards lost. Some old en-gravings of a portion of this work are, however, extant, and give us a fairly exact idea of it.[1] Still, in order to form any judg-ment of these works, we have to rely on the descriptions and criticisms of contemporary writers.

Michel Angelo had chosen the moment when the Florentine soldiers bathing in the Arno were startled by a call to arms. There is marvellous life and beauty in the attitudes of the men hurriedly springing up the bank, dressing and seizing their weapons to hasten to the aid of their comrades, who have already begun the fight in the distance. Vasari tells us that all artists who came to admire this divine handiwork of Michel Angelo, declared, "that such divinity of art had never before been seen, and that no other genius could ever equal it." We ought to believe him, he adds, because "all those who studied from that cartoon, and designed similar subjects, became excellent artists."[2] And Cellini tells us that this was the first great work in which

---

[1] We have engravings of some parts of the design by Marcantonio and Agostino Veneziano. At Lord Leicester's seat of Holkham Hall there is an old copy of the battle engraved by Schiavonetti and afterwards reproduced by Harford, but it is uncertain if it is an exact copy of the original. Springer suggests that it may have been composed with the aid of the fragments previously engraved.

[2] "Vasari," the Le Monnier edition, vol. xii. pp. 177–179.

Michel Angelo put forth all his marvellous strength, "with so many splendid movements that no work was ever seen, either ancient or modern, attaining to so high a degree of excellence." In his opinion it was even superior to the ceiling of the Sistine Chapel. Regarding the other cartoon, he remarks, that "the admirable Leonardo da Vinci had chosen to delineate a cavalry skirmish, with an assault on the standards as divinely executed as words may express." [1] These cartoons, he says in conclusion, were the school of the world ; and, in fact, tradition tells us that Rodolfo Ghirlandaio, Andrea del Sarto, Francesco Granacci, and Raffaello d'Urbino were numbered among the many artists who studied from them.[2] Neither work has not the solemn calm we admire in the Pietà, in the David, and in the Cenacolo ; on the contrary, both depict the most stirring energy of action, movement, and life. In Leonardo's cartoon, so great is the fury of the fight, that horses as well as men are engaging one another in mortal combat. And in Michel Angelo's, as we see by the engravings, there is no figure that is not a masterpiece of action and *ensemble*. Draughtsmanship had at last succeeded in not only rendering human form and expression ; but also the very tumult of life's passions, in all their infinite variety. The human form, so laboriously studied during several centuries by so many generations of artists, at last stood out from the canvas, and freely moved in space. Art and artist had alike achieved independence ; Prometheus had ravished fire from heaven, and given life to his creation. Leonardo, having conquered the first difficulties, threw aside the work, and devoted himself, as usual, to the solution of novel and no less difficult art-problems. But Michel Angelo, although much influenced by Leonardo's genius, and although in some of his drawings showing diligent study of Leonardesque expression,[3] never imitated, and did not follow him through his ever-varying phases of fresh artistic enterprise. On the contrary, to his life's end he kept to the path first traced by this cartoon, and in which he had first discovered his artistic freedom. He no longer dreaded any

[1] Cellini, "Vita," Le Monnier edition, 1852, pp. 22–23.

[2] Springer, however, denies that Leonardo's influence upon Raffaello is to be dated from the latter's study of these cartoons. In his opinion the Madonnas and portraits executed by Raffaello on his arrival in Florence, prove that the painter of Urbino had not yet acquired the grand manner that he afterwards adopted. Springer, *op. cit.*, p. 57.

[3] This is especially noticeable in the drawings preserved at Oxford.

obstacle, either of form, material, or subject ; for all things issued spontaneously from an imagination trained to obey solely those laws of art to which he subordinated everything. It is true that each day brought him face to face with fresh difficulties ; but he was always ready to attack them with victorious vigour, and the struggle gave birth to ideas and creations of increasing originality. His almost excessive exuberance of vitality prevented him from ever attaining to Leonardo's Olympian calm, and still less did it allow him to arrive at the serene harmony of Greek sculpture. In his more audacious works lies hidden the germ of the future corruption and decadence of Italian art, and the germ becomes plainly visible in the productions of his clumsy imitators.

In those days Raffaello Sanzio d'Urbino (1483–1520), pupil of Perugino, the chief representative of the Umbrian school, was already far advanced in his training. This school, inaugurated by the works of Giotto and his followers in the sanctuary of Assisi, was, notwithstanding certain eminent qualities peculiar to itself, in reality derived from the Florentine school, from which it constantly received fresh aliment. Raffaello himself, although remaining at Perugia until the end of the fifteenth century, was early in indirect communication with the art world of Florence, thanks to his master's frequent visits to that city. And even in his earliest works he showed little willingness to submit to all the conventional fetters of the Umbrian school, and displayed a native delicacy and originality capable of raising its standard to an unexpected level. But on coming to Florence (1504–6) he perceived that art had made a mighty stride, and lived in a new atmosphere of which he soon felt the effects. Study of Masaccio drew him nearer to Frà Bartolommeo della Porta, who at once led him beyond the Quattrocento. This master, whose influence over Raffaello was undoubtedly great, and who was the first to indirectly communicate to him certain qualities of Leonardo's manner, was, as we have already noted, a skilful harmonizer of broad masses of light and shade, and surpassed all other painters in the architectural grouping of his figures and in unity of composition ; he also had great breadth of touch, especially in draperies, and a singular sweetness of expression, rendered still sweeter by the example of Leonardo. At a later period, about 1508, his colouring was much improved by a visit to Venice. The effect of Raffaello's sojourn in Florence was quickly visible in his Madonnas, of which at this period he painted a large number, seeking to give them the expression, at once human and divine, that is one of the most eminent merits and peculiar characteristics of his style. Studying his virgins, not only in his pictures, but also in his sketches, which are more numerous and frequently of equal beauty and originality, we can trace the gradual transformation of the Quattrocento Madonna, in adoration of the divine infant, into the happy mother contemplating her own child and joyfully treasuring him in her arms ; it is a complete cycle of maternal love.[1] We feel and see the propinquity of Frà Bartolommeo, and the more remote presence of Leonardo, whose manner is distinctly visible even in the portraits, which, together with Virgin Mothers, constituted Raffaello's chief occupation while in Florence. It is impossible to look at his Maddalena Doni without calling to mind the Gioconda ; and his portraits during this first period, in which no reminiscence of Leonardo can be traced, are much weaker and more tentative. Michel Angelo prepared himself for his gigantic Roman works by studying anatomy and the most daring postures and movements ; Raffaello, on the other hand, first applied himself to expression and grace ; then, by study of the two celebrated cartoons, the example of Frà Bartolommeo and the aid of his own genius, he finally devoted himself to great compositions. Leonardo had been the first to strike out the new paths, which the other two rival geniuses quickly invaded and triumphantly pursued.

And now, when Leonardo returned to Lombardy, Raffaello and Michel Angelo were summoned by Julius II. to Rome, which by his means became the literary and artistic capital of Italy, and consequently of the world. Here ancient and modern culture touched hands, Christianity and Paganism, all the diverse forms of the fine arts, seemed suddenly brought into substantial harmony. It was a solemn moment ; the mind of man had just awakened to fullest consciousness of its own power in the harmonic unity of mankind's intellectual life ; was inspired by a new happiness, and a divine confidence in its future. In the midst of this harmony, which seemed like music suddenly shed from heaven, there was an ever-increasing exuberance of grand creations of art, such as the world had never

[1] "Durch Raffael ist das Madonnenideal Fleisch geworden." Springer, *op. cit.*, p. 58.

before, will never again, behold. New forms, new images, new types arose, in which Greek mythology and Christian sentiment, learning and inspiration, the real and the ideal, mingled together and joined in forming a world of art—a world revealing a nation's soul at the moment of its becoming, as it were, the conscience of the human race, the centre of light illumining the future. In this intellectual atmosphere, in presence of those mighty monuments of Rome and the Campagna, reducing to unbearable insignificance all things devoid of true grandeur, the minds of the great Tuscan artists were lifted to a higher plane and showed their greatest might.

Raffaello was in Rome in the September of 1508, after having already won his first laurels in heroic composition ; but it was now that the smouldering fire of his genius suddenly shot up into liveliest flame. His was a genius revelling in spontaneous harmony, a genius developing without struggle, without pain, without uncertainties or obstacles of any kind. All loved him, all yielded to the fascination of his gracious nature. His prodigious creative strength was equalled by his power of assimilation, so that everything the various schools of Italian painting had brought forth was united and reproduced by him, as a new art, to which he imparted a grace and delicacy hitherto unconceived. His life was no conflict, but a happy and spontaneous intellectual evolution ; his art was no effort, but a natural symphony. It uplifted the mind from which it emanated, no less than it uplifts the mind of him who contemplates it. We cannot pause to give prolonged consideration to all the more celebrated achievements of Raffaello's brush. That would lead us too far from Florence and from our principal theme. Fortunately, however, the great works of art of this decade are thoroughly known, and Raffaello's painting needs little comment : to see it is to understand it. We may, therefore, hurriedly pass on, only staying to note what is necessary to our aim. Between 1508 and 1511 the first of the Vatican Stanze was completed, that known as the Stanza of the Segnatura. These frescoes are a true poem. On the vaulted ceiling are symbolical figures of Philosophy, Theology, Poetry, and Jurisprudence ; on the walls beneath are four great compositions—the School of Athens, the Dispute of the Sacrament, the Parnassus, and the representation of canonical and civil law. All the accessories, in every part of the Stanza, accord with this grand synthesis. It is hard to believe that it was conceived and put into shape by

Raffaello alone, who at that time, being in his first youth and entirely devoted to the study of art, could not have possessed the varied knowledge required to compose and carry out the work with such admirable success.   Possibly he received no little assistance from Pope Julius II., who gave him the commission, and whose portrait is to be found in one of the frescoes.   It is certain that contemporary scholars had some share in the work ; but it is not easy to discover the direct prompter of the noble theme, for the reason that it was in fact the thought of the age transmuted in Raffaello's mind into an art creation.   In that alone consists the originality and individuality of this masterpiece, which no one else could have accomplished.   The champions of religion disputing on the Sacrament and the real presence of God, the Greek philosophers discussing the highest scientific truths, Apollo and the Muses, Justinian, Tribonianus, and Pope Gregory IX., are all collected in the same room, all joined in the same artistic conception.   Neither do they present themselves to our eyes as mere faithful transcripts of historic and poetic personages of the past.   No ; they have risen from the grave, have come to life, beings real and breathing as the men around them.   We may say that all the living Greek element that will live for ever in the world, now, after long burial and oblivion amid the misty sophisms of the schools, reappeared in its immortal youth, illumined by the rays of the Italian sun, which, sweeping away mediæval clouds, once more displayed to mortal eyes the peaks of Olympus clear cut against the azure Hellenian sky.   If the creative might of genius endued this world evoked from past ages, these Divinities called back to earth, with the special colour of the age, and almost with a new nationality, what of that ?   It only brings them still nearer to ourselves.   Italian art, joining past and present, and teaching us their harmony, exhibits in the gods and heroes of antiquity the human element they had in common with us ; teaches us to find in them, as it were, a part of ourselves.   This it is that constitutes the peculiar character and historical value of Italian art.

It would be impossible to describe in words the numerous works now completed by Raffaello with truly prodigious rapidity.   He had touched the culminating point of his art, and was in the full vigour of his strength.   Grandeur of composition, nobility of conception, breadth of colour, variety of style, skill in draughts-manship, grace and harmony of colour, disputed the palm in his

GROUP IN THE "TRANSFIGURATION" OF RAPHAEL.

productions with a wealth of fertility such as the imagination can barely grasp.

The Stanza della Segnatura was succeeded by that of Heliodorus, this again by the Conflagration of Borgo, and finally by the Stanza of Constantine. Meanwhile, in the Loggie of the Vatican, new compositions, rapidly designed by the master's hand, were painted by his pupils on the vaulted ceilings and on the walls ; fantastic arabesques inspired by the antique were reproduced in an ever-varying form, demonstrating another of the thousand aspects of the Renaissance spirit. Whenever the artist indulged in a short rest from the fatigue of fresco-painting, it was only to depict on panel or canvas other unrivalled gems of art. Who could express in words how infinite a source of intellectual joy the Madonna Della Seggiola, and the still more beautiful Virgin of San Sisto, have been and will ever be to mankind ? In these, the primitive type so carefully and studiously sought by Raffaello is enriched by more grandeur of composition and breadth of execution, without losing anything of its ineffable grace.

In 1509 the banker Chigi, finance minister to Julius II., charged Baldassan Peruzzi with the construction of a villa in Rome, and shortly afterwards (1514) Raffaello came there to paint his Galatea, and design the compositions for the legend of Psyche, executed by his pupils. So the little villa, at present known as the Farnesina, was converted into another temple of art. All who have had the good fortune to feast their eyes at leisure on these paintings, turn away with an intense desire to see them again, convinced of some mysterious charm in them potent to soothe the most troubled spirit.

Raffaello was unresting in labour, and his genius, instead of becoming exhausted, seemed to gain fresh strength in every new effort. But his physical force was of less enduring quality, and at the age of thirty-seven years he passed away while engaged on his Transfiguration. This, although finished by the hand of Giulio Romano, is always accepted as Raffaello's mightiest work, both for power of design and the Michelangelesque boldness of its figures and composition. At length he had submitted in some degree to the overmastering influence of the rival artist who was urging art to the more and more daring enterprises, more perilous heights from which it was finally cast down by feeble imitators lacking the power of the great man who knew how to observe necessary limits.

In order to form a just idea of the inexhaustible artistic fecundity of the first quarter of the sixteenth century, we must remember that, at the time when Raffaello was painting the Stanze and Loggie of the Vatican, Michel Angelo was engaged on the vault of the Sistine Chapel. The latter artist had already been commissioned by Julius II. to prepare for him a tomb of gigantic proportions, and instantly produced one of the most colossal designs ever conceived by the mind of man. It was to be an epic poem in marble, representing the spirit and might of the Papacy triumphing over all human limitations. About forty statues of marble and bronze were to be grouped on the steps of the enormous mass, on the summit of which heaven and earth would uphold the sarcophagus in which was to repose the image of the slumbering Pontiff. Julius II. adopted the idea with so much enthusiasm, that, in order to find a suitable site for the monument, he determined to rebuild St. Peter's from its foundations, so as to make it the grandest temple of the Christian world. On the 11th of April, 1506, notwithstanding his advanced age, he went down a hazardous rope-ladder to a great depth, whither few dared accompany him, to lay the foundation-stone of the monstrous edifice. But the envy of rival artists, the eccentricity and impatience of the Pope, who perpetually gave him fresh commissions, compelled poor Michel Angelo to continually suspend his labours on the monument, and tormented him to such a degree, that, as he said in his letters : " It would have been better to set myself to the making of sulphur matches. . . . Every day they stone me as though I had crucified Christ. . . . I have wasted all my youth bound to this sepulchre." Worst of all, the great work was never executed ; all we have of it are the statues of two shackled prisoners, and the Moses. But in the latter work the whole soul of the great sculptor seems to live and breathe. In a sitting attitude, with one hand resting on the tables of the Law, the other grasping the long tresses of his beard, the Lawgiver appears to be fixing his indignant eyes on the worshippers of the golden calf. The low forehead with the two symbolic horns, the terrible glance, the colossal proportions— the entire figure, in short, is so awe-striking—that were Moses to rise to his feet, the whole people would take to headlong flight ; none able to withstand the awful menace of his glance.

Instead of completing this monument, Michel Angelo was now compelled by the Pope to paint the vault of the Sistine Chapel

THE MOSES OF MICHEL ANGELO.

THE PROPHET JEREMIAH OF MICHEL ANGELO.

and only at a later date found leisure to finish the Moses. He began the ceiling in 1508, and towards the close of the following year, daily spurred on by the indomitable impatience of Julius II. —who once even threatened to throw him down from the scaffolding—he unveiled a considerable portion of it. In 1512 the whole was completed. Nothing like it had ever been seen in the world. The movements, the superhumanly grandiose lines, and artistic *motif* of every figure, display such terrific energy, that the vault seems about to open to give it more freedom of action. Some of the figures are moving, coming towards us, others soaring on high. The chapel enlarges as we gaze. We are no longer looking on a painted surface. Michel Angelo has peopled this ceiling with Titans. The characters of Holy Writ, of history, allegory, sacred and Pagan tradition, are all transformed here. His fancy, discovering a mythology of its own, raised an Olympus, which, although created by one man, seems the work of a whole nation, and will ever remain immortal in the kingdom of art, and the history of the human intellect.

Glancing at the *ensemble* of the various schools of art which we have rapidly noticed, it will be observed that while seemingly obedient only to the unshackled and almost capricious inspiration of individual artists, these schools were really evolved one from the other by an inevitable and logical process ; so that their every development and aspiration reached their natural fulfilment in Raffaello and Michel Angelo, who, in raising art to its highest level, seemed only to amalgamate the labours of their predecessors. All appeared prepared, nay, predestined, for the lofty attainment. Julius II., when urging artists to noble tasks, became inspired by their ideas ; took a very lively part in their most famous works, and promoted them with the feverish ardour of a mind imbued with true Roman greatness. He was constantly on the scaffolding of the Sistine Chapel ; he had a passage made to enable him to go straight from the Vatican to Michel Angelo's studio ; he seemed to think that upon him lay the vast responsibility of leading Italian art to the topmost pinnacle of success. And the men and means needed for this end arose spontaneously on all sides. To Raffaello and Michel Angelo may be added Bramante, who, without entirely transporting architecture beyond the limits of the Quattrocento school, nevertheless led that school to its highest perfection. Julius entrusted him with the construction of the Vatican Loggie, and of the Museum, to which he contributed the chief treasures of his palace at the Santi Apostoli. These were the Belvedere Apollo, and the Laocoon, discovered in 1506, in a vineyard among the ruins of the Baths of Titus. Further excavation revealed the Torso of the Belvedere and the sleeping Ariadne. Earth itself opened to give new life to antiquity. It was also Julius II. who commissioned Sansovino to execute Rome's most celebrated funeral monuments : those in memory of Cardinal Girolamo Basso and Cardinal Ascanio Sforza. What other Mæcenas did so much for art, or can be even distantly compared with this Pope ?

Should the student, while admiring the superhuman beauty of Leonardo's, Raffaello's, and Michel Angelo's works, again repeat the question we have already mooted : how it came about that this divine power of uplifting and purifying the spirit of mankind should have been granted to men born amidst such depths of moral decay and corruption, there would be much to say in reply. First of all we might remark, that as yet the links between the intellectual and moral development of nations are too imperfectly understood for us to arrive at any complete solution of the arduous problem. It might, however, be added that we have frequently seen how the undeniable, if often exaggerated, corruption of the Italian Renaissance was chiefly prevalent in the upper and more cultivated classes of society, especially among. politicians, often among literary men, but had penetrated much less to the lower orders than is generally believed by many modern writers.[1] And this explains why history, while so pródigal in narrating the crimes of that age, can seldom record any really condemnatory facts concerning the morality of those who touched the summits of art, and who, like artists of all times, were usually of somewhat lowly origin. Michel Angelo, although descended from an ancient family, was born in very humble circumstances. In all relations, whether as son, brother, or citizen, he showed many rare and noble qualities, of which his letters, his poems, his whole life, down to its simplest details, furnish abundant proofs. Who can fail to

---

[1] We believe we have found a new proof of this assertion in the "Lettere di Allessandra Macinghi negli Strozzi," edited by Cesare Guasti (Florence Sansoni, 1877). These letters of a Florentine mother of the fifteenth century, show very clearly that family affection was still sacred, at least among citizens unspoiled by public life. In reading this book we see that there still existed a society very different from that described by historians, who seldom concern themselves with domestic life, although it is in the family circle that education begins and moral principles are established.

admire him, on seeing how he cast aside his all-powerful chisel to tend the dying servant, whose loss he so bitterly mourned, and to whose kindred he gave such loving counsel and consolation as to win the title of their second father?

Frà Bartolommeo, the son of a muleteer, had a most gentle and benevolent character, was a faithful and devout admirer of Savonarola, and was animated by genuine religious zeal. Concerning Leonardo, the natural son of a notary, and Raffaello, the child of a mediocre painter, history only tells us that, apart from certain obscure and rather irregular love affairs, they were solely absorbed in the study of beauty and truth, and in the contemplation of the noblest and most exalted ideas. This course of life could have no deteriorating effect, and their characters, in fact, appear to have been uniformly harmonious, well-balanced, and serene. It is true that there was much corruption in those days, even among artists. Their manners were very loose, their eccentricities infinite, jealous, frequently virulent. No one would wish to take Benvenuto Cellini for a model of conduct. Yet, as a class, they seem to have shared the characteristics of the masses, who were less corrupt than literati and politicians, and had still less to do with public life where demoralization had reached its highest pitch.[1]

As a proof that true greatness of soul was still to be found in

---

[1] On the history of Italian art at this period, besides the best known Italian works and those already quoted by us, see also : Grimm, "Michelangelo's Leben" (we have no knowledge of the last edition) ; Clement, "Michelangelo, Leonardo, und Raffael deutsch bearbeitet," von C. Clauss (Leipzig, Sumann, 1870) ; Crowe and Cavalcaselle, "History of Painting in Italy," a work very generally known. Very valuable as a short history of Italian art is the volume on the "Fine Arts," forming a part of "The Renaissance in Italy," by John Addington Symonds (London, Smith, Elder & Co., 1875-1877). The biography of Michel Angelo, written by A. Gotti, and already quoted by us, is the first in which use is made of the great sculptor's "Lettere," edited by G. Milanesi (Florence, Le Monnier, 1875). "The Life of Michel Angelo," by Mr. C. Heath Wilson (London, Murray, 1877), is founded on the lines of Gotti's work, but with the addition of many independent judgments, and much original research, especially on the frescoes of the Sistine Chapel. Copious notices on the fine arts are to be found in the Roman histories of Gregorovius and von Reumont ; the latter also treats the subject in his work on Lorenzo dei Medici. The following books also merit examination : H. Janitschek, "Die Gesellschaft der Renaissance in Italien" (Stuttgart, Spemann, 1879) ; Hermann Hettner, "Italienische Studien zur Geschichte der Renaissance" (Brunswick, Vieweg, 1879). In the *Nuova Antologia* (issue of the 1st of June, 1880) there is a valuable study on the "Scolari di Raffaello" from the pen of Marco Minghetti.

those days we have only to cite the career of Christopher Columbus. In 1492 this navigator first left Europe and crossed unexplored seas, to attempt the discovery of the New World ; and in 1504, at the age of sixty-four years, he returned from his fourth voyage, beset by a series of horrible storms, and closed his eyes on the 20th of May, 1506. The grandest element of his life and of his truly heroic character is neither the intrepidity with which he braved known and unknown perils, nor the steadfastness with which he confronted mockery, persecution, calumny, and ingratitude of the blackest dye. The determining feature of his character, and hence the chief source of his moral greatness, was his unshaken faith in the inductions of science—the spirit enabling him, amid the turmoil of Atlantic waves, and the rebellion of mutinous comrades, to persist in recording every new phenomenon that he beheld. This it was that gave him strength to pass safely over trackless waters, and this, too, was the genuine spirit of the Italian Renaissance, without which no such man could have come into the world. That Italy should have given him birth proves that, notwithstanding her depth of corruption, our country would have been able to find in her own intellectual grandeur a natural basis for the construction of a new moral world had not foreign invasions assaulted her at the very moment of transformation, and at once changed and shattered the course of events. Hence the mistaken belief of many that the undeniable contrast between the nation's intellectual and moral state was permanent instead of transitory, inherent, as it were, to our character and inseparable from it.

But certainly this contrast is continuously before our eyes in the fifteenth and sixteenth centuries, and we must again note its presence in the history of our literature now that this had ceased to be classic and learned, and become national and modern. This literary transformation was mainly brought about by the Ferrarese poet Ariosto, who composed his "Orlando Furioso" at this period, and contributed more than all others, as Capponi says, "to render the Tuscan tongue the language of the nation."[1] We have already seen how the romances of chivalry of the cycle of Charlemagne, after winning much popularity in Tuscany during the fifteenth century, acquired literary shape in the "Morgante" of Pulci. Together with these, and even more than these, the romances of the Arthurian cycle and the heroes of the Round

[1] Capponi, "Storia della Repubblica di Firenze," bk. v. chap. viii.

Table had become popular among the castles in the valley of the Po, where, once upon a time, it had been the custom to write and sing in Provençal, and where, later, poems were written in a hybrid form of Italianized French or Frenchified Italian. This dialect, however, soon disappeared before the rapid spread of Italian and Latin elements, and at a later date the learned men made Ferrara the chief centre of classic culture in Northern Italy. The Este family and the Universities helped to bring this about, but above all the incessant activity of Guarino Veronese, whose numerous pupils speedily diffused the study of Latin and Greek. Owing to this double current, this engrafting of the classic and the romantic, even as the "Morgante" had appeared in Florence, so now Boiardo's "Orlando Inamorato" came forth at Ferrara. Versed in Greek and Latin lore, an ardent admirer of knightly romance, singularly, and almost extravagantly, hopeful of the resuscitation of chivalry, Boiardo showed true poetic ideality and original power in the construction of his poem, by mingling the Arthurian cycle with that of Charlemagne. Such were the forerunners of Ariosto in Ferrara, the which city was now the rival of Florence and the centre of chivalric poetry and refinement.

Nevertheless, the streets of Ferrara, and its ducal castle in particular, were not solely quiet havens of peaceful study—they were likewise the scene of most atrocious crimes. Alfonso I., who became lord of the city in 1505, was a skilful captain ; her foundries produced the best artillery in Europe, and, notwithstanding a gloomy and ferocious disposition, he played the patron to poets and painters. His wife was Lucrezia Borgia, who, from fear, prudence, or the altered condition of things, seemed now to have become a different woman. She was frequent in her devotions, gave largely to the poor, promoted charitable institutions, and passed her days among men of letters, who lauded her beauty and chastity, her piety and her theological attainments. But, as if by some horrible fatality inherent to her name and blood, strange and terrible tragedies went on around her, even in Ferrara.

One of her waiting maidens named Angiola Borgia,[1] was courted by two of the Duke's brothers, the bastard Don Giulio and Cardinal Ippolito. The latter was a bishop at seven years of age, a cardinal at fourteen, loved field sports, fighting, women, and high

---

[1] Our purpose requires us to give details of these events, although briefly noticed earlier in this volume.

living better than the Church, and died at the age of forty-one, from a surfeit, it was said, of roasted crayfish and excess of *vernaccia*, a strong white wine that he kept stored in a coal cellar. So impetuous was his temper that he once caused a flogging to be given to an envoy bearing him an admonition from Pope Julius II. To this man Angiola Borgia incautiously admitted that she could not resist the fascination of his brother's—and rival's—eyes. Thereupon the Cardinal repaired to Belriguardo, lay in wait for Don Giulio, and, on the latter's return from a hunting party, had him dragged from his saddle by four *bravi* and his eyes torn out in the presence of the woman he loved. The Duke was furious, but quickly pardoned the offender; for he was never inexorable, save to kinsmen who sought to usurp his power, and nothing of that sort was to be feared from a cardinal. But the bastard, Don Giulio, thirsted for revenge. He had regained the sight of one eye, which had not been entirely wrenched from the socket. Accordingly he joined with another brother, Ferrante, who aspired to the lordship of the city, and planned the assassination of both Cardinal and Duke (1506). The plot being betrayed, Don Giulio fled to Mantua, and Don Ferrante foolishly threw himself on the Duke's mercy, who this time knew no relenting. With a blow from the staff he held in his hand, the Duke knocked out the suppliant's eye, in order, as he said, to make him match his brother and accomplice. He then cast him into a dungeon. There Ferrante died, and there Don Giulio, afterwards languished, until restored to liberty by Alfonso II. in the year 1559. Three confidential friends of the conspirators were quartered, fragments of their corpses suspended above the castle gates, their heads spitted on lances and exposed to public view. A priest named Gianni, likewise concerned in the plot, escaped execution in consideration of his robe; but he was placed in an iron cage hung from a turret, so that all men might see him. A week later he was strangled, to induce the belief that he had committed suicide. His corpse was mutilated, dragged through the town, suspended by one foot from a stake, and there left to fall to pieces from decay.

Yet this Court of Ferrara was the home and centre of literary men, who praised in elegant verse the magnanimity of the Duke, the chastity of the Cardinal, the gentle piety and purity of Duchess Lucrezia! At the head of this Court circle was Bembo, not yet a cardinal, but young, handsome, an accomplished gallant, a great admirer of Lucrezia's charms, a learned Greek scholar, a polished composer of Latin prose and verse and at the same time one of those who mainly contributed to bring into credit the use of the written vernacular. But the favourite of all Ferrara, the most gracious and pleasant cavalier, sought by every one and cherished by all, was the poet Ercole Strozzi. His Latin verses met with great favour, and some, dedicated to Madonna Lucrezia, were in celebration of Cæsar Borgia's sanguinary deeds. Encouraged by Bembo, and inspired by his passion for Barbara Torello, he also penned a few Italian sonnets. At daybreak on the 6th of June, 1508, this brilliant youth was found dead in the street close to the church of San Francesco, his throat cut, his body pierced with twenty-two wounds. Several locks of his long curly hair had been torn from his head and lay scattered on the stones beside his corpse. All Ferrara wept for him, but no one's grief was so eloquently expressed as that of the bride, whom he had publicly espoused just thirteen days before: " Why can I not go down to the grave with thee ? "

> " Vorrei col foco mio quel freddo ghiaccio
> Intorpidire, e rimpastar col pianto
> La polve e ravvivarla a nuova vita :
> E vorrei poscia, baldanzosa e ardita,
> Mostrarlo a lui che ruppe il caro laccio,
> E dirgli: amor, mostro crudel, può tanto." [1]

Amid the perennial chatter of Petrarchian rhymesters, and the tedious and sickly conceits of the schoolmen, the despairing love-cry of this woman, who, although without naming him, seems, as Carducci expresses it, to point her finger at the crowned assassin of her spouse, strikes on our ears like a voice of nature, a genuine inspiration of poetry that was once more Italian. Rumour declared that Lucrezia Borgia had been jealous of Barbara ; but everything points to the conclusion that the jealousy was the Duke's, and that he revenged himself on the unfortunate young poet for repulses received from the latter's mistress and wife.[2]

---

[1] "Oh that my fire could warm this rigid ice ; my tears restore this dust and rouse it to new life ! And then with daring joy I would approach the man who snapped the cherished tie, and exclaim : ' Ferocious monster ! see what love can do ! ' " (" Rime scelte dei poeti ferraresi." Ferrara, Pernatelli, 1713, p. 55).

[2] Carducci, "Delle poesie Latine edite ed inedite di L. Ariosto." Scrotti, "Vita di L. Ariosto." Ferrara, Camerale Printing Office, 1773 ; Carducci, *op. cit.*, p. 202.

Such was the society frequented by Ariosto, when secretary to the haughty and dissolute Cardinal d'Este, and even his own home afforded no better example. He could not fail to know that his father Niccolò had been sent to Mantua by Duke Ercole I., for the purpose of poisoning Niccolò d'Este, the would-be usurper of the government, and that the plot was discovered barely in time to prevent the elder Ariosto from administering the draught. The assassin found safety in flight, but his accomplices were hanged. And while holding the office of Captain of the fortress at Reggio d'Emilia, where Lodovico Ariosto was born in 1474, Niccolò had satisfied his greed for wealth by pilfering the stores of his unlucky soldiers. Summoned to Ferrara in 1480, the populace almost openly revolted against him, and poems appeared, fiercely attacking and branding him as a thief, traitor, and assassin. One of these poems represents his wife lamenting that she cannot cross her threshold for fear of hearing herself styled the wife of a thief, while her husband cynically replies :—

> " Io rubo e ruberò chè in fra le genti
>   Chi è senza roba matto dir si suole." [1]

At Lugo in 1496 he was deprived of his office of Commissary for having unjustly put a nobleman to the torture. Fortunately his son was too much absorbed in his own thoughts to notice what went on around him. When his father harshly reproved him for neglecting his legal studies, he listened very attentively, but only in order to turn the lecture to account in the " Cassaria," a comedy he was then writing. The poet Strozzi gives a description of Ariosto out hunting, and of how he uncoupled the hounds while pondering his elegies.[2] One day in a fit of abstraction he walked all the way from Ferrara to Carpi in his slippers. Entirely immersed in his art, even the greatest events of the time failed to arouse him. When, in 1496, Charles VIII. was preparing a new descent into Italy, Ariosto was engaged upon a Latin ode in imitation of Horace. " Me nulla tangat

---

[1] " I thieve and will thieve, for in this world, he who has nothing is called mad." *Vide* "Sonetti giveosi" di Antonio da Pistoia, and " Sonetti satirici senza nome d'Anton," Bologna, Romagnoli, 1865. No. lviii. of the collection of " Curiosità Litterarie."

[2] Carducci gives Strozzi's verses at page 92 of the work to which we have already referred.

cura." "What signifies to me the coming of Charles and his hosts ? I shall rest in the shade, hearkening to the gentle murmur of the waters, watching the reapers at work. And thou, oh my Phillis, wilt stretch thy white hand among the enamelled flowers, and weave me garlands to the music of thy voice."[1] The death of the poet Michele Marullo seemed to him a worse misfortune than the foreign invasion. What mattered it, to be subject to a French instead of a Latin king, when the oppression remained the same ? "Barbarico ne esse est pejus sub nomine quam sub moribus ?"[2]

From 1495 to 1503 he devoted himself with tremendous ardour to the study of the classics, and wrote Latin verses full of movement and fervour ; thus refining his taste and strengthening and fortifying his style, which was still tentative and insipid in Italian. He knew little or no Greek. Having entered the service of the Cardinal d'Este, he wrote verses in praise of his patron's goodness and purity ! He narrated the atrocious incident of the blinding of Don Giulio, exculpating his murderous master, and denying his relationship to the victim, whom he accuses of malice, envy, and adultery.[3] But he could affirm the kinship later, when it became a question of lauding Alfonso's magnanimity in sparing the lives of brethren guilty of conspiring against their own blood, and only condemning them to imprisonment.[4] He even celebrated the purity and holiness of Lucrezia Borgia. But all this was the conventional language of the Court, and sometimes a simple imitation of Horace. When, however, Ariosto vented his real feelings, as in the satire on his brother Galasso, he seems another man, and expresses sentiments almost worthy of Tacitus. Burning with indignation, he describes the licentious and ambitious lives of prelates, who are ever trying to mount higher, and covetous of temporal power alone. "What will ensue if one of these men should fill St. Peter's chair ? He will instantly remove his sons and nephews from the sphere of private life. But even to give them kingdoms, he will never be moved to make war upon the Infidel. That would in some sort be worthy of his office."

[1] This ode is given by Carducci in *op. cit.*, pp. 81–82.
[2] *Vide* same work, p. 130.
[3] L. Ariosto, "Opere Minori." Florence, Le Monnier, 1857. Two volumes. Vol. i. pp. 267–76.
[4] "Orlando Furioso," canto iii. st. 62, and canto xlvi. st. 95.

" Ma spezzar la Colonna e spegner l'Orso,[1]
Per torgli Palestina [2] e Tagliacozzo
E dargli a suoi, sarà il primo discorso.
E qual strozzato, e qual col capo mozzo
Nella Marca lasciando ed in Romagna,[3]
Trionferà del cristian sangue sozzo.
Darà l'Italia in preda a Francia e Spagua,
Che sozzopra voltandola, una parte
Al suo bastardo sangue ne rimagna." [4]

But even events such as these failed to disturb Ariosto's serenity. His whole life was devoted to the Muses ; all things served as themes for poetry ; he polished and repolished his verses until he had brought them up to the desired pitch of perfection. Then his cares were at an end. Corruption stirred him to no lofty wrath, but, if little moved by it, he escaped its infection. When Cardinal d'Este insisted that he should go with him to Hungary, he replied that he did not wish to turn horseman instead of poet, and, quitting the Court, regained his freedom and applied himself to his studies with fresh ardour. This step was no sacrifice, for so modest were his tastes, so simple his mode of life, that, as he said, he deserved to have been born in the days when men fed on acorns. " Rather than seek wealth I desire quiet, to carry on those studies which cultivate the mind and render me too heedless of poverty ever to renounce liberty in order to avoid it. I feel no envy on seeing my lord and master beckon to another instead of to me. I go alone and on foot whither my affairs call me, and when I ride my own hands buckle the saddle-bags on my horse's back." [5] Thus it came about that while in his writings he

---

[1] The Colonna and Orsini families.

[2] He means Palestrina, an estate of the Colonna.

[3] An allusion to Cæsar Borgia's wars in Romagna, and more especially to the slaughter at Sinigaglia.

[4] Ariosto, "Opere Minori," vol. i. satira i. pp. 159–60. The lines may be roughly rendered :—

" But to break the Colonna and crush the Bear,
To seize Palestrina and Tagliacozzo
And give them to his own, will be the first affair.
And this one hung and that beheaded,
Down the Marches and in Romagna
He will triumph with Christian blood well sated.
Italy will he give in prey to France and Spain,
And they, overrunning all, some share
To the race of his bastards may remain."

[5] "Opere Minori," vol. i. satira ii. pp. 166 and fol.

frequently went with the times, he was never contaminated by
them. Accordingly, no unworthy act can be imputed to him,
although certain of his verses had been best left unwritten.
He was unfailingly affectionate to his kindred, but incon-
stant in his loves, until Alessandra Benucci bound him to
her for life. He appears to have married her secretly, in
order not to forfeit his right to certain family benefices. He
was never so happy as when dividing his life between his study
and his garden. In the latter, as his son Virgilio tells us,
"he worked on the same plan as in the composition of his
poems, for he never allowed anything he planted to remain
more than three months in the same spot; if he sowed peach-
stones, or any other seed, he so often stirred them to see whether
they had sprouted that he ended by destroying the shoots. . . . I
remember that once, after planting some capers, he went daily to
look how they were getting on, and was vastly pleased by their
vigorous growth. In the end he discovered them to be sumachs,
and that no capers had come up." [1] For a man of this temper
Court life was advantageous, since it forced him from his solitude
into contact with the world. He was entrusted with various
diplomatic missions to Rome and elsewhere; acted as governor
in Garfagnana, where he had much to do and experienced many
annoyances; he accompanied his patron, the Cardinal, not only
on hunting excursions and journeys, but even on military campaigns. It is also said that during the fight of Polesella in 1510,
he succeeded in capturing a Venetian vessel on the Po, and thus
contributed to the Duke's victory. [2] Certainly these events were
of use to the poet, who was soon to write such admirable
descriptions of nature and mankind.

Down to 1503 he continued to pen Latin verse, but then, at last,
began the poem of the " Orlando Furioso," and speedily showed
the marvellous results of his long study. He had now acquired,
without loss of spontaneity, singular vigour, elegance, and dignified sobriety, and all these qualities had been absent from his
former Italian writings. The genius of Ariosto was developed
and hewn into shape by dint of perseverance and unflagging
application. He corrected and recorrected his verses over and

---

[1] *Vide* the "Memorie," written by Ariosto's son, and included by Barotti in his
"Vita di L. Ariosto." Ferrara, Camerale Press, 1773; Carducci, *op. cit.*, p. 202.

[2] Baruffaldi, "Vita di Lodovico Ariosto," p. 137; Antonio Cappelli, "Lettere
di L. Ariosto con prefazione e documenti." Bologna, 1866, 2nd edition, pp. xlv.-vi.

over again, with a carefulness specially remarkable in a writer whose chief merits were simple spontaneity and elegance. He had gained these gifts by infusing the terse Latin element into the Italian poetry of his period, and was thus able to regenerate and make it immortal. And the coupling of the two elements was accomplished in Ariosto's verse with the same perfection and harmony visible in Raffaello's frescoes of the Galatea, the school of Athens and the Parnassus.

The epic material of the " Orlando Furioso " is no more than a continuation and development of Boiardo's " Orlando Inamorato." The manner, however, in which the poem is built up, its various sources, its characters, and the question of its ironical or non-ironical meaning—a much-disputed point—are all extremely important to literary history and criticism, but need not be discussed at this moment. Here we have only to remark that the originality of Ariosto principally consists in the novel form of poetry created by him on the plan we have mentioned. Let us turn the pages at random, for greater delight is gained in this fragmentary fashion than by steady perusal. Let us glance at the adventures of Cloridano and Medoro in the enemy's camp ; let us admire their friendship, their fidelity, and the courage with which Medoro defends the body of his king :—

> " Come orsa che Valpestro cacciatore
> Nella pietrosa tana assalita abbia,
> Sta sopra i figli con incerto core,
> E freme in suono di pietà e di rabbia, &c." [1]

Medoro was already a prisoner, and Zerbino, enraged by the blows inflicted on his men by the unseen Cloridano,

> " Stese la mano in quella chioma d'oro
> E strascinollo a sè con violenza ;
> Ma come gli occhi a quel bel volto mise,
> Gli ne venne pietade e non l'uccise." [2]

But before our emotions are too much excited, the poet transports us elsewhere on the winged steed of his fancy, and we find the fainting Medoro supported in the arms of the beautiful Angelica. We pass from adventure to adventure, from one description to another, and even objects seen a thousand times before appear

[1] " Orlando Furioso," xix. 7.   [2] Ibid., xix. 10.

full of life and freshness, as though the world were just issuing from chaos before our eyes. The rose so often sung and described by poets seems to shoot from the soil for the first time, radiantly blossoming, fresh and virgin, endued with new beauty in a garb of immortal verse—

> " L'aura soave e l'alba rugiadosa,
> L'aria, la terra al suo favor s'inchina."

Chargers, knights and ladies, storms, forests, enchanted lands, incidents and personages, both possible and impossible, pass before our fascinated gaze with the force of reality and nature. How is it that in reading this poem we seem transported to the Loggie of the Vatican? Why do Galatea, Psyche, the figures of the school of Athens and the Parnassus, seem to start from the walls and hover around us, while the poet's varied fancies become living forms moving, breathing, and smiling upon us like old acquaintances? It is because this poetry is a mirror reflecting the whole life of the age, both outer and inner, both moral and æsthetic, with all its splendours and all its contradictions. And this mirror finally makes it all clear and intelligible to us, tracing, nay, almost moulding its physiognomy, and adorning it with its myriad changing tints. In the " Orlando Furioso," knightly romance puts forth its fullest strength, and thus spends its vigour ; from this moment it begins to decay, and can do little else than subsist on the remains of its old vitality.[1]

---

[1] Besides the histories of Italian literature and the life of Ariosto by G. Baruffaldi (Ferrara, 1805), see the " Notizie per la vita di L. Ariosto, tratte da documenti inediti," and edited by G. Campori (Modena, Vincenzi, 1871, 2nd edition) ; Panizzi, " The Life of Ariosto," prefacing his edition of " Orlando Furioso," published in London, 1834. Leaving aside many other works which might be quoted, we will only mention two of the more recent that have been of much use to us, and to which we have frequently referred : *i.e.*, Carducci's work on the " Poesie latine edite ed inedite di Lodovico Ariosto ;" and that published by Cappelli, " Lettere di Lodovico Ariosto, tratte dall' Archivio di Stato a Modena, con prefazione, documenti, note, ec." Another very valuable work is Professor Pio Rajna's " Le fonti dell' Orlando Furioso " (Florence, Sansoni, 1876). The contents of the poem and its sources are treated in this volume with all the author's well-known learning. In his introduction he gives a brief history of the poems of chivalry, and maintains that Ariosto's inaugurated the imitative period, and marked the close of " the fortunate period in which classic lore served to promote originality." Professor Rajna places Boiardo in the latter period. We, on the contrary, hold that Ariosto's poem proves that at that time classic lore did promote poetic originality, for it was in this quality that he pre-eminently excelled. There are no signs of decadence in Ariosto, but rather the most splendid

It is a singular fact that in the first twenty years of the sixteenth century nearly all the master works of Italian genius came to light, and it was within this period that the minds of their authors attained to maturity. All Machiavelli's principal works were likewise written during these years, and many of those of Guicciardini, although more pressing occupations compelled the latter to defer to later times the composition of his great History of Italy. But he now wrote several of his numerous Ambassadorial Reports, his Florentine History, and other works which would have alone sufficed to give him enduring fame. And these works plainly illustrate his character—certainly one of the most typical of the age, and one that brings it most clearly before us. As we shall frequently meet with Guicciardini again, and be introduced into his intimacy, it will not be amiss—now that he has appeared upon the scene—to give some particulars of his life, derived from his "Autobiographical Reminiscences." Unfortunately these give exact and minute details of his early years only, and are then interrupted. He was descended from a very old race of Florentine nobles. The majority of his ancestors were active and keen-witted men, but addicted to the pleasures of life, self-interested, and greedy of power. He tells us that Messer Luigi, his great-uncle,

---

and mature flowering of art, which only began to wither after his time. Touching the subject and plot of the poem, Boiardo certainly showed greater originality since he was the inventor of both, while Ariosto only continued and worked them out. However, in art, form is a substantial part ; therefore I cannot join with Professor Rajna in asserting that Boiardo shows us how classic lore brought forth true poetic originality. Still more impossible does the assertion become when we reflect that the subject of the poem of chivalry has little or nothing in common with the classics. Their influence was advantageous to style, for Boiardo's style was far from correct. Professor Rajna compares Ariosto to Raphael, the painter of very human virgins, and contrasts him with Frà Angelico, the painter of truly celestial beings. Would he then maintain that the classics promoted less originality in Raphael than in Frà Angelico? All that can be said is that the religious sentiment is more lively in the Friar's saints and virgins. As, in our opinion, both Ariosto and Raphael show greater and truer originality, we cannot subscribe to the following judgment of the illustrious author : "Besides the bent of his genius, Boiardo had the good fortune to come into the world at the right moment. Neither before nor after could even he have succeeded in uniting the freshness and dashing spontaneity of the popular poet with the chasteness, the clear and exact knowledge of scope and means, proper to the artistic poet. In the later-born Ariosto the artist is supreme ; *but classic learning is no longer transformed into living strength ; the process of re-creation is replaced by imitation* " (Rajna, *op. cit.*, pp. 33, 34). It seems to us, on the contrary, that in Ariosto classic imitation promotes instead of destroying spontaneous creation ; it is no reproduction, but a true and actual renascence.

was several times Gonfalonier of the Republic, had four wives, and was so given to women, that even in his old age he would run after serving-maids and stop them in the streets. He had no legitimate male issue, but had one natural son by a slave, and left his whole fortune to him. This son afterwards became Bishop of Cortona. Like his father he was of licentious habits, even when advanced in years, " and in gluttony followed the example of other Churchmen who stay in Florence taking their ease, and whose chief concern is thought of their dinner." [1]

Guicciardini's grandfather, Messer Jacopo, also given to gluttony and dissipation, was a keen and daring if unlettered man, a declared partisan of the Medici, and held in turn all the principal offices and dignities of the Republic. It was he who, while filling the post of Gonfalonier, favoured Lorenzo dei Medici's schemes by passing the law upon wills that he knew to be equally unjust and dangerous, and that afterwards led to the terrible conspiracy of the Pazzi in 1478. It was he, too, who kept the people quiet when Lorenzo had to go to Naples to avert the war brought on by the conspiracy. This Guicciardini's son, Piero, father to the historian, had a certain amount of literary culture, was acquainted with philosophy, and the Greek and Latin tongues, and acquitted himself honourably of various embassies and other political offices. He was an admirer of Savonarola, attending his sermons and even making a compendium of them ; he had little friendship for Soderini, and, like all the Guicciardini, was an adherent of the Medici. But he never let himself be carried away by party spirit, being an honest, temperate man, benevolent to the poor and peaceful both in counsel and action. In fact, his son, in celebrating his many merits, has only one fault to find with him—that of being too quiet and reserved.

This son, the historian, was born in 1482 ; he coupled the prudence of his father with the energy of his grandparent, while surpassing both in intellect and culture. Of temperate habits and dignified manners, selfish and very ambitious of power, he was also covetous of wealth, although not to the extent of seeking it by dishonest means. Indeed he and the Guicciardini in general enjoyed the reputation of having always kept their hands clean. He early applied himself to serious study. He was a good Latin scholar and versed in what were then the first rudiments of mathematics ; he also studied Greek, but, as he tells us himself,

[1] " Ricardo Autobiografici," in the " Opere Inedite," vol. x. p. 32. and fol.

entirely forgot it. Thus the three great writers of that learned age, namely, Ariosto, Machiavelli, and Guicciardini, either knew no Greek at all, or so little as to quickly forget it. In 1498, the year of Savonarola's execution, Guicciardini was a lad of sixteen. He began the study of Roman and civil law, first in the Florence studio, then from 1500 to 1505 at Ferrara and Padua, with the addition of canonical law. During this period, Florence being in a very disturbed state, Guicciardini's father thought it well to commit 2000 crowns—a large sum for those days—to his son's safe keeping in Ferrara; and the latter, notwithstanding his youth, rendered scrupulous account of the whole. This is not only a proof of his prudence, but likewise of the confidence reposed in him by his father. About the same time, his uncle, the Bishop of Cortona, fell seriously ill and died shortly after in 1503. Instantly his nephew determined to throw learning aside and enter the priesthood, requesting his uncle, who seemed disposed to consent, to immediately resign in his favour the benefices he held. This step, Guicciardini tells us, was not caused by any vocation for the religious life, nor from love of the indolence so general among the wearers of ecclesiastical robes ; but solely in order to make his way in the world, and end by becoming a cardinal.[1] These facts are sufficient to show from the beginning the good and bad qualities of the youth, and to foreshadow the character of the man. Fortunately for him it happened that Piero Guicciardini, although the father of five sons, renounced all idea of retaining ecclesiastical benefices in the family ; he had no wish that any child of his should be a priest, since, as he expressed it, the Church " was too thoroughly gone to the bad." In fact these were the days of Alessandro Borgia.

Accordingly, on the conclusion of his university career, Francesco Guicciardini came to Florence, as appointed teacher of law, took his doctor's degree, and speedily became one of the first Professors of the Studio. But in 1506 the Studio was closed, and he then practised with success the profession of advocate. He was very eager to make rapid way in the world ; to further that purpose he even planned a suitable marriage, and, in 1508, took to wife Maria Salviati. His father opposed the match, not so much because he preferred and hoped that his son should choose a richer bride, as because he was unfavourable to an alliance with the Salviati, who were too fond of luxury, too hostile to the Gon-

[1] " Ricordi Autobiografici," p. 68.

falonier Soderini, and too much moved by party spirit. "However," writes the younger Guicciardini, "I deemed that five
hundred crowns more or less made but little difference, and I
wished to ally myself with the Salviati, exactly because, in addition
to their wealth, they surpassed other families in influence and
power, and I had a great liking for these things." [1] His plans
were successful, for he was quickly entrusted with many offices,
missions, and affairs all of which brought him no less profit than
honour.

The same year saw the beginning of his first works, for on the
13th of April, 1508, he began to write his "Ricordi Autobiografici
e di Famiglia," [2] and almost simultaneously his "Storia Fiorentina,"
which was more than half finished by February, 1509. [3] The first
of these two productions has no great literary value, since, being
chiefly composed of notes and detached fragments, it was soon
interrupted. Yet the admirable faculty of observation, and exactitude of psychological inquiry, which were the dominant merits
of the writer's maturity, are already evident in these "Ricordi."
They have likewise the same simple, direct, and spontaneous style
characteristic of all his "Opere Inedite," whereas that of the "Storia
d'Italia," is exceedingly artificial. Here, too, the writer's feeling
for and instinctive need of truth and reality are sometimes pushed
to the verge of cynicism—as, for example, when he quietly notes
facts, little to the credit of himself and his ancestors, with the same
calm and indifference as though he were writing of purely historical
personages.

His Florentine History, on the contrary, is a work of sound
literary merit. Starting from Cosimo dei Medici, whom he quickly
passes over to begin upon Lorenzo, it finishes with the battle of
Ghiara d'Adda, where the Venetians were defeated by the French
on the 14th of May, 1509. Thus, it may be said to be a history of
events either contemporaneous with, or little removed from, the

---

[1] *Op. cit.*, p. 71.

[2] "I began to write on the 13th day of April, 1508." These words occur at
the beginning.

[3] At p. 250 of this work, in mentioning the institution of the Tribunal of the
Ruota in 1501, he says: "It still exists at this date, 23rd of February, 1508,"
which according to the new style is equivalent to 1509. We may remark that
throughout this history Guicciardini follows the Florentine style, that, as every
one knows, dated the beginning of the year from the 25th of March (*ab
Incarnatione*). In his "History of Italy," on the contrary, he follows the Roman
style, dating the new year from the 25th of December (*a Navitate*).

author's day. Its pages mark the transition from the old chronicle to modern history, which here takes shape for the first time. It is true that the author still follows the plan of noting the beginning of each year, as though it were the necessary beginning either of a new historic period or of new events ; but this is done in so fugitive a manner that the reader hardly perceives it. The contents, however, are divided into chapters, according to the nature of the subjects and events, the which are narrated and developed with admirable regularity. This work shows a lucidity, an elegance, and above all a penetrating judgment and experience of mankind that are positively astounding in a writer of only twenty-seven years, and who had as yet taken no part in public affairs. His acumen in the definition of character, in the descrip-tion of the vicissitudes of party strife, and the personal motives and passions provoking or leading up to events, his impartiality towards the Medici, the enthusiasm with which he renders justice to Savonarola ; in a word, the objective truth and historic precision of his narrative are beyond all praise. When the events he recorded had not passed before his eyes, or been derived from credible witnesses, it is ascertained that he was careful to refer to the original documents. It was with their aid that he expounded the laws, reforms, and diplomatic missions of the Republic, and sometimes in almost identical words. So far he had not entered, as in the History of Italy, on a wider and more complex field of events ; and, as frequently occurs in his other works, he sometimes fails to perceive the impersonal concatenation of events, through trying to refer all things to selfish passions and individual efforts, to diplomacy and political intrigue. Nevertheless he has furnished us not only with the first instance of modern civil history, but likewise with one of the first and most brilliant models of the new Italian prose : a lofty, simple, lucid, and elegant prose, spontaneous without triviality, dignified and correct without ever falling into the snare of Latin circumlocution. And we may at once remark that Guicciardini never allowed himself to be carried away by his own imagination, as was sometimes the case with Machiavelli. He is no lover of poetry, can neither write comedies nor " Decennali," seeks no theories, and has no ideals to transport him beyond the bounds of reality. For the same reason his exactitude in the description and narration of events is, as we shall frequently have occasion to observe, very superior to that of Machiavelli, to whom in other respects he was inferior. It would be hard to find in the literature of any other nation, especially of that period, any historical picture at once so lucid, elegant, and precise, or with so sure and deep a knowledge of men and things, at all equal to this Florentine History. Also, notwithstanding certain divergences, it is so nearly akin to Machiavelli's writings, both in matter and manner, as to strengthen our conviction that these authors' works, albeit the individual creations of two men of genius, are none the less the necessary product of their age, and mark an epoch in the history of national thought.

CHAPTER X.

Machiavelli superintends the drilling of the Militia—His journey to Sienna—General condition of Europe—Maximilian makes preparations for coming into Italy, to assume the imperial crown—Machiavelli's mission to the Emperor—His writings on France and Germany.

(1506–1510.)

URING the years 1506 and 1507, Machiavelli was employed on a series of petty details. His whole time was now given to the organization of the new militia, a task devolving entirely upon him and undertaken with much ardour and cheerfulness. He was daily employed in writing to the Podestà, or Mayors of different towns, instructing them to draw up muster rolls of all able-bodied men, form battalions, and provide funds for the expense of levying and drilling the men on the lists. He forwarded weapons and instructions; was apprised of all serious riots, and took measures to quell them, either by adjudging suitable punishments, or, in extreme cases, despatching Don Michele and his company to use violent means. Frequently, however, the great brutality of Don Michele, instead of extinguishing disorder, only inflamed it, and other remedies had to be sought. Machiavelli attended to all this business in the name of the Nine (the Balìa of War), to whom he was secretary; but in point of fact was held responsible for everything. Consequently the captains of the militia showered upon him an immense number of letters,

many of which are still in existence.[1] Nor was this all. He had
to make frequent journeys through the territories of the Republic,
and personally contend with a thousand fresh difficulties ; he had
to make levies of foot soldiers,[2] select the captains of the bands,
and send lists of their names to Florence, where their nominations
were at once confirmed, as *chosen and revised by Machiavelli*.[3]
The first trial made of these foot soldiers was to despatch several
hundreds of them to the camp before Pisa ; but no sooner had
they gained a little reputation as good soldiers, than agents came
from the Free Companies or from neighbouring States, tempting
them by liberal offers to desert their flag. Hence fresh anxieties
and fresh precautions, to prevent the difficult work from being
undone as soon as it was started.[4]

But all this unceasing labour did not prevent him from being
occasionally sent by the Ten or the Signoria on military business
to the camp before Pisa, or on diplomatic missions of more or less
importance. Soderini was always ready to employ him in this
way, on account of the great confidence he reposed in him.

In the August of 1507 he was sent to Sienna, to report on the
suite accompanying the Legate Bernardino Carvajal, Cardinal of
Santa Croce, and on that prelate's reception there. The Cardinal
had been sent by the Pope to meet Maximilian [5] in the belief that

---

[1] For an example of this correspondence, although of little importance, *vide*
document i. of the Appendix (II.) of Italian edition, giving some of those comprised in the " Carte del Machiavelli," case iv., Nos. 57, 58, 79, 80, 113. There
are many more among the same " Carte," and in private Florentine Archives, as we
shall later have occasion to note. See to the " Opere " (P. M.), vol. v. pp. 339,
353.

[2] " Opere " (P. M.), vol. i. pp. 68, 69, and vol. v. p. 249.

[3] Between November, 1508, and February, 1509, he proposed and obtained the
nomination of no less than 584 men. Canestrini, " Scritti Inediti, d. N. Machiavelli," p. 339 and following of the notes.

[4] Canestrini, " Scritti Inediti," pp. 283–365. We have already noted that this
work is very confused, and the choice of documents seems to have been made haphazard. Much superior, because arranged on a fixed plan, is the portion (pp.
383–395) concerning the Florentine Militia, first published by Canestrini in vol.
xv. of the " Archivio Storico." But the document LXI. at p. 258, asserted, without proof, to be written by Machiavelli, seems to us to afford no internal evidence
of his authorship. There are many other letters by Machiavelli still remaining
unedited, though of slight importance, regarding the Militia (Florence Archives,
class xiii. 2, No. 159, sheet 15–161). *Vide* Appendix (II.) of Italian edition,
documents ii. and iii.

[5] Maximilian I. not having yet been crowned, only bore the title of King of the
Romans. The following year he was elected Emperor, and in Germany King.
Thus he was sometimes styled King and sometimes Emperor.

the latter was truly coming to assume the imperial crown. Machiavelli's task was to use every endeavour to extract from the Legate the Emperor's real views as to the serious political complications then brewing.[1]

We accordingly find the Florentine secretary engaged in the very humble office of inditing reports from Sienna concerning the hundred and ten horses and the thirty or forty mules brought by the Legate; and also recording how many calves, flayed lambs, pairs of fowls, geese, young pigeons, flasks of wine, and melons had been presented to him by the Siennese.[2] He adds how it was rumoured that Pandolfo Petrucci was in reality vexed at the coming of the Emperor, deeming it useful only to the Pisans, although feigning to be pleased. Also, that the Legate was commissioned to dissuade the Emperor from continuing his journey, and had therefore, together with another German Cardinal, been empowered to crown him elsewhere than in Italy. But even these few and scanty particulars were mere floating reports.

Nevertheless, the Emperor's progress kept all minds in suspense. At Florence it was viewed under many aspects, and one of its results was that before long Machiavelli had to leave Italy on a foreign mission. Not only was it known that wherever the Emperor passed he exacted large sums of money; but also so serious and manifold were the elements of European complication, that the smallest incident might lead to the gravest and most unforeseen consequences. The death of Queen Isabella and the revolt of Castile in favour of the Archduke Philip and his wife Joanna, the daughter and legitimate heiress to the Queen, had compelled Ferdinand of Aragon to pursue a more cautious and less aggressive policy. He had therefore made truce with France, had signed the treaty of Blois with that country in October, 1505, and had come to Italy to make a closer inspection of the state of affairs. The death of the Archduke, which occurred at this time, the insanity of Joanna, and the regency of Castile consequently entrusted to Ferdinand, tranquilized that monarch to some extent.

---

[1] In the "Opere," vol. vii. p. 146, there is an epistle of the Ten, dated 18th of May, 1507, despatching him to Piombino, to make friendly overtures to the Lord of that State, whom, as a near neighbour of the Pisans, it was necessary to conciliate. But on reaching Volterra, another letter, dated 20th of May, summoned him instantly back (*vide* "Carte del Machiavelli," case iv., No. 141), on account, it was said, of there being no longer any necessity for the mission.

[2] "Opere," vol. vii. pp. 147-155. The letters are dated on the 10th, 12th, and 14th of August, 1507.

These events, however, gave him much to do at home, where there was no lack of causes of disorder, and no lack of malcontents. The latter might easily find a leader in the great Captain Gonsalvo, now living in retirement on his own lands, on account of the jealousy and mistrust the monarch had conceived of him, by reason of his enormous popularity with the army and with all Spain, whose forces had reaped great glory under his command. All these things were to the advantage of France. Her good fortune and restless power were again in the ascendant, and a speedy opportunity for gaining fresh laurels was afforded her by the desperate revolt of Genoa. This was quelled by Louis XII. at the head of his own army, and with much bloodshed, in the first days of 1507.[1]

The assertion of French prowess immediately called upon the scene another rival of France, in the person of Maximilian. This fantastic monarch, with his changeable character, and greed for adventure, found himself at the head of a nation not wanting in strength, but considerably weakened by the ravages of political disturbance. The Holy Roman Empire had been transformed into the Germanic Empire, by the formation of nationalities in other States which had achieved independence. Over Italy the Empire had but little influence ; and none at all over Spain, France, or England, who were now indeed its formidable rivals. The princes, bishops, and free cities forming its components were likewise animated by a spirit of independence, that greatly undermined the authority of Maximilian. For, whereas he was supreme in the Archduchy of Austria, and his other proper States, and also as feudal lord in Alsatia, Suabia, and elsewhere, he was of small account as King of the Romans. Even in Germany a feeling of nationality was now in process of formation, tending to unite all scattered elements under a central authority, and favourable to any representative of the unity of the Empire. But there was one obstacle. Maximilian wished to reconstitute the Empire in the interest of the Hapsburgs, by means of a Council nominated by and dependent upon himself, whereas the German patriots desired an oligarchy placing all power in their own hands, and making the emperor himself their subordinate. Thus, there were stirring at the same time the interests of the

---

[1] Henry Martin, "Histoire de France," tome vii. liv. 45 (4th edition) ; Dareste, "Histoire de France," Paris, Henry Plon, 1866, tome iii. liv. xix. p. 410 and fol.

House of Hapsburg and those of the States in its possession, the need of local independence, the growing sentiment of nationality and Germanic unity, and the still potent traditions of the Empire : and all these constituted a medley of elements that could neither be separated nor brought into harmony.[1]

At the head of these very complicated and difficult political conditions was the yet uncrowned emperor, still, therefore, entitled the King of the Romans. Maximilian I. was a man of very curious and contradictory character. Of pleasant and affable manners, not exactly handsome, but with a strong and well proportioned person, he was lavish of his money, was skilful in war, especially in the command of artillery, and was therefore beloved by his soldiery. His brain seethed with the strangest and most fantastic designs, which he could never bring to fulfilment, since no sooner did he begin to execute one, than he felt impelled to start another.[2]

Still imbued with mediæval ideas, he wished to bend the world beneath the sway of the Empire ; to reconquer Italy ; to go to Constantinople to fight the Turks and liberate the Holy Sepulchre : sometimes, he even dreamed of becoming Pope, an idea that would seem incredible, had he not expressed it in some of his letters.[3] Nevertheless, this man, with his schemes for the subjection of the East and West, had to endure daily disputes as to the number of soldiers and amount of money due to the Empire from princes and free cities ; nor could he always succeed in obtaining obedience, even from the subjects of his own special States. Money often failed him for the payment of his troops, and he made vain appeals and in vain assembled diets to get supplies. Thus he was reduced to pledge the crown jewels, and even to take service under petty potentates, and receive pay almost as an ordinary free captain. All this, notwithstanding, he never abandoned his vast projects, in which Germany sometimes affected to second him, and then un-

[1] W. Maurenbrecher, " Studien und Skizzen zur Geschichte der Reformationszeits," Leipzig, 1874, p. 101 and fol. ; Bryce, " The Holy Roman Empire," London, ch. xvii. ; Ranke, " Deutsche Geschichte in Zeitalter des Reformation " ; Berlin, " Duncker und Humblot," 1852.

[2] Albèri, " Relazioni degli Ambasciatori veneti," series 1, vol. vi. pp. 26, 27 ; Quirini's " Relazione."

[3] Gregorovius, vol. viii. pp. 68, 69 ; Alb. Jäger, " Über Kaiser Maximilians I. Verhältniss zum Papstthum " (Sitzungsberichte der K. Akad. d. Wissenschaften, xii. Band, Wien, 1854) ; Brosch, " Papst Julius II.," Gotha, 1878, Funftes Capitel, p. 144.

expectedly left him in the lurch. But even this did not prevent him from plunging into deeper schemes and perpetually planning fresh ones. Thus he stands before us as the last knight-errant of a world on the point of extinction, and, in spite of his sterling qualities, often appears in a grotesquely comic light.

In his foreign policy Maximilian constantly found himself in antagonism with France, who, by dint of maintaining clandestine relations with many princes of the Empire, created continual difficulties for her adversary. The interests of the two powers were perpetually clashing both in the Low Countries and in Italy. For this reason, Ferdinand and Isabella of Spain had stood by Germany in order to injure France. But after the treaty of Blois, Louis XII., feeling safe from Spain, took courage, and Maximilian perceiving that war was inevitable, tried to collect men and money.

France had not kept her promise of giving Charles, nephew, and, afterwards, successor, to the Emperor, the king's daughter, Claude, to wife ; and thereupon Maximilian refused the investiture of the Duchy of Milan, in order to gain that State for himself. The submission of Genoa, and its encouraging effect upon the French, induced him to hasten his descent into Italy, for the purpose of taking possession of the crown, becoming lord of Milan and re-establishing everywhere the Imperial dominion. Julius II. watched these movements with an anxious eye, wishing to direct them according to his own desires, which all tended to one end. This was the re-acquisition of the territories he considered to have been torn from the Church, particularly those occupied by Venice, towards which State he appeared to nourish an inextinguishable hatred. Already, by means of keen-witted legates, he was laying the threads of his future policy. So far, however, his designs had failed, for it was impossible to reconcile Germany with France, who on her side was drawing nearer to Venice. Maximilian still persisted in his scheme of coming to seize the crown, even though he had to encounter both French and Venetians on the road. Thus men's minds in Italy were kept in perpetual tension, the Pope's no less than the rest, for he could not tolerate that the course of events should proceed independently of his influence. And if the rumour of Maximilian's wild idea of becoming Pope ever reached his ears, it must have caused him much annoyance, however incredible and puerile the notion was in itself.

But to enter Italy Maximilian required both men and money ;

and both were lacking. To obtain the first he might turn to Switzerland, for that country, since her fierce and heroic resistance against Charles the Bold, Duke of Burgundy (1476–77), had become a rich mine of fighting men. However, Switzerland was now only nominally a portion of the Empire, and Maximilian himself had been obliged, after the obstinate struggle of 1499, to recognize the independence of the Helvetic Confederation. This was speedily joined by Basle and Schaffhausen, by Appenzell a little later. It thus comprised thirteen cantons, to which other small republics were bound by ties of varying strength, among them that of the three Rhetian Cantons, known in Italy as the Grisons League, and which at the present time are an integral part of the confederation under the name of Canton Grisons. All these republics were now ready to send their excellent infantry to join in any war for the defence or offence of any State ; but their services had to be bought. Louis XII. had gold, but Maximilian had none, and vainly endeavoured to obtain it. Thus, even among the Alps, Germany and France were in conflict, and in a country that but a few years before had acknowledged the supremacy of the Empire every advantage was on the side of the rival power.

In 1507, Maximilian demanded an army from the Diet of Constance, in order to reconquer the Milanese territory, seize the crown, and re-establish the Imperial authority. The Diet declared itself in favour of the enterprise ; but wished it to be undertaken in its own name, and with generals of its own choice, whereas Maximilian desired to lead it himself in the name of the Empire.

From this, one of the usual matters of dispute in Germany, the usual consequences arose, namely, temporary and insufficient arrangements. The Emperor was granted 8,000 horse and 22,000 foot soldiers, but for six months only, dating from the middle of October, and 120,000 Rhenish florins for artillery and extraordinary expenses.[1] With Maximilian's well-known vacillation and lavishness, it was to be expected that by the end of the six months he would be again without money or men, and without having even commenced his campaign. Nevertheless, finding himself, as Guicciardini phrased it, "on board ship, with scanty store of biscuits," [2] he seemed on this occasion determined to act

---

[1] Guicciardini, "Storia d'Italia," vol. iii. bk. viii. p. 281.
[2] Ibid., chap. xxx. p. 346.

promptly. In fact, he at once divided his army into three detachments : one to march on Besançon to threaten Burgundy ; the second into Carinthia to threaten Friuli ; the third towards Trent, whither he went in person, to hold Verona in check. According to his usual custom, he arranged these manœuvres with the utmost secrecy, remaining in retirement, and directing that all ambassadors accredited to him, should not pass beyond Botzen or Trent. He was much enraged against Venice ; for that State, instead of joining with him, had allied herself with France, who had guaranteed her territories on the mainland, and to whom in return she had guaranteed those of Milan, and promised to oppose armed resistance to the passage of the Imperial troops. Louis XII., therefore, having provided for the defence of Burgundy, despatched G. J. Trivulzio at the head of 400 lances and 4,000 infantry to reinforce the Venetians, who had sent the Count of Pitigliano with 400 men-at-arms towards Verona, and Bartolommeo d'Alviano with 800 men-at-arms into Friuli.[1]

All now seemed prepared for a vast conflict, that might have the gravest consequences for Italy. Little wonder, then, that great agitation should prevail, especially in Florence, whither Maximilian, in the name of the Empire, had sent a demand for the sum of 500,000[2] ducats, as a subsidy towards his coronation journey. The Florentines were totally unable to pay so exorbitant a sum ; but even had it been much diminished, they would still have been in an extremely difficult position. On the one hand, they could not absolutely reject the demand, for fear of being exposed to the Emperor's wrath, if he really came to Rome ; on the other, they knew that any concession would cost them the friendship of France, for which they had already made many sacrifices. Soderini, being a declared friend of the French alliance, his enemies made use of this uncertainty to attack him, and were further incited to do so by the Imperial ambassador, who said evil things of "the Gonfalonier's tyrannical rule," and promised that his master would soon find a remedy for it.[3] This gave rise to an animated discussion, concluding with the proposal to follow the example of other

---

[1] Guicciardini, Leo, Sismondi.

[2] Guicciardini, " Storia d' Italia," vol. iii. chap. vii. p. 299.

[3] Parenti, "Historia Fiorentina," Biblioteca Nazionale of Florence, cod. ii. 134 (copy), vol. vi. sheet 145. As in the case of Parenti, as well as Cerretani, we have sometimes made notes from two ancient copies, and sometimes from the original works, we are obliged to quote different codices.

Italian States by sending ambassadors to Maximilian ; but first of all to despatch some one to ascertain if he were really on the advance, since otherwise there was no necessity for coming to terms with him. Soderini, having the fullest confidence in Machiavelli, wished him to be the envoy, and even caused him to be elected by the magistrates. But so loud an outcry was raised against what was deemed an act of undue favouritism, that it was found needful to send Francesco Vettori instead, although even this measure hardly allayed the popular irritation.[1]

For now a party hostile to the Gonfalonier was in course of formation, and all pretexts were seized for attacking him. It was asserted that Florence had only nominal freedom, since all power was in the hands of one man, who gained adherents among the populace and men of little account, in order to put aside citizens of higher standing of whom he was jealous. The official director of the Mint had the strange idea of issuing florins stamped with the portrait of Soderini instead of the lily of Florence. Soderini disapproved of it and caused the coin to be withdrawn, but this did not save him from reproofs and satirical comments.[2] Some time after, it became necessary to dismiss Don Michele, the Bargello (or commander) of the infantry, because his dishonesty and violence plainly showed the evil results of employing rogues in the service of the Republic. Even this measure excited ill-natured remark. No one, it is true, defended Don Michele, but it was said "that it would have been well rather to put him, secretly to death, than to send him away too much our enemy." Fortunately it was not in his power to do further harm, for in the February of the following year, while leaving the house of Chaumont one evening, he was murdered by some Spaniards who had been present ; and thus "'ost his life, as he had made many others lose theirs."[3]

---

[1] Guicciardini, "Storia Fiorentina," chap. xxx. p. 340.

[2] Parenti, "Historia," &c. (copy), *loc cit.*, June, 1507.

[3] Parenti, "Historia," &c., cod. ii., iv., 171, sheet 2, October, 1507 (original MS.). Parenti's words teach us the kind of morality then prevailing in public affairs. Soderini was blamed and attacked, for not having put to death secretly and without trial, a man up to that moment in the employment of the Republic. Strange, too, that this infamous assassin (known as the Strangler), so long one of Valentino's most faithful instruments, should not only have obtained official employment in Florence with so much ease, but should have enjoyed the protection of many Cardinals. In fact, at the time when he was a prisoner in the hands of Julius II., who hesitated what to do with him, the Florentine ambassador, Giovanni Acciaiuoli, wrote from Rome to the Ten, under the date 20th October, 1504 : " I

Still more lively disputes were excited by the despatches of Francesco Vettori. He wrote that for the present Maximilian would be content with only fifty thousand ducats ; but that he demanded instant payment of that sum, otherwise the Florentine orator would not again be admitted to his presence. And Vettori added, that it was positively necessary to come to a decision, since German affairs became daily more inflamed. Therefore Florence must either pay the tribute and make an enemy of France, or refuse to pay and make an enemy of the Emperor. Accordingly, discussion in Florence grew more and more furious. After a lengthy debate, the *Pratica* decided on sending ambassadors, and the choice of the Eighty fell on Piero Guicciardini and Alamanno Salviati. Then, opposition was made to the Embassy in the Council of Ten and the Council of Eighty on the part of Guicciardini himself. He declined the post, alleging that it was useless to send ambassadors without authority to conclude an alliance, and that to conclude one amidst so much uncertainty was dangerous, inasmuch as they would lose the friendship of France without being assured of German assistance.

In this conflict of opinion the Gonfalonier deemed it best to carry the question before the Great Council, and allow every one to express his mind freely. At that time this was a very unusual measure, and being considered a violation of liberty, no one spoke a word. Usage demanded that the government should bring forward its proposal and that the citizens should decide

will not omit to inform your Excellencies, that by reason of not having, *ut aiunt*, found Don Michele guilty of any crime deserving death, and because ten Cardinals have interceded for him, all Rome declares that he will be set at liberty." Rumour was verified by the event (Florence Archives, ch. x. d. st. 4, No. 82 at sheet 46*t*).

We have elsewhere noted (p. 305) how this man, styled by nearly every one Don Michele the Spaniard (Parenti frequently alludes to him under that name), was by some erroneously supposed to be of Venetian birth on the strength of a letter by Niccolò degli Alberti, Commissary of Arezzo. We then said that the letter, alluded to in a note to the "Opere," was not to be found, and that even were it found, its statements could not hold good against the testimony of chronicles and official documents. Since then we have by chance discovered this very letter in a file of autograph letters written to Machiavelli, belonging to Signora Caterina Bargagli, *née* Countess Placidi, and kindly placed at our disposal by that lady. Although this letter offers no evidence that can change our opinion, and has no historic value, yet as it has often been quoted, and is very brief, and refers to the time of Don Michele's dismissal, we have included it in the Appendix (II.) document iv. of the Italian edition. For a curious letter from Don Michele himself to Machiavelli, taken from the same collection, and giving some idea of the man and of his time, see Appendix (II.), document v. of Italian edition.

from the benches (*pancate*)—each of which elected a representative, who had either to speak in support of and vote for the law, or remain silent if he intended to oppose it. To grant freedom of speech to all, appeared then, according to Parenti's expression, "an actual loss of liberty disguised under a show of wider liberty." [1] At last, as the best thing to be done, it was decided to fix an ultimatum of some feasible arrangement and forward it to Vettori, not however for immediate conclusion, but only to be used at his judgment, in case of urgent need. Thereupon the Gonfalonier, catching the ball on the rebound, succeeded in persuading the Ten of the imprudence of employing ordinary couriers for the conveyance of instructions of such exceptional importance. The despatches might be intercepted ; it was therefore expedient to send a trusty messenger, able at need to deliver the instructions by word of mouth. Thus he gained his point of sending Machiavelli and establishing him beside Vettori, as he had long most ardently wished. The Florentines grumbled, of course, and it was said that Soderini had chosen Machiavelli because the latter was his puppet (*mannerino*), and could be made to write anything he liked, "as best suited their ends and designs." [2] The truth was that the Gonfalonier had greater confidence in Machiavelli than Vettori, and did not wish to be involved by the latter in a dangerous course of policy.

Therefore, in the December of 1507, Machiavelli set forth on his journey, bearer of the following instructions : that 30,000 ducats should be offered to Maximilian, and that, in case of absolute necessity, the sum should be increased to as much as the 50,000 now demanded by him. Payment, however, was only to begin when his journey to Italy was decided, and would be continued as he advanced. Machiavelli was obliged to destroy his

---

[1] Parenti, "Historia," &c., cod. ii. iv. sheet 171 (original MS.).

[2] Cerretani, cod. ii. iii. 76, sheet 316 (copy). Cerretani's hostile feeling towards Soderini is proved by his assertion that the Gonfalonier sent Machiavelli in order that he should write in the manner agreed between them "with advices very similar to those of Francesco Vettori, which confirmed the coming of the Germans in the strongest terms." Had this been true, it would have been superfluous to take so much trouble to have Machiavelli chosen as messenger. Besides, it was generally known that Soderini's sympathies were on the side of France, not Germany. In any case it is worthy of remark that Parenti, Cerretani, and Guicciardini, all show in their Florentine histories equal animosity against Soderini, without, however, being able to cast any slur on his political integrity. The opposition party formed against him was gaining strength.

despatches [1] on the road, for fear of their being found on him in Lombardy, where indeed, as he had foreseen, his person was rigorously searched.

This Legation—of which only sixteen letters remain—three signed by Machiavelli, the others written by him, but bearing Vettori's signature—was of no great importance in itself, since its sole purport was to drag on negotiations with Maximilian, in order to give him nothing in the end.[2]   But it is rendered valuable by the observations Machiavelli had occasion to make on the Swiss and the Germans, and owing to the information it contains of events which had just taken place in North Italy.   On the 25th of December he passed through Geneva, reached Botzen on the 11th of January, 1508, and thence on the 17th despatched two letters.   In the first, signed by Vettori, he relates that the offer of 30,000 ducats having been by no means well received by Maximilian, they had quickly raised it to 40,000, whereupon he had shown a much more friendly spirit, although always suspicious that the Florentines were using their wiles to keep him at bay. The Emperor was at seven leagues from Trent, and was already hard-pressed for money ; there would be therefore little difficulty in inducing him to be satisfied with a moderate sum, provided it were paid without delay.   But this was exactly what neither Vettori nor Machiavelli had power to do.[3]

The second letter, written the same day in Machiavelli's own name, gives minute details of his journey ; and we note the remarkable care and attention with which he observed the countries through which he had so rapidly passed.   " Between Geneva and Constance," he writes, " I made four halts

---

[1] He gives an account of this in the letter of the 17th of January, 1508, written by him and signed by Vettori (" Opere," vol. vii. p. 163).   As early as the 21st of November, the Ten had written to Vettori that Machiavelli had started, " in order to bear thee our decision, and should anything happen to the despatches, he will give thee the same news by word of mouth ; and we hope he may arrive in safety."   On the 29th of January, they expressed their annoyance at the loss of the letters, which would have been useful for the better explanation of their views. See "Opere" (P. M.), vol. v. pp. 251 and 272.

[2] The editors of the " Opere " (P. M.) declare that they have verified the autographs, but it is plain that they have only done so occasionally ; otherwise they would have noted, that instead of a few only, all the letters of this Legation are in Machiavelli's handwriting.   (Florence Archives, " Dicci di Balìa, responsive," files 87, 89, 90, 91.)   Had they verified these autographs, they would not so frequently have reproduced the errors of former editions.

[3] See the letters dated 17th and 24th of January, both signed by Vettori.

on Swiss territory, and have applied my best diligence to the investigation of customs and characteristics. I have heard that the chief mass of the Swiss is composed of twelve Cantons, bound together in such fashion that all decisions of their several Diets are respected by all.[1] Therefore, it is an error to say that four (Cantons) are with France, and eight with the Emperor. The truth is, that France has kept men in Switzerland who, by means of gold, have poisoned the whole country, both publicly and privately. If the Emperor were rich he might gain the Swiss, who do not wish to excite his enmity, but are unwilling to aid him against France, who has so much gold. Besides the twelve Cantons there are other Swiss, like those of the Valais and the Grisons League, who are on the Italian border, and not so strictly united with the former as to be unable to act independently of the deliberations of the other Diets. Nevertheless, they are all agreed as to the defence of their liberties. The twelve Cantons each contribute four thousand men for the defence of the country, and from one thousand to one thousand five hundred for foreign service. And this because, in the first case, all are by law compelled to bear arms ; in the second, namely, when it is a question of going to fight elsewhere, no one need go, save of his own free will." [2] There is

---

[1] In a short memoir read before an historical Society of one of the Cantons of Switzerland, in 1875, by M. Alexandre Daguet, the author says : " Machiavel en personne est venu en Suisse. Il a passé quelques jours sur nôtre territoire, bien peu de jours, il est vrai ; mais un temps suffisant pour donner à cet esprit pénétrant par excellence l'occasion de se faire une idée exacte de l'organisation politique des Confédérés, du fort et du faible de leurs institutions, et pour qu'il ait appris à connâitre les traits distinctifs du droit public qui unissait les 12 *Ligues* ou cantons, dont se composait en ce moment le corps helvétique." " Machiavel et les Suisses, Etude d'histoire nationale et étrangère" (extrait du " Musée Neuchâtelois," Juillet-Août, 1877), Neuchâtel, Wolfrath et Metzner, 1877. The Cantons numbered twelve at that period, Appenzell not having yet joined them.

[2] Second letter of 17th of January. At that time the Venetian Ambassador with Maximilian was a certain Vincenzo Quirini, whose despatches are still unedited at Venice ; but his Relation was published by Albèri (Series I., vol. vi. pp. 5–58). In this (at pp. 39–41) we find other remarks upon Switzerland, which it may not be amiss to compare with those of Machiavelli. According to Quirini, the twelve Cantons could send abroad 13,000 foot soldiers, after providing for the defence of the country. The Grisons League could give 6,000 men, the Valais 4,000, St. Gall and Appenzell 3,800. Each Canton had its own banner, the twelve one in common, and the Grisons League the same. No one could fight against his own flag or that of the Confederation without incurring the penalty of death and confiscation of his property. These flags could only be borne by soldiers sent abroad by agreement with the Cantons, or with the Confederation. Lodovico Sforza, the Moor, when attempting to reconquer his own State (1,500), hired many

no cause for surprise in Machiavelli's interest in studying a Republic maintained by its own strength, and sending the minutest particulars to the Ten, when we remember that he wished to see Florence established on a similar basis. Meanwhile, in order to conclude even this second letter with some point related to his mission, he mentions how at Constance he had diligently questioned one of the Duke of Savoy's orators as to whether Maximilian's enterprise would or would not be carried on, and had been told in reply : " Thou wouldst learn in two hours more than I have been able to comprehend in many months. The Emperor acts with great secrecy ; Germany is a very wide land, people arrive at different spots from very distant provinces ; to know anything for certain, it would be needful to have many spies on all sides." [1]

Four letters follow, two of which, *i.e.* of the 25th and 31st of January, written almost entirely in cipher, contain insignificant and scarcely intelligible news, or else indecent illusions. In fact, they were merely written so that, in case of being intercepted by the enemy, it might be easier to save the two others giving intelligence of the persons surrounding Maximilian and of the stratagems employed by them.[2] Then, on the 8th of February, he sent a letter from Trent, signed by Vettori, relating how Maximilian, having arrived there and being authorized by Julius II. to assume the title of Emperor elect, had marched on the fourth day of the month, with drawn sword and preceded by heralds, to the cathedral, where his Chancellor, Mathias Lang, Bishop of Gurk, had

Swiss mercenaries of the kind designated as *Freie,* because they took service in small bands with all who would pay them, and had no flag of their own. It was for this reason that they refused to fight against the mercenaries of Louis XII., who bore a flag. For had they done so, they would have forfeited both their citizenship and their property. Lodovico's defeat and ruin was caused by their defection, at least according to the account given by Quirini, who adds that the men of the Valais, the Grisons, Appenzell, and St. Gall would all have acted in the same manner.

[1] Letter of the 17th of January, signed by Machiavelli, and previously quoted.

[2] The two letters of the 25th and 31st of January are published in the " Opere " (P. M.), pp. 271 and 276 ; but in fragmentary fashion, since no interpretation is given of their principal portions in cipher. The following words are quoted from the letter of the 25th of January. (They, too, were in cipher, although the editors do not mention it.) " For this reason it is needful for me to tell you that this letter contains nothing ; but is only written that the true despatches may be saved if this be found." We have ascertained that the other fragments in cipher contain, as the editors mention, nothing but jokes, indecencies, and nonsense.

harangued the people and officially proclaimed that the Emperor was on his way to Italy to take possession of the crown.[1]

The same letter went on to relate the very singular manner in which the expedition had begun. The Marquis of Brandeburg had marched on Roveredo with 5,000 foot and 2,000 horse, and then suddenly retraced his steps. The Emperor, with 1,500 horse and 4,000 foot, had marched towards Vicenza, and had taken and sacked the Seven Communes which enjoyed self-government under the protection of Venice. It was rumoured that he was laying siege to a castle, when it became known that he, too, had returned by Trent, and was stationed ten miles from the city on the road to Botzen. " Now I would fain inquire what the wisest man in the world could do, if employed on the mission with which your Excellencies have charged me. Had your letters[2] arrived three days ago, I should have immediately paid (the requisition), in the sure belief of the Emperor's coming, and I should have been approved, only to be condemned to-day in view of what has actually happened. It is difficult to forecast events. The Emperor has many and worthy soldiers, but he has no money, neither is it apparent from what quarter he will get any, and he is too lavish of that which he has. Now, although in principle it is a virtue to be liberal, it is no use satisfying a thousand men when one needs twenty thousand, and liberality has no effect save on its objects. He is skilled in war, patient of fatigue, but so credulous that many have doubts of the expedition, so that there is matter both for hope and fear. What renders credible his success is that Italy is on all sides exposed to rebellions and vicissitudes, and has no good soldiers ; so that there have been miraculous victories and miraculous defeats. It is true that there are the French with good soldiers ; but as they are now deprived of the Swiss, who usually won their victories for them, and as the ground is trembling

---

[1] In this way the Emperor's coronation was then rendered independent of the Pope. " In dieser späten Neuerung sprach Maximilian den Grundsatz aus, dass die in Deutschland fortdauernde Kaisergewalt von der Krönung durch den Papst unabhängig sei" (Gregorovius, "Geschichte der Stadt Rom," vol. viii. p. 48).

[2] On the 19th of January the Ten had written to Vettori that he might promise 40,000 ducats, paying the first instalment of 16,000 whenever Maximilian put his foot on really Italian soil. Trent could not be regarded as Italian territory, since the Emperor was free to go there whenever he liked, as though it were his own land. Vettori was also empowered to promise even 50,000 and pay 20,000 at Trent ; but only in case of extreme urgency and when the Emperor's coming was certain. Vettori was to be judge of the measure of urgency. " Opere " (P. M.), vol. v. p. 272.

beneath their feet, one is doubtful of them. Therefore, in considering all these things, I dwell in uncertainty, inasmuch as for the accomplishment of your mission, the Emperor should attack and be victorious." To this letter, written as usual by Machiavelli and signed by Vettori, the latter added a few lines in his own hand, saying that in his judgment " it would be the most inopportune thing in the world to recall Machiavelli : that it was necessary for him to remain until everything was settled." [1]

Every despatch of this Legation treats of the same theme. The Emperor insists upon receiving the money immediately, and the Florentines raise disputes to gain time and give nothing, and profit by the increasing uncertainty and confusion of the state of affairs. An army of 400 horse and 5,000 foot entered Cadore, which was devoted to the Venetians, and on being joined by Maximilian with a body of 6,000 infantry, invaded and ravaged about forty miles of Venetian territory. Then suddenly the Emperor found his purse empty and hurried to Innsbrück to raise money on his own jewels. The two Florentine orators followed him thither and learnt that as he had not paid his Swiss soldiery, the Cantons had allowed France to hire infantry, and that this power had already 5,000, and the Venetians 3,000 Swiss in Italy. Meanwhile Bartolommeo d'Alviano surrounded the troops left in Cadore, and after slaughtering a thousand of them, captured the remainder by seizing the fortress of Cadore. He then continued his march, the enemy retreating before him, captured Pordenone, which he held in fief, Goritzia, Trieste, and Fiume. The Germans hazarded an attack between Trent and the Lake of Garda, but although partially successful, it led to no results. The two hostile armies remained fronting each other in the valley of the Adige ; but before long the 2,000 Grisons men, receiving little pay from the Emperor, deserted the camp. Their example was quickly followed by others, and on reaching Trent they all dispersed. Maximilian had never been able to obtain from the Empire more than 4,000 foot soldiers at a time, and always for six months only ; so that when one set joined him the others went away ; and to collect a

---

[1] "Opere," vol. vii., letter of the 8th of February, pp. 186, 187. The words written in Vettori's hand were given very incorrectly in several editions ; but in the " Opere " (P. M.) they were given in accordance with the original. For instance, where the old editions say : " Machiavello is in want of much money, for my part there shall be no lack even for him," it should stand thus : " As long as I have money for myself, neither shall Machiavello be in want of any " (" Opere " (P. M.), vol. v. p. 288).

larger army would have required funds which he could not procure
He called a Diet at Ulm to demand fresh subsidies, and hastened to
Germany ; but suddenly vanished from sight and went into hiding
at Cologne, where he received intelligence that the Diet had been
prorogued without coming to any decision.[1]

Machiavelli's letter of the 22nd of March, 1508, from Innsbrück,
after giving some of this news to the Ten, concluded thus : "You
tell me that I may pay the sum offered, if I can believe, at fifteen
soldi the *lira*,[2] that the Emperor will persist. But I believe at
twenty-two *soldi* the *lira* that he will persist ; I cannot, however,
foresee whether he will conquer or if he will be able to go on ;
since up to the present, one of his two armies of six or seven
thousand men each has been beaten, and the other has accomplished nothing. On the other hand, Germany is very powerful,
and may, if she choose, gain the victory. But will she choose ? "
And Vettori added, that not being very well, he had decided to
send Machiavelli to the Diet and as envoy to the Emperor. This
proposal was immediately accepted by the Ten ;[3] but could not
be carried into effect, because persons about Maximilian, and in
his confidence, sent them word that it would be better neither to
go nor to send any one.[4] Accordingly the two orators remained
where they were, to carry on the usual shilly-shally business, of
which they were heartily tired. "Your Excellencies," they wrote
on the 30th of May, "have spun so fine a thread that it is impossible to weave it. If you do not catch the Emperor in his
extremity, he will claim more than you offer ; yet if you catch him
in this extremity, one cannot, as you wish, foretell his coming at
fifteen *soldi* the *lira*. You must come to a decision, divine the
less dangerous course, and entering upon it, settle your minds in
God's name ; for by trying to measure great matters like these
with compasses, men are led into error." [5]

Nevertheless, events showed that the thread had not been spun

---

[1] Leo, "Storia d'Italia," bk. xi. ch. ii., § 5.

[2] We have elsewhere explained that these words signify : *with fifteen chances to
twenty*, there being twenty *soldi* in the Florentine *lira*.

[3] "Opere" (P. M.), vol. v. p. 317, in the letter of the Ten to Vettori, 9th
April, 1508.

[4] Letter of the 29th March, misdated 28th March in the "Opere" (P. M.).
Both the original letter and official duplicate are to be found in the Florence
Archives, "Dieci di Balìa carteggio, responsive," file 90, sheets 423 and 429, with
the deciphered copy in Buonaccorsi's hand, sheet 434, always with the date 29th
March.   [5] Letter of the 30th May.

so badly as the orators thought. On the 8th of June, they sent word that a truce had been concluded between Maximilian and Venice for a term of three years (6th of June, 1508). The Pope, England, Hungary, and the States of the Empire were parties to it on the one side ; on the other, the Italian States, Spain, and France. This latter power, however, not having been consulted or advised on the matter, showed great discontent, and afterwards made it a pretext for her iniquitous conduct to Venice, in being induced by the Pope to join the League of Cambray, which aimed at the destroyal of the Republic. But meanwhile, in consequence of all these changes, the Emperor received nothing more from the Florentines, who thus obtained their intent. Vettori asked for his recall, urging the inutility of remaining any longer at his post ; while Machiavelli, who felt threatenings of an internal malady, at once took his departure. He had left Trent on the 10th of June, and on the 14th he was already at Bologna, whence he indited the last news respecting the truce gleaned by him on the road.[1]

He had been absent from Florence 183 days. He had left it the 17th of December, 1507, was at Geneva on the 25th, and started thence the following day for Constance, at that time a week's journey, during which, although always on the move, he was able to see almost the whole of Switzerland, and make the best of his opportunities for observation and inquiry. On the 17th of January, 1508, he wrote from Botzen, and up to the 8th of June, when he left Trent on his return towards Florence, divided his time between that city, Botzen and Innsbrück.[2] He there

---

[1] Letter of 14th of June. At the end he relates how a certain Serentano, about the Emperor's person, had told Vettori that there was room to include the Florentines in the truce, and that if they wished, the Emperor would name them as his adherents. They must, however, decide quickly. At this point there is a passage in the original letter which has been omitted from every edition, including that of Passerini and Milanesi. It begins after the words, " and the French began to send their troops there," and runs as follows : " Francesco believes that this fellow (Serentano) has put this thing on foot, thinking to better his own interests by it ; and believes that it could be managed by giving a thousand ducats to be divided between him and another. And therefore he prays your Excellencies to advise us quickly on the matter. Francesco will depart from Trent to-morrow, to go to the Court. God be with him." Florence Archives, " Dieci di Balìa, carteggio, responsive," file 91, at sheet 342.

[2] From the documents in the Florence Archives, published by Passerini, " Opere " (P. M.), vol. i. pp. 69, 70, it appears that Machiavelli's election was decreed by the Ten, on the 17th of December, 1507, *cum salario alias declarando.* He started the same day, and returned the 16th of June, 1508. For current expenses he received 110 broad gold florins, of which 80 florins and 10 soldi were,

witnessed the continual going and coming of Germans of every grade and condition : soldiers, generals, princes, prelates, diplomats ; and thus found an opportunity for studying that people, and bequeathing us a brief description of them. The Florentine orators were not, as the Venetians, required to draw up, at the close of their embassy, a general report on the state of the country to which they had been sent. But occasionally they found space in their despatches for very shrewd notes and considerations. Indeed, it was in work of this kind, that men like Guicciardini and Machiavelli took the first rank ; and they also, either for their own pleasure or for the advantage of the magistrates, sometimes wrote full reports without being obliged to do so.

We have an " Istruzione " (or paper of instruction) written by Machiavelli in 1522, long after he was out of office, for his friend Raffaelo Girolami, who was accredited ambassador to the Emperor in Spain. In this, while giving advice on the best mode of conducting an embassy, he clearly indicates the method pursued by himself. "You must," he wrote, "carefully observe everything : the character of the prince and of those around him, of the nobility and of the people, and then furnish full details." He proceeds to offer rules as to what should be more particularly noticed in Spain, and tells him that an ambassador should gain a reputation as a man of honour, and not think one thing and say another. "I have known many who, in order to be deemed sagacious and wily men, have in such wise forfeited the prince's confidence, that it has afterwards been impossible for them to carry on negotiations with him." He also adds several suggestions on the smaller tricks of the trade. On this head he says, that when it is a question of drawing general inferences and trying to divine men's intentions or the more secret current of affairs, it is very odious to express your own opinion in your own name, therefore better, if only to give greater weight to your words, to put them in the mouth of well-known personages, saying, for instance : "Considering all that has been written ; sagacious persons here present, deem that such and such results must follow."[1]   In fact, we continually meet with this expression in his

as seen by his accounts, spent upon the journey to Innsbrück.   During his absence, his salary consisted of 10 small lire net per diem, including his usual salary of 2 lire, 4 soldi, 11 denari per diem.   Thus he received a daily addition of 7 lire, 15 soldi and 1 denaro ; and thus was paid 1419 lire for his 183 days' absence, besides his ordinary stipend.

[1] " Istruzione fatta per Niccolò Machiavelli a Raffaello Girolami," " Opere,"

reports, and are now able to appreciate its full value. But minute and practical as were the counsels given to Girolami, Machiavelli himself did even more and better than he advised. Especially so on this mission to the Emperor, when having no affairs of much gravity to occupy his time or attention, he devoted himself chiefly, and by his own desire, to an attentive and conscientious study of the country in which he was detained.

We have already seen how carefully he observed and described the general condition of Switzerland even when travelling in great haste. And now being again in Switzerland he began immediately, on the 27th of June, the next day after his arrival, to write his Report on German affairs (" Rapporto di cose della Magna "), in which he gave a very faithful portrait of the Emperor, and a general sketch of the country. To this sketch he subsequently attempted to give a more literary form, under the title of Portraits of German things (" Ritratti di cose dell' Alemagna "). It would appear that after the battle of Ravenna, here recorded, he had the

---

vol. iv. pp. 177–182. This letter is dated 23rd of October, but no year indicated. However, Ferdinand of Aragon died in January, 1516, and was succeeded by Charles, nephew of the Emperor Maximilian. The latter died on the 12th of January, 1519; in the same year Charles went to Germany as his successor in the Empire, and in 1522 returned to Spain, whither Girolami was sent to him. Herr H. Heidenheimer, in a valuable study (" Machiavelli's erste Römische Legation, Dissertation zur Erlangung der Doctorwürde," &c., Darmstadt, 1878), also mentions (at p. 59 and fol.) this " Istruzione," and giving it, as it seems to us, an undue importance, not only examines it diligently, but almost as though it were a really scientific treatise. He seeks in it a mathematic precision of language, finds in some words a hidden signification they do not possess, and meets in this fashion difficulties that have no existence. Machiavelli says : " Every one who is *good* can faithfully execute a commission ; the difficulty lies in executing it *sufficiently*." So at p. 60 Herr Heidenheimer disputes on the true meaning in this passage of the words *good* and *sufficiently*, whereas it is very clear that the author means to say that in order to be faithful it is enough to be good ; but that to succeed *sufficiently*, or with requisite ability, something more is needed, namely, aptitude, prudence and sagacity. When Machiavelli says : " That to put your opinion in your own mouth would be odious," Herr Heidenheimer examines the signification of the word *odious*, the cause of this *odium*. " Worin dieses *odium* aber bestehe, wird nicht gesagt. Jedenfalls aber ist auf den ausserordentlich starken Ausdruck *odioso* sehr zu achten " (p. 64). But even here there can be no doubt of the meaning of the words quoted, which merely signify, that to express judgments in your own name, regarding the countries and personages to whom the ambassador is accredited, and regarding probable events, may generate odium, that is may offend some one's pride, may appear presumptuous, &c. For this reason those who are practised in the business are accustomed to write in similar cases : "Sagacious persons here deem that," &c. But notwithstanding some too finely drawn subleties, Herr Heidenheimer's work shows admirable industry and scholarship.

intention of composing a longer and more important work upon Germany ; but soon afterwards threw it aside, without adding any fresh matter to the fragment that remains to us. Neither is his Discourse upon German things and the Emperor (" Discorso sopra le cose d' Alemagna e sopra l'imperatore ") of any importance. It dates from 1509, when Giovanni Soderini and Piero Guicciardini were accredited to the Emperor, and only consists of two pages, in which he merely refers to what he had already said in his Report. Accordingly the latter, substantially a brief relation in the Venetian fashion addressed to the magistrates of the Republic, is the only original and important work written by him on the subject, with the exception of a few small additions to be found in the fragment of the " Ritratti." [1]

The Report has been variously judged by German writers. Gervinus affirms that both this and another similar composition, of a little later date, upon France, prove the acuteness with which Machiavelli " could probe national characteristics, and the profundity with which he judged the political conditions and internal state of foreign countries, and the nature of nations and of governments. His statistical notices upon France are excellent ; perhaps nothing better has ever been said regarding the Emperor Maximilian and the German government." [2] This opinion has been frequently expressed in Germany, down to the present time.[3] One writer, however, pronounces a very different verdict, *i.e.*, Professor Mundt, author of a work upon Machiavelli, far more recent but also far inferior to that of Gervinus. In his opinion, Machiavelli's estimate of Germany and the Germans is a phantasy partly inspired by the " Germania " of Tacitus, but without any

---

[1] See the three compositions upon Germany in the " Opere," vol. iv. p. 153 and fol.

[2] Gervinus, " Historische Schriften," p. 97 : " Seine *Ritratti* von Frankreich und Deutschland beweisen wie scharf er in die Eigenthümlichkeiten der Völker einzugehen verstand, wie eindringend er die politische Lage, den innern zustand fremder Länder, die Natur der Nationen und der Regierungen beurtheilte. Seine statistischen Notizen über Frankreich sind ganz vortrefflich und über den Charakter des Kaisers Maximilian und des deutschen Regiments ist vielleicht nichts besseres noch gesagt worden, als was er in seinen Berichten und gelegentlich sonst vorbringt."

[3] " Wie dürfen es heute beklagen, dass einer Ausländer schon in kurzer Frist dazu gelangte den zustand des Reiches vor vierthalbhundert Jahren so zutreffend zu erkennen, ohne dass die Deutschen etlichen Nutzen daraus gezogen haben " (" Der Patriotismus Machiavelli's," a paper by Herr Karl Knies in the " Preussische Jahrbücher of Berlin, June, 1871 ").

connection with things as they really were during the early years
of the sixteenth century.[1] The financial conditions described by
him, the purity of manners, the liberty and equality for which he
demands our admiration, are nothing, according to Mundt, but an
idyl spun by Machiavelli's own fancy ; since it is impossible to
discover whence he derived the portrait that he offers us.[2] It is
enough, says Mundt, to read the works of Luther, and the writings
of his contemporary Fischart, to be convinced that virtuous
German simplicity was only a dream at the commencement of the
Reformation.

We have already noted, and shall often have occasion to repeat,
that as regards statistics and minute exactitude in the definition
of special facts, Machiavelli is often surpassed by the Venetian
Ambassadors, who sometimes also surpass him even in scrutinizing
the characters of personages with whom they were in contact, and
divining their most secret intentions. But he is, however, unrivalled in defining the tendency and political value of peoples
and princes, the general action that the latters' personal qualities
exercise upon contemporary events, the essential nature of institutions and the effects produced by them. But, when it is necessary
to divine what course the King of France or the Emperor will
probably pursue from one day to the other ; what passions or
desires will move them at a given moment ; then the Florentine
Secretary is inferior to the Venetians and even to some of his
fellow citizens—to Guicciardini, for instance. This was probably
the reason why he was outstripped by many in the race, and
never succeeded in attaining to the office of Ambassador. But
whenever it was needful to define the elements of the political
force of France or of Germany, of the King or of the Emperor,
then his intellectual might asserted itself clearly, and he soared
far above other men.

[1] " Dabei scheinen die Erinnerungen an Tacitus und dessen frische naturglück-
liche Urgermanen zuweilen die Phantasie des Machiavelli unwillkürlich bestimmt
und verwirrt zu haben. Jedenfalls sind ihm darauf unabweisliche Einflüsse ange-
flogen, die ihm zu einer so wunderbaren, schon mit der damaligen Wirklichkeit
durchaus nicht mehr harmonirenden, sondern zu einer politischen Fata Morgana
verflüchtigenden Malerei verfuhren konnten " (Theodor Mundt, " Niccolò Machiavelli und das System der modernen Politik." Berlin, Otto Janke, 1861, p. 218).

[2] " Man weiss in der That kaum, wodurch Machiavelli darauf geführt werden
konnte, die Deutschen seiner Zeit auch in ihren Lebenssitten in einem so fabel-
haften, der Wirklichkeit nirgend entsprechenden Lichte zu sehen. Ein Original
zu seinen Schilderungen, konnte er selbst nicht geshen, noch aus irgend einer
anderen Mittheilung übernommen haben, &c." (Ibid., p. 220).

In Italy, observation of political and social facts is certainly of very ancient date ; for we find as many examples of it among the Chroniclers of the fourteenth century, as among the men of learning and ambassadors of the fifteenth century, who have bequeathed to us some admirable photographs of the countries they visited and of the political personages with whom they were thrown. Machiavelli, however, was the first to discern the cohesion of social facts in a marvellously organic unity. For although Guicciardini, in his youth, collected many precious data upon Spain, and transcribed them with wonderful lucidity and precision, yet when he tried to amalgamate them in order to pronounce a comprehensive judgment on the character and political strength of the country and its government, his power failed him to a certain extent, as we shall have occasion to show later on. So it may be said that the immense material of observation, accumulated by Italy during many centuries, was first co-ordinated in Machiavelli's mind, thus laying the foundation of his future science of politics. Forecasts of this were already visible in his Report upon Germany, and in the similar Report he shortly after wrote upon France. In both, and especially in the former work, we also detect another quality, seldom ascribed to him, but without which many of his writings would be inexplicable. He was a follower of certain ideals, which so completely possessed his imagination that he sometimes beheld them where they did not exist. This gave a kind of personal colouring to the facts he narrated.[1]

Readers acquainted with the descriptions of Germany by Bracciolini and Piccolomini, who—particularly the second—had lived long in the country and minutely depicted it, with unceasing laments over its ignorance, roughness, and barbarism ; or those who have read the Travels in Germany[2] by the same Francesco Vettori who had been with Machiavelli in Tirol, and which contains little else than a collection of indecent stories, will find themselves in a new world on perusing the brief but eloquent pages in which Machiavelli records his hearty admiration for the same country. It is impossible not to be struck by the acumen with

---

[1] As we have previously remarked, Burckhardt was one of the first to notice this point in his work, "Die Cultur der Renaissance in Italien," dritte Auflage, Leipzig, 1877–78, two vols. *Apropos* to Machiavelli he observes : "Seine Gefahr liegt nie in falscher Genialitat, auch nicht im falschen Ausspinnen von Begriffen, sondern in einer starken Phantasie, die er offenbar mit Mühe bändigt, vol. i. p. 82.

[2] " Viaggio in Alemagna," published in Paris and Florence, Molini, 1837.

which, while extolling the simplicity of life and the military training of Germany, he recognizes the real strength of that nation even in the midst of the prevailing anarchy and political impotence, and demonstrates the weakness of Maximilian despite that monarch's good qualities, military valour, great popularity, and the vastness of his empire. And all this confirms the judgment pronounced by Gervinus.

We must, however, repeat that Machiavelli only passed through Switzerland rapidly, and had not gone beyond Innsbrück during his stay in Tirol. It is true that he had seen many Germans there, and conversed with some who spoke Latin and Italian, but he had not visited their country, and knew nothing of it from personal experience. And although knowing how to distinguish Switzerland from Germany, he seems often to consider them rather as portions of the same country than as two different regions, peoples, and nations. We have noted that, as Commissioner with Albizzi to the camp before Pisa, he almost always spoke of the Swiss as Germans. And in the report we are now examining, it is evident that when he speaks of Germany he not only includes Switzerland and Tirol, but also, these being the only two German-speaking countries he has visited, attributes to all the manners and modes of life he had observed there. His enthusiasm was roused by the spectacle of those proud, sober, warlike populations ; in the " free freedom " (" libera libertà ") of the Swiss Republics he recognized his ideal of an armed nation, and consequently held them up as examples to be imitated by Italy. The continual arrival of German troops, whose departure was the signal for the coming of others ; the information he received from them of the many republics flourishing in their land ; their martial aspect, and their military prestige, so strongly impressed his imagination, that in Germany he beheld a sober, liberty-loving country, entirely devoted to arms. Thus, then, he described it ; and more than once attributed to it the customs of Swiss and Tirolese, with whom it had certainly some points of resemblance and relationship. And this may serve to explain the inexactitudes noted by Mundt, who failed, however, to trace them to their real causes, and therefore arrived at no clear conception of Machiavelli's work.[1]

[1] Herr H. Heidenheimer, in his before-mentioned pamphlet, pp. 70–74, excuses Machiavelli for not having remarked the agitation of Germany, and the real state of the multitude, on the score that he had been little or not at all in the country,

"There can be no doubt," says the Secretary, "of the power of Germany, with her abundance of men, money, and arms. The Germans spend little on administration, and nothing on soldiers, for they train their own subjects to arms.[1] On festival days, instead of playing games, their youth seek diversion in learning the use of the petronel, the pike, and of other weapons. They are frugal in all things, for they affect no luxury either in their buildings or their attire, and have but few chattels in their dwellings. It suffices them to have abundance of bread and meat, and to have stoves to protect them from the cold; and he who owns no other possessions, does without them and desires them not. Therefore their country exists on its own produce, without needing to buy from others; they sell things fashioned by their hands, which are scattered over nearly the whole of Italy, and their gains are all the greater because earned by labour with very little capital. Thus they enjoy their rough life and liberty, and for this cause will not go to war, excepting for great recompense; nor would even that suffice, but for the decrees of their communities." Here we seem to be listening to a reminiscence of Tacitus in his "Germania." There is, as it were, a tone of pain, betraying a soul wounded by the unexpressed comparison that Machiavelli is instituting between Italy and the country he describes. It is as though he cried impetuously to the Ten: Behold how you should order the Republic if you truly desire its freedom and strength! The splendour of Italian arts, letters and wealth, that had blinded the judgment of so many of our writers, who therefore despised foreigners, never dazzled the eyes of Machiavelli. His keen glance pierced straight to the primary source of things; and in the corruption of his country he discerned the inevitable cause of her future woes.

But as he goes on he comes nearer to reality, and describes it

had no knowledge of the German tongue, and was acquainted with the grandees and the Courts but not with the people of Germany. This is true, but the omission remains the same.

[1] At p. 15 of Quirini's "Relazione," from which we have before quoted, the author, with a view to practical issues, discusses German men-at-arms, and compares them with the Italian, examining in what respects they are superior, in what inferior; concluding with a remark, which, as the official utterance of a Venetian ambassador, proves that Italians had already begun to lose their self-confidence. "All Germans like these are naturally more ferocious than our men, and have less fear of death than the Italians; yet they are neither so prudent, nor so disciplined as the latter, neither are they so skilful."

with greater fidelity. " All Germany is divided between communes and princes, who are the enemies of one another and all enemies of the Emperor, to whom they will not give too much power, lest he should subjugate their land as the kings have done in France. And this is understood by all ; but few understand for what reason the free cities of Switzerland show so much hostility, not only to the princes and Emperor, but likewise to the communes of Germany, with whom they share both the love of liberty and the need of self-defence against princes. The true reason is that the Swiss are enemies, not merely of the Emperor and princes, but also of the nobility of Germany ; since in their own country there is none, neither any distinction among men, saving of those acting as magistrates, and all enjoy a free freedom. Thus it comes about that the German nobles do their utmost to keep their communes divided from the Swiss. On the other hand, the Emperor, being opposed by the princes, aids the communes, who are Germany's backbone, and thus they (the nobles) find themselves weakened, being attacked on both sides, and their States divided among many heirs. And added to this are the wars of the princes and communes among themselves, against one another, and of both against the Emperor ; so that it is easy to comprehend why, notwithstanding the great strength of the country, it is in fact much enfeebled." [1]

All these reflections are to be found almost identically worded, both in the " Ritratti," [2] which contain little else, and in the second

---

[1] Even in his " Discorsi " (book i. chap. lv.), Machiavelli greatly extolled Germany, recording a law existing in some of those republics, according to which the citizens were put upon their honour to declare the amount of their property and pay a proportionate tax without any official investigation ; and this was carried out without any ill results, so great, in his opinion, was the good faith of those citizens. Mundt makes some sarcastic remarks on this head. But we may quote the words of an old and trustworthy German writer on the subject : " Egregia vero laus ab homini extero, et eo qui, institutorum et morum civilium diligens esset atque elegans spectator. Sæpius autem ille res Germanorum præ patriis laudare solitus erat. Quod valde probat tributi a civibus accipiendi ex fide inventum, ad Norimbergensium præclarum civitatem, imprimis, opinor, pertinet : qui illum conferendi in publicum modum appellant *die Losung,* et præcipuæ dignitatis magistratum, quæstores ad id constitutos, *die Losunger.* Aliqua facultatum pars iureiurando promissa, pro censu cuiusque pecunia æstimato, ærario inseritur, sed clanculum : ne scilicet modus divitiarum aut inopiæ cuiusque, utrumque autem sedulo occultare solent cives, facile reliquis pateat. . . . Nobile millum adeo et memoratu dignum morem a Vuagenscilio, in elegante copiosaque eius de hoc urbe commentatione, nusquam descriptum extare, dolendum est" (Joh. Frid. Christii, " De Nicolas Machiavelli, libri tres." Lipsiac et Halae Magdeb. 1731, p. 108).

[2] " Opere," vol. iv. pp. 153-160.

part of the " Rapporto." [1]   The latter, however, being, as we have
seen, almost an official report, speaks first of the state of affairs
and the character of the Emperor ; saying of him, that notwithstanding his apparent greatness and power, he was practically very
weak, because Germany, being so divided and so jealous, never
granted him necessary supplies.   " They say that his States return
him a net revenue of 600,000 florins, and that his imperial office
brings him 100,000. This should suffice for the pay of many men ;
but, owing to his great liberality, he is always without soldiers and
without gold ; nor can one see what becomes of his money.   Prè
Luca (the priest Luca dei Renaldi), who is always about his person,
told me that the Emperor never took advice of any one, yet is
advised by all ; that he wishes to do everything himself, and does
nothing in his own way, because whenever, in spite of the
mysterious secrecy assumed by him, the course of events unveils
his designs, he is always guided by those about him.   His liberality and lavishness while obtaining him the praises of many,
are his ruin, since all take advantage of him, all deceive him.
And one who is about him told me that, although when once
made aware of it he does not allow himself to be deceived anew ;
yet in so great variety of men and circumstances, it might happen
to him to be deceived every day of his life, even if he always discovered the fact.   But for these defects he would be an excellent
prince, for he is virtuous, just, and likewise a perfect captain.[2]

" His coming into Italy gives alarm to all men ; for it is known
that his needs would grow with victory unless his nature were
entirely changed.   And if the trees of Italy bore ducats for him
instead of leaves, they would still fail to meet his requirements.
Note, also, that from his frequent prodigality proceed his frequent
needs, from his needs his frequent demands, and from these the
frequent Diets ; just as his feeble resolves, and their feebler execution, are the fruit of his scanty judgment.   However, had he come,
you could not have paid him by means of Diets." [3]

The Portraits of French things [4] (" Ritratti delle cose della
Francia ") are chiefly detached thoughts written after his last

---

[1] " Opere," vol. iv. pp. 168–173.

[2] The portrait of the Emperor, drawn by the Venetian ambassador Quirini, at
pages 26, 27 of his " Relation," answers precisely to this by Machiavelli, and concludes by saying " that he always leaps from one decision to another, and thinks
of so many improvements to each, that he misses both the time and opportunity
for accomplishing anything."

[3] " Rapporto," &c.   " Opere," vol. iv. pp. 165–168.   [4] Ibid., p. 133 and fol.

mission to France in 1510. Nevertheless, he remembers to note in them the increasing power of France, in consequence of her great centralization, resulting from the union and submission to the crown of the different provinces and the Barons. Thence a political strength within, a military strength without the kingdom, superior to the social and real power of the country ; precisely the reverse of what he had observed in Germany. " All the nobility are devoted to military life, hence the French men-at-arms are of the best in Europe. The foot-soldiers, on the other hand, are bad, being composed of rabble and labouring folk subject to the Barons, and so oppressed in every act of life that they are vile. Exception, however, must be made of the Gascons, who being near to Spain, have something of the Spaniard, and are a trifle better than the others, although in recent times they have proved themselves rather thievish than valiant.[1] Yet they behave well in the defence and attack of fortresses, although badly in the open field.[2] In this, too, they are the reverse of the Germans and Swiss, who are unrivalled in the field, but worth nothing in attack or defence of fortified places. For these reasons the kings of France, putting no faith in their own infantry, hire Swiss and *landsknechts*. In point of fact, the ferocity of these men is greater than their bravery and skill, and if the enemy withstands their first onslaught, they become so timid as to seem like women ; the which indeed was noted by Cæsar, who said of them, that at first they were more than men, at last less than women. And therefore, he who would overcome them must play with them and ward off their first attacks. They cannot endure prolonged hardship ; therefore, in such case, it is easy to rout them when they have been thrown into disorder, as we have seen proved on the Garigliano during the last war with the Spaniards.

" The country is very rich in agricultural produce, but poor in money, everything going into the hands of the nobles and the bishops ; these latter absorb two-thirds of the riches of the

[1] " Opere," vol. iv. p. 153 and fol. The Gascons, and more particularly the Basques, who were often confused with them, formed a light infantry that had high repute in France.

[2] Even during the last Franco-Prussian war, the Germans accused the French of behaving indifferently in the open field, and of always preferring to fight behind cover of some sort. "Always to fight behind cover, and always to be covered by their fortresses, such are their tactics," was what we read in the German journals of the period, although the wars of Napoleon had caused a different opinion to be formed.

kingdom, and have exceeding political power, being very numerous in the Councils of the throne. The people of France are humble and most obedient, and hold their King in great veneration. They live at very slight expense, through the great abundance of animal food, and every one also has a little land.[1] They dress coarsely, and in garments of small price ; they do not wear silk of any kind, neither they nor their womenkind, for they would be marked by the nobles." [2] And at another page of these "Ritratti," always written in detached paragraphs, Machiavelli says : " The French nature is greedy of others' goods, and then prodigal of its own and others' property. And therefore, the Frenchman would steal with his very breath in order to devour and waste and enjoy it with him from whom he has stolen : a nature contrary to that of Spaniards, who never let you see any trace of what they have robbed from you." [3]

Evidently Machiavelli had no sympathy either for the French or for France, with whom he was much better acquainted than with Germany ; but the Republic had no reason to be pleased with the French. And we find another proof of this antipathy, even in the few and brief detached reflections in his works entitled : " Of the nature of the French" [4] (" Della Natura dei Francesi "). " They are very humble in bad fortune, insolent in good. They are rather cavillers than men of prudence. They weave well their bad and roughly laid warp. They are vain and frivolous. No Italians get on well at Court, save those who have nothing more to lose, and fish in troubled waters."

In the " Ritratti " he also passes in rapid review the various States bordering on France, in order to show that she has no great danger to fear from any one. He alludes to the imposts, to the revenues of the country, speaks of the forms of government, of the army, the universities, of the administration, and above all of the royal prerogative and power, which were almost unbounded. They

---

[1] "Opere," vol. iv. p. 142. This shows that even in those days small holdings were general in France.

[2] "Opere," vol. iv. p. 142.

[3] Ibid., vol. iv. p. 139. Guicciardini, in his "Relazione sulla Spagna," 1512–1513 (" Opere Inedite"), vol. vi. p. 277, says of the Spaniards : " Being astute, they are good thieves ; and therefore it is said that the Frenchman is a better lord than the Spaniard, for both despoil their subjects ; but the Frenchman spends (his money) directly, the Spaniard accumulates it ; and also the Spaniard, being keener witted, must know better how to thieve."

[4] They consist of little more than a single page. " Opere," vol. iv. pp. 151, 152.

are hasty, brief, detached remarks, resembling notes jotted down on a journey.

But the principal point demanding our attention in this, as well as in the discourse upon Germany, is the author's continual, almost involuntary and irresistible tendency to accumulate special particulars regarding a few general facts, such as the nature of the country, the character of the people, the tendency of the government. Thus, these become the centre from which his observations diverge, and to which they return, the key explaining the social and political conditions under his notice. In France he pauses to contemplate the association of all men and all national activities under the unity of one supreme command, and sees that this leads to an augmentation of political and military strength. It does not, however, escape him, that all this may be dangerous in the long run, inasmuch as individual liberty is sacrificed by it, and the mass of the people oppressed. Many centuries have gone by, many different and famous events, many revolutions, yet the justice of his verdict is still unassailed. To this day France suffers from her centralization, which, as Tocqueville [1] showed us, and as we find in these notes of Machiavelli, is of far older date than is generally believed. To this day, also, has endured the excessive power of the clergy that he observed in his time. Even the great prevalence of small landholdings, upon which so much has been written, declared by so many to be the direct outcome of the Revolution and entirely modern, is of far older origin, and, as we have seen, did not escape the Secretary's eye. In fact, nothing ever escaped him that was of any political, real, or general importance.

In describing Germany he started instead from the point of view of the great variety of customs and interests, of local passions and franchises. Even if these generated confusion and deprived the government of unity of action, they did not sap the strength of the country, which even in the midst of disorder was nourished by individual independence and military training. For centuries this has remained the dominant fact and characteristic in the history of Germany, who to this day maintains the federal form, and notwithstanding her many triumphs is exposed to internal struggle by the diversity of her constituent elements. That which totally escaped Machiavelli, that of which he has no word to say, was the vast religious agitation then in course of preparation.

[1] In his excellent work, "La Révolution et l'Ancien Régime."

This may be explained, not only by his never having sojourned in the interior of Germany proper, and by his ignorance of the language, but still more by his profound indifference to religious questions, and very scanty knowledge of them. This defect, however, was common in his time to the majority of Italians.

CHAPTER XI.

(1508–1509.)

N the outbreak of the Genoese revolution in
1507, Louis XII. had promised the Florentine
ambassador, Francesco Pandolfini, that, in the
event of having to bring an army into Italy to
reduce that city, he would also halt in Tuscany
to accomplish the subjection of Pisa to the
Florentines. And this he asserted and caused
to be asserted with so much persistence, that it was even agreed
what sum should be given to him when all was completed. But
after subduing Genoa, he went back to France, as usual failing to
keep any of his promises to the Florentines.[1] Therefore, as soon
as the latter were free from fear of Maximilian, who had withdrawn
after making truce with the Venetians, they felt that they had a
right and were in a position to attend to their own affairs, counting
only upon their own resources. They decided to make a beginning
by ravaging the Pisan territory, a measure neglected by them
during the previous year. The antagonists of the Gonfalonier
immediately raised a lively opposition, and were joined by others,
who began to perceive the cruelty of the thing, and felt pangs of
conscience on seeing the extreme misery to which the Pisan
peasantry were reduced, and particularly the sufferings of the

[1] See the Legation of Francesco Pandolfini in Desjardins, " Négociations diplomatiques," &c., vol. ii. p. 199 and fol.

women, many of whom died of exhaustion.[1] Nevertheless, the project was carried through, for it was now decided to bring the affair to an end, and the fitting moment seemed to have come.

The Pisans were much cowed by the devastations inflicted upon them in June ; and to reduce them still lower, the Florentines engaged Bardella, the Genoese corsair, at 600 florins the month, to blockade the mouth of the Arno with three vessels, and thus prevent any supplies from reaching the besieged city on that side.[2] Machiavelli, who during March and April had been sent about the Florentine territory to enlist infantry, was stationed in the camp from August to November as paymaster to the troops. There he pushed on the operations of the war and ordered the continuation of the work of destruction ; moved about collecting reinforcements and proposing the election of regimental corporals. At his instance, we find that the Nine nominated about four hundred in a very short space of time.[3] The Ten seemed to have entrusted him with the entire conduct of the campaign. In fact they wrote to him on the 18th of August : " Thou art prudent, and being in the secret of everything, it is unnecessary to further explain our wishes to thee."[4] And in October, not only did he repeat the

[1] Guicciardini, " Storia Fiorentina," p. 351.

[2] Buonaccorsi, " Diario," p. 134 and fol. ; Guicciardini, "Storia Fiorentina," pp. 351, 352.

[3] " Opere " (P. M.), vol. v. p. 343, and "Scritti Inediti del Machiavelli," pp. 339–341.

[4] Letter of the 18th August, 1508, " Opere " (P. M.), vol. v. p. 338. With it they sent him 500 ducats. See at the same place the patent dated 16th of August. These Commissions to the camp and through the territory are to be found in the " Opere," vol. vii. Other documents relating to the same subject are to be found in the " Scritti Inediti " and in the " Opere " (P. M.), vol. i. and vol. v. These documents show that in March and April, 1508, Machiavelli employed 34 days in travelling about the territories of the Republic, " to collect foot soldiers, and received 17 broad florins for his expenses." (" Opere " (P. M.), vol. i. p. 69.) Eight hundred broad florins were sent to him on the 18th of August, for payment of the men and for the devastation of Pisan lands. (Ibidem, p. 71.) In October he was sent round to recruit soldiers and lay waste the crops of millet and oats. (Ibidem, p. 71.) In March, 1508–1509, he received 12 broad florins for the expenses of 24 days' travel with three horses, to elect the corporals of the companies. Then further sums were sent to him for the pay of the infantry : at one time 283 broad florins, 6 soldi, and 10 denari ; at another, 285 florins and 5 lire, and so on. In the month of May we find him at Pescia and Pistoia to collect bread and provisions. In June he received a payment of 8 lire the day, for the 89 days he had been travelling hither and thither. (" Opere " (P. M.), vol. i. p. 72.) All this shows the accumulation of business to which he had to attend, and how he was always on the move.

August ravages on the Pisan lands, but even laid waste the lands near Viareggio belonging to Lucca. In this way he compelled the Lucchese to make an agreement for three years, solemnly binding them to give no more help to the Pisans, either in men, money, or provisions.

But when France perceived that in this way the Florentines were bringing the war with Pisa to an end without her help and without any advantage to herself, she hastened to protest. She protested against the devastation carried on without the previous permission of the King ; protested against the treaties of agreement with her enemy the Emperor ; and threatened the instant despatch to Pisa of General G. J. Trivulzio, with three hundred lances, so that the surrender might not take place without her assistance, and she might thus be able to urge fresh and greater pretensions. It was easy for the Florentines to prove that France had not the least right to complain, and that her pretensions were absurd ; but it was not possible to withstand the pertinacious demands of the King, who was determined to have money at any rate. They already knew that Julius II. had finally succeeded in his long meditated design of the League of Cambray, by which, in December, 1508, Pope, Emperor, Spain, and France joined hands for the destruction of Venice. It is true that this event, by distracting general attention and schemes of war from Tuscany, left her freer to do and dare ; but on the other hand, the obligation contracted by France of marching a numerous army into Northern Italy, rendered that power still more greedy of money, more dangerous, and more dangerously near.

For this reason the ambassadors Alessandro Nasi and Giovanni Ridolfi were now at Blois, with instructions to come to terms and pay as little as possible to France and to Spain, who had quickly asserted equal pretensions. The latter power was ready to sell the ancient friendship for the Pisans which, as she now affirmed, she had always preserved ; while the former was disposed to sell to her ever faithful allies, the Florentines, their own undeniable right to provide for their own interests with their own resources. Nevertheless it was necessary to yield. The negotiations proceeded slowly, for disputes arose, not only upon the sum to be given, but also as to the method of payment. And meanwhile it was needful to make donations to Rubertet and the other ministers of France and Spain, who, after graciously accepting them, asked for more, and showed no haste to bring matters to a conclusion.

At last Nasi and Ridolfi wrote, that on the 13th of March, 1509, a treaty had been signed by which the Republic was bound to pay 50,000 ducats in several instalments to the King of France, and as much to the Spanish monarch, to whose ambassador they had also been obliged to promise a fee of 1,500 ducats, on his refusal to be content with one thousand only. Nor was that all. They had been obliged to sign a second treaty with France alone, promising to pay her another 50,000 ducats under pledge of the strictest secrecy, to avoid rousing the jealousy of Spain, who would then have insisted on receiving the same amount.[1] In short, the Republic was to disburse over 150,000 ducats to her friends, to gain their permission to exercise the rights naturally belonging to every State.

Meanwhile, however, Florence had pushed on the war. Machiavelli was still at the camp, and the Ten wrote to him on the 15th of February, authorizing him to give all requisite orders, "inasmuch as we have placed all this charge upon thy shoulders."[2] It was an immense responsibility for a man like himself, untrained in war ; but he accomplished miracles, by attending to everything with feverish energy, and matters progressed very satisfactorily. The Genoese had ordered the withdrawal of the corsair Bardella, and their merchants instantly sailed in with corn ships to carry help to the Pisans up the Arno. On the 18th of February, however, they were repulsed, for some men-at-arms, 800 militia infantry and a few guns had been sent to San Piero in Grado, in time to hold the mouth of the river.[3] A band of equal strength was sent into the valley of the Serchio, to guard the mouth of the Fiume Morto, a canal by which boats passing by Osole or Oseri brought succour to Pisa. Afterwards, the celebrated architect, Antonio San Gallo, came with a band of axemen and sawyers and a quantity of timber, to construct a dam across the Arno to exclude future supplies. Machiavelli ordered the instant construction of a similar work across the Fiume Morto.

In conducting these affairs he corresponded directly with the Ten, without paying much deference to the Commissary-General Niccolò Capponi, who though but ill-pleased, remained quietly at Cascina. Soderini therefore sent a friendly remonstrance to

---

[1] Desjardins, "Négociations," &c., vol. ii. pp. 256–297. See more particularly the letter of the 13th of March, 1509, at p. 293.

[2] "Scritti Inediti," pp. 347, 348.

[2] Buonaccorsi, "Diario," p. 138.

Machiavelli, bidding him to try and save appearances at all events.[1] Accordingly Machiavelli wrote at once to inform the Commissary that he was at the mill of Quosi, "to watch lest any other boat should try to enter, in order to stop it, as they had stopped the first."[2] But after this he went on as usual, for there was no time to think about etiquette. He hastened to Lucca to protest against the help continually sent thence (to Pisa), and obtained a promise that a stricter guard should be kept.[3] By the 7th of March he had completed the barricade across the Fiume Morto, consisting of three rows of iron-bound piles under water, and was staying in the camp at Quosi to superintend the raising of the bed of the river Oseri by means of three small vessels captured from the Pisans, in order to make it fordable for the Florentine troops. And on the 7th of March he wrote to the Ten, "that Jacopo Savelli had twice crossed and recrossed it with eight horses ; and when our troops can cross, and carry fifty fascines with them, why then even the army of Xerxes might ford it." The same letter showed that his hopes ran very high. "The militia companies were excellent, and gave no trouble whatever. He believed that this time the Lucchese would keep their promise not to send succour, and prevent both private individuals from bringing supplies, and the Pisans from coming to fetch them. Otherwise, as he had told them, it was useless for them to make treaties with the Florentines, who could well make one weapon serve for two purposes.[4] His meaning was that the same precautions would have prevented succour from being sent by the Lucchese, or received by the Pisans.

Matters having reached this point, the army being divided, and various operations about to be carried on, it appeared very strange that the weight of all things should still rest on the shoulders of Machiavelli, who was neither a General nor Commissary of War, but merely the trusted confidant of Soderini. Accordingly, the Council of Eighty elected two other Commissaries[5] in the persons

[1] Letter of Andrea della Valle, 19th of February, 1508-9. "Opere" (P. M.), p. 353.

[2] "Opere," vol. vii. p. 240. Letter of the 20th of February.

[3] Ibid. (P. M.), vol. v. pp. 373 and 378.

[4] Letter of the 7th of March, 1508-9. "Opere," vol. vii. p. 240.

[5] Guicciardini, never very well inclined towards Soderini, says that this choice was made so that "things might be conducted with better order and more reputation, since the only public official in the camp was Niccolò Machiavelli, Chancellor to the Ten" ("Storia Fiorentina," p. 381). Yet, as we have seen, Capponi also was there.

of Antonio da Filicaia and Alamanno Salviati, who on the 10th of March came to Cascina to confer with Machiavelli and Capponi in order to settle what steps were required to bring the expedition to a speedy end. They decided to form three camps. One at San Piero in Grado, where Machiavelli and Salviati were to remain with Antonio Colonna to guard the Arno, the nearly finished bridge over the Fiume Morto, and the bastion erected for its defence. A second was to be established at San Jacopo, to prevent the Lucchese from sending help to Pisa by the valley of the Serchio ; and here, Commissary Antonio da Filicaia was to be stationed. The mountain paths, however, by which the Pisans could fetch provisions from Lucca on foot were still open ; therefore a third camp was formed at Mezzana, whence other tracks could be watched, and Capponi was sent there as Commissary. Each of these blockading camps, depriving Pisa of all possibility of help, was to contain one thousand men, two-thirds of whom were of the Florentine militia.[1]

Before all these plans could be carried into effect, Machiavelli received orders by a despatch of the 10th March, to go to Piombino, where a Pisan delegation was coming with a safe conduct, to propose terms of surrender.[2] As it was feared that this was only a pretext of the Pisans to gain time, the Ten commissioned him to come to a clear understanding of their purpose, with instructions to insist upon unconditional surrender, and to instantly withdraw should the envoys be unauthorized to agree to it.[3] The city of Pisa was reduced to positive extremity. By the formation of their three camps, the Florentines had cut off every chance of help from without, either from Lucca or the coast ; and now, after the sums paid to Spain and France, enjoyed full liberty of action. The great war now impending, in consequence of the League of Cambray,

---

[1] Guicciardini, "Storia Fiorentina," ch. xxxiii. pp. 387, 388 ; Buonaccorsi, "Diario," pp. 138, 139.

[2] The embassy was composed of citizens and country folk. Guicciardini tells us, at p. 332 of his "Storia Fiorentina," that they were twenty in number : Ammirato ("Istoria Fiorentina," vol. v. ch. xxviii. p. 497. Florence, Batelli, 1846-49) tells us that a safe conduct was granted to twenty-four persons. In the printed edition Machiavelli is made to say that with their followers "they were a string of 164, or more." "Opere" vol. vii. p. 255 ; and in the "Opere" (P. M.), vol. v. p. 392, we read "a string of 161, or more.". The original MS., however, says : "a string of 16, or more." The stop after the 16, always placed after figures by old writers, had been mistaken for the figure 1.

[3] See letter and commission of the Ten, dated 10th March, 1508-9, "Opere," (P. M.), vol. v. p.384.

kept both the forces and attention of the great potentates, including the Pope, concentrated in Northern Italy, and therefore left the Pisans without hope of assistance even from that quarter. Thus far, it is true, they had maintained a long, heroic, and successful defence, and would certainly have continued it longer, had not serious internal disorders, no longer to be warded off, been added to all their dangers from without.

The obstinate energy of their defence was mainly attributable to this, that, whereas the Florentines had hitherto carried on the war by means of mercenary or auxiliary troops, they had not only armed all their citizens, but even the inhabitants of the outlying territory, and also granted the latter a share in the government. This union, unprecedented among our Republics, had enormously strengthened the defence, and evoked instances of virtue, self-denial and heroism, such as were seldom witnessed in the Italian history of that period. In fact, even Pisa's antagonists were filled with admiration at such examples, and Machiavelli saw in them fresh grounds for hopeful expectations of the national militia that he was now organizing. But the prolonged war had also given birth to other consequences. The peasant class, being always the first to be attacked and daily compelled to greater sacrifice of life and property, necessarily obtained a preponderant share in the government of the city. This, in short, had now become a military government of public defence ; and naturally the chief power fell into the hands of those who showed most vigour in repulsing the enemy. But notwithstanding this, the citizens having more experience of public affairs, and greater political acumen, still continued to be able to direct matters according to their will.

Thus by slow degrees a genuine conflict of interests had arisen, for which it was difficult to find a remedy. The country round was all laid waste and exhausted ; the Florentines showed that they no longer entertained any wish for revenge ; they demanded unconditional surrender, but would treat all with the same humanity, as their own old subjects. There was no reason why these conditions should not be acceptable to the inhabitants of the territory, who knew that, the war once ended, they would be treated as subordinates even by the Pisans, according to the general custom of all Italian Republics. Such conditions, however, were not at all agreeable to the inhabitants of the city, to whom an unconditional surrender implied loss of the independence that was dearer to them than all else in the world. Hence the disaccord of citizens and rustics. The latter asserted that their lands were reduced to such a state that it was no longer possible to prolong the defence, and that they were ready to surrender; the citizens, on the contrary, were still obdurate, and created endless delays for the sake of gaining time. Now they proposed ceding the territory only, then they tried to terrify its inhabitants by asserting that these would bear the chief brunt of the Florentine vengeance. But the latter proved in a thousand ways their intention of showing clemency to all. Besides, the idea of ceding the territory alone was acceptable to no one, for in that case the war against the city would still continue, and the requirements of the siege would involve fresh devastation of the country round.[1]

Hence, the embassy sent from Pisa to Piombino consisted of country folk and citizens, who were not of the same mind, and Machiavelli already knew this and was soon to have fresh proof of it. On the 15th May, he wrote a report of his mission to the Ten. The Pisans, who had arrived in great numbers, had complained that instead of two or three influential citizens, there was no one to meet them but an ordinary Secretary, not even one sent expressly from Florence. In any case they sued for peace, with security of life, property and honour; but they were not authorized to conclude terms. Upon this Machiavelli, being much dissatisfied, turned, after a few words, to the Lord of Piombino, and said " that he could make no answer, because they had said nothing. If they wished a reply, let them say something. Your Excellencies desired obedience, demanded neither their life, their property, nor their honour, and would allow them reasonable liberty. " Then the Pisans brought forward their proposal of yielding the territory and being left shut up within their city walls. " Do you not see," replied Machiavelli, again addressing himself to the Lord of Piombino, " do you not see that they are laughing at you ? If it is not intended to give up Pisa to the rulers of Florence, it is useless to enter into negotiations; and as to the security, if it is not intended to keep faith, there is nothing to be done." And afterwards he told the country folk, "that he regretted their simplicity, for they were playing a game in which, in any case, they must be the losers. If Pisa had to be taken by force, they would lose property, life, and everything. If, on the contrary, the Pisans were victorious, then the citizens would treat them not as equals, but as slaves, and would drive them back to their ploughs."

[1] Guicciardini, " Storia Fiorentina," p. 387 and fol.

At this point, one of the citizens present began to cry out that the terms were not suitable, since they tended to create division among them ; but the country folk instead seemed ready to consent to the terms, and expressed a desire for peace. Machiavelli took no further concern in the matter, and left the next day, although on two occasions, even after he was already mounted, the delegates came back to him to try to renew the discussion.[1]

He was compelled to go instantly to Florence, to obey the imperative summons of the Ten.[2] But we soon find him once more at the camp of Mezzana, whence he wrote to the Ten, on the 16th of April, in reply to their invitation to go to stay at Cascina. After minute details of the condition of the army, stating that the infantry equalled any that could be had in Italy, he concluded by urgently praying them to leave him where he was, otherwise he should not be able to attend either to the infantry or anything else, whereas it did not signify whom they sent to Cascina. He added that he was aware that to stay at Cascina would be much less fatiguing, much less dangerous for him ; " but if I wished to avoid fatigue and danger, I should not have left Florence ; therefore, I beg your Excellencies to permit me to stay among these camps, and labour with these Commissaries on necessary matters ; for here I can be good for something, and there I should be good for nothing, and should die of despair ; therefore I again pray you to fix upon some other man."[3] The Ten replied, giving him leave to stay where he thought his presence most useful,[4] and he went backwards and forwards

---

[1] " Opere " vol. viii. p. 249 and fol. Letter of the 15th March, 1508–9.

[2] The letter of the Ten is dated 5th of April, and bears the inscription C^{ito}_{ito} (or) sia per via. It ordered Machiavelli to be in Florence the same day, with all the men he had with him : " Haste as much as possible, for the case is urgent." This letter is published in the " Opere " (P. M.), among the documents of the " Commission to the camp before Pisa." Machiavelli, however, had already started, nor could he have been at Pisa if the order was to be in Florence the same day. To this letter the editors of the " Opere " (P. M.) add others found among the " Carte del Machiavelli," written from Florence in the name of the Ten, addressed to Machiavelli at the camp, yet signed with his name, without any explanation of how Machiavelli could write letters from Florence to Machiavelli in camp before Pisa. It would seem that, as he still retained the office of Secretary to the Ten, the chancery sometimes continued the custom of placing the secretary's name at the end of official letters, either in full, or only in initials, even during the absence of the bearer of the name. Of course, neither letters nor signature are in Machiavelli's handwriting.

[3] " Opere," vol. vii. p. 258. Letter of the 16th of April, 1509.

[4] Ibid. (P. M.), vol. v. p. 401. Letter of the 17th of April, 1509.

between the three camps, watching how things went on, and always being where his help was needed to see that the soldiers were properly cared for. At one moment he was paying the men, at another sending off provisions, at the next advising and directing the blockade operations, for cutting off supplies from the city.[1] On the 18th of May, he was at Pistoia to hasten the despatch of a delayed supply of bread, and giving stern orders against any repetition of the blunder.[2] And this unrelaxing vigilance at last produced the desired effect, for the Pisans were so hemmed in on all sides that they were driven to agree to surrender.

In fact, on the 20th of May, the three Commissaries wrote to the Ten,[3] announcing the arrival of four Pisans to ask for a safe conduct, in order to send ambassadors to Florence to arrange the capitulation. And on the 24th, the ambassadors, five citizens and four countrymen,[4] appeared in the camp, and travelled so rapidly with Alamanno Salviati and Niccolò Machiavelli, that they reached San Miniato the same evening.[5] On the 31st, Machiavelli had returned to Cascina, and the ambassadors, after arranging in Florence the terms of surrender, which was, in fact, unconditional, although clemency was assured to them, returned to Pisa without delay. There was no time to be lost. On the 2nd of June three hundred starving people had sallied from the miserable city, and flocked to the camp at Mezzana, praying for bread, which was given them. The next day more famished bands poured from every gate of the city, and it was necessary to drive many of them back, or the whole camp would have been thrown into disorder.[6] On the 6th all was arranged for the entry of the Florentines the following day. The three Commissaries came to

---

[1] Letter of the 21st of April, from the camp of San Piero in Grado, "Opere," vol. vii. p. 262.

[2] Letter of the 18th of May, from Pistoia, "Opere," vol. vii. p. 265.

[3] It is in the Florence Archives, and is published in the "Opere," vol. vii. p. 267, and in the "Opere" (P. M.), vol. v. p. 413. It was written from the camp in the valley of the Serchio, by Machiavelli, who added in his own hand the three signatures of the Commissioners.

[4] The letter of the 21st of May, written by Machiavelli and signed by Salviati, mentions that there were to be five countrymen and four citizens ; but the mistake is corrected in the credentials given by the government of Pisa, "Opere" (P. M.), vol. v. p. 415.

[5] Letter of the 24th of May, 1509, from San Miniato, written by Machiavelli and signed by Salviati, "Opere" (P. M.), p. 417.

[6] Letter of the 3rd of June, 1509, "Opere," vol. vii. p. 279. Letter of Antonio da Filicaia, 3rd of June, 1509, "Opere" (P. M.), vol. v. p. 423.

the camp at Mezzana to meet Machiavelli, who had received three
thousand ducats for the soldiers' pay.   An order was also received
leaving to the Secretary the choice of the soldiers who were to
enter the city, and these were to receive in anticipation a third
of their pay, so that they might have no pretext for committing
excesses.[1] They waited a day, in order to enter on the 8th.
Probably, although we have no certainty of it, astrologers were
consulted in fixing the day and hour.   All that we know is that,
among the many letters then received by Machiavelli, we find
one from his friend Lattanzio Tedaldi, earnestly advising him not
to commence the entry into Pisa before half-past twelve, and, if
possible, a few minutes after thirteen o'clock, an hour that had
always been of good omen to the Florentines.[2]

According to the unanimous verdict of contemporary historians,
from that moment everything was carried on with the greatest
humanity and kindness towards the unhappy city that had fought
so well and suffered so cruelly.[3] Not only did the Florentines
abstain from all violence, not only did they carry in large stores
of provisions and distribute them among the starving inhabitants,
but they also restored to the Pisans all the real property they
had previously confiscated, scrupulously calculating to the advantage of the original proprietors even the profits of the last year,
up to the day of the conclusion of peace.   The statement of the
accounts was entrusted to the historian, Jacopo Nardi, who said
that they were drawn up in a manner so favourable to the Pisans
that it was as though the latter had dictated, instead of submitting
to the conditions of the peace.[4] For the Pisans regained their
old privileges, and the re-establishment of their administrative
magistracies ; their former freedom of commerce was restored
to them ; in law suits they were granted right of appeal to the
same judges as the Florentines.   But if all these things did
honour to the conquerors, especially to Soderini and Machiavelli,
who had had the chief share in making and carrying out the
decrees, still they could not avail to satisfy the conquered.

---

[1] " Opere," vol. vii. p. 284 and fol.   " Opere " (P. M.), vol. v. p. 427.

[2] " Carte del Machiavelli," case iv. No. 40.   " Opere " (P. M.), vol. v. p. 429.

[3] Guicciardini, " Storia d'Italia," bk. viii. ch. iii.   " On this occasion, the
good faith of the Florentines was worthy of note ; for, although full of so much
hate, and exasperated by many injuries, they were no less faithful in the fulfilment
of their promises, than easy and clement in making them."

[4] Nardi, " Storia di Firenze," vol. i. pp. 409, 410.

Liberty, independence, and political rights were for ever lost !
No Pisan could again hope to share in deciding. the fate of his
city, and therefore the principal families emigrated to Palermo,
Lucca, Sardinia, and other parts. Many took service in the
French army, then fighting against Venice in Lombardy, and
afterwards sought in the South of France a home reminding
them of their soft Tuscan clime.[1]   Among these exiles were the
Sismondi, ancestors of the illustrious historian of the Italian
Republics.

In these days, Nardi tells us, many thought of Antonio Giacomini, the first to place the war with Pisa on the right road
towards a successful ending, and who had then, from others'
envy, been left on one side ; so that now, in his old age, blind
and infirm, he was pining in neglect. By a strange caprice of
fortune, the victory had been achieved by Machiavelli, who was
no soldier.   But his conscience could not reproach him, for he
had never been one of those who despised Giacomini ; on the
contrary, he had always felt a sincere admiration for him, and
lost no opportunity of declaring it.   For it was the example and
excellent military success of that General that had encouraged
him to organize the militia, to whose efforts the surrender of Pisa
was attributed.

At any rate, all things had gone well with the Secretary, and
the clemency shown in taking possession of the city, increased
his reputation for prudence and the influence of his name.
Letters of congratulation poured in upon him from all quarters.
One dated the 8th of June, from Agostino Vespucci, his colleague
in the Florence chancery, told him that bonfires had been burning
in the city since twenty-one o'clock, and that it was impossible to
describe the public rejoicing : " every man *quodammodo* is going
mad with delight. . . . *Prosit vobis* to have been present at a
glory of this kind, *et non minima portio rei* . . . *Nisi crederem
te nimis superbire,* I would venture to say that you, with your
battalions *tam bonam navastis operam, ita ut, non cunctando sed
accelerando, restitueritis rem florentinam.*   I hardly know what
I am saying.   I swear to Heaven, so great is our exultation, that
I would pen you a Tulliana (a Ciceronian oration), had I the

---

[1] Sismondi, " Hist. des Répub. Italiennes," Bruxelles, 1838–39, vol. vii. p.
244.   " Capitolazione per la resa della città di Pisa sotto il dominio della repubblica Fiorentina," in Flaminio Dal Borgo's " Raccolta di diplomi pisani," pp.
406–28, in 4°, 1765.

time, *sed deest penitus.*" [1] And on the 17th of June, his friend, Commissary Filippo da Casavecchia wrote to him from Barga : " May a thousand good fortunes result to you from the grand gain of this noble city, for truly it may be said, that you personally have had a great share in the matter. . . . Each day I discover in you a greater prophet than the Jews or any other generation ever possessed." [2]

Nevertheless, all these triumphs were not unfraught with danger for the future of Machiavelli, nor even of the Republic itself. On the one hand, he naturally became the object of increased jealousy and envy. Had not he, a simple Secretary, superintended a siege with almost greater authority than that of the War Commissioners ? Had he not, too, had the good luck to achieve success, and thus put an end to the obstinate struggle that for so many years had exhausted the resources of the hostile cities ? Then, on the other hand, this fortunate success made all men conceive the highest opinion of the new ordinance ; so that Machiavelli and the others placed such unbounded faith in it, as to make it later the source of great and bitter disillusions. No one seemed then to perceive that all that the militia ordinance had really accomplished, was to lay waste the country, without encountering the enemy in battle ; and keep strict watch to prevent supplies of provisions from reaching a city already so worn and exhausted by famine as to be no longer able to bring an army into the field. Neither did any one reflect that things might have gone very differently had it been a question of confronting disciplined and able soldiers in a pitched battle. This was an experience to be made at a later date, and then Florence learned to her own cost the danger of building on illusive hopes in time of war.

---

[1] " Carte del Machiavelli," case vi. No. 43. This letter of Vespucci was published in the " Opere " (P. M.), vol. v. note to p. 431.

[2] *Vide* " Appendix " (II.), document vi. of Italian edition. The original is among the " Carte del Machiavelli," case iv. No. 45 ; part of the fragment given above was published in the " Opere " (P. M.), vol. v. p. 431.

CHAPTER XII.

(1508–1510.)

HE 10th of December, 1508, had witnessed the conclusion of the League of Cambray, that Julius II. had so carefully planned and so ardently promoted. The Emperor, Spain, France, and the Pope had united, apparently, to combat the Turks, but really to gratify their revenge by the destruction of Venice, and were already agreed as to the division of the territory. The Pope was to receive the coveted lands of Romagna ; the Emperor, Padua, Vicenza, Verona and Friuli ; Spain, the Neapolitan territory on the Adriatic ; and France, who had to bear the brunt of the war, Bergamo, Brescia, Crema, Cremona, Ghiara d'Adda and the Milanese States. Hostilities immediately began, and from the beginning it seemed as though both nature and mankind had conspired to the injury of Venice. The powder magazine exploded ; a thunderbolt struck the fortress of Brescia ; a boat carrying 10,000 ducats to Ravenna was wrecked ; certain of the Orsini and the Colonna, who had engaged in the Venetian service and pledged themselves to bring a considerable force of foot soldiers and cavalry, kept the instalment of 15,000 ducats they had already received, and then broke the contract by order of the Pope. But the indomitable Republic remained undismayed, and despatched a powerful army of native and foreign

troops to the Oglio under the command of Niccolò Orsini, Count of Pitigliano, and Bartolommeo d'Alviano. Orsini, however, being excessively prudent, D'Alviano excessively daring, and neither willing to yield to the other, the conduct of the war was very uncertain.

Their adversaries, on the contrary, went straight to the mark. On the 15th of April, Julius II. issued his bull of excommunication against the Venetians and all who assisted them, empowering any one who could to make slaves of them after stripping them of their possessions. On the 14th of May, the French advanced guard, commanded by G. J. Trivulzio, passed the Adda and met the rearguard of the Venetians under D'Alviano. This commander, by making a halt while the remainder of the army marched on, found himself isolated, while the enemy on the contrary was continually reinforced by freshly arriving troops. Seeing this, D'Alviano despatched messages to the Count of Pitigliano; but he replied, with his usual timidity, that the Senate did not wish any pitched battles at present, and that his colleague would do well to continue the march. Nevertheless D'Alviano attacked the enemy and behaved with valour, but met with the ill luck that usually marred his career. Brisighella's Italian infantry fought like heroes, six thousand of them maintaining the struggle until the last man was cut down. Twenty pieces of artillery were lost; and D'Alviano himself was wounded and taken prisoner. His army was completely routed; but a portion of the cavalry escaped, and the main body of the Venetian army under Pitigliano, having continued the march, took no part in the conflict. This battle, known as that of Vailà or Agnadello, was the first of the great and sanguinary struggles of which thenceforward Italy was to be unceasingly the scene, and in which the Italian soldiers and captains of either side fought with equal valour, binding their country more and more firmly in the bonds of foreign domination. The French held Caravaggio, Bergamo, Brescia and Crema in their power; they also seized Peschiera, and thus within a fortnight Louis XII., who had entered Italy at the head of his army, was already lord of the territory promised to him at Cambray. Accordingly his ardour in the prosecution of the war soon began to relax. The Count of Pitigliano had shut himself up in Verona.

But meanwhile the Papal army, consisting of 400 men-at-arms, as many light horse, and 800 infantry, advanced rapidly into

Romagna without encountering other obstacles. Soon, too, it was further strengthened by 3000 Swiss, commanded by the Pope's nephew, Francesco Maria della Rovere, now Duke of Urbino in virtue of his adoption by the deceased Duke Guidobaldo. When the tidings of the battle of Vailà reached the Duke Alfonso d'Este, he threw aside his neutrality, drove the Venetian Visdomino from Ferrara, sent thirty-two of his celebrated guns to the Pope's army, and repossessed himself of certain lands formerly taken from the Este by the Venetians. The Marquis of Mantua behaved much in the same manner. In expectation of the Emperor's arrival, the imperial feudatories in Friuli and Istria made attacks on the humbled Republic of St. Mark, whose only hope now lay in sowing dissension among her adversaries by yielding to a few of them the full extent of their demands.

There was no longer anything more to be given up to France, since she had already seized all that she desired ; so the Venetians restored to Spain the small Neapolitan territory held by them on the Adriatic. But that was a very trifling matter under present circumstances. They sent Antonio Giustinian as ambassador to the Emperor with *carte blanche* to give up all that should be required of them. And Giustinian, who had always proved himself an influential and haughty diplomat, prepared a Latin speech, so humble in tone, that it may be called positively cowardly ; and for this reason Venetian writers have sought to deny its authenticity.[1] But the discourse did not serve its

---

[1] "This oration Ad divinum Maximilianum Romanorum Imperatorem," translated by Guicciardini in his "Storia d' Italia," was thought by many, down to our own day, to be an invention of the enemies of Venice. But as we have elsewhere stated, Ricci had discovered an old copy of it among the "Carte del Machiavelli," where it is still preserved (case vi. No. 53), and transcribed it in his "Priorista," stating that it had not been written to calumniate the Venetians as they had asserted, but was really the composition of Giustinian. Machiavelli alludes in his "Discorsi" (bk. iii. ch. xxxi.) to the deep abasement of the Venetians, "who sent ambassadors to the Emperor to declare themselves his tributaries, and wrote letters full of cowardice to the Pope." Signor Saltini, of the Florence Archives, recently discovered another old copy of this same oration of Giustinian, sent to the Signoria by Messer Piero dei Pazzi, Florentine Ambassador at Rome, together with his letter of the 7th July, 1509, in which he said : To give a proof of the humiliation to which the Venetians are reduced, I send "the enclosed oration which they have published here as having been pronounced *coram Imperatore*." See "Antonio Giustinian e i suoi dispacci di Roma," in the "Archivio Storico," series iii., vol. xxvi. issue iv. 1877, p. 72 and fol. See also Preface to the "Dispacci di A. Giustinian," edited by P. Villari, 3 vols. Florence, Le Monnier, 1876.

purpose, for Giustinian could not even obtain audience, the Emperor having declared that he must first come to an agreement with France. On the other hand, Venice succeeded in her negotiations where she least expected to do so, namely, in Rome. Thence the Florentine Ambassador wrote that "it was a miserable thing to behold the Venetian orators bènt to the earth, so was their pride sunk in humiliation." [1]

In fact, the Pope, too, had changed his designs. Now that he held the lands of Romagna, although he still made a show of great anger, and demanded from the Venetians repayment of the revenues drawn by them in past years, yet it was easy to see that his wrath was beginning to be turned against the French, whom he hated, as he hated all foreigners in general. For they, having gained all they desired for themselves, no longer showed any intention of prosecuting the war. He was already thinking of joining Maximilian against France ; but the Emperor, although now provided with funds, and although many imperial States had declared themselves ready to make their submission, still delayed crossing the frontiers of Italy. All these things might change the face of events at any moment. In fact, the Bishop of Trent formally took possession of Verona and Vicenza, and Padua also surrendered without striking a blow ; but at Treviso matters went differently. The nobles there, as in all the cities under Venetian sway, were most hostile to the Republic, and proposed immediate surrender to the Emperor's representatives ; but the people, who both at Treviso and elsewhere always sided with Venice, rose in revolt, and with cries of *Viva San Marco*, sacked the houses of the nobility and expelled the Imperial envoys. [2] Venice, being in no condition to defend her subjects, and seeing that although the nobles inclined to the foreigner, the populace flew to arms to maintain their union with the Republic, chose this moment for decreeing that the latter should be allowed to defend themselves, by releasing them from their oath of obedience. It has been much disputed whether this conduct was the result of deep policy or of pusillanimity, and the historian Romanin positively denied the fact, on the strength of having found no document confirmatory of the decree. [3] But without the issue of any positive

---

[1] See the letter of the Ambassador dei Pazzi quoted above, and published at the end of Signor Saltini's article on "Antonio Giustinian," &c.

[2] Sismondi, "Hist. des Répub. Italiennes," vol. vii. ch. vii.

[3] Romanin, "Storia documentata di Venezia," vol. v. bk. xiii. ch. iii. p. 217.

decree, this resolve may have been the natural and inevitable result of the impotence to which Venice was then reduced ; and the energetic defence maintained by the inhabitants of her cities would in this case serve to prove, not the depth of her policy, but the greatness of the affection with which she had inspired her subjects.

This affection, of which surer proofs were daily given, and the increasing discord among the leagued powers, at last restored the courage of the Venetians. On the 17th of July, 1509, they entered Padua by surprise, and during the seizure of the city and surrender of the fortress, the peasants plundered the dwellings of the nobility. The whole of the Paduan territory followed the city's example ; and Verona, occupied by the Bishop of Trent with very scanty forces, was on the point of doing the same, especially when, after having begged of the Imperials the help of the Marquis of Mantua, this general was captured on the road by the Stradiotes of Venice. Meanwhile, Louis XII., instead of recommencing the war to assist his allies, was on his way back to France, leaving La Palisse on the Veronese boundaries with 500 lances and 200 noblemen. And this was after having concluded with the Pope a treaty of mutual defence for their own States, by which he left the vassals of the Church to their fate ; and the chief of these, his whilom ally, the Duke of Ferrara, was now exposed to the full brunt of the attacks of Julius II.

At last, however, Maximilian decided upon action, and came to the siege of Padua, which town the Venetians had garrisoned with all their available forces. The two sons of the Doge Loredano brought a body of infantry at their own expense to share in the defence. They were followed by 176 other gentlemen of Venice ; and all the country folk hurried within the walls, bringing their crops with them. The Emperor led the most powerful army that had been seen in Italy for many centuries. There were the French troops of La Palisse, Spaniards trained to arms under Gonsalvo de Cordova, Italians, Germans, adventurers of all nations, and two hundred guns. In all it comprised from eighty to one hundred thousand men.[1] Siege operations were quickly begun and a breach was made ; but when the army tried to storm the walls, the Venetians fired the mines they had laid, and the greater part of the assailants, including several leaders of renown, were hurled into the air. Accordingly, on the 3rd of

[1] Sismondi, "Hist. des Répub. Italiennes," vol. vii. ch. viii.

October, the siege was raised. Then fresh quarrels arose among the allies, especially on the part of the Emperor, who having exhausted his exchequer begged money from all, and more pressingly than ever from the Florentines. He reminded them of the sums they had authorized Vettori to promise him, as soon as he came to Italy, where he now was.

The Florentines were obliged to despatch two ambassadors to meet him at Verona, Giovan Vittorio Soderini and Piero Guicciardini, the historian's father. Machiavelli called their attention to what he had already written upon Germany and the Emperor, and advised them to keep their wits about them, because the Emperor "very often undid in the evening that which he had done in the morning."[1] So the ambassadors hastened to sign a treaty (24th of October, 1509), by which the Florentines bound themselves to pay 40,000 ducats to Maximilian, who promised them in return his friendship and protection.[2] The gist of the matter, however, was that they were to pay, and the payment was to be made in four instalments : the first at once in the present month of October, the second by the 15th of November,[3] the third in January, and the fourth in February of the following year.

A decree of the 10th of November nominated Machiavelli bearer of the second instalment, with instructions to be at Mantua by the 15th, and after delivery of the money to go on to Verona, or wherever he thought best to obtain intelligence. And Machiavelli fulfilled his mission, and immediately began to seek for news in Mantua, not omitting the remark that that was "the place where lies are born, and even rained down ; and that the Court was fuller of them than the public streets."[4] On the 22nd he was at Verona, and wrote thence on the 26th, instantly grasping, in his usual way, the essential facts required to form a just idea of the state of things there and of public opinion. "The nobles," he wrote, "do not love Venice, and incline to the allies ; but the people

[1] "Discorso sopra le cose di Almagna e sopra l'Imperatore," to which we have already made allusion. It consists of two pages only. "Opere," vol. iv. p. 174.

[2] Nardi, "Storia Fiorentina," vol. i. pp. 419, 420. Signor Gaspar Amico, in his book upon Machiavelli (p. 326, note 2), quotes the original treaty, which is in the Florence Archives, parchment, 24th of October, 1509.

[3] Buonaccorsi, "Diario," p. 144, says "25th of November;" but in Machiavelli's commission we find the words "not later than the 15th."

[4] Letter of the 20th of November, from Mantua. "Opere," vol. vii. p. 297.

—the populace, and the country folk—are all *Marcheschi*.[1] The Bishop of Trent is at Verona with a few thousand foot and horse ; Vicenza has already rebelled and given herself to the Venetians ; the Emperor is at Roveredo and will not receive ambassadors ; the Veronese nobles look to France, who in the end has only sent 200 Gascons and 200 men-at-arms. But these reinforcements are of no use, for they are too scanty ; and meanwhile the allies devastate and pillage the country in a way that cannot be described." " And thus so great a desire of death or vengeance has entered into the souls of these country folk, that they are become more hardened and enraged against the enemies of the Venetians, than were the Jews against the Romans ; and it daily happens that some one of them, being taken prisoner, submits to death rather than deny the name of Venice. Only yester-evening there was one brought before this Bishop, who said that he was a St. Markite[2] and would die a St. Markite, and otherwise would not live ; therefore the Bishop had him hung, for neither the promise of his life, nor of other advantage, could turn him from this opinion : therefore, all things considered, it is impossible for those monarchs to hold these lands so long as the peasants have breath."[3]   The energetic and sometimes heroic resistance of these peasants recalls the very similar resistance made by the Pisan peasantry, and is another proof of the vigour and energy still existing in the lower ranks of Italian society, to whom recourse was seldom made, and to whom historians have accorded scanty attention.

Machiavelli's letters proceeded to say that " things cannot long go on in this fashion. The more slowly the war proceeds, the more will the love for the Venetians increase, since the inhabitants both within and without the walls are eaten up by the allies, who rob and pillage them, whereas the Venetians, although making continual skirmishes and raids, yet respect their property and cause them to be treated with the utmost consideration.[4]   Meanwhile Louis XII. and Maximilian are by no means in accord, and it is feared that in the end the latter will join the Venetians. Of these two sovereigns the one can make war, but will not, and therefore lets things drag on ; the other wants to make war but cannot. If, however, in this fashion they nourish the desperation of the peasantry and the existence of the Venetians, it is believed,

[1] That is : *faithful to Saint Mark.*   [2] That is : *faithful to Saint Mark.*
[3] Letter of the 26th of November.   [4] Letter of the 29th of November.

as I have before said, that from one moment to another something may happen to make Monarchs, Popes and every one else repent not having done their duty in due time.[1] In all these places which the Venetians take possession of, they have a St. Mark painted, grasping a sword instead of a book ; therefore it would seem that they have discovered to their cost that to keep their States neither studies nor books are sufficient."[2]

On the 12th of December Machiavelli was at Mantua, whence, the war about Verona being already near, he sent a long and minute description of the latter city ;[3] and shortly after, having received permission from the Ten, returned to Florence.

During this short journey, which lasted nevertheless almost two months, Machiavelli had little to do, and seems to have turned his spare time to account by beginning the second of his Decennials, that he afterwards left unfinished. In fact, the fragment of it remaining to us, treats of events happening between 1504 and 1509. And in a letter he wrote to Luigi Guicciardini during these days, and of which we shall have more to say presently, we find a postscript saying : " I expect Gualtieri's reply to my *cantafavola*." Now this was the title frequently applied both by himself and his friends to " The First Decennial."

Machiavelli begins the second by announcing that he shall venture to relate recent events, although

" Sia per dolor divenuto smarrito."[4]

After invoking the Muse, he alludes to the rout of Bartolommeo d'Alviano in Tuscany, accomplished chiefly by means of the valiant Antonio Giacomini, whom he highly eulogizes. After still briefer notice of a few general events in Europe, he recalls how Pope Julius II., not being able " to restrain his ferocious soul," began the war against the tyrants of Perugia and Bologna. Thus at last he speedily arrives at the League of Cambray. This he seems to attribute chiefly to the victories of the Venetians

---

[1] Letter of the 1st of December.　　　[2] Letter of the 7th of December.
[3] He repeated this description with some merely stylistic variations in bk. v. of his " Istorie Fiorentine " (" Opere," vol. ii. p. 45), as Ranke has already observed in his " Geschichte der romanischen und germanischen Völker von " 1494 *bis* 1514—zweite Auflage. Leipzig, 1874. See page *153 of the second part of the volume, entitled : " Zur Kritik neuerer Geschichtschreiber."
[4] " Although his brain be bewildered by grief."

over the Emperor in 1508, and to their having then deprived him of certain States :

> " Le qual di poi si furon quel pasto,
> Quel rio boccon, quel venenoso cibo,
> Che di San Marco ha lo stomaco guasto." [1]

Then the Florentines, turning the opportunity to account, starved Pisa into submission, by compassing her about in such fashion that none could enter " without wings ; " so that although her obstinacy had long endured,

> " Tornò piangendo alla catena antica." [2]

But nothing could be concluded without first satisfying the covetous desires of the potentates, who continually found new pretexts for obtaining money.

> " Bisognò a ciascuno empier la gola.
> E quella bocca che teneva aperta." [3]

Afterwards the allies weakened the power of Venice at Vailà, and then it was clearly seen how little avails force without the prudence that discerns and provides for evils beforehand.

> " Di quinci nasce che 'l voltar del cielo
> Da quello a questo i vostri Stati volta
> Più spesso che non muta il caldo il gelo.
> Che se la vostra prudenzia fusse volta
> A conoscere il male e rimediarvi,
> Tanta potenzia al ciel sarebbe tolta." [4]

And after these verses, which, though certainly neither elegant nor harmonious, attest the unbounded faith he always placed in political craft, and the art of government, that in his opinion

---

[1] " Who later became that fare, that fatal mouthful, that poisonous cheer, that has disordered the stomach of St. Mark."

[2] " Weeping took up her former chain."

[3] " It behoved us to fill the maw of every one,
And their ever gaping mouths."

[4] " Hence it comes that the face of Heaven is turned from this to that of your States, more often than the heat and frost return. For if your prudence were directed to knowing the evil and remedying it, much power would be [taken from Heaven."

could never miss success, he comes to the moment when Maximilian having failed in the assault of Padua,

> " Levò le genti, affaticato e stanco :
> E dalla Lega sendo derelitto,
> Di ritornarsi nella Magna vago,
> Perdè Vicenza per maggior despitto." [1]

And with this event, which occurred at the time that Machiavelli was at Verona and Mantua, "The Second Decennial" comes to a stop. It is a short fragment and even less valuable than the first.

The letter dated 8th of December, from Machiavelli in Verona to Luigi Guicciardini in Mantua, to which we have already alluded, shows that he did not dedicate all his leisure to writing very indifferent verse. It would seem that Guicciardini, brother to the historian, had sent him an account of an indecent adventure that had happened to him ; and the Secretary, in return, related another of so revolting a nature, that we should not notice it at all, were it not that the letter containing it having been printed almost *in extenso*, it is necessary to say a few words about it. He relates, then, how once at Verona he found himself in the squalid abode of a woman of evil fame. She was so horribly dirty, ugly, and foul, that when, in going away, the light of a lantern enabled him to see her clearly, he was so disgusted at having approached her as to be seized with a fit of vomiting. Now the hastiest perusal of this anecdote, which it would be preferable to entirely ignore, clearly shows that in order to excite his friend's laughter, Machiavelli indulged in more than his usual exaggeration, and went considerably beyond the bounds of probability. Such exaggeration makes us deplore that a man no longer in his youth, father of a family and husband of an affectionate wife, could even jestingly dip his pen in such rank impurity.[2] Neither is he sufficiently justified by the usual excuse of the temper of the times. Fortunately, he afterwards had too much important business on his hands to find leisure for imagining or writing other indecencies of the kind.

[1] " Weary and tired he withdrew his men ; and being forsaken by the League, and yearning to return to Germany, to his greater despite he lost Vicenza." " Decennale Secondo," in the " Opere," vol. v. pp. 374-80.

[2] The original of this letter, of which a few eccentric persons had made copies, is in the Florence Archives, " Carte Strozziane," file 139, sheet 216. Parts of it were given, with many errors of the press, at p. 1142 of the edition of Machiavelli's works in one vol. published by Usigli, Florence, 1857.

His friends often emulated him in the most unseemly discourses, but at this period their correspondence from Florence treated solely of his domestic affairs and complications. His kinsman, Francesco del Nero, wrote to him at length on the 22nd of November, of a family quarrel. He did not enter into particulars, but it seems to have been an affair of some consequence, as many weighty personages were quoted and consulted on the subject ; among others the Gonfaloniere Soderini and his brothers, who showed themselves interested in Machiavelli's favour.[1]   Soon after, on the 28th of December, another and still more serious communication reached him from his faithful friend Biagio Buonaccorsi. " A week ago," he wrote, " a certain person introduced himself masked,[2] and with a couple of witnesses, to the notary of the Conservators, protesting that you, as the son of a father who, &c.,[3] are not qualified for the post of Secretary. And although the law, frequently before quoted, is entirely in your favour, yet many make a great noise about it, and it is spoken of in all quarters, even in the houses of ill-fame." This letter, after advising him, in the name of his friends, to keep out of Florence for the present, says in conclusion : " I make entreaties and return thanks for you here, things that you are not adapted to do for yourself. So it is better for you to let pass this storm, which has kept me sleepless for days, not neglecting anything that could be done for you, since, though I do not know why it should be so, there are very few here disposed to help you." [4]

It is difficult to guess the exact point of this long discourse. It may have been a question of taxes or debts to the State left unpaid by Machiavelli's father, who may thus have incurred prohibition from holding any public office, a prohibition that the malevolent were perhaps desirous to enforce in his son's case.[5] This is a

---

[1] " Carte del Machiavelli," case iv. No. 55. Appendix (II.), doc. vii. of Italian edition.

[2] The original says *turato*, *i.e.*, with his face hidden.

[3] The original letter leaves the sentence unfinished in this way.

[4] This letter, included in the " Carte del Machiavelli," was published by Passerini in the "Opere " (P.M.), vol. i. p. 74.

[5] It was not unusual in Florence to make sons suffer penalties to which their fathers had been sentenced. About the same period, Filippo Strozzi, as we shall see later, incurred punishment for having married the daughter of Piero dei Medici, who was a rebel. And in his " Storia Fiorentina," p. 377, Guicciardini observes that another question was raised on the same count : namely, whether as Piero had attempted to enter the city by force, " and by virtue of one of our statutes had incurred the punishment of a rebel, both in his own person and that of his

mere hypothesis, but it is supported to some extent, not only by the circumstance of the quarrel spoken of in Francesco del Nero's letter quoted above ; but also by the fact, that in June, 1508, according to an arrangement with his brother Totto, Niccolò Machiavelli had assumed possession of the whole paternal inheritance, together with the considerable debts and obligations by which it was burdened. In 1511 the officials of the Monte, or Exchequer, regularly debited him with the due amount of tithes, and he was afterwards obliged to pay large sums to the creditors.[1] It is not surprising that disputes and quarrels should have arisen under these circumstances, and it was also perfectly natural that the Secretary's enemies, whose number was much increased by envy of his good fortune, should seize the occasion as a pretext for annoying him. But whether he had already started before Buonaccorsi's letter came, or whether, assured of the Gonfalonier's good will and the law's favour, he did not attach much importance to his friend's fears, it is certain that on the 2nd of January he was already in Florence, engaged in the usual affairs of his office.[2]

descendants, Filippo Strozzi should not be punished, not only for having married a rebel's daughter, but for having married a rebel." Passerini, in editing Buonaccorsi's letter, above quoted, says in a note to the words, *per essere voi nato di padre*, &c., "Bernardo, father of our Niccolò, was an illegitimate child." But, as usual, he has no proofs to give of this assertion, which seems to us entirely unfounded, judging from the ancient " Records " of the Machiavelli family in the Marucelliana Library. These " Records," quoted at the beginning of this work, show us that Bernardo inherited as a legitimate son, and that the illegitimate children are mentioned apart. Neither Ricci in his " Priorista," nor any other author, ever alleged this charge of bastardy. Besides, to the best of our knowledge, neither Florentine statutes nor Florentine historians assert that the legitimate son of a father of illegitimate birth would be disqualified from filling the modest post of Secretary. It was barely forbidden to natural sons to be elected to the highest offices of the State : to the Gonfaloniership or the Signoria.

[1] See the two documents published in the " Opere " (P. M.), vol. i. pp. 58 and 59. From these we learn that, on the 21st of June, 1508, a compact had been arranged by arbitration, between Niccolò Machiavelli and his brother Totto, and in consequence the paternal estate, formerly divided between the two, all passed over to Niccolò with its accompanying charges and taxes. On the 15th of April, 1511, the officials of the Monte " deliberaverunt quod onus X.ᵉ (Decimæ) domini Bernardi de Machiavellis . . . describatur et ponatur poste domini Nicolai domini Bernardi de Machiavellis, et quod dictus Nicolaus gaudeat beneficio dello sgravo delle bocche, com'era sotto la posta di M. Bernardo suo padre, si in effetto cancellinla da conto di decto M. Bernardo, e ponghinla alla posta di Niccolo suo figliuolo, sanza alcuno loro prejudicio." "The same property," observes Passerini, " was registered in the name of the children of Niccolò Machiavelli in 1534, which was the first *catasto* (or census) made after this one."

[2] On the 28th of February, 1509-10, he received 54 gold florins, as payment at

By the 13th of March he was at San Savino, settling a question of boundaries between the Siennese and Florentines ;[1] in May we find him in the Val di Nievole reviewing the battalions, and also continually occupied with the organization of the militia in Florence.[2]

Meanwhile the Venetians, who had entered Vicenza, arrived too late at Verona, where the Imperial forces were already entrenched. They captured several places in Friuli and the Polesine ; but their fleet, which had been sent up the Po to take Ferrara by assault, was defeated and almost destroyed owing to the cowardice and inexperience of its commander, Angelo Trevisan. Soon after, namely at the beginning of 1510, the Count of Pitigliano died ; and thus, Alviano having been taken prisoner, the Venetians had no commanders for their army, and could find none better than Giovan Paolo Baglioni of Perugia. But at this moment help reached them from a most unexpected quarter.

The Pope's jealousy of France was daily increasing. He had summoned a host of foreigners into Italy in order to combat Venice. But now that Venice had humbled herself at his feet, yielding to him in all things, he not only showed a disposition to leniency, but had granted her absolution, and, as the Venetian ambassador to Rome said in his Report, had actually said " that if there were no such State " (as Venice) " it would be necessary to create one." [3]   And even at this moment he began to raise his well-known cry of *Fuori i barbari.* The Florentine Orator in France, Messer Alessandro Nasi, who for some time had reported, in speaking of the Pope and the King, how it was his belief "that there was no small suspicion between them, and little good faith," now began to write that the anger of the French had become very vehement.[4]   But even for Louis XII. it was no slight affair to be at war with the Pope, especially with a Pope of the temper of Julius II., who, in the words of the ambassador Trevisan, "wished to be lord and master of the game of the whole world." [5]   In

---

the rate of one florin a day, above his regular salary "for the 54 days, beginning from the 10th of November and ending with the second day of the last month of January, when he returned to Florence " ("Opere," P. M., vol. i. p. 83).

[1] "Opere" (P. M.), vol. i. p. 75, note 27.

[2] Ibid., note 28.

[3] "Sommario della Relazione di Roma," of Domenico Trevisan, 1st of April, 1510, in Albèri's "Relazioni degli Ambasciatori Veneti," series 11, vol. iii. p. 36.

[4] See Nasi's Legation in Desjardins, "Négociations," &c., vol. ii.

[5] "Sommario della Relazione di Roma," before quoted.

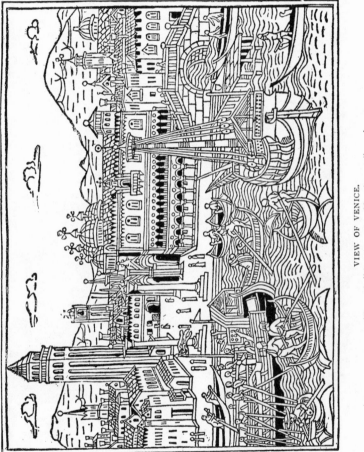

VIEW OF VENICE.

(*From the "Supplementum Chronicarum," 1490.*)

addition to this there was the circumstance, that the Swiss, esteemed by far the best infantry in the world, and always needed by France, now claimed such exorbitant terms that the King was enraged, and obliged to content himself with making some separate arrangement with the men of the Valais and the Grisons. And meanwhile Cardinal Mathias Schinner, Bishop of Sitten, or Sion, gained their ear and went about among them offering money for the hire of troops in the Pope's service.

Soon the war broke out again, although languidly, between the French and the Emperor on the one side, and the Venetians and the Pope on the other. The Venetians with their feeble army, commanded by a leader of so little note as Baglioni, would have been in no condition to oppose the enemies' united forces ; but the Emperor continued undecided, and in France, on the 25th of May, 1510, occurred the death of the Cardinal d'Amboise, who had been the instigator and guide of Louis XII.'s policy. This monarch now left his affairs in the hands of Rubertet, or else, which was worse, tried to act on his own impulses ; wherefore all men looked forward to evil days. Chaumont, who owed his elevation to being the nephew and tool of the deceased Cardinal, immediately received orders to retreat upon Milan, leaving the Emperor 400 lances and 1,500 Spanish foot soldiers.[1] And another cause of all this was, that the Pope's influence was beginning to be felt in France. To the clergy, and to the whole country, it seemed a serious matter to be at war with the Head of the Church. Nor did the latter suffer the grass to grow beneath his feet, but was already trying to excite Genoa to revolt, to which end Marcantonio Colonna had, under false pretences, left the service of the Florentines and marched thither with 100 men-at-arms and 700 foot soldiers.[2] A great deal was said at the time about this mysterious attempt ; for at first no one understood the purport of Colonna's movement, nothing being known of his secret agreement with the Pope. His expedition, however, came to nothing, being stopped half way. But the army of Julius II., under the

---

[1] Sismondi, " Histoire des Républiques Italiennes," vol. vii. ch. viii.

[2] Buonaccorsi, " Diario," p. 148, says 700 men-at-arms and 700 foot soldiers ; but several private letters give other figures, and 700 men-at-arms seems an improbable number. *Vide* Appendix II., of Italian edition, in document viii., a few letters written by friends of Machiavelli, showing that this Colonna affair long remained a mystery for the Florentines and caused them much annoyance. It also brought on them the unjust reproofs of France, who either suspected, or feigned suspicion, of their good faith in the matter.

command of Francesco Maria della Rovere, reduced the Duke of Ferrara to such straits, that he must have surrendered had not Chaumont sent him a timely reinforcement of 200 men-at-arms. And another serious danger now threatened the enemies of the Pope, for 6,000 Swiss had come down from the Alps to his assistance. Suddenly, however, for no apparent reason, they unexpectedly withdrew to their mountains. Some said that they had gone back because, as usual, unprovided with cavalry or artillery, and without hopes of obtaining any from the Pope. Others declared that after receiving 70,000 crowns for this expedition, as much more was given them by France, to persuade them to abandon it. For some time past their reputation for loyalty had become very doubtful, since every one knew that they only fought for gold.[1]

Owing to these new complications, the Florentine Republic was now in a position of great anxiety. As the old ally of the Popes and of France, it could neither separate itself from Louis XII. nor from Julius II. ; yet these rulers were actually at war and would not allow it to remain neutral. Division from France, for whose alliance it had made so many and continual sacrifices, and to whom Soderini was so much attached, implied isolation and dependence on whichever power gained the mastery in the important conflicts that were now unavoidable. Division from the Pope already in arms, and whose States touched so large an extent of Florentine frontier, signified exposure to immediate attack, without strength to resist it. Yet France persisted in demanding that the Republic should come to a speedy decision, and send contingents to take part in the war, while the Pope was in arms and on the alert. Soderini therefore had recourse to what was his usual remedy, when uncertain upon which course to decide : he despatched Machiavelli to France, with credentials instructing him to collect intelligence, and to assure the King that both he (the Gonfalonier) and his brother the Cardinal were still faithful to him, and desired to support the French ascendency in Italy. Machiavelli was also to persuade him, that for this end it was necessary either to defeat the Venetians in a short and energetic campaign, or to exhaust them by delay ; that it was necessary to keep on friendly terms with the Emperor, so that he might harass them continually, and, if requisite, even cede Verona to him ; but that his Majesty

---

[1] Sismondi, "Histoire des Républiques Italiennes," vol. vii. ch. ix. p. 320.

must not come to open rupture with the Pope, since that might prove very dangerous to the interests of France.[1]

Machiavelli pursued his journey very slowly, for he understood the vanity of these unasked counsels, and also because, as he wrote to the Ten from Lyons on the 7th of July, he clearly perceived that his journey could lead to no result, " save that of keeping your Excellencies well informed of all that happens from day to day." [2] The first news sent by him from Blois on the 18th of July, was precisely that the King declared himself willing to defend Florence ; but that Florence must decide to be either friend or foe, and if the former, must instantly send some troops to the camp.[3] As regards the Pope, then added Machiavelli, it is easy for you to imagine what they say of him, since to deny his authority and subject him to a Council, to ruin him both as to his temporal and spiritual state, are the smallest disasters with which they threaten him.[4] All here disapprove of the Pope's expedition, thinking that it bodes evil both to Italy and Christianity ; and they hope that after his failure to stir Genoa to rebellion, things will come to a stop. Impossible to have a more honest cause against a potentate, than to show that in attacking him it is wished to defend the Church ; and therefore in this war his Majesty might have all the world with him.[5] The King would wish to come to an agreement, but would not be the first to propose it. When the Orator from Rome suggested it to him, he replied : If the Pope will make one step towards me no bigger than the black line on a finger nail, I will make one towards him the length of an arm ; but otherwise I will do nothing. They still hope that your Excellencies may be able to use your offices in the matter, and I have not rejected the suggestion, judging that no more frightful misfortune could befall our city, than that of incurring the enmity of these two potentates. Nevertheless, great preparations are being made. The King has decreed a Council of

---

[1] " Opere," vol. vii. p. 320 and fol. The documents of the Legation are missing, but there is Soderini's letter.

[2] This is also apparent from the decree of 20th of June, 1510, fixing his salary, published by Passerini, " Opere " (P. M.), vol. i. p. 76. This states that Machiavelli was sent as envoy, " there being no ambassador in that place, and for as long as it may be necessary for him to remain there, to give daily information to their magistrature (that of the Ten) of everything that may occur."

[3] Letter of the 18th of July, from Blois.

[4] Letter of the 21st of July, from Blois.

[5] Letter of the 26th of July, from Blois.

the prelates of the kingdom to be held at Orleans ; he has engaged the Duke of Würtemberg in order to have German troops ; he is trying to come to terms with the Emperor, whom he wishes to accompany to Rome with 2,500 lances and 30,000 foot soldiers ; and he has sworn upon his soul that he will accomplish one of these two things : either to lose his kingdom, or crown the Emperor and make a Pope after his own fashion.[1]

Then on the 9th of August he related how, having gone with Rubertet to see the King, and having conversed with him on Italian matters in general, he had perceived that the French felt no confidence in the Florentines, excepting when they saw them with weapons in their hands ; and indeed trusted them the less because of the belief in Florentine prudence. He added in conclusion : " Your Excellencies may believe, as they believe the Gospel, that should there be war between the Pope and this sovereign, you will not be able to avoid declaring for one side or the other. And therefore it is judged by all who wish you well, to be necessary for your Excellencies to consider the matter and decide, without waiting for the crisis to come upon you, and be pressed by necessity. The Italians who are here believe that it were best to seek peace ; but that if it cannot be obtained, the King should be shown that to keep a Pope in check, neither many emperors nor much noise may be needed. And discoursing with Rubertet on this matter, I showed him all the knotty points of the question, and how, if they make war alone, they know what they bring upon themselves ; but that if they engage in it with allies, they will have to share Italy with them, and therefore be involved in a greater and more dangerous war among themselves. Nor would it be a desperate enterprise to impress these knotty points on their minds, if there were more than one influential Italian here who would take the trouble to try." [2]

The King had decreed a Council at Orleans, to see if he could overthrow the authority of the Pope and create another. The which thing, observes Machiavelli, " if your Excellencies were elsewhere, might be desirable, so that even these priests might have some bitter mouthfuls to swallow in this world." [3] But things did not turn in that direction ; and meanwhile the probability of war increased, and the French insisted more than ever on

[1] Letter of the 3rd of August, from Blois.
[2] Letter of the 9th of August, from Blois.
[3] Letter of the 18th of August, from Blois.

the Florentines taking arms without delay. Machiavelli held a long discourse with Rubertet on the matter, to make him understand that the Florentines having exhausted their resources, and being surrounded on every side by the States of the Pope or of the Pope's friends, might be immediately attacked from various quarters ; and that in such case the King, instead of receiving help from them, would have to send troops for their defence,[1] and simultaneously provide for the safety of Genoa, Ferrara, Friuli and Savoy.[2] And he so repeatedly insisted upon these points, even in the royal Council chamber, that at last Chaumont received orders to demand no armed assistance from Florence, but this did not prevent him from speedily returning to the subject, and with his accustomed insolence.[3]

The King was now intent upon the idea of coming to Italy, and in thinking of the future neglected the present. At Ferrara and Modena things were going very badly with his friends. The Pope's army had entered Ferrarese territory, and Modena had opened its gates to Cardinal di Pavia. Reggio was ready to do the same ; half the Duchy of Ferrara would have been already invaded, if Chaumont had not despatched 200 lances, who were sufficient to arrest the course of events.[4] This drew from Machiavelli the just remark, that everything might have been remedied, if thought of in time. But as we have seen, this great neglect of business was a consequence, foreseen by every one, of the death of Cardinal de Rohan. He had devoted attention to these small affairs, which were now conducted haphazard. "Thus," Machiavelli wrote, "while the King thinks of other things, and his people neglect him, the sick man is dying.[5] Nevertheless, all here are agreed that should he come to Italy, it will be necessary for him to increase your Excellencies' power. If he comes and you remain in your present condition, although you may have to support hard rubs and much expense, yet you may also hope for much benefit."[6]

---

[1] Machiavelli continually received letters from the Ten, the Gonfalonier, and friends, treating of these dangers of the Republic. Many of these have been published, together with those of the third Legation to France, in the "Opere" (P. M.), vol. vi. See also the Appendix (II.), document ix. of Ital. ed.

[2] Letter of the 27th of August.

[3] This is proved by other letters to Machiavelli, also published in the "Opere" (P. M.), vol. vi. See in the Appendix (II.), document x. of Ital. ed.

[4] Sismondi, "Hist. des Répub. Ital.," vol. vii. ch. ix. p. 318.

[5] Letter of the 2nd September.   [6] Letter of the 5th September.

Meanwhile the new ambassador, Roberto Acciaiuoli, was on the point of arrival, with more definite proposals, and Machiavelli, who as usual had no money, asked urgently for a remittance, and made preparations for departure.[1]   By the 10th of September he was already on the way, and wrote from Tours that great efforts were being made in France to assemble the Council, and that it was already settled on what points to ask its judgment.   It was to be questioned as to whether the Pope had the right to make war upon the most Christian King, without either challenge or warning ; whether the King had the right to make war in return for his own defence ; whether one who had purchased the Papacy, and committed infinite scandals, could be deemed the true Pope.[2]

During his journey back to Italy, Machiavelli was obliged to make frequent halts, so that we only find him in Florence on the 19th October, and from the instalments by which his salary was paid to him, we learn that his absence had lasted 118 days.[3] During this period he received, as usual, many letters from friends who kept him informed of Italian matters.   Very few of these, however, were from the pen of his faithful friend Buonaccorsi, who at that time was distracted with grief owing to the long and serious illness of his wife.   In fact, on the 22nd August, after excusing himself for his silence, he wrote in conclusion : " I have reached such a pitch, that I desire death rather than life, seeing no channel for health, should she be torn from me." [4]

---

[1] Letter of the 5th September.   [2] Letter of the 10th September.

[3] His stipend was of 10 lire a day, inclusive of his salary as chancellor, " which thus was given again when he was sent to the above place."   This sum equalled that of 12 small lire, from which deduction was made of 2 lire, 4 soldi, and 11 denari for the ordinary salary he received in Florence.   On the 12th November, having made up his accounts, there was found to be owing to him a total of 1416 small lire.   He had already received 700 on account ; his regular salary for those days amounted to 264 lire, 17 soldi, 2 denari ; therefore he still had to receive 451 lire, 2 soldi, 10 denari, which were paid to him.   See the " Stanziamenti," published by Passerini, " Opere " (P. M.), vol. i. p. 76.

[4] " Carte del Machiavelli," case v. No. 23.   These also comprise a few letters from Roberto Acciaiuoli to Machiavelli, after the latter's return to Florence, alluding to the merry life they were then leading.   For Buonaccorsi's letter, see Appendix (II.) of Italian edition, document xi.   We do not know if his wife's illness ended fatally.

CHAPTER XIII.

(1510–1511.)

OW in 1510 it was clearly seen that storms were slowly but relentlessly gathering over the Florentine Republic. The Pope, with irresistible pertinacity and ardour, laboured to isolate France by leaguing against her, with Spain and Venice, and possibly with the Emperor also. Events seemed to favour his efforts, and nòthing worse could have befallen the Republic and the Gonfaloniere Soderini, whose policy had always been founded on the friendship of France, which he neither could nor would relinquish. Therefore Florence might be encompassed by foes at any moment. This critical state of things naturally swelled the ranks of Soderini's antagonists within the city. All those who were discontented with, or envious of him, joined to the no small number of those who always slide with the stream, daily drew farther away from him. They had no accusations to bring against his political rectitude, or his excellent administration ; but they could now cry aloud the often-repeated complaint, that his government was too personal, in that he had excluded men of credit and influence for the sake of exalting others of low degree who were useful instruments in the execution of all that he and his secretary Machiavelli desired. This, they said, naturally weakened the government, and its effects

were visible even in the diminished authority of the magistrates, and the insecurity of the streets by night. The chronicler, Giovanni Cambi, adds, that licentiousness had increased, and that women of evil life had become so insolent that they defied the laws by lodging in all parts of the city and showing themselves everywhere. Also, by means of their adherents, they threatened personal injury even to the Eight of the Balìa, who went about in fear of their lives.[1]

But this was not the worst. The Medici party, favoured by the Pope, daily gained ground. During Piero's life, his coarse manners, dissipated conduct, vindictive and despotic character, and his repeated attempts to re-enter Florence by force of arms, had alienated men's minds from him and his family. But after his death by drowning in the Garigliano, towards the end of 1503, the aspect of things began to change. The headship of the family had now devolved on his brother, Cardinal Giovanni, who resided in Rome, and was of a very different disposition. Of cultivated and pleasant manners, he was always surrounded by artists and literary men, and in all things followed the old traditions of Cosimo and Lorenzo, of whom—both for good and for evil—he was the worthy descendant. He took the greatest care to maintain the semblance of a modest private citizen, showing himself free from all craving for rule in Florence. The experience of his forefathers had taught him that he too might more easily achieve power the better he preserved an appearance of shunning it. He was a ready and generous benefactor to all applicants ; so that he gradually came to be considered the natural representative of the Florentines in Rome. For he gave indiscriminate assistance to all who were there, making use of his influence in the Curia and the favour he enjoyed with the Pope, who was well pleased to witness the elevation of an adversary and rival to Soderini.[2]

In this way, although far off, the Cardinal was already recognized in Florence as the head of a party whose numbers were daily increased by all the malcontents and all the enemies of the Gonfalonier. And as soon as he felt his position sufficiently assured, the Cardinal began to lay aside his apparent reserve. In

---

[1] Giov. Cambi, "Istorie," vol. ii. p. 253 and fol. (In the "Delizie degli Eruditi Toscani" di Frate Ildefonso, vol. xxi.)

[2] All this is admirably analyzed and described by Guicciardini in his "Storia Fiorentina," ch. xxxii. ; and also in his "Storia d'Italia," vol. v. bk. x. ch. i. p. 27. The other historians and chroniclers of the time testify to the same effect.

1508 one of the first signs of this was to be seen in his success in arranging the marriage of Filippo Strozzi with Clarice, daughter of Piero dei Medici. This alliance caused great excitement in Florence, because it was contrary to the laws affecting the children of rebels, and also because it was vigorously opposed by Soderini and his friends. Yet notwithstanding the clamour raised about it, Filippo Strozzi was let off with a fine of 500 gold crowns, besides being *ammonito* for five years, and banished for three to the kingdom of Naples.[1] This sentence was considered very mild, in a case of violation of the Statutes ; and it was not apparently carried out in full, since we find Strozzi again in Florence before the three years had expired. The Medici party was stirring now, and becoming more and more audacious.

This caused Soderini so much anxiety, that on the 22nd of December, 1510, he insisted on rendering to the Council an exact and minute account of his administration during his eight years of government, in which period the expenses had amounted to about 908,300 gold crowns. He delivered accounts of the savings made, of the sums expended ; exhibited his books, and then deposited them in an iron box.[2] It was plain to all that the Republic had never enjoyed so regular and economical an administration. Yet directly afterwards a plot against the Gonfalonier's life was discovered, and it was rumoured that the Pope himself was implicated in it. On the 23rd of December, namely the day following that on which Soderini had publicly rendered up his accounts, a certain Prinzivalle della Stufa went to Filippo Strozzi with a proposal for murdering the Gonfalonier and overthrowing the government, and added that the Pope had approved of the design and promised the help of some of Marcantonio Colonna's men. Whether Strozzi was really, as he said, averse to mixing in affairs of State at that moment, or whether he had no confidence in the speaker, it is certain that he indignantly rejected Prinzivalle's proposal, and after allowing him time to escape, revealed the affair to the Gonfalonier. So all that could be done was to summon and interrogate the fugitive's father, bring him to trial, and exile him for five years.

Soderini was much disturbed by the matter, and on the evening of the 29th, when the Gonfaloniers of the Companies were to be nominated, he came before the Council and stated that the plot seemed to be widely spread in the city, and that a second attempt

[1] Cambi, " Istorie," vol. ii. pp. 221–223.   [2] Ibidem, pp. 242, 243.

might easily be made. His murder, he said, had been planned in order to immediately close the Council and change the government, by convoking the people in Parliament in defiance of the strictest prescriptions of the law. In the course of this speech he entered into many details ; and again gave a long exposition of his political conduct, of his method of government, his impartiality and his justice. He was so overcome by emotion that his eyes often filled with tears, especially when speaking of the unjust accusations urged against him, and of the threatened danger to liberty, which, as he said, it was sought to destroy under cover of hatred to himself.[1] The Council showed their resolve to maintain a free government, and proved it, not only by their reception of the Gonfalonier's speech, but also by voting a law for the defence of liberty, which he had many times brought forward and advocated, but never succeeded in carrying. This law[2] provided for the case of a sudden deficiency—from conspiracy or other unforeseen cause—of the legal number constituting one or

[1] Cambi, "Istorie," vol. ii. p. 243 and fol. Ammirato faithfully follows Cambi. Guicciardini, in his "Storia d'Italia," at the end of ch. iii. bk. ix. vol. vi. p. 202, alludes to the conspiracy, saying that "some infamy attached to the person of the Pontiff, as he had been aware that by means of Cardinal dei Medici, it had been arranged with Marcantonio Colonna and certain young Florentines, that the Gonfalonier, Piero Soderini, should be killed in Florence," &c.

[2] Cambi, "Istorie," vol. ii. p. 249. Ammirato, following Cambi, speaks of this law and repeats the same mistakes, among others that it abolished the Parliament, which had instead been abolished long before, namely, in the time of Savonarola. The "Provvisione," dated 20th of January, 1510-11, is in the Florence Archives, "Consigli Maggiori, Provvisioni," reg. 201, sheet 41-43. Its preface, given below, clearly indicates how the mistake arose of the pretended abolition of Parliament in this year : "The magnificent and most excellent Signory desiring to establish and consolidate the present peaceful condition of the people, their lives and liberty, and provide that it should not be imperilled nor stained by any accident, however grave ; and reflecting that if by any accident, ordinary or extraordinary, some one of the three chief offices and magistracies of our city might not be of the legal number, or might be so diminished as not to comprise a sufficient number, namely, the two-thirds, or that the purses of some members should be (by those who seek to do evil) either damaged, stolen, burnt, or hidden, so that the new names could not be drawn ; thus all the actions of the present state and liberty would be suspended and cease ; and as this would furnish a reason, not being otherwise possible to re-establish things, that a Parliament should be convoked, which, having to be done by force, would be done in favour of whomever should be most powerful, not of those desiring good and peaceful life ; they therefore . . . provide and ordain," &c. The clauses of the Provvisioni also provide for the method of election to incomplete or omitted magistracies, and for the nomination of the substitutes, and the renewal of the purses, always by means of an extraordinary convocation of the Great Council.

more of the chief magistracies (Signory), Gonfaloniers of the Companies, and Worthies (Buoni Homini), and also provided against any tampering with the purses for the purpose of preventing the regular extraction of names, and then convoking a popular Parliament in order to upset the government. Should the purses be left intact, or at least the registers of the names preserved, the new law obliged those remaining in office to proceed at once to the work of election, by drawing the names. Should the purses have been destroyed or carried off with the registers, then the Great Council was to be assembled, and at its second meeting, the members present, no matter how few, were to instantly begin the election. As to the office of Gonfalonier, the only thing done was to reinforce the regulations previously passed on the 26th of August, 1502, when it was, as they said, declared perpetual, and the new method of electing the Gonfalonier minutely defined. Yet all this signified nothing. However much the number of malcontents in Florence had increased, they were still in a minority that could not possibly succeed in overthrowing the government, so long as they had only their own resources to depend upon. The real danger to the Republic came from without, and there was no time to be lost. For this reason, it was Machiavelli's great object to place the Republic in a state of defence, and solely reliant on its own forces. More convinced than ever of the utility and efficaciousness of his militia infantry (*ordinanza a piedi*), he now laboured with great energy at the formation of a mounted militia, armed with crossbows, lances, or matchlocks. For the present he placed it on a temporary footing, almost as an experiment, in order later, after successful preliminary trials, to get a law passed for its permanent establishment, as had been already done in the case of the infantry ordinance.

During the two last months of 1510 Machiavelli travelled through the Florentine dominions, for the purpose of enrolling light horse ; he then went to Pisa and Arezzo, to visit the two fortresses and report upon their condition ; in February, 1511, he was at Poggio Imperiale, to investigate the state of that place. In March we find him employed in the upper valley of the Arno and in Valdichiana, giving payment in advance to a hundred light cavalry, whom he brought to Florence in April ; and in August he made another journey to engage a second troop of the same number.[1] In the interval between these tours he had gone twice

[1] " Opere " (P. M.), vol. i. pp. 77–79. For these journeys he received nothing but his travelling expenses.

to Sienna, first to repudiate a continuation of the truce expiring in 1511,[1] and the second time to confirm it by another truce for twenty-five years, stipulating, however, on the one hand for the surrender of Montepulciano to the Florentines, and on the other, offering pledges that Florence would support the sovereignty of Petrucci in Sienna. This treaty, officially proclaimed at Sienna in August, was concluded through the mediation of the Pope, who wished to prevent the Florentines from proceeding to summon the French into Tuscany.[2] And Petrucci himself had besought the Pontiff's assistance, being in terror of the popular discontent, at that moment much increased in consequence of the unavoidable cession of Montepulciano.[3] On the 5th of May Machiavelli was again on the road, on a mission to Luciano Grimaldi, lord of Monaco, and returned thence on the 11th of June, after having concluded a treaty of friendly alliance and commerce for ten years.[4]

Meanwhile the Council of Tours gave Louis XII. the desired reply, namely, that he had complete right to make war on the Pope. The latter, however, without waiting for answer or counsel from any quarter, had already begun the war, and was carrying it on with the ardour of a youthful commander. On the 22nd of September, 1510, he had entered Bologna, with an Italian and Spanish army led by the Duke of Urbino and Marcantonio and Fabrizio Colonna, before Chaumont had time to oppose any resistance. Neither did the approach of winter check his progress, for, burning with wrath against the Duke of Ferrara, he pushed on and captured Concordia ; then he attacked Mirandola, held by the widow of Luigi Pico, the faithful adherent of France who had only sent a feeble reinforcement to his aid. In the first days of 1511 the old Pope had himself carried in a litter from Bologna, and remained within gunshot during the assault. Snow

---

[1] Sienna Archives, "Deliberazioni della Balia," vol. lii., 2nd of December, 1510 : "Messer Niccolò Machiavelli, the Florentine envoy, arrived, and after presenting his credentials, repudiated, in the name of the Florentines, the truce described in the book of treaties between the Florentines and Siennese."

[2] Guicciardini, "Storia d'Italia," vol. v. bk. x. ch. i. p. 8.

[3] Buonaccorsi, "Diario," p. 162, copied by Nardi, vol. i. p. 448 ; Sismondi, vol. vii. p. 353 ; Ammirato, *ad annum ;* Gaspare Amico, "Vita di N. Machiavelli," pp. 348-50.

[4] Machiavelli, "Opere," vol. vii. p. 391 ; "Opere" (P. M.), vol. i. pp. 77-79 ; Gaspare Amico, at p. 352, note 3, and at p. 353, note 1, gives two documents relating to this mission, and, with the exception of orthographical errors they are faithful transcripts.

was falling heavily, the rivers were frozen, and a cannon ball struck the quarters where he lodged. Another day, having gone a little distance from the camp, he nearly fell in with a French ambuscade, and would certainly have been captured had not the snow prevented his return at the appointed hour. Mirandola was valiantly defended by Alexander, the nephew of G. J. Trivulzio ; but as Chaumont, from jealousy, sent no help, and the enemy had opened a breach, it was at last obliged to capitulate on the 20th of January, 1511, and also to pay 6000 ducats for exemption from the sack and pillage promised by the Holy Father as a reward to his troops.

So great, indeed, was the Pope's impatience, that instead of waiting to enter by the gate, he had himself drawn up through the breach in a wooden box, and gave possession of the State to Giovanni Pico, cousin of the deceased lord, and who had always been the enemy of France.

For the French, the death of their general Chaumont, on the 11th of February, was a fortunate event. He had allowed Modena to be seized by the enemy, had failed to reach Bologna in time, had sent no succour to Mirandola, and thus all things had been ruined by his fault. Now that he no longer enjoyed his uncle's most efficacious protection, he could not hope for the same indulgence as before, and therefore adversity drove him to such despair that he died of grief. The command of the army was then once more entrusted to the veteran G. J. Trivulzio and the young leader Gaston de Foix, who was destined to do great deeds during the few months of life still remaining to him. In fact, the fortunes of the war speedily changed. In May, G. J. Trivulzio brought his army close to Bologna, and the Pope, who had previously rejected the offers of peace proposed by the Congress at Mantua, and even urged by the Emperor, now fled almost in a panic to Ravenna, hoping that the Bolognese would undertake the defence of their city. He had left there the Cardinal Francesco Alidosi, formerly bishop of Pavia, as Legate of Romagna ; and the Duke of Urbino and his army were not far off. The Cardinal, in great favour with the Pope (a point that gave rise to strangely indecent rumours), was, however, much detested, and considered as a man in whom little confidence could be placed.[1]

---

[1] As early as April, 1510, the Venetians had warned the Pope that the Cardinal was a friend of the French, but their warning was disregarded. See Brosch. "Papst Julius II.," p. 224.

The moment it was known that Trivulzio was approaching the city with the Bentivoglio, the Bolognese rose to arms ; on the 21st of May they threw down Michel Angelo's statue of Julius II. and shattered it to fragments, which were afterwards carried off and converted into a cannon by the Duke of Ferrara. The Cardinal immediately fled to Castel del Rio ; the Bentivoglio and the French entered the city ; the Duke of Urbino, surprised by the sudden revolt, and hard pressed by the French, made so hasty and disorderly a retreat, that he lost all his artillery and baggage. This the enemy carried away in donkey loads, and for that reason the fight was called the day of the Donkey-drivers.[1] Mirandola again changed its master, and the Duke of Ferrara retook all the lands from which he had been ousted.

The Pope was at Ravenna when he received news of all these events. Although the public voice hurled accusations of treason against the Cardinal—who certainly had neither made due resistance, nor sent any warning to the Duke of Urbino—yet it was against the latter that Julius II. turned his rage, exclaiming, If he fall into my hands I will have him quartered.[2] Encouraged by this, the Cardinal came to Ravenna, and kneeling at the Pope's feet, did not content himself with obtaining pardon, but tried to cast all the blame upon the Duke. Urbino was only twenty-one years of age, but was already stained with crime, and now the Pope's anger, the dishonour of defeat, and the Cardinal's conduct, stirred him to such fury that, chancing to meet this

---

[1] Sismondi, vol. vii. ch. ix. ; Gregorovius, vol. viii. ch. i. pp. 65-7. These facts are also mentioned by all the Venetian historians, such as Bembo, Friuli, Marin Sanuto, &c. Also by Paride dei Grassi, who shows more hostility than the others to Cardinal Alidosi : " qui pastor servare Bononiam debuit et potuit, prodidit et perdidit, die iovis xx. Maii, hora circiter xx." In his opinion the Cardinal was in league with the enemy, but this is not stated by the other historians. Paridis Crassi, " Diarium Pontificatus Julii II.," vol. ii., at sheet 146*t* (Florence National Library, MSS. Magliab. ii. 11, 145). Farther on, at sheet 147, it is said that the more faithful citizens wished to defend the gates of Bologna, and hastened to him : " sed is qui ad malum natus est, et qui populum et civitatem ac pontificio honorem barbaris vendere statuit, blande respondit : non timendum esse, quoniam optime rebus omnibus et saluti omnium consuluisset. Itaque, cum alii ad eum confugerent hoc idem annuntiantes, ipse Judas proditor, simulato habitu, cum suis satellitibus fere centum aufugit ex palatio."

[2] " Si in manus meus veniet dux nepos meus, quadripartitum eum faciam ex merito suo." But when he was told of the loss of the city and the Legate's crime, he announced these things to the Cardinals in very few words : " Uno verbo captam esse Bononiam ab hostibus indicat, non tamen legatum dixit in hoc peccasse " (" Diarium " *cit.*, at sheet 147*t*.)

prelate in the streets of Ravenna, he killed him with his own hands, splitting his skull with blows of his staff. Paride dei Grassi—the continuer of Burchard's Diary—hated the Cardinal, and believing him a traitor, approved of this murder, exclaiming : Oh, good God, how just are Thy judgments ! We must render thanks to Thee for the death of the traitor ; since, although he was killed by the hand of man, yet it was Thy work, or, at least, approved by Thee, without whose consent no leaf may fall to the ground.[1] But the Pope was inexpressibly grieved at so horrible a crime, committed by his own nephew against a Cardinal whom he dearly loved and cherished.[2] He threatened to make an example of great severity, and, in fact, soon deprived his nephew of his office, and subjected him to trial by four Cardinals.

But there were other events causing him still more pain during this year of ill fortune. The affair of the Council tormented him as a continual menace to his authority. And although scarcely a subject for real anxiety, it was no laughing matter to a man who had so often threatened to use the same weapon against Alexander VI., and who, like the predecessors he had so harshly censured, had failed to maintain his solemn promise of assembling the Council within two years after his election. When at Bologna, in the September of 1510, the Pope had shown great indignation

---

[1] "Bone Deus quam justa sunt judicia tua, unde tibi omnes gratias agimus, quod de proditore perfido dignas predictionis suæ poenas sumpsisti, et licet homo hoc fecerit supplicium, tamen a te sine quo nec folia in arbore movetur commissum aut saltem permissum credimus, ideoque gratias rursus tibi agimus." ("Diarium" *cit.*, at sheet 148*t.*) The skull of Cardinal Alidosi is still preserved at Ravenna. Besides the authors quoted above, see also Reumont, "Geschichte der Stadt Rom," vol. iii. part ii. p. 40 and fol. ; Brosch, "Papst Julius II.," p. 222 and fol.

[2] It is very difficult to find fitting words in which to hint at the rumours then afloat, and openly mentioned, concerning the relations of the Pope with the Cardinal. They merely testify to the corruption of the times, and the very bad estimation in which the morals of Julius II. were held. Certainly his youthful career fully justified many accusations; but the particulars to which allusions were made, were often totally unsupported by proof. This is confirmed even by Brosch, although his book is conceived in a spirit of hostility to Julius II. On more than one occasion, after having carefully related and examined these charges, he concludes with the remark that they only prove how bad was the Pope's reputation as to his moral and private character. *Apropos* to what was said in those days about his relations with the Cardinal, he finishes with these words : "Die empörenden Beschuldigungen, welche deshalb auf Julius Namen gehaüft wurden, fallen zurück auf die Lästerer jener zeit und sind unzweifelhaft ein Nachklang ihrer Reden, während es höchst fraglich ist, ob der Papst solche wirklich verdient habe" (p. 224).

at the unexpected news that five of his Cardinals had changed
their course, and were on the way to Florence in order to go to
Pisa, where the Council, or *Conciliabolo*, as he called it, had been
convoked after the meeting at Tours.   Louis XII. had himself
demanded of the Florentines that they should at least offer one
proof of fidelity to France, by allowing it to be held within their
dominions.   This demand caused a lengthy debate in the Council
of Eighty, at a meeting attended by more than one hundred
members.   They had no desire to offend the Pope, but neither
did they wish to forfeit the French alliance, and this second consideration prevailed, being supported by the suffrage of the
followers of Savonarola, who had always urged this plan of a
Council.   So, as early as the month of May, it was decided to
consent to the King's request ; but it was also agreed to keep
their decision secret.   The only effect of this secrecy was that the
Pope for a time preserved a show of mild and temperate intentions
towards the Republic, upon which, however, he was resolved to
wreak vengeance at the earliest opportunity.[1]

Meanwhile a summons to the Council of Pisa, placarded on the
doors of various churches, had been prepared by the Cardinals of
Santa Croce, San Malò, and Cosenza, who declared themselves the
mouthpieces of their colleagues, and invited the presence of the
Pope himself.   On the 28th of May, the Pontiff, with the utmost
surprise and indignation, beheld this notice nailed to the door of
the principal church in Rimini.

Although the matter went on slowly, it was steadily pursued,
and Julius felt that he must strike a counter-blow.   In March,
1511, he nominated eight new Cardinals.   Two of these, Mathias
Lang and the Bishop of Sitten (or Sion), were chosen for political
reasons ; but the others, each of whom paid from ten to twelve
thousand ducats, were nominated partly to obtain funds much
needed at that moment for the war, partly to fill with trusty
adherents the gap caused by the desertion of others.   Besides this,
he at last decided to call a Council at the Lateran in opposition to
that of Pisa, and on the 18th of July, 1511, he convoked it for the
19th of April, 1512, threatening the schismatic Cardinals with
immediate degradation from their dignity, unless they rendered
immediate submission.   Nevertheless preparations for the *Con-*

---

[1] Filippo dei Nerli, "Commentarii dei fatti civili occorsi dentro la città di
Firenze."   Augsburg, 1728, bk. v. pp. 102, 103 ; Guicciardini, "Storia d'Italia,'
bk. ix. ch. iv.

ciliabolo made progress, being urgently pressed on by King Louis XII. ; and in September even gained the adhesion of the ever fickle Maximilian. At this moment the Emperor was recurring to his fantastic dream of having himself proclaimed Pope,[1] and therefore, as Emperor, issued mandates to the different States bidding them send their Orators to Pisa.[2] At the same time the Pope despatched to Florence the Bishop of Cortona, a Florentine by birth, to warn the Republic against allowing the *Conciliabolo* to meet in its territories, by hinting at the serious calamities which would inevitably ensue. But the Republic, already placed between two fires, and already bound by promises to Louis XII., neither dared to consent nor refuse, and only hoped to delay matters by temporizing.

The disturbance and irritation caused by these affairs twice prostrated the white-haired Pontiff on a sick bed, first in June and again in August, when he was actually believed to be dead. Already, according to custom, the pillage of his private rooms had begun, when the Duke of Urbino, who was still in Rome awaiting the judgment of the four Cardinals, hastened to the Vatican, and found his uncle alive. The city had risen in revolt, and Pompeo, nephew of Prospero Colonna, condemned by his family to assume the cowl, notwithstanding his vocation for the sword, came to the front for a short time as a new Stefano Porcaro. But just as a republican form of government was being organized, it was learnt that the terrible Pope had regained his full strength, and all plans dissolved in air.

In fact, Julius II. plunged into action with greater ardour than before. Both Pisa and Florence were placed under interdict for having sanctioned the preliminary formalities of the Council on the 1st of September, and he only absolved the Duke of Urbino, in order to make use of him in the war. He then concluded a so-called Holy League with Venice and Spain against France, leaving the Emperor the option of joining him. The Pope was to collect 400 men-at-arms, 500 light horse, 6000 infantry ; Spain 1200 men-at-arms, 1000 light horse, 10,000 infantry ; Venice 800 men-

---

[1] See Gregorovius, "Geschichte," &c. P. Lehmann, "Das Pisaner Concil von" 1511, "Inaugural Dissertation." Breslau, Jungfer, 1874.

[2] L'Amico, "Vita di N. Machiavelli," in note to pp. 356 and 357. There are two letters, with some misprints, one dated 7th of September, 1511, from the Pope against the Council, the other dated 27th of September, from the Emperor in favour of it. The originals are in the Florence Archives.

at-arms, 1000 light horse, 8000 infantry. Besides this the Pope was to contribute 20,000 ducats the month, Venice the same amount, and also fourteen light galleys, and Spain twelve light galleys.[1] The viceroy of Naples, Don Raimondo de Cardona, was nominated Captain General. The objects of the League were: the union of the Catholic Church; the extirpation of the *Conciliabolo;* the recovery of Bologna and all other territories, Ferrara included, belonging or presumed to belong to the Church; the recovery of the Venetian territory in Northern Italy; and war against all opposing these schemes, that is against France. The 5th of October, the Holy League was solemnly proclaimed in the church of Santa Maria del Popolo at Rome. On the 24th, the schismatic Cardinals of Santa Croce, Cosenza, St. Malò and Bayeux were stripped of their dignities and benefices. Cardinal San Severino was for the moment spared; but it was soon his turn to feel the weight of the Pope's anger.[2] Besides these measures his Holiness, the better to show his hostility towards the Florentine Republic, nominated Cardinal dei Medici as Legate, first at Perugia and then at Bologna.

The Florentines felt that the storm was upon them, and tried to shelter themselves as they best could. They had succeeded in obtaining the departure from Pisa of the three procurators who had on the 1st of September accomplished the purely formal preliminaries of the Council.[3] By a Commission dated 10th of September, they then despatched Machiavelli on various errands, first to try and meet the Cardinals on the road to Pisa and persuade them to wait; then to hasten to Milan with the same message to the viceroy; and finally to France, to expound and explain the true state of affairs. "No one," so ran his instructions, "shows any wish to attend the Council, and therefore it only serves to irritate the Pope against us; and for this reason we make request either that it shall not sit at Pisa, or shall at least be suspended for the present. No prelate seems to be coming from Germany; from France very few and very slowly. And it is a matter of universal astonishment to see a Council proclaimed by three Cardinals only, while the few others who were said to adhere to it, dissimulate their opinions and defer their arrival. Notwithstand-

[1] Guicciardini, "Storia d'Italia," vol. v. p. 29.

[2] Lehmann, "Das Pisaner Concil von" 1511; Brosch, "Papst Julian II. und die Gründung des Kirchen Staates," p. 234 and fol.

[3] Buonaccorsi, "Diario," p. 163.

ing this, it is said that the fortress is to be occupied and the city filled with men-at-arms, for the which reason disorders have already occurred at Pisa, which even lies under the Papal interdict, and wherein the chief ecclesiastical authorities have declared against the Council. If, therefore, there should be no hope of agreement between the Pope and the King, and if the latter cannot be persuaded to desist altogether, he should at least be induced to delay for two or three months." [1]

On the 13th of September, Machiavelli sent a letter from San Donnino, where he had found the Cardinals of St. Malô, Santa Croce, Cosenza and San Severino, who informed him that they were going to Pisa by Pontremoli, without touching Florence. But before going on, they intended waiting ten or twelve days for the arrival of prelates from France. On the 15th, the Florentine ambassador, Francesco Pandolfini, wrote from Milan that Machiavelli had already arrived, and been presented to the viceroy, Gaston de Foix, to whom he had explained his object. He declared to him that the Florentines did not refuse the Cardinals a safe conduct, as these had immediately given the viceroy to understand ; but merely begged them to consider the dangers to which they were exposed by the Pope's preparations for war. And Gaston de Foix gave the soldier-like answer that a safe conduct ought to imply an escort of five or six hundred lances.[2] From Milan, Machiavelli went straight to France. And on the 24th of the same month Roberto Acciaiuoli wrote from Blois, that he had gone with him to the King to read his Majesty a memorial they had together drawn up. "The King earnestly desired peace, would feel grateful to those helping him to bring it about, and had convoked the Council for the speedier attainment of this aim. It had not been possible to persuade him that dread of the Council was urging the Pope to war instead of peace. It was the King's desire that the Council should commence where it had been convoked, but he had added that it would not meet before All Saints' Day, and would shortly be transferred elsewhere."[3]

---

[1] " Opere," vol. vii. p. 394. The original is among the " Carte del Machiavelli," case v. No. 155, and is in the handwriting of one of the scriveners of the principal Chancery.

[2] Desjardins, *op. cit.*, vol. ii. pp. 528–32.

[3] " Opere," vol. vii. p. 407. Two copies of this letter exist in the Florence Archives (class x. dist. 4, No. 109, now lettered " Dieci di Balìa, carteggio, Responsive," No. 105), one copy in Machiavelli's hand at sheet 99–100 ; the other in a different hand (with an addendum containing the transcription of the cipher) at

After this colloquy Machiavelli immediately set out for Florence, was there by the 2nd of November, and left for Pisa on the following day.[1]

The vacillating behaviour of the Florentines neither satisfied France nor conciliated the Pope. When struck by the interdict, they had appealed against it to the General Council, without specifying whether they meant that of Pisa or that of Rome. They compelled the priests of a few churches to perform divine service, so that all who wished might attend it. Nor did they stop at this point, but brought forward and carried a law strongly seconded in Council by the Gonfalonier, empowering the magistrates to levy a tax on the clergy. This tax, to gradually amount to the sum of 120,000 florins, was to be exacted in the event of the Pope making war upon the Florentines, and was to be paid back within a year if no war took place, and within five if it should.[2] This proved that if it came to the worst the Florentines were determined to protect themselves ; and Pandolfo Petrucci turned the circumstance to account by persuading the Pope to march with his army towards Bologna, which was in no condition for defence, instead of passing through Tuscany, where he would have found himself in a mountainous region, and would have been obliged to encounter Florentines and French at the same time.

Petrucci urged these measures most strongly, not only because war in Tuscany was always hurtful to all whose States were within its frontiers ; but also, because according to the treaty already concluded with them, he would have been bound to assist the Florentines.[3] For this reason he also begged the Pope to consider that they had consented to the Council with the utmost unwillingness, and solely from fear of the French, in whose arms

sheet 94–97. This file comprises ten more of Acciaiuoli's letters, from the 2nd to the 30th of October, and there are several others in the following file ; but none in Machiavelli's handwriting.

[1] The journey occupied fifty-four days, as he had started from Florence on the 10th of September. He received the usual pay of twelve small lire a day, inclusive of his ordinary salary, and also sixty gold florins for his travelling expenses. "Opere" (P. M.), vol. i. pp. 80, 81.

[2] Cambi, "Istorie," vol. ii. (xxi. of the "Delizie" ecc.) p. 268 and fol. ; Guicciardini, "Storia d'Italia," vol. v. bk. x. ch. ii. pp. 34–41.

[3] In fact, when at a later period the Florentines were in peril of attack from the Spaniards, they reminded him, although in vain, of his sworn promises. See in the Sienna Archives ("Lettere alla Balìa"), the letter dated 24th of August, 1512.

they would certainly have to throw themselves, in case of attack.[1] This was all true, as it was truer still that their temporizing, hesitating policy, at the moment when a great conflict was rapidly drawing near, might endanger the very existence of the Republic. Yet this policy was forced upon them by the knowledge of their own weakness, by internal dissensions, and even by the uncertainty of the intelligence forwarded by their ambassadors from different parts. Pandolfini, who was with Gaston de Foix, wrote in October from Brescia : "The designs of the King of the Romans take so much time to colour, that often no sooner are they coloured than it becomes necessary to alter them, on account of the change of conditions and preconceptions upon which they were formed. Therefore, as regards him, we must wait upon events.[2] Then, too, French affairs are carried on here in such wise, that sinister results may be expected at any moment, for in the long run the bad government of men has never given birth to any good thing. The King is very hot for the Council ; but if your Excellencies could get it delayed for a month, it would be very easy to avoid it altogether, since by that time flames will have burst out elsewhere. Haste would perhaps kindle a blaze in our own house, with no possibility of extinguishing it even if the Council were quenched." [3]

So it came about that the Council was sanctioned, although most reluctantly ; all sorts of obstacles were placed in its way and it was turned into ridicule. When the Cardinals wished to come to Pisa, accompanied by three or four hundred French lances under the command of Othon de Foix, Lord of Lautrech, the Florentines instantly despatched Francesco Vettori, who plainly informed the Cardinal of St. Malô, that should they arrive accompanied by men-at-arms, they would be treated as foes. Upon this they came escorted only by Othon and Châtillon with a handful of bowmen. All requisite precautions were taken to maintain order in Pisa and the neighbouring cities, and the Pope showed so much satisfaction that he suspended the interdict until the middle of November.[4]

---

[1] Guicciardini, " Storia d'Italia," vol. v. bk. x. ch. ii. pp. 41, 42.

[2] Desjardins, *op. cit.*, vol. ii. pp. 533-37. Pandolfini's letter from Brescia, 13-14th of October, 1511.

[3] Ibid. pp. 537-40. Letter from the same, 15-17th of October.

[4] Guicciardini, " Storia d'Italia," vol. v. book x. ch. ii. pp. 45, 46 ; Buonaccorsi, " Diario," p. 164 ; Nardi, vol. i. p. 452.

As we have said,[1] Machiavelli, on the third day of November, left Florence for Pisa, where other Florentine envoys had already arrived, taking with him a few soldiers to guard the Council, which had held a preparatory meeting on the 1st, attended only by four of the cardinals and about fifteen prelates. The clergy of the cathedral had refused them the use of the church vestments and would not even yield them the right of officiating in the church, of which the doors were actually locked. But the Florentines ordered that the use both of cathedral and vestments should be freely granted, without any obligation on the local clergy to attend the Council if they had no wish to do so.[2]

Thus at last the first meeting of the Council could be held in the cathedral on the 5th November, and after the celebration of high mass by Cardinal Santa Croce, in the presence of his three colleagues, four decrees were proclaimed. These declared the validity of the present Council, declared the Pope's censure of it to be null and void ; also proclaimed the nullity of the Lateran Council, on the ground of its being neither free nor independent, and finally decreed the condemnation and punishment of all those who, having been invited to be present, had failed to appear.[3]

The following day Machiavelli wrote that he had spoken with Cardinal Santa Croce in order to persuade him, as if of his own impulse, to transfer the Council elsewhere. " By removing it to France or Germany," he had told him, "they would find the Pope much less adverse to it, and would also gain more adherents, and greater obedience : matters of much weight in an affair of this sort, where one willing follower would be worth more than twenty dragged by force." [4] The second meeting was held on the 7th November, and the third, fixed for the 14th, took place instead on the 12th, after which it was decided that the fourth should be held

---

[1] See p. 526.   [2] Guicciardini, *op. cit.*, vol. ii. pp. 45, 46.

[3] Letter of Machiavelli from Pisa, dated 6th November. " Opere," vol. vii. p. 414 and fol. In note to p. 415 and fol. will be also found the reports of the meetings of the Council, at which Machiavelli was present. A note at p. 178 of vol. vi. of the " Opere" (P. M.) might lead the reader to suppose that Machiavelli had shared in the compilation of these reports, but this was not the case. In the letter accompanying them, the compilers merely say : " As to the solemn mass . . . we send your Excellencies a brief summary of as much as we could retain, relying for the rest unknown to us on the sagacity of Niccolò Machiavelli, who was also present, and is more skilled than ourselves in these matters." The Reports and letter are in the Florence Archives, class x. dist. 4, No. 110, now lettered " Dieci di Balìa, Responsive," No. 106, at sheet 54-55, 102 and 148.

[4] " Opere," vol. vii. p. 414 and fol.

on the 13th December, at Milan. The indifference, or rather patent disapproval of the Republic, the hostility of the mass of the people, and a serious riot that had consequently occurred between the Pisans and the Florentine soldiers on the one side, the French and the lackeys of the Cardinals on the other, the which riot was only with difficulty suppressed by Othon de Foix and Châtillon, who were both wounded, were the reasons leading to the speedy removal of the Council to Milan.

In that city the Cardinals slandered the Florentines in every way, trying to irritate the minds of the French officers against them. But even in Milan the Council encountered the same general indifference, the same aversion on the part of the clergy, who, on the Cardinals' arrival, refused to celebrate divine service. The lesser clergy only gave reluctant obedience to the orders of the Senate; the Canons and others continued their resistance until they were threatened with exile, or Frenchmen were sent into their houses.[1] The truth was, that as Guicciardini justly observed, all perceived that these Cardinals were merely ambitious men, stirred by personal interests, and that they stood in " no less need of being reformed than those whom they intended to reform."[2] The Council served as a weapon of war in the great contest so soon to be decided by arms, and therefore public attention was fixed on to that contest alone, to the exclusion of everything else. Accordingly, the Florentines, although finally freed from the annoyance of the Council, experienced no relief, for they had now to study if it were possible to preserve the bare existence of the Republic in the flood of coming disaster.

---

[1] Desjardins, *op. cit.*, vol. ii. pp. 543–5 ; Pandolfini's letter from Milan, dated 1–7th December.   [2] " Storia d'Italia," vol. v. bk. x. ch. ii. p. 46.

END OF VOL. I.

APPENDIX.

APPENDIX.

DOCUMENT I.

An Autograph Letter of Machiavelli, though not written in his name, and without signature, date or address, relating to family affairs.[1]

Carissime frater. Sabato fece 8 dì, ti scripse,[2] dandoti notitia come e' ci pareva da pensare di far San Piero in Mercato litigioso,[3] come hauto da messer Baldassarre per simonìa perchè 'l piovano vechio non volle mai cedere alla renuntia, se non haveva cento ducati da Pèro, et di questo ce ne è tanti testimoni et sì autentici et sì disposti al provare, che se questa cosa si dà in accomandita ad chi voglia la golpe, el priore ci ha una speranza grandissima, et crede che sia costì chi ci attenderà. Messesi innanzi messer P°. Accolti o el Cardinal di San Piero in Vincula o messer Ferrando Puccietti.

Ad me pare che tu ti ingegni di tòrre huomo che *non solum* sia atto ad favorire la causa, ma anchora ad splendere di suo, et che dal canto nostro non corra spesa ; et più tosto convenire collui grassamente, purchè e' titoli una volta rimanghino : dell' altre cose . . . mettile ad tuo modo, perchè la spesa si lievi da dosso ad noi, et che altri [4] . . . colli favori et con la industria et con danari. Dal canto nostro puoi offerire la simonia

---

[1] " Carte del Machiavelli," cassetta i. n. 54. It was written in cipher, is deciphered in Machiavelli's handwriting, but refers to him as a third person. Neither does its style afford any proof that it is his. We give it as a simple curiosity, and because it has some relation with his two first letters. See text, book i. chap. i.

[2] It was first written thus : *ti scrivèmo el priore et io ;* this was afterwards cancelled and the words : *ti scripse* substituted.

[3] In the " Quaderno di Ricordanze," quoted by me in book i. chap. i., it is recorded that in 1393 Ciango dei Castellani left, among other legacies, to Buoninsegna and Filippo, son of Lorenzo Machiavelli, all the rights of patronage in the parish of San Piero in Mercato. [4] Gaps in the original which is torn at this point.

certa, la contenteza de'2/3 de' padroni, la possessione facile, le pruove della simonìa vera et autenticha, le quali son tucte cose da farci correre un di cotesti cortigiani, che non sogliono attendere ad altro che ad simile imprese, quando e' ne possono havere. Et tu sai che per la soddomia, che è causa più ingiusta, sono molti che hanno e' benefitii litigiosi, et assai li hanno perduti. E costì messer Giovanni delli Albizi, che è huomo d' animo : penserai se ad questo tu potessi valertene in cosa alcuna. Nicholò nostro ci farà tucti quelli favori che saranno possibili, et parli mill' anni vetere el fummo di questo fuoco. Le altre lettere si mandorno per la via dello 'mbasciatore, et harai ricevuto la cifera, con la quale hora ti scrivo. Di nuovo ti ricordo el mettere in questa impresa huomo che spenda et habbi favori da sè. *Vale.*[1]

DOCUMENT II.[2]

Letter of the Ten of Balìa to Paolo Vitelli urging him to take Pisa by storm.—15th August, 1499.

Illustri Capitaneo Paulo Vytello. Die xv augusti 1499. Anchorchè la Signoria Vostra, per mezo de nostri Comissarii, habbi più volte inteso lo animo et desiderio nostro, et che quella per la sua innata affectione verso della nostra Excelsa Repubblica non habbi bisogno di essere altrimenti pregata et exortata ad expedire quelle chose chi ci habbino a tornare in utilità et honore maximo ; *tamen* per lo offitio et debito nostro non vogliamo omettere di scrivere alla Signoria Vostra, et monstrarle come li infiniti oblighi habbiamo con seco, e' quali non sendo necessarii, non rianderemo altrimenti, richieghono di corroborarsi con questo ultimo della recuperatione di Pisa, per la quale *potissimum* li fu concesso lo arbitrio delli exerciti nostri. Et veramente quando noi pensiamo con noi medesimi la somma sua virtù, et quanto felice exito habbino auto e' preteriti sua conati, noi non dubitiamo in alcuno modo di conseguire questa desiderata victoria. Dall' altra parte, el desiderio che habbiamo di conseguirla, ci fa stara dubbii assai che la dilatione dèl tempo non rechi tale incomodità et disordine seco, che non sia in nostro potere el ripararvi ; nè ci darebbe mancho dispiacere quando tal cosa seguissi (*quod absit*), l' honore di che si priverrebbe Vostra Illustrissima Signoria, che lo utile, commodo et

---

[1] At the back of the letter there is written in another hand : "O' trovato *virum bone conditionis, qui vocatur* messer Bartolbleo (*sic*) Scaranfi, che expedisce *gratis*, et serviracci senza voler chosa alcuna. Farassi la impretatione ; dipoi, avanti si pigli piato, lo consiglereno bene."

[2] Florence Archives, cl. x. dist. 3, No. 91, a. c. 77. In the margin the amanuensis has written : *Exortatoria pulcherrima.* As we have mentioned in the body of the work, we have excellent reason to believe that this and the two following letters are by Machiavelli ; nevertheless we cannot positively assert them to be his, not having discovered the original manuscript, but only the copy preserved in the Chancery registers.

sicurtà dello Stato nostro, di che saremo privati noi, perchè non mancho habbiamo a core la grandeza sua che la preservatione nostra, di che sappiamo non bisognare farle altra fede che le opere che si sono facte sino a qui, le quali sempre si accresceranno con li meriti suoi. Sia adunque Vostra Signoria contenta et pregata volere prima coronare sè di cotanta victoria quale è cotesta, con admiratione nan solo di tutta Italia, ma di tutto el mondo; et dipoi, con satisfactione et nostra e di tutto questo popolo, preso supplicio di cotesti nostri ribelli, et reintegrati delle cose nostre, possiamo voltarci a chosa che facci la città nostra felicissima, et la Signoria Vostra non seconda ad alcuno altro, benchè antico et famosissimo capitano. A la quale del continuo ci offeriamo.

————

DOCUMENT III.[1]

Letter of the Ten to the Florentine Commissaries at the Camp of Captain Paolo Vitelli.—20th August, 1499.

Comissariis in Castris contra Pisanos. Die xx augusti 1499. Noi veggiamo, et con tanto dispiacere nostro quanto si possi mai sentire per alcun tempo, differirsi in modo cotesta giornata, che noi non sapiamo più che si sperare di bene ; perchè, nonobstante che voi scriviate che per tutta stanocte futura saranno ad ordine tutte le cose disegnate ; *tamen* per le parole del Capitano, non ci pare ancora vedere terra, nè ad che porto noi habbiamo ad applicare questa barchetta. Et se Sua Signoria dice che è per fare quello di bene può, et che elli è necessario che ancor noi lo aiutiamo, etc. ; noi non veggiamo in che cosa noi li siamo mancati, perchè e' ci pare havere infino a qui et concedutoli ogni cosa che Sua Signoria ci ha adomandata in sua particolarità, et provistolo in tutto quello ci ha richiesto a benefitio della impresa ; et per ultimo con quanta celerità ci è suto possibile, vi habbiamo provisto delle balle della lana, delle palle del fuocho lavorato, et della polvere in qualla quantità si è possuto ; et questa mattina, per non mancare del consueto, vi habbiamo mandato le lame del ferro stagnato, secondo ne richiedete ; et e' danari per rinfrescare e' soldati vi si sono promessi ogni volta ci advisavi il dì della giornata. Ma veggiendo con varie cavillationi et agiramenti tornare invano ogni nostra fatica, et ogni nostra diligentia usatasi anihillarsi,[2] sentiamo dolore infinito ; et se la honestà o le leggi el permettessino, egli è più giorni che due di noi sarebbono venuti costì, per vedere con gli occhi et personalmente intendere la origine di cotanti aggiramenti, poi che voi o non ce li volete scrivere o in facto non ve li pare conoscere. Et veramente noi credevamo, et ancora non possiamo se non crederlo, che cotesti Signori volessino più presto tentare la fortuna, et essere

1 Florence Archives, cl. x. dist. 3, No. 91, a c. 81.
2 In the margin is written : *O quantus moeror* !

ributtati per forza da cotesta expeditione, che per socordia et inertia, consumando il tempo, essere necessitati, per la diminutione della reputatione et delle forze, partirsi di costì con una inhonesta fuga. Il che succederà ad ogni modo, se passa due giorni da oggi che la forza non si sia tentata ; perchè, venuta la pagha nuova, cotesti pochi soldati vi restano, haranno iuxta causa di partirsi, et e' nostri cittadini, per parere loro essere dondolati, non saranno per volersi più votare le borse, veggendo non essere del passato suto alcuno utile alla loro città. Noi vi parliamo liberamente a ciò che con la prudentia vostra possiate tocchare fondo, et a noi fare intendere apertamente come ci habbiamo a governare, se hora non succeda la cosa secondo l' ordine dato.[1] Parendoci non havere mancato in nulla, saremo in ferma opinione di essere trastullati, et faremo tutta quella provisione per la salute et honore nostro che ci occorrerà. Et perchè dal canto nostro, come insino ad hora si è facto, non resti ad fare alcuna chosa, siamo contenti che il Capitano facci venire costì a' soldi sua messer Piero Ghambacorti,[2] et riceva *etiam* e' balestrieri a cavallo sono in Pisa, secondo che voi ne scrivete. Il che facciamo contra a nostra voglia ; per molte ragioni, le quali noi vi habbiamo per l' adrieto significate : pure il desiderio habbiamo fare piacere a Sua Signoria ci fa non pensare se non satisfarli ; et così confortate Sua Signoria satisfare a noi di questo unico et singulare benefitio, di fare questa benedecta giornata, della quale voi, per nostra parte, con quelle parole vi occorreranno più efficaci li pregherrete, et con ogni instantia graverrete.

Le genti del Signore di Piombino si potranno in parte satisfare alla giunta de' danari vi manderemo, et con questa speranza li intracterrete.

Habbiamo questa mattina lettere da Milano, come e' Franzesi hanno expugnato Annone, castello populato assai, forte di sito, di munitioni et di presidio, in uno dì, et noi siamo già con cotesta obsidione a dì 20, et non sapiamo qual successo seguirà.

Da Lucha intendiamo come Rinieri della Saxetta è tornato in Pisa, sì che vedete quello possiamo sperare, poi che luy vi creda stare sicuro hora, et per lo adrieto ne dubitava. *Valete.*

DOCUMENT IV.

Another Letter of the Ten to the Florentine Commissaries with Paolo Vitelli.—25th August, 1499, attributed to Machiavelli.

Comissariis in Castris contra Pisanos. Die xxv augusti 1499.[3]—Se voi vedessi in quanta mala contenteza et afflictione di animo è tutta questa città, non che a voi che siete membri di quella, ma a qualunche altro verrebbe istupore et admirazione grande ; ma chi sapessi come le

---

[1] Here in the margin is written : *Verba minantia.*
[2] This is he who was afterwards arrested and tried in Florence.
[3] Florence Archives, cl. x. dist. 3, No. 91, a. c. 85t.

cose fino a qui sieno procedute, et con quale spendio conducte, et di che speranza nutriti, non se ne maraviglierebbe, perchè conoscerebbe noy et questa città dopo una lunga fatica et dispendio, quando aspectava indubitata victoria, essere minacciati di manifesta ruina ; et sì de repente la vedrebbe menare da uno extremo all' altro, che più tosto la iudicherebbe animosa per non si prostèrnere et invilire in tanta augustia, che altrimenti. Et veramente e' ci dorrebbe manco ogni damno che di cotesta impresa fussi resultato a la città nostra, quando e' si fussi un tracto secondo el desiderio nostro tentato animosamente la forza ; perchè, se ne fussino suti ributtati, si sarebbe da' nostri cittadini con più prompteza reparàta tanta forza che si fussi al nemiço superiore. Ma sendosi consumata tanta fanteria, et preparata con tanti danni, in otio et sanza farne alcuno experimento in favore della nostra città non sapiamo nè che ci dire nè con qual ragioni exscusarci in cospecto di tutto questo popolo, el quale ci parrà havere pasciuto di favole, tenendolo di di in dì con vana promessa di certa victoria. Il che tanta più ci duole quanto più ce lo pare havere conosciuto, et con ogni efficacia ricordata alli antecessori vostri.[1] Pure, poi che Dio o la fortuna e qual si fussi altra causa ha condocto le cose in termine che bisogna o soldar di nuovo fanteria, o perdere con perpetua infamia coteste artiglierie, ci sforzeremo di non mancare di fare quanto ci fia possibile.

Et perchè nel fare nuovi danari, per havere a fare nuovi provvedimenti, andrà più tempo ; et desiderando che in questo mezo coteste cose si salvino, habbiamo scripto per tutto el territorio nostro, per numero di comandati, de' quali buona parte dovevano essere costì subito, et noi seguiremo col provedimento, per poterci valere di buon numero di fanti freschi e pratichi come ci scrivete. . . .

Siamo a hore 3, et habbiamo differito la staffetta, perchè desideravamo pure con quella mandarvi somma di danari. Ma per essere hoggi domenica, et tutto il giorno suti occupati nella pratica, non ne habbiamo possuto expedire alcuna somma ; ma domattina di buon' ora vi se ne manderà quelli ci fia possibile.

—

DOCUMENT V.[2]

Letter of the Ten to the Commissary Giacomini Tebalducci.
1st July, 1502.

Commissario generali, Antonio Iacomino. Die prima iulii 1502.—
Hiarsera ti si scripse quello ci occorreva in risposta di più tua ; haviamo dipoi ricevute l' ultime di hieri, et per quelle inteso cosa che ci satisfa,

[1] Their two predecessors had been seized by malarious fever, and one of them, Piero Corsini, had died of it. They were therefore succeeded by Paolo Antonio Soderini and Francesco Gherardi.—*Vide* Guicciardini, "Storia Fiorentina," ch. xx. p. 207.

[2] Florence Archives, cl. x. dist. 3, No. 101, a. c. 2 : Machiavelli's autograph.

et questo è come Anghiari si tiene, et come e' nemici non lo possono molto sforzare per mancamento di palle, etc. Et havendo dipoi ricevuto una lettera da M.re di Volterra,[1] el quale pochi dì sono mandamo ad Urbino ad el Duca Valentinese, della quale ti mandiamo copia, et per quella intenderai quello che lui giudicha et advisa delle genti di quello Duca. El quale adviso, quando fussi vero, ci renderebbe più sicuri, et più facile ci farebbe la recuperatione delle cose nostre. Ma desidereremmo bene che la perdita di quelle non fussi maggiore che la si sia suta infino ad qui, ad ciò che si cominciassi dipoi più facilmente ad racquistare la reputatione, et non si continuassi in perderla. Et per questo se si possessi soccorrere Anghiari o monstrarli qualche speranza di soccorso, ci sarebbe sopradmodo grato, et tornerebbe molto approposito alle cose nostre : il che ci fe' più desiderare uno adviso haviamo hauto da huomo prudente, che ci scrive dalla Pieve ad San Stephano, significandoci prima come gli Anghiaresi si difendono ingenuamente ; et che se si mandassi un cento cavalli et qualche fante, admonendogli che facessino spalla ad quelli della Pieve et ad altri del paese, sarebbono per molestare intanto e' nemici, che sarebbono necessitati levarsi de campo. Et per questa cagione ci è parso mandarti la presente volando, ad ciò veggha quello si può fare in questa cosa, et non manchi del possibile. Et ad noi pare che, havendo hora la gente franzese alle spalle, si possa governare le cose costì più audacemente, et con più fiducia mettersi avanti ; et però di nuovo ti ricordiamo, se possibile è, se non in facto, *saltem* in demostratione, rincorare quelli nostri fedeli d' Anghiari, si per dare animo loro ad stare forti, si *etiam* per non lo tòrre ad li altri, et per non dimostrare ad li subditi nostri che noi li lasciamo in preda et si vilmente nelle mani d' un semplice soldato : et di questo ne aspectiamo risposta, et lo effecto se li è possibile.

Noi attenderemo ad sollicitare e' Franzesi, e' quali fieno ad Sexto domani ad ogni modo, et di mano in mano li respigneremo secondo che ad voi occorra o al capitano di epsi, con el quale speriamo di essere domattina ad Lugho. Scriverete oltre ad di questo ad Poppi, alla Pieve, et se voi potete, ad Anghiari et al Borgo, confortando, monstrando gli aiuti propinqui et che presto con loro satisfactione et danno delli adversarii saremo liberi da ogni molestia. *Bene valete.*

DOCUMENT VI.[2]

Letter of the Ten to the Commissary at Borgo la S. Sepolero.— *14th May,* 1503.

Petro Ardinghello Commissar. Burgi. Diex iiij maij 1503.—Noi haviamo questo dì ricevute tre tua, l' una di hieri et l' altre d' avanti

[1] Francesco Soderini, Bishop of Volterra, at that time ambassador to Valentinois.
[2] Florence Archives, cl. x. dist. 3, No. 103, at sheet 172 : Machiavelli's autograph.

hieri; et commendiamoti della diligentia che usi et hai usata in intendere
et advisarci. Et perchè tu desideri sapere prima quello che delle genti
venute ad Perugia non ne intendiamo, et dipoi quanto noi confidiamo
nella natura et fortuna di quello Duca, ti rispondiamo, che da Roma di
coteste genti nè dell' altre non se ne è mai inteso nulla; et se ci haves-
simo ad rapportare ad quelle lettere, ad Perugia non sarebbe un cavallo;
nè ce ne maravigliamo come fai tu, perchè le ven, gono di verso Roma
et non da Roma, sendo sute alloggiate 30 o 47 miglia discosto; et moven-
dosi *ad nutum Principis*, et ad hora che lo Oratore nostro non ne può
havere notitia, non ce ne ha possuto advisare. Pertanto conviene rap-
portarcene ad te, del quale crediamo li advisi essere fedeli e ben fon-
dati; nè possiamo di coteste cose fare altro iuditio che si possa chi è
costì, nè dartene altro adviso.

Et se noi habbiamo da pensare alla natura et fortuna di quello
Signore, non crediamo che la meriti disputa, perchè tucti gli andamenti
et cenni suoi meritono di essere considerati et advertiti da chi è discosto,
non che da noi ad chi lui è addosso. Nè manchiamo di pensare che
quelle genti conviene sieno venute là, o per venire alle stantie, o per
assicurarsi di quella città, o per assaltarci per divertire el guasto, o per
darci tali sospecti che noi o non diamo el guasto a' Pisani, per paura di
essere divertiti, o, dandosi, non si dia gagliardamente, come si farebbe
quando fussimo liberi da ogni sospecto. Le prime dua cagioni ci dànno
piccola brigha, la terza pensiamo che el Duca ne habbi voglia grande
et che la desideri, quando e' non habbi ad havere altro rispecto che l'
nostro. Et perchè noi non veggiamo però che sieno cessate tucti e' ris-
pecti, ne stiamo alquanto sollevati con lo animo, perchè nè lui nè el Papa
sono sì pochi obbligati ad el Re, nè el Re ha tanti impedimenti, che loro
non li debbino havere, non vogliamo dire reverentia, ma respecti grandi,
o che lui facciendo loro qualche temerità non li possa correggere. Et
benchè noi conosciamo quello Duca volonteroso, giovane et pieno di
confidentia; *tamen* non lo giudichiamo al tucto temerario, et che sia per
per entrare in una impresa che facci alla fine ruinarlo, come delli altri
che infino ad qui vi sono entrati. Non siamo però ostinati in questa
opinione, anzi crediamo che facilmente ci potremo ingannare, et per
questo si pensa ad non lasciare cotesto paese al tucto abbandonato di
forze. Diciamoti bene questo, che se si ha da dubitare di assalto mani-
festo ad 12 soldi per lira, e' se ne ha da dubitare ad 18 soldi di furto,
et acciò che lui sotto qualche colore potessi nascondersi, come sarebbe
di fare rebellare una di coteste terre, et possere excusarsene. Et perchè
ad questo si ha ad pensare più noi, più te lo haviamo sempre ricordato,
et di nuovo te lo ricordiamo, che ti guardi dagl' inganni, et di non essere
giunto incauto in modo, o che di nocte non ti truovi e' nemici in corpo, o
di dì non sia ad tempo ad serrare le porte.

Nè possiamo dirti altro in questa materia, nè dartene altri advisi, perchè
quanto ti si discorre et scrivetisi, ti si dice in su li advisi tuoi; et quando
quelle genti vi fussino venute perquella quarta cagione di farci o risolvere

la presa o ire freddamente, siamo disposti che ci facci male la forza et non la opinione. Nè voliamo desistere, nè allentare un punto da lo incepto nostro ; perchè ci conforta ad questo el malo essere de' Pisani, el desiderio di toccarne fondo, la causa iusta et li conforti della Maestà del Re, el quale non vorrà che le cose cominciate sotto gli auspitii suoi habbino altro fine che honorevole. . . .

DOCUMENT VII.[1]

Letter of the Ten to the Commissaries at the Camp before Pisa.—
27th May, 1503.

Commissariis in Castris. Die 27 *Maij* 1503.—Questo giorno occorre fare risposta alla vostra di hiarsera, data ad 2½ di notte, per la quale restiamo advisati della cagione perchè hieri non passasti Arno, et come hoggi disegnavate ad ogni modo passarlo, et noi crediamo lo habbiate facto. Et quanto a' fanti da pagarsi di nuovo, vi si mandorno hieri e' danari, et con lo adviso come havessi ad soldare et pagarli, et così come e' danari dovettono arrivare hiarsera di buona hora, così questa sera debbono essere arrivati Lazzero di Scaramuccia et il Guicciardino, perchè così ci promissono. Et perchè voi ci dite circha el capo da darsi ad quelli cento fanti da farsi costì, non vi parere ad proposito Bernardo di messere Criacho, rispecto alla emulatione, ci conformiamo facilmente nell' opinione vostra ; et se per la nostra vi se ne scripse, fu più per ricordo che perchè ne fussimo al tucto resoluti ; et però ve ne governerete come vi parrà, et noi tucto approverremo.

El discorso che voi ci fate del passare in val di Serchio, et la prontepza dello animo vostro, non ci potrebbe più satisfare, il che tanto più vi si adcrescerà, quanto voi vi vedrete provisti di quella forza più per li fanti 200 nuovamente ordinati. Nè vi potremo più confortare ad procedere animosamente et tirare la 'mpresa avanti ; perchè veggiamo el tempo fuggirsi fra le mani, et essere in preiuditio nostro et in favore de'nemici, e' quali si vede che non pensono ad altro, se non come e' possessino temporeggiarci. Voliamo nondimancho ricordarvi più per el debito dello ofitio nostro, che per credere che bisogni farlo, che noi equalmente desideriamo et stimiamo la salute di cotesto exercito quanto il danno dell'inimici, et però vi confortiamo ad adoperare in questa parte animo et in quella prudentia, et ad pensare bene ogni accidente che potessi nascere, non perchè vi facci stòrre dalla impresa, nè dal procedere avanti ; ma per farvi entrare ne'periculi con maggiore securtà et più cautamente. Le cose che noi vi havemo ad ricordare in questa parte sarebbono molte ; ma non ci pare da dirle per giudicarlo superfluo, sapiendo voi el paese come egli è facto, le fiumare come le stanno, quello possete temere da Pisa per la disperatione loro, quello da Lucha per la invidia et odio

---

[1] Florence Archives, cl. x. dist. 3, No. 107, at sheet 24t : Machiavelli's autograph.

naturale di ogni nostro bene. Et havendo innanzi ad gli ochi tucte queste cose, potrete facilmente pensare ad li rimedii, e' quali noi giudichiamo facili, stando voi ordinati sempre, et ciascuno sotto le bandiere sua, non permettendo ad alchuno che esca dell'ordine, o per cupidità di preda, o per altra insolentia che suole disordinare e' campi, et fare spesso ruine grandissime : di che stiamo di buona voglia per conoscere e' capi, et sapere che tenete bene el segno nostro, et vi fate obbidire.

Noi, perchè la desperatione de' Pisani non ci offenda, haviamo provedute quelle tante forze havete con voi ; ma perchè l' odio de' Luchesi non vi nuoca oltre alle forze vi trovate, come più dì fa vi si dètte notitia, si mandò Andrea Adimari in montagna di Pistoia, L° Spinelli in val di Nievole, et prima si era mandato Girolamo de' Pilli in Lunigiana, con ordine tenessi parati tucti gli huomini delle loro provincie et in su quella frontiera di Lucha, per assaltare e' Luchesi da quella banda, quando e' movessino contro a di voi in su la factione del val di Serchio. Commissesi loro s' intendessino con voi, et colli cenni, ordini et consigli vostri si governassino. Non si sono dipoi altrimenti sollecitati, per volerli lasciare disporre ad voi, e' quali scriverrete quanto sia necessario, componendovi con quelli del modo, acciò che altri stia a' termini, et che disordine non segua sanza bisogno.

Et perchè voi ci dite, che non potendo condurre con voi in una volta tante vectovaglie in val di Serchio, che voi potessi fare quella factione, et che, bisognandovi ritornare per esse, è bene pensare di farne una canova o ad Bientina o ad Monte Carlo ; vi si risponde che questa cura ha ad essere vostra, et di quello di voi che ha ad rimanere ad Cascina, dove è bene rimanghi tu, Pierfrancesco, ad ogni mòdo, perchè una volta havete la Comunità obbligata ad portare el pane, havete costì la farina, havete e' ministri che ne hanno caricho, a' quali potrete ordinare dove le habbino ad volgere et ad farne canova, per rinfrescarne lo exercito, anchora che ad noi paressi che fussi più ad proposito fare capo con quelle a Bientina che ad Monte Carlo, per potervi servire del lago, et condurvele co' navicelli incontro.

Noi crediamo che vi sia venuto in consideratione in questa passata d'Arno, ch' e' Pisani non possono havere altro expediente ad molestarvi, che assaltare Cascina o qualchuno di cotesti luoghi nostri ; et siamo certi, havendovi pensato, vi harete anchora proveduto. Et noi, stimando questa cosa, disegnavamo mandare ad Cascina gli huomini d'arme di Luca Savello, e' quali questa sera in parte debbono essere comparsi ad Poggibonzi. Ma non volendo noi *etiam* abbandonare in tucto le cose di sopra, per esservi pure qualche cavallo del Duca, c'è parso fermarle ad Poggibonzi, per potercene servire ad un tracto, et ad Cascina et di sopra. Haviamovi voluto scrivere la verità, et voi darete nome che decte genti habbino ad venire subito costì ad Cascina, per tenere e' nemici addreto, et valervi di questa reputatione. . . .

DOCUMENT VIII.

Letter of the Ten to Antonio Giacomini.—29th August, 1504.[1]

Antonio Jacomino. Die xx augusti 1504.—Hiarsera ti si scripse della deliberatione facta da noi circha el voltare Arno alla torra ad Fagiano, et come noi volevamo fare questa factione subito dopo el guasto, et che per questo egli era necessario che tu pensassi dove, dato el guasto, stèssi bene el campo, per rendere securo chi lavorerà ad tale opera. Di nuovo ti replichiamo per questa el medesimo, perchè tale deliberatione è ferma, et voliamo ad ogni modo che la si metta innanzi ; et però bisognia che oltre allo aiutare tale cosa collo effecto, la si aiuti *etiam* colla demostratione. Questo ti si dice, perchè se fussi costì alcuno condottiero ad chi non paressi, voliamo tu li possa fare intendere quale sia lo animo nostro, et che noi voliamo unitamente et con le parole et co' fatti la sia favorita.

Et perchè noi non voliamo che si perda punto di tempo, domattina mandereno costà Giuliano Lapi e Colombino, ad ciò sieno teco, et, mostroti el disegnio, possiate ordinare quanto sia necessario. Et acciò intenda qualche particolare, e' si è ragionata che bisognino dumila opere il dì, et che gli habbino le vanghe et zappe : voliamo pagare questi huomini ad dieci soldi el dì per ciascuno. Bisogna adunque pensare se di cotesto paese all' intorno se ne può trarre tanti, perchè bisognia che siano buoni, pagandogli noi nel modo soprascripto. Et havendo ragunato costì 1000 marraioli, secondo lo adviso di Francesco Serragli, potrai examinare fra loro quali sieno sufficienti all' opera soprascripta, et li farai fermare et provedere degli instrumenti loro ; et el resto provedere in quel modo che ti occorrerà meglio. Et non ti bastando ad adempiere el numero questi luoghi convicini, te ne andrai ne' luoghi la propinqui ; et quando non si potessi el primo di cominciare più opera con dumila huomini voliamo si cominci con quelli più si può, et così quanto prima si può, adempia el numero decto.

Ragionerai tucte queste cose con Giuliano Lapi, et ti varrai dell' opera sua per comandare ad quelle cose che in tale factione sono necessarie. Mena decto Giuliano seco tre o quattro huomini per valersene, et noi facciamo conto che tu ti vaglia, oltre ad quelli, di Pagolo da Parrano et altri simili, che fussino in cotesto campo buoni ad essere soldati, et ad indirizare una simile faccenda. Nè ti scrivereno altro in questa cosa, ma ci rimettereno ad quello che ad bocca ti discorrerà Giuliano Lapi. Et el disopra ti si è scripto, acciò che intenda avanti allo arrivare suo, e' meriti di questa cosa, vi volga l' animo, et ti prepari ad quella con ogni modo possibile.

Fara' ci scrivere appunto da chi ne ha la cura, quante marre, vanghe, pale, et libbre d' auti si truovono costì in munitione' et di tucto ci darai adviso. Potrai cominciare ad fare comandare e' Comuni che venghino

---

con quelli huomini ti parrà, et un dì, quale tu giudicherai che si possa, principiare l' opera ; et farai che portino seco la metà vanghe, et l' altra metà meze pale et meze zappe.

————

DOCUMENT IX.

Letter of the Ten to the Commissary T. Tosinghi, 28th September, 1504.[1]

Tomaso Tosinghi, Commissario in Campo.   Die 28 *septembris,* 1504.— Questo dì si sono ricevute tre vostre lettere di hieri, le quali, perchè ci confermavano in quello medesimo che voi ci havevo scripto per la de' 26 dì, accrescendo le dubitationi et le difficultà circa el fornire coteste opere, deliberamo haverne consulta del Consiglio degli Ottanta, et di buon numero di cittadini, per vedere come havamo ad procedere. Et insumma loro consigliono che per ogni respecto si debbe ire avanti et non abbandonare l' opera, anzi raddoppiare la buona diligentia, perchè l' habbi el fine si desidera, et non perdonare ad alcuna spesa, nè disagio ; et lo hanno consigliato con tanta caldeza che non si potrebbe stimare. Pertanto è bene che si faccia in modo che nè per voi, nè per noi manchi, et se sturbo veruno habbi ad seguire, nasca dal tempo ; perchè desideriamo, avendoci addolere di alcuna cosa, dolerci del tempo et non delli huomini. Et per non mancare dal canto nostro, questa sera mandereno danari per li operai, et così sollecitereno le altre cose che per noi si hanno ad sollecitare. Ma perchè e' danari et el tempo si spenda utilmente, ci pare che non si spenda ad nessuno modo danari in quelli operai che voi giudicate disutili, così di quelli che si truovono costì, come di quelli vi venisseno per lo advenire. Et però potrete tali disutili licentiare, perchè voliamo piuttosto habbiate 500 huomini che sieno buoni, che 1000, et che ve ne sia 500 inutili.

Vorremo, oltre ad di questo, che si pensasse come infinite volte si è decto, che quando pure el tempo sforzassi ad levarsi la opera restassi meglio et più perfecta che fussi possibile, il che ci parrebbe seguissi quando voi ordinassi in modo quello è facto, che tucto operassi qualche cosa. Et però vorremo che con sollecitudine si attendesse ad ridurre la pescaia in modo che la facessi qualche operatione, et che le piene la fermassino et facessino più forte, et così che si sboccassi ad ogni modo el secondo fosso. Et se non si potesse detto secondo fosso condurlo ad Arno tucto largo come e' fu cominciato, vi si conducessi con quella largheza si potessi, acciochè per qualche modo e' pigliassi le acque, et non havessi ad rimanere una buca in terra senza fructo. Parrebbeci anchora che voi facessi la sboccatura di quel fosso fornito, largo almeno cento braccia, ritirando la largheza in verso dove havessi ad essere la bocca del secondo fosso ; et se voi non potessi fare questa tale sboccatura

---

[1] Florence Archives, cl. x. dist. 3, No. 112, at sheet 152 : Machiavelli's autograph.

quadra, la farete smussata, faccendo che el più largo fussi dalla parte del fosso fornito. Questa cosa ci parrebbe che dèssi la via più facilmente all' acqua, che non maggiore empito entrassi nel fosso, et togliesse facilità a' Pisani di chiudere la sboccatura, sendo largha. Di nuovo vi si dice che noi desideriamo che l' opera si tirassi innanzi infino al fine, servendo el tempo. Ma perchè el tempo può guastarsi ad ogni hora, vorremo che si lavorasse in quello che facessi l' opera più utile, il che ci pare che sii il fermare la pescaia, sboccare *quomodocunque* el fosso secondo, et al fosso primo fare una sboccatura. Noi pensereno in questo mezo dove debbino andare cotesti huomini d' arme alle stanze, et te ne manderno listra, acciochè, bisognando levarsi in un subito, tu sappi dove si habbino ad distribuire, et non segua disordine. Ma terrai questa cosa in te, acciochè, sappiendosi pel il campo, e' non cominciassino a levarsi prima che tu non ordinassi o che non fussi el desiderio nostro. Et perchè tu ci scrivi che il sig. Marcantonio desiderrebbe essere alloggiato in Maremma, potrai nel discorso del parlare dirli, come tu credevi che si fussi pensato qui, per honore della sua persona ; et per riputatione delle cose nostre costà, di alloggiare la persona sua et li cavalli leggieri in Cascina, do le genti sue d' armi ne' luoghi convicini et commodi.

Intendiamo oltre ad di questo quello tu scrivi delle castagne, el quali noi desiderreno tòrre ad li Pisani ad ogni modo ; et però vorremo pensassi ad questa cosa, et ci scrivessi el modo come ti paressi da procedere, et se andandovi con una scorta grossa et con li huomini del paese ad ritorle, e' bastassi. Communicherai questa ad Giuliano Lapi.

———

DOCUMENT X.

Letter of the Ten to the Commissary T. Tosinghi, 30th September,
1504.[1]

Tomaso Tosinghi in Castris Commissario. Die xxx septembris 1504.—
Hieri et avanti hieri et questa mattina ti si scripse particularmente quale fussi il nostro desiderio circa il procedere nelle cose di costà, et di nuovo brevemente ti replichereno, come noi vogliamo si stia tanto in campagna et si seguiti cotesta opera, quanto el tempo ci serve, el quale, per essere questo dì bellissimo, ci dà speranzá che, se non mancha da voi, cotesta impresa debbi havere el fine desideriamo. Et vi si ricorda particular-mente el fortificare la pescaia, et ridurla in termine che la facci qualche fructo, et così che voi diate la perfectione ad quel secondo fosso, et lo riduciate in termine che pigli dell' acqua ; et sopra ad ogni altra cosa, vi si ricorda fare l' abboccature de' fossi larghissime, in modo che fra l' uno et l' altro fosso presso ad Arno, almeno ad cento braccia, non rimanghi punto di grotta, anzi sia sgrottato ogni cosa, se non infino al piano de' fossi, almeno quanto più giù si può, acciò che venendo Arno grosso, et

———

[1] Florence Archives, cl. x. dist. 3, No. 112, at sheet 156 : Machiavelli's autograph.

non trovando chi lo ritengha, e' rovini più facilmente verso quella parte donde se gli è cominciato ad dare la via. Noi ve lo replichiamo spesso perchè lo desideriamo, parendoci che, potendosi finire l' opera o non si potendo finire, questa sia una delle più utili cose et delle più necessarie che voi dobbiate fare. Non voliamo manchare farvi intendere come e' ci è venuto ad notitia, che in Barbericina et *etiam* da cotesta parte d'Arno donde è il campo, si truovono anchora ritte buona quantità di biade ; di che ti diamo notitia, perchè vorremo che ad ogni modo le si togliessino o guastassino a' Pisani. Et se non si potessi nè guastare nè tòrre quelle di Barbericina, si guastassino almeno quelle che fussino da cotesta parte del fiume ; però intenderai dove le sieno, et vedrai ad ogni modo di privarne e' nemici. *Vale.*

Sendosi dato per il Consiglio Grande della nostra città, autorità amplissima a' nostri Excelsi Signori di potere per arbitrio loro perdonare et rendere e' beni ad qualunque Pisano, ti mandiamo, in questa, copia d' uno bando, per il quale si possi pubblicare tale loro autorità ; el quale bando vorremo che tu mandassi ad quella hora ti paressi più comodo, in lato che chi fussi in sulle mura di Pisa lo potessi udire ; et dipoi lo mandassi anchora in cotesto exercito nostro. *Vale.*

Per parte de' Magnifici et Excelsi Signori Priori di Libertà et Gonfalonieri di Iustitia del Popolo Fiorentino, si fa bandire et pubblicamente notificare, come egli è stato ad loro Excelse Signorie conceduta amplissima autorità et facultà dal Popolo et Consiglio Maggiore della città di Firenze, di potere concedere venia per arbitrio loro ad ciascuno di qualunque grado, stato o conditione si sia, el quale al presente habiti nella città di Pisa, et restituirli e' suoi beni, et adsolverlo da qualunque delitto, maleficio o excesso, per alcun tempo infino ad questo dì havessi commesso.

DOCUMENT XI.

Letter of the Ten to the Captain of Leghorn.—10th January, 1504 (1505).[1]

Al Capitano di Livorno. Die x ianuarii 1504.—La Excellentia del Gonfaloniere nostro ci ha mostro una tua lettera che tu li scrivi, dandogli notitia delle cose di costà, et della buona et diligente guardia che per te si fa in cotesto luogho, il che ci è suto sommamente grato, perchè in vero non habbiamo al presente chosa che noi desideriamo più che cotesta. Et i tale tua diligentia ci fa assai buona testimonianza, lo esservi stato ropto la carcere, et tractone el prigione sanza che da te o da altri per tuo ordine sia suto sentito, et dipoi sanza essere visto se ne sia per le mura fuggito, in modo che ogni poco meno di diligentia che per te si fussi usata, posseva costì nasciere caso di maggiore importanza

[1] Florence Archives, cl. x. dist. 3, No. 116, at sheet 23 : Machiavelli's autograph.

e per adventura inremediabile ; perchè chi può uscir fuora per le mura sanza esser visto, può *etiam* sanza esser visto entrar drento ; et così chi sanza esser sentito può rompere una prigione, può *etiam* fare delle altre cose più pernitiose, le quali non hanno per adventura bisogno di tanto aiuto, et con mancho strepito si possono condurre. Pertanto noi non restereno mai satisfacti della tua diligentia, infino non intendiamo che tu l' habbi in modo raddoppiata, che costì non si possa muovere una foglia che la non si veggha o non si senta ; et perchè noi speriamo che ad questa hora tu harai ritrovato chi è suto autore della roptura della carcere et della fuggita del prigione, voliamo ce ne dia subito notitia, scrivendoci chi furno et di quale compagnia sono et da quali cagioni mossi. Et quando tu non li havessi anchora ritrovati, userai diligentia in cercarli per poterci satisfare in darcene notitia.

Tu accenni, oltre ad di questo, nella preallegata lettera al Gonfaloniere nostro, come haresti da dire altre cose, oltre ad quelle scrivi che ragguardano alla salute di cotesta terra, et sono d' importantia grande ; ma non lo fai per esser cose da riferire ad bocha. Donde e' ci pare che in questo caso tu non usi minore prudentia che ti habbi usata diligentia in quel primo ; et veramente le cose d' importanza si debbono tener segrete, ma non tanto che per ignoranza di quelle non vi si possa provedere. Et però era bene considerare che tu parlavi di Livorno, et che bisognia parlar chiaro, et le cose d' importanza dirle, maxime scrivenda allo Excellentia del Gonfaloniere in particulare, del quale ragionevolmente doverresti confidarti. Et però se tu hai da dire alcuna cosa, dilla et scrivila larghamente, acciò che vi si possa fare provisione, et che noi non restiamo in aria per li advisi tuoi.

DOCUMENT XII.[1]

Machiavelli's Report on the Institution of the New Militia.

Voi mi havete richieste che io vi scriva el fondamento di questa Ordinanza, e dove la si truovi : farollo ; et ad maggiore vostra cognitione, mi farò un poco da alto, et voi harete patienza ad leggierla.

Io lascierò stare indrieto el disputare se li era bene o no ordinare lo Stato vostro alle armi ; perchè ognuno sa che chi dice Imperio, Regno, Principato, Repubblica ; chi dice huomini che comandono, cominciandosi dal primo grado et descendendo infino al padrone d' uno brigantino, dice iustitia et armi. Voi della iustitia ne havete non molta, et dell' armi non punto ; et el modo ad rihavere l' uno et l' altro è solo ordinarsi all' armi per deliberatione publica, et con buono ordine, et mantenerlo. Nè v'

---

[1] The original of this document is among the "Carte del Machiavelli," case i. n. 78. It has not been given in any edition of the "Opere" ; but was published in marriage pamphlets, first by Ghinassi, then, with greater accuracy, by Professor D'Ancona

ingannino cento cotanti anni che voi sete vissuti altrimenti et mantenu-
tivi; perchè se voi considerrete bene questi tempi et quelli, vedrete essere
impossibile potere preservare la vostra libertà in quel medesimo modo.
Ma perchè questa è materia chiara, et quando pure la si havessi addis-
putare, bisognerebbe entrare per altra via, la lascierò stare indreto. Et
presupponendo che la sententia sia data, et che sia bene armarsi, volendo
ordinare lo Stato di Firenze, alle armi, era necessario examinare come
questa militia si avessi ad introdurre. Et considerando lo Stato vostro,
si truova diviso in città, contado et distrecto; sì che bisognava cominciare
questa militia in uno di questi luoghi, o in dua, o in tutti ad tre ad un
tracto. Et perchè le cose grandi hanno bisogno d'essere menate adagio,
non si poteva in nessuno modo, nè in dua, nè in tucti ad tre e' sopraddecti
luoghi, sanza confusione et sanza pericolo introdurla : bisognava pertanto
eleggierne uno. Nè piacque di tòrre la città, perchè chi considera uno
exercito, ad dividerlo grossamente, lo truova composto di huomini che
comandono et che ubbidiscono, et di huomini che militano ad piè et
che militano ad cavallo ; et hauendo ad introdurre foima di exercito
in una provincia inconsueta all' armi, bisognava, come tutte l' altre
discipline, cominciarsi da la parte più facile ; et sanza dubbio egli è
più facile introdurre militia ad piè che ad cavallo, et è più facile im-
parare ad ubbidire che ad comandare. Et perchè la vostra città et voi
havete ad essere quelli che militiate ad cavallo et comandiate, non si
poteva cominciare da voi, per essere questa parte più difficile ; ma bisognava cominciare da chi ha ad ubbidire et militare ad piè, et questo è el
contado vostro. Nè parse pigliare el distrecto, anchora che in quello si
possa introdurre militia ad piè, perchè non sarebbe suto securo partito
per la città vostra, maxime in quelli luoghi del distrecto dove sieno nidi
grossi, dove una provincia possa far testa ; perchè li humori di Toschana
sono tali, che come uno conoscessi potere vivere sopra di sè, non vorrebbe
più padrone, trovandosi maxime lui armato, et il padrone disarmato : et
però questo distrecto bisogna, o non lo ordinare mai all'armi, o indugiarsi
ad hora che l'armi del contado vostro habbino preso piè, et sieno stimate.
Quelli luoghi distrectuali che sono da non li armare, sono dove sono nidi
grossi, come Arezo, Borgo ad San Sipolcro, Cortona, Volterra, Pistoia,
Colle, Sangimigniano : li altri dove sono più castella simili, come la
Romagna, Lunigiana, etc., non importono molto, perchè non riconoscono
altro padrone che Firenze, nè hanno particulare superiore come interviene
nel contado vostro ; perchè el Casentino, Valdarno di sotto et di sopra,
Mugiello, etc., ancora che sieno pieni di huomini, *tamen* non hanno dove
fare testa, se non ad Firenze ; nè più castella possono convenire ad fare
una impresa. Et però si è cominciata questa Ordinanza nel contado,
dove, volendola ordinare, bisognava darle ordine et modo, cioè segni
sotto chi e' militassino, armi con che si havessino ad armare ; terminare
chi havessi ad militare sotto ciascuno segno, et dare loro capi che li exer-
citassino. Quanto alle armi, quelle che sono date loro sono note : quanto
a' segni, è parso che le sieno bandiere tucte con uno segno medesimo del

Lione, ad ciò che tucti li huomini vostri sieno affectionati di una medesima cosa, et non habbino altro per obiecto che 'l segno publico, et per questo ne diventino partigiani; sonsi distinti e' capi ad ciò che ciascuno riconosca la sua: sonsi numerate, perchè la città ne possa tener conto, et comandarle più facilmente. Era necessario dare ad queste bandiere termine di paese; et ad questo bisognava, o terminare el paese vostro di nuovo, o pigliare de' termini suoi antiqui; et perchè e' si truova diviso in Capitaneati, Vicariati, Potesterie, Comuni et Populi, parve, volendo andare con uno di questi ordini, da terminare queste bandiere con le Potesterie, sendo li altri termini o troppi larghi, o troppo strecti. Et però si è dato ad ogni Potesteria una bandiera; et ad dua, tre, quattro et cinqua bandiere si è dato uno conestabole che li struisca, secondo la commodità del ragunarli, et secondo la moltitudine delli uomini descripti sotto tali bandiere; tanto che trenta bandiere che voi havete, sono in governo d' undici connestaboli; et li luoghi dove le sono messe, sono Mugiello, Firenzuola, Casentino, Valdarno di sopra et di sotto, Pescia et Lunigiana. Pareva bene, anchora non si sia facto, scrivere sotto ogni bandiera, cioè in ogni Potesteria, più huomini si poteva, perchè, come dixe messer Hercole in uno suo scripto, questo ordine vi ha ad servire sempre in reputatione, et qualche volta in fatto; nè può servirvi in reputatione poco numero di huomini; nè *etiam*, in facto, del poco numero di huomini, quando pure bisognassi, si può trarre lo assai, ma sì bene dello assai, el poco. Nè impedisce cosa alcuna el tenere ordinati ne' paesi assai huomini, non li obbligando ad fare più che 12 o 16 monstre lo anno, et dando loro libera licentia d' andare dove vogliono ad fare e' facti loro. Et però el tenerne ordinati assai è più prudentia, con animo di non havere poi adoperare, nè levare da casa chi ha honesta cagione di starvi, o chi si conoscessi inutile. Et così alla reputatione ti giova il numero grande, al facto il numero minore e buono; perchè sempre si potrà farne nuova scielta et meglio, havendogli visti più volte in viso, che non li havendo visti.

Voi dunque vi trovate scripti ne' sopra scripti luoghi, et sotto 30 bandiere et undici connestaboli, più che cinquemila huomini; havetene facto mostra in Firenze di 1200;[1] et sono procedute le cose, sendo nuove, assai ordinatamente; ma le non possono stare più così, perchè e' bisogna, o che la 'mpresa ruini, o che la facci disordine; perchè, sanza dare loro càpo et guida, non si può reggiere contro alli inimici che la ha. El capo che bisogna dare loro, è fare una leggie che ne dispongha, et uno magistrato che l' observi; et in questa leggie bisogna provvedere ad questo, che li scripti stieno bene ordinati, che non possino nuocere, et che si remunerino. Ad tenerli ordinati, bisogna che questo magistrato habbi autorità di punirli, et facultà da farlo, et che la leggie lo necessiti ad fare tucto quello che è in substantia della cosa, et che, stralasciandola, le facessi danno; et però bisogna constringerlo ad tenerne armati un numero, almeno ad tenere

---

[1] Here the manuscript has these words, afterwards scratched out: *Et ne havete mandati già cinquecento in campo.*

le bandiere ; et e' connestaboli ad provvedere all' armi, ad far fare loro le mostre et vicitarli, ad rivederne ogniunno cento, et cancellare in certi dì et in certo tempo, et rimetterli, ad mescolarvi qualche cosa di religione per farli più ubbidienti. Quanto ad ordinare che non possino nuocere, si ha ad considerare che possono nuocere in dua modi : o fra loro, o contro alla città. Se fra loro, possono ferirsi l' uno l' altro particularmente, o fare ragunate per fare male, come sogliono. Nel primo caso si vuole duplicare loro la pena, et maxime quelli che ferissino in su le mostre ; ma ferendo altrove, si potrebbe observare le leggie vechie. Quando e' facessino ragunate in comuni, bisognerebbe fare ogni viva et grande demostratione contro ad chi ne fussi capo, et uno exemplo basta uno pezo nella memoria delli huomini. Contro alla città costoro possono fare male in questi modi : o con ribellarsi et adherirsi con uno forestiero, o essere male adoperati da uno magistrato o da una persona privata. Quanto ad lo adherirsi ad uno forestiero, li huomini ordinati nelli luoghi sopraddecti non lo possono fare, et non se ne debbe dubitare. Quanto allo essere male operati da uno magistrato, è necessario ordinare le cose in modo che conoschino più superiori. Et considerando in che articulo loro hanno ad riconoscere el superiore, mi pare che li habbino ad riconoscere chi li tenga ad casa ordinati, chi li comandi nella guerra, et chi li remuneri. Et perchè e' sarebbe periculoso che riconoscessino tucte queste autorità in uno solo superiore, sarebbe bene che questo magistrato nuovo li tenessi ordinati ad casa ; e' Dieci dipoi li comandassino nella guerra ; et e' Signori, Collegi, Dieci et nuovo magistrato li premiassi e remunerassi : et così verrebbono sempre ad havere in confuso el loro superiore, et riconoscere un pubblico et non un privato. Et perchè una moltitudine sanza capo non fecie mai male, o, se pure lo fa, è facile ad reprimerla, bisogna havere advertenza alli capi ad chi si dànno le bandiere in governo continuamente, che non piglino più autorità con loro si conviene ; la quale possono pigliare in più modi, o per stare continuamente al governo di quelle, o per havere con loro interesse. Et però bisogna provedere che nessuno natìo delli luoghi dove è una bandiera, o che vi habbi casa o possessione, la possa governare ; ma si tolga gente di Casentino per il Mugiello, et per Casentino gente del Mugiello. Et perchè l' autorità con el tempo si piglia, è bene fare ogni anno le permute de' connestaboli, et dare loro nuovi governi, et dare loro divieto qualche anno da quelli governi primi ; et quando tutte queste cose sieno bene ordinate et meglio observate, non è da dubitare. Quanto al premiarli, non è necessario ora pensarci ; ma basterebbe solo darne autorità, come di sopra si dice, et dipoi venire a' premi di mano in mano, secondo e' meriti loro.

Questo ordine bene ordinato nel contado, de necessità conviene che entri ad poco ad poco nella città, et sarà facilissima cosa ad introdurlo. Et vi advedrete anchora a' vostri dì, che differentia è havere de' vostri cittadini soldati per electione et non per corruptione, come havete al presente, perchè se alcuno non ha voluto ubbidire al padre, allevatosi su per li bordelli, diverrà soldato ; ma uscendo dalle squole honeste et dalle buone educationi, potranno honorare sè et la patria loro : et il tucto sta nel cominciare addare reputatione ad questo exercitio, il che conviene si faccia di necessità, fermando bene questi ordini nel contado, et che sono cominciati.[1]

[1] The MS. finished with *contado;* then follow two erasures ; then *et che sono cominciati.*

On the cover are the following words in Machiavelli's hand : "1512. La cagione della Ordinanza, dove la si trovi, et quel che bisogni fare. *Post res perditas.*" It is plain that these words were written at a later date, namely, after the fall of the Republic.